That Alone, the Core of Wisdom

"My brain is only a receiver, in the Universe there is a core from which we obtain knowledge, strength and inspiration. I have not penetrated into the secrets of this core, but I know that it exists."

— Nikola Tesla, Scientist

That Alone, the Core of Wisdom

A Commentary on

Ātmopadeśa Śatakam

the One Hundred Verses of Self-Instruction of Narayana Guru

by

Guru Nitya Chaitanya Yati

PRINTWORLD

Publishers of Indian Traditions

Cataloging in Publication Data — DK

Nityacaitanya Yati, 1924-1999, **author.**
That alone, the core of wisdom : a commentary on Ātmopadeśa śatakam, the one hundred verses of self-instruction of Narayana Guru / by Nitya Chaitanya Yati. – Third impression.
pages cm
Reprint. Originally published: 2003.
Includes index.
ISBN 9788124602409

1. Narayana Guru, 1856-1928. Ātmōpadēśaśatakaṁ. 2. Ātman. 3. Vedanta. I. Narayana Guru, 1856-1928. Ātmōpadēśaśatakaṁ. II. Title.

LCC B132.A8N58 2021 | DDC 181.48 23

ISBN: 978-81-246-0240-9
First published in India 2003
Second impression, 2013
Third impression, 2021

Narayana Gurukula website: http://www.narayanagurukula.org.
e-mail: tapovana@hevanet.com

Published and printed by:
D.K. Printworld (P) Ltd.
Regd. Office: 'Vedaśrī', F-395, Sudarshan Park
ESI Metro Station, New Delhi – 110 015
Phones: (011) 2545 3975, 2546 6019
e-mail: indology@dkprintworld.com
Website: www.dkprintworld.com

Foreword

Narayana Guru once asked a young novice, "Do you know Vedanta?"

The young man answered, "No. What is there to know about it?"

"Do you know what water is like?" replied the Guru.

"Yes."

"Do you know what wave is like?"

"Yes."

"Do you know that water and wave are not two?"

"Yes."

"That is all."

"If Vedanta is so simple, why do people spend so much time studying it?"

"Because people forget the wave is water."

"Why do we forget?"

"Because of maya."

"How do we get rid of maya?"

"By knowing that wave and water are not two."

"What is the use of knowing they are both the same?"

"So you won't put such questions!"

This story was told to me by my Master, Nataraja Guru. As he himself was a disciple of Narayana Guru, it is even possible that he was the novice mentioned.

The point, however, is that truth is so very simple we don't need to make any effort to know it, but an undetectable ignorance conceals what should be obvious. Then we take a lifetime of beating around the bush to arrive once again at what is already known to us. Once the lost truth is regained, the search comes to a close and there is no need to utter another word.

Between the effortlessness of the obvious and the silent wonder of regaining the forgotten truth, there are many hurdles to be cleared.

The truth we speak of is neither fact or fiction. It is not the object of immediate perception or the subject of mediate inference. Either you unconditionally know it or you do not. This is the knowledge which cannot be taught but, paradoxically, it dawns upon you on listening to one who knows.

There is no assurance you will know because you listen, and there is also no assurance you will know if you do not listen. What one listens to is a word symbol of that which cannot be adequately symbolised or represented. To rectify this defect, a series of mutually complementary symbols can be presented by the knower. One or all of these analogies may prepare the listener to have a state of mind which can suddenly get the jolt of confronting the Absolute. There is no guarantee, but it is in the compassionate nature of gurus to offer any number of chances to those who are willing to listen.

In the *Ātmopadeśa Śatakam*, the polarising of the Self and the non-Self is therefore presented with one hundred variations.

Narayana Guru (1854-1928), composed these hundred verses in Malayalam in the year 1897. For about half a century it was only read by a few scholars, and no one thought of translating it into any other language. The first English translation and commentary was written by Nataraja Guru in the Fifties, though it was not published until 1969. During that time three Malayalam commentaries and one Sanskrit translation and commentary were written and published. One of these was based on Nataraja Guru's English commentary. Of late, the works of Narayana Guru have attracted many scholars, and new translations and commentaries are appearing year after year.

Narayana Guru's basic stand is that of a non-dualist visionary. At the same time he could appreciate the value of the traditions that entered into the aggregate rightly or wrongly called the Hindu religion. He was not a partisan in favour of any particular religion. This made it possible for him to have a neutral stand and to view all religions with the attitude of a devoted lover of beauty, goodness, love and truth.

It may seems superfluous for me to write a new translation and commentary when my own Guru has already written one which is undoubtedly a bona fide translation and authentic commentary.

However, when Nataraja Guru instituted a hierarchy of teachers, a parampara, for the Narayana Gurukula, his intention was to have an unbroken chain of the continuators of wisdom teaching. He personally told me on several occasions to develop and enlarge on points and aspects of the work which he had only hinted at and which he had had no time to elaborate.

In the Malayalam language there are no words more simple than the ones the Guru has used. Thus, one cannot escape the fault of meddling with the obvious and making each verse a conglomeration of confusion by commenting on it. Yet we take that risk in the hope that our listener or reader will ultimately leave us and take refuge in the compassion of the Guru, developing a proper attitude which is more likely to help him or her to see the Guru's wisdom-gesture, imprinted in his every word, of the forgotten truth which everyone is seeking all the time.

Beginning in the Fall of 1977 and continuing through the Winter and early Spring of 1978, the students of the Narayana Gurukula in Portland, Oregon, USA agreed to participate in a meditation on *Ātmopadeśa Śatakam*. The idea was to learn one verse a day and to give full attention to external events and internal life, understanding and molding them in the light of the meditation that ensued from each verse. This book is a transcription of the morning meditation I gave on the meaning of each verse. We have decided to publish it because it complements the translation and commentary of Nataraja Guru. The Guru's translation faithfully adheres to the original word structure of Narayana Guru's Malayalam composition. In the present translation we have taken the freedom to rearrange words to enable the reader to have an easier reading of the meaning, but we have taken every care not to deflect from the original intention of the author. An even freer translation will be found in the Appendix of this work.

As Nataraja Guru's commentary will always remain as the most authentic, we have not repeated what is so ably expounded by him. However, we hope that the present book will be seen as complementary to his. It is our wish that the reader will find this book a helpful guide to meditating on the One Hundred Verses of Self-Instruction.

Nitya Chaitanya Yati

Contents

Errata

pg.	*line*	*printed*	*read as*
14	4	*varēṇa*	*varēṇam*
24	1	*p̈mānta*	*pumānta*
25	10	*p̈māntam*	*pumāntam*
27	10	intensity if	intensity of
28	4 fr b	behaviour	behavior
59	12 fr b	conse-quential	consequential
95	6	ashes, the	ashes of the
98	10	its	it's
135	3	*jaḍamity*	*jaḍamitu*
165	11 fr b	everyday	every day
167	8	everyday	every day
197	20	programme	programme.
203	14	having lost	have lost
213	8	a expansive	an expansive
263	8	*kāla*	*kala*
263	15 fr b	*kāla*	*kala*
263	14 fr b	*kāla*	*kala*
263	12 fr b	*kāla*	*kala*
266	15 fr b	*maitrī*, compassion	*karuṇā*, compassion
266	11 fr b	*kāla*	*kala*
305	11 fr b	*ētum*	*otum*
327	11 fr b	everyday	every day

fr b = from bottom

330	2	own itself	own self
330	2	to be misery	to be in misery
330	5	maximum	maxim
330	14	'the inherent principle'.	"the inherent principle."
330	16	shinning at once	shining at once
331	19	God, is the self	God, the self
331	20	factor, derived	factor, is derived
334	4 fr b	(provide extra space before the para to have a break)	
347	1	ontological errors,	axiological errors,
348	6	you own existence	your own existence
354	2	A . . . U . . . M.	A . . . U . . . M . . ..
397	4 fr b	with the its	with its
466	10 fr b	goods aromas.	good aromas.
468	4	little things".	little things."
522	5	body is form,	body is foam,
540	14	"functioning". one	"functioning": one
563	9	sometime	some time
566	2	into it.	in to it.
566	9 fr b	in to the immanent.	into the immanent.
607	1	flame of a candle, is the	flame of a candle. Is the
620	4	*annbhavam*	*anubhavam*
620	15	He is helped	You are helped
635	16	itself misleading.	itself is misleading.
639	5	everyday	every day
653	2 fr b	opportunity the enter	opportunity to enter
664	5 fr b	wont last forever.	won't last forever.
675	4 fr b	reality or	reality of
689	15	you teeth	your teeth
691	9 fr b	exists with us.	exists within us.
720	13	dispair	despair
726	5 fr b	angry	anger

Acknowledgements

THIS book began as a series of talks given in Portland, Oregon, USA beginning in late 1977. For one hundred consecutive mornings, Guru Nitya commented on the verses one at a time, impeccably transmitting the eternal spirit of the Guru in traditional Upanishadic fashion.

The approximately thirty students spent their days relating the teaching to whatever occurred in the course of their activities, and in the evening met to discuss their experiences. Thus a group spirit infuses the book to a certain extent, and is responsible for some of the direction the commentary took.

The morning class was tape recorded, and Nancy Yeilding spent each day transcribing the tape and correcting the Malayalam and Sanskrit terminology with Guru Nitya, after he had finished preparing a shorter version of the verses that was published earlier as *Neither This Nor That, But. . . Aum.* Without her dedicated time and attention, this work would very likely have disappeared in the mists of time.

Scott Teitsworth edited the work prior to publication.

Introduction

A thin, intense-looking man sat quietly next to a small pond hidden in the wilds near the southern tip of India. The man's legs were crossed in lotus pose and his body remained quiet, but his thoughts were intense and penetrating. A bright sun shone brilliantly on the surface of the water, and each tiny wave carried a burning image of the solar disk on its crest. The pond was alive with the dancing, shimmering wavelets, undulating hypnotically in a way that would have mesmerised anyone less wakeful.

The soil in this region is sandy in all directions, to the south and west joining the shore of the Arabian Sea with a barely noticeable break. Palms and scrub undergrowth are sparse in the desert soil, gnarled and twisted by heat and prevailing winds. At the foot of the nearby mountains, increased nutrients allow the jungle to grow more thickly, while the tropical climate favours an exuberant outburst of life. Vines engulf the trees, epiphytes blossom on every branch, and insects swarm in profusion. Snakes, many of them poisonous, lie camouflaged in branches fallen to the ground.

As the day wore on a light breeze sprang up, and sand and dust sifted onto the pool's surface. The man watched carefully as the dirt slowly sank into the crystalline water, swirling downwards as myriad speckles of light, until lost in the darkness of the depths. He knew that in time the little lake would fill totally with sand, becoming as dry and barren as much of the land around it, but that the wind would also scour out new hollows in other places which the monsoon rains could fill up in turn.

As the young man critically studied the scene the depth of his contemplation intensified. The wind sang through the vine laden trees nearby. The multiple sun-images gradually merged together, increasing the light to a dazzling degree. Suddenly, like a dam giving way, his awareness was flooded with insight rushing upon insight, and he was enveloped in a gloriously all-embracing happiness. In the face of such meaningful brilliance, all he could do was incline in reverent adulation towards the source of all his wonder.

Deep in his state of blissful contemplation, the man's mind reeled with the implications of the scene before him. Not a single insight, but a full flood of them prevailed on all sides, filling him with a sense of understanding. The wayside pool became a perfect symbol of humanity's eternal situation. Whatever elements were present in the surrounding world the winds blew about, scattering them into the pond. This meant that if an individual self was likened to a neglected pond in a waste land, the winds bringing in dust from the surroundings were like the forces of nature or maya presenting perceptual and conceptual material. Each of these sensory elements affects consciousness by producing some kind of reaction, as an agitation of the surface of the pond. By its very existence the material affects the clarity of the water, and as it sinks to the bottom its accumulation alters the terrain in the same way that samskaras condition individuals, by gradually changing the shape of their inner landscape.

To the blissful meditator the one sun above clearly represented the Absolute, the giver of all light and life which remains unaffected by the rotation of the earth, cloud activity, storms, or any other terrestrial phenomenon. To him, this was the Self with a capital 'S'. The multiple images reflected by each separate wave, mirror, dewdrop, or other surface on the earth below were like the endless parade of changing individuals, selves with a small 's'. Each of these images reflected the true sun in a beautiful and uniquely distorted manner. When the pond was still the images grew more and more perfect, though no one would be so foolish as to mistake even the most perfect of them for the sun itself. When wind rippled the surface the images became increasingly agitated, until at their most extreme the image of the sun was entirely obscured. But no amount of clouding or evaporation had even the most negligible effect on the sun above. It was exactly like the individual self's relation to the Self: close and harmonious in moments of peace, farther from sight as one became more agitated.

The man was Narayana Guru, and many profound revelations like these came to him as he sat alone in the wilderness of south India. Through him the fruits of his realisation would begin to spread out in ripples of wisdom which would eventually impact the whole world. But before that happened he wanted to allow the inner principle that was instructing him to teach him as much as possible.

Like a grand book, the whole universe is a symbolic expression of higher truth, and the guru principle is a name for the way in which this truth reveals itself to the seeker. For Narayana Guru the world of nature around him was the medium of this invisible wisdom transmission, so that everywhere he looked he saw meaning. The vines climbing into the trees spoke of the pattern of our lives where the accretions of memories slowly choke and submerge our original form. The red hot ember of a stick from a cooking fire being twirled around to produce virtual images became an analogy for the course of our lives, with its bright, moving spark of the present leaving a virtual afterimage of shapes in memory. Spinning oil lamps hanging in the dark of a simple place of worship spoke to him of the inner structure of the human body. Waves rolling in to the shore whispered of individual existences sweeping across the depths of the Real. Each grain of sand became for him a precious jewel of value beyond price. He was overwhelmed by intense happiness and gratitude for this oceanic awareness, and knew he must share it with anyone who might also wish to embrace it. The time of teaching was no longer far in the future.

Sitting quietly in the midst of this torrent of meaningful images, the Guru began to formulate a new and revolutionary philosophy. While the prevailing belief of most of humanity is that this world is either unreal or merely a practice ground for a future life in another place, he knew from inner assurance that it was the whole, and this was many times over more than enough. That Absolute, which everyone spoke of in different ways, was itself manifesting as all This. Everything was here, at this very moment. But when it was conceived of as having a specific form, people tended to forget its connection with the original mold from which it came — its Karu — and focus only on the form. This led to fantasies and projections about the past and the future, which in turn led to endless arguments and disputes. But those who remembered the source had no need to quarrel: they were content to know and share their knowledge.

This was not so much a casting down of gods and the religions that paid homage to them, as an emancipation from illusory ideas. The apparent loss brought about by the dissolution of imaginary deities was more than offset by the gain through the understanding of one's own being. If people could truly appreciate the unity of the created with the creator they would at last be freed of all constraints, and happiness would be seen to be their own essential nature. This would free everyone from so many delusions and release them from misery. The Gurū's heart went out to everyone and everything: he must bring this insight to the world.

Filled with intense happiness and a boundless compassion for humanity's suffering, Narayana Guru moved from his wilderness retreat to the fringes of civilization, where he soon attracted the attention of sensitive souls. All who came to associate with him felt a pervasive peace in his presence, and found their minds becoming activated in ways that solved problems rather than manufactured them. Very rapidly his followers became numerous, and his influence began to spread.

It is mysterious how one person can act as a catalyst for social change, while others who might uphold the same beliefs remain unknown and ineffective. Narayana Guru spoke gently and lived simply, but his message went directly to the heart of the people and began to have important consequences. The populace felt moved to action by his words and presence as nothing had ever moved them before. Life in South India began slowly to improve, though as with all change it was a slow and challenging process.

Everywhere he went the Guru rhetorically asked people, if, as taught even in the scriptures, we are one in essence and the Absolute is equally the source of all things, why should there be high and low castes, why should women be treated as unworthy, and why should humanity treat the environment — in a sense the body of the divine — as either an evil to be eradicated or a mere waste receptacle. Why indeed? Such logic appealed to people's common sense, and the Guru's ideas began to have an impact. In a land where the downtrodden and fortunate alike had come to accept their places as divinely assigned, and the social code was rigidly enforced by fear of mundane as well as divine retribution, sea changes began to occur. The various castes began to have contact with each other, with some radicals, led by the Guru himself, even maintaining that castes should be abolished altogether. Schools for girls were instituted, and a more universal education began to chip away at inequality based on privilege. Only in the area of man's relation to his environment did the Guru's message fail to move the rock of habitual behaviour, but considering the magnitude of the task of totally reorienting a society it is understandable that this was put off until the most egregious human wrongs could be attended to. Humanity as a whole has barely begun to address this issue, though it looms large in the near future, as the health of the earth begins to seriously decline from overpopulation and pollution.

* * *

Narayana Guru directly embodies the ancient ideal of the lone seeker experiencing the "flight of the alone to the Alone." The smattering of stories that have been passed down about his early life show that he was an unusually wise and sensitive child, with strong tendencies towards absolutism and the courage to follow his own instincts with little regard for social pressures. Though perhaps instructed by his family, no one speaks of his having had a guru. When the time came to leave home, he plunged into solitude. He rediscovered his true nature on his own, far from any ashram or school, by sitting quietly and contemplating alertly. He went deeply into his own core and there discovered the Core of all, what he calls the Karu in the present work. Later on, when he studied the classics, he could see he was allied with ancient rishis like Śaṅkara, Rāmānuja, and Patañjali. As he himself said, "First we experienced it in ourselves and then we found it was written in books."

Such relevant insight was a key reason that Narayana Guru became widely known and tremendously influential during his lifetime. His philosophical revaluation of the weak points of the ancient wisdom teachings, such as the issues of caste and orthodoxy, bringing them up to par with the rest, places him in the forefront of the great Indian teachers of history. The insight he experienced transformed those around him, flowing outwards like the ripples on a pond to affect society as a whole. Such was the power of his influence that today Southwestern India is celebrated as one of the most advanced societies in the world.

Throughout his long lifetime of introspection, Narayana Guru's philosophy evolved from one virtually indistinguishable from the classicism of Śaṅkara to a radical vision that was uniquely his own. Whereas the ultimate analysis of India's ancient schools was that this world is unreal and the Absolute alone is real, the Guru decided that falsifying the world around us was not only invalid but led to a state of mind which allowed all the evils of religious corruption to overwhelm the world's innate beauty, in the same way that parasitic vines engulf and often kill the trees on which they grow.

In the ninth verse of the One Hundred Verses of Self-Instruction, Narayana Guru presents one of his favourite images: that of a contemplative sitting alertly under a great tree. Growing on the tree and simultaneously reaching out to engulf the contemplative is a proliferating vine: the beauteous profusion of creation. Many of us have become mesmerised by the swaying branches of the creeper, and have forgotten the magnificent tree which supports it, giving it shape and providing its nourishment. We surrender to the embrace of the enfolding vines. India in Narayana Guru's time, the late nineteenth century, was a stultifying example of this, a tremendously oppressive social structure held rigidly in place by fatalistic acceptance, with all people's hopes for happiness deferred to heaven worlds and future lives.

When we do this to ourselves we can feel lost and confused, because we have substantially limited ourselves by identifying with only a part of the whole. Therefore the Guru counsels us not to run away and not to try to destroy the creeper, but to sit alertly, uncaught, remembering the tree and renewing our freedom at every moment, while simultaneously appreciating how wondrously the situation remains in balance.

It is not easy to maintain a balance between the real and the unreal. It requires intense contemplation. We must remain awake to the changing situation, walking a fine line as it were, a razor's edge of equilibrium. When we relax our vigilance we drift to one side or the other, becoming caught in the deceptions of worldliness or, on the other hand, drifting away from involvement with the world, considering it of less importance than some abstract, hypothetical notion. Only a dynamic interplay between our assessment of the tree and the creepers produces a living, creative philosophy.

So instead of dismissing the world as an illusion born of maya, Narayana Guru's vision embraces the world as simultaneously true and untrue, both real and unreal at once. Resistant of but not impervious to scientific analysis, these elements mix together in a way that can only be described as a wonder, a wonder so perfect as to deeply inspire the contemplator of the mystery of existence. The dialectical solution to this paradox is the key to a lifetime of freedom.

Guru Nitya speaks to this point towards the end of his commentary:

> There is a generally held belief that because Vedanta treats this world as maya it dampens one's interest in everything here, making one ineffective. Many European critics think even now that the progress of India is retarded because of Vedanta's emphasis on maya as explaining away the need to do anything in this world. Narayana Guru restates Vedanta in such a way that every individual reaction, every aspiration which is ontologically valid, has a relevant place in life. There is no shying away from any responsibility or any efficient action, as long as it is done at the right time and in the right place. In this way we can say he corrects the notion of Vedanta in these verses.
>
> Now by verse 92 the proper status of the transactional world is well established. Life is valid. It only lacks validity when we are confused regarding the *pratibhāsa* and the *vyavahāra,* or everyday, aspects. *Pratibhāsa* means that within the transactional world there are possibilities for illusion. It's true those illusions are to be avoided, but this doesn't mean that because it gives rise to illusion we should neglect the necessary aspects of the ontologic world. That would be an unwarranted extrapolation.

This way of looking at the world charges us to engage in our own life to the maximum degree. Reality is not a substitute for something else — it is exactly what it is. There is no other place, no heaven or hell to which our actions are leading us. The implications of such a philosophy are profound, and indeed the Guru's life as one of the great emancipators of the human race clearly demonstrates the potential of those implications. Unfortunately, it is such a radical belief that few have been bold enough to embrace it. Humans are all so deeply grounded in escapist belief systems that even when we encounter such an example we are unconsciously drawn back to our fantasies of future payoffs, diverting and diluting our capabilities from involvement in the crucial issues of the present. Even within the mystery school of the Guru's own philosophy, the Narayana Gurukula, there is only an incipient appreciation of this revolutionary outlook.

Narayana Guru clearly foresaw the importance of a demonstrable ideology in keeping with the tenets of science, so that people all over the world could understand his message of unity and tolerance. With this end in mind, he sent one of his three preeminent disciples, P. Natarajan, the future Nataraja Guru, to do graduate work at the Sorbonne in France, in order to become well-versed in Western philosophy and science. The combination of Vedantic reductionism and scientific mental discipline had a profound effect on him, and he was later able to make a philosophic breakthrough, expressing the elements of Self-realisation in a revolutionary scheme of correlation that was free from localised or limiting elements. This allowed him to interpret the mystical truths of his guru in academically strict, scientific and mathematical terms. In order to perpetuate the teachings of Narayana Guru he started the Narayana Gurukula, loosely based on the model of the traditional Indian ashram.

Nataraja Guru was succeeded by his disciple, Guru Nitya, who excelled at interpreting the teachings in human terms, expressing them clearly and simply on the level of daily life. It was his role as a teacher of all who approached him with sincerity, including the Americans to whom the present commentary was given, that assisted him to hone his communication skills to a fine point. Through these three teachers, the parampara or hierarchy of the Narayana Gurukula has brought over 100 years of continuous contemplation to bear on the present work.

* * *

Ātmopadeśa Śatakam, the One Hundred Verses of Self-Instruction, is Narayana Guru's best known large-scale work. In it the timeless wisdom of Vedanta is presented in a loosely organised, somewhat informal manner reminiscent of the Upanishads. It was written in 1897, at the request of Narayana Guru's disciples, notably Sivalingadasa Swami, around the time he moved to Sivagiri, the ashram near Varkala at which he centered the last stage of his life. The imagery of the natural world from Narayana Guru's years in the wilderness makes up the core of its analogies. Each image, developed in from one to a small group of verses, is more an angle of vision or point of view than a finalised statement of absolute truth. The work is a sum total of many of these points of view. Originally there were some sixteen or eighteen more verses which the Guru later edited out, streamlining the work to a "modern" one hundred. It is widely read today in Kerala and surrounding areas, forming a significant part of the philosophical heritage of Southwestern India.

In his earlier writings, Narayana Guru had couched his vision in terms of the Hindu pantheon, whose symbols saturated every aspect of life in South India at that time. With further contemplation and insight, he moved steadily throughout his life towards a universal, scientific appraisal that would not be limited to any particular time or belief system, but would harmoniously take all of them into account. The present work was composed towards the end of this development, and so is nearly, but not completely, devoid of religious references. It was only with his last great book, *Darśanamālā,* along with some shorter works, that Narayana Guru's philosophy became fully scientific and completely free of regional imagery. A knowledge of the complex pantheon of Indian iconography is unnecessary for the appreciation of these later works.

It is a common idea in the modern world that lack of faith, meaning the lack of belief in a god or gods, is tantamount to moral and ethical collapse, and that humanity must live in fear of eternal punishment in order to behave correctly. The *One Hundred Verses* dispels this notion, demonstrating that a proper unitive understanding is all that is needed for the highest ethical standards to prevail.

Even in systems in which faith is not considered a valuable or even important element, a certain amount of faith *is* necessary in order to enter into a programme in the first place — the faith that the study will produce results. This is the faith exemplified in the opening verse, where a kind of mental obeisance is paid to a principle and a set of ideas which it is hoped will lead the aspirant to a return to the wisdom of the Self. This is a significant revaluation of the traditional Indian structure wherein a deity is invoked at the outset of any work. By the 100th verse the two counterparts — the individual and the Karu or cosmic core — are reunited as one in the embrace of the celestial pulse of aum, and the necessity for faith is gently and peacefully extinguished.

Humanity has a long history of listening to inspiring words of wisdom, nodding indulgently in vague appreciation, and then continuing on unchanged, wandering in confusion and bringing misery and fear upon itself. This stems from the methodological error of attributing authority to an outside agency, such as a hypothetical god or gods or worse yet a priestly caste, and relegating humans to an automatic and unremitting state of sin.

This unwarranted duality is effaced in Narayana Guru's philosophy. Each of us is seen to be of an equal status with all other elements of creation, and the responsibility for action and understanding lies solely within the individual. The world is unassailably united with the perceiver of it, and what is done to it is done to oneself. This is a radical revaluation that bestows a great freedom coupled equally with an unlimited responsibility.

* * *

The brightly shining centre of *Ātmopadeśa Śatakam* is the core or Karu. Unitive and singular, it is a dimensionless point. Like a seed it sprouts and grows into the flowers of the endless dualities of existence: day and night, the self and the other, sleeping and waking, pain and pleasure, and so on. The gist of the practice involved with this study is meeting and neutralising the manifold dualities by attuning oneself to the nondual core, the Karu, that infuses them with life. Dualism is surprisingly persistent and difficult to disarm. As it comprises practically everything conceivable and perceivable, it is almost always met on its own terms. Only by a profoundly mysterious act which cuts through the dualism, like the inward obeisance recommended by Narayana Guru at the very outset of this study, can the Karu be apprehended.

Arriving at the point where such a gesture is even possible, meeting and overcoming each obstacle, is where there is much work to be done. This is paradoxically why, despite the instantaneous dawning of insight, the road is at the same time long and arduous. The result of this effort, though, is the transformation of perception, the harmonisation of activity, and the infusion of happiness or bliss into every aspect of life.

The One Hundred Verses truly is a work that will transform dedicated students of its teachings, not necessarily by putting them in touch with some mysterious external force, but by helping them do away with excess mental baggage, replacing it with a wise and compassionate philosophy. A careful reading of the commentary, combined with an honest assessment of its relation to everyday life, will surely bear the fruit of increased happiness and satisfaction.

Because *Ātmopadeśa Śatakam* was intended as an instruction for Narayana Guru's disciples, it reveals a great deal of the way in which a guru imparts knowledge. In fact, it is difficult to imagine a more perfect medium for guru instruction. It is uniquely suited for use as a template or course of study. But unlike most tracts for individual use, there is a real necessity for the elucidation of a wisdom-preceptor, someone who has already explored and grasped the depths of the work, to guide the student. In this, Guru Nitya Chaitanya Yati is most eminently qualified. As he says in verse 98:

> Many people do not retrospect and examine all the significant aspects of their life in order to learn and grow. They just walk on. They are not confused only because they don't think about things, not because they have resolved them. But they are really no better than the person who retrospects and is confused.
>
> Such kind of a non-reflective way of life leads you to the most agonising kind of experience. The bright moments of

> life bring you, for a while at least, satisfaction in what you are doing. The next moment the whole thing appears to be futile, meaningless. Then come a few bright moments. Then doubt assails. The net result is living in a vicious circle.

The cryptic verses reveal many layers of meaning to the thoughtful contemplative; happily, the more casual reader now has Guru Nitya's own meditations, products of a lifetime of contemplation and study. Just as no perspective can totally encompass the Absolute, no commentary can fully explore the potentials in each of these verses. While Nitya's versions are by no means exhaustive, they are excellent examples of what can be gained from the verses by reflection.

Since no one angle of vision is sufficient to fully appreciate the Self or the Absolute, the work presents it in a number of perspectives. The visions are not strongly organised as with modern scientific treatises, but rather loosely affiliated along the lines of more ancient texts, such as the Upanishads, of which this could easily be considered a modern example. (For those who are interested in such matters, an in-depth structural analysis of *Ātmopadeśa Śatakam* is supplied in Nataraja Guru's commentary.)

There is always some degree of limitation in describing the indescribable. This is particularly to be expected when the subject of the study is affirmed at the outset to be "incomprehensible, indescribable, and indeterminate," as it is in this work. Because of this fluidity, any non-poetic, fixed statement of "truth" regarding the Absolute tends to be untrue to the extent it is inflexible or circumscribed. A more subtle and open-ended style is called for, which in its turn can bring about a greater depth of insight and certitude than any linear course of instruction.

To overcome this limitation of mental imagery a guru will often give example after example, some of them overlapping or even mutually contradictory, to be dialectically assembled until wisdom dawns in the disciple's mind. In the One Hundred Verses, Narayana Guru is presenting the indescribable Absolute from various angles of vision, piling up allusions and analogies until the reader can achieve a breakthrough in understanding. Guru Nitya uses this approach in his commentary also, so that the reader will find certain ideas that contrast with or even contradict previous ones, but are nonetheless true in their particular context. Contradiction is considered an important technique to force the disciple to seek his own interpretation, and to dig deep beneath the surface to find hidden areas of agreement between seemingly diverse factors.

There is a well-known story of some blind men and an elephant. A number of sightless people are trying to determine what an elephant is really like. The one touching the ear says, "Ah, it is like a rug!" The one touching the tail says, "No, it's more like a rope!" A third with a leg says, "It feels like a tree trunk to me!" They argue more and more vehemently about it, with each unwilling to give up his own limited point of view. Of course, each perspective is true up to a point. The blind men are a wonderful metaphor for religious dogmatics, kept ignorant by their arrogance in believing the small part they are in contact with is in fact the whole. But what if they decided to share their views with each other and incorporate as many perspectives as possible? In that case the more people involved, the more angles of vision brought to bear, the better the picture they would be able to develop of the beast they were examining.

Narayana Guru spent his life mediating exactly this kind of confusion among roomfuls of disputants, patiently demonstrating to everyone how their opinions could be coordinated and made into a useful programme. His motto was that people should always be prepared to "know and let know, rather than to argue and win." Such a plan underlies the structure of the One Hundred Verses as well. In it there are many angles of vision, all very carefully and thoughtfully coordinated and assessed. In other words, there are so many "blind men" here, that an accurate depiction of the elephant actually becomes possible.

This multifaceted approach is in fact an essential method of instruction in this type of work, being more abstract and less rigid than either a classical academic approach or a vocational course of instruction. The latter aim to reestablish pre-existing ideas, whereas Narayana Guru seeks to bring the student to an orientation from which he can discover truth for himself. Because of this, *Ātmopadeśa Śatakam* is not a book that offers a mechanical programme of steps to take to achieve some predictable result. Rather, it reveals the reader's own inner nature from a series of metaphysical perspectives. It is up to the individual to make as much as possible out of it. Remembering the reality of the Self is sufficient in itself to bring about a dynamic change of orientation in one's whole being. With the addition of Guru Nitya's commentary, the implications of such a reorientation in one's everyday life are made clear with an irrefutable certitude.

* * *

The commentator of the One Hundred Verses of Self-Instruction, Nitya Chaitanya Yati (1924-99), grew up on a matriarchal, communal plantation in rural South India, where his parents and relatives encouraged and inspired him in his intellectual and artistic endeavours. After many years of wandering and seeking, which brought him in contact with Mahatma Gandhi, Ramana Maharshi, G.H. Mees and others, he became the disciple of Nataraja Guru, a primary disciple of Narayana Guru and a thoroughgoing absolutist in his own right. After a stormy apprenticeship, Nitya became the third of the gurus in the lineage of Narayana Guru. He spent his lifetime teaching, writing, and interacting with many thousands of disciples worldwide. Among other things he established two ashrams of the Narayana Gurukula in the Western United States. Over time he became conversant with the unique needs and modes of thought of the West, which actually overlap the traditional Indian world very little.

In 1977, a mere two years after declaring categorically that he had only one student and that was himself, Nitya and a group of disciples moved into one floor of a house on the side of a hill in Portland, Oregon. Nitya was giving classes at nearby Portland State University, writing books and keeping up his voluminous correspondence, reading widely and studying science, art and philosophy, and all the while instructing a sizeable group of seekers. The place hummed with activity all day and most of the night. Towards the Fall, a plan was made to begin a course of instruction in *Ātmopadeśa Śatakam*, the One Hundred Verses of Self-Instruction of Narayana Guru. The students agreed to spend 100 days committed to the project, examining one verse in depth each day.

Nitya's plan was to meet for an early morning class, where one verse would be introduced and its meaning elucidated. Then, throughout the day, the students would ponder the implications in the midst of whatever activities they were engaged in, striving to bring the truth of the Guru's words into their everyday lives. In the evening they would all return for a discussion of what they had observed. This gathering usually had all the hallmarks of Upanishadic instruction, with disciples asking probing questions and the Guru expounding at length, often bringing personal elements to bear as well. Unfortunately, the evening sessions were never recorded. The morning meditations were taped, however, and transcribed later the same day. This book is the result.

A guru's talk is similar to a teacher's lecture, a more or less extemporaneous presentation with the background of memories and insights substituting for written notes. At times a guru is able to go further, practising a form of prophecy, or 'forth-speaking'. By gently lowering and quieting the ego, the wellspring of intuition is tapped and allowed to flow naturally to the surface. Coming from such trans-conscious depths, it is as if the ancient traditions are speaking directly through him to meet the needs of his disciples. The essence of this programme is described by Nitya in his commentary on verse 89:

> The whole universe is like a book, in that everything in it is a symbolic expression of higher truth. We are getting educated in that truth day after day. That truth grows, sustaining the meaning and value of life. If you turn to it, you see there is nothing devoid of knowledge. Such knowledge brings you to the oneness of everything.

In the classes that make up the present study, Nitya first led the group in several short chants to bring a state of attunement, then meditated intensely for a few minutes before beginning the talk. On many mornings the result was nothing short of revelatory, having a profoundly transformative effect on the gathered disciples, who then went about their daily tasks in a state of wonderment and ecstasy.

The students who came together at the incipient Portland Gurukula for the class represented a diverse sampling of Westerners of 1970s America. For those unfamiliar with that heady time, a brief sketch is perhaps in order. The social climate in America was very intense. People believed their beliefs with a vengeance and often preached them aggressively. The fact that humans in many parts of the world were visibly suffering and dying due to ideological turf wars lent an air of desperation to nearly every discourse. Young adults were everywhere filled with passion; many had left their homes in what was called the Generation Gap, to wander the country or gather in loose communal groups. Disbelievers in the Vietnam War clashed with true believers from World War II and the Korean War over issues of patriotism, and the young refused to accept the time-honoured hypocrisy of racial prejudice as well. Unquestioning obedience to authority was being supplanted by an as yet unguided independence, and drugs and multiple love-affairs accelerated the excesses of youth to a fever pitch. All socially accepted standards, the good along with the bad, were thrown away. Even those who sought sanctuary in meditative groups and retreats were quiet with a passionate intensity. In the anarchic moral psychosphere of the West, few realised that their lives were being shaped by their desires and personal beliefs as much as by external events. It was a time of chaos and excitement almost unimaginable now, in the sedate years of the twenty-first century.

In the midst of this moral hodgepodge and shimmering dream nightmare, Guru Nitya arrived in 1970. With a commanding presence and a visible inner certitude that marked him as unique, he began teaching in a side room of a church in downtown Portland, Oregon. Such was the interest in Indian philosophy in those days, that fledgling KBOO radio taped and broadcast his class on the Bhagavad Gita to listeners all over the city. It was quickly clear that his intensity was more than a match for the confusion around him, and he built a small but focused group of followers.

Some years later this group, augmented by seekers from around the United States, and Australia and India as well, gathered together and rented a house in Hall Street, less than a kilometer from the site of Nitya's first Gita class in Portland. The heterogeneous group was made up of doctors, teachers, writers and other artists of various stripes, blue collar workers, householders, and mendicant wanderers.

Early in his adulthood, Guru Nitya had been told by an

astrologer that throughout his life he would be surrounded by women, artists and madmen. To an Indian in mid-century, the idea of women following a guru was much more unbelievable than even artists or madmen, but in this case the stars turned out to be right. Many women were attracted in part by Nitya's charisma and the Narayana Gurukula's philosophy of sexual equality, and became a powerful presence there. Women, artists and madmen would be a fair assessment of the makeup of the disciples at Hall Street. In fact, many fell into more than one category! A number of students lived in the house, and many more came from all over the area to spend their days in the congenial environment, rising in the dark to arrive in time for the six o'clock morning class.

The one uniting factor in all the students was a strong desire to understand themselves and their place in the universe. But in a situation where so many different people are brought together in such an intense environment, there are often a number of problems that come up. Intrapersonal and interpersonal conflicts form part of the backdrop of the commentary of the One Hundred Verses. The Guru often addressed these issues directly at other times, but he also took pains to point out the relevance of the day's verse to the problems that were raised by the people around him. This brought the value of the teachings home in terms that could be easily understood by everyone. Without this process of relating subtle truths to the world of concrete dilemmas, the teachings remain an academic exercise, to a degree sterile and abstracted. Their very importance is measured by how much they influence a student's actual life.

Although he transcended religion for himself, Narayana Guru always embraced its value for others. He repeatedly said, "Whatever the religion, it is good if it makes a better person." The implication is that abstract beliefs are of no value in themselves, only in whether and how they lead us to improve ourselves. Drawing direct connections between ideas and their implementation was also a keynote of Nitya's teaching style.

So, why do we make a search for truth in the first place? What is it that motivates some people to leave their comfortable habit patterns and seek self-improvement? Nitya describes this situation with great economy in his commentary on verse 92:

Because of the obscuring aspects of prakriti we spoke of earlier, the true nature of the Self is veiled to different degrees on different occasions. At times the veiling principle can be easily removed, and at other times it persists for a long time, leading you to get involved in more action.

There is no time when the aspiration to be with our own true nature is not with us. Our seeming alienation from it comes not in reality but in the individuated forms of our consciousness. When the Self manifests itself with a body, the body identity acts as a colouring or conditioning agent. This is the first veiling principle. Because of it, part of consciousness feels as if it is segregated from its true field, its true home, so it is always seeking to return to its native nature.

The inner quest continues in us, never leaving, perpetuated by the conditioning of the physical body. In reality nothing is alien to us, everything belongs to the Self and the Self is existence through and through. So in every existential factor there is a possibility of discovering the ananda aspect of the Self. This is why the mind is again and again drawn to individual things, people, events, possibilities. The existential aspect and the ananda aspect have become linked in our awareness, and are continuously operating within us.

So we have a great bifurcation or division into two: an outer manifestation where action never ceases, and an inner manifestation where the quest for being with our own true Self is also going on continuously. The Guru says what seems to be action outside is only an external reflection of this incessant quest we are feeling inside. All actions which happen outside mirror in themselves what is happening inside, that is, the eternal quest.

Regarding Guru Nitya's own inner quest, he himself underwent a transformation during the teaching of the Hundred Verses, finally emerging from the long shadow of his brilliant guru Nataraja to shine in his own light. Although he had been a first rate teacher for many years, it was always with at least a tinge of presenting the wisdom of someone else. He was a preeminent interpreter of the great thinkers of history. One can still sense this in the first six or seven verses: while exceptional they nonetheless have a *constructed* feel, with Nitya bringing in Kant and Sankara and the Upanishads to bolster his carefully thought out arguments. After this there is a loosening up, a freeing of the style, as an inner force begins to surge to the fore. Somewhere around the fifteenth verse, psychic gravity has increased to the point where a fusion reaction commences. Ideas of supreme brilliance pour out in a lucid cascade. A carefully prepared pyre has finally been fully ignited. Nitya is no longer mediating the guru-expression, he has become the Guru.

* * *

The format of the 100 verses is used to instruct disciples as much as to elucidate the text. This also shapes the commentary, with the guru heightening and bringing focus on certain areas while de-emphasising certain others, simultaneously bringing it to life in a way an academic version never could. Such a technique provides an interesting "inner commentary," while at the same time using the work as it was truly intended to be used: as a method for a guru to instruct disciples and other aspirants.

The careful reader should be able to deduce the inner teaching being presented to the students in the class, by visualising the images which are being evoked, and how they are put together to make an almost symphonic composition on top of the structural material. Taking the time to make the images come alive in the mind is the only way to reveal the full depth of the subject. For the listeners in the original class this visual imagery was often more real than the actual words that were heard. Not infrequently the flow and clash of the images, presented in the lively fashion of a highly animated teacher, produced a state of exaltation or sense of great peace by the end of the class, at other times jolting the students out of their complacency to spend the day in critical self-inquiry.

Occasionally there is a reference which seems to have no referent. During the time of the class in the Hall St. house, meetings and discussions were underway all day long. After meditating on the verse of the morning throughout the day, the class would meet again in the evening for another talk and group discussion. Some of the seemingly ungrounded references are to ideas brought up in these other encounters, and are left in because they are valuable points to ponder even without a specific connection to the text.

Another element that distinguishes this commentary from dry philosophy is the pervasive underpinning of love between the teacher and the taught, and the deeply felt concern and respect between friends in the class. To retain a sense of this in the present work we have included some of the colloquial elements that are an inevitable component of any oral course of study.

Much is lost in transcribing an oral presentation to a written form. Intangible elements like gestures, smiles and frowns, and so on, were a very important part of the class, and are impossible to indicate with the written word. For the maximum appreciation of this commentary, the reader should read slowly and with mental "inflections," which will perhaps bring out some of what was originally conveyed by gesture or tone of voice.

The most profound of these invisible elements were the moments when the Guru severely criticised the students as a group. The sense of tension and alarm imparted to the class resembled that of an immanent thunderstorm, and literally galvanised the class into a more concentrated attention.

Perhaps the most lamentable loss, though, is the tremendous amount of humour with which Guru Nitya taught. Lightheartedness and humour nearly always infused the commentaries. A number of statements, which might otherwise appear rather severe, were given with a disarming laughter or an obvious physical exaggeration that added an invisible but essential dimension. His jokes were wry and amusing rather than obvious, and are very likely to be missed when read over. What may look like a straightforward, illustrative story was probably told with an air of delight and vivaciousness. Some intense and pointed truths were mitigated by a lighthearted tongue.

The twinkle in his eyes at those times was occasionally counterbalanced by a look filled with lightning bolts. The ego is very clever to annex almost any teaching to its own glory, even teachings advocating its own dissolution. In this regard the spiritual ego is said to be most powerful and tenacious of all. One of the most important roles of a guru is to destroy this seemingly indestructible form of ego, since the individual is virtually helpless to do it on his own. The disciple implicitly grants the guru the right to try to at least shrink his ego, which often requires drastic measures. A few of the verse commentaries have this tone, which may strike the reader as a far cry from the safe and unchallenging environment of the modern schoolroom.

This almost ferocious self-examination stands in decided contrast to the ego-friendly approach, as in much of the so-called New Age spirituality, for example. The former exemplifies the kind of critical thinking that has long been considered essential to a successful search for truth, while the latter is often characterised by nothing more than a superficial interest in intriguing concepts. Those who uncritically accept tantalising or lurid ideas are easily duped by exploiters of all kinds, of which the modern era abounds. The history of religious thought is as often a tale of battles against the dubious manipulations of a priestly caste for its own material benefit as it is a portrayal of a philosophical search for truth.

In this light the One Hundred Verses is a secret bomb aimed to destroy the hypocrisy and false ideology we carry around with us all the time. It appears on first impression safe and peaceful, a bit like a house cat sleeping in the sun, but it is in reality a powerful blast aimed at the root of our own false sense of a separate self. Not only does it attack the social mask we maintain for the dubious benefit of others, but, it exposes the taproot of our own self-delusion as well. Such self-delusion is the starting point for all the other masquerades and deceptions we obtrude into the social arena, and with its demise all other pretenses wither and fade.

* * *

Ātmopadeśa Śatakam is widely known in South India, and its implications are certainly more apparent to someone with a background in Indian ideology, but a work like this can only be fully appreciated with the help of a commentary from one who has thought about it for many years. For Westerners the cryptic nature of many of the verses, even after several generations of refining their translation, makes them almost totally obscure standing on their own.

The verses do make much more sense in their original Malayalam than when they are translated into English. Their koan-like appearance is due in part to the difficulty of encapsulating a rich terminology into a language which lacks words for many of the concepts involved. Sanskrit and its modern offshoot, Malayalam, often require paragraphs of explanation to reveal the nuances implicit in them — one of the main reasons for an extensive commentary.

Historically, the interpretation of word meanings has been an important element of Indian spiritual life. Since words convey ideas, and ideas lead to action, a slipshod interpretation of word meanings indicated an undeveloped orientation to the whole of life. From this perspective, the student is only learning to read the verses properly, coming to understand their meaning as the concepts are correctly sorted out. All the same, the number of Malayalam and Sanskrit terms dealt with in detail in the class has been reduced in the present work, in order to make the commentary more readable.

* * *

The most significant structural feature of the One Hundred Verses is its division into halves between verses 49 and 50. The first half deals with more or less pragmatic considerations of the seeker's relation with the world, while the second half is more focused on introspection and the contemplative's inner unfoldment. Nataraja Guru summarises this in his own commentary.[1]

> With this fiftieth verse which marks the centre of the hundred verses of the composition, when read together with the immediately previous one, we have to note that there is a change-over from one aspect of Self-instruction to another. The change-over could be described philosophically as passing from the ontological to the teleological.
>
> Verse 49 ended on the note that one should settle down in inner peace of mind. Those aspects of Self-realisation that

1. *One Hundred Verses of Self-Instruction*, Gurukula Publishing House; Varkala, Kerala, p.167.

> are most conducive to this peace as understood in this contemplative context have been treated of by the Guru in a certain methodological and epistemological order. In both the halves of the work we notice that the topics discussed are around factors of subjective import as the subject-matter of the whole composition would warrant. Introspection however becomes affirmed deeper in the second half as deeper recesses of the Self are brought up into view and scrutinised more carefully where again the reader would profit by noting the inward approach to the subject-matter. Cosmology and psychology enter into the structure of the verses in their own manner, and one is to be understood in terms of the other. A contemplatively neutral psycho-physical method and theory of knowledge, besides an axiology or science of values, all viewed in an absolutist sense, are implied in the verses as they now pass on to the latter half of the work.

Despite Nitya's deferring to his Guru's commentary in the foreword, the present book is the definitive one for the Western reader, at least. Nataraja Guru made few concessions to the beginning student, and spoke the language of serious philosophy rather than everyday English. His work is more properly viewed for most as an adjunct to the present one, which someone seeking another layer of insights might seek out for its structural analysis and contemplative rigour. Nitya himself has also written a shorter commentary on the One Hundred Verses, *Neither This Nor That But . . . Aum*, which, by pinpointing the essence of each verse, can be a very useful addition to the study as well. But without any doubt, the commentary in *That Alone* goes to the heart of this epochal work.

* * *

Ātmopadeśa Śatakam literally means 100 verses of Self-instruction in Sanskrit. A *śātakam* is a work of 100 verses. The word atma, here translated as Self, is used by Narayana Guru as it was used in the Upanishads. Often translated as soul or oversoul, meaning a universal spirit, it is here understood as a neutral matrix in which everything comprising the world has its existence. The states of consciousness are mere epiphenomena flickering through it. In this work at least the individual concept is written as 'self' while the more general or absolute is written 'Self'.

Upadeśa is an instruction given by a guru to a disciple. (When the 'a' and the 'u' are combined between *ātma* and *upadeśa* in Sanskrit they become an 'o'). *Ātma-upadeśa* is by no means referring to self as an ego or individual. The work is not intended for teaching oneself, as in "self-help manual." Rather the reference is to instruction *on* the Self or the Absolute.

It is important to understand the distinction between self and Self, which at some level is arbitrary or even false. This is a key concept in the 100 verses. The Self is akin to the collective unconscious, coequal with God or the Absolute, while self refers to the ego or the individual. Curiously, the word atma carries this same dual character in Sanskrit.

From a dualistic perspective, the terms appear very wide apart, as in God and the individual. As the ideas become increasingly refined they move closer together, eventually converging in unity. They have become identical, in the same way the individual in essence *is* God or the Absolute.

The following description by Dr. Peter Oppenheimer from his foreword to Nitya's book *Meditations on the Self* is an excellent summary of the differences between the self and the Self:

> Light is one. Though it can radiate as many rays, reflect its image onto many mirrors, and become multicolored when passing through prismatic mediums, it remains one self-same light. . . .
>
> When we say, 'my mind'; 'I change my mind'; 'I witness my mind', we are recognizing a central core of the light reflected in the mind which radiates its light outwards and to which in turn all impressions converge. This point of reference is, in the West, called the *ego*. It may be referred to as the self with a small 's'. It can be compared to the image of the sun mirrored on the surface of a lake; it is not the sun itself. When ripples and waves disturb the surface of the lake, the bright image of the sun throbs, changes and gets distorted.

> Similarly, when the mind is restless and subjecting itself to the many possible surface agitations, then the light of the Self mirrored in it becomes distorted, and the notion of I becomes unclear and unstable. Thus one's self-identity expands and contracts. Because it is circumlimited, changing and transient, we give this notion of I the label of self with a small 's'.
>
> The Self with a capital 's', on the other hand, is unlimited, unchanging and eternal. Like the sun in the firmament, the Self is never tainted or colored by the prismatic mediums through which it passes; it is never dimmed by the opacity of the mirrors that reflect it; and it is never disturbed by the surface agitations of the bodies on which it shines. It is this one pure *light* that is lending its absolute reality to all realities; it is this one all-witnessing *eye* that is lending its total vision to illuminate all partial visions; it is this one unchanging *value* that is lending its pure bliss to be the value behind each and every value.
>
> Darkness has no positive existence of its own. It is merely the absence or negation of light. In the same way, ignorance is nothing but the absence of knowledge, and suffering is the negation of beingness. It is only the self-luminous light of the Self that can dispel all darkness and burn away the dross of all ignorance, so that what remains is the existence of the knowledge of a joy of fathomless depth.

A group of terms, sattva, rajas and tamas, appear here with no introduction, since they had been discussed extensively prior to the beginning of the study of this particular work. They are the three states or modalities of nature, the gunas, and as such are all reflections, effects of the one cause. Sattva is the transparent mode, clearly reflecting the essential nature of things and situations; rajas is the translucent mode of colourations and interpretations; and tamas is the opaque state of darkness and regeneration. The effect of the alternation and intermixing of the gunas on one's state of mind is very important. Seekers traditionally have emphasised adherence to *sattva* and attempted disassociation with rajas and tamas in an imagined purificatory process, but in the philosophy of Narayana Guru (and indeed going back to at least Patañjali) each is to be seen as having a rightful place in a balanced interpretation of life. The subtleties of their interrelations are discussed throughout the work, receiving a final clarification in verse 88.

Narayana Guru's placement of rajas and tamas on a par with sattva is another significant revaluation in his philosophy. Overemphasis on sattva, the so-called "spiritual" behaviour, is an essential building block of the spiritual ego. What others have decried as "mirror-polishing," perfecting one's ability to flawlessly reflect the divine through non-attachment, Narayana Guru has described in his down-home vernacular as an attempt to wash the lather out of soap. Lather is a part of soap's true nature, so no matter how long you wash it, the lather keeps on coming just as long as there is still soap.

The idea is that "getting rid" of much of life is a tragic misunderstanding. Life is the very expression of the divine, and as such is to be exalted rather than transcended. Where spiritual novices seek to kill off their own desires, the Guru wants us to reattune ourselves to the Karu shimmering at the heart of every aspect of life, including our needs and desires. Guru Nitya sums up this point in verse 93:

> The way the Absolute manifests is through each individual desire. In the desire you can see the mark of the Absolute. So all desires are to be seen in the Absolute, and the Absolute is to be seen in each desire.
>
> Of all earthly pleasures for human beings and other animals, the one that most excels is when a couple is in the deep embrace of love, experiencing orgasmic ecstasy. But the Upanishads say that experience is as nothing compared to the coupling of the cream of your intellect with the Self in the cosmic embrace. When that happens it is as if you have all the embraces of the world. You are in eternal union. It is this eternal union with the Self that you should see reflected in all other forms of embrace.

> It may be just the eye caressing a flower or the finger giving a tender touch of loving care, but you should be able to see in it the coming together of the essence of your own life with the totality. The individual essence and the cosmic essence merge into one another. What pulls these two together is desire — a *priyam* or endearment — but it is that which brings you to the ultimate release, the absolute perfection.
>
> In this verse, from an ontologic ground the teleologic finality of the soul's search is brought to its complete perfection. As the Brihadaranyaka Upanishad says, "This is a man's highest path. This is his highest achievement. This is his highest world. This is his highest bliss."

Preparations are now complete, and the reader is invited to enter the mystical path of *Ātmopadeśa Śatakam*. It is a pathway of great beauty and growth, a way that changes the explorer as it is followed by stripping away excess baggage and lightening the load at every stage of the journey. It can be entered into easily, with a modest effort coupled with the determination to push through the accretion of undergrowth clogging its first few steps. Beyond, the way becomes clearer the farther it is followed. The path can be tread for a little way or for a lifetime. All that is gained upon it can never be lost, while all that is lost should have been thrown away in any case. Aum.

Scott Teitsworth
Portland, Oregon, 2003

Verse 1

aṟivilumēṟiyaṟiññitunnavan ta-
nnuruvilumottu puṟattumujjvalikkum
karuvinu kaṇṇukal añcumuḻḻatakki-
tterutere vīnuvaṇaṅṅiyōtiṭēṇam

Permeating the knowledge which brilliantly shines
at once within and without the knower
is the *karu;* to that, with the five senses withheld,
prostrate again and again with devotion and chant.

The first verse begins with *aṟivilumēṟiyaṟiññitunnavan,* one who transcends empirical knowledge. Empirical knowledge is knowing something through personal experience or direct perception. First meditate on this. Watch your awareness pass through you as a stream of consciousness. Identify your status as the knower. For instance, when you say "I know; I am the knower," have a conscious awareness of yourself as the knower of both the 'I' in you as well as the object of your awareness.

As you read, notice how your consciousness penetrates into the meaning of what is written here. It is as if you are entering a room and becoming acquainted with whatever is in it. Similarly, you enter into the word content and become familiar with the concept it presents. When you look at an object you are not only seeing a form, you are also entering into the essence of it and knowing it as transformed states of your own consciousness.

In English, the word 'experience' implies an interaction between the knower and what is known. In Sanskrit the word for experience, *anubhava,* means becoming likewise. It is not an interaction between the subject and object, but a transformation of the subject. You as the knower are transforming your consciousness of the moment into what is known. In the present context, experience should be understood as a subjective transformation. It is "in-formation" in the true sense of the word.

There is a state of knowing in which you become oblivious of your personal involvement as the knower. When you are fully engaged in an experience you are not simultaneously thinking of yourself. Ideas such as "I am knowing, I am enjoying," etc., only come when you ruminate on your mental states or communicate them to someone else. Otherwise there is just knowing by itself. It is the structure of the language into which we put our thoughts that creates differences between thoughts and things. For example, if you see a bird in a tree you don't think it is happening inside your head as an occurrence of knowledge, you see it as a bird "out there." Then the known itself is both the knowing and the knower. It is as if the knower is interjected into the known. You don't have to struggle in order to bring what is known into you, or to fuse the knower into the known. It all happens spontaneously and instantly.

In this verse Narayana Guru refers to the dichotomy between the world outside and the world inside. The best way to understand your inside world is to close your eyes and restrain your other senses. When your senses are not put into operation you experience only the subtle sensations of passing ideas, inner urges and conscious volition which constitute your inner world.

Closely watch your consciousness and examine what takes place when you say "I am the knower," "This is knowledge," and "This is known." What do you experience that is called the knower within you? Where is the separate thing called knowledge? The object of knowledge may be seen as everything other than the subject. Although these are seemingly separate entities, in terms of consciousness there is no differentiation. On all such occasions, what you experience is a single consciousness undergoing different modulations. Here knower, known and knowledge refer only to aspects of your personal and private experience. They take place within your own awareness as mere transformations.

The key word in this verse is *karu*, which is both definable and indefinable. It is ultimately to be understood as the Absolute, the primeval cause, the universal Self, and the "nature that is naturing." Its literal meaning is 'mold'. The blacksmith uses a mold into which he pours molten metal to form a cast of an image or vessel. In a bird's egg there is a kind of mold contained in its genetic code. Out of this mold comes the fledgling bird, which eventually transforms into an adult. Human beings also come from a mold that has in it the blueprint of the chromosomes. Any effect has a mold — its cause. The mold of an actualisation is its potential. The mold of knowledge is consciousness. The mold of articulated thought is language. Words are the mold of meanings. The mold of material things is energy. The mold of energy is the law that controls and directs it. Thus everything in this world, ranging from the most subtle to the most gross, has its own corresponding mold. The generalisation of all of these is called Karu.

In another sense, that which gives truth and meaning to consciousness and fills it with content is Karu. When it is understood as that which manifests, or as the "nature that natures," it has the status of immanence. As references to the mold cannot always be confined to its specificatory aspects, it is also to be understood as the transcendent. It is immanent in universal consciousness and it transcends individual comprehension.

The Guru wants us to understand Karu in both these senses at the same time, without shifting the emphasis from one to the other. If we can do this, the earth we see here is really earth, water is water, man is man, and tears and smiles are tears and smiles. This is what Guru describes as that which shines brilliantly outside. All these external facts belong to the universal concrete. Just as the Himalayas, the Alps and the Rockies have been "out there" for millions of years, physical, chemical and biological transformations have been going on for billions of years with unbroken continuity. The traditions and social customs of comparatively later periods are also part of the same external reality. When the classical scientists termed matter as everything external, it was meant more or less in a metaphorical sense. The word 'matter' is derived from the Latin word *mater*, which means 'the mother'. The mother is another form of Karu. She gives birth to new possibilities.

At this stage we can ask, "What is it that makes a mold a mold, a Karu a Karu?" In the order and meaning of things we see a correspondence that tallies with the operation of our reason. We can understand a mold or a cast only in terms of the meaning it presents to our reason. When we reduce the visible in terms of the calculable, we can see a meticulous adherence of reason to a mathematically precise harmony. We are compelled to think that there is something similar to reason operating in whatever we understand as the mold. Later in these verses we will come across a definition of the Self as the knowledge that knows, even when there is nothing else to illuminate it other than itself. In that sense we can say the Karu is the Self.

In Narayana Guru's *Guhāṣṭaka,* he defines Karu as (1) the truth that has no other foundation while itself being the foundation of the entire world; (2) that which is modulating as the attributes of the flux of becoming, both as the known and the knower, and at the same time transcending all modalities; (3) the womb of all while having no womb for itself; and (4) the pure duration that is generating the flux of time.

The philosophy of Spinoza is very close to what is contained in the first verse of *Ātmopadeśa Śatakam.* What Narayana Guru calls Karu appears in the philosophy of Spinoza as substance. The substance of Spinoza is self-founded and self-established; it includes within it all matrices of causes and effects. Spinoza gives two attributes to substance: extension and cogitation. In Vedanta, extension is called *vyāpti.* Spinoza's concept of extension appears in the Guru's verse as 'outside', and his idea of cogitation is akin to 'knowledge' as it is used here. The phrase "at once brilliantly shining," comes in Spinoza's philosophy as *omnia.* Furthermore, what Narayana Guru terms as *arivilumēri* is the same as Spinoza's *intellectus infinitus; uruvilum* is the same as *motus et quies; purattu* corresponds to r*es particulares; ottu* is the equivalent of *facis totius universi.*

The unitive vision expressed in this verse is becoming more and more recognised by modern day scientists. It is very similar to the Copenhagen interpretation of quantum theory given by Heisenberg and Niels Bohr. As a starting point they divide the physical world into an observed system, which is identical with Guru's term *puṟattu*, outside; and the observing system, which combines in it what Guru terms *aṟivilumēṟi*, permeating knowledge, and *uruvil*, within. Even David Bohm, one of the main opponents of the Copenhagen interpretation, expresses a position which comes very close to the world vision presented in this verse by Narayana Guru:

> One is led to a new notion of unbroken wholeness which denies the classical idea of analysability of the world into separately and independently existing parts. . . .We have reversed the usual classical notion that the independent 'elementary parts' of the world are the fundamental reality, and that the various systems are merely particular contingent forms and arrangements of these parts. Rather, we say that inseparable quantum interconnectedness of the whole universe is the fundamental reality, and that relatively independently behaving parts are merely particular and contingent forms within this whole.[1]

You are obstructed from knowing this continuous process because of the intervention of the constant awareness "I am, I am, I am." You have to tame and humble this aggressive 'I'. Think of the 'I' as of no worth other than that of an excellent tool. It has no power of its own to create anything. It is only a speck of total consciousness that becomes ego-identified. Let that I-consciousness prostrate before this one supreme cosmic consciousness which is becoming everything. That will help bring about the normalisation of your perspective.

Narayana Guru tells us: "the supreme knowledge is shining at once as the inner world and the outer world with great resplendence." It is blazing as this universe, as the Self, as knowledge, as emotions, as value-appreciations. We are to turn with reverence to that universal yolk, to that cosmic egg of consubstantiation.

If you want to meditate on this verse, focus its light on whatever happens during the course of the day. Repeat the verse in your mind. Feel the great wonder of your own consciousness that is continuously modulating as the world outside and the idea inside. Do this while

---

1. D. Bohm and B. Hiley, 'On the Intuitive Understanding of Nonlocality as Implied by Quantum Theory', *Foundations of Physics*, vol. 5 (1975), pp. 96, 102.

you are looking at things, talking to another person, and doing your daily routines. When you sense that wonder, it will spontaneously produce in you a great reverence for the universal within you. This will naturally make you grateful that you can think, see, feel, know and do, and thus participate in the cosmic manifestation of the Absolute. Is it not wonderful that the manifestation outside can reciprocate your innermost dreams and desires?

In the process of our sophistication we have lost our natural innocence, our capacity to stand in awe and wonder. We have to cultivate that sense of wonder once again. It is a wonder that this body that was lying like a log of wood on a bed a few hours ago is now sitting here and reasoning. It is a wonder that it can witness a multidimensional universe which was not present during that sleep. The subtle depths from which the contents of dreams themselves come are a wonder. It is a wonder that I can talk to you and you can listen to and understand me.

You have done away with all your sense of wonder through acts of analysis and labelling. After having filled the pigeonholes of your mind with hoarded labels, you think you have become wise. But these labels are blocks which only increase your blindness. You have become devoid of the sense of the numinous. If you say 'God' and there is no feeling in you, if you say 'Absolute' and you don't become overwhelmed, be sure you have no idea of God or the Absolute. You need to rehabilitate your numinous essence.

For a baby every moment is a wonder. Out of their wonder-filled minds, small children can create so much beauty. It is yet a wonder, a joy, that we can see and touch each other. The thrill of that wonder is the adoration I am speaking of. You have to cultivate an attitude of devotion to that known and unknown Magician who makes all this possible. Śaṅkara says that of all the things which can bring emancipation to a person, there is nothing like devotion. It is the supreme way to liberation. Devotion is wholeheartedness; it is absolute love.

See this wonder that is being manifested around you and within you moment after moment without turning away from any of your normal duties. Through the whole day — while you eat, walk, work, go to sleep — ponder over this wonder with devotion. If you make notes of what you see and feel, and then read them in the evening, you will be surprised to discover how many treasures you have admired in a single day.

With this verse you are entering into an intense spiritual discipline.

Verse 2

***karaṇavumindriyavum kalēbaram to-
ṭṭaṟiyumanēka jagattumōrkkil ellām
paraveḷi tanniluyarnna bhānumān tan-
tiruvuruvāṇu tiraññu teṟiṭēṇam***

The inner organ, the senses, the body,
the many worlds known by direct perception —
 everything, when contemplated,
is the glorious embodiment of the sun that shines in
 the sky beyond;
this should be known through relentless search.

Take your mind back a few hours to when you were in deep sleep. At that time there was no consciousness. This can be analogically related to the world being completely merged in darkness. As dawn comes, things slowly begin to appear. Similarly, the deep unconscious in you slowly moves, and a vague awareness of consciousness comes. When that awareness becomes assertive, questions come to your mind. "Is it morning? What time is it now? What am I going to do today?" There is always some question coming up in your mind. This interrogative aspect of consciousness is called *manas*.

According to Vedantins, there are four categories of wakeful consciousness. The first is this questioning aspect, which is an attempt to assign meaning to whatever confronts you. Meaning is given to sense impressions or stray ideas by relating them to something already known. A new impression or idea is oriented in relation to previously experienced situations. When it is thus given a formal fixation, it finds a place in your scheme of understanding. In order to do this, you recall the memories which seem to be associated with what is being presented to your senses or mind. This faculty employed in the recall of memory is called *cittam*. It is the second category of consciousness.

After the relevant memory associations are revived, they are then used to decide the nature of the current impression or idea. The third category of consciousness is a faculty used to predicate the subject appropriately. It is called *buddhi*.

You are in a state of suspense until you make a judgement on the value of the new stimulus. Once its nature is decided, you feel either satisfied or disturbed by it. This feeling affects your personal identity in a variety of ways. The fourth category of consciousness is the affectivity of the ego, called *ahamkāra*. *Aham* means 'I'. You relate your personal experience to a central consciousness in you called 'I' which is affected in terms of pain, pleasure or indifference. With this, one unit of impression has been almost instantaneously processed regarding its significance to you. Taken all together, these four aspects — *manas, cittam, buddhi,* and *ahamkāra* — are called *karaṇam,* the dynamism of the psyche.

After going through the process of questioning, recollecting, reasoning and being affected, you pass on to the next stage: reacting to the situation. For this you need the use of your organs of perception and action. The senses, body and mind all come together in a confection which becomes a holistic action, monitored by the major urge, drive or interest that dominates that particular moment of your life. Each action-inaction complex contains a whole universe of interest. After one interest is fulfilled or thwarted, your mind moves on to another; thus you go from one world of interest to another in a continuous sequence. These worlds spring up from the awakening of the latent urges lying buried in the unconscious.

The external world is revealed to your eyes by the sun or some other physical source of light. All the visual images you see are only transformations of light. Similarly, there has to be a light from within for you to actually become aware of these visual images and other impressions. Just as visible things are transformations of light, what you experience as other persons, things and interests are all transformations of your consciousness.

You can profitably use this verse to detect your latent urges, hidden propensities, and even your basic drive. Your senses are bombarded with countless millions of stimuli, out of which only a very small percentage are consciously recognised and grouped together into meaningful patterns. Our minds cannot attend to many ensembles at a time. Usually only one is promoted to interact with an item of interest. In each encounter, you need to learn to detach your mind from its fixation with the heart of the situation, so you can make a mental note of the dominating interest that motivates either an action or a reaction. It is both intriguing and educational to discover the hidden motivations and strategies of your mind. This will loosen the compulsive hold that unconscious predilections have on your conscious ability to choose. The chain of associated ideas which your recall of memory evokes can even bring to light many childhood shocks that have become cankerous. When you come across the same attraction or interest recurring again and again with assertive and irrepressible dynamics, you can recognise it as your major drive.

Your basic drive expresses the principle characteristics of your matrix of vasanas, or incipient memories. Vasanas are the essences of consolidated memories, called samskaras. A samskara is a processed or cultured impression that remains with you for the rest of your life. When you are born, you do not come to this world as a clean slate, as John Locke presumed. According to geneticists, we carry many hereditary factors in our chromosomes which form the blueprints of our lives. In Sanskrit these are called vasanas. The Indian concept of vasana is a little more complex than the geneticists' version. Vasana roughly corresponds to what psychologists call instinct. The rishis believe that each of us inherits both a body from our parents and a preconditioned, individuated self from a previous incarnation. Thus there are vasanas that correspond to certain factors found in one's parents, such as propensities to mental diseases or physical ailments, and those that correspond to what is brought over from a previous life as refined causal factors processed out of the impressions, or samskaras acquired in that life. Both the genetic factor and the causal consciousness constitute the foundation of the present personality. Genetically, one's heredity is billions of years old. Psychically, heredity is ageless, because ultimately it is an integral part of universal consciousness, *saṁvit*, represented in this verse by the symbol of the sun shining in the sky beyond.

In the present verse, Narayana Guru is effecting a transformation of the individual's personal experience into a cosmic phenomenon. The author's intention becomes evident when this verse is read in the light of the opening verse of the first vision of his *Darśanamālā*:

> In the beginning there was non-existence indeed.
> Dreamwise then again, by mere willing,
> everything existent created He, the Lord Supreme.

Here, he attributes the manifestation of this universe to the latent potentials in God's mind, which he refers to as vasanas. In *Darśanamālā*, Narayana Guru pairs theology with cosmology, whereas in the present verse he is blending cosmology with psychology.

The psychic dynamism with which verse two begins, when traced back to its origin, will be revealed to have its archetypal mode in the very foundation of the natural order. In what we call cosmic evolution, Narayana Guru sees the operation of a universal intelligence instead of accidental events leading to random mutations. In the third and fourth lines, he instructs the aspirant to see all the items enumerated in the first and second lines as aspects of a cosmic principle which is both effulgent, as light, and a provider of substance for everything to manifest.

The Karu spoken of in the previous verse refers to that which is here called *bhānumān*. *Bhānumān*, sun, is derived from the word *bhān*, which means shining or brilliant. *Bhānam* is a word that can mean both 'light' and 'knowledge'. In St. John's Gospel, the Word is equated with God, and is described as both the material and the efficient cause of everything that is manifested here. The Guru is using the same concept of the primordial cause which has within it the intelligent scheme of the universe, and the substantiality that can be infinitely expanded into the myriad forms of the universe. The only difference is that he has dropped the theologic allusion to God. Instead, he uses an absolute principle which implies within it a cosmology and a psychology that have the same pattern or design for their respective unfoldments. The Guru expects the student to reflect as diligently as possible in order to understand all the minute details of the instruction given in each verse.

We have already seen that psychic dynamism includes the quaternion of mind, memory, intellect and the ego-factor. If these are to be seen as the gracious embodiments of "the sun that shines in the sky beyond," we should first of all fix the meaning of the words 'sun', 'sky' and 'beyond'. According to the order of the words in the original Malayalam, *para* comes first. We have translated *para* as 'beyond'. Although the word, when taken alone, can mean 'other' or 'beyond', it is also used in the sense of *param*, which means 'the highest', 'most excellent', 'greatest' and 'the Absolute'. *Veli*, the word translated as sky, also means 'the open'. The sky in which we see the physical sun is a closed system, whereas the sky or space to which the Guru calls our attention is infinite: the open, spaceless space in which there is no difference between the Absolute and the space in which it shines. It is a space that is spatialising, and not a space that is spatialised. It is in this material cause that we have to place the finalised expression of our mind, memory, intellect and ego.

The potential cannot be discerned in the way the actual can. By merely looking at a gene, one cannot say if it is going to be a black bee, a barley kernel, or a burly hippopotamus. Mind, which is the primary cause of all psychological phenomena, is similarly indiscernible.

Regarding memory, a crystal does not forget its geometrical form. You can dissolve and re-culture it a million times and it will always adhere to its previous shape. In the cosmic order of manifestation, the repetitive process reveals a built-in memory of everything which the entire sequence of physico-chemical transformation has previously undergone. The human mind belongs as much to nature as the design on the wing of a butterfly belongs to the gene structure of the caterpillar from which it emanates over and over again. Thus, the memory that functions within us is only a continuation of the cosmic principle of the economy of acquired know-how.

The intellect faces the problem of making categoric decisions. The laws of nature are imperative. They are precise to the most minute detail. The areas of indecision and heterogeneous functioning we see in human intelligence show the inadequacy of our methodology, which is unable to explain the more evolved in terms of the less evolved. The intelligence operating at lower levels of biochemical, physico-chemical and psychophysical levels is of a predetermined nature. At a higher level, the factor of free will arises. The free expression of the human mind should be seen as both the cream and the scum of the final unfoldment of nature. The nature we are referring to here is not infra-nature, but that which includes meta-nature and supra-nature as aspects of the nature of the cosmos.

We have already explained how the interest of an individual decides the selective structuring of the data coming from the senses. There is an instrumentality which decides the division of a cell and then governs its development from a fetus to a mature human being. Without this instrumentality, nothing can manifest. The same continues in a person as the ego. We have to see *karaṇam*, the psychic dynamism, as a gracious modulation of the primordial light which has transformed into this universe. We are using the term 'transformation' rather than 'evolution', because we are aware of the conceptual limitation that is now imprinted on that word after the advent of a theory of evolution which does not attribute to the cosmic principle of transformation an intelligence that is ontologically universal and teleologically purpose-oriented.

Verse 3

veḷiyiliṛunnu vivarttaminnu kāṇum
velimutalāya vibhūtiyañcumōrttāl
jalanidhitanniluyarnniṭum taraṅgā-
valiyatupōleyabhēdamāy varēṇa

Existing outside and, as specific modes, seen within,
the five elements, like sky, when contemplated,
should become like waves rising in rows
from the treasury of the watery deep, without any
separate reality whatsoever.

The symphony of music, the feast of colours, the fondling and gentle caressing of an affectionate friend, the relishing of delicious food and sweet aromas, make life on earth an unforgettable experience. Who would not want to come to this magnificent world again and again just to hear its music, see its beauty, be enticed by its fragrances, drink to the lees the sweetness of its promise, and cuddle it in a big hug of fond affection? Yet this is not all. When the head aches and the limbs are worn out, the heart is restless and the mind is murky, gentle sleep comes with sweet solace to throw a magic spell over the soul. Every impression of the world fades out. There is deep and profound silence. Not a thing stirs. Nothing is known. Peace reigns supreme. No one would regret it if that peace lasted forever. How blessed are we that we can go from the world of bounty and variegated richness to the world of profound silence and peace.

The uninformed minds of little people make a mess of this wonderful world because they take the wrong for right and right for wrong. There is a tricky blind spot somewhere in man's fate that makes him stumble and go into real tangents; this makes most things go badly with him. The world to which he has come to have a feast and celebrate his individuation turns into a nightmare. He sees around him only spiteful people with pitiless hearts, scornful of his intentions. The extremes of nature are against him. Diseases of all sorts plague his body and mind. He sheds pails of tears, curses fate for being born a wretched creature, and seeks to drown his disasters in the bottomless pit of the unconscious. This is the lot of most people, unfortunately. The Upanishads say: "Those who stray away are 'killers of themselves', and find themselves in a diabolic state enveloped by a blinding darkness."[1]

Here are the philosophers, who have sharpened the blades of their logic and are equipped with the laws of grammar and the regulations of rhetoric. They want to examine minutely the knower, the known and knowledge. The great master Śaṅkara proclaims that the effect has no reality other than that of the cause. Do you want to go all the way with him and have a scrambled egg instead of a chicken roast? Who doesn't know that the chick comes from the egg? If he is understood as sneering at the poor wretch who is fantasising a possible feast of phantom chicks, which is only in the phenomenal world of effects, who cannot say that the transcendentalist is not a wee bit wrong in the proper application of the sound laws of logic?

It might sound as though the philosopher is going too far, but don't be too impatient. Let us stay with him until he has his final say in the matter. Could there be two truths? That is a logical impossibility. Could truth be one thing in the morning and another in the evening? Certainly not. At least in principle we can agree that a truth without a second, without change, cannot have a beginning or an end. If there is not a second thing to compare it to, no qualities can be predicated of truth because predication implies the principle of comparison. If you cannot compare, you cannot judge. Further, such a truth does not permit any dichotomy within it, such as of knower and known. So we should excuse Śaṅkara for making an attempt to illuminate the source of illumination. As it has become imperative at this point to dismiss the duality of the subject and

1. Dr.K.B.Ramakrishna Rao, *Isavasya: An Invitation to Infinite Living* (Mysore University, 1977), p.13.

object, both Śaṅkara and his argument fade out into nothingness. Nor are we there, to know the rest of the procedure.

What now? Hmmm . . . .

No, there is hope. Here comes the philosopher Rāmānuja. According to his way of looking at truth, the chick walks, squeaks, cocks its head, looks hither and yon, scratches the dirt, pecks at grains and swallows worms. All these efficient functions are not seen in the egg. That means cause is not the whole reality. The whole, the total, should include not only the egg and the chick, but even the whole genealogy of the chicken family and the inestimable future of its propagation. According to him, truth is identical with experience and should not be tampered with by the limitations of logic. This makes things much better! Once again the world is restored, with all its gaiety, pomp and colours. Once again we can gather around the table and taste the delicious goodies.

Rāmānuja, however, lands us in another sort of trouble. This whole universe, from the far-off stars to our fingernails, is to be seen as the physical body of the Supreme Lord. Every atom of it is animated by the one divine principle, *nārāyaṇa*. If you are sensitive, this philosophy will raise your blood pressure, because you cannot put the kettle on the fire and boil a part of the Divine in it. When a man eats a man, he is called a cannibal. Has anyone coined a word for eating God?

But wait a minute! That cannot be true. No one would mistake a hard stone for strawberry ice cream. The world of experience cannot be a homogeneous whole. A pinprick on top of your nail is hardly noticeable, but a pinprick under your nail will make you howl. That means there is a qualitative difference between the degree of consciousness in a nail and the nerve endings of the skin or muscle. We do not think with our feet, but with our brains. The software of the brain is such a superb system that it can even appreciate and produce subtle values, like beauty.

We should not be fanatical in our craze for unity. It is far more convenient to think of a spirit that knows and a matter that is known. We can have a subject and an object clearly marked out. It is a neat arrangement that each of us has our own autonomous system with which to digest our food, and we can think our own private thoughts without them being peeped into by someone else. Madhva is the philosopher who agrees that the independence of truth prevails without being compromised by countless specifications of the differentiae which operate to account for all names, forms and functions, provided they are all treated as dependent factors.

As a separate individual I can boil my vegetables and drink my apple juice, while my friend cooks his steak and drinks his beer. This is certainly a clear indication of our freedom of will. How I wish I could have the same freedom in deciding not to grow or in deciding to suspend time for all eternity or have my own sunrise and sunset specially programmed, just like the little prince of Antoine de Saint-Exupery! Well, there is a limit. I cannot push my free will to that extent. This means I am not my master. Who is the master then? Here Madhva agrees with Rāmānuja that this world show is run by the one independent Absolute, which both call Narayana or Vishnu. What Rāmānuja calls *vibhūti*, or the innumerable spiritual, psychic, moral and physical qualities of the body of the Lord, are simply renamed by Madhva as dependent factors of the one independent Absolute, which he calls *tattva*.

Śaṅkara now reappears with a smile. He does not speak, but his profound silence gives assent to what Madhva says: "That alone is." At this point Narayana Guru whispers to us in his gentle voice, "Know all this: individual gold-crested waves, surging on the surface of consciousness, are inseparable from the oceanic treasury which is at once the independent and the dependent, the spirit and the body, the effect and the cause." What a relief! Now we can agree with all the great masters, and also appreciate our personal stands in relation to the transpersonal and intersubjective world of experience, as well as the nondual truth of transcendence.

In the present verse, Narayana Guru calls our attention to the external world with a reference to the classical notion of the five elements: ether, air, fire, water and earth. These are actual, objective realities, as well as symbolic representations of all that we experience in life.

Earth is the most gross of all the elements. The term refers to the actual solid ground, and also symbolically represents the physical and concrete aspects of life. Certain attitudes are even described as being earthy or "down to earth."

Water is not stiff and static like earth. It has the quality of flowing, and assumes the shape of its container. It easily mixes with liquids of like nature. It represents both the actual element water and the vital fluids. Our emotional life is sometimes compared to water. It has depth like the ocean, and yet our emotions fluctuate like surging waves. Jesus spoke of the water of life and the water that quenches the eternal thirst. The famous story of Jesus converting the water contained in six earthen jars to wine of great excellence is a good study of a symbol of transformation.

As we pass on from water to fire, we encounter a still more rarefied element. Fire is indispensable in our lives. Apart from visible fire, like the flame of a candle or the sun in the firmament, the whole universe undergoes transformation in the alchemic fire called thermodynamics. Just as a fire consumes everything in its path, our lower mind is ever curious, wanting to taste everything. The lower mind goes on licking the unconscious into conscious shapes. We have the gastric fire in our stomachs to digest our food, and the divine fire known as the warmth of the heart.

Next in the series is the element air. Just as fish live in water, we swim around in an ocean of air. It carries our life-giving breath, *prāṇa*. Air symbolises our psychic life. Its quality is touch. All the other elements share in this main characteristic of air. Smell is a stimulating touch in the nose, taste is a tickle on the taste buds of the mouth, and sight is the contact of light on the rods and cones of the retina. Even hearing is effected by sound vibrations touching the eardrums. No other quality has a wider span than touch. We experience it on the entire surface of the body.

Crossing the threshold from air to ether, we enter a world of mystery. It both is and is not. In a sense it is the space that allows objects to exist separately and distinctly. Space keeps items from all being squashed into a single dimensionless point in the same way that time is nature's way to prevent everything from happening at once. The Michelson-Morley experiment failed to prove that ether exists as a physical element, yet we cannot localise objects and juxtapose them into picturesque ensembles without somehow conceiving of space. In ether or *ākāśa* we find the link between the psychic world of the configuration of sound ensembles and the physical world of vibrations.

On the whole, the physical manifestations of earth, air, fire, water, and space, are taken for granted as objective phenomena. When we see each other, speak and listen to each other, fondly embrace or hatefully push away, we are sure we are interacting with an objectively valid physical world. But the study of a little science immediately topples these conventional notions. The various kinds of sound we seem to hear, whether musically resonant or dissonant, turn out to be manufactured mostly inside our brains as an interpretation of the vibrations that have tickled our eardrums. Sound vibration, as such, can never be studied in isolation from its interference with the psychochemistry of the brain. What is true of sound is also true of the other four senses. The vast space in which we see and hear all the objects of our perception is also projected by the mind. The whole process is called *vivarttam*, meaning the superimposition of mental images on an elusive ground which at best can only be inferred. This inference in most cases is no more than a presumption.

In spite of the subjectivity of the phenomena belonging to each person's private mind, there is an astonishing degree of public agreement with regard to the homogeneity of what we experience as the world. You seem to see what I think I am seeing; this prevents the world of transactions from collapsing in ruins. To account for this universality, philosophers imagine that all individuals' minds are made up of what Spinoza called the "thinking substance."

Instead of leading us into a metaphysical speculation of hair-splitting and logic-chopping, the Guru introduces us to the sense of wonder that can evoke in us a feeling of reverence and devotion to the Unknown. The Unknown presents itself to us as our own consciousness, which is continuously fed with a visual world of colourful panoramas and an enjoyable world of musical symphonies. The key word used here to describe the Absolute is *jalanidhi*, the oceanic treasury of inestimable value. Although Narayana Guru supports Śaṅkara's nondual philosophy, in the present instance his idea of the Absolute is very closely akin to

Rāmānuja's concept of the Supreme as a repository of all auspicious values.

The world of the five elements, which is experienced within yet recognised as being outside by an act of superimposition, should be understood as a series of waves of modifications of consciousness rising one after another from the divine treasury of an ocean of cosmic consciousness. Such a recognition will inevitably bring a mystical feeling of poetic appreciation that is bound to touch our spiritual heart.

The part we play in the creation of the world is not insignificant. We are co-creators with the Divine. Without us, the world would be without colour, sound, or any of the sensory qualities that we know. It would be an inert mass of no meaning. Yet, when individually taken, each of us is nobody. The possibility of a collective consciousness in which we participate should necessarily fill us with deep reverence and devotion for that which is at once the unknown and the only known.

The world we experience is like a feast of immeasurable abundance. The common man sees in it recognisable forms, admirable shapes, beautiful colours, and a perennial supply of things to gratify his several needs. Apart from the world's immediate presence, we also experience our memory of the past and imagination of the future. This gives it a vertical aspect of depth and height. If you are a poet you can find an infinite variety of symbols, allegories and ideograms with which to interpret the rich meaning of life. Artists will never exhaust the themes of inspiration presented by nature. Philosophers can endlessly ruminate on the world's hidden cause and its hypothetical purpose. For the scientist, every atom is literally a challenge to probe and investigate. The fact remains that no one goes outside their mind to experience or prove anything other than what is conceptually produced within their own prodigious brain. Sir Arthur Eddington recognises this fact and agrees that the physicist is not studying any physical entity as such, but only what can be conceptualised as a rational entity.

In Newtonian physics, the ultimate entities of matter were the autonomous and self-monitored atoms that were like loose grains of sand on a shore, just touching each other but getting no closer than that. As Fritjof Capra says in *The Tao of Physics*:

> The stage of the Newtonian universe, on which all physical phenomena took place, was the three-dimensional space of classical Euclidian geometry. It was an absolute space, always at rest and unchangeable. In Newton's own words, 'Absolute space, in its own nature, without regard to anything external, remains always similar and immovable.' All changes in the physical world were described in terms of a separate dimension, called time, which again was absolute, having no connection with the material world and flowing smoothly from the past through the present to the future. 'Absolute, true, and mathematical time,' said Newton, 'of itself and by its own nature, flows uniformly, without regard to anything external.'[2]

Today, the picture given to us is very much more like half-melted salt crystals in a saturated saline liquid; a boundary line can no longer be drawn between one thing and another:

> At the subatomic level, matter does not exist with certainty at definite places, but rather shows 'tendencies to exist', and atomic events do not occur with certainty at definite times and in definite ways, but rather show 'tendencies to occur'. In the formalism of quantum theory, these tendencies are expressed as probabilities and are associated with mathematical quantities which take the form of waves. This is why particles can be waves at the same time. They are not 'real' three-dimensional waves like sound or water waves. They are 'probability waves', abstract mathematical quantities with all the characteristic properties of waves which are related to the probabilities of finding the particles at particular points in space and at particular times. All the laws of atomic physics are expressed in terms of these probabilities. We can never predict an atomic event with certainty; we can say only how likely it is to happen.[3]

This is not only true of the inner structure of matter, but also of the

---

2. F. Capra, *The Tao of Physics* (Bantam Books, New York, 1975), p. 55.
3. *Ibid.*, p. 68.

boundary between matter and consciousness. It is as if everything is in everything else. It is from such a unitive philosophy or unified view of science that Narayana Guru calls our attention to the adorable Absolute.

Before us are two main possibilities, two directions we can go with our life. One is, we can retire from our consciousness and enter into the unfathomable depth of the unconscious. Every night we taste the joy of remerging with the totality, at least for the little while we are in deep sleep. Actually, joy is not the right word exactly, because in that state there is no pleasure or pain. The only quality is undisturbed peace. If sleep is very peaceful, death should be a state of everlasting peace. Unfortunately, though, we are afraid to die. The yogis have an alternative to death. They promise us an immortality which has the same quality as deep sleep, with one major difference. While sleep is retiring into the total inertia of matter, the yogi's absorption is one of entering into the boundless realm of spirit's unmodified consciousness. In both cases — sleep and spiritual absorption — bodily functions are reduced to a minimum.

To worldly-minded people, the prospects of sleep or spiritual absorption can look like poor substitutes for the excitement and promise of an outwardly directed life. The wakeful world of transactions has great visual attraction and many and varied rhythms and harmonies of music. We can get into communion with the co-dwellers of our earth. It is up to us to cultivate our liking for what can be painful or hazardous.

In the first verse, Narayana Guru asked us to turn to the Supreme, which he compared to a mold that is seen as manifesting into everything, both the world outside and the psychological reality inside. We were asked to prostrate before that nondual reality, which is neither cause nor effect and yet is always a cause changing into an effect. In the second verse, he compared it to a sun of supernal glory in the void of consciousness. In the present verse, the Guru wants us to know that we are emerging from the depth of the Absolute's treasury of immeasurable value as a wave of its manifestation, only to fall and merge once again with the Absolute.

To see life as a series of waves rising up and merging back to the ocean of All fills one's mind with beauty, peace and joy. If you do not know the world this way, then other people become symbols of threat or hostility. A unitive vision makes each of us the keeper of our brothers and sisters. Our hearts attract each other and souls merge with one another. In every person we meet we see a new opportunity, a new possibility, and a fresh avenue of friendship. In this verse, the Guru leads us to a meditation that can free us of all sense of separation. There is no longer any boundary between the self and the other. Gleefully we can jump and immerse ourselves in the oceanic treasury of wonder.

These are our two paths, the world of physical awareness and the world of spiritual absorption. If we are not in one, we are in the other. It is both beautiful to live and beautiful to die.

Verse 4

aṟivumaṟiññiṭumarthavum p̈mānta-
nnaṟivumorādimahassumātramākum;
viral̥taviṭṭu vil̥aṅṅumammahattā-
maṟivilamarnnatu mātramāyiṭēṇam

Knowledge, the object of interest,
and one's personal knowledge are nothing other than
mahas;
merging into that infinite, Supreme Knowledge,
become That alone.

Consciousness is like an ever-flowing stream. We do not always know the whole of it, since we tend to ignore causes and focus on effects. We hardly notice the contours of the riverbed, tending to look only at the effect it has on the surface. Within a limited purview this is not disastrous, but a river will occasionally enter into a gorge or a ravine and drop out of sight. Our experience is similar to this.

"Oh, here is my child," a mother thinks without thinking. It is not a mere idea. It fills her with a great joy. Although she does not say "I am rating this experience as a value," that is exactly what is happening. In this example there are three phases: cognition, connation and affection. The initial cognition or registration of the child in the mother's awareness can be summarised as "here is," or *asti*. Then follows the recognition that this is her own child, known as connation, *bhāti*. Her unspoken and spontaneous joy is at once a knowledge and an affectivity, *artham*.

The Sanskrit term *artham* has two definitions which are relevant in this context: value and meaning. What immediately strikes a person is an intuitive recognition of the value. The rationale for it comes only later when one can sit back and ponder over the experience and assess its meaning. Although psychologists prefer to say that the experience of affection follows connation, here the Guru has changed that order. In the term *aṟiññiṭumartham*, "the captivating lure of its value," he combines the intuitive recognition of the meaning and the value one confronts in the wake of an experience. His reference is not merely to *bhāti* but to the flash of consciousness that comes with the affective impact of the situation. Thereafter the person cools down. Next the Guru brings in pure connation as such, which he describes as *p̄māntam aṟivum*, one's personal knowledge. Affection is called *ānanda* in Sanskrit. It does not stand alone, which is why he identifies it as the conscious experience of being affected.

Countless latent urges lie buried in a person's causal consciousness. What we call causal consciousness roughly corresponds to what Jung calls the personal unconscious. He speaks of "the longing of the unconscious, of its unquenched and unquenchable desire for the light of consciousness."[1] Not all of our urges are pleasure-giving. Very many of them are born of fear, and motivate us to avoid or flee. The rest are pleasure-seeking, ranging from the gratification of sensual desires to the achievement of sublime beatitude, the peak experience of a yogi or mystic.

In the present verse we are facing three problems of epistemological importance. First of all, we should know what prompts the mind to move from one universe of interest to another. Vedantins attribute this to the latent urges or incipient memories, which we have approximated with Jung's personal unconscious and its motivation. The second question is how do the latent urges get into consciousness? Here the Guru traces their origin to *mahas*, the primeval stuff. Thirdly why is consciousness fragmented into the knower, the known and knowledge? From the second part of the verse we can deduce that a dissipation of interest causes the fragmentation of consciousness. In other words, unity comes about through a merging process occasioned by the total focusing of the mind. When that intensity is relaxed, the mind returns to its habitual

1. C.G. Jung, *Symbols of Transformation* (Bollingen Series XX, 1956), p. 205.

attitude of a knower having knowledge of the known.

Let us now go into each of these problems in more depth. The individual ego has no independent existence of its own. What is termed 'he' or 'she' is only a relative factor. The only independent reality is the Absolute, which is defined in Vedanta as *sat*, *cit* and *ānanda*. *Sat* refers to the ground of all things, whether physical or psychic. *Cit* refers to the source of illumination. It comprises both luminosity and what is illumined. *Ānanda* is the ground of all values. When conceived of as the Absolute, there is no division between these attributes, which are verbalised only for the sake of convenience. Also, within each of these three aspects — the ground of being, consciousness and the ground of value — there is no innate division.

Individuation is experienced only because of an obscuration of the original unity. In Vedanta a negative principle is postulated as a counterpart to the Absolute. The relation between this negative entity, maya, and the Absolute is the same as that between light and shadow. Shadow has no existence and cannot maintain itself in the presence of light. Yet shadow is experienced by everyone, just as light is.

What is referred to here as shadow is to be understood clearly to appreciate its function. When Plato said that the visible world was a shadow of the archetypes in the world of the intelligibles, people thought he was speaking in terms of allegory. But in our own days, physicists and physiological psychologists insist that all of our sensory experiences and subjective emotions are made up of a series of projected images, which are the same as shadows. For example, let us take the experience of seeing a thick blue book, which we identify as the Bible. We can trace the source of this experience from two sides. We can go from the side of the object, which in the present case is a book. Or we can go from the side of consciousness, which recognises it as the teaching of Jesus Christ and some ancient Jewish prophets. Vedantins prefer to look at it from the side of consciousness, whereas scientists would rather give credence to measurable external data.

Let us first lend our ears to the scientists. According to physicists, there are no colours such as blue and red. We see only material things that are illumined by light. Light is electromagnetic energy, believed to be constituted of photons. These energy-carrying photons can be heterogeneous or homogeneous. The quality of light is decided by the length and amplitude of its waves, as well as its purity. Visible sensations are directly connected with these three qualities of light: length decides hue, amplitude causes brightness, and purity brings saturation. For example, if a number of homogeneous photons come together, the light is called pure. Depending on the variations in wavelength, it will appear to be indigo, blue, red or whatever. The amplitude is caused by the intensity if the photons. Light waves are measured in millimicrons. The human eye can see only the frequencies varying between 380 millimicrons, which marks the border of the ultraviolet, and 760 millimicrons, where the infrared begins. Waves outside these dimensions, such as X-rays and gamma rays, can be measured by machines although they are not visible to the naked eye.

In visual experience there are three distinct phases of the channelling of energy. The initial phase has two parts. First external light, such as that of the sun, illuminates an object. Then the rays of the sun, affected by the physical and chemical properties of the object, are reflected, with considerable alterations in the length, amplitude and purity of the original light. Even at this stage the light has changed into a shadow, so to speak. This altered or physically conditioned light is radiated in all directions. A minute fraction of it falls on the lens of the eyeball. Whatever light enters the visible span converges on the retina. Thereafter we cannot make any reference to light. Light stops at the retina.

The retina is lined with rods at the periphery and cones at the centre. From these, light kicks off electrical impulses which are conducted to the brain. This is the second phase, when light casts its shadow in the form of nerve impulses. Once the impulses reach the cortex they are further processed and related to a previously registered and maintained coding of experience. Some strange phenomenon in the brain interprets the experience as seeing an object; a book for instance.

From the scientists' own verdict, it is clear that there is no way to decide the equivalency or one-to-one correspondence between the third version of an object given by the brain mechanism and the original object, because what we "see" is a shadow of a shadow of a shadow.

In relation to each of these stages, physicists, biochemists, neurologists and physiological psychologists have collaborated, proposed hundreds of postulates, and coined a vast number of impressive technical terms in Greek and Latin to explain the phenomenon of vision. With all that, the simple fact of seeing a book continues to be both a mystery and a wonder.

The mechanism of cognition is very elaborately dealt with by scientists, but they are at a loss to tell us how we recognise. To meet this contingency a new branch of science has been developed, genetics. It is coupled with paleontology in the attempt to make a breakthrough in the understanding of latent memories. It is now postulated that the mind is not a *tabula rasa*, as Locke suggested. What we call mind is, according to the behaviourists, only an epiphenomenon caused by the collective functioning of the central nervous system. The human brain contains about ten billion nerve cells, or neurons. These neurons are connected by synapses, across which chemicals diffuse, providing the means by which messages are conducted from one cell to another. According to Carl Sagan, an average human neuron has from 1000 to 10,000 synapses. He tells us that "the human brain is characterised by some 10^{13} synapses" and that

> The number of different states of a human brain is 2 raised to this power — i.e., multiplied by itself ten trillion times. This is an unimaginably large number, far greater, for example, than the total number of elementary particles (electrons and protons) in the entire universe. . . . These enormous numbers may also explain something of the unpredictability of human behaviour.[2]

Scientists also tell us that each neuron, like every other cell, contains a chromosome with a DNA molecule in the form of a helix, composed of five billion pairs of nucleotides. These nucleotides are considered

2. Carl Sagan, *The Dragons of Eden* (Random House, New York, 1977), p. 42.

to be the storage of knowledge going back four billion years. Again Sagan reports,

> The information content of any message is usually described in units called bits, which is short for 'binary digits'. . . . Since there are four different kinds of nucleotides, the number of bits of information in DNA is four times the number of nucleotide pairs. Thus, if a single chromosome has five billion (5×10^9) nucleotides, it contains twenty billion (2×10^{10}) bits of information. . . . How much information is twenty billion bits?. . . If a typical book contains five hundred such pages (300 words), the information content of a single human chromosome corresponds to some four thousand volumes.[3]

Although these are conjectures, scientists have at least come to the conclusion that in each individual body there must be some mysterious element of inestimable age, to account for the mind's capacity to readily recognise the rudiments of sensory experience.[4] One can easily see that the substance they refer to cannot give us any imaginable attributes of matter. The only reason they do not call it spirit is a simple prejudice born of the tussle between the Grand Inquisitor and the scientist, in which the Catholic church persecuted scientists like Galileo and progressive thinkers like Bruno. Scientists give heredity prime importance, postulating that incipient memories can belong to any member of one's hierarchy, such as a grandfather, a monkey who lived ten million years ago, an algae of two billion years ago, a bacteria of three billion years ago, or even a virus of four billion years ago. When you read all this in a science text, you feel a compulsion to accept it because you are already impressed by science's technological achievements. But this is only half the story.

The real question remains "What is consciousness?" To make it more exact, why is there a mathematically precise logic and order,

---

3. *The Dragons of Eden*, pp. 23-25.
4. Please refer to the commentary on *Jñāna Darśana*, v.7, in *The Psychology of Darśanamālā* of Narayana Guru by Guru Nitya Chaitanya Yati (Gurukula Publishing House, Fernhill, 1987) for further elaboration of memory processes.

both in the structure and function of the physical world, which can be accurately detected and favourably interpreted by a homogeneous human intelligence, and shared by any rational being anywhere in the world? If, for the purpose of a unified normative notion, science can uphold a mythical "matter," what prevents a Vedantin from postulating an all-pervasive consciousness, which has both the intelligence to modify itself into the structured universe and the capacity to constantly appreciate itself, and which manifests as the individuated consciousness with varying clarity and levels of appreciation? When the scientist postulates the accumulation of information through billions of years, faithfully held together through millennia to be eventually activated across our synapses, the Vedantin attributes to primal consciousness the capacity to dream, the ability to imagine, the power to compute, the skill to design, and the sense of humor to perpetuate a universal sport. If both are myths, why don't we accept a laudable, pleasant one, rather than admit a pessimistic hypothesis which both begins from and terminates in uncertainty?

Both the Vedantin and the scientist agree that there are latent urges in us, that these urges are multitudinous, and that only one of them can hold the stage of the mind at a time. This accounts for the short span of a single universe of interest. Martin Heidegger's assessment of experience is admissible at this stage. Each experience takes place as if the individual is placed in a prefabricated world of continuance. This is what he called 'facticity'. The individual acts, refuses to act, or reacts in some manner to the facts that are presented, partly due to heredity and partly through the structuring of the environment. When one takes up the challenge, one gains an existential profile; one's interaction becomes existentially motivated. A wave in the ocean cannot remain stationary, because of the pressures of other waves which are eager to take its place. In the same manner, an interest either burns out through gratification or fizzles out as frustration. This is what Heidegger calls 'forfeiture'. The net result is one universe of interest giving way to another. We have already explained in the second verse that Narayana Guru recommends selective structuralism in sensory experience, in tune with one's innate disposition.

To understand the insertion of latent urges in our system, we can get a clue from the term *ariññiṭumartham*. We have already mentioned that *artham* means both meaning and value. The configuration of sensory data, and the conscious reading of meaning into it, come from the objective and subjective aspects of consciousness arising as gestalt formations. *Artham* is the same as gestalt. Like an implied figure in a jigsaw puzzle, there is in this seemingly chaotic world an overall normative principle which enables the orderly structuring of both things and ideas.

If we take sound as an example, we select, out of the full spectrum of possible sounds, fundamental notes at discrete intervals for our vocal and musical expressions. These are the musical notes, which can be arranged in scales and combined with different pitches and frequencies to form complex harmonies. They are universal and timeless in their resonance and dissonance. There is no limit to the variety of combinations that can be organised from them. In fact, all the words we use are coined by structuring resonating sounds. In music we can see a perfect example of psychophysical organisation creating meaning or value.

Sound is just one factor which is at once physical in its content and aesthetic in its potential. There are many other potentials in us that can be traced back to the very origin of this universe. We are all born with certain basic potentials, and undergo the recurrence of environmental feasibility and accidental or deliberate actualisations of these potentials, which build up the history of our experience. Experience, in the present case, is to be understood as a hierarchy passing through several generations in the physical sense and several cycles in the psychic sense.

A child already has the ability to distinguish one from many, above from below, and dark from light. These are like its fundamental notes. By continuous composition the child can increase the number of concepts, ultimately becoming familiar with vocabularies and ideas that might fill an entire dictionary and encyclopedia. Any piecemeal approach to this process, such as that attempted by behaviourists, will only mutilate the holistic experience of knowledge and lead to awkward conclusions. It would be like trying to understand a Beethoven symphony by carefully studying the constituent parts of a violin. Again, in a negotiation using a bank check, what is important is the purport of negotiation and not the instrument as such. Obviously, the paper check, the instrument, is visible, objective and easy to handle. But that does not justify the transference of our attention from the essential to the nonessential, since the physical form of the check is intrinsically worthless. What Narayana Guru is presenting is a science of the Absolute, not an analytical treatise on a delimited area of relative interest.

The third question to which we want to return is why consciousness is fragmented into the knower, the known and knowledge. We have already seen that all experiences are composite productions which are consciously or unconsciously organised. The will to live is seldom actualised to its fullest and final satisfaction. In each unit of experience, the individual makes a thrust to approximate the final meaning or value which he or she is envisioning. In lower forms of life there is no conscious visualisation of purpose; it manifests only as an instinctive motivation. In people it can range from a vague hunch to a clear vision like that of a prophet or an enlightened scientist.

Living can be compared to an ambitious musician playing an unwieldy instrument. The haunting possibility of a musical composition gives him the urge to play. As he plays, there is no separation of man, instrument or music. When he is finished, he leaves the instrument and ponders over the accomplishment. Now he, his instrument and the music each have an independent existence. Like this, we cannot always remain at a peak experience. When there is a dimming or dilution of value, there comes a separation back into the knower, known and knowledge.

What makes a musician is that person's capacity to generate a symphony of ecstatic value. Similarly, those who seek the realisation of the Self should be able to experience the unitive wholeness of knowledge in which there is no separation of the knower, knowledge, and the meaning or object of knowledge.

Verse 5

ulakar uṟaṅṅi uṇarnnu cintaceyyum
palatumitokkeyumuṟṟupārttu nilkum-
vilamatiyātaviḷakku udikkayum pin-
polikayumillitu kaṇṭu pōyiṭeṇam

Worldly people, having slept, wake and think many thoughts;
ever wakefully witnessing all this shines an unlit lamp,
precious beyond words, that never fades;
ever seeing this, one should go forward.

It is said that the British philosopher Bishop Berkeley had a maxim: "Think with the learned and speak with the vulgar." Those he referred to as 'vulgar' were people who are not philosophically inclined or disciplined. In the present verse Narayana Guru speaks of *ulakar* in somewhat the same sense to mean those who are not philosophically critical in examining life and pondering on high values. Most people live in a world of getting and spending, where their only lot is to wake and sleep and conduct themselves as their fancies dictate.

In verse two the Guru spoke of *jagat*, the several worlds of interest that come and go. In the same vein, the term *lokam* is to be understood as "the passing universes of interest." Like many other biologic species on earth, human beings are caught between alternating spells of geotropism and heliotropism. When the sun sets, our energy wanes and we go to sleep. When the sun rises, our energy returns and we wake up to engage in the day's activity.

We do not know who puts us to sleep and who wakes us up. Where does our motivation come from, and who supplies us with energy to carry out the intentions of the mind? The Guru speaks of a light that intently looks on whatever we do. What could that light be? A picturesque mention of such a light is made after the narration of a legendary episode in the Maitri Upanishad:

> Verily, the gods and the devils (Asuras), being desirous of the Self (Ātman), came into the presence of Brahma (the Creator). They did obeisance to him and said: "Sir, we are desirous of the Self (Ātman). So, do you tell us."
>
> Then, meditating long, he thought to himself: "Verily, these devils are desirous of a Self (Ātman) different (from the true one)." Therefore a very different doctrine was told to them.
>
> Upon that, fools here live their life with intense attachment, destroying the saving raft and praising what is false. They see the false as if it were true, as in jugglery.[1]

There is a recurring idea in several Upanishads of the two kinds of knowledge that influence our life on earth. One is called *avidyā*, ignorance, and the other is *vidyā*, knowledge. Living according to the motivations of one's ego-centered interest is called avidya. It is mentioned in the Isa Upanishad that such people are living in darkness. Giving one's attention to transcendental ideas is called vidya. Paradoxically, it is mentioned in the same Upanishad that those who are attached to transcendental ideas live in even greater darkness, as it were.

It is hard to determine when someone is wise and when they are not. A passage to this effect comes in the Katha Upanishad (2.5), the Mundaka Upanishad (1.2.8), and the Maitri Upanishad (7.9):

> Those abiding in the midst of ignorance,
> Self-wise, thinking themselves learned,
> Hard smitten, go around deluded,
> Like blind men led by one who is himself blind.[2]

---

1. Robert Ernest Hume, *The Thirteen Principle Upanishads* (Oxford University Press, New York, 1971), p. 456.

2. *Ibid.*, p. 456.

The Guru's reference to "people of the world (who) sleep, wake and think many thoughts" should be seen in the light of these Upanishadic passages. He instructs us to turn to that which witnesses all our thoughts and deeds, which he compares to an unlit lamp that is nonetheless mysteriously shining. In the Maitri Upanishad we read the following description:

> Assuredly, the nature of the ether within the space (of the heart) is the same as the supreme bright power. This has been manifested in threefold wise: in fire, in the sun, and in the breath of life.
>
> Verily, the nature of the ether within the space (of the heart) is the same as the syllable OM.[3]

What is referred to here as fire, sun, and breath is not three separate entities, because in the same Upanishad it says:

> Adoration to Brahma, who dwells in all, who remembers all! Bestow all upon this worshipper!
>
> With a golden vessel
> The Real's face is covered o'er.
> That do thou, O Pushan, uncover
> Unto the Eternal Real (*satya-dharma*),
> the Pervader (Vishnu).
>
> He who is yonder, yonder Person in the sun — I myself am he.
>
> Verily, that which is the sunhood of the sun is the Eternal Real. That is the pure, the personal, the sexless (*a-liṅga*).
>
> Of the bright power that pervades the sky (*nabhas*) it is only a portion which is, as it were, in the midst of the sun, in the eye, and in fire. That is Brahma. That is the Immortal. That is splendour. That is the Eternal Real.[4]

In the commentaries of the previous verses we have seen how our minds are influenced by the three modalities of nature which are

3. *The Thirteen Principle Upaniṣads*, p. 449.
4. *Ibid.*, p. 449.

triggered by our incipient memories. In the present verse, the difficult problem of transcending these modalities is broached. In Chapter XIV of the Bhagavad Gita, Arjuna is confronted with this same problem. He asks Krishna:

> By what marks, O Master, does he who has transcended those three modalities of nature become (recognised)? What (is his) conduct and how does he transcend those three modalities of nature?[5]

To this question Krishna answers:

> Light and activity and delusion when present, O Pandava (Arjuna), he is not dissatisfied nor hankers for them when absent.[6]

The Karu mentioned in verse one appears in the Bhagavad Gita as *bhūtātman*, the manifesting Self. The three aspects of the Karu are its self-luminosity as knowledge of knowledge, its manifestation as the psychodynamics that animates a person, and the eidetic world that is presented to the knower. These three aspects are described in the verse from the Gita quoted above as light (*prakāśam*); activity (*pravṛtti*) and delusion (*moham*). Although the Absolute does not undergo any change, the negative principle of the Absolute gives rise to a superimposition of these triple aspects.

In Vedanta, this kind of modification is called *nirvikāra*. Narayana Guru is preparing our minds to arrive at the notion of the unmodified Absolute, which he is going to present in verse seven. In this verse and the next he focuses our attention on the alternating phases of consciousness. The natural state of the Absolute is its self-founded brightness. The Guru equates this with the lamp which is neither lit nor ever dies. Activity and delusion, which are also attributed to the manifesting Self, *bhūtātman*, in this verse of the Gita, constitute the changing world in which the common man is caught as if in a snare.

In *The Consolation of Philosophy* of Boethius, Philosophia describes the unfortunate state of man:

5. *The Bhagavad Gītā*, tr. and comm. Nataraja Guru (R & K Publishing House, New Delhi, 1973), p. 590.

6. *Ibid.*, p. 590.

> Alas! How this mind is dulled, drowned in the overwhelming depths. It wanders in outer darkness, deprived of its natural light. Sick anxiety, inflated by worldly winds, swells his thoughts to bursting.[7]

The remedy for this tragedy which the Guru suggests here is to see the light within that witnesses everything. In the Mundaka Upanishad it says:

> Two birds, fast bound companions,
> Clasp close the self-same tree.
> Of these two, the one eats sweet fruit;
> The other looks on without eating.
>
> On the self-same tree a person, sunken,
> Grieves for his impotence, deluded;
> When he sees the other, the Lord (*īś*), contented,
> And his greatness, he becomes freed from sorrow.
>
> When a seer sees the brilliant
> Maker, Lord, Person, the Brahma-source,
> Then being a knower, shaking off good and evil,
> Stainless, he attains supreme identity (*sāmya*) [with Him].[8]

The experiencing sensory-mind complex and the animating Self in us, born of the same principle, are described as two birds that are like intimate friends clinging to each other. According to Śaṅkara, they are the individuated self and God. They dwell in the subtle body, which holds in itself the tendencies and impressions created by desire, ignorance and action. Of the two, the individual soul enjoys the fruit of action. The other, God, who is by nature eternal, pure, wise and free; who is omniscient and has maya as his limiting adjunct; does not taste, but merely looks on.

As the individual self is totally immersed in samsara, the world of delusion, it repeatedly becomes despondent. It is believed that such a soul, degraded by its own false identification, is born again

7. *The Consolation of Philosophy of Boethius*, tr. Richard Green (The Library of Liberal Arts, New York, 1962), p. 5.

8. Hume, p. 374.

and again in inferior wombs. Perchance with the compassionate guidance of a blessed one, the individual may some day, by purification, discipline and meritorious life, achieve the sameness of vision to see the true light that shines within, recognising: "I am this Bright Person who is the Self of all and is the same in every being." Then he or she would shake off all notions of duality, such as merit and demerit and the two kinds of action that constitute bondage. Having become freed of all blemishes, the self will attain the absolute equality that transcends all duality. The Gita says of such a state:

> Those however in whom that unwisdom in the Self
> has been destroyed, to those wisdom shines
> sunlike as the Ultimate (the Absolute).
>
> Those having That (Absolute) for reasoning,
> That for the Self, That for finalised discipline,
> That for supreme goal, they go to a state of
> final non-return, all their (relativistic) dross
> being cancelled-out by wisdom. (V.16, 17)[9]

Compare the opening clause of the second verse given above, "Those having That (Absolute) for reasoning," with the opening line of the present verse, "Worldly people sleep, wake and think many thoughts." Martin Heidegger says that the common lot of all human beings is their facticity, existentiality and forfeiture. But in the Gita it is specifically mentioned that there is no forfeiture when one's reasoning is unitive. Unitive reasoning is well-founded, regulated and directed to its object, as opposed to discursive reasoning, which is accompanied by the dissipation of interest. Nataraja Guru, in his commentary on the Gita, says, "Such a reasoning establishes a direct bi-polar relationship with the object of its search. It does not get lost in endless ramifications. Bi-polarity, once established, is conducive to further reasoning along the same lines, culminating in the highest good, in the Self."[10]

---

9. Nataraja Guru, pp. 270-71.
10. *Ibid.*, p. 149.

The instruction given by Narayana Guru in the present verse is to establish a bipolarity with that ever-wakefully witnessing Absolute, the unlit lamp in us, which is precious beyond words. However, the Guru knows how difficult it is for an uninstructed and undisciplined person to raise himself or herself to that sublime state of perfect attunement with the Supreme. In the next verse he grieves for the sad state of man.

Verse 6

uṇaraṇaminniyuṟaṅṅaṇam bhujiccī-
ṭaṇamaśanam puṇarēṇamenniváṇṇam
aṇayumanēkavikalpamākayālā-
ruṇaruvatuḷḷoru nirvikāra rūpam?

One has to wake up, then go to sleep,
has to eat food and embrace; thus, in this way
many ambivalent urges arise; therefore,
who is there to comprehend reality's one changeless form?

This verse ends with a rhetorical question: "Who is there to realise the one changeless form?" Both the problem and the solution that are going to be elaborated in the rest of the work are here set forth. In the world of spirituality, there are many antinomies such as God and Satan, good and evil, the numenon and the phenomenon, the transcendent and the immanent, *brahman* and dharma, and the absolute and the relative. The antinomies presented in this verse are the changing life urges and the unchanging form of the Absolute.

As soon as we enter into any field of inquiry, what impresses us as paradoxical is the receding of the familiar and the certain into a world of vague ambiguity and incertitude. Sir Arthur Eddington gives the example of a table. He says that a physicist who is using a table has before him two tables. One is phenomenal and the other is real. The phenomenal table can be seen, touched and used. All the same, as a physicist, he knows that it is not real. What is real to him is an aggregate of fast-moving molecules that are invisible to the naked eye and are in a state of flux, ever agitated with the swirling force of entropy. Thus even a familiar table can vanish into an incomprehensible world of assumptions when one becomes serious about assessing its reality.

The position of the Vedantin is not very different from that of the physicist. He also has to tackle the paradox of appearance and reality vying with each other. The senses are easily affected by appearance, while the real is elusive and contrary to the very nature of the mind which is actively engaged in pursuing it. However hopeless this case may look, one cannot let go of the pursuit and accept the appearance as a *fait accompli.*

We are worldlings. It is the functional nature of the earth to rotate on its axis and revolve around the sun. As a consequence we experience the alternation of day and night. The earth is called *dharā,* that which supports. There are many things on earth which are supported by their latent potentials, their dharma. Dharma is both the structural and functional secret of all forms of individuation. Although the structural and functional system in an individual is a self-governing unit, it is part of a more complex system. The shimmering star in the sky and the eye that gazes upon it with delight have a physical cohesion that cannot be easily explained.

The psychosomatic effect of day and night was dealt with in the previous verse. Whether we are wakeful or sleeping, there is in us an essence that does not change. The Upanishads call it *brahman,* the all-embracing unitive principle. All the major functions of the body and mind are supervised and kept operating, even when we are asleep, by a governing intelligence that is constantly adjusting and tuning the individuated system to its maximum harmony. This harmony is experienced as peace, happiness and unity. Our basic nature is this changeless essence, referred to in the previous verse as the witnessing light of the unlit lamp.

Dharma is our second nature. It has the paradoxical characteristic of coupling the changeless with an ever-changing course of becoming. As individuated beings, we are modulations of dharma.

Waking and sleeping is only one of the major binary functions of the complex mechanism of our nature. When we wake, the demands for nourishing the body and amusing the mind are keenly felt. For many, the main pursuit in life is in finding bread and butter and distractions that can save them from boredom. There are many words in Malayalam for eating, but in this verse the Guru has carefully chosen the word *bhujiccītenam* to reflect this idea. *Bhū* means that which manifests. *Bhuj* is that which causes becoming. It is also related to *bhoga*, enjoyment.

One who enjoys is called a *bhoktā*. We experience a sense of agency in three ways, as the knower, the doer and the enjoyer. From verses one to four, our attention was focused on the knower. In verse five it was turned on the doer, and now in the present verse the focus is on the enjoyer.

Seeking nourishment for the body is only one of our several life urges. Jesus said that man does not live by bread alone, meaning that a person is not merely a body. The body is animated by an energy that knows, thinks, discerns and evaluates. This phenomenon is called the soul or spirit. The nature of the spirit is to pervade. It is characteristic of the spirit or the self in us to return again and again to the pure being of the universal Self to which it belongs. It does not feel at home when it is confined to the limitations of a body. Just like water finding its own level, the self is always in search of the boundless. The individual's attempt to cater to the necessities of the body is a relativistic form of dharma, while the spirit's need to transcend the limitations of the individual's body, family, clan, tribe and nation is its absolute dharma.

The spirit's affinity for the Absolute is like a child's attachment to its mother. Both have a compulsive need to relate to one another. Although the child and the mother have separate bodies, they were one for nine months. The period of the child's confinement within the mother's womb conceals many secrets of the spirit and its manifestation. Even before the formation of the fetus, a part of the child and the mother was together for ages, millennia, even from the very beginning of the universe. The child feels at home only when it regains its 'at-one-ment' with its seedbed, the mother. The mother feels the same way. She suckles the child, embraces and kisses it. When they are united they forget themselves. Paradoxically, the soul's search for its freedom through expansion binds it at every step. The mother introduces the child to the father, from whom the child got its equally timeless other half. The child's love is extended to the father and later to brothers and sisters. In this way, love expands the domain of interest and also creates new bondages.

The dharma that sustains the life-giving energy that fosters the characteristics of the individual and unfolds as the growing personality, has several levels of formation and shades of meaning. As the sole ground of individuation, it is undifferentiated from the Absolute. As the primeval cause of manifestation, it is the temporal function that introduces motion into the field of spatial extension. As the existential base of individuation, it is an evolutionary process that channels and organises indistinct and undifferentiated energy to assume definite forms of structural integrity that can function with physical, chemical, biological and, at the human level, psychological propensities. As the dynamics of a living organism, it is a retentive store of memory that is used as a ready reckoner with which to decide courses of action and reaction that are conducive to both the organism's self-preservation and to the furtherance of its life term as a stable system. As the propensity of life urges, it is an amalgam of a pleasure-seeking collective will and a continuing process of individuation, in which every blind drive and conscious effort is controlled and decided upon by its longitudinal history. And as the immediate interacting agent that recognises itself with the self-awareness of an I-consciousness, it is a homeostasis that governs reflexive and instinctive behaviour, acquired habits, adaptation, and willed actions that serve the self-regulating system which is intent upon maintaining its fluid equilibrium.

Such is the complex sense in which dharma is to be understood. It is this dharma that decides the meaning of persons, things and events that are objectivised, from time to time, as the counterparts of the knower, the doer and the enjoyer in a person. Reading meaning into a situation is the same as promoting a life urge or securing the system against attack or damage. The eidetic cohesiveness which one sees as meaning is what creates the togetherness of an ensemble or gestalt. Formulating a gestalt is identified by Indian psychologists as the configuring of *artha*. When dharma and *artha* come together, they impel the individual to desire, *kāma*. The desire can be for union, *rāga*, or for separation, *dveṣa*. This double-faced compulsion is essentially libidinal.

The thirteenth chapter of the Bhagavad Gita outlines seven modifications that influence the course of our lives: *icchā*, desire; *dveṣa*, hatred; *sukha*, pleasure; *duḥkha*, pain; *saṁghāta*, the interrelatedness of properties; *jīva*, the biotic principle; and *sthairya*, the will to live.

Another pertinent reference is found in the *Yoga Aphorisms* of Patañjali, in which he lists five hindrances to spiritual union. The *kaivalya* or aloneness aspired to by the yogi, and the realisation of non-differentiation with the Absolute aspired to by the Vedantin are not doctrinally different. They vary only in their methodological approach. So by examining the hindrances enumerated by Patañjali we can get a clearer understanding of the seven modifications of the Gita. Patañjali's five hindrances, or *kleśa*s are: *avidyā*, ignorance; *asmitā*, egoism; *rāga*, attraction; *dveṣa*, repulsion; and *abhiniveśa*, clinging to life.

According to the Gita, the two constituent factors of our lives are the triple modalities of nature, prakriti, and the consciousness that is characteristic of the spirit, purusha. Nature is seen as being responsible for the aggregate of cause and effect, and the consciousness of the spirit as being responsible for the search for happiness. As the spirit is imprisoned in the body, which is dominated by nature, the search for happiness is vitiated by the distorting and veiling principles of rajas and tamas. Even sattva has a tendency to create a sense of attachment to anything pleasure-giving.

In the diagnosis and treatment of these defects, yogis and Vedantins hold different views. In Patañjali's *Yoga Aphorisms*, chapter 2, sutra 17 says: "the cause of that which is to be avoided is the union of the seer and the seen." The Gita does not recommend withdrawal or turning away from the world that is seen, but the cultivation of a transparency of vision by which one sees the Absolute alone as the one reality residing in all. Perceiving the Self alone in everything is given as the ideal in the sixth and seventh mantras of the Isa Upanishad:

> Now, he who on all beings
> Looks as just (*eva*) in the Self (Ātman),

And on the Self as in all beings —
He does not shrink away from Him.

In whom all beings
Have become just (*eva*) the Self of the discerner —
Then what delusion (*moha*), what sorrow (*śoka*) is there
Of him who perceives the unity![1]

In Narayana Guru's *Yoga Darśana*, he combines the positions of the Vedantins and the yogis when he says:

That which always unites the mind
With the reasoning Self, and also gets united with it,
And which is in the form of restraint,
That is praised as *Yoga*.

Where the seer, the sight and the seen
Are not present, there the heart
Should be joined, as long as incipient memory-factors
(are present);
Such is *Yoga* (says) the knower of *Yoga*.[2]

Although the nature of consciousness is to seek liberation, the instrument at its disposal defeats that purpose. The serial order in which experience comes is: awareness, then activity, followed by a consolidation of the total effect as a conditioning. Such conditioning inevitably leads to a future recurrence of the same experience, which will be dominated by a reaction of flight or combat if the accompanying emotion is painful, or attraction if the accompanying emotion is pleasure-giving. Identification of consciousness with the modalities causes forgetfulness of one's true nature. This is what the Guru laments in the present verse.

1. Hume, p. 363.
2. Nataraja Guru, tr., *An Anthology of the Poems of Narayana Guru* (Gurukula Institute of Aesthetic Values, India, 1977), p. 71.

Verse 7

uṇararutinniyuṟaṅṅiṭātirunnī-
taṇamaṟivāy itininnayōgyanennāl
praṇavamuṇarnnu piṟappoḻiññu vāḻum-
munijanasēvayil mūrtti nirttiṭēṇam

Do not wake any more, and without sleeping remain
as Knowledge;
if you are unfit for this,
then keep yourself in the service of those
contemplatives
who live free from birth, awakened to *aum*.

This verse sounds paradoxical, at least when we hear it for the first time. Narayana Guru instructs the seeker to remain steadfast, merged in knowledge, without having the need to alternate between the states of waking and sleeping. To be wakeful during the day and to sleep at night is an experience which man shares with most living beings. Is it within our power to inhibit the automation of Nature that governs our sleeping and waking habits? Is it possible to rid our consciousness of its tribasic fragmentation and keep it blazing without flickering?

The word the Guru uses repeatedly from the opening verse to the present is *arivu*, meaning the Word or Knowledge. We often think of knowledge as merely pieces of information. To correct such a faulty notion at the very outset, the Guru qualifies this knowledge as *aṟivilumēṟi*, the Knowledge that surpasses all knowledge. It is further described as that which is seen as the outside world and experienced within as one's subjective awareness.

In the six previous verses there are indirect references to six possible differentiations within the field of one's experience. In the first verse it is given as the inner world, the outer world, and the knowledge that knows both. In the second verse the Guru presents a graded hierarchical series: the psychic dynamics, the senses, the body, and the many worlds that are the objects of perception. These together constitute the total body of experience.

In the third verse, the reference is to the eidetic world of perception where each sensory experience produces a mental image. It is difficult to discern whether or not the image has a genuine one-to-one correspondence with the original model whose presence can, at best, only be presumed. In verse four, consciousness is shown to be split into three basic elements, the knower, the known and knowledge. These are essentially the psychological version of the cosmological structure given in verse one.

Our attention is drawn in the fifth verse to the alternation of consciousness between waking and sleeping, and the tendency of the mind to become discursive and scattered during the wakeful state. The sixth verse highlights the shift of interest from one item to another in a continuous sequence.

It is only after covering all the things that can kick the mind out of gear, making it eccentric or off-centered, that the Guru places before the seeker two alternative disciplines from which to choose. The first is: "Do not wake any more, and without sleeping remain as Knowledge." Even a cursory look at the differentiating forces enumerated in the six previous verses will convince anyone how difficult it is to remain as pure Knowledge, let alone to escape the automation of waking and sleeping.

The seeker Narayana Guru addresses throughout this book is the Self within each of us. He is careful to underline the essential unity of the Self, even when describing its possible differentiations. In fact, his main interest so far has been to convince the seeker that his or her essential being is not in any way separate from the one Knowledge that permeates all.

In verse one the Guru asks us, as a mark of initiating the search for Self-realisation, to prostrate ourselves with devotion and with senses restrained before that shining principle which he calls Karu.

This does not mean lying down before an external God or a Creator outside, but committing ourselves to the truth that is here and now as this all-filling Knowledge, the Total Reality. The secret of equalising the outgoing attention and the incoming stimulus is to be seen as the interiorisation of the five senses and the filling of one's self with a sense of wonder for the adorable Absolute. The surrender suggested is an exhortation to return to one's own real wholeness.

In verse two we are invited to share the glory of the effulgent Self, adored by contemplatives as the unitive inner cohesiveness of all things, and the homogeneity of the one Knowledge to which all names and forms and states of consciousness belong. The Guru especially mentions that one should be relentless in one's search. Any compromise, at any level, can unwittingly lure the mind off on a tangent. The various 'isms' and 'ologies' are historical testimonials to the sidetracking that has occurred through the millennia. He further cautions that unity, which is a marvel, can be comprehended only when contemplated. Only one in a million succeeds in this search, and even then only after extensive lapses. Implicitly, the Guru attributes our failure in this to the selective structuralism of the persona, which causes the search to be initiated on the basis of whatever incipient memory is stimulated at any given time by the changing ensembles of life situations.

We become aware of a psychic compulsion pushing us in a certain direction only when it becomes pathologically exaggerated, such as in obsessions, inhibitions, phobias and manias. Still, the so-called healthy mind is not as free to act on its own as one might wish to believe. Even a scientist who is firmly wedded to a creed of honesty in observing facts is likely to miss negative data when he is otherwise encouraged by some positive observations.

Another interesting discipline which Narayana Guru recommends may escape our attention if we do not give sufficient consideration to every word he uses. After bracketing the psychic dynamism, the senses, the body, and the many worlds known by direct perception, he looks beyond to the sun, representing the Self, which is to be understood as both the immanent and the transcendent taken together. The Guru does not elaborate his methodology of bracketing, suspension, and phenomenological reduction, as

Edmund Husserl takes so much pain to describe in his voluminous writings. He does, however, make an effective polarisation of the here and now with the ever and everywhere, by resorting to an analogy for which the entire philosophy of Spinoza can be given as a satisfactory interpretation.

The secret of all polarisation is that the counterparts of the dialectical situation share a common value, which has made the polarisation feasible or even imperative. Mother and child, teacher and taught, ruler and subjects, lover and beloved, all are examples of dialectical bipolarity. The common interest in all these cases can be reduced to the experience of happiness. The counterparts are individuals who can reciprocate their thoughts and feelings. But the bipolarity suggested in this verse is not between two individuals. Rather, it is between one's personal awareness and the totality of Knowledge. As one of the counterparts is impersonal, the question of reciprocation does not arise. However, bipolarity makes sense only if there is a free flow of the essence of one into the other and vice versa, as in exosmosis and endosmosis.

By giving the analogy of the inseparability of waves from the treasury of the oceanic depth, the Guru has already given us the secret of sharing one's essence with the total, even when that total is of an impersonal nature. The example of the wave is not given to dismiss our individuality as a mere phantom, like the form of a wave, but to stress that the seeming separateness of the wave does not deprive it of its vertical relationship with the ocean. The constant awareness of this depth reestablishes one in the lost heritage of union with the Absolute.

In verse four, without resorting to any analogy, Narayana Guru explicitly describes one's true being as pure Knowledge, and exhorts the self to become identical with it. Pure Knowledge transcends the altering states of our physical organism, so it is no more than legitimate to say: "Remain as pure knowledge and do not become afflicted with any bodily state such as waking or sleeping."

The Guru knows that such a rare identification with the Absolute is not within the easy reach of most people, so he offers an alternative: to engage oneself in the service of a contemplative who has no more questions to be answered, and who sees this grand drama going on but is not assailed by it. Thus, with the seventh verse we are brought to the threshold of entering into a bipolar relationship. It is up to each of us to choose with whom we wish to establish our bipolarity. It can be with a living person in the sense of seeing the Word manifesting through one who is physically present. Or, if we have the power of relating to the impersonal, then the living Word is always present in our hearts. Either way, the important thing is that we are committed.

If we plant a seed, it needs to remain in one place to grow. It won't survive if it is pulled up every day and put in another place. Bipolarity has the same secret. There has to be contiguity, a continuation of natural flow. The sap of a tree has an ascending and descending movement. Like that, there has to be a reciprocal flow between the master and the disciple, between the seeker and the light that is sought.

In establishing bipolarity with a master, you should begin the discipline at a physical level, such as making your service directly available to your teacher. This provides you with an opportunity to decipher the meaning of the wakeful world by observing your teacher's reaction to various aspects of it. By pondering upon the words of instruction, you can decode the conceptual images of the world of subjectivity. By observing your teacher's neutral silence, you can learn the secret of abolishing incipient memories. From the teacher's overall identity with the transcendental, you can discover the nonduality of the transcendence to which we all belong.

Again and again in the path of the profound, there appear brilliant souls of deep understanding and infinite mercy who are looked upon by the world, rightly and gratefully, as the true saviours of mankind. Romain Rolland speaks of them as midday suns that shine at the zenith and remain with the destiny of man even after their physical disappearance. The Buddha, Socrates, Jesus Christ and the prophet Muhammad are well-known examples of such masters, who go on shaping the minds and lives of people long after their deaths, despite the vicissitudes of human history.

The Buddha was originally Prince Siddhartha, the son of a chieftain in the foothills of the Himalayas. Like any other person, he spent his childhood and early youth waking and sleeping, utterly lost in the confusion of his mind. Although he was pampered by his royal father and was given every form of indulgence, he was stricken with grief when he saw the misery of people all around him. Old age, poverty, disease and death, which are taken for granted by most people, appeared to the young prince as shameful mistakes that challenged his compassionate disposition. He took the responsibility upon himself to find a lasting remedy to these ills of humanity. To find an answer to the secret of suffering, he renounced his royal palace, dear wife and beloved child, and passed through discipline after discipline with the hope of becoming awakened to a higher truth. That is the remedy: to wake up from the wakefulness of our everyday life. From the hedonistic indulgences of a royal harem, he went to the other extreme of mortifying his body and mind, but found in that discipline the same despair he had encountered in the pleasurable days of his palace life. Finally he gave up all hope of waking up from the dreadful dream of phenomenality and its uncompromising demand for karma. Like a miracle of miracles, a strange homeostasis brought him to the neutral zero that balances good with evil, pain with pleasure, the wakeful with the sleeping, and light with darkness. On touching this point, Siddhartha became awakened and recognised himself as the blessed Buddha, who had discovered the golden middle path which is neither of waking or sleeping, fasting or feasting. He became very much like the proverbial bird of the Svetasvatara Upanishad, which silently witnesses the activities of its mate without succumbing to the temptation of any phenomenological urge.

The state of the awakened one is described differently in various religions; the models are not always similar in their external characteristics. In the Bhagavad Gita, the state of the awakened one is described in the second chapter as *stithaprajña*, well-founded in reason (Ch. II, v. 55-68); in the fourth chapter as *jñānī*, seer (Ch. IV, v. 18-24); in the fifth as *brāhmīsthiti*, one established in the Absolute (Ch. V, v. 23-28); in the sixth chapter as *yogi* (Ch. VI, v. 27-32); in the twelfth as *bhakta*, a true devotee (Ch. XII, v. 13-20); in the thirteenth as *kṣetra-kṣetrajña viveka*, a true discriminator of the field and its knower (Ch. XIII, v. 27-32); in the fourteenth as *guṇātīta*, one who has transcended the three modalities (Ch. XIV, v. 22-26); and in the eighteenth chapter as *brahmabhūtaḥ*, the perfected contemplative (Ch. XVIII, v. 50-57). Even a cursory glance at the verses referred to here will give us some idea of a contemplative who has sundered all doubts by becoming awakened to the secret of the alternating phases of consciousness, cryptically epitomised in the sacred syllable *aum*.

There is a passage in the Chandogya Upanishad which says if a person is kidnapped from his home town and taken to another city, blindfolded, and then released, he would still find his way back home. He could just get help and directions from one or several other people along the way. Like that, the bipolarity suggested in this verse for arriving at the true nature of oneself can happen with the help of one person or many. The real, essential bipolarity is with the quality of the person's knowledge. That knowledge is specifically stated here as "being conversant with the secret of aum." Aum is otherwise known as *praṇava*. In the Bhagavad Gita, *praṇava* is praised as the supreme essence of the Vedas, the revealed scriptures. Krishna identifies it with the Absolute. The Chandogya Upanishad says:

> Now then, the Udgitha is *Om*, *Om* is the Udgitha. And so, verily, the Udgitha is yonder sun, and it is *Om*, for it is continually sounding *'Om'*.[1]

Aum in this context is called *anujña*, meaning 'the word of consent'. People wake in the morning when the sun comes up. That is allegorically cited here as the sun giving consent to everyone to get up and engage in various activities. In a world of relative good and bad, pain and pleasure, and truth and untruth, one finds it difficult to agree with others in matters of contradictory values or situations which spell personal loss. But an absolutist who has transcended all such dualities does not feel restricted or restrained by inhibitions. He gives consent to all. No one is in greater agreement with the world than a realised person.

In the Mundaka Upanishad, aum is looked upon as an efficient tool to realise the Absolute:

> Taking as a bow the great weapon of the Upanishad,
> One should put upon it an arrow sharpened by
> meditation.

1. Hume, p. 182.

> Stretching it with a thought directed to the essence of That,
> Penetrate that Imperishable as the mark, my friend.
>
> The mystic syllable *Om* (*praṇava*) is the bow. The arrow is the soul (*ātman*).
> Brahmā is said to be the mark (*lakṣya*).
> By the undistracted man is It to be penetrated.
> One should come to be in It, as the arrow (in the mark).[2]

In the Svetasvatara Upanishad also, aum is looked upon as a means to meditate on the Absolute:

> By making one's own body the lower friction-stick
> And the syllable *Om* the upper friction-stick,
> By practising the friction of meditation (*dhyāna*),
> One may see the God (*deva*) who is hidden, as it were.[3]

In the Maitri Upanishad, aum is identified with a number of triads: *'A'*, *'U'* and *'M'* as the sound form of the Self; feminine, masculine and neuter as the sex form; fire, wind and sun as the light form; Rudra, Brahmā and Vishnu as the Lordship form; the Rig Veda, Yajur Veda and the Sama Veda as the understanding form; earth, atmosphere and sky as the world form; past, present and future as the time form; and breath, fire and sun as the heat form. All these are honoured as aspects of aum.

The reference to the knower of aum as a wise person, worthy of adoration, is made in the opening passages of Gauḍapāda's *Kārīkā* on the Mandukya Upanishad. According to the Mandukya, the word aum is constituted of the sounds *'A'*, *'U'* and *'M'*, followed by silence. The *'A'* represents *viśva*, the empirical world of name and form; *'U'* represents the dream world, *taijasa*, which is a self-luminous and self-regulated world of subjective consciousness; and *'M'* represents an undifferentiated mass of consciousness, *prajñā*, the presence of which one infers from one's experience of deep sleep. The silence that follows is the final aspect. Of this, the Upanishad says:

---

2. Hume, p. 372.
3. *Ibid.*, 396.

> The fourth is without an element, with which there can be no dealing, the cessation of development, benign, without a second.
> Thus *Om* is the Self (Ātman) indeed.
> He who knows this, with his self enters the Self —
> yea, he who knows this![4]

Commenting on this mantra, Gauḍapāda says:

> The knower of Brahman, who has realised the highest truth, has entered into the Self by burning away the third state of latency; and hence he is not born again since *Turīya* has no latency (of creation).[5]

This agrees with Narayana Guru's description of wise contemplatives as "those great ones who ever live free from birth, in silent contemplation, awakened to aum." To become fully conversant with all the implications of knowing *praṇava,* we recommend that the reader make a detailed study of the Mandukya Upanishad with Gauḍapāda's *Kārīkā,* keeping in mind all the implications of the *udgītha* given in the Chandogya Upanishad.

Aum is said to have both a lower form and a higher form. The lower form, represented by our wakeful and dream experience, tends to horizontalise the affiliation of consciousness. As a result, both the senses and the mind are assailed by the dualities of pain and pleasure and good and evil. The higher form of aum, however, represented by *prajñā* and *turīya,* has the power to verticalise consciousness so that it can free itself from all bondage. In the next verse, Narayana Guru gives us the secret of verticalisation.

---

4. Hume, p. 393
5. Swami Gambhirananda, *Eight Upanisads,* Vol. 2 (Advaita Ashram, Calcutta, 1966), p. 227.

Verse 8

oḻimutalām paḻamañcumuntu nāṟum-
nalikayilēṟi nayēna māṟiyāṭum
kiḻikaleyañcumariññu kīḻmaṟikkum-
veḻivuruvēntiyakam viḻaṅṅiṭēṇam

Enjoying the five fruits, such as beauty,
mounted on a foul-smelling gun and evasively flying back and forth
are five birds; having brought them down, through an inversion,
that radiant inner awareness should fill one's entire being.

The first ten verses mark the introduction to the One Hundred Verses of Self-Instruction. Among these, verse eight is of crucial importance. In it, an ontological assessment is made with a teleological goal. Metaphysics comes to grips with aesthetics and ethics. Further, this verse exemplifies the structural plan of the work as a whole. The reader with a careful eye can see the circulation of libidinal energy, which explains many secrets of human woe and happiness. There are also several paradoxes to resolve, which we will examine one by one.

First of all, let us get a picture of the structure of the allegoric gestalt of this verse. The metaphor is of a tree with birds hovering around its branches and a hunter standing beneath it. The fruits above and the hunter below mark a vertical parameter. The tree has five kinds of fruit, symbolising the objects of the five sense interests. The birds are said to be flying back and forth evasively, enjoying the sensuous fruits. The range of their movement should be understood as a horizontal perimeter within which life urges become actualised at an ontological level. The Guru is using a mixed metaphor, alternating the tree with a foul-smelling gun evocative of the alimentary canal. As we go into the details of this metaphor, we should notice some of the glaring paradoxes which are placed side by side. A tree symbolises life, growth and fruition. On the other hand, a gun is a symbol of fate, uncertainty and destruction. Both of these aspects are merged by the literary device of depicting their outlines as vaguely as possible. The person standing beneath the tree is the enjoyer, and the five evasive birds are none other than his or her own sense interests. This person is required to act with hostility towards the intention of the sense appetites. Thus, two contrary intentions are bracketed by the implied relationship between the person beneath the tree and the birds playing hide-and-seek in the branches. It would seem that the annihilation of one's senses would spell great disaster, plunging one into a grievous darkness. Instead it is pointed out that one becomes filled with a great light by striking down the five birds. So this metaphor has in it six factors to reckon with: the birds and fruits, the tree and gun, and destruction and illumination.

In this verse, Narayana Guru lays the groundwork for both the aesthetics and the ethics he wants to develop in the rest of the book. Aesthetics will be considered first in the Kantian sense, and then in the context of the historical transformation that the concept has undergone.

Our knowledge has two aspects. We arrive at one through intuition; the other is what we experience as our sensibility. In a number of cases, these two aspects go hand in hand. When intuition aids us in deciphering the meaning of a sensation, we arrive at an empirical notion. Our common experience is to put sensation on the side of what is generally looked upon as matter: the realm where names and forms are important. Intuition, on the other hand, is taken as a natural device of operational efficiency, with which the mind structures the logical relevancy of the connectedness between things and ideas within the matrix of cause and effect and other relation-relata complexes. According to Kant, there are a priori principles governing both intuition and sensation. In fact, he even calls the pure form of sensibility pure intuition. He says:

> Thus, if I take away from our representation of a body all that the understanding thinks as belonging to it, as substance, force, divisibility, etc., and also whatever belongs to sensation, as impenetrability, hardness, colour, etc., yet there is still something left us from this empirical intuition, namely, extension and shape. These belong to pure intuition, which exists *a priori* in the mind, as a mere form of sensibility, and without any real object of the senses or any sensation.
>
> The science of all the principles of sensibility *a priori,* I call *transcendental aesthetic.* There must, then, be such a science forming the first part of the transcendental doctrine of elements, in contradistinction to that part which contains the principles of pure thought, and which is called *transcendental logic.*
>
> In the science of transcendental aesthetic accordingly, we shall first isolate sensibility or the sensuous faculty, by separating from it all that is annexed to its perceptions by the conceptions of understanding, so that nothing be left but empirical intuition.[1]

It is important to understand the fundamental nature of sensuous knowledge as Kant explains it in his *Critique of Pure Reason.* It comes very close to the unique role that a person's subjectivity plays in their appreciation of an empirical experience:

> In order to prevent any misunderstanding, it will be requisite, in the first place, to recapitulate, as clearly as possible, what our opinion is with respect to the fundamental nature of our sensuous cogitation in general. We have intended, then, to say that all our intuition is nothing but the representation of phenomena; that the things which we intuit, are not in themselves so constituted as they appear to us; and that if we take away the subject, or even only the subjective constitution of our senses in general, then not

1. *Great Books of the Western World,* ed. Robert Maynard Hutchins, vol. 42: Kant, (Encyçlopedia Britannica, Chicago, 1952), pp. 23-24.

> only the nature and relations of objects in space and time, but even space and time themselves disappear; and that these, as phenomena, cannot exist in themselves, but only in us. What may be the nature of objects considered as things in themselves and without reference to the receptivity of our sensibility is quite unknown to us. We know nothing more than our own mode of perceiving them, which is peculiar to us, and which, though not of necessity pertaining to every animated being, is so to the whole human race. With this alone we have to do. Space and time are the pure forms thereof; sensation the matter. The former alone can we recognise *a priori,* that is, antecedent to all actual perception; and for this reason such cogitation is called *pure* intuition. The latter is that in our cognition which is called cognition *a posteriori,* that is, *empirical* intuition. The former appertain absolutely and necessarily to our sensibility, of whatsoever kind our sensations may be; the latter may be of very diversified character. Supposing that we should carry our empirical intuition even to the very highest degree of clearness, we should not thereby advance one step nearer to a knowledge of the constitution of objects as things in themselves. For we could only, at best, arrive at a complete cognition of our own mode of intuition, that is, of our sensibility, and this always under the conditions originally attaching to the subject, namely, the conditions of space and time; while the question: 'What are objects considered as things in themselves?' remains unanswerable even after the most thorough examination of the phenomenal world.[2]

In the first line of verse 8, *o̥ḷimutalām, paḻamañcum* and *untu* should be carefully examined to understand their aesthetic interconnectedness. *Oḷi* means light, with an affective quality. It does not stand by itself as an abstraction. It immediately suggests its counterpart: the 'I' that is attracted by the light. The word *mutalām* implies the initiation of the chain of events that are imperative whenever the attraction of light is registered in an appreciating eye. It is followed by the

2. *Ibid.*, pp. 29-30.

suggestion *paḻam*, an edible fruit. The allegorical force engendered by putting the images of the attracting light and the edible fruit side by side subjectively creates a pleasurable situation through the complementary interaction of the two images. Even at the word level of suggestion, the Kantian intuition of transcendent aesthetics — the a priori — is maintained.

Thus, in this verse a psychological phenomenon comes on the heels of an ontological urge, and is followed by its own pattern which is typical of each person concerned. The subtle nuance of the suggestion is so forceful that one wants to hide from oneself on hearing these words, because the hint given by them recalls to one's mind many anecdotal memories one might well want to bury or forget. Then, like the bang of a rifle shot, comes the reminder of death. From an attitude of playfulness one is abruptly called to consider the serious eventuality of death. This is like suddenly calling the attention of a clown who is doing pranks in a circus arena to the grim reality of the gas chamber. Even when a person is indulging in the trivialities of life with an outward show of gaiety, he is often reminded of the possibility of tragedy that may be encountered at any moment. This is a peculiar context, but so very common in life. Two imperatives come from opposite sides, as it were, and both claim the pursuance of their path by the ego consciousness, which is caught between the conclusive compulsions of incipient memories and the moral dictates of a volition that cannot be superseded without aggravating the tragedy of one's placement in a conse-quential chain of events. One says "enjoy;" the other says "withdraw." It is a perennial dilemma.

Some of the deeper aspects of the problem which is presented in a muted form in this verse will be further explicated in verses 69 and 70. In verse 69, the organs of perception, such as hearing, are compared to horses that are yoked to a chariot of libido. The ego which rides in it is described as a shadow of the Self, which is always drawn towards objects of pleasure. Irresistibly, the chariot is driven in pursuit of these ephemeral items of interest. In verse 70, the same libido is presented as a phenomenon of magical potency that unfolds itself as the inner organ, the senses, and the body and its very many hedonistic urges. We should bear these descriptions in mind when we think of the five birds who are enjoying fruits such as visual beauty.

The movement of the birds is qualified as *nayēna*, evasive. The word *naya* has several shades of meaning. The tactics of a diplomat are called *naya*. The implication is that in outward form one seems to be upholding ethical norms and correct behaviour, while at heart one is maneuvering with conceit. The defense mechanism of concupiscence is *naya*. In the Holy Koran one can find hundreds of passages decrying this kind of conceit. For a spiritual or moral life, one is asked to be straightforward and simple.

The Freudian concept of the clash between the id and the superego being reflected in the neurotic behaviour of the ego, can be used to more fully understand the connotation of the term *naya*. The operation of the moral authority of the superego is a kind of mirroring within oneself of a false image of public expectations. One then tries to conform to the requirements of that pattern with continuous deliberation, while at the same time indulging in a secretive enjoyment of forbidden pleasures, privately painting them with altruistic motives to look as bright and acceptable as possible. The ethical considerations of trying to please both oneself and the public are as enigmatic as the Sphinx. The kind of morality upheld by this kind of attitude is what Henri Bergson describes as closed and static. It is opposed to the morality of an absolutist, which is both open and dynamic. In *The Devil's Disciple,* George Bernard Shaw tries to show the distinction between these two kinds of morality. The dharma that Narayana Guru wants adopted is what the Isavasya Upanishad describes as the ethics of a truthful person, *satya dharma*.

The final instruction given in this verse is to subvert one's interest in the gratification of desires, which was exemplified in the first two lines of the verse by the tactual enjoyment of the fruits by the five birds or sense interests. The straight, literal meaning of *kīḻmaṟikkum* is 'bringing down'. There is also an implied sense of 'inverting the situation'. This can be better understood in the light of the Freudian concepts of the topography of the unconscious, preconscious and conscious factors, and the movement of psychic energy either horizontally or vertically. In the present context, the Freudian id is to be taken as the incipient memories which have within them the potencies of karma in various stages of maturation.

Although Freud speaks of the topology of consciousness, the situation is so mobile that the landscape is constantly fluctuating. There are two kinds of energy spoken of here which have a mutual affinity. One is the light that is revealing the presence of an object of enjoyment, which is recognised by behaviourists as a stimulus affecting the receptors. The other is a quantum of energy, which Freud recognised as a libidinal cathexis coming from the depth of the individual's unconscious and flowing towards the source of physical stimulation.

To understand this a bit better, let us take the example of a certain variety of sesame seed grown in South India. Usually it is sown in February and blossoms in April. If, by mistake, the same type of seed is sown in May, you still have to wait until April of the next year for it to blossom. So it is not merely the physical environment that makes the seed unfold its characteristics. It has within it a genetic encoding of its programme. Similarly, each incipient memory has its own inner rhythm of releasing its libidinal energy.

In this process, every instance of experiential encounter with an object of interest results in the diffusion of energy. When energy is taken from one area, it naturally loses that much energy. Understood in this sense, the overt enjoyment of pleasures is a continuous process of the exhaustion of one's reserve of psychical energy. So there is a paradoxical element of self-destruction involved.

In certain cases the expression of libidinal energy circulates inwardly rather than being directed toward an external object. Freud had occasion to notice this only in some pathological cases where a person was indulging in autoeroticism. Freud here confuses the body and the self, a common misunderstanding. But limiting pleasure to autoeroticism is still directing the energy to an objective expression and not to the core of oneself. Thus, his was only a partial view.

What Narayana Guru recommends here is a healthy way of turning one's energy inward: conserving and directing energy by concentering all interests within one's own self. This brings about a process of sublimation, which unfortunately has not been explored very much by psychologists. Alfred Adler, who had an intimation of this depth, tried to pinpoint it by examining the insights of Dostoevsky, who he quotes as saying, "I have a mad love of penetrating to the limits of the real, there where the phantastic begins." Adler continues:

> His attacks he describes as making him feel as though an intoxication of joy enticed him to the furthermost limits of the sensation of living, where he felt himself near God, so near indeed, that only one step would have sufficed to cut him off from life. This picture recurs again and again in all his heroes and has a profound significance.[3]

Going to this depth can be either pathological, bordering on the symptoms of epilepsy, or it can be one of the highest forms of spiritual absorption, so powerful as to make one's body tremble when external consciousness is withdrawn into such a profound sense of inward ecstasy. Once, when Sri Ramakrishna casually viewed the flight of some white herons against the background of a dark cloud, the beauty of the birds gliding in harmony was so telling that he entered into an ecstatic spiritual absorption. In such an experience, the energy is not going outward to the object. Rather, it is received into the vortex of the soul or psyche in an inversion of the energy flow. Instead of a sensuous experience triggered by an external stimulus, the entire psychic field spirals centripetally to the core of one's deepest consciousness. One experiences both the inside and the outside as a continuous whole of the same blissful Self. Dhan Gopal Mukerji, in *The Face of Silence*, speaks of another such experience of Sri Ramakrishna:

> Wherever Rama Krishna looked, he saw Light, Light, Light. "I have found you, I have found you." Crying, he dashed out of the temple. Wherever he went he saw nothing but light. The Ganges curved at his feet like a sickle of gold. The shore on which he stood was but a rock of solid flame. The trees in the distance, the boats and their boatmen in the middle of the river, the birds coursing through the sky, and the very sky itself sang possessed of the Divine Light. "I

3. Alfred Adler, *The Practice and Theory of Individual Psychology* (Routledge & Kegan Paul Ltd., 1964), p. 283.

have found you, I have found you!" He cried with the Rishis of old:

"Harken unto me, ye sons of Immortality.
I have found Him the Person Supreme!
Even the Gods — those dwellers in the
highest spaces — are humbled now that I
have found Him the sun-clad One!"[4]

Although in these words of Dhan Gopal Mukerji's there is a poetic exaggeration of the seer's inner sense of wonder, it is nonetheless a portrayal of the true experience of the spiritual inversion which Narayana Guru wants us to understand. Between the object of interest and the pleasurable experience of the self, there is a numerator/denominator relationship. The object of interest is the numerator, and the ego-oriented self which seeks gratification is hiding in the unconscious as the denominator. When the situation is inverted with the envisioning of the Supreme Self as the occasion of all happiness, the Self is pushed into the forefront as the numerator. The object that was initially instrumental in verticalising the self, its awareness, and its blissful nature into a unitive whole, effaces its individuality and goes into the denominator as the existence that precedes the essence.

4. Dhan Gopal Mukerji, *The Face of Silence* (E.P. Dutton & Co., New York, 1926), pp. 37-38.

Verse 9

irupuṟavum varumāṟavasthayeppū-
ttoru koṭivannu paṭarnnuyarnnumēvum
taruvinaṭikku tapassuceytu vāḻum-
naranu varā narakam ninacciṭēṇam

Growing on both sides, in a blossoming state,
is the one vine which has come, spread out and risen
to the top of a tree;
remember that hell does not come
to the man dwelling in contemplation beneath it.

In the last verse there was also a reference to a tree. It was bearing five kinds of fruit. Five birds, representing the five senses, were flying around and enjoying those fruits. In a note of drastic action, a hunter belonging to the same context as the tree shoots at the five birds and brings them down. This implies an inversion to verticalise the horizontal tendencies of the 'birds'.

Now we have the same picture revised in a more peaceful, contemplative manner. The whole life situation is once again symbolised by a tree. In a sense the tree represents the historical duration of consciousness. We are already familiar with the four alternating states of consciousness: the wakeful, dream, deep sleep and the transcendental. The wakeful and the dream states are conceived horizontally, while we think of a vertical core rising from the deep sleep state to the transcendental. We do not know anything in deep sleep, and the transcendent state passes unnoticed. What remains is the alternation between the wakeful and dream states.

Thus, the space of our everyday living is filled either with wakeful experience or dream experience. Our wakeful experience cannot make any sense if the external items are not meaningfully related to an inner consideration of their worth or value. A glorious sunrise comes. You turn to it and say "how wonderful!" Outside is the sun, inside is the wonder. The love for the beautiful is embedded in us. Even when no beautiful thing is being presented, the capacity to appreciate beauty is still within us. Everything which happens in wakeful life has a corresponding urge, interest or value vision lying buried in the deep unconscious. This is the causal factor which produces the effect of what is experienced, called *suṣupti*, or *suptam*.

Suptam is the state of the unconscious, but it is not by any means empty. Like a seed pod, it has many seeds embedded in it. These are called vasanas. Some of them are cyclic in their manifestations. For instance, there are certain kinds of lilies which flower only in a particular season. You can bury the bulb in your garden anytime, but it will lie there dormant until its proper season comes. Then it will flower forth. There are other kinds which are not seasonal, they just go on blooming. Whether seasonal or unseasonal, the seeds of all our experiences lie buried in the garden of our unconscious.

Now let's talk about the dream state. Where do all these images in our dreams come from? There is a myth-creating tendency within us, which is capable of finding appropriate symbols to make a language like that of a fairy tale. This is lying buried in the same place as the urges of the wakeful state. It is a common repository from which wakeful life and dream life are both manifesting. The wakeful and the dream are both causally related to the deep unconscious, where the seeds of all these concepts are lying in wait, seeking to be promoted in one way or another, either as an actual experience or, if an actual experience cannot be promoted, then as a dream experience. Freud and others think that a dream is the expression of an incomplete wakeful experience, a wish-fulfilment, or a prophecy or premonition of the mind.

There is a secret in all this. Where is it all happening? It all happens in the individuation of consciousness. The individuated consciousness comes from the non-individuated consciousness. Non-individuated consciousness has no time; time is a factor which only comes as a part of the structured functioning of the mind itself. The human mind can act only through a series of interrogations, *manas*. After *manas* comes *cittam*, association with memory; *buddhi*, judgement; and *ahamkāra*, affectivity based on the value-assessment. This completes one unit of mental activity. Almost immediately the next unit comes. We cannot attend to two units at a time, we can only go from one to another. In this way the mind becomes sequential, and the idea of duration is created. Time is essentially a way of looking at the movement of the conscious mind. We have made devices like clocks and sundials, but these are not time. Time is a kind of memory knot or an aid solely fabricated out of the human mind.

The mind also needs to be able to place things in some kind of setting. If there are three objects before us, they should be placed in a certain way so they can all be separate from each other. Composition is another of the mind's functions. It is like an artist arranging items when he wants to paint a still life. He puts the vase and flowers in a certain way, with some other object on the table placed just so. If he puts them all in one place it would be difficult to distinguish the outlines of one from another. So he has to spatially separate everything. If the same artist wants to paint a forest or a panoramic view, he still has choices to make, although the scene has been composed by nature already. He may not choose to paint many small shrubs and trees. He might isolate one big tree, then two other trees, a stump, the lake, and a part of the hill. Out of the many elements he selects some and omits others; then he structures them to suit his sensibility. Similarly, the mind structures its own spatial and temporal compositions, basically for its own convenience or to suit its level of understanding.

This goes on within a grouping of several minds as well. The world is already a complex phenomenon, structured by the compositions of many minds. This is the world tree to which we have come, to sit before it in contemplation and also to send our twin vines of objectivity and subjectivity on the journey of growth and extrapolation along its trunk.

The Guru begins the verse by referring to the six states. These are: the state of being before birth, birth, growth, transformation or evolution, degeneration and final extinction. Everything comes out of the state of eternal being. Then it is born into the process of becoming as an individual; it grows, changes, gets old; and finally it dies, disappears, vanishes. This is true of everything that transpires within the waking state. It is also true of our dreams. Before a dream comes, the elements of it and the reason for it are lying buried as a necessity in the seed state. When the seed is expressed as a dream, it sprouts into fantastic forms full of meaning. After a time, as another seed presses forward for expression, interest in the previous one wanes, and it disappears.

In our wakeful life, a particular necessity arises out of many potential necessities. It assumes a certain reality, a certain form. At that point the necessity becomes very categorical, a hard and fast imperative that can move us to action. Finally it is either fulfilled or its importance is slowly lost, and the interest dissipates and is gone.

In this verse, a certain creeper is branching into two and flowering forth as these wakeful and dream experiences. The deep sleep state lies hidden within us as a ground or seedbed of tremendous potentials. It is an unconscious mass. Like Pandora's box, we do not know what good things and bad things lie buried in it. When once life begins to function, the creeper comes up out of its seed. A new baby, like Deva here, says "my time has not yet come. Leave most of it buried. Every day I will express just a little bit." She programmes little smiles for two minutes. Then one scream, then back to a smile. Then she has fifteen minutes of loud screams with a variety of expressions, and then she goes back to sleep. But next year, she won't sit in anybody's lap. She will push everyone away and be busy exploring everything.

In the process of the realisation of the Self we are always trying to attain the state of the transcendental. The transcendental, or the witness, is here separated from the tree. The Guru symbolises it by a contemplative who sits under the tree of manifestation. About him many things are happening. He sees that all these things are going on, but he just sits there, seemingly unconcerned. He is not sitting there as a careless hobo, though, because the creepers are always growing in all directions and covering everything. Along with his detachment he is very awake to the situation around him, so that he doesn't become entangled in it. If you are not alert as you sit there, if you don't sit in just the proper way, you will also be caught and covered. And yet, you do not run away from it. You sit right under it, doing tapas.

What is tapas? In the Bhagavad Gita certain examples of tapas are given. For instance, I have these hands with which I can wreak a lot of destruction. I can also use them to create beneficial things or to help others. When my actions are withdrawn from anything negative, and my potentials are allowed to operate for the well-being of the world and to contribute to the perennial virtues of life, it is a tapas or ascetic discipline of the body.

Likewise, I can use my tongue to fabricate many lies, manipulate the minds of people, create difficult situations, cause agony for others, make two people quarrel or make whole groups of people fight. I can become a pedagogue of the streets, cause mass movements and revolutions and bloodshed, even create a situation where one country goes to war with another, or start a world war.

The great war of the Mahabharata, in which so many people were killed, began with one man, Yudhiṣṭhira. He was challenged to gamble. With a rightful stand, he could have said "no, I don't want to gamble." But he said "Okay." From that simple beginning the whole war started. A woman was ill-treated during the gambling. She said to her husband Arjuna, "I will not tie the knot of my hair until you tie it with the blood of the man who mistreated me." So he promised her, and for the fulfilment of that vow the great war was fought.

The Ramayana is similar. Sita asked Rama to go and get a golden deer. Lakṣmaṇa was protecting her, but she abused him and sent him away. Then Rāvaṇa came and kidnapped her, and the whole epic began.

These are instances where the words used caused great misunderstandings and tragedies. On the other hand, we have Sophia or Sarasvati, the goddesses of wisdom, and Vāgdevī, the goddess of the word. With them, words are rarely used. When they are, it is to console or inspire someone, to express a noble idea, to bring about something beautiful. They are used for a friendly assurance or to give courage. When we use our words only for these purposes, otherwise keeping silent, we are said to be doing tapas with our tongue or our word.

When the mind is withdrawn from all the horizontalities of life and is geared to a perception of higher truth and the manifestation of its beauty, we are doing tapas with our mind. The contemplative who is sitting quietly under the tree is not just wasting his time. Although he looks somewhat unconcerned, he is actively engaged, concerned with everyone and everything. He is full of love and full of consideration. If he wants to be able to save anyone, he has to keep from being entangled in the creeper, to keep himself detached.

If three people are drowning and a fourth takes pity on them and swims into the middle of the three, they will catch hold of him from three sides and all four will drown. So he needs to do it intelligently, first taking one to safety and then going back for the next. Only chance determines whether he can save all three. At least he won't be killed along with them.

Your compassion should be such that you are not caught in a snare in the name of compassion. You have to detach yourself. Martin Luther King spoke of having a cause for which you are willing to die. We want to change that to a cause for which you are willing to live. Dying is not a great virtue. Living is the great virtue, and not only living now, but living forever.

Have you ever noticed that when you dream you can be conscious of the dream being a dream, but that awareness does not prevent the dream from manifesting. You cannot get out of the dream until it is over, even when you know you are dreaming. A dream may be very fascinating, though, or very eerie; anything can happen in it. But it does not overwhelm us, because we know it will vanish as soon as we wake up. Our wakeful life can be very similar. Things may look so important, but there is another consciousness which says, "The world is like that, and it is just a passing phenomenon. We really cannot do anything about it."

This aspect of consciousness is symbolised by the person who is sitting under the tree. We are the tree. There is no other. In this tree, time and space are getting filled by our wakeful experience on one side and our dreams on the other; they are both originating from our own deep unconscious. While this is going on, the witnessing aspect of consciousness is removed from it and made to sit contemplatively under the same tree, watching all the many events of life taking place.

This is the imagery of the verse. Look for the creeper within you which is blossoming as your wakeful life hour after hour. Watch for your fantasising aspect that is blooming in another direction. Also examine the root, the seeds of all this in your transactions in the wakeful and in your fantasies. Decide how much total participation you should have in these two kinds of functioning. If you involve yourself too much, it will pinch you. That pinching is here called *narakam*, hell.

Now turn inward and watch the silent depth of the unconscious. See how from that depth, into which we cannot penetrate, ideas spring up, concepts come as mental pictures. However much we try, we cannot go beyond a certain limit of consciousness to fathom the depth from which these thoughts and images come. Now add to that unconscious depth the many autonomic functions going on in the body, of which we do not know anything, either. By studying textbooks we know the inferential guesses made by people who call themselves scientists about what they think the functions of the kidneys, pancreas and many such vital organs are. But we are none the less ignorant about the reality of those functions.

We are, though, conscious of our breathing. Although respiration goes on most of the time without our being aware of it, we can do it consciously. Yet we cannot consciously hold our breath for a long time. Something beyond our consciousness compels us to give up that deliberation. A struggle of life and death comes, and we are forced to live.

When we add the unconscious in us to the unknown in us, the sum total remains at the causal source. We have as its counterpart our conscious experiences, and also those aspects of our behaviour pattern which we do deliberately. There are aspects of our psychophysical organism that are known, and there are conscious reasoning, sensation and volition. Putting together the conscious and the known with the unconscious and unknown, we get a total picture of our individuation.

Let us go a step further. Retrospectively look into your life and recognise certain emotional patterns, beliefs, ways of looking at life and the like, which are similar or identical with those of your parents. Also consider the skills and talents you have learned from them. Next, call to your mind whatever you know of your parents, such as their physical forms, voices, special mannerisms, and skills. Consider certain of their behavioural patterns, their beliefs and prejudices, which make no sense to you. We very much want them to behave differently, think differently, or have different beliefs, but they are holding onto patterns we do not appreciate. We really do not know anything of their motivations, what is going on within them. We also do not know the genetic similarity they have with our grandparents and great-grandparents.

Here we have a conscious picture of the continuation of the life of our parents in us. When all this is added up, you will find an extension or extrapolation of the unconscious causal factors in you. You can see the depth of that unconscious timewise, ranging back through the millennia of the evolution of life. This gives us some idea of the depth of the unconscious, which we experience here and now within ourselves.

Next, call to your mind a picture of the world. What is it that we call world? The world map may come to mind. Some of the recent satellite photographs of Earth may also come up. We may review pictures we have seen in astrophysics texts, ranging from formations of nebulae to the various constellations of the Milky Way, our own solar system and the planetary systems. Then we think of the Earth itself, with its oceans, mountains, political regions and national boundaries, and the historical rise and fall of cultures, dynasties and civilisations. Our present moment is structured out of all this. But apart from the concepts, do we know anything about the reality behind these images and pictures? No, we don't.

So, first we pictured the depth of our unconscious, and now we have a peripheral vision of the horizontal breadth that is historical, geographical, mythological and legendary. It is the world we appreciate poetically and aesthetically, the world we love and abhor, the world where we feel roots, and the world we want to demolish, change, reform.

Now place yourself as an individual in that world, which has a peripheral dimension of many conceptual images and also a great depth of the unconscious extending from you to the very origin of the universe. What you are now doing is an act of witnessing. Experience this aspect of consciousness calmly and uniformly, with no special interest. Just watch it and see it. Then compare this neutral state of mind to your consciousness when you very badly want to do something. See how enthusiastic you become, how much energy you put into it, how your whole system becomes animated with that enthusiasm. This is to be distinguished from the witnessing consciousness. Whenever we are self-pitying, or when we are enjoying all the changing, passing states of mind, this one consciousness is always looking on. It is never affected. Some other aspect in us gets affected and afflicted, and the witness sees how we are afflicted.

All this is pictured in the allegory of a tree covered with a blossoming creeper which has two vines. One vine represents the perceptual order of our conscious, wakeful transactions; the other the conceptual order, including all our subjective fantasising and imagination. The depth we have referred to is understood as the seed of the creeper. Its flowers are our individual experiences which have become permanent expressions, as well as what we have taken on from the recorded experience of mankind in the form of history, art, literature, and all the manifestations of human workmanship like the formations of cities and monuments.

The person sitting under the tree symbolises that tiny bit of consciousness that witnesses the unfolding of life all about itself. Compared to all that, the witnessing consciousness is like a shimmering star lost in an oceanic universe of conglomerations. There is every chance of losing track of it at any time. Although it looks insignificant, it is the centre on which all activities of our life find their ground and their motivation.

Long ago in bucolic India it was not uncommon for people to sit under a tree in contemplation. Nowadays this can only happen in ideal situations. When we try to locate that very peaceful witnessing centre, we become aware of a terrible noise and a kind of restlessness in the atmosphere. When this kind of demand is made on the senses and the mind, it can evoke in us many strange emotions tied up with our latent potentials and incipient memories. Our curiosity is aroused and we become distracted. It is a real struggle to keep our balance and remain in absolute resonance with the passivity of the centre. We sit for five minutes waiting for the noise to quit or go away. Then we become impatient. We get up to go investigate, and become entangled in whatever is going on. But for one who wants to go deeper into the reality of the Self, this is to be taken as a real challenge. How much forbearance can you cultivate, and how are you to remain unruffled in spite of the situation?

Our vulnerability to distraction produced the element of exasperation we noticed in verse seven. There the Guru pointed out that the many demands of nature, such as sleeping, waking, eating, mating and so on, come to us continuously. This flux leaves us little chance to know the changeless reality in which all the changes are mirrored. Yet while the mirror may be filled with the many turbulences of the external world, it remains unaffected. Similarly the pure witnessing consciousness, while seemingly being modified, really does not undergo any modification. In verse eight, the Guru recommended a rather drastic attitude to refocus our contemplation, which can bring it to a position of great stability as exemplified in the present verse by the contemplative beneath the tree.

The challenge here is both real and unreal. It is unreal in the sense that it comes and goes, but it is real in the sense that it can cause genetic potentialities to perpetuate whatever misery and joy we experience as individuated beings. The psychophysical organism used as a tool by the Unknown definitely undergoes substantial change, and it persists even beyond the individual's lifetime. Biologically it is proliferated and continued from generation to generation. This is why the Guru said, "Oh, who is there to know this unmodified state of the Self?"

Then he brought us to an enigmatic situation where we have two definite alternatives. One is to go beyond all these transient changes, to identify with the changeless and remain as that knowledge, *arivum*. As verse seven pointed out, this is not at all easy for most of us. And if it is not possible to do it, we should then turn to those who have succeeded, establish bipolarity with them, and through that bipolarity also attain to the changeless state.

The instruction of verse eight is to adopt a drastic attitude. You should not allow your mind to be like a wandering dog in the street. You should become its master. This little awareness which is just witnessing has in it at least the potential for omniscience. In most of us, the omniscience of the witnessing element is a bit like the United Nations. The U.N. sees what is going on all over the world, but it has no power to stop a nation from indulging in any stupidity. It can only advise, "Don't do it." We also have a Unified Notion in the omniscient witness in us which sees everything. If we cultivate it, if we give it a volitional power, it would be like handing over all the world's militaries to the United Nations and giving it a mandate over the so-called sovereignty of the individual states. It would then be able to prevent atrocities.

This could actually happen, but at present it does not. There are certain individuals, though, who do practice it. They combine their witnessing consciousness with their volitional consciousness. This is extremely effective as long as the witnessing consciousness is established on a normative notion of good for all, highest beauty, supreme truth and unlimited commitment.

There is an element of fakery and deception when a preconceived, prefabricated version of life is presented to us. It disguises the essential true nature behind it. Freud and people like him did great service to humanity by pointing out that both situations and the people who are confronted by situations wear masks, and we should tear them away in order to be fully alive. When you are centered in the witnessing consciousness you can clearly see the painted masks worn by people and events. Very few people, however, know the nature of the reality hidden behind them.

We are here in a search to see what is behind the masks. What is immediately behind them are the very many urges which we call incipient memories, or vasanas. For these forces defense is absolutely necessary, and the mask itself is the defense mechanism. Unfortunately, while these masks protect society, they also blindfold the individual from seeing his own reality.

In the present verse, Narayana Guru implores us to come out of this deluding situation, to sit outside it and watch the game. Once your mask is gone, it is easy for the witnessing consciousness to establish itself on the ground of an absolutist norm, such as universal truth, universal goodness, universal beauty. That's why he said the person sitting under that terrible tree can do tapas. The need to be austere was already suggested in verse eight; here that austerity is made a permanent feature and not just a single action. The single act of bringing down the birds progresses to a habitual performance of tapas.

Many methods have been taught by the great Masters to achieve detachment from the ensnaring creepers of the world tree, and to cultivate an absolutist vision which can turn individuation into a tool to serve the purpose of higher truth, goodness and beauty. The Buddha said we should have the right mode of seeing, of thinking, of speaking, of behaving, of feeling. How does one find the right mode? By taking refuge in the Buddha, by taking refuge in the four-fold truth, by cultivating the five virtues. In the morning, a Buddhist monk gets up and repeats three times that he is taking refuge in the Buddha, the dharma and the sangha. Then he takes five pledges:

> I take the vow that with this hand of mine I will never hurt any sentient being.
> I take the pledge that I will not grab anything which does not come to me as benevolently apportioned by nature.
> I take the pledge that I will not waste even a second in worthless talk or gossip.
> I will not allow desires to take me out of the path of righteousness. I will always stick by the right path.
> I will not allow any kind of narcotics or addictive substances to pollute the comprehension of my mind.

Then he will study the scriptures in company with his fellow monks, probing deeply into the life and teachings of the Buddha. This is one way to detach oneself from the entanglements of the world and become liberated. There are many others.

Another way is to walk into the open arms of Jesus Christ and feel the warmth of his love in your heart. He says, listen to the Word of my Father, listen to the Word which comforts and saves. He enunciates the nature of the kingdom of God and how one qualifies to enter it. Then he gives the assurance that he will show us the path and the goal, the light and the life, death and resurrection.

Or you can take the Islamic way, which is so beautifully given to us by the Sufis, of making Allah your beloved. Lao Tzu exemplifies the witnessing Self which remains at the neutral zero. A most wonderful way is to examine the paradoxes of life and try to understand their inner cohesion.

Still another way is as the rishis have taught. From ancient times down to, say, Ramana Maharshi in our time, they have all taken the question, "Who am I?" and diligently followed the track of where it led them. That path took them away from all the superficial disturbances to the pure light, which we have just now placed under the tree as the contemplative witness. Such a seer is by no means a derelict, though those preoccupied with masks and surfaces might call him one. In terms of value, he is working harder and more effectively than most very busy people. He is exercising and experiencing great purification.

There are really only three states, the waking, the dreaming and the unconscious. Witnessing is not in itself a state, or *avasthā*. It is the one which is seeing all the states. It is more like a catalyst in bringing dramatic changes to them. From now on we will be concentrating our attention on knowing more of this witnessing Self, which can detach itself from the three aspects of consciousness and remain pure.

Verse 10

"iruḻil irippavanāru? colka nī" ye-
nnoruvan urappatu kēṭṭu tānumēvam
aṟivatināyavanōṭu "nīyumār" e-
nnaruḻumitin prativākyamēkamākum

"Who is sitting in the dark? Speak, you!"
In this manner one speaks; having heard this, you also
to know, ask him, "And who are you?"
To this as well, the response is one.

If you close your eyes and try to visualise your existence from inside, it is hard to decide where the boundaries and limitations of your body actually are. You can feel certain vague sensations here and there, but from inside with your eyes closed you cannot see where the outer periphery of the skull is. In fact, everything merges into a kind of total darkness. Yet the clarity of your idea of existence is not the least affected. It remains the same. We are asked to imagine a situation where we can reduce the input of all our sensory data to just the voice that we hear. Touch, smell, taste and sight are to be removed from our mind.

In such a situation you are fully aware of your own existence, and you recognise it by saying "I." In this special state, suppose you sense that another person is also present. To make sure you ask, "Who is there?" You get an answer, "I." How do you understand what you heard when you heard "I?" You understand it by turning to your own concept of 'I'. The other person understood your 'I' by comparing it to his experience of the term. With this understanding, have you gone beyond your own knowledge to any extent? Not at all.

There is a great demand on our consciousness all the time for it to transmute and transform into whatever conceptual idea is presented to us through the perception of the five senses. For instance I may say, "I have seen a blue lotus. It was very beautiful." On hearing this, you have to think of a lotus flower and also of the colour blue. You have to recall an experience when you enjoyed something, possibly not even a flower at all, and transfer that enjoyment together with the other concepts. Then you make a composition of all of them in your mind before you can imagine how I experienced the blue lotus. Only then can you say, "Yes, I understand. It must have been very beautiful."

This process sounds a bit intellectual, but the inner perception involved is not entirely intellectual. It is to be approached from within, and not from outside in the academic manner. It can be fully understood only by silently absorbing oneself into the all-knowing, all-seeing, all-feeling greater psyche which belongs to everyone. This opens up the floodgates of love, and you become one with all. The counterpart of this is to close doors and create exclusions and inclusions.

If a child comes to its mother and says, "Mom, my ear hurts," she understands. But how does she understand it? Her own ear is not hurting. Instead, she has had a previous experience of that kind of pain. When the child says "my," the mother sympathetically repeats in her mind "my." Then she introjects her own concept of a painful ear into this "my." Finally she projects the understanding thus gained back onto the child. So there are simultaneous functions of introjection and projection operating in the process of understanding, and both belong solely to our own 'I' consciousness. A series of memories are called up and structured around this 'I' consciousness. This is the only way the mother can have an idea of the particular kind of pain the child is actually experiencing. In fact, it is impossible for her to go outside of herself to know anything about what the child actually feels.

It is only a small step to realise that the child which the mother sees is itself a composition of her own perceptual data, to which are added other conceptual memories. In the transactional world we have every evidence that the mother and child are two separate entities: the child with its pain and the mother with her own sensibility; the mother attending to the child and the child appealing to the mother. All these are of course valid, but when we philosophically examine the situation, we have to reduce the seeming difference between the child and its mother to just one witnessing consciousness.

This is the same witnessing consciousness which was placed under the tree of life in the previous verse. It reappears in this verse as a homogeneous principle which contains within it all our seemingly divergent experiences. When you call me "you," I understand it as "I." When I call you "you," you understand it as "I." The 'you' and 'I' we speak of are only understood conceptually. This is a special kind of enigma, called maya. Only one consciousness is operating, but it is capable of differentiating parts of itself from itself to structure personalities, things, ideas and events, which then seem to stand apart from it and become a separate reality. It then interacts with what it generates.

Every mother thinks that she understands her child, while actually she understands an aspect of herself and imagines she is understanding the child. There is nothing wrong with this. In fact, it is the true nature of things. If the consciousness which functions through our organisms were really different, there would be no homogeneity. Mutual understanding and interpersonal transactions would not be possible. The mere fact that we understand shows that we are actually the same, in the same way that the mother and child are the same. Everything we experience is the same.

We are now seeing the witnessing self a little more closely. We need to also be looking at how it can become afflicted and non-afflicted. When the child says "I feel pain in my ear," the mother doesn't have the pain but she has the idea, "this is my child." My body, my hand, my eyes, my mind, my child — in each case the 'my' becomes the centre of a circle of awareness. What is inside the circle is of special importance to us because it is 'ours', and what falls outside the circle becomes 'the other'. Thus we separate I and the other, mine and not mine, me and not me. This is purely arbitrary. You can contract or expand the circle; you can include or exclude anyone. When you include it is called love, and when you exclude it is not-love. Hatred is another kind of inclusion, as in "my enemy."

When her child has a pain, fear suddenly comes to the mother. "Is it serious? Should I consult a doctor?" Then she thinks of all the terrible diseases which can come to children. If she is fearful by nature she may even become hysterical about it, but if she is calm she will intuitively know the proper course of action to take. So on one hand, our identity in consciousness can have the liberating effect of seeing oneself in all. Knowing the witnessing consciousness as the same in all beings is an enlightening experience. But when we are obsessed with the circumlimitation of what is "mine," we are heading for trouble. That attachment brings all the bondages which are described in the previous verse as the twofold creeper of external and internal ramifications. Externally it may lead you to many actions which are not warranted, bringing unnecessary complications and even misery; internally it may lead to delusory fantasies and fearful thoughts, which can cause confusion or great unhappiness.

The Guru has now brought us to the very core of our consciousness, which can spread out in all dimensions and include everything in itself. We can see the whole of experience as an experience of total awareness, or we can have a highly coloured experience of 'I' consciousness, afflicted and affected, with all the seeming variegations of conceptual knowledge produced by perceptual data. We should go back again and again to the pure witnessing consciousness, so that we can both remain undeluded by the superficial turmoil of manifestation and at the same time be completely available to participate in the necessary aspect of life.

It is quite difficult to maintain a balance of these two reciprocal functions, witnessing and activity, to remain detached while at the same time all the data are coming to you through your senses and being processed. It is like being split inside, with one personality sitting quiet and another doing all the activity. Psychologists call this schizophrenia, a disease. For the Vedantin it is not a disease; it is a very natural thing. We have to admit there is a twofold function in us. If we educate our psychologists a little better about the inner functionings of the psyche, at least they will no longer torture people by confirming them as schizophrenic patients. Later on we will go into this in greater depth, but for now we should not exceed the scope of the present verse. Narayana Guru had a sublime scheme in mind for *Ātmopadeśa Śatakam* which we want to adhere to as closely as possible.

In the Isavasya Upanishad, we are asked to become familiar with the secret of ignorance, where I consider 'you' and 'I' as two. We are also asked to become familiar with the secret of wisdom, that 'you' and 'I' are the same. If we do not know these secrets, we can be led into ridiculous situations. Unitive understanding does not mean you can jump out of the transactional world and become something else. The world does not evaporate away when you realise the one 'I' that pervades everything. It continues to be there, so you have to come to terms with it.

All the same, the truth is that there is no world other than the one you construct out of your own concepts. It is something like a novelist or playwright who makes characters out of his own imagination, and then discovers after a few chapters that he is bound by the limitations of his creations. He has become so committed to the characters that he can't make any changes. The members of the cast refuse to allow any enlargement of scope or vision by the author. It is his own creation, but the creator has become fully dominated by his creations. In the same way we create our own world and then we become afraid of it, or we get caught up in it and we don't know how to deal with it. It is an enigmatic situation.

The meditation that one should engage in with this verse is to see the oneness, which you know through the witnessing consciousness, and also the curious way in which the world created by you makes things difficult for you.

Verse 11

***"ahamaham" ennaruḷunnatokkeyārā-
yukil akamē palatallatēkamākum
akalumahantayanēkamākayālī
tukayil aham poruḷum tuṭarnniṭunnu***

"I, I", thus, all that are spoken of,
when carefully considered, inwardly are not many;
  that is one;
as the receding I-identities are countless
in their totality, the substance of I-consciousness
  continues.

We have before us the picture of pure knowledge, as given in verse four. When we came to verse five, the Guru pointed out how it was difficult for us to remain identified with that pure state of knowledge because of the many recurring identifications such as the sleeping one, the wakeful one, and the possessor and promoter of urges. It was shown more explicitly in verse six how the necessities of life, like sustenance of the body, pressure the mind to make us seek different activities and involve us in different situations. These come to us day after day and night after night. It was noted how challenging it is to remain in the pure state of knowledge. We can either transcend all the necessities of life and remain unaffected, without any transformations or transmutations, as the ever-abiding, pure knowledge of consciousness; or we can seek the company of one who has learned the secret of transcending all the changing forms of the eternal flux.

Now we know where we stand. We admit to ourselves that it is very difficult to remain unchanged. We are constantly being dragged away by the flood of events in spite of our great desire to remain unaffected. Some terrible force is carrying us along from situation to situation. Then we were asked to examine this force which distracts us, and we realised that we are attracted by things like beautiful objects, sweet sounds, gentle touches, fascinating fragrances and delicate tastes. It is as if we are constantly being enchanted by the varied and countless distractions presented to us by our senses.

Just as we were given a choice earlier to seek the company of a liberated, realised Master, we are here given another choice. It is whether to just be helplessly swept away, or to make an absolutist break from the tendency to succumb to these kinds of pulls by discerning the value implied in each such pull. When you are attracted towards the beautiful, that thing by itself has no power to attract you if you are not already alive to the quality you see in it. Before you see beauty in something, there must be within you an idea of beauty, a power to see it, and a love for it. The occasion only awakens that dormant sense of beauty in you. If your inside was not thus stimulated and aroused to be projected onto the subject, you would not have been pulled in that direction in the first place.

So instead of projecting your inside onto an outside object and then clinging to the object, why not use the essence of the object as an opportunity to examine what is lying within you? In other words, you can make the object a mirror to reflect your inner beauty. Then you are not distracted; the very object of distraction serves as a tool for you to go deep inside and see the beauty in yourself. The knowledge of the pure knowledge which we are becomes enriched with its own *vibhūti*, its own possibility of showing its many natures. This kind of verticalising all tendencies, breaking away from the external objectivity of the pull and reversing the value vision, is a continuation of sitting at the feet of a wise one.

We are still dealing with a problem which surfaced earlier. In verse eight, the five kinds of distraction were given. In the next verse we went a little deeper, to the very cause of why the dormant tendencies in us wake up at all. Then we saw that our life is a kind of nursery ground, filled with the seeds and seedlings of millions of tendencies which are all lying buried in an apparent deep sleep called *suṣupti*. They germinate and sprout in two directions. One is the conceptual world of subjective fancies, dreams, imaginations, thoughts and reasoning. The other is actualisation in the world of space and time, name and form, action and reaction. In this way an inner world and an outer world are filled with the bountiful blossoms of various expressions. These grow to form a tree of life with its six-fold changes of being: birth into a special form of existence, growth and change, replication, decay and disappearance. An aspect that is different from all this is pictured as the one who sits and watches. The pure aspect of knowledge likewise persists, while the changing, impure state proliferates. It does not proliferate to such an extent that the pure state is completely annihilated, however.

Then we were brought to a situation to focus our attention on that pure state. If the five senses are deceptive, and if the five organs of action are giving you various promptings toward doing, let us keep them all aside except one. We turned away from all the senses other than hearing, and all the organs of action other than speaking. We tried to see what the content is when we say "I," and what it is when we say "you." 'You' and 'I' are different because I am myself and you are the other. But when I say "you" you say "I," the same as what I say. An 'I' here and an 'I' there. It sounds strange. Even in what we expect to be the other, there resides in its very core an 'I'. I understand the 'I' of the other by reference to my own 'I'. Thus, this 'I' is a great secret. In it is pure knowledge. It is also tainted by what is not pure, and can thus differentiate between 'I' and the other. The secret of the other is in 'I', and the secret of 'I' is also in the 'I'. The One is in it, and the Many also originate from it. In the present verse we are asked to look for an 'other' within ourselves. For this, the *aham* or I is to be seen as *ahanta*, the *ahanta* of this moment and the *ahanta* of the next moment.

Ahanta may be translated as 'I-consciousness', but it has a larger implication. To understand it, we must first understand *abhimāna*. *Abhi* means in the present situation; *māna* means measurement. Your 'I' measures the present situation as that which belongs to this moment and has these characteristics. Whenever you experience something there is a kind of knowledge content by which you measure its worth, you assess its meaning and what kind of affectivity you have for it. This value assessment determines the depth and kind of identity you have with that situation. This is the implication when we say *ahanta*, ego-identity.

Now you are sitting here and listening to this commentary, so your ego-identity is that of a listener. When you got up from sleep this morning and decided to come for class, you had a different kind of mind; you were thinking of all the things you needed to do to get ready. The content of that time was different from the present context. Yesterday, when you were sitting here and listening to another verse, you were thinking of some other ideas. When you were at your workplace you had another kind of ego-identity. In the passage of time, you go from one 'I' identity to another, which is here described as *akalum ahanta anēka.*

Over the course of a day we move continuously from one set of interests to another. While our ego-identities are many, we do not think that the person we are in the morning is different from the person we are in the evening. Nor do we think we are in any way different than what we were two or ten or twenty years ago. Why? There is a continuity when we put together the essence of the differing 'I' identities. All together, as Narayana Guru describes it, "Despite countless receding I-identities, in the totality of their substance the one 'I' continues," unbroken.

What is 'I' then? 'I' is a consciousness or knowledge *of* a knowledge of the present moment in the nature of that knowledge. In other words, knowing that you have knowledge of the present moment in nature, which itself is an expression of that knowledge. This is very important to know. And what is the content of 'I'? The content of 'I' is the knowledge of the knowledge of this moment that that knowledge is of such and such a nature. Where does the 'I' idea reside? It resides in the presentness of the time factor and also the content of what is presented in this moment. Without time and without content, that 'I' does not occur to us.

The content of this moment is one of listening, one of being attentive. Absorbed in contemplation, there are no sensual ticklings, no relishing of anything such as eating or drinking. We are not disturbed by someone coming and threatening us. Thus, this moment has its own quality. We live in that quality. We know it. Therefore, 'I' as an *abhimānī*, as a measurant of this moment, has its own qualitative uniqueness. Yesterday when I was in the marketplace, did it have the same quality we are experiencing now? No, it had another quality. The 'I' of the past was of that time with that nature. Now it is this time with this nature. After two more hours, it will be of that time with another nature. Within me I am seeing several different "I's": the 'I' of now, the 'I' of a previous moment, and the 'I' of a moment which is yet to be.

Do I really, seriously think that these are all different "I's?" No, I don't. Why? Because I have an assurance from inside that there is no break. If I have such an assurance, am I reasoning it? No, it is an intuitive perception. I really do not know whether it is reasoning or imagination or intuition. I just have a clarity, an absolute certainty from within that I am the same. Where does that sameness remain unbroken? It remains in the essence of all I have measured in the past, as my memory. It is in my experience of measuring this moment and my expectation of what I will be measuring in the next moment. There is a contiguity in my memory, experience and expectation. My unitive state is a continuum of memory, experience and expectation.

Now we have a scheme, a method by which we know how relata give us a clue about unification or unitive understanding. Within 'me' are many worlds of interests, which can all be linked together as my world, my life story, my biography. They are all tied together with this centerpiece: "this is what I have lived, the great matrix of my memory." So I have a method to unite things which seem to be different from each other. All that I have to look for is one homogeneous principle that resides in everything.

In the previous verse, this pure aspect of me was shown sitting under a tree. It was very cautious, so as not to be caught by the twin aspects of the creeper growing upon the tree. This creeper is like an octopus, with its tentacles extended on all sides: it might catch me and swallow me up. But I wanted to become a contemplative, and broke loose from it by sitting under the tree cautiously and vigilantly, giving up all activity. Now it cannot catch me. I have become a seeker with great diligence, relentlessly looking for the unbroken inner unity. I cannot find it in my ego identity, but I can see a thread of pure consciousness going through all.

Now we have the correlating secret of the one and the many within ourselves. The one and the many are also lying in the transactional world of time and space where my whole unit becomes one. There are also others with similar kinds of bodies, with different kinds of value-visions and value-formations and different behavioural patterns. The problem becomes complex, but I am not afraid because now I have a scheme to deal with it. It is with this preparedness we are entering into the arena of life, fully armed with a correlative scheme to live out our unitive understanding.

Verse 12

toliyumelumpu malam durantamantaḥ-
kalakaḷumēntumahantayonnu kāṇka!
poliyumitanya poliññu pūrṇṇamākum
valiyorahanta varā varam tarēṇam

See the skin, bone, dirt and inner urges which end tragically
to which the I-identity is conjoined;
this which perishes is the other; oh, grant the cherished boon
that the great I-identity increases to perfection.

We have been describing in the previous verses two juxtaposed aspects. One is the witnessing self. The other is the consciousness that is caught in these bodily functions and various kinds of modifications of the mind. When a person wants to discover his reality, it is likely he will be caught either in his physical identification or in his spiritual identification. Most of us, when the idea of 'I' comes to mind, think of the body and its mental functions. This is a fictitious 'I'; it does not exist. It is only developed as a convenience to hold together the many biologic functions and mental ideations taking place. The growing child has no idea of an 'I' when it first comes to this world. People refer to it as 'you'. Afterwards the child, imitating older people, says "I". Eventually this 'I' identity takes hold in the child.

The body is part of all that is within the 'I' identity. Outwardly, what we see is skin. Inside, the anatomical structure is made of bones, and is filled with all kinds of dirt, *malam*. In America, you might prefer to call it blood and guts. But however much you try to preserve all this, it will come to a tragic end.

The inner organ in us belongs to this organism. Within it are so many previous conditionings, called vasanas or incipient memories. When these come up they provoke the interrogating aspect of consciousness, and awareness bubbles up in the form of questions. Then memories are associated with these questions, and we make certain judgements. This leads to our affective volition, the actualisation of many desires. The ego-identity, *ahanta*, carries all this.

The body is covered with skin, and skin is sensitive. It is a sense-organ which covers our whole body. From all around us, our sensations are always producing the awareness of our bodily existence. The eyes, ears, nose and tongue are also only modified forms of skin. The skin in the eye is made extra sensitive to light; the skin in the ear is made into a drum which vibrates; the skin in the nose has its olfactory nodules; the skin in the tongue has its taste buds. After all is said and done, it is only skin. Narayana Guru here uses skin to represent the sensory system. It is a very ingenious way of combining the physical entity with the mental. The skin belongs to the mind because it is a sensory organ, and it is also the most peripheral cover, like an envelope, for holding together the muscles, tissues, nervous system and bones.

The skeletal system gives the body its specific form. When we are alive, we can run and jump and do all kinds of acrobatic feats. It looks like the system is very well structured. The bones are all well arranged and held together in their sockets. But if our very simple breath leaves the body, all these bones will come apart. If we were to go to the burial ground and dig up an old body, there wouldn't be any flesh, any skin on it. None of the organs would be seen, and even within the skull the brain and everything would be gone. It would have all been reduced to clean bones. If we were to try to pick them up, they would all come apart. Anatomists have to tie the bones together with wires to make them stand. In life, what is holding them together? Only this breath. The physiological organism of ours is very perishable.

Between the skin we spoke of and the consciousness of 'I', which in the present case means the ego, many desires arise. According to Freud, the seedbed of our desires is in the rapture of the skin, in the various visceral areas of the body. These are easily tickled. The child gets an erotic pleasure when the inside of its mouth, the skin of the inner part of its lips, is rubbed. When it sucks the mother's nipple, there is an erotic stimulation in the nipple which sends electrical charges through her to produce lactation. She secretes milk into the mouth of the child. When the child is having this rapture of the lips it is having a pure erotic pleasure, and sweet, nourishing milk also comes as a reward. It is encouraged to do more of it.

When the same milk goes to the other end, the child urinates and purges its bowels. It experiences an anal pleasure with each purging. So the child's first pleasures are sucking the mother's milk, urinating and excreting. Then the mother adds to it by touching the cheeks and under the chin. She tickles its sides, hands and legs.

All over the body there are ticklish areas. The pleasures people crave mostly come from tickling. Seeing something beautiful is an erotic pleasure where the sensitivity of the eye is tickled. The ear has harmonic pleasures from the tickling vibrations of voices and music. The nose is tickled by various odours. On the whole, we live for the pleasure of the skin. The urges for these pleasures are deep down, but they are lived at the level of the skin. So, in a sense, the pleasures of life are only skin deep.

We are very fond of touching, but if we get burned or the fingers are scalded, we are afraid to touch anything. If a thorn pricks us in the toe or the sole of the foot, it makes us nervous about touching the ground. Where pleasure is, there pain is also, living very close by. The pursuit of pleasure often brings us pain.

As if physical pain were not enough, religious people have added moral pain through the invention of guilt. In modern man, many of the pleasures of the skin are intimately connected with a moral conscience of great sin, great guilt. In America and some other places, if two men or two women are found sleeping together a lot of fuss is made about it. Instead of being praised as friendship, it is condemned as homosexuality. The whole issue of skin touching skin leads to so much fuss and so much guilt. "God in heaven will be mighty upset if skin touches skin!" whine the pious. Is it really such a big deal? Its just a small affair on a minor planet, someone's skin touching somebody else's, but we have penal codes and moral codes with so many items, labelled *a*, *b* and *c*, on and on endlessly. And lawyers argue in the courts, "Did touch, didn't touch," and show proofs and evidence.

The whole world is a mess. Mostly it is a mess because of the destruction towards which it naturally trends. The rest is due to our own foolishness: the whole affair of the ego is essentially a stupid business. What little of value remains?

Guru here says *itu poliyum*, this will perish. From the skin to all the dynamisms of all the inner urges which are seeking pleasures, this whole system will come to an end. Meditating on it won't help us much. That wouldn't give us the idea of *sarūpasiddhi*, of attaining one's own nature. You won't find the eternal by meditating on the body or the mind or any of the senses or sensory pleasures that disappear after a while.

One should turn to the pure awareness that was present even when one was in the mother's womb as a fertilised ovum, a developing fetus, and as a child who was pushing itself out through a strange kind of interaction between itself and the mother, finally to come to its own liberation. All these things are done by another awareness residing within. It is the same in the mother, the child, the father, and all the living beings all over the universe. It is a common life principle, a homogeneous principle of life, which can remain dormant, come into a form of manifestation, and assert itself in all shades of awareness, yet it is never itself affected. It is immortal; it never dies. It is called the *ātman*.

To meditate on it, the ancient wise ones made a formula, *ayam ātmā brahma*. It means, this *ātmā* is *Brahman*; this self-luminous awareness that resides in all beings is the Absolute. That which is other than that which lies between the skin and all the other urges, it never perishes. When we contemplate this, when we meditate on it continuously, there comes the perfection of that awareness.

The highest form of devotion is called *bhakti*. In his *Vivekacūḍāmaṇi*, Śaṅkara defines bhakti as the continuous contemplation of one's true form. And what is our real form? That is what realisation is: the apprehension of our own true beingness.

"That increases and becomes Absolute", *anya poliññu pūrṇṇamākum.* In this process, we must continue to maintain our primary identity, "I am the body." Otherwise, we are putting together two incompatible things: the ego-identity born of the body and mind, with the suggestion given by the rishi that "you are the Absolute". The meaning then becomes that this embodied ego is the Absolute. This is the strange position which many religious and even spiritual people unfortunately assume. Then they become megalomaniac, saying "I am Christ," "I am God," "I am an incarnation," "I am Bhagavan," or "I am an avatar." And what is that "I am" there? It is the perishable stuff which we were denouncing just a little while ago.

Śaṅkara calls this filling the dog's skin with sacred milk. In India and Arabia, people make a kind of bucket for carrying water by sewing up the skin of animals — cows, camels or dogs. Arabs use them for drinking purposes, while Indians usually use them only for carrying water at construction sites. They are considered to be very dirty, so if you bring milk in one nobody will drink it. The milk is no longer sacred when you put it in a dog's skin. Like that the ego is a dirty, foul thing. It should not be identified with the Absolute, but by mistaken notions people often do it. This not only obstructs their path to realisation, but causes them to swell up with pride, become arrogant and aggressive, and create a lot of nuisances for the world. They become very fanatical, create various kinds of personality cults, and make everyone kowtow before them. It is hard to be sure of the difference between surrender to the Absolute in the guise of a guru, and servitude to some aggressive fellow. Unknowingly we think we have chosen the right one when we have really chosen the other.

I was reading a friend's journal yesterday. She was struggling with this very problem regarding her teacher. Quite rightly, she asked herself "am I his slave in servitude, or is he an image of the Divine to whom I am surrendering myself?" This is where big trouble comes in. A person may think that this man with a beard is the guru or God. This pot-bellied, bearded man, or this bald-headed scarecrow who are called gurus are not gurus. They are perishable creatures, full of dirt like anyone else. They smell as much as anyone. It is only the light shining through the words of wisdom that is imperishable. Fortunately or unfortunately, sometimes the sound comes through an instrument which otherwise is reeking with all its dirt. This is a great warning against false identification, both for spiritual adepts and their associates.

So Narayana Guru says that if we just look at this body, we can understand how impermanent it is. On the other hand, it is not difficult to see that the Absolute never perishes. But he foresees a great danger in this perishable ego hitching itself to the imperishable Absolute, and then falsely believing that it is the Absolute. "Oh, God! Here I really need your help. Please come and give me the great blessing that I won't become a megalomaniac, that I won't have a false, bloated ego. I am unable to help myself here. You, God, should come and help me." He says "O, God, give me this great boon, that I won't become a spiritually egoistic person."

The spiritual ego is very hard to overcome. If ten people bow before you and show reverence, you may be able to retain your sanity, but it will soon leave you when more and more people show an attitude of reverence. It is extremely difficult to maintain a proper attitude.

We have a story in India that some people decided to make fun of a simpleton. He wanted to sell a small goat, so he was carrying it to the market. These people stood at different places along the way, knowing that he would soon be passing. The first man said, "What kind of a joke is this? Where are you going with that dog?"

The simpleton replied, "Dog? This is a goat."

"Goat, eh? Can't you see its a dog?"

"Dog?" He looked it over and said, "Its not a dog, its my goat." He took the first man for a fool. But when the second man asked him about his dog, he began to suspect something was wrong. He wasn't sure if the problem was with himself or the other people. When he came to the third man who called it a dog, he was all the more troubled. How can you disagree with three people? He thought, "This is probably neither a dog or a goat; it must be a devil. The devil may be showing itself to me as a goat, and showing itself to others as a dog."

When he came to the fourth man, who said "Hey, man! Is that dog for sale?" he thought, "This is really a dog. I am absolutely mad, thinking a dog is a goat. This is a real devil, and I am carrying it around!" He walked a little farther, and when nobody was around he threw it down and ran away. That was just where the fifth man was hiding; he picked up the goat and went to join his friends.

Like that, when the first man comes and says, "Oh, great guru!" you say "No, man! Don't make fun of me." Then two people come and say "great guru!" "Eh? Am I? No, I am not." Then ten people come and bow and call you a great guru. You look at yourself and ask, "Am I a great guru, or not?" Then a hundred people come, then ten thousand in seven jumbo jets. Now you cannot deny that you are really a great guru, it's all confirmed. So you have to say, "God, come and save me. This is where you are needed. I won't be able to get over this temptation by myself."

The New Testament begins with the same idea. The very first event is Jesus being taken to the top of the tower and told to jump. "See the whole world. It will be yours!" Jesus said, "Satan, get thee behind." This kind of firm attitude is what is needed. "Satan, get thee behind; you should not tempt your Lord. I am here to bow before my Lord and not before any worldly temptation." If we substitute the term 'ego' for the devil or Satan, we will never go far wrong in our interpretation of the old scriptures.

This verse asks us to discriminate between the perishing self and the imperishable Self. Identity with the imperishable Self comes by divine grace. It is not by mere intellectual pursuits or internal argumentation that we come to it. It is a divine gift, and it has to come by grace. So here, out of the philosophical scrutiny and analysis, the Guru is bringing us closer to an attitude of piety, of adoration even, of one who is helpless without divine grace. This verse instructs us to resort to prayer, to prayerfully seek divine help in knowing the true nature of things, and not to be misled by the world of phantoms.

Verse 13

triguṇamayam tirunīṟaṇiññorīśa-
nnakamalriṭṭu vanaṅṅiyakṣamāṟi
sakalamaẓiññu taṇiññu kēvalattin-
mahimayumaṟṟu mahassilāṇiṭēṇam

Having offered the flower of your mind to that Lord
smeared with sacred ashes, the three *guṇa*s,
having cooled down the senses, unwound everything,
and become calm,
when even the glory of aloneness has gone, become
established in *mahas*.

The theme of this meditation is one of the major subjects taught and discussed in all the major world religions. In the Semitic religions it is presented as an external temptation which comes to man to distract him and cause him to deviate from his divine nature and get caught in the snares of the external world. After indulging in this for some time he discovers he has fallen, and is filled with remorse and regret. He desperately wants to get back to his divine state, frees himself from temptation, and regains his divine state. This is the theme of Fall-Repentance-Return. Fall of course refers to falling away from the original divine state. Repentance means becoming once again pensive or thoughtful, reconsidering your present situation. Then you make a pilgrimage from the world of sensuality back to the domain of the spirit.

This same theme occurs in a very picturesque, allegoric way in *Saundarya Laharī,* one of the major works of Śaṅkara. In it, Nature is considered as a great divine urge of creation, like a mother who is giving birth to many things, a mother of great creative intelligence.

She is called *devī*. *Deva* means Light. An embodiment of Light is called *deva*, and in its feminine aspect, *devī*. So *devī* is the mother of all creation. Of course, this is poetic license. Its not that there is an actual person somewhere creating everything, but that we can see the whole universe as a divine intelligence of creativity.

The Indian mythological personification of the Creator is called Brahma, who gathers the dust of the feet of the mother of creation. This dust is the existence that can become manifested in the various individuated forms, and the awareness of this individuation brings about interaction between one created being and another. We see creation exemplified at many levels. At the chemical level, it may be seen in molecular functions, chemical combinations, and various forms of synthesis. At the physical level, matter is patterned and directed by gravitational and electromagnetic fields and thermodynamics. On the psychological level, creation is revealed through our mutual attractions and repulsions.

The three qualities, or *guṇa*s — sattva, rajas and tamas — are necessary for any creation. Sattva, the transparent, is the capacity to clearly represent existence. Rajas is kinetic, dynamic, activating — the energy that does the making and unmaking. Tamas represents the inertial force that stabilises and solidifies creation. According to the legend, the Creator uses the three gunas to create the whole world. If you philosophically understand the process, you don't have to think of any external creator. Our mind is the creator. It has the ability to present anything to itself. When something is presented and experienced, it exists. Thus, the mind creates forms of existence, one after another.

After creating the existence of something, the mind assumes the role of the seer, with the creation as the seen. An interaction is unleashed between the seer and the seen. Then the mind thinks, "I am the knower." After developing an affection for the known or the seen, it perceives "I am the enjoyer." Yet it is all the same mind. There is an ego centre which measures the situation, evaluates it, and says "I am its knower, I am its enjoyer. I am seeking enjoyment. I know what is pleasurable which is not yet present. I want to actualise it." Here the same ego assumes one more position, that of an actor.

"I am the seer; I am the actor; I am the enjoyer." When all three of these come together, we are in a single world of interest. A world of interest remains sometimes for only five seconds, sometimes for two minutes, sometimes for the whole day, a few days, months, or even years. Its length varies, but we go from one world of interest to another in a continuous series. This is allegorically portrayed in Śaṅkara's *Saundarya Laharī* as the several worlds created out of the three gunas by Brahma. When we understand it in our own life, our mind is a creator which goes on taking these three modalities and making world after world.

Śaṅkara uses a second allegory. The Lord of preservation is Vishnu, and his consort is Śrī or Lakshmi. Here the Lord is none other than the interests in our mind. When a world is created, there should be an interest in it, a central joy to keep you glued onto it. There needs to be one value in it which is glowing with attraction, and Lakshmi is the glowing value that captivates our interest.

Take, for example, breakfast. The taste of it, the way in which it is lovingly served, along with your appetite, makes it very fascinating. Once you have eaten it though, that value factor, the fascination, is gone. You are now satiated. You can't sit there all day eating your breakfast. So, however great the value of an individual world is, it cannot remain long. You have to be presented with another value: now office work, now school, now friends, now something else. Śaṅkara says the Lord of preservation, Vishnu, has a terrible job to do. He has to keep supplying you with interest after interest. Yet he somehow manages to preserve these millions of worlds, which are called *anantam*, endless. Endless are the worlds of interest.

In spite of what the mind creates and the values presented by the various qualities, time devours all these things. So the Supreme or the Infinite is described again by Śaṅkara as the great Lord who crushes all these worlds of interest in his palm, turning them into ashes. He smears his body with them. What we see as a great reality is only ashes smeared on the transcendental God. It is not even skin deep.

The enjoying self in you has many concepts of attraction, but when you turn to your inner reality all these seem false. At that point you begin a return. It is a pilgrimage from unreality to reality, from your sense orientation to the realisation of your most divine centre. And when does this take place? Every day, all the time, whenever our senses are drawn outward to get glued onto objects, and the great surge of excitement comes. This is the time to hitch it to the central core of our own divine being, rather than identifying the excitement with an objective, external situation, as we invariably do. Each time a pretty thing is attracting you, you become a beggar: haggard, poverty-stricken, wanting, desiring, stretching your hand, crying for it. You become miserable. Once you get it, you realise you have wasted a lot of time in pursuing this trifling thing. Now that its yours, you just put it aside.

I do the same thing sometimes. I wait for the Book-of-the-Month Club to send me some big book. I get very excited in anticipation of its arrival. But when it comes, I look at it and say, "Oh beautiful, wonderful! Put it on the shelf." Do I read it? No, I don't have time for it. I have other things to do. And what happened to that great value, that great excitement? It is transferred to the next month's offering. This month's book is already mine. I can take it from the shelf any time.

This happens between people also. Before someone is possessed as a friend, as a lover, as a wife or husband, many days and nights are spent thinking and worrying about how to get together with them. So many intrigues and posturings take place. But when they are finally yours, it can become a stalemate. Often you feel trapped, unable to extend your sense of adventure to the next person. Friends are not as easily stuck on a shelf as books.

God made Adam and Eve and gave them the bounty of Eden. They lacked nothing. Then their attention turned to the fruit of sensuality. They looked and tasted, and then they felt miserable. Suddenly they discovered they were naked and needed clothes. From that moment they knew shame, fear, anxiety — all the torments of exteriorised consciousness. They had been living in absolute freedom and great innocence, but they became subjected to guilt by entering into the world of necessity. Their descendants have yet to return to the heritage that was given them in the beginning by the Lord.

So, at the very height of the excitement and joy of gaining something, you are asked instead to relate it to the very core, to spiritualise that experience. You are not asked to kill the joy, but only to look for its essence. You have to realise that it is not produced by objects, but is an essential part of your own divine nature. If the joy we see in a person, in a desirable thing, opens a window for us to see the Lord, the Absolute, the Divine, which is our own truest Self, then everything becomes a door for us to enter into our innermost sanctum. This critical process is described in the first two lines of the verse: "Gather your mind-modalities as flowers and make an offering of them to the Supreme, who transcends all the necessities of the world."

You are not asked here to withdraw from everything, but to transcend everything. This is accomplished by spiritualising, by seeing everything as divine. A sense of reverence should come and fill your whole being. You are standing before a child, your own child, and thinking of it only as a child which has come from you. But when you look with this new vision, it is no more a child. You see the divine manifestation in it. You can see your union with the divine in that which makes your heart go to the child's heart, and the feeling of trust the child has in you. When you see that union it is no longer a discomfort, it is a devotion. You are not bound. Otherwise you feel obligated and bound to everything to which your senses take you. Now it is glorious that you are given an opportunity to be with your own real being. With that reverence which comes and fills you, your work becomes a devotion. It is a service, an offering, a dedication.

Sakalam aẓiññu means you are no more a person bound within the shell of this human mortal coil. You become expanded. Your expanded being fills everything, embraces everything. The spirit encompasses everything, and you are one with it. Now you are liberated; you have become free because the spirit is free.

When you become intoxicated with this oneness, you may become funny for some time. You want to declare this to everyone, and you run after them saying, "Do you see what I see? I have found the Way! I got it, and you want it!" In this way we become not helpful but a menace. Cool down. Cool it. There is nothing to be excited about: you are just becoming real. If you have found it, others will find it. They are already in the process. Let them take their own time and do it in their own way. Don't get excited.

The world becomes much better. A demonic world is now transformed into a divine world. A bound person has become a free being. The worlds of interests just come and go like dreams. They are enjoyed, as dreams are enjoyed. You know that it is only a passing show. Even a passing show should have its merit, so you give it that much credit. Then you own the world, and along with it you become one with the Divine that is behind all that. Right in the world of immanence, you see transcendence.

This is the theme for today's meditation. When we leave this place we will become involved in several worlds of interest. Each time a world of interest is created, watch how you come to it and what the central interest is. Then see how it wanes and you get into another one and another one. Each time you enter a world of interest, relate its central value to the Divine, to the one reality behind it all. This is your pilgrimage. In the evening, examine the pattern that flowed and unfolded through the whole day. The spirit of this is to become a continuous living reality. Call it back to mind again and again.

Verse 14

tribhuvana sīma kaṭannu tiṅṅiviṅṅum-
tripuṭi muṭiññu teḷiññiṭunna dīpam
kapaṭayatikku karasthamākuvīle-
nnupaniṣadukti rahasyamōrttiṭēṇam

Going beyond the boundaries of the three worlds, with all-filling effulgence,
when the three-petaled knowledge has faded out, ever brighter shines that light;
a pretentious seer will never grasp this;
thus, the Upanishads' secret word should be remembered.

The Catholic Church begins with the laity, then there are novices, priests — called brothers or fathers — bishops, archbishops, cardinals, senior cardinals, and finally the Pope. There is a certain maturisation implied in this hierarchy. Each one is trying to pass beyond a certain boundary to enter the next category. There is an increasing approximation of perfection. Even when we come to the Pope, though, his approximation is far from perfect. Transcending his position is the saint, and beyond the saint is Christ himself. Even beyond the personal aspect of Christ is the eternal spirit of God: the Word or the Holy Spirit. Beyond that is God itself.

So we have to pass through several approximations before we come to the final all-filling reality. For example, a man gets initiated by a spiritual master into the wisdom tradition. If it is the Hare Krishna movement, he will be asked to shave his head, just keeping a little tuft, wear ochre cloth and chant *hare kṛṣṇa* a certain way. While it is true that he has decided to someday become like Caitanya

Mahāprabhu, or like Sri Krishna himself, or the Absolute, this only says he is tending to become them. In the present state he is only pretending.

When you are pretending, don't say you have already become what you are tending towards. Tending to become something and actually becoming it are two totally different things. It is a long way. Don't think you will fully understand it in only a day. It's for a whole lifetime. Take it easy, but also take it seriously.

We have two difficulties here, in respect to being unified with the Absolute. One is a cosmological hindrance and the other is psychological. Our cosmological hindrance is that this body is a separate unit. It is physiologically structured, so it is subject to physical laws and chemical operations.

The three worlds of this verse are the earth, atmosphere and sky. Gravitation pulls us down onto the earth, so we are earthlings and always feel the solid ground under our feet. We undergo a variety of daily experiences, always seeing the one and the many on this earth of ours. Regarding atmosphere, when we see the sunshine we say, "Oh, wonderful!" but when the day becomes dark it affects our mind negatively. The clouds and rain can alter our mood. The sky is the home of the sun, moon and stars. First we probe the sky with an appreciative eye, and then with telescopes. The telescope extends our eyes farther than they can see. Now we are extending our arms and legs also by sending missiles to the nearby planets. All of it produces a great sense of wonder.

Thus we become fully convinced of three external worlds. After first achieving this conviction, we now have to erase it from our minds and see everything as a manifestation of one truth. We have to undo whatever has been learned, which is not at all easy.

The cosmological world which we perceive is structured in a certain way. Thanks to our many years of familiarity with it, we are divided from our inner nature by many boundaries and separations. To see it unified again has been the dream of many people, among them Albert Einstein. He thought there must be a unified theory by which the general and special aspects of relativity could all be unified in a central scheme. From ancient times mathematicians and physicists have been measuring things, and by the time the Euclidean age arrived they knew exactly how to measure everything as a three-dimensional structure. Since the time of Descartes they have wanted to understand the relationship of things which were previously divided, coordinating time with space, geometry with algebra, and so on. This led up to Einstein giving the world-view of the classical physicists a major jolt, by adding time as a fourth dimension and replacing a fixed universe with a relative one. Then we started seeing the physical world differently. Not as differently as it would appear on paper, however. The Empire State Building was built with a three-dimensional outlook, and when Einstein said no, it should be four-dimensional, the building did not break apart and fall down. It continued to stand. So in what way does the new way of looking at things actually affect anything?

Even now if you take a pencil and draw a triangle on a piece of paper, you will have three straight lines and three angles totaling 180°. If you take a piece of paper as big as the whole universe, though, and then try to draw three straight lines, you can't do it. The lines will curve and their angles will be greater than 180°. But this curvature on a universal scale does not nullify for an instant the straight lines a carpenter uses to measure as he builds. Classical physics still works fine at the everyday level.

Somewhere we have to relate these two things: what is universally true is not true in a particular sense, and what is true in the particular sense is not true generally. The macroscopic world around us can only be arrived at through mathematics. There is no other way to reach it. We can see some of it, but we have to perform calculations in order to really understand it. Then there is the microscopic world, which we cannot see at all. It is also mostly appreciated through mathematics. A chromosome can only be seen with the aid of a microscope. Within that is the DNA, which has twenty billion pairs of nucleotides on each strand. It is impossible to visualise, and yet scientists are even beginning to be able to manipulate it.

The world is separated into the macrocosmic, the empirical, and the meta-microscopic. How can you have a unified view? Narayana Guru is asking here not for a unified view, but for a unitive one. Unified means taking this and that and putting them together to have a comprehensive view. A unitive view, on the other hand, is where from inside you see it all as part of one awareness, one experience. Then alone are you transcending the limits of the three modes of the physical world. What you may call the objective world is existing or standing divided into three compartments. We should have a unitive understanding from within which will wipe away all these distinctions.

In subjective consciousness there are also three barriers, constituting our psychological hindrance. The first is I know that I know. Secondly, in what way do I know? I know that you are all sitting here and who each of you is. Thirdly, I know I am glad that one of you who sometimes has to work can be here today. These are three aspects within my own psychological experience. So the world is cosmologically and psychologically divided, and objectively and subjectively divided. How can you transcend all of these?

Today you can make a preparation, but you are only pretending to the state of transcendental awareness. The idea of pretending should not be taken in a wholly negative sense. You can say the Pope is a pretender because he is not crucified, but he is not hypocritical. He is trying his best to reach the level of the Apostles, to have their attitude and acceptance of the dictates of the spirit of God, and then even go beyond that and identify with God.

In India we use an image of light and shade. Light drives away the shadows of the tri-basic divisions such as knower, known and knowledge. The secret of this is not known to the pretender called *kapaṭayati*. *Kapaṭa* means false; and *yati* means a seer. In Sanskrit, *paṭam* means cloth, and *ka* means what or why is it? People might ask "why do you put on this cloth?"

"Because I am a yati", I answer.

"You become a yati just because you've put on peach coloured robes?" If you are a yati only because of this cloth, it is meaningless. People who become ascetics just because of the *paṭam*, the cloth, are focusing on the external aspects, and they won't get any special knowledge. But we are not speaking of the yati of cloth alone in a disparaging way. We only say that he has not arrived yet, he's on the way, he's in the queue. One can get into the process and slowly move forward, and some day unitive understanding will come from inside.

Scientists sometimes arrive at impossible findings, such as when light exhibits the characteristics of both particles and waves. We say it is made up either of particle-like waves or wave-like particles. When you say wave-like particle, you have to conceive of two very different concepts and then unite them in your mind in an impossible way. How can something be a particle-like wave or a wave-like particle? And yet, if you want to understand quantum physics you have to accept this impossible stand. Otherwise the result is two separate camps of physicists who don't agree, the particle physicists and the wave physicists. Physics should have one unified standard, so they come to a compromise that the wave is like the particle and the particle is like the wave. But this compromise is only in words. Square circle? Yes, a square-like circle and a circle-like square. These are all only intellectual games.

What we are asked here is not to make an intellectual game by renaming all our concepts, but to feel from within the unity of the external world and the unity of the internal world. Both these unities are to be found only in a mystical state; they cannot be arrived at intellectually. Narayana Guru is going to present a mystical state in the next verse. For now, though, we can only appreciate it as a mental image. Maybe some day you may actually get it.

What are you expected to do? Certain schemes to become a yati, or seer, are given to us by the wise. One is *amānitvam,* meaning that you don't say "I am better than you." When you take a measuring rod and measure yourself and measure another and another, and then examine the differences, you will assume a certain sense of superiority that is contrary to your unitive vision. You shouldn't think of yourself as a separate reality; you are belonging to the commonality. This is *amānitvam.*

Another idea is *aḍambhitvam*. Often we experience an egotistic thrust, saying "this is what I can do." We should curb that pride. Then there is *kṣānti,* having forbearance. We are all living in darkness, and as we move around in the dark we may stumble over one another. Don't get annoyed by it; forbear, take it easy. Next is *ārjavam*. Straighten up your mind, be vigilant, wakeful, upright. Do not compromise when it comes to truth. You have to intellectually appreciate truth and emotionally sustain it. *Ārjavam* is cultivating this uprightness of character.

Then *sama* and *dama:* settle down to your own chosen pursuit in life, and do not let any distraction come and take you out of your seat. Do not let any internal disturbance push you away either. You should make yourself invulnerable to internal as well as external distractions. Let the interest you are cultivating become all-filling, so that your whole joy of life is in it and it becomes meaningful every moment. Day and night are then filled with the joy of living the one truth to which you have dedicated yourself. In this, even if slips come, failures come, put up with them. Don't lose your centre. Stand firm. In order to be able to do this, you must have a clear notion of what your intention is, and how to go about your business every step of the way. In this process, see that you are not grabbing things away from others, but are only using the resources that are apportioned to you by nature in its benevolence. There is perfect sharing of life with all. Thus you transform and get into a mode of life, a behavioural pattern, where there is total sharing with the rest of the world. Full cooperation is given. You include in your happiness the happiness of all, but you do not tread upon your own happiness. You make yourself as much your own friend as a friend of others. You don't alienate yourself and become hostile to yourself. No hostility to others and no hostility to yourself. Do not be disturbed by the world and don't disturb the world. Get into greater and greater harmony.

The wise ones who have gone before us are still sharing their wisdom with us through their recorded experiences given in scripture, poetry, literature, and historical chronicles. Derive light from them; be benefited by spending some hours in study, pondering, meditating, passively contemplating. These methods are given in some form in all religions by all the masters. So we don't lack for advice, we have only to clear our desks and put things in the right places and start. Then we progress day after day.

In ancient times there was a method of finding out an honest man. If a thief was brought before the king, an iron ax was put into the fire, and when it became red-hot the thief was asked to pick it up. If he was an honest man it wouldn't scald or burn him, if he was a real thief it would. This is given in the Chandogya Upanishad as a test of one's truthfulness. Truth and untruth are a subjective thing while grasping a red-hot iron piece is objective, but the rishis believed there is one truth governing the subjective and objective worlds together, and that if someone was truthful nothing would happen to them. That's a unitive way of looking at it. It sounds silly to us, but still there are people who walk on fire and do not get burned. Somatic changes can come about because of a psychological attitude. Both psyche and soma are controlled by another state which is capable of uniting them.

In the Brihadaranyaka Upanishad it says *satyam* means truth. The word has three component parts, *sa, ta* and *ya. Sa* means that which is, *ya* means that which is, and *ta* means that which is not. Thus, on one side is truth, on the other side is truth, and in the middle is untruth. The word *satyam* is structured with truth on either side and untruth in the middle. It says that if there is truth on either side, untruth cannot remain there, so don't bother about it. Our world is also structured like this. There is a great truth; and there is a great truth in us. These two truths can abolish whatever untruth occurs in our everyday life.

Verse 15

***parayuṭe pālu nukarnna bhāgyavanmā-
rkoru patināyiramāṇṭoralpanēram
aṟivapara prakṛtikkadhīnamāyā-
lara noṭiyāyiramāṇṭupōle tōnnum***

To the blessed ones who have sucked the milk of *para*
ten thousand years is but a moment;
but if knowledge succumbs to *apara prakṛti*
half a second seems like a thousand years.

Some people are always caught in one difficult situation or another. They need to have something to cry about. There is always darkness surrounding them. And yet we cannot say they are bad people. They have very tender minds, highly suggestible. They are compassionate. Mostly they suffer because of their relationship with someone; or else they have economic difficulties, physical diseases, mental aberrations. Even if you try to help them, as soon as you pull them out of one tight situation they slip into another. After some time you become fed up with them. It looks as if they can never be helped. What is wrong with them? They are caught in the necessities of a relativistic world.

In a moderate way we all suffer from this same problem. We are human beings, so our lives are all intertwined and interrelated. Naturally we have to be sympathetic to the needs of those whom we love. Our own needs can also be very pressing. When the day breaks, several necessities come and stand before us, asking for our attention. There are many obligations: we have to oblige this friend or that relative. If you have a sensitive mind which exaggerates situations, then even little things will appear very urgent, needing to be done immediately, and you can get into an anxiety neurosis. Afterwards you regret what you have done in haste. The regret over what you have done, the anxiety over what is yet to be done, and the darkness in which the present moment is caught, assault you from all sides, and then all you can do is sit and suffer.

In the present verse, this state is described as getting caught in *apara prakṛti*. *A* means not, *para* means the Absolute. When a situation proliferates, or something multiplies and recurs, it is prakriti. Most of the things in our life are recurrent. We have breakfast, but by noon we are hungry. Then we have lunch, but by evening we are hungry again. Hunger is recurring. Our needs, most of which have to do with the body and the mind, can all multiply in this way.

In an earlier verse we were discussing another element in us, the witnessing consciousness. There is a flickering light which is like a spark somewhere in us which is not afflicted or affected by any of the passing qualities of life. This is actually the spark of the spirit in us. It is our Self. The necessities of life can easily overpower and veil this subtle light. Suppose you befriend it. If you are in search of yourself, be friends with that little shimmering spark in you. In fact, the love that you give to others comes from it, and the love you enjoy arises when it is touched by another person. If your mind is conjoined with the divine spark, you begin to experience a more beautiful world within yourself. This is what Jesus was referring to when he said the kingdom of God is within you.

We have such a very rich treasure in us! When you find it, the remorses of the past do not bother you any more. You cannot do anything with the past; it is gone. Let the dead bury the dead. Along with the past, bury your regrets also. Catholics go and confess to a priest. With the confession, a feeling comes that now whatever it was is over. That's a fine thing. But even without going and telling another person, you can say "what is done is done; I can't do anything about it. If it has no value, I won't repeat it." That's all you do; then it leaves you.

Regarding the future you can say "let it come. When it comes I will see." Its not that you should not plan your life, but instead of seeing a hundred problems all at once, make ninety-nine problems wait while you take up the one problem that is most relevant. Then if your mind does not exaggerate it, it won't look particularly unnatural. And what could your problem be anyway? If it is of the body, people are always being born, while others are dying. This is only normal. Growth brings other problems. A child cries when a tooth is coming in — there is nothing we can do about it. We cannot prevent the pain. Our sitting and crying with the child doesn't do any good. You just understand that the child is having a tooth come in. Then after some time gray hair comes, wrinkles come, the face changes, teeth fall out — what of that? Are these not natural? We shouldn't exaggerate them.

In the course of a day we may have to do many things, or we may have very little to do. Many of the things which look imperative are not. They can be avoided, dropped off. The growth of the mind brings many problems. The seeming needs of the mind are multiplied by TV and other advertising; everyone is trying to catch your attention because you are the consumer. To make you consume the goods they manufacture, greed is to be generated and lust to be stimulated. Thus there is an external influence which is trying to make your mind thirsty, hungry, haggard, all the time with a sense of poverty, thinking "I don't have this, I don't have that." These can all be dropped one by one.

We need to be doing two things simultaneously. One is going inward and befriending our own spirit, our dear friend that is the Divine. We are realising the Self within; in other words, seeking the kingdom of God within ourselves. The other is in regard to the outer world, the world of necessity: we need to give up all exaggerations and become more matter-of-fact. We are still sympathetic, but we are changing the mode of our sympathy. Perhaps your most beloved friend is in a state of crisis. He or she is in great darkness. Instead of adding your own darkness to theirs, you should try to bring them to your joy. Share your joy with them and not your sadness.

This does not appeal to most people. As soon as they see the other person's face, long and sad, their countenance falls and they also become sad. They think it's a must that if their friend is crying they should be too. It is not necessary. When Arjuna was caught in the most terrible situation between two armies, and the missiles were flying, he stood there in tears. Krishna was also standing right next to him in the same situation, but he smiled. This implicitly showed that there was a way out of the seemingly insurmountable difficulties. It was with this smile that Krishna started Arjuna's programme of correction. So you should offer your smile and not your tears. This is not something that can be accomplished in just one day, but it definitely can be accomplished.

When our friend comes and plays the piano, he is lost in it. He does not know how time passes. Those of us who sit and listen also forget everything. What is happening? There is music in all of us and our life is music. Our life has in it a rhythmic flow, a rhapsody, a melody; it is harmonious. When the harmony in us is evoked, the spirit comes to prevail. Our deeper nature becomes more prominent than our outer nature. The outer nature and the inner nature come together in a state of harmony. We go into our own depths. For this brief time we are not in this world. After playing for some time, our friend gets up from the piano. We all feel that we were in another world, and now we are returning from it. We are sitting on the same couch in the same room with the same people, but we were all different for a time. The seat was more comfortable and restful. All this magic was done by music.

Another friend is in her studio getting into her day's work. Its not work to her, its a creation of beauty. Each stroke of the brush is opening up a new joy. What was never seen before is now coming from her. It is an opening up, an unfoldment. This unfoldment is rich with wonder, the revelation of beauty. The centre of the soul is resonating with what the eye sees. Thus the objective world and the subjective world become related in the spark of joy. It is this spark we should be friends with.

Two lovers meet. They look into each other's eyes. They are never tired of seeing each other; again and again they gaze with a sense of wonder. They are absolutely oblivious of everything happening around them. They are only two people — there is nothing else in the world. They look into each other's eyes as if they are swallowing each other. They touch. They hold each other. There is ecstasy, nothing but ecstasy.

When a child is playing with a toy, he does not know how time passes, either. In his rapture, he is just like the others, or rather they are like him. But when all of them come out of their state of unity, the world of misery is again outside, waiting to pounce on them. The musician is no longer a musician, the lover is not a lover, the artist is not an artist, the child is no longer engaged in his child's nature — all are once again the victims of necessity.

Yet it is possible to retain continuous joy, by getting into companionship with your own real Self. Call it whatever name you want; call it God, Krishna, Jesus, Beloved, whatever. It is your own. It is all the time with you.

We see some rare people who have no money, but who have risen above their entanglements in the world of necessity. They may live in rags and be physically unhealthy, but they have a twinkle in their eyes, a joy in their heart, a smile on their lips, a tenderness in their attitude, and a kind word to say. They can always cheer you up. Even at the moment they are passing away, it is a great joy just to sit by them. They are like a light that shines before you. We cherish the company of such people. They are the real light of this world. They don't need anything, and yet they have a richness by which they can enrich the mind of everyone. Why should you not be that person? You don't have to invest anything for it, only change your attitude of life a little. Then when your life is changed, it changes the lives of others too.

Many people used to ask Ramana Maharshi what they could do for the world. He always asked them, "Who is doing for whom?" Thus their focus was turned to their own selves. If I want to make you happy, I myself should be a happy person. If I am sad, how can I make you happy? To make you smile, I should first of all know how to smile. I should know what peace is to bring peace to you. We have to discover the peace within ourselves, the joy within ourselves. This can be done only if the friendship that we cultivate with the spirit within becomes continuous, unbroken.

This is like magic: your world tomorrow won't be the same. You live in exaggeration. This world is not as bad as you paint it. What is madness? Madness is a positive or a negative exaggeration of the mind. If you see a thing in its natural value or worth, not more or less, it is a sane attitude. But we tend to exaggerate.

If somebody is busy doing something and you pass by and they do not smile or greet you, you say, "Oh, he does not like me any more. That's why he didn't greet me." You are so self-conscious and poverty-stricken, wanting somebody's attention all the time.

What kind of a terrible disease is this? If you didn't have such a disease you would say, "Oh, my friend was very busy today, so absorbed in himself that he didn't see me." It amuses you. "He didn't even see me!" The other attitude is, "He deliberately ignored me." One thing is seen two different ways. One hurts you and the other amuses you. So why should you be on the side of being hurt rather than amused? I am speaking of you, not some far away people. You can make your world a real heaven. This is the paradise; there is no other. This is a happy world, right in the palm of your hand, every day. But you throw it away.

This is the promise Narayana Guru gives us in this verse.

Verse 16

adhikaviśāla maru pradēśamonnāy
nadi perukunnatupōle vannu nādam
śrutikaḷil vīṇu tuṟakkumakṣiyennum
yatamiyalum yativaryyanāyiṭēṇam

A very vast wasteland suddenly
flooded by a river in spate — thus comes the sound
that fills the ears and opens the eyes of the one who is never distracted;
such should be the experience of the seer *par excellence.*

To many people, this world is like a desert. When they retrospect and look for what they have achieved in life, they see nothing worthwhile that they have attained. It fills them with great sorrow. When they look around to see what they can get, they also do not see anything. Their future is bleak. Thus their past, present and future are all filled with meaninglessness. Their life may be considered to be like that of one who is lost in a desert land. Everywhere there is only sand, sand and more sand. Then they see a canal with clear, blue water in the far distance. They go running to it, but it disappears. It turned out to be only a mirage. After running from one mirage to another, they give up the fruitless chase and become utterly hopeless and desperate.

Some people realise this only at the very last moment, when the call of death comes. As they lie helpless on their death bed, the whole life they lived appears as totally wasted and worthless, and they are filled with great remorse. Of course it is far too late to rectify the situation. But some people realise this earlier in life. They are so blessed that even at an early age they sense that there is something wrong with the world of values with which we are surrounded. These wise ones suspect the validity of these seeming values.

When the eyes are turned outward we see several forms of attraction. Naturally we are drawn towards them. We use our ears only to find our way to these attractions, in a way making our ears subservient to the cause of the eye. But if we close our eyes and sit at the feet of a blessed one, he may give us the secret key that all masters have: the key to the kingdom of God, as Jesus put it, or the key to the cave of the heart where Krishna says he resides.

There is a musical symphony going on unbroken, continuous, in each one of us, but we don't hear it. Its not hard to hear. We have only to listen. Our body is not an inert mass, it is like a great city. Its music is like the city traffic, which we only hear when we listen for it and are not interested in something else. There are so many things happening within us all the time. Each subatomic particle makes a musical note as it whizzes around, and each organ has its own melodic line. So, millions of musical notes arise in us, blending into a magnificent symphony that never stops. If we turn inward, we can hear this music of ours. To different people it sounds different. I always hear it as the tuning of a tambura or someone playing on a harp. This inner sound is called *nādam*. The *nādam* can become several times more meaningful when we sit at the feet of a master and listen to his word.

When the multitude went to the Mount to listen to Jesus, he gave a sermon which changed the lives of his listeners. Even two thousand years afterwards, that which came from his lips still goes deep into our hearts and touches us. What we hear is called *śruti*. The Upanishads are called sruti because when a disciple sits with veneration at the feet of a teacher, as was done in the ancient days when they were composed, what he seeks is sruti, that which is heard. Sruti is the music of the whole universe, the symphony of its creation, how it is sustained, and where finally it dissolves back into oneness.

A guru says "That thou art." When a disciple hears this, he understands the purport of the guru's words as "I am That." Before coming to this realisation, though, the disciple has to give up his present concept of the 'I'. The present concept is "I am this body, I am this mind, I am these senses, I am known by such and such a name, I belong to such and such a country and such and such a family." These are all limiting conditionings of the 'I'. They are to be dropped one after the other. This false identity has betrayed us. The guru is giving us our genuine identity, "You are That." This is known as *upadeśa vākya*, the dictum of instruction.

Once there was a young man named Śvetaketu. He was sent to a gurukula, a forest university of ancient days, for study. He studied twelve years. When he came back home, he was very proud of his graduation and went to his father to show off his knowledge. He said, "Father, ask me anything you want to know about astronomy or economics or archery. I know all these things now."

His father responded, "My dear son, many have gone from our family to the gurukula before you, but nobody returned with such conceit. What happened to you? Please tell me — what is it, knowing which you know everything? And what is it, not knowing which you do not know anything?"

Śvetaketu was stunned. "Father, please repeat the question. I never heard such a question before. You please tell *me* what it is, knowing which you know everything, and what it is, not knowing which you do not know anything. My dear father, I think my teachers also do not know this. Otherwise they would have taught me. So I prostrate at your feet. Accept me as your dear disciple. Teach me."

"Ok, I shall teach you. Go and bring a fruit from a fig tree," said his father. He went and brought one. "Now cut it. Look into it. What do you see?"

"I see very tiny little seeds. Each seed is so small — smaller than a mustard seed."

"Cut that." So he cut it. "What do you see now?"

"Almost nothing; just a little white stuff."

"From where does a fig tree come, my son?"

"From that."

"So this is that which becomes the fig tree?"

"Yes."

"*Tat tvam asi*, Śvetaketu. That thou art, my son. That which looks invisible and yet becomes all this, you are That."

Then Śvetaketu was asked to put some salt crystals in a vessel of water and bring it. His father asked him, "Where is the salt?"

"Father, it is dissolved."

"Now touch on the surface and taste it."

He tasted it. "It is salty."

"Now touch the side and taste."

"Salty."

"Put your finger at the bottom and taste it."

"It is salty."

"The salt, which is invisible and yet pervades every drop of water, That you are, my son. *Tat tvam asi*, Śvetaketu."

The father went on taking a number of examples, showing over and over how one reality pervades everything and seems to be many. When the fig seed changes into a sapling, leaves come from it which are very different from its roots, very different from the seed itself. Then flowers come which are different from the leaves. The fruit is again different. So many formal variations come from one source, yet they are all one.

So this is *upadeśa vākya*, the dictum of instruction. For meditating on the instruction two other dictums are given. They are called *manana vākya*, the dictums for meditation. One of these is *prajñānam brahma*. When you are deep asleep, consciousness is filling that state which has within it no division of subject and object, and yet it has all the possibilities of becoming the dream or the wakeful through the slightest stimulation. *Prajñā*, or the seed ground of all this universe, is within you as the basis of consciousness. It opens up as every form in the dream, and it unfolds as everything seen in the external world. Knowing this you say, "All these variations which I see here are all modifications of my own *prajña*. *Prajñānam brahma:* all the variations that I see in the form of this cosmic universe are none other than the Absolute."

This universe is not a separate thing, it is an extension of our own self. It is not something that can be rejected. It is to be endeared to us. This world is our Self.

When I see everyone here as my own self, I become many times more responsible. My responsibility is an unlimited liability: I owe everything to everyone. I am not only my brother's keeper, I am responsible to the whole universe in preserving its truth and maintaining its law, its rhythm. I am fully committed. I turn inward and meditate. I don't see any sun or moon, no vegetation, no human beings, no birds or animals. This is the subjective world of pure thoughts and feelings.

All this is coming from a light within me which is like a ceaseless spring, a fountain from which the stream of consciousness flows. This is my *ātman*, my soul. The other *manana vākya* is *ayam ātmā brahma*, the soul is *brahman*, the Absolute. If you open your eyes, that world is yours and you are That and That is Brahman. If you close your eyes, that's Brahman too. Inside and outside, all the time, you see only That. This reverberates in your mind: "My guru said 'you are That, That thou art'." Through relentless meditation, participating in the world with the meditation *prajñānam brahma*, or by withdrawing from the world meditating on *ayam ātmā brahma*, one comes to the secret of the unity of all.

This is the *rahasya*, the secret, which was referred to in verse 14, when it was mentioned that a person who is a yati only by outward appearance does not get this secret. As he does not get it, the world outside still appears to him to be threefold: the world of sky, the world of atmosphere and the world of earth. It remains divided into the past, present and future. And his inside will remain as three broken bits: the knower, knowledge and the known. But when one gains this inner secret he is no more a *kapaṭayati*, no more a yati in appearance alone. He is a *yativaryan*, a noble seer of a restrained life.

The unbroken symphony which one hears in one's own physical body, and the new realisation which comes from the word of the Guru that everything is One, extends the song, extends the symphony until it fills the three worlds with a great resonance. It is like the rumblings of an ocean. You hear your inner world filled with this one music.

Earlier we were told that there is a light which is not kindled, not lit. When you are sleeping and waking and thinking many thoughts, this light is looking on intently, seeing everything, witnessing everything, and illuminating everything. That eye is always within you, but as you were running after the mirage in the desert you were turned away from it. Instead, you were using two external eyes of distraction. When you hear this all-filling sound of musical ecstasy, the eye of wisdom opens. When it opens, you see everything through it. Now all your desires are absolved, you have no more any desire. Your happiness is such that it can be compared to no happiness. There is no greater happiness than this. Such a seer should be the model for our minds.

In this sixteenth verse, there is a quintessence of all that was taught in the previous fifteen verses. We began with:

> In and beyond the knowledge which shines
> at once within and without as the knower
> is the *karu;* to that, with the five senses withheld,
> prostrate again and again with devotion and chant.

One who is withdrawing the eyes is called a yati. The restrained seer is given in the very first verse.

Ordinary knowledge is the desert of this verse. When you transcend ordinary knowledge and go beyond, then alone you see the one reality which is shining outward and inward all at once, both as the cosmos and the psychic world.

In the second verse we were told that it is one sun in the firmament which is seen as all this. When you listen to the Word and meditate, it opens your eye, the eye that is not only seeing all but has created all this for you. The Upanishads say, "What eye, that world." What you see, that is your world. The British Scientists' Association says, "We believe what we see." The fact is, we see what we believe. We always try to see to establish our belief. So if you become one with the Absolute, you see the Absolute everywhere.

Then we were told of the surface of the ocean and the grand treasury of values in its depths. Here, when wisdom prevails like a flood, the wasteland of your life becomes an oceanic treasure. What were previously only grains of sand are now transformed into pearls of priceless worth. Everyone you meet, everything that happens — previously it was only a grain of sand, now it's a pearl of great price. Life becomes so enriched by the change in our attitude and in our vision. What could be more wonderful, more beautiful, than this?

Verse 17

aẕaleẕumañcitaḻārnnu raṇṭu taṭṭāy
cuẕalumanādi viḻakku tūkkiyātmā
niẕaluruvāyeriyunnu neyyatō, mun-
paẕakiya vāsana, vartti vṛittiyatrē

Having two tiers of five petals, whence pain arises,
rotating, beginningless, hangs the lamp of the self,
burning as the shadow (of true being), with the oil
of latent urges and mental modifications as the wicks.

Here a picture is given of our individuated self. It also holds true for the universe in general. In fact, one is interlaced in the other. So the verse can be understood cosmologically as well as psychologically.

Light and darkness are two counterparts which make a total reality. In the last verse the emphasis was on the bright side, but there is also a down-to-earth aspect which we should notice to have a well-balanced view of life. Narayana Guru does not want to be unrealistic in appreciating the whole situation, so now he is calling our attention to the background of whatever we see and experience here.

When we look at a beautiful form it is very pleasing to us. One way of putting it is the form is visible because it is highlighted. On the other hand, we may say that the figure is projected on a background of darkness and it is in contrast to the shadow that it stands out.

When we say we are seeing something, it is the dark shadows that provide us with the figure. If we remove all the shadows from a painting or a photograph, nothing is left. Similarly, when we are watching a film projected on a screen, the screen itself is white and the film is casting shadows on it. These shadows are where the bright light of the bulb in the projector is screened off. So what we look at is not the light so much as the shadows. They are what create all the meaning for us. This is not only true for the eyes, but for the other senses also. When we consider this, the world is a shadow play.

Sense experience is described in this verse as being pain-filled. Sensation in Sanskrit is called *samvedana*. This has two implications. *Vit* means to know; *veda* is that which is known; *veditam* is that which makes you know. In this sense, *samveditam* or *samvedana* mean that which enables you to know properly. At the same time, *vedana* means a pain; *samvedana*, a pain which you have become reconciled with. When you tickle a child, the child laughs, but if you tickle it too much, it cries. When two lovers meet and unite, they consider love's consummation as the greatest bliss. Yet a rapist's assault brings the most terrible pain. In both cases it is essentially two people having intercourse, but in one case the experience is wonderful and in the other it is horrible. Exactly where the joy of life resides, there pain also resides.

When you want to meditate and not to read, you turn off the light. Then you feel more comfortable. When you want to appreciate something through visible contact, you turn on the light. But if you turn on too much light, the object loses its charm. To properly appreciate a painting you have to put it at a certain distance and have the light properly balanced. Then alone does it have beauty. In old age, when the eyes are becoming weak and the light seems to grow dim, you can no longer see things properly. It is as if the soul itself is going blind. You feel so sad. Or perhaps you have an eye disease and the bright light is painful to you, so you need to wear dark glasses to filter the light. In so many ways, the light which is a great joy to us can equally be a source of pain.

All the five senses contain a mixture of pain and pleasure. If there is too much noise you want to shut it off, but if it's good music you want to listen. Real music comes only rarely. Most of the time you have to put up with the many terrible noises of the world. At times we exalt in the fragrances wafted to us by gentle breezes, but we are often breathing in the pollution of smoke, exhaust and carbon monoxide. A gentle caress is delightful, but it quickly becomes irritating when carried on for more than a short while. This is why the Guru began this verse with the word *aẓhaleẓhum*, pain-filled.

Next, our five senses are compared to the five petals of a lamp. Nowadays we have only electric lights and we don't have a feel for the image. In ancient India they used to hang an oil lamp, with tiers of petal-shaped wick holders, in the middle of the room. With the wicks lit it resembled a simple candelabra, which would swing gently and rotate with the movement of air in the room, casting fantastic shadows over the walls and furniture. Our life is here compared to such a rotating light with five burning petals of the senses. The burning brings a kind of pain, but our attention is focused more on the play of light and shadows on the walls.

The pain and shadows are the important things to examine. The biophysical and biochemical aspects of sensation are agitations in the nervous system, which put the molecular system of the brain in a quandary each time a stimulation comes in. Every item of knowledge has an agitation behind it. All the sensations we have are agitations in our system. On the other hand, when we don't have any sensations and our system is peaceful, we don't know anything. Literally our experience is based on agitation: nervous agitation from chemical stimulation and electrical impulses, and electrical vibrations and reverberations. We are aware only when these disturbances are taking place, so no one was there to know when the process first started; the Guru therefore calls it *anādi*, beginningless.

In the cosmological view we have five elements: earth, water, fire, air and space. Each of these corresponds to one of our senses: sound travels through the *ākāśa*, touch is of the air, visual forms are illuminated by fire, taste is produced by water and smells come from the earth. A physical organ is especially attuned to each of these sensations: the eye, ear, skin, nose and tongue. Thus, in us there is a physical reality and also a psychic reality. We may say there are two tiers. The physical tier translates incoming data into the electrochemical language of the brain, while the psychic tier is concerned with interpreting the significance of each sensation.

According to Western physiologists, we have a physical system that is generating a psychic condition. Indian psychologists, on the other hand, say we have a psychic condition which animates the physical system. If you are lying unconscious or fast asleep, you won't have any taste of honey, you won't feel what touches you. All the pleasures of the senses cannot be stimulated if consciousness is not present, even though the physiological system is intact. When a person is asleep and you speak to them, their ears still remain open and the sound still falls on their ears, vibrations still beat on the tympanum. It is a physical thing, and the vibrations necessarily act on the eardrum. Yet the person doesn't hear a thing. What is the block between his consciousness and the external stimulus? The coordination has to come from inside. This is why the Indian psychologist points the arrow from the side of the psyche to the physiological system.

The Western psychologist nonetheless puts the arrow from the entry of the stimulus into the system, and afterwards from inside comes the response. Instead of this, Narayana Guru thinks in terms of a selective structural response, where deep down in you are incipient memories or latent potentials and urges. It is only in correspondence with what is already within you that yo ı can make sense of anything coming as a stimulus from outside. For you to understandably recognise everything you see, touch, taste, smell and hear, there should be a corresponding concept within you. That concept is lying latent within you as a vasana. Here the study of physiological psychology, which governs the entire field of memory and learning, experience and education, is to be examined to get a proper picture of what the Guru wants to convey to us.

The whole thing is summarised here in a very simple way: you can look at the universe as being constituted of the five elements, which are just matter. Then why do we call it a cosmos? Because of the great wonder that we see definite laws operating. The sun stands in the centre of the solar system, and the planets are moving in the same kinds of orbits around it at constant speeds. From our perspective they are always crisscrossing, and yet their separations are maintained so that they never collide. They are all lying in vacant space, but they don't fall down or go running off. We have so much water on the Earth and the Earth is rotating and revolving, and yet the water never falls off. Even though it is not held in any receptacle, the water just sticks on despite all this movement. What keeps everything in its proper place? It is amazing. An Australian does not know at all that he is walking upside down. When a Russian or a Northern European is standing on his feet, a New Zealander is actually hanging with his head down and feet up, and the people in India are walking sideways. Isn't it a tremendous joke? When you really consider all the cosmic laws, how everything is regulated without our even being aware of it, it is totally wonderful.

So there is a certain cosmic law operating in everything. On the bright side is this law, while on the dark side are the inertial masses of things. Recently, we were very hopeful of finding some kind of intelligent life on Mars. A lot of money was spent to send instruments there to send back the information. And what did we find there? Nothing. Just huge piles of inert dirt. So, cosmologically there is a two-tiered system. The bright side is the subtle mathematical laws which are so precise we can land an instrument package on a distant planet, while the other side is all this dark, heavy matter.

We also have these two tiers individually. We are made up of masses of dirt, yet how much do we love that dirt when a little love is generated in us! Then we don't say we are dirt. We hug the other person and press harder and harder, because our bodies are preventing the soul of one from merging into the soul of the other. We feel like, "I want to become one with you, but this body is between us. Let us merge." The bright aspect, the light aspect, is wanting to merge, but the body is in between. Our two tiers are our body and soul, matter and spirit.

There is an afferent aspect and an efferent aspect; there is stimulus and there is response; there is a sensory system and a motor system. We have all these dualities and ambivalences within our system. Narayana Guru summarises all this by just saying "two tiers", leaving us to discover for ourselves its many ramifications. We can find any number of pairs of tiers operating in us, such as the external and the internal, motor and sensory, material and spiritual, physical and psychic, and so on.

The tragic note in all this is that the present is a product of the past and its tentacles are stretching into the future and we are caught within this web. Before the development of modern science we were threatened only with the religious superstition — some call it religious belief — of sin, that we were all carrying the sins of our fathers. Adam erred and sinned against God, and that original sin is shared by all humanity. The divinity of man and original sin are what we are asked to believe by religion. From the first man to the present there is a continuation of the darkness as well as the divinity that was in Adam.

Previously we were believers, back when the apocalyptic threat of the world crashing one day was enough to make everyone believe in Christ. The message was "believe soon, because tomorrow the world is going to end." Now we are no longer influenced by theology. Its place has been taken by science fiction. Its the scientists who are now afraid that the whole thing is going to burn out.

When we pushed religion away, science came in to fill the vacuum. Are its fairy tales any improvement? I read somewhere that in everyone of us are at least seventy-eight atoms that were once in Julius Caesar. Everything that has happened is so intermixed in us! Who can compute next how many of Judas' atoms and how many of Christ's atoms are in us?

Christians have carefully calculated that man was created on 22 October, 4004 BC. Now we have Carl Sagan saying that bacteria are three billion years old and viruses are another two billion years older than that. Man is about ten million years old, although they have yet to fix the exact date. Then he says in every chromosome there is DNA, and in every DNA are twenty billion pairs of nucleotides. So we have twenty billion pairs of nucleotides, carrying the information accumulated over five billion years, sitting inside us to cause trouble whenever we do anything. This is far worse than religion, which only threatened us with original sin.

Of course, I am mostly joking. When you strip away the semantic differences, the myths of science and religion are remarkably similar.

In any case, Narayana Guru does not want to go into these kinds of fabulous theories. He just wants us to know there are ancient vasanas which serve as the oil feeding the lamp which is burning in us. The principle itself is very simple. And what is a vasana? I am holding two theories in my hand, one for the consumers of the theory of reincarnation and the other for those who do not believe in it. For disbelievers, the theory of genetic inheritance expresses the gist of it. I shall tell the theory for those who do believe.

Our friend comes here and gives us very good music on the piano. I lie in my room listening to it. It gives me such wonderful sensations of delight! I melt into it and I sleep; I wake and still enjoy it; I drift in and out of pleasant states all the while listening. This is a new thing. Last year I did not have this luxury, but now he comes quite often. The next time I go to bed he is not here, so I feel "Oh, not a good sleep today. There is no musical background for it."

Another friend goes and gets me a special kind of cookie. At the very sight of it my soul wakes up. "Ah! There it comes." If you have them twice or thrice you cannot give them up. On the Japanese sesame cookie it is written "Warning. Habit forming." Then they say, "But what of that? It's good for you."

These are called samskara, when an experience is received by the sense organs, and the quality of that experience is condensed and kept in the system as a memory bit. Samskara in Sanskrit means cultured, that something is cultured within you. A raw experience is made into a culture and kept there. If I want to have a full experience of a piano, there should be such a big thing, occupying so much space; but when it is cultured and put on a magnetic tape I can carry it in my pocket. If it is further condensed, it can be received as a radio wave by small crystals, which can produce the whole effect of an orchestra. This economy of space is one of the most wonderful things.

When what was sung by someone is sent from the radio station through the atmosphere, it is not transmitted as music. It goes as a radio wave. Similarly, whatever I have experienced in this life is kept in a condensed form in me as my samskara. When I take the essence of all those to my next life, they are further condensed. First the physical was made subtle, now it becomes causal. This causal element is called vasana.

Whatever has come to me from my previous lives is my present vasana, and my present samskara is added to it. My samskara in its turn will someday become vasana when I am passing to the next life. The vasana of previous lives and the samskara of this life are the past which is bearing on the present. That present is aspiring to experience the future. I look into the future with desire, and also with anxiety because of the painful experiences I previously had. Even as I get into the car to go to the dentist, I am already anticipating all those terrible things going on. Ouch! It's in the future, but the pain and the unpleasantness of it start from just going out the door. Past, present and future are all filled with the impact of vasana. The present is actually a manifestation of this vasana as it is being burned through the five senses. The *varti*, the wicks of the lamp, are the five senses; while the *vṛtti*, the flames, are the modifications that come as our experiences.

In this verse, we are brought back from the high state of spiritual ecstasy to where we fit into this world. It is from all these actual, necessary aspects of existence that we have to rise to that higher state. We are not to forget that we have a body that can give us pain, a mind which can give us pain, sensations which, when exaggerated or stimulated too much, can cause us pain, and that we are carrying all the garbage of the past with us all the time. These are all real.

It is on this we have to build our own joy and understanding of the Absolute. The lamp is hanging in the Self, in total knowledge. Within the total knowledge situation we have both our physical and psychic selves. What we call experience is shadow, so it is darkness; and the real is the Self. As we are so tuned into this shadow, we never know the light of the Self at all. We just go from one shadow to another shadow.

Those of you who want to have further illumination on this subject should read Plato's cave allegory. He speaks of a cave in which some people are living. They are watching their shadows being cast on the wall on the opposite side of the cave. By long association with these shadows they have come to identify themselves with them. When a shadow moves its head, they think they have moved their head. They have created a whole theory centered around their shadows. When one of them wants to turn around and look at the light source that is casting the shadows, he finds that he is riveted in place, he is bound in such a way that he cannot turn. He starts howling, "I am bound, I am bound!" Everyone else laughs at him, "What a stupid fellow! He says he is bound. He claims he's not a shadow." They think they are sane and he is mad.

He continues to try to turn around, and the more he struggles, the more he feels the bondage. But finally he frees himself from the shackles and sees there is a light behind everyone that is casting the shadows they were watching. As he walks towards the light he notices it is a fire burning. He goes past the fire and out of the mouth of the cave. There he sees the real sun shining in the firmament.

When he looks at the sun, he becomes dazed and cannot keep on looking. He has never seen such a bright light before. It's too much for him. He is blinded. But finally his eyes get used to seeing in the sunlight, and he can see the actual world with actual beings all around him. He thinks, "My God! I was seeing only the shadows of these things before. My poor brothers and sisters are still in the dungeon, suffering. I should go back and tell them." And so he reenters the cave.

This is exactly what a guru does. First he goes and finds the real light, then he takes pity on those who are still caught in the shadow world and comes back to teach them. Usually he is met with hostility when he tells them there is another world more real then what they are seeing. He may even be crucified. But it is essential for us to somehow come to the understanding presented in this verse of exactly where we are now and what true possibilities lie before us.

Verse 18

ahamirulallirulākil andharāy nā-
mahamahamennaṟiyātirunniṭēṇam
aṟivatināl ahamandhakāramalle-
nnaṟivatininṅaneyārkkumōtiṭēṇam

The "I" is not dark; if it were dark we would be in a state of blindness,
unable to know even "I,I";
as we do know, the "I" is not darkness;
thus, for making this known, this should be told to anyone.

Occasionally we get into a state of emotional crisis. A kind of depression comes, and we feel very wretched. At such moments we may even say, "I don't see any light. I am in a state of absolute darkness." Because of the negative attitude we are in, we do not see the contradiction in this statement, which is that for us to know we are in a state of ignorance implies a degree of knowledge. If there is no knowledge at all, one would not even see that one was in a state of darkness. At least there is that much faint light.

This light of knowledge, which is always shimmering like a spark within us, is not brought from outside. It is self-luminous — it is our own awareness. With this awareness we can at least say "I am." When we say "I am ignorant" we have to first say "I am." Then it is not ignorance.

When Descartes was assailed by great doubt, he became very confused. He wanted to find out if he knew anything for certain. First he examined the many general laws which were the foundations of his knowledge, such as: this world is created by God, and the world exists and can be perceived with the senses. He started doubting all this. For instance, how do I know the world is created by God? Because the Bible says that God created the world in six days and rested on the seventh. How do I know that what is said in the Bible is true? Because it is a book of revelation. How do I know its a book of revelation? It is stated in that book. Is this not begging the question? The authenticity of the Bible cannot be revealed by the Bible itself. That isn't authentic. If the Bible is not authentic, I cannot put my trust in it. If I cannot put my trust in it, I don't have to believe that God created this world. In this way Descartes rejected idea after idea as unexamined statements.

Socrates said the life that is not examined is not worth living. Descartes felt the same way, so he wanted to examine everything critically. In the light of reason, the testimony of the revelations seemed to be dogmatic, arbitrarily made, so he saw it as conjecture. Then he turned away from word testimony to sensory perception. A man with jaundice sees everything with a yellow cast, but it is a defect of the eye and not of the world. Even when our sensory systems are of normal health and without defects, we see many optical illusions. We see blue in the sky when there is neither a sky as such nor any blue colour. It doesn't exist. There is only vacant space filled with invisible air, but because of a certain diffraction of light coming from the sun we see a blue dome-like thing above us. If you're travelling by road and speeding along in a car, nearby things seem to run by very fast while far away objects look stationary. How can the world move and not move at the same time? We cannot believe our eyes. Again we may see a man hammering in the distance. We see the hammer falling on the object, but only later do we hear the sound. They are not synchronised. How do we know, then, that the sound is produced by the hammer?

In this way Descartes doubted everything. One thing he could not doubt, though, was that he was doubting. Everything else can be doubted, but you cannot doubt that you are doubting. From this he came to the conclusion that there is something imperative in knowledge. There is even a categorical imperativeness, and there is a logical necessity in accepting this categorical imperativeness in reasoning. Thus he arrived at an axiomatic basis for philosophical thinking. He said *cogito ergo sum*, "I think, therefore I am." Or *dubito ergo sum*, "I doubt, therefore I am."

In this verse, Narayana Guru is using a similar argument, which says that even in your darkest moment don't you say "I am?" Of course you do. When you sit with your eyes closed in a dark room, are you not absolutely sure of your own existence? Don't you see that very clearly? What kind of light is that? From where does that awareness come? When we look at the clarity of the awareness "I am," we are astonished by the self-luminous principle which seems to reside within us. This inner light is called *cit*, or *caitanya*, gnosis.

There is another work by Narayana Guru, called *Arivu*, or *Knowledge*. It is a very beautiful work. In it he presents such questions as when you know a thing, what is the knowledge with which you know? If you take away that knowledge, is there any known remaining with you? When you consider carefully, can you differentiate the knowledge by which you say "I am" from this knowledge? What constitutes the knowledge of the known? Don't you see that there is only one knowledge, which is seen to be the knower, the known and knowledge?

So when you say "I am," it is a very clear case of self-evidence. All the proofs that we use in science are in order to bring a certain certitude to us. The highest form of certitude is one you don't have to prove. In mathematics this is called axiomatic. Axiomatic knowledge requires no proof, because it is self-evident. What we are saying is it is evident to our self. Thus, self becomes the measuring rod of all knowledge; in other words, the self is the normative notion with which we measure truth. All other truths are derived only by using this normative notion.

Until an experience becomes your own, it remains extraneous to your real knowledge or wisdom. You have to own your knowledge: it must become part of your own experience. And nothing is more clearly experienced than the awareness "I am." Even a simple person knows this. From a little child to the most profound philosopher or scientist, this knowledge is common to all.

We have seen in the previous verses' meditations that our experience can have within it a bright spot and a dark spot. Between the range of these two extremes there can be many gradations of consciousness. When we turn only to the dark element, life appears full of crises. It may look negative, depressing, bleak, meaningless. Even at such dark moments it is with the consciousness of 'I' that we say it is bleak and dark. Turn to the very self with which you say this, and that brings you back to the brightest spot within yourself. Then you won't lose the stable footing of your life. You are reclaiming your own self-awareness. If you habilitate yourself in the bright centre of your own self, then you can withdraw from that which frightens you, that which makes life dark.

Most of us think that realisation is very hard to achieve, that it is a rare attainment of only a few people. The Guru wants us to know it is not so. Realisation is of all people; everybody is already experiencing it in some measure. It is just that we do not know it is Self-realisation. We are under the impression that some day this world is going to disappear and some other kind of reality is going to assert itself, but this is just another of the many illusions created by the exaggerations of religious people. Such beliefs only increase unhappiness by convincing people they are ignorant and unrealised. It is a very simple thing to know you exist. This can be the starting point for you to reclaim more and more of your world into the realm of awareness, into the light of the Self.

After we realise that the knowledge we have within us is Self-knowledge, Narayana Guru wants us to go one step farther and tell it to another person. When you do that, the other person at least knows that someone is speaking to him. When I say "I know I exist," the other person says "yes, I also know I exist." There is a homogeneity in the understanding of two people of the concept 'I'. Just as I say "I exist," you also say "I exist." There is an identity involved: the quality of awareness of the 'I' in me is identical with the 'I' in you; in a third person, fourth person, of all the people in the world. So at least we all have one common knowledge — we all recognise "I am."

In this basic awareness "I am," the Guru wants us to see the unity of all awareness. This is the common platform on which we can link ourselves as part of the one binding knowledge of all beings. You can't talk to your dog about Shakespeare, but you can communicate by looking into its eyes. It understands. One friend of mine even writes letters to her dogs. There is communication in their souls, even though the dog does not read the letters. As she writes, she somehow feels that within their souls there is some kind of resonance or union, a oneness. In all living beings there is this one awareness. First we know it ourselves, and then we make it known to others.

Siddhartha, called Gautama, mortified his body for six years, going from teacher to teacher to look for truth. He became very disheartened. Finally he thought of giving up the pursuit. He said, "There is no meaning in this life, there is no truth. I don't see anything. It's all dark. I'll just sit under this tree. Let me die; let the body fall off. I won't get up from this seat unless I come to know truth."

Then a girl named Sujata came. She thought it was some kind of tree spirit sitting there. She wanted to make an offering to the spirit, so she brought some milk pudding and gave it to Gautama. He was very hungry and accepted it. After a while, he was miraculously filled with a great light. He became awakened. When he was so awakened, he marvelled at the truth he saw. He said to himself, "What a wonderful truth this is! So magnificent; so perfect! But will anyone have an open mind to receive it? The whole world is steeped in ignorance. I don't see one person worthy of receiving this great knowledge, so I will not speak of it to anyone."

At that point the Lord, Brahmasampati, came and said, "O Blessed One! Now you have become an Awakened One, the Buddha. What you have come to know is a great knowledge which can heal all the ills of the world. Be compassionate. Look at this world. The people are not dirt as you seem to think; they are not blind as you seem to think. There is only a little stupor. You can wake them. A little dust of ignorance is veiling the truth from them. You can brush that off their eyes and they will all clearly see. Just as you have now come to know the truth, they will also come to know it, because the truth is already within them."

Jesus said the Kingdom of God is within you. It is this truth which is within you. We must first discover it, and then we know that the same truth is in the heart of all people, of all beings. Thus your own self-awareness will bring you to the awareness of, and the kinship of, the Self of all. "If you once know the Father, then you know the brethren." Here what is equivalent to the Father is the most certain knowledge which is within you. Then you see the same certain knowledge within all the brethren. You see your own self in all, and in all your own self.

From the knowledge of the Self, you go to the sharing of the same knowledge. What is vertically true becomes also a horizontal fact. *Prajñā*, the known; *karuṇa*, compassion; and *maitrī*, fellowship: each one follows from its predecessor. First I know that I exist. Using the same principle, I know that you also exist. If you do not see and are wailing and carrying on, and I see there is no reason for it, that it is only because you don't see the divinity and imperishability of your own being, then I feel compassionate. Then I come to you and say, "Now look here my brother, my sister, why should you cry like this? You are all light, imperishable and immortal." So we get into friendship and fellowship. With our fellowship we mutually recognise each other as belonging to the same truth. We get into a bond of love based on truth. Like the warp and woof that make up a whole cloth, I have my Self-knowledge and the knowledge that the same Self is also in you. The whole universe can become part of our own Self, and all can come to realise it together.

Verse 19

aṭi muṭiyaṟṟamatuṇṭituṇṭatuṇṭe-
nnaṭiyiṭumādima sattayuḷḷatellām
jaḍamity sarvamanityamām; jalattin-
vaṭivīne vittu taraṅgamanyamāmō?

The bottom, the top, the end, that is real, this is, no,
that is —
in this way people quarrel; the one primal reality is all
that is;
all this inertial matter is transient;
except as a form of water could a wave ever arise?

In the Sermon on the Mount, Jesus said, "Blessed are the peacemakers, for they shall inherit the Kingdom of Heaven." One great need in this world is peace and peacemaking. There is always a tendency to fight. Another precious teaching from the Bible is "Peace on earth and good will among men." Seemingly there are so many reasons to lose our peace and come to blows. Even the words of the greatest seers and saviours have caused bloodshed. In their great names and in their great love, man has shed more blood than in the name of cruelty. Such is the sad state to which we have come. The philosophy we learn in this study of *Ātmopadeśa Śatakam* is a philosophy of life. Its aim is to unite in peace rather than divide by endless arguments.

In the previous verse we were asked to share, but when we come to share something we want to do it on our own terms, in just the way we like. Fights come when someone else wants to have it their way. When R.D. Laing speaks of the 'I' and the 'other' he is touching on these same elements, where the 'I' becomes solidified as an individual with a personal interest. He and his interest are the same. It is in that sense Laing calls it the self. The 'other' is the other person, who has a similar vested interest. He is wholly identified with his interest. However limited it may seem, they each have their own philosophy and vision to guide their actions.

Narayana Guru begins this verse with *aṭi* and *muṭi,* the alpha and omega factors. Philosophers who give primacy to intelligence generally look at the source of things: what causes this effect? The fundamental question is very important to them. The early Greek philosophers, from Thales to Heraclitus, all asked where the universe came from and what its nature was. Philosophers like Socrates asked "Who am I?" In the Indian context, Śaṅkara said these effects have all come from a cause. What is not in the cause can never become an effect. In the effect we see so many ramifications and elaborations of differences. If you go back to the cause you do not see all the separations. For example, a seed does not tell us what kind of leaves, flowers, roots and branches will develop from it. It is just one single item, where all that is to come is the same. Thus from the effect you should go back to the cause. That means you go back to your own alpha, your roots. So Śaṅkara is a philosopher of *aṭi,* the base.

After Śaṅkara came Rāmānuja, who did not feel impelled by a logical necessity to reason. He had a greater need to experience love here and now, to experience the love of God as a person. He didn't want to think of impersonal facts like pure existence or pure knowledge. He thought if there was a Lord, he should be able to see him with his own eyes. He should be able to touch him and serve him. For Rāmānuja to see, the Lord should manifest visibly; to listen, the Lord should come and speak to him.

In the Christian context we have God, the Word, and the Word that becomes flesh. Only when the Word becomes flesh and stands before us as a person, as in Jesus Christ, can we look into his eyes, see his smile, and have the touch of benediction. Then we can carry in our minds his sweet image, his tenderness, his calmness, his soft speech. We can have a number of recollections of that personal aspect. Rāmānuja said, "This is what I want. I want my Lord to be Vishnu. I should be able to see his lotus eyes, his pearl-like teeth, his cherry lips, his gentle touch, the lotus in his hand." He went on with a full description: "This is the final thing to which I am aspiring, the omega, to see and serve my Lord, to be with him. My Lord should be inside me as well. I should experience the Lord in every atom of my being as the indwelling immortal reality. There is no maya; everything is real. All these effects are the effects of the Lord. Don't say this is inertial matter. There is no inertial matter. Matter is constituted of atoms, and every atom is animated. The heart of the atom is the supreme Indweller of the psyche. Thus everything becomes divine to me." So Rāmānuja's is the philosophy of *muṭi*, the omega, where the effect is as real as the cause.

There are other philosophers who say, "You claim that your God is omnipotent, omniscient and omnipresent, but this is a finite world. How can there be an infinite in the finite?" Aristotle asked the followers of Plato, "Have you ever seen an archetypal horse? You don't see any archetypal horse anywhere. You don't see the universal. You are there; I am here. You and I are particular realities. It's only for the sake of language that you are abstracting and generalising and saying 'we' or 'horses'. There are only white horses, brown horses, black horses, lame horses and galloping horses. All these are individual factors. The infinitude you speak of is only a theorisation. Everything is finite; everything has an end."

Previously in classical physics we thought of an infinite space in which the cosmos was set. At present there are several notions. Most say that space is very big but not infinite; it must have an end. Others maintain you cannot say anything definite. You can argue whether we are in a big bang or a steady state. Is it a particle or a wave? Red shift or violet shift? Black hole or white hole? They go on fighting in a pool of uncertainty.

So scientists argue as much as philosophers. But what is really important is our daily life. The often-forgotten purpose of philosophy is to give us a philosophy of life, a framework to orient our lives by. Fritz Perls once formulated some basic presumptions into a prayer: "I do my thing and you do your thing. I am not in this world to live up to your expectations and you are not in this world to live up to mine. You are you and I am I. And if by chance we find each other, it's beautiful. If not, it can't be helped." This is one way of not quarreling. However, it is not the compassionate way of looking at life. You are not only you, you are also me. I am not only myself, I am also you. I should care to live for you, and you should be able to care for me. Otherwise the world will fall to pieces. It will become a chaos of opposed interests and opinions vying with each other. If we fight over everything, about the alpha and the omega, finitude and infinitude, and the self and the other, for example, we will have the confusion of tongues of the Tower of Babel. We will have the divided self and the politics of the family, as described by R.D. Laing.

Narayana Guru says there is a key to resolve this situation. We must look for the animating principle, the numinous factor, as well as that which is inertial and dead. The inertial matter, *jaḍa*, is the basis for differentiation. The animating Self is the unifying factor. Even physicists have to think of a unifying matter rather than the myriad individual cases of its manifestation. Then they don't have to bother whether something is a piece of iron or a piece of cheese. It can all be reduced to a primal substance from which it has sprung, in other words, the Mother of all phenomenal things, the *mātṛ*. The word matter is derived from *mātṛ*, meaning mother or the Mother of all beings, all things. You have to reduce everything to one principle, without which there cannot be any physics, or chemistry, or whatever. That is the animating principle, while all the specific instances are the *jaḍa*.

In our personal life also we are presented with a flux of everything moving and changing. Even as we sit quietly our blood is surging through us. A tidal flood of air passes in and out of our lungs. Body cells are dying and being replenished. The carriers of energy in the circulatory system are exchanging dead matter for new energy at a tremendous rate in the alveoli. Within the body are so many separate, individual items, yet there is a unifying consciousness which rules the whole organism as one single piece. Everything in the body mutually aids and supports the rest, even the will, which is a collective motivation for the benefit of the entire organism. In the same manner, society is a collective whole to which each individual belongs, and the physical universe is a collective factor of which life on earth is a part.

When you look at these things from the numinous side it unites everything, while if you look at them from the phenomenal side it separates them. There has to be a conscious effort on our part to recall our drifting interest and drifting mind to come back again and again to the numinous centre. Then in our relationships with the rest of the world there will always be the consideration of unity.

In corporate life we tend to become very critical of others' attitudes or behaviour, we go about trying to trap people in their opinions, building up cliques, groups within groups, blowing things out of proportion and pitting one against the other. There is an old saying that "two is company, three is a crowd." Two people can get into a bipolarity fairly easily, but when a third comes it is easy to become confused. Ideas proliferate geometrically. Now we have to choose, and we may become unsure of what is right. But after all, it isn't very difficult. We should easily be able to accommodate the third factor, the triangularity.

This verse has a very practical bearing on our life. It encapsulates the art of living together, the art of reconciliation, the art of harmony. Narayana Guru here presents the example of the ocean and the wave. What makes a wave look different from water? It is only the formation of a crest on the surface of the water. The essence of the wave is the same water. It is the form we are fighting and not the essence. We should discipline ourselves in such a way that we can turn from the form to the essence every day, all the time.

Two strangers see each other. They look at each other spontaneously. One feels an attraction to the other, and the same attraction is felt in the other heart also. Unknowingly, the joy of seeing wells up in their hearts and they both open up with smiles. Something pulls them together. They introduce themselves; they talk; they discover common interests. They become animated with their interest. When the time comes to say good-bye, they have already developed tentacles to hold onto each other. They exchange addresses and phone numbers. So even when they leave, they have not really left. When each goes home they are more lively than ever, feeling closer than when they were talking face to face. Even in absence, their presence becomes more meaningful. That presence has a profound influence on them. It grows. They carry the memory of the other around with them wherever they go. They want to speak of that person to their other friends and have their friends meet them.

What is this strange phenomenon? This mutual attraction is what has been keeping the world going through the millennia. Although countless people have been born, lived and died on this earth, the heritage of mankind is maintained by this simple sharing. We have not seen the Buddha, we have never met Jesus Christ, nor Socrates. We have never seen Kant or Spinoza, Shakespeare or Shelley, Kālidāsa, Vālmīki, or the philosophers of far-off China. Bach, Mozart and Beethoven were isolated within a tiny section of our planet. Still, our human heritage is molded by the brilliant thoughts of all these wonderful people from all around the world: the poets, storytellers, those who made the myths and legends, the inventors, composers, scientists and discoverers. Whatever they have contributed is still present in our lives, guiding us, teaching us, and helping us every moment. But they are not here. Only the friend next to you is here, the friend who exemplifies and incorporates all those wonderful qualities and insights. And we can all share this tremendous inheritance and even more with each other, to make life an ecstatic and joyful experience.

Even when you do something as simple as sip a cup of coffee or tea, think about what you are doing. Your morning tea begins in some far-off land, where very poor people get up at 4 o'clock. They crowd onto a battered bus, then walk to the plantation where ripe leaves are waiting to cut into their fingers. Leeches climb on them to drink their blood. All day long they fill their baskets, then they go home to a meager supper. The tea leaves are hauled to huge mills employing hundreds of people, where they are cleaned, dried, and made into the kind of blend you want. Then it is put in tins or boxes, and sent by truck down the mountains and out to the coast. The shipyard is filled with more poor labourers, who load the tea onboard ships. Then across the ocean it comes to your port. The distributors parcel and package it and send it to your local market, where you buy it and take it home. Thus the whole world participates in one cup of tea. If you like sugar with your tea, there is another world of production and distribution behind that spoonful of white grains you tip into the cup. So should you not look into the numinous aspect of just a cup of tea?

If you become sensitive to the numinous aspect of life, gratitude will naturally fill your whole being. Each time you put a morsel of food in your mouth or sip your tea or coffee, you will become so grateful to the corporate life of mankind for giving you so much for so little effort. You will see nothing but the unity underlying the many forms of the world. Great will be your joy to share, to give, to receive. Then you won't fight. The belligerency comes in where you see only your own personal interests — "my home," "my family," or just "my self." The superficial form of your self interest should be subsumed in the ocean of the general interest, and you should feel the world is your country, your home. That humanity is your family, filled with your brothers and sisters.

The Guru wants us to really feel this: to stand united, to find peace and become peacemakers. We have to first be peacemakers in our own lives. We bring peace to ourselves. By putting all the peaces together, we make peace with the world. If you fragment it, you lose it. So let us gather all the peaces together in one meaning, in one divine thread of love and compassion and understanding.

Verse 20

ulakinu vēṟoru sattayillatuṇṭe-
nnulakar urappatu sarvamūhahinam
jaḻanu vilēśayamennu tōnniyālum
nalamiyalum malarmāla nāgamāmō?

Other than this the world has no reality;
"there is" — all such that people say is without reflection;
even if to a numskull it appears to be a snake,
will a fresh flower garland ever become a serpent?

Occasionally this world we inhabit will appear to be very dark. We feel like running away from it. We think that somewhere there could be another world, one where everything is as it should be.

"I should run away from this wretched world to a more spiritual place." With these kinds of thoughts people have made conceptual hells and heavens. They comfort themselves by thinking that as miserable as they are now, someday they will go to heaven and everything will be set right. At the same time, a lot of their motivation comes from the threat of a hell somewhere. Even great philosophers like Plato thought of a world of intelligibles where all the archetypes are, in contrast to this world of shadow — the shadows of the archetypes.

Narayana Guru says this kind of duality is unwarranted. It cannot be justified. What is is only this world.

It is how we understand the world that makes all the difference. Either you can think of it as a sea of tears, full of misery, or you can see in it the possibility of actualising all the dearest values. We have seen certain analogies in the previous verses, like the transient waves on the surface of the ocean which, when you dive deep into it, is found to be a repository of sunken treasures. Or a desert land where the passing moments are like meaningless particles of sand, but when you gain a better understanding every grain becomes a priceless jewel.

After examining these analogies, we had a closer look at life and saw that we have a double arrangement within our system for knowing things. From the side of the world come certain forms of energy, such as light or sound waves, to stimulate our sensory system, while from the side of our psyche there has to be a self-luminous consciousness to lend itself to be modified by the stimulation coming from the external world. This modification does not happen haphazardly. It is manipulated by the latent urges in us. Time here has a great significance. A certain impression that has been lying buried in us for several years or even many lives becomes potent to take over the present moment, synchronising the light from within and the stimulation from outside in order to produce a certain effect. That effect can be pleasurable or painful. It can be attractive or threatening. Thus this complex situation is structured like a pearl, in which there is both light and darkness. The pearl has a kind of smoky translucency as well as a general opacity, even as it reflects pure light. So like the modalities of nature — sattva, rajas and tamas — we can see in it transparency, translucency and opacity. We can see a light which gladdens our heart as well as a mystery which makes it difficult to evaluate its full worth.

So after giving a structure to the awareness of each passing event, we have seen the possibility of converting every experience into a living moment of priceless worth. This should be clearly in our mind when we consider the present verse.

The analogy given here is of a snake and a garland made of fresh flowers of great beauty. A man walks into his dimly lit bedroom. He is tired and wants to go to bed and rest. Reaching out his hand, he touches something cold and wet. He is greatly startled. In the dim light he sees something long and thin with dots on it, like a coiled up snake, and nearly faints with terror. Then he turns on the light and sees it is a garland made of the finest flowers dipped in rose water. It is fragrant, cooling, and very beautiful. Each flower has been especially chosen and arranged with great artistic skill as an offering of love.

Nothing is more valuable to a person than life itself. When the nature of the garland was hidden away for a moment, it appeared to be something which could take away life. Once it is clear there is no threat, however, the garland only enhances the value of one's own life. Dear life and the garland are two positive values, which become integrated into one sense of endearment.

Pavlov's dogs were conditioned to salivate whenever a bell was rung. Like that we are conditioned to many threats and attractions from our surroundings. The Guru specifically uses the word *ulakar* here, which means those who are conditioned by the pains and pleasures of this world. In another of his works, *Advaita Dīpikā*, or *The Lamp of Non-Dual Wisdom,* he says:

> To the wise man the world has substance,
> and mind-stuff represents the value-form of delight.

This is contrary to what most Vedantins say. Usually they think that this world is unreal, but Narayana Guru asserts this is the only reality. There is no other.

Ramana Maharshi had a kind of sarcoma, a very painful form of cancer. His left side was tearing away from his body. Thousands of people were sitting around in deep despair. They themselves had no cancer; they were not suffering from anything physical. Only one man had this dreadful disease, but there was no joy in anyone. All were very sad. Even the ashram peacock's cry was like a terrible lamentation, as though it were voicing the anguish of all the thousands of people sitting there. Among them were people from America, Japan, all over the world. There were Hindus and Muslims, Catholics and Protestants, children and old folks, beggars and millionaires, heads of government, doctors. This huge variety of all kinds of people were united in having a very painful time.

Maharshi's sister came to his bed and started screaming. She was crying aloud. Maharshi looked at her and said, "What is the matter?" She said, "It's you! It's you! You are going away!" She had no disease, but she was the one who was crying and he was sitting there serene, calm and unaffected. As she cried, he added, "Going?

Where? Where can I go? And where is to go?" He did not see any place to go nor did he see anyone going anywhere. This is the only place. There is nowhere else to go.

When I was a student, I felt very miserable. The whole college situation seemed meaningless, so I wrote a letter to my principal stating I was going away. He sent back a note asking me to come and see him before I left. When I went to his office, he invited me to lunch with his wife and him. He said, "It's a fine thing that you want to leave on finding that this place is not meaningful to you anymore. That's very good. But tell me, when you go away, are you going to take your mind with you also, or are you going to leave that here?"

"Surely I take my mind with me wherever I go," I said.

"That means you'll be taking the same sorrow, sadness, suspicion, doubts, misery, everything with you. It will be the same in the place where you go because you are taking all this with you. If you can leave your mind here and run away from it, fine."

This is so true. I get letters almost every day from people who say that they want to get away, to run away. Go away where? We think all the misery is because we are with certain people and certain situations. When we move away it will again be a wonderful world. If you can create a wonderful world in another place, you can create it where you are now, too.

Ultimately, what is? Only the light from within you, which is illuminating your life. What is illuminated becomes coloured, darkened by the venom that comes from within your own previous conditionings. You become entangled in your conditioned misconceptions. But if we look back to the source of illumination, we become less affiliated with the murkiness around us.

It's up to us to make our world miserable or beautiful. When the shift is more and more on the sensory side, we are drifting into the shadow. When the emphasis is more and more on the spirit, we are reclaiming and rehabilitating ourselves in the values that are imperishable. We can be assailed by doubt, fear, a sense of strangeness, difficulty in communication, and lack of understanding of the motivations of people. Here we are removed from the centre, the spirit.

We have to reconcile with the fact that on the sensory side of life

— the physical, biological aspect of life — there are inevitable changes. There are transformations such as birth and death, growth and decay. We cannot do anything about them. They have to be accepted. Once they are accepted, what is left can be absolutely beautiful.

You can also find beauty in the changes themselves. I've been reading about the life of Karl Jaspers, a man who was very sickly from childhood. He was always threatened by heart disease and bronchiectasis, but he was able to accept them, saying, "These are my limitations. I have to go to bed every now and then. But then I can again get up and work." He saw the bright side of life, the truth. First he saw truth as a scientist would see it. He studied jurisprudence, then medicine, followed by psychiatry, the methodology of doing research, and the pure philosophy of life. Finally he became a full-fledged philosopher. He did all this by always putting the bright side of life first, while his diseases were pushed to the background. Jaspers' life was very beautiful. Despite his condition he lived a rich life for almost eighty years, learning to see the world as a wonderful reality of great beauty.

There have been many people who were even more unfortunate than Jaspers. Friedrich Nietzsche, for instance. He had migraine headaches, a very small percentage of eyesight, and terrible pain and spasms all over the body. He couldn't eat any spices — the slightest trace would give him stomach cramps and make him vomit. Often he couldn't sleep. His doctors didn't want him to use his eyes for reading, but he would sit ten hours at a stretch and write before he was pulled down by his ailments. Great pain and torment filled his life, but he treated it as a shadow behind and put his own light before him. He drew great strength from this light, and accomplished a great deal.

When you consider examples like these, do you realise how fortunate we are? Our plight is not so terrible. We have comparatively much better health and faculties. Our medical care is humane and even correct much of the time. Our food and the comfort of our surroundings exceed even the wildest dreams of medieval kings. Where is there cause for despair?

The passing moments of our lives are to be made lively and rich.

One thing I have learned in my life is that the moment that comes will not come again. It's gone. You can see the moment approaching. Receive it with open arms. Glorify it by enriching it with your joy, finding a new value, a new sense of direction in life. Have a renewed sense of wonder. Thus, that moment becomes eternalised in your life, it is a moment to be remembered and to be proud that you could live it so well. Then you can move on to the next moment; this one has already been immortalised in you. What you have achieved in that moment is your eternal repository. Wonderful! You feel fulfilled. You are filled with gratitude: "Oh, I lived this moment so wonderfully!" This is your own life, in this very world, with all these amenities given to you in the here and now.

With this understanding you are eager to race to the next moment because it is going to be wonderful, going to be beautiful. It will yield so much. You see the promise of the future already in it. It's going to be still more wonderful than what you have already lived. Then you pass on to the next with joy and grace. The day opens up with such beauty, such promise. There is nothing like life, nothing like this world, a world where you can make friends, a world where you can create beautiful things, a world where you can share beauty with others and where you can make others part of your own self. A world where there is such an abundance of love and sharing.

The only thing is that you shouldn't drift into darkness. Don't look at the world as something horrid, but as beautiful, divine. Every bit of it. Then we know we are the creators of our own fate. Not through this individual ego with all its vagaries, but through a full affiliation with the eternal, supernatural light that enriches everything. Only then will we have the strength to become masters of the situation, the whole beauty of creation, the beauty that has painted the petals of the flowers, which has given shape to the butterflies and birds, which makes the mountains look awe-inspiring and the oceans look vast, which makes the clouds float so gracefully overhead. This is where we find our true freedom.

You belong to the same overmind of beauty. Not with your ego but with your spirit. Participation in it will reveal to you the divine artist in you, the divine musician in you, the divine intelligence, the divine creator, the divine lover, the divine unifier, the divine peacemaker within you. It's such a blessing to be in this world, to be born here and to live here. This body of ours will fall away just like a candle burning out. But before it burns out the candle gives off a lot of light. What does it matter that it is eventually extinguished? It has lived its moment of light. We live surrounded by smoke and darkness. Make up your mind that you will live this day, each coming moment, in all its worth and beauty, and that you will share it with all. This is the great teaching the Guru offers us.

Verse 21

priyamoru jātiyitenpriyam tvadīya-
priyamapara priyamennanēkamāyi
priyaviṣayam prati vanniṭum bhramam; tan-
priyamapara priyamennaṟiññiṭēṇam

Endearment is one kind; this is dear to me;
your preference is for something else;
thus, many objects of endearment are differentiated
and confusion comes;
what is dear to you is dear to another also; this should
be known.

Experience falls into two categories, the internal and the external. In the external world we interact with things, people and various kinds of events. Inside us, we entertain ideas, recall memories, and experience certain sensations. Yet all of these experiences can be grouped together in one category as the object matter of experience.

The subject in each case is what you call 'I'. I see this orange outside. I like it. I have an idea and I like it very much. Here the idea is inside me and the orange is outside me, but both are objects of my interest. There can be a thing outside which I like and you do not like. I may also have an idea that I like but you do not like. You like another idea. You have a subjective feeling or notion as well as items outside, which are all the objects of your interest. So now we have three things: 'I', my idea, and what is not 'I', or what is outside me.

There is one more factor also. There is a pure light in us, a pure Self, which has been described in this work in so many ways. In the very first verse it was described as the one cosmic yolk which is transforming into everything, the Karu. After that it was compared to a supernal sun of pure awareness shining in the firmament of consciousness. Again it was compared to an oceanic treasury. We treated it as the one knowledge behind all knowledge, which unifies the knower, the known and knowledge within itself. Then it was compared to a light which was never lit and which will never be extinguished. Apart from shedding light, it illuminates things and it is always looking on as the eternal witness.

Next we tried to see it as the one changeless truth behind all changes. That was further understood as the truth that is revealed to a contemplative person who knows the secret of the sacred syllable, aum. After that it was pictured as the supreme light which fills our inside so much that all the horizontal interests in life become verticalised by the experience.

Again the same light was described as the neutral consciousness of the witnessing self sitting under the tree of life, and not being caught by the tendrils of the phenomenal creeper which is overladen with the flowers of individuation. Thereafter we saw it as the oneness, the uniting factor, which allows one person to understand another, and is the homogeneous reality in our recognition of different things. Again, we saw within us the continuity from one 'I' identity to another; it is the golden thread which passes through all separate notions of 'I'. In this sense it is the unifying factor in the 'I' consciousness of different people. Then we saw it as the one reality which comes to its fullness and perfection when the consciousness associated with an individuated self in the form of an embodied being is liberated by the fall and decay of the body. It never perishes: it comes to perfection. We saw it as having a likeness to that supreme Lord who remains unaffected by the three modalities of nature. We were asked to turn to it and affiliate ourselves in a bipolar attitude of love and devotion whereby we can offer to that Lord all that sprouts in our mind. In this way we remain one with the unchanging reality.

What comes in between us and this wholesome experience? The threefoldness of the things outside. Past, present and future; here, there and far beyond on earth, the atmosphere and the sky; all are introduced to trifurcate our experience. Triadic experience occurs inside as well as outside, with the knower, known and knowledge;

enjoyer, enjoyed and enjoyment; and actor, action and what is acted upon. A person with a unitive understanding can see the sameness outside and inside. It is again and again that sameness we are referring to in this course of study.

When our life is fragmented and bits of it are lying scattered around meaninglessly, the light of this One can come like a flood to overwhelm our divisions and charge every event with great significance. Every grain of sand becomes a pearl of priceless worth. It has been described as absolute joy, experiencing which you transcend the passing of time. Everything becomes a timeless, eternal reality.

We have also seen that in the same world, even people endowed with great wisdom will put their emphasis on different aspects of truth. One will say the cause is real; another that the effect is real; while yet another will say it is neither the cause nor the effect, but what you derive from it that is real. Such varying approaches are what lead to fighting among people. After showing us this danger, Narayana Guru warned us to be careful, that this world can indeed be threatening. It can be dark, frightful and depressing. If your mind is already tainted with the dark colours of fear, since it is through that very mind you look at the world, this world will also look very frightening. But if your mind is free of such taint, then you see it as a fresh garland of newly picked flowers, very beautifully strung together. Thus in its structure, function and value this becomes a world of great endearment, full of truth that can be adored as vast wisdom.

These are some of the analogies that Narayana Guru has presented to us in the first twenty verses of *Ātmopadeśa Śatakam*.

Now the Guru tells us to look again at that light within. It is always shining forth with the same kind of brilliance, but it passes through a kind of mechanism of different gears. The gears can make the light seem brighter or darker. It can even be turned off for a time. When that happens you are in state of tamas. Light is still within you, but it is as if you are in the dark. You are helpless. Then it can be turned on a little. It is your own little light. And it can be turned up to its fullness also.

When you turn your light on, it illuminates your world of experience, whether inside or outside, as if through a shielding glass. The glass is your mind. It's not a very faithful device for giving you a transparent vision; it is clouded in various ways. It is already coloured with your interests, which have come to you because of previous conditionings. You yourself have experienced pain or pleasure previously in conjunction with something you are now encountering, so you are already coloured in favour or against it. Several of these prejudices or preconditionings are already present in you. And the conditionings need not necessarily be previous ones. Someone can put into your mind a prospective expectation, which also colours the mind. All these bring about differentiation.

Reality has three unifying aspects. One is called *sat*, existence. I exist, you exist, this couch exists, the house exists, the sky exists, the world exists. All these can be brought under one common heading of existence. All that exists is a genuine existence which implies the existence of all. It's called *sat*.

I am aware of my existence, of your existence, of the existence of the world. Thus I have an all-embracing awareness that includes everything. What is not in it, I will never know. This awareness, which includes in it good and bad, far and near, one and many, big and small, irrespective of all variations, is just one knowledge, *cit*. So we have one all-inclusive existence and one all-inclusive knowledge.

I value my beingness and you value your beingness. Everything tends to become valuable in one way or another. All these values are measured by our own happiness. This is called ananda. So we have *sat*, existence; *cit*, knowledge; and ananda, the primordial value. Taken all together, the whole of reality is therefore called *saccidānanda*.

One can be permeated with the consciousness of *saccīdananda*. It can be blissful if it is not differentiated, but instead of this generic sense of existence, subsistence and value, we tend to see things individually. When they are broken into bits we have instead *asti*, this is; *bhāti*, I know it; and *priyam*, I love it. In Western terms these correspond to cognition, connation and affection. In the fragmentary notions of *asti*, *bhāti* and *priyam* there is scope for a great deal of confusion. We can have "This is, I know it, I dislike it"; or even "This is, I do not know what it is, therefore I do not know if I like it or not." Only when we cultivate an ever-prevailing sense of unity are we out of this confusion. When we identify with the egoistic self we see only through this fragmentation and do not experience *saccidānanda*.

If we can approach life from the point of view of the all-seeing witness, which is not tainted with incipient memories or proliferating interests, then we will see the good of all, the general good, in which what pleases me is also included. This is not attained, as some mistakenly think, by summarily dismissing what pleases me as an individual.

Often there arises a tendency for us to become self-critical if what we like is not liked by others. Yet if we are all human beings, there should be an underlying happiness regarding what we like. I like vegetarian dishes, and some of my friends like non-vegetarian dishes. So should I give up my vegetarian diet in deference to the others' non-vegetarian tastes for the sake of unity? Of course not. We have to think more generically about what we like. Vegetarian food and non-vegetarian food are both essentially food. I love to have food, and my friends also love to have food. At this level we are not different. So I can go with my friends to a restaurant and I'll have what I like and they can have what they like. We are all partaking of food. Basically, our need is the same and our fulfilment is the same. The differences are only in the particular details. Of course, the differences are also important and can't be overlooked. When I am hungry and you are hungry, I cannot just say that as both of us are one, I will eat for you also. You have to take care of your side of the business.

We have to distinguish how we cater to the general happiness, and what implications it has in its particular aspects. A husband and wife may love each other very much. They live a unified life, but that does not mean that they do not have two toothbrushes. Having separate toothbrushes does not take away from their friendship in the least. When we shift our focus from particular objects back to the Self, we will stop getting so confused on this issue.

Four elements are involved from this perspective: the Self, the ego, objects, and our interest in them. An interest usually comes between the ego and the object; actually it is the interest lying buried behind the ego that directs it to the objects. All this happens in the light of the Self. Unfortunately, the light is the part we completely forget. It is in this light of the existence of the Self that we derive the idea of the existence of the object. It is from the knowledge of the Self that we derive the notion of what we know. And it is from the value of the Self that we derive the enjoyability of the object. These three basic facts we forget when we are concerned only with the objects themselves.

Even after we learn this wisdom, when we go out in the world our life is again governed by preferences. 'My' comes instead of 'our'. "He is my friend, my guru. I have a right to protect my friend." "No, no. He is *my* friend; he is my guru. I see it like this." Then they fight. The combat is in the ego field. From there if you can get into the spirit field it is very wide; there is enough room for everything. When Alice wanted to join the tea party, all the animals said, "No room! No room!" Alice was indignant. "There is plenty of room. Why do you say there is no room?"

There *is* plenty of room. You don't have to fight and say that because that person is there you don't have any space now. Your space is not taken away by anyone. The space you occupy is always there for you, and the space occupied by the other is there for them. The Absolute is big enough to include everything and everyone.

Jesus said, "Don't bother about the flocks. My sheep can be outside the flock also. Why do you bother about a person being in a different church? If I am really the Good Shepherd, I will go where he is. It doesn't matter if he wanders away from the group. In my Father's mansion there are many chambers." That's a beautiful way of putting it. There is not just one chamber in God's mansion; it has such variety that there are unlimited possibilities.

We have to reorganise our lives and make our visions wide. The more interests that are there, the more wonderful it is. You paint and I sing and another person dances: it will only enrich our lives the more. Why should everyone do the same thing? In contrast to the Soviet communists, Mao Zedong once said, "Instead of one flower, let there be a million flowers blossoming. Why should there be only the red flower? Let there be a million flowers with a million hues, flourishing." That's wonderful. Even when a million flowers of a million hues flourish, it is the flowerness that we glorify. In other words, if we know the essential value that is lived out differently by different people, and if we glorify that, it is one. Let us cultivate that insight by which the oneness is immortalised.

Verse 22

priyamaparanteyatenpriyam; svakīya-
priyamaparapriyamiprakāramākum
nayamatināle narannu nanma nalkum-
kriyayaparapriya hētuvāyvarēṇam

The happiness of another — that is my happiness;
one's own joy is another's joy — this is the guiding
principle;
that action which is good for one person
should bring happiness to another.

Watching the lives of various beings, anything from worms to the most contemplative yogi or seer, it is easy to see that all actions are motivated by the desire for happiness. Our motivations can be conscious or unconscious. Even so minor a thing as shifting your position as you sit here is only to make you more comfortable. If you cough, it is because there is an irritation you want to remove so you can feel better. The slightest movement we make is in search of a better adjustment for greater happiness, because happiness is the main goal of life.

In the search for happiness, and in the actualisation of it, our primary tools are the senses, the organs of perception, the organs of action, and the mind. Our hands itch for doing something. When we sit somewhere for a long time, we feel like getting up and walking. We cannot be silent for very long before we wish to talk and express ourselves. The five organs of action and organs of perception are all to be engaged in something. We find our happiness in engagement through these organs.

We have five senses, so there are five kinds of happiness. In seeing alone there are millions of varieties of things to be seen. We look at very minute things, we look at very large things, we look at bright things and dark things, at the colourful and the colourless. In the same way, each sense organ has its own world of variegation. Our affectivity lies between our perceiving mind and the things that are perceived.

There are two real causes of happiness. One is obvious and the other is hidden. First let us discuss the former, which is when the cause is known to us. We have many latent urges in our mind, all waiting for a favourable environment to provide an opportunity for their actualisation. Hunger is a biological urge of this type. A hungry person is looking for an opportunity to get some food. It may begin as an unconscious motivation, but it soon becomes conscious. So we go to a place where food is available, such as a kitchen or restaurant. Inside is hunger; outside is the availability of food. When these are brought together, we are satisfied.

Of course, we don't want to just stuff something in our mouths. The whole presentation is important. We like it to be served on a neat table, properly set with nice utensils, by someone who is friendly. It should please the eye, and smell delicious. In India people enjoy eating with their hands also. When foods are mixed with the fingers they have a special kind of feeling, so even before the food hits their mouth they can enjoy its touch. Then it is tasted. Finally the food becomes nourishment, creating metabolic changes in us, and we have sensations of satiation and relaxation. This whole range of pleasures is involved in the simple act of just satisfying hunger.

There are many preferences involved in this priyam, or this main item of the fulfilment of an urge, to make us really happy. We prefer to eat in a certain restaurant, to be served by a certain person, to eat food prepared in a certain way. Some people like their food boiled, others steamed, and still others fried. We stress the quality of the object as the main condition for happiness. Happiness is thus considered as an external factor which is coming in to us. Our desire is inside; happiness is manifesting outside. So it becomes a conditional factor. Narayana Guru tells us that we become confused by thinking of happiness as an external factor.

The Guru begins this verse with a word that has an equivocal meaning, *aparan*. When you see a total stranger, that person is entirely different from you. You have your own body and that person has theirs. But when you look at each other, you find something pleasing. That person becomes an object of happiness. Now you greet each other and enjoy each other's company. Each of you says, "I am so-and-so." There are two separate I's. I and you. You and I. Two separate people. Then later you say, "Let us sit here and talk." The 'I' has now been transformed. There is an 'us' where before were two I's. The other is now melting into the not-other. *Paran* is other; *aparan*, not other. When 'I' and 'you' change into 'we' or 'us' the other has changed into no more another. This is the implication of the word the Guru uses. We are no more others.

"Now let us both go to the restaurant and eat something." You both go. One asks, "What do you want?" "You tell me what *you* like." "No, no, no. You please say what *you* like." "How about this particular dish?" "Yes, let's both have that." So they order it. Each wants to make a great concession to the other, conceding to their wishes. At least five minutes will be wasted finding out what the other person likes because each is being a kind of martyr in the cause of love. It's very beautiful.

I read in a novel about two middle-aged women who were living together. One wanted to get up first so she could make tea and bring it on a tray to the other before she woke up. She stealthily got up and tiptoed to the kitchen, where she was surprised to find the other one already making tea for her. All through the story they were making little martyrdoms to please each other like that. This is called *svakīya priyam*. Let my own happiness be your happiness; let your happiness be my happiness. It is this commonality of happiness that unites two people; then there is no more the other.

When we desire something, it is because of a latent urge. In the coming together of two people there is a need to love and a need to be loved. There are needs to eat, to do some work and to find fellowship. All these motivations come from urges. When an urge becomes strong, it becomes a desire. When a desire is promoted it becomes a wish, and when a wish is promoted it becomes a will. A will when actualised becomes an action. Thus it begins with desire and ends in action. All actions in which we are engaged have behind them a motivation, and they involve things or persons outside us, so to speak. This entire process is implied in the term priyam.

If things and persons outside us are within the scheme of our action, we have to see that it is not unilateral. We must make bilateral arrangements in the action set-up. A brute is only motivated by its own urges; it does not look for a bilateral agreement. It unilaterally charges at the object of pleasure.

Lovers do the same things that rapists do with their victims. Physically, there is no difference in what they are doing. The distinction is that one is unilateral and the other is bilateral. In rape, the happiness of the other person is not looked into. One is only caring for his own happiness. What was beautiful then becomes an abominable crime, instilling fear and revulsion in the victim.

There is also a hidden cause of happiness. We are not merely the senses, the mind and our latent interests. Behind all this is a self-luminous light, which assures us of the existence of everything. In fact, it is the primeval existence. It is the ground of all existence. It is only because of this existence that anything is possible. Yet we only see the existence of a person or the existence of an object, and not existence as such. We forget that it is through our participation in the general existence that we become existent. This existence is the existence of knowledge, of a great awareness, of an illuminating consciousness which covers the knower, the known and knowledge.

The existence of one thing and another thing have between them a homogeneity. I can present you with an existing apple and an existing pear in the same dish because the apple exists, the pear exists and the dish exists. When I poetically say, "Here is an apple, a pear, and also my love for you," you can see the fruit but you do not see what we call 'love' in the dish. In the words "I am giving you my love," is an idea. The other person who feels sentimental about this expression becomes resonant to it inside, experiences a similar sentiment, and replies "Yes, truly this is offered in love." The existence of the pear and the existence of love are not of the same order, yet because of the knowledge of love in you and the other person there is a homogeneity of that particular kind of knowledge.

The pear and the apple can come together as pure existential knowledge, and the love with which they are offered comes phenomenologically. The existential and the phenomenological are different and yet they become one. In anything you see or experience, all your concepts and ideas, and your entire social, moral and spiritual history, also come along as part of your perception. Therefore, all existential experiences automatically change into phenomenological experiences.

There is still one more aspect here. The overall existence, this all-embracing consciousness of knowledge, is also revealing how one happiness pervades everything. The happiness of seeing a sunset, the happiness of eating a good breakfast, of holding the hand of someone we love, of reading or writing poetry, of painting, of listening to beautiful music, the happiness in all the variety of things you enjoy through the five senses or that are performed by the five organs of action, conceived by mind and enjoyed by mind — are all part and parcel of one universal experience of happiness. You are That. When you realise yoûr real nature from within, there cannot be another because what is seemingly another is only due to external diversity. In reality it is part of the same existence of the same consciousness and the same happiness. Thus, the *paran* or the otherness, ceases. There is no other; there is only That. Calling attention to this, the Guru says, "That thou art." You are That.

Through a realisation of the Self, we come to know there is no other. I cannot pinch my left hand with my right and expect to not feel it since they are separate things. I still feel the pain. If I hold my left hand in the right one, the tenderness, the happiness is neither of the left hand or the right; it is my own happiness. Thus from inside, when you see the oneness of all things, there cannot be a separation of my happiness and another's happiness. For a realised soul, an awakened one, whatever he or she is doing is a spontaneous expression of Self-love. It is not an ego-centered love; it is the love of the supreme Self for itself.

The reason God created the universe, if you believe in that, is for God's own joy, not for anyone else's. This is why it is said in the Brihadaranyaka Upanishad: "No husband loves the wife for the sake of the wife, but for the sake of the joy of the Self. No wife loves the husband for the sake of the husband, but for the sake of the joy of the Self. No parent loves the child for the sake of the child, but for the sake of the joy of the Self. No man loves wealth for the sake of wealth, but for the sake of the joy of the Self." In none of these places is the reference to the ego as the self; it is to the universal Self, the Self that is in all.

Two things, then, can bring us together. One is the actualisation of an interest or an urge in us, and the other is the universality of the Self. When someone like Jesus Christ or the Buddha comes to the world and engages in an action, they are filled with the universal sorrow of mankind. They engage in activity in order to reverse this pain and suffering. This can be compared to and contrasted with our individually oriented actions. Take for instance a person who takes delight in becoming a physician. It fulfils a certain drive in him to find self-expression through service to others. In addition, it is a means of livelihood and a way to express his talent. In the orientation of an ordinary person who does not have the deep insight of the spirit, it is only the motivational urge to be a physician that is getting actualised here.

There is another person who is ill, and there is a need for him to be cured and recover from his illness. He comes to the doctor and asks, "Please heal me. I am suffering." The doctor replies, "I am most pleased to render my service to you. I want you to be cured. You should not suffer." Thus the physical, personal need for a patient to be cured and for a doctor to render his service bring them together. They enter into a bipolarity. They are no longer two separate entities, they belong to one common context of therapy from which both benefit. By rendering the service the doctor becomes happy, and by receiving the service the patient becomes happy.

If the physician also has the mind of the physician of all physicians, like Christ, Buddha or Krishna, then he is not only seeing his action as a means of livelihood and expression of talent, but as a correction which he is bringing to his own universal body that is now ailing. He is curing only himself. If the patient is also oriented this way, he sees that the universal benevolence is acting in the form of a doctor. He is filled with gratitude, not especially to this doctor — though that's also there — but to the universal benevolence in the manifestation of this world.

An engineer has his skill and the need to perform it. He invents a machine. Then he makes it, sells it, or installs it for someone who has a need to be relieved of some kind of work. That person feels happy for the engineer's service, and the engineer has the satisfaction of doing his job well. Whatever role we are playing, whether carpenter, smith, plumber, teacher, anyone, there is a bipolarity involved in it. In that bipolar situation we become dialectical counterparts in which a common interest fuses us together. Then the other person ceases to be just another; there is a coming together. So we can come together from the side of the latent urges as well as from the side of realisation.

Narayana Guru, as a realised person, is revealing to us: "Oh Man, please do not think that there is any other. It is only seemingly so. Let all your actions be directed to universal happiness, to the universal actualisation of happiness." When you engage yourself in an action, look for your counterpart. That comes from above. From below you also realise that this counterpart is your own Self. In this way you get a double correction and a double incentive to ensure the happiness of all concerned.

Verse 23

aparanu vēṇṭiyaharnniśam prayatnam
kṛpaṇata viṭṭu kṛpālu ceytiṭunnu
kṛpaṇan adhōmukhanāy kiṭannu ceyyu-
nnapajaya karmmamavannuvēṇṭi mātram

For the sake of another, day and night performing action,
having given up self-centered interests, the compassionate person acts;
the self-centered man is wholly immersed in necessity,
performing unsuccessful actions for himself alone.

When a person looks at his own life, he sees certain topological limitations. He draws a circle around his own ego consciousness and marks in its centre his ego. He places everything especially dear to him inside the circle, calling them 'I' and 'mine'. Outside he places everything alien. This circle is the ego boundary spoken of by existentialist psychologists.

There are many kinds of ego boundaries. There is a "home front" where, if you are not certain of your neighbour, you make a strong barricade. Of course, as Robert Frost has said, you are fencing yourself in as much as the other out. You only think you are keeping an alien world outside, when actually you are putting up a wall and imprisoning yourself.

So there is a personal ego boundary and one for your home. Then you make a powerful boundary for your prejudices. Religion can never be meaningful to one who has such a boundary. His religion is only a fanatical dogma in which anyone who does not share the same faith is a rival and an enemy, and so they are pushed outside the circle of his beliefs.

There are some Frenchmen who will not speak English, even though they know how, because of a kind of linguistic patriotism. If you travel with one of them from Paris to Marseilles they will speak no English. Yet as soon as you cross the Belgian border, they become normal and begin to speak English with you. This kind of fanaticism exacerbates language barriers. So there are several topological boundaries with which people imprison themselves. Narayana Guru uses the term *kṛpaṇan* to describe someone caught in these self-centered limitations.

On the other hand, for the person who sees his counterpart as frontierless, the whole world is his. He cannot brook any kind of differentiation, whether by caste, race, colour or creed. Even though for the sake of communication such a person uses the word 'I', in his mind it means 'we' or 'all of us'. Such a person is here called a compassionate one, *kṛpālu*.

All of us, whether compassionate or selfish, have to do action. Even breathing is an action. The Bhagavad Gita says that no person remains for even a moment without engaging in action. Our actions are of three kinds. One is *nitya karma*, the daily activities which you have to perform necessarily for the maintenance of your own life. In the morning you have to wake up, clean yourself, eat and evacuate your bowels. No one else can do these things for you. They are imperative actions, because you yourself have to perform them.

The second kind of action is called *niyata karma*. This refers to your placement in society, where you have accepted a certain role due to your vocation or career. You may be a doctor, a lawyer, an engineer, businessman, teacher or whatever; you have some work assigned to you by your own option or a contract. It requires you to do a certain kind of work for certain hours each day, and if you don't do it there is a breach of contract or somebody will suffer. You and everyone else expects you to do it. This type of daily, expected work is called *niyata karma*.

The third kind of action is *naimittika karma*. It is incidental. There is no regularity to it. Say you go for a walk or a ride and you see someone fall down unconscious. This is not a daily occurrence. If you are a compassionate person, a good samaritan, you stop and see what happened. You call for help or try to get him to a hospital or his home. Perhaps you cover him with your coat or administer first aid. All this is done incidentally, and little or none of it is prescribed. This is *naimittika karma.*

Of the three karmas, *nitya karma* is common to all people. It is for one's own creature comfort. There is nothing good or bad about it. You don't eat because it is a great virtue: you have to eat. And you don't consider someone's morality or immorality just because they are breathing. They have to breathe.

Leaving this type of action aside, there are really only two kinds, *niyata* and *naimittika*. The motivation to act in either of these ways can come from two entirely different sources, namely selfishness and compassion. This is where your whole life pattern is decided. The person who is basically selfish has to limit the world around him to make himself secure. The more he thinks of himself, the more glaring is the contrast with what is his non-self. An increasing strangeness comes between him and the rest of the world. He becomes suspicious of the outside, which brings feelings of insecurity. The suspicion and insecurity compel him to build a fortress around himself. As this becomes exaggerated, he becomes paranoiac. He needs to always cover up, to do things secretly and calculatingly. He holds his cards away from others and secretly senses what profits everyone is going to make. Then he wants to play tricks, as his only concern is how to gain. He does not believe others, and so others do not believe him. As he is feeling insecure, he cannot be open with others, and this lack of openness makes him unacceptable to others. Thus everyday he is losing some ground. He makes his life more and more difficult by shunting himself away from others. Ultimately his life becomes very shallow. He cannot have any real truths or any great culture or tradition. There is no sublime height to go to. His world of interest is very cramped.

We see millions and millions of such unfortunate people all around us. It's just terrible. They live within their own prison walls, incarcerated by their own selfishness. I see hundreds and thousands of families who live this kind of wretched life — no meaning, no value before them. All day and all night long they think only of their eating and drinking and their one particular family's interest.

Everyone else can go to the dogs. They are always in trouble. Each day they further cut off their vital links with the rest of the world. Such miserable beings.

The Guru says here that their face is always down, they cannot face the world. They are living in shame, living in vulgarity, shame and greed. They are engaged in actions which will never succeed. They are living only for their own sakes. Even if you try to help such people, they can never be helped. As soon as you lift them out of one quagmire, they get into another. This is the terrible situation where both daily and incidental actions are monitored by selfishness.

Compare this to a compassionate person. The dominant theme in his life is "we are one. I care for you. It doesn't matter who you are, I care for you." In Victor Hugo's *Les Miserables*, there is a bishop who knows nothing but love for mankind. He lives for all. He uses his office, his position, everything, only for the sake of redressing the pain and agony of his fellow man. Reading Hugo's great work and getting into the spirit of the bishop is many times more profound than reading religious scriptures. What a wonderful character; what a beautiful life! You shed tears for him. You want to go live with him. At least once in your life you want to meet a person like him, who can inspire you for the rest of your life.

The compassionate one. As he has no ego boundary, he uses the word 'I' only for the sake of centralising thoughts and relating ideas. It is only a philosophical reference point, a focus for consciousness, not a fixed social structure. It's not an ego. For this reason he can relate literally anything to the central notion called 'I'. As he is not putting walls around himself, he comes into relationship with the rest of humanity and all kinds of animals, birds, and plant life.

When you read the poems of Robert Frost, you are so thrilled that he can get into an easy conversation with a bird, a flower, a tree, bush, brook, stone, road, anything. Wherever he turns, he sees nothing but friendship. The whole world is open to him. What a wonderful way to live!

We don't have to just think of saints. Saints are living all around us. A man may be very humble but yet open up many windows, many life interests, so he can commune with everyone around. He keeps his door open for people to walk in. He boils his pot not for himself alone, but for anyone who is hungry or thirsty. Jesus said "Ye come to me, those who suffer. Leave your load on my shoulders." Such a compassionate one easily relates himself to others. In his word, the world finds consolation. He is their light and inspiration. Anyone who encounters such a person easily affiliates themselves to him. Naturally, his base is becoming stronger than that of the selfish person: "I love you; you love another. Therefore your friend becomes my friend." Thus, everyday his influence grows, his friendship spreads. He is generous and gives everything without question.

In a reciprocal way, everything wants to pour into him. Whatever he gives, ten-fold, a hundred-fold, it comes back to him. So he is always successful. He is always influential. His word is taken with honor by everyone. They believe him and trust him. He has no axe to grind. Therefore what he says rings true. It is hard to resist the word of such a one.

These are the two contrasting principles underlying our actions. One is the selfishness of the self-centered egoist, the other the compassion of the spiritually open person. These are the two possibilities before us, and it is up to us to choose between them. It's a pity that most people make themselves lost to the world by opting for the egoistic stand. It is equally easy to be compassionate, to be open, to not push away.

Previously we saw how our joy should also be the joy of the other. Here we are bringing this same idea to a deeper level. Begin by looking for your counterparts in life. If I am a teacher, those who want to learn are my counterparts. If I am a doctor, the patients are my counterparts. If I am a businessman, those who will be benefitted by the things I want to supply are my counterparts. If I am a parent, my children are my counterparts; if a husband, my wife; and if a friend, another friend is my counterpart. Everybody has their counterparts in life. It is not just one person, but so many people and so many fields. And between ourselves and our counterparts we can open up a floodgate of reciprocal relations based on compassion.

You may be doing a strict business deal, but once you are in the situation you can open up to the other person as a human being. Instead of just scheming how you can make a profit off of him by exploiting the situation, you can look at how you would want to be treated if you were in his place. Then it would be easy to imagine what kind of security the customer should have and what kind of benefits he should receive. If you look from both sides, from the side of the business executive *and* the side of the customer, you can come to a neutral position which is optimally beneficial to both. When you take this approach, you are not afraid of what you are doing. There is great moral support for it, looking out for the well-being of your brother. And the customer trusts you and feels encouraged to always come to you in the future as the person to provide his supplies. The good will always increases.

This will never fail in any field. When a doctor cares for a patient by thinking first of the fellow human coming to him and not just of the money to be made, the very look or word or touch he uses is like nectar. The patient may be healed even before any medicine is administered. In this way we are all saints and we can be saints, here and now in our daily life. This is the great lesson Narayana Guru is giving us for our meditation today: how to move away from selfishness to compassion, and how to break down the barriers around us.

As a footnote I want to say something to all of you. Some of the letters I get here from very beautiful people are full of darkness. The only cause for their darkness is the lack of compassion and the self-centeredness in their egos. In the last couple of days, I received word about two families breaking up, each of the women with two children and the man finding it impossible to live with her. The woman finds she is caught up in darkness. Innocent children suffer tremendously because of this lack of compassion on the part of their parents.

I sometimes wonder, is there anything called love which unites people in this country? How shallow, uncouth, rotten is the thing called love here. It is terrible, selfish to the core. Dark souls, never caring for anything but their personal interests. Brutes. And yet how beautiful they look. It is so painful to see.

Only this morning I wrote a letter to a young friend to get back immediately to his wife and two little ones. It is shameful, an utterly shameful situation. And these people have been running after swamis and gurus for years. They have been claiming to live a spiritual life. Still they claim to be spiritual, yet not caring the least for each other. What a painful, shameful thing. Where is compassion in them? Why do they speak of love? Do they understand what love is?

A little baby not six months old to be thrown away by a father, saying "I don't care for that child any more." Is he a father? This is a rotten place. I think this country has lost something very, very precious. It is high time a search should be made in the heart to discover the treasure called compassion. Instead we run after fantasies and never want truth at all. I am not just here philosophising. I am speaking to you of hard facts of life, of stark realities of life.

I am not asking you to become such a great saint as living for the Eskimos or saving the whales. Save your own child before you go out to save the whales. You are so compassionate that you want to preserve rare species. Your child is a rare species. Why don't you show some compassion to her? Americans are very clever to find out what is on Venus, but they are not clever to find out what is in their own child's mind.

Allow this to percolate deep into your soul, then make a serious self-examination. You can make your life many times more precious, more worth living.

Verse 24

avan ivan ennaṟiyunnatokkeyōrttā-
lavaniyil ādimamāy orātmarūpam
avan avan ātma sukhattinācarikku-
nnavayaparannu sukhattināy varēṇam

"That man," "this man" — thus, all that is known
in this world, if contemplated, is the being of the one
  primordial self;
what each performs for the happiness of the self
should be conducive to the happiness of another.

When we look around, we see other human beings just like us. We also see other kinds of living beings with some of the traits of humans. For instance, they all want to eat, drink, sleep and reproduce. In these categories, man is not an exception. He is conforming to some laws of nature.

Now we have access to know a little more of these natural laws with regard to the control of things which have physical existence. If for some reason the whole universe is blasted apart and it goes back to its original state, then scientists believe there will be only hydrogen left. Hydrogen is considered to be the basic element because it has only one proton and one neutron. These are held together, and their electron is held in orbit, by an inherent law. Even when two of these hydrogen atoms combine with one of oxygen to make a molecule of water, the hydrogen and oxygen retain their distinct qualities, their characteristics that make them what they are. Basically nature restricts the qualities of a thing through the operation of innate laws.

From a materialistic point of view, as we pass through all the stages of evolution from the primordial substance to man, we see the operation of physical laws. As we approach man on the evolutionary scale we see there is a greater freedom in choosing between options. A monkey, for instance, has a much greater range of choices than a snail.

In his *Nicomachean Ethics*, Aristotle takes up the question of the meaning of life. He begins his study by putting the question, "What is it that distinguishes man from the rest of beings, and that determines the meaning of his life?" One thing that separates us from the rest is that we are the only animal that writes poetry, that builds schools and colleges, writes books and stores them, and has developed a vocabulary consisting of thousands of words covering all shades of meaning and embodying a large number of concepts. In short, we can say that man excels in his knowledge. In a sense we can say he *is* knowledge.

Next, Aristotle puts forward a very beautiful idea. He says although we are all aware of what is good, the word 'good' by itself does not have any special meaning. It is a word like 'is'. What is the meaning of 'is'? The meaning of 'is' is, you are judging something to be or not to be. It is or it is not. To say something is, there has to be a light within you which discerns the existence of something. Essentially, it is the power to discern an existence. If you cannot discern that by yourself, you cannot live that truth. Aristotle quotes the substance of a verse from Hesiod, which says a man is excellent who can perform all his activities with no confusion in his mind, making his own judgements always right. Those who cannot do that should at least turn to others who are wise enough to counsel them. Those who do not even turn to the wise are good for nothing.

Thus, you are good for yourself only when you can discern. Discerning means gaining a certitude of the Self. It becomes evident to your self. When it is self-evident, then alone can you say 'is'. This evidence of the Self that comes to us operates in the hydrogen atom as a principle of determination. If I am a hydrogen atom, I should only have one electron and one proton. I should have only the correct atomic weight and my characteristics should be such and such. And if I am a man I should have awareness, a discerning power.

After establishing this much, Aristotle goes a step further. He says if a man decides to be a flautist or a harpist, will he not set for himself the highest possible standard in that particular art? If a man chooses to be a carpenter, will he not put before himself the highest standards of carpentry? Unfortunately, this idea is an unwarranted extension to a specious conclusion.[1] The main reality is the knowledge of the Self. If you choose to be a fully developed person, you should naturally put before yourself the highest possible standard of the attainment of pure knowledge. The highest possible truth is continuous and contiguous from the very first form of reality to you. It is whole, without part, and without any possible division. This makes one not only a brother to all fellow humans, but also in kinship with all of existence.

If everything manifested is our own Self, and we are considering the happiness of the self, such happiness lies in being harmonious with our own nature. If we are dislodged from the harmony of our physical well-being we become sick. If we are jolted out of our moral integrity, we become morally sick. If we are pushed away from the proper functioning of our minds, we become either retarded or subnormal. If our understanding is clouded, we become stupid.

From the most minute atom to the foremost philosophy, there is a natural harmony that maintains its beingness. Each has a harmony within itself and a harmony in its relationships with other things. Nature maintains its harmony, and we are by no means foreigners to it. The most beautiful part of it is that nature reveals itself in its own unfoldment of consciousness, which manifests as our consciousness. We who are the knowers of nature are really nature knowing nature.

Because we are the knowers of nature, we know how an atom is constituted. We also know how to fission an atom, blast it apart. Knowledge can be good to maintain and appreciate harmony, and also to destroy it. If I have knowledge of an actual event, I can then distort it or conceal it in such a way that no one will be able to detect it. Knowing the whole truth enables me to distort it. For instance when a man kills someone, he knows the circumstances under which that person was killed, the weapon used, the place the body was disposed of, and where the weapon was thrown away. Because of

1. Cf. John Ralston Saul, *Voltaire's Bastards* (New York: Vintage Books, 1992) p. 506ff.

his full knowledge, he can then distort the evidence to conceal his crime, and if he does it well he will never be detected. So knowledge for a wise man is a great tool for being good, but for an evil man it is a tool which makes possible tremendous destruction.

Thus, knowledge by itself is amoral. There has to be more involved than factual, rational knowledge. The truth that you are seeking to discover is not only a rational truth, it should be a truth which is rich in its content of love. You love your Self. You have not only a knowledge of the Self, but also a great love for it. If your Self is the Self of all, there has to be an extrapolation of the same principle of love going to everyone. You cannot say "I know that you are my Self, but I cannot love you."

Protagoras put forward the claim that knowledge need not necessarily be a virtue. Socrates said knowledge is virtue. Protagoras replied, "No. A man who knows truth can also distort it." Socrates said, "In that case he does not know truth. If he really knows, he has to be virtuous. A man who says he knows and is not virtuous knows only one part of it." In the Upanishads this is called knowledge that walks on only one leg. For the Self to walk on two legs it must have knowledge and also love. Love for what? For itself. Nature reveals itself in a human self so that it knows it is all, or that it belongs to all. If you are concerned with the happiness of the Self, that binds you to commit yourself to live always for the happiness of all.

This verse introduces the concept of *svadharma*, performance in accordance with your true nature. In deciding this nature, the Guru wants us to know there are two aspects. One is our specific nature, and the other is our general nature. As humans, you and I should have the same general nature, while our specific nature is to function in society in certain different ways. For instance, my specific nature is of a teacher, and my general nature is of a man. As a teacher I teach and as a student you learn. So there is a complementarity in our interpersonal relationships, while from inside you and I are just beings, human beings. If this is extended to all biological manifestations our general nature is life itself, while our specific nature is exemplified by the species to which we belong.

Aristotle also thinks this is very important. You are not just an individual, you are a political and social being. As a social being you have to live with groups. You cannot say if an isolated person is good or bad because he has no occasion to interact with anyone else. Only when he expresses himself in relation to others can we decide whether he is good or bad. The way Aristotle puts it is the self has not only to be but also to activate. It is not a knowledge which you are storing up, but a knowledge you put into operation. And the knowledge you should put into operation is that you are everyone, that other people's happiness is your concern. Whatever you do, it should be to assure others' happiness as well as yours. To whichever society you conform, if your everyday life is not bringing out the best in you and promoting the happiness of those around you, you are not functioning at all.

That's very beautiful. Aristotle continues with an example of a musician who sings very well. Everyone is very pleased and says he is a great musician. After some time he develops an ailment in his larynx and loses his voice. Now it is horrible to sit and listen to him even when he speaks, but he is still honored as a great musician. 'Is' really means 'was' but out of consideration for the person we don't take away his musicianship, although it is not presently factual. As a kind of past testimony we honor him. Aristotle says the greatness of that man is not in himself, it is in the donor. Someone who says he is great gives that honor to him. For it to be truly justifiable he should still be able to sing.

A person may be a very good poet at the age of 50 or 60. Then at 70 he becomes senile and goes mad, but he is still called a great poet by virtue of what he once did. But, as Aristotle goes on to say, we won't give this kind of honor to someone when it comes to the matter of being good. If a man is bad today, we do not say he is a good man because he was once good. A single swallow or one sunny day do not make a spring. If it is spring there should be a songbird singing every morning. Like that, good means being consistently good.

So how do you become consistently good? By being fully aware of yourself all the time. There is no vacation permitted here. If you are concerned with the highest happiness of the Self, it has to be inclusive of all selves without exception. All the time, whatever you do should be governed by the principle of aiming for the total good of all with whom you interrelate. That's the minimum requirement.

Ultimately you should relate yourself to the whole universe, where there is nothing outside you. But the minimum is to show this recognition toward the group in which you are moving around, and to which you are committed.

If a child is sick, the mother cannot sleep. She could say, "I am not sick, only the child is sick. So why should I keep on waking?" But this is not possible. The mother instinctively keeps a vigil all through the night to see that the child is as comfortable as she can make it. Until this is attended to, she won't be able to sleep at all. In a small sense, mothers have the self-realisation that their self is greater than their body. Their self includes the child, and if the child is sick it is as if they themselves are sick. There is an extension of the self beyond the body — to that extent a mother is a realised person. It is only a small step in realising the fullness of the universe, but at least it is a step.

It is the same with lovers. Total strangers meet, become fascinated with each other, and fall in love. After that, what one of them experiences the other also feels. There is a Japanese story in the book *Zen Flesh, Zen Bones*, by Paul Reps, about a man who was a good musician. He had a harp which he would play, and his best friend would say things like, "Oh, I understand what you are playing. This is a butterfly flying." Then he would play something else and his friend would say, "Oh yes! I know. This is a fountain," or "this is spring." The musician was playing, and his friend was always appreciating and enjoying it. Then one day the friend caught pneumonia and died. The musician took up his harp and smashed it to pieces, saying "I cannot play any more. My best friend is not here to appreciate it. Without my friend, what joy is there for me in playing?"

The legend is such that even now in Japan when a good friend dies someone breaks a musical instrument. Whether that is important or not, the essence of the story is very beautiful. You want to share happiness with those whom you love. The one you love most is your own Self. If you truly know your own Self, it is not confined to your body, it permeates all beings. Your life should be a consecrated life, dedicated to the happiness of all. That's why the previous verses said that such a person, whether he is healthy or not, all day, all night, whatever he does is motivated to make life a little brighter for others, to bring a little more light on things which are concealed, to make a little more harmony where there is chaos and disorder. This is Narayana Guru's very basic fundamental of social ethics, which is based on Self-realisation. Realisation and doing good are not two separate things, they are one and the same.

Verse 25

oruvanu nallatum anyanallalum cē-
rpparu toẓil ātmavirōdhiyōrttiṭēṇam
paranu param paritapam ēkitunnō-
reri narakābdhiyil vīṇeriññiṭunnu

What is good for one person and brings misery to another
such actions are opposed to the self, remember!
those who give great grief to another
will fall into the fiery sea of hell and burn.

After presenting the positive approach to the happiness of all in the previous verse, Narayana Guru here counterbalances it with the negative approach, which brings in the problem of evil. All lovers of mankind throughout history — saints, philosophers, saviors and masters — have given consideration to the problem of evil.

In the last three or four verses, whenever the Guru referred to the 'other' he used a special word, *aparan*, meaning one who seems to be another, but when properly considered is not. Here, however, he uses *paran*, meaning one who definitely is another. When such a dichotomy comes into our life and we do not see any kinship with another person, even the compunction against doing evil doesn't go very deep. A kind of morbidity comes to the mind; we become dull and insensitive to the pain we cause others. To that extent we shrink into our egoistic shell and lose touch with the transcendent aspect of reality and its all-permeating beauty.

One definition of the Absolute is *satyam śivam sundaram. Satyam* means the all-pervading truth; *śivam* the auspicious, peaceful calm which is absolutely harmonious; and *sundaram* is that which is positively experienced as beauty *par excellence.* To have a comprehensive vision of the Self, one should experience the overwhelming beauty of the Absolute in both its manifested and unmanifested states. When there is a deficiency in this vision, ignorance is casting its shadow on us. When the shadow of ignorance becomes more and more pronounced, we see less of truth and become increasingly identified with our physical entity, which separates us from our divine nature.

This question is taken up and elaborated on in one of Plato's dialogues, *Timaeus.* In it the whole story of creation is discussed in a mythological way, and when you read it, it has a profound effect on your mind. It seems the Creator at the time of creation wanted to make a universe teeming with all kinds of life. He mixed together the essence of the four elements with his own immortal essence. His spirit, the divine, is indissoluble; it will always be immortal. The elements, however, are not: they come together and separate.

The elements have their own qualities, such as the fire burning and the air moving as wind and causing hurricanes. Similarly the water can be blown into great waves, and the earth can become morbid. These elements and their qualities are also present within each individual. When your elements are affected, sensations come from that side into your Self or spirit. On the other hand, the capacity to know and to animate flows from the spirit into the four elements. There is a two way circulation from the elements to the Self and from the Self to the elements.

This theory of Plato's is used by St. Augustine in developing his own study of evil. He considers evil to be a negative principle, unable to stand by itself, like a shadow cast by the sun. It is akin to a deficit intelligence in place of positive intelligence; it is also a deficit cause.

This is given in another way in the Bhagavad Gita. In Chapter Six, verses 5 and 6, we are given the instruction that the Self should be raised by the Self, and the Self should never let down the Self, the Self is the best friend of the Self, and the Self can also become its own worst enemy. Whenever you consider part of the Self as non-Self, that non-Self itself will become your enemy, it will behave as if it is your enemy.

We can experience this in our everyday life. If I consider a certain person as my very Self then it will be a great joy to have him around. Everything we do brings great joy to my heart: seeing him, talking with him, admiring him. The joy does not happen anywhere else than in my heart, so I am bringing joy to myself by giving my love to him. But if I consider him as not being a part of me, as not belonging to me as part of my Self, he may become my enemy. He is an 'other', and the very fact of seeing him walk into my room fills me with rage. My body starts shivering and trembling with anger. I cause myself great pain by hating him in this way, pain which may not affect him at all. Then I feel fear that this fellow has come to do some evil to me. I avoid him because I fear for my safety: he is my enemy and may become violent. He may take away my possessions. I start living in fear.

Of course, its all just an attitude within me. I can make myself happy in my friend's presence, or I can make myself very miserable just by changing my attitude. This is what the Gita calls making the *anātmā*, the non-Self, behave as the enemy. In considering part of your own Self as non-Self, you make that part a potential enemy. In one way or another we are all doing this every day by alienating people, by negating people, by cultivating discontent within ourselves. It is a scourge, a plague. If we do not like the presence of certain people, their very look or sound, we don't have anything to do with them. In this way we chop up our world into so many small bits and poison several of them.

So when this friend we are speaking of comes to me, I turn to my other friend and say look, our good friend is here. Then her mind also brightens up. Another friend asks who is here. Oh, it's our friend! — and she also becomes happy. Happiness is contagious. On the other hand, if I say, "Here comes that idiot, I don't like him at all," my enmity also is contagious. My other friends do not have any problem with that person, but when they hear me talk like that they also become negative. They wonder what that guy has done for me to hate him and they become suspicious. My negativity spreads like a cancer from one heart to another. Thus all the time we create smoke and fumes, poisonous pollution of the mind, and enmity everywhere. Then bickering, gossip and backbiting appear on all sides. The *narakābdhi,* the ocean of hell the Guru speaks of, is not anywhere far away, it is right where we are.

Narayana Guru's disciple Nataraja Guru, in his commentary on this verse, says that when a spark of fire goes into a pile of sticks, it does not just burn one tiny bit of it. It will affect the next piece and the next until it becomes a conflagration. Like that, when we sow the seeds of discontent it is contagious. In a very literal sense it can become a hell fire, even when small discontentments accumulate.

An example of this is the little pamphlets printed and circulated in Japan prior to World War II that said, "America is our worst enemy. Our fleets and manufactured goods are rivaled by American mercantilism and American capitalist expansion, so they are our enemies. Spread this to every corner of Japan." In America the same kind of rumor was spread: "Japan is our own worst enemy. If we allow that country to go on expanding, there won't be any America left." In each country, stereotypes and prejudices were fostered and reinforced. Soon American minds were filled with venom, and Japanese minds were filled with venom. A terrible war was fought, culminating in atom bombs being dropped on two Japanese cities. That was real hell fire: tens of thousands of people burned in no time, and many more slowly suffering horrible pain and death.

It is not just a story Narayana Guru is telling us. It can become actual at any moment. It all begins from just one spark of discontentment or one wrong notion, and we have millions of them from which to choose. America has a huge stockpile of deadly weapons, enough to annihilate the entire planet many times over. Until recently, Russia's stockpile was almost as large, and at least a half dozen other countries have nuclear arsenals. What are we doing? Accumulating the ability to devastate the whole universe? It all begins as paranoia in the mind of one person expressed to another. Someone in the CIA or the Pentagon says, "I really see the possibility of Russia or China attacking us tomorrow," and then we go mad, preparing to do more destruction than ever before. Unfortunately it is not only in the matter of realisation that the oneness of the Self operates. It also works very efficiently in becoming polluted with negativity.

St. Augustine took two ideas from Plotinus and Plato, deficient causation and the aesthetic conception of evil. Man has free will.

The freedom of his will, when it is in resonance with a universal will of goodness, is a salvaging factor. Free will can also become a free expression of the ego which is cut off from the light of the spirit. When it is cut off, it places sensory pleasures or physical well-being as more cherishable than spiritual excellence. This is the idea of deficient causation.

Nature itself is against such kinds of excesses which the egoistic will brings upon life. When a person relishes his food too much and goes against nature's laws by becoming gluttonous, the excessive food poisons his physical body. He eats more than he can digest properly, and accumulates toxins that are absorbed and that cause him physical disease. Plotinus and St. Augustine say here that nature is coming to our aid to save us from the excess of free will originating from the dark side of the self, which is the ego.

Like physical disease, other kinds of excess bring war, pestilence and so many other problems. The exclusive growing of vast areas of one type of crop, for instance, has brought about an explosion of damaging insects and plant diseases. The pollution we release in the air has devastated forests, caused cancer in humans, and even eroded buildings. The list of such excesses is very long. All of them are considered as the evil which originates from man's free will.

Man should learn how he can exercise a true free will, which is when he is freeing himself from the clutches of his sensuality, from the demands of his vasanas, and when he is seeing the oneness of all from inside. Only after getting free of these conditionings does true freedom of will come. Otherwise, you think you have free will, but you are a slave to your senses and your urges. You make your reason a kind of donkey upon which evil rides to its own destruction.

The second thing St. Augustine shows us is also in the Bhagavad Gita, which says you can only free yourself by being the Absolute. As St. Augustine poetically puts it, if you can see the grand beauty of the panorama of creation and sing with the mind of the Creator, you make a beautiful world for yourself. The gorgeous sun which rises in the east as a golden disc, the gentle breezes that come from the salty oceans and the breezes from the mountains laden with the aroma of spices, the clouds that bring rain to our gardens, the singing birds and the blooming flowers, the variety of plants that provide food for man and other beings — when we see this grand beauty everywhere we are having a panoramic vision of the Absolute. We become so saturated with the sense of its magnificence that we cannot alienate ourselves from the wonderful goodness of the Absolute.

This is where the aesthetic cause of evil comes in. When you have lost the sensitivity to appreciate things aesthetically, when you become incapable of seeing the beauty of creation, you become a corrupted person.

One possible misunderstanding that can arise from this verse is to think of action in a linear way. If we consider all the actions that we do in life and their virtues, we may be filled with a sense of self-righteousness and see injustice in our suffering for things which we have seemingly never done. This is a linear vision, and karma is not to be understood as linear. It is highly complex. Our actions make one composite whole, and our responsibility to each other is unlimited. If we do not understand our unlimited liability to each other and make it a partial one, then our thinking becomes relativistic. Our understanding is no longer that of an absolutist.

Any deficit in any one of us is also a deficit of the whole. The deficit action of one can weaken the whole system to an extent. The contributory effect of that kind of karma is like a carbuncle, which is a localised disturbance but the poison it generates circulates throughout the body. In a sense it is the poison of the whole body that comes and accumulates as a carbuncle in one place. Similarly, through specific people the poison of our collective activity is manifested. If that person retrospects about his own personal life, he may not see anything to justify the pain coming particularly to him. Here it is not the individual but the collective Self which is suffering.

Only if you take it in this way will the suffering of Christ make any sense. Otherwise, how can his crucifixion be a matter of concern to anyone after two thousand years? How does that help? It was not just one person's action: a sacrifice was given in a collective sense. Although the sacrifice was of one person, in it we see the essence of the entire universe.

We have to see it both ways: one person's sacrifice as a sacrifice for all, and the evil of many people as the evil that affects each person. I recommend to you both Plato's *Dialogues* and St. Augustine's *City of God* (Chapter XII, 6-7) and *Confessions* (Chapter VII, 13) for further reading, because this is more than a fascinating study. It is our daily problem. It is good to have some insight into it. Some of the finest souls on earth have given their best thoughts to this subject, and these books do a great amount of searching.

With this verse and the previous one, Narayana Guru gives the world his contribution of social ethics based on Self-realisation. It should become a cardinal principle of our own lives. It is not confined to any creed. On the positive side you are asked simply to see the Self in all and befriend it. From the negative angle you are told that if you make your own Self alienated from you, you will cause a boomerang of the same evil upon you. Thus, for your own peace and unbroken joy it is necessary to contribute to the general good every day and every moment. We take upon ourselves unlimited liability to bear the cross of all; we commit ourselves to be our brother's keepers. The best teaching of all the world's scriptures is epitomised here in eight brief lines.

Verse 26

avayavamokkeyamarttiyāṇiyāy ni-
nnavayaviyāviyeyāvariccitunnu
avan ivan ennatināl avan ninaykku-
nnavaśatayāmavivēkamonninālē

Holding the limbs together, remaining like a bolt,
the limb owner envelops as vaporous being;
for this reason, "that man" and "this man" arise in
this way —
so that man believes, due solely to the weakness of
non-discrimination.

This body of ours, which is constituted of many parts, is held together by the living entity. Everything is kept together by the agency of breath, which is vaporous. As one such constituted body looks different from another, we fail to discriminate the living entity that is pervading all beings as one and the same.

It is commonly believed that there are no two snow crystals that look alike. Similarly, we never come across two human beings who are exactly alike, although they all have the same kind of body. The police take advantage of this fact when they record people's fingerprints for security purposes. It seems impossible that with so many billions of hands in this world, multiplied by ten for all the fingers, no two fingerprints are the same. We make a big deal of this difference, which we see only on the skin of the thumb, for instance. The whole world attaches so much importance to such a superficial variation solely to find out who did something wrong. But no matter how much you study these prints you won't learn who did something right. A thumb print is only useful for finding out a wrongdoer; it won't help you to find the good or discern truth.

If you look at a big wrestler's body it is so round; the muscles look like they are made of steel. He moves around with so much confidence in his strength, but if he does not breathe for a couple of minutes that is all it will take for him to lose consciousness and fall down, crashing to earth as if he has no strength at all. If he does not resume breathing quickly, his body becomes stiff. Then it swells up and all the cells break. The body decays and soon becomes part of the earth. Is it not a great wonder that that little breath in us is maintaining all the functions of the body? It causes us to cerebrate, circulate blood, respire, digest food, grow and change, and learn and retain our memory. All this depends on a tiny bit of vapour: the incoming and the outgoing breath.

So what is it within us that goes on doing everything for us, expanding and contracting the lungs, keeping up the throb of the heart? We walk around in this body all day and we live in it all the time, and yet we do not know anything of these functions. Physiologists, neurologists and biologists are all running around looking at every synapse, cell and protein formation, thinking that from this they will get some clue. They know something is altering proteins, something is making synaptic changes and cells are growing and dying, but what is that something? Nobody knows. John Lilly asked the question, who is the programmer? There is a grand programme going on in this human biocomputer, but who is the programmer?

The programmer is called in this verse *avayavī*, the one who owns all the separate parts of the body. The limb owner is making this vapourous thing operate, and this operation causes weakness in the power of discrimination.

You are sitting here. The life in you did not come from a piece of stone or out of thin air. It came from two living people, your father and mother. Go backward in your mind and retrospect. See how you were lying as a fetus in your mother's womb. Go beyond that. Before the union of your parents were you not still potentially in them? Yes, sure. So then what is your age now? It is from your birth date to now, plus your gestation, plus your parents' age. And behind your two parents are four other people, your father's and your mother's parents, so add in their age. If you go on like this for twenty generations, you already have more than two million people and hundreds of years behind you. Over two million people involved in producing you in just twenty generations. Now go back even before the appearance of human beings, to other species. Who then is an alien to you?

This very life which is now functioning in you is spread out through all these forms of beings. It is one and the same principle in all. Do we have eyes to see it? No, we are too weak to discriminate that way. The Guru says *avaśatayām*, we are weak so we cannot discriminate. Since we cannot discriminate we can only take into account the immediate changes within this one system.

What is knowledge or awareness? As scientists understand it, it is only a specific change that happens chemically in our brain matter. Recent studies of synapses have shown that in learning they undergo a plastic change of shape and size, and then retain the change by molecular function. This is understood as a constituent part of a general experience of pain or pleasure caused by the agitation of the nerves. When you say two and two make four, this is what happens. Also when you get a pinprick this is happening. And again when you say "I am thinking of God," this is what is happening. Thus, substantially, there is no difference between your knowledge of comprehending the Absolute and having a pinprick. At the nervous level it's all useless, superficial agitation. Such an understanding may bring us total dismay.

We soon come to a dark chamber and stand outside its door, unable to penetrate into it to know the secret of how this agitation is manifesting. Who keeps this order? Who decides what kind of plastic change should occur to represent an idea? Who decides how it can be retained? Who decides what kind of protein to make and when? Even our clumsy research has isolated and named more than twenty varieties of protein, but no one knows what is behind it. Our knowledge is coming and standing at the portals of this wonder, unable to penetrate beneath the surface. Beyond lies a great darkness. The greatest of all wisdom, all knowledge, is happening behind that door and in that darkness. It keeps the whole universe proliferating and multiplying endlessly. What a great wonder it is!

When we look at it this way this very earth on which we walk is the great mother from which all this has come. How many times should we kneel with gratitude that all this was made possible from mere dust! It may look superstitious to say that out of dust God created man, but it is the perfect truth. Forget God if you like, but you can certainly see that out of the dust of the earth came all of you who are sitting here, listening to another clod of earth who is articulating. Seen from inside like this, how can we be different? And yet our little pains are so very important to us. Our life is not ruled by wisdom but by pain: little, little pains and agitations.

Narayana Guru is lamenting the weakness which makes it difficult for us to go beyond the darkness and see the wonder of all this. He is preparing our minds to receive his definition of the Self, which he gives in the next verse. This is not something you discuss and know by your reason. You have to lay down your tools and watch the game for a little while with the attitude of a silent witness. Retire.

If you like, you can try to imagine the two million, ninety-seven thousand, one hundred and fifty people who were your progenitors in the last twenty generations. Line them up behind you and look at everybody's face. See how you have come directly from their scrotums and ovaries. None of them were aware of producing a child, they only found out when the woman vomited and had terrible pains that something had happened to her. You and I came in secret and in ignorance. Nobody knew, but unfailingly it was going on all through the long years. The unfortunate genes that happened to get into me as a sannyasi, a celibate person, may perish with me, but that won't stop the world. I can only stop my part of it. Life, which was to be perpetuated for millennia to come in my scrotum, I can put an end to it and give it peace, peace, peace. But so many others have already contributed to perpetuation. After their children will be another twenty generations, another two million people lined up.

Behind us we see not only human beings. As Carl Sagan has said, we can also see the dragons and dinosaurs as our great-grandfathers. I do not even know all the species involved, which means I have forgotten my own great-grandfather. Sagan even speaks of the possibility of a gnat mating with a giraffe and becoming an ostrich because the life-bearing genes of each are not bigger despite the proportion of their bodies.

Thomas à Kempis, in *The Imitation of Christ*, says that all the learning you have gained here has helped you only to increase your vanity. How can you ever gain your sanity again? He claims you have become profound in knowing all the theological explanations of the Trinity, but you have lost your humility. We become humble just as soon as we come to know that there is nothing to be proud of. We do not yet know who we are. When you say "I do not know," that's the temple in which dwells your real being. The door of that ignorance has to open. There is someone within the dark chamber saying "I know." When the sound "I know" comes outside, it changes into "I don't know" because it is a knower who is saying "I do not know." This is a big miracle, the knower who is sitting behind and saying, "I do not know."

In the Kena Upanishad it says one who does not know claims that he knows, and one who knows keeps quiet. The wonder is too much for him even to acknowledge what he knows.

While I am speaking to you, countless millions of bacteria are having breakfast inside my lungs and my heart. They are all separate beings with their own personalities. If you look through a microscope at a dab of spittle you can see that each bacterium walks around with its own programme, some with a shirt or pants, shades, clean-shaven or with a beard. Yet with all this inside me I behave as if I am only one person. So either I am millions of people or we are all one person.

Now think of this magical bolt by which all these corporeal entities within the body are held together as if they are one. Meditate on this. What is it that keeps your whole body united? Why doesn't it fall apart?

Once a good friend of mine in Australia came to see me. She was so overjoyed about meeting me that she was driving madly and her car struck a lamppost. After the big shock, she found something was missing. She could find only one hand. The other one had come off and was lying behind her. She couldn't believe that a hand could come off just like that. She was fully in her right mind when people came running up to help, but she told them not to worry about taking her to a hospital. She said, "My friend can heal it just by touching it," and insisted on going to a chiropractitioner who could put it back in its socket. Then she was brought to me. She said, "It's all right, just touch me." None of us know how it really happened, but after some time she was all right. Just as the hand came off it came back. Who healed it? How did it heal by itself so easily? We don't know.

Where is this bolt we are speaking of? There is actually no nut and bolt; it is all held together just by supposition. When you are walking on your two feet you do not realise you are performing a great circus feat, balancing a body upright on just two legs. This wonder called life — that is what you should meditate on.

See how that wonder is the same in a slug as well as in you. When you come to this place for meditation, don't trample on all the poor slugs. They cannot walk fast. Like you they want to be around us, and come up the stairs little by little. But before they reach the meditation hall, some pious meditator tramples them. We have a spider sitting here in the corner meditating with us. All these seemingly insignificant creatures are part of the same web of life to which we also belong.

Verse 27

iruḷil irunnaṟiyunnatākumātmā-
vaṟivatu tānatha nāma rūpamāyum
karaṇamotindriya karttṛ karmmamāyum
varuvatu kāṇka mahēndra jālam ellām

Sitting in the dark, that which knows is the self;
what is known then assumes name and form,
with the psychic dynamism, senses, agency of action
and also action;
see how it all comes as *mahēndra* magic!

When we look at a deck of tarot cards, it begins with the card symbolising the Fool and ends with the Magician. Along the way from the Fool to the Magician we come across various representations of life, including even the Judge and Death. Like that our life also begins as an untutored fool and ends in the wonder of magic, *jālam*.

In this verse, the Guru is equating the Self and the world to a grand magic. Here the magic is in the way things are experienced. When we experience things they are there; and when we do not experience them they are not there. Ultimately we cannot say whether they are or are not. They are, otherwise we would not experience them. But at the same time they are not: if they really existed they should continue, but they don't. That's a great magic.

At one moment, two lovers hug each other and whisper in each other's ear how much they care and what wonderful love they are having. In the next moment they behave like strangers. Everything said up to then no longer has any value. They cannot even remember it. Then again their mood fluctuates and changes. They are willing to bury everything for a new deal. And so, on and on.

The Magician comes with his five children for entertainment. He is the mind itself, and his children are the five senses: onlookers as it were. Together they start a big magic show. The senses are really more like angels than children, so they are called *indriya,* a name derived from Indra, the shining one. Even though the eye, for instance, is made up of inertial matter like skin, water and nerves which by themselves have no ability of knowing anything, the eye is sensitive to sunlight and it can clearly see everything. It is like a *deva,* a luminous angel. So all five senses are called indriyas or devas.

Mind is a superluminous thing that sees what the eye sees, hears what the ear hears, touches what the hands touch, smells what the nose smells, and tastes what the tongue tastes. In addition, it is capable of producing all these effects even when the senses are out of commission, such as in a dream state. Thus mind is called *mahēndra; maha* means great, and *indra* means that which brings ideation. This *mahēndra* in us, the mind and the senses, is producing the world jugglery, the world magic.

Everything we experience comes within the scope of this magic. If we go backwards from the effect of the magic to its cause, the first thing is of course the magic itself. Behind it we see the senses and the mind. When we examine the mind, we see that we experience everything as a series of events. All kinds of activities are going on. Somebody is running, walking, sitting, talking, coming to you, having interactions, loving and hating. One of the main features of this magic is endless activities, karma.

Behind each activity you can sense yourself as an actor: "I talk; I look; I see; I do." And doing all this either pleases or displeases you: "I am very happy to see this; I am ashamed of this; this is horrid; I am getting bored; I don't want anything; I want all this." Someone is going on shouting all the time "I, I, I," as the actor, the knower and the enjoyer. It is always the same 'I' but the emphasis changes to accommodate the various angles.

The actor, the knower and the enjoyer have their negative aspects also: "I am not the actor; I do not know; I do not enjoy this." So the 'I' takes roles and denies roles, which leads to questions of identity. In an action situation you either identify yourself or you do not identify yourself with it.

So just who is this 'I' which clamors and makes so much noise? When you scrutinise it you will find that its nature is consciousness and that consciousness has a centralised notion where "I, I" is throbbing all the time. It is an 'I' consciousness, *ahamvṛtti*, that is affected by whatever is going on. There is an affective ego, an affective 'I' consciousness, engaged in this grand magic.

When we look further at this 'I' consciousness that engages in activity, feels pleased or displeased, wonders and gets frightened, we are amazed to see that it is not just one static, identical consciousness functioning as all this. It is much more like a stream of water. In the stream of consciousness, before the 'I' consciousness decides upon something it moves around propounding arguments. Endless arguments are going on within it: "this is such and such; this is related to such and such, and therefore such and such." There is a judging quality, and affectivity comes only as a consequence of it. Before it decides what a thing is, its affectivity is not yet decided. Whether it is going to be positive or negative, painful or pleasurable, is held in abeyance.

This is the stream of consciousness as it is used for reasoning. When we look into it, we see there are hundreds of memories, associated ideas, everything of the past recalled in order to understand the present situation. After these are recollected and used to identify something, they don't disappear. They go back and hide where they were before so they can be used at a later time. Thus an affective judgement is coming as a consequence of active reasoning. Active reasoning is facilitated by a series of memories and memory recall. Something is stimulating this memory recall, these questions and affectivity. There is a compulsion to judge, to compare, recollect, examine. That compulsion is called *manas* or mind.

Where does this compulsion come from? It is like the Fool of the tarot. The Fool does not know anything, but it wants to know. We begin, not from the Magician's magic, but from the Fool who is crying out, asking, "What is this? I don't know anything. Tell me please!" The Fool comes in the form of an interrogation on the surface of consciousness. Consciousness itself is frothing out like a white foam made up of many tiny bubbles. The bubbles are coming up from the depths of the unconscious. If we try to look beyond these bubbles rising up into consciousness, it becomes very frustrating because we cannot see anything clearly there. One idea bubbles up, is examined and lived out, and then perishes. Even before it perishes another idea is already in the mind, enlarging, growing into an activity, an affectivity, and then it also is forgotten. As these come sequentially, one after another, you can definitely distinguish what was, what is, and what will be. It is played out in a time sequence. So there is not only mind, there is also time.

There is a vastness in which what sequentially arrives is all placed in various ways, either one above the other or beside each other, or three things put in a triangular relationship or intertwined or even separate. For all these, space is required. The time operation is functioning within space.

So there is a time-space continuum. Within the time-space continuum, individual bubbles of interest are coming and bursting into meaning. Meaning is registered in the form of a language symbol, such as a name. Once we have left behind the stage of the newborn, the Fool, no ideation comes into the mind without its being presented with a label, a name. And when you call out a name, a corresponding form comes to mind. Seemingly out of nowhere all these factors, all these categories have come: names and forms; time and space; actors and action; the doer, knower and enjoyer; and the interrogating faculty, memory, judgement and affectivity.

Let us go to the prime source which has produced all these. We don't know where they all came from, so all this knowledge is resting on non-knowledge. Or, as someone once described it, there is a cloud of unknowing. It is from the heart of the cloud of unknowing that all this knowing is happening. Is it total unknowing? We cannot say. If there was total ignorance, how could all these things come? We see them clearly, so the light with which we know them must have come from that cloud of unknowing. Behind the cloud of unknowing is an all-knowing principle. It is never known as itself, it is known as all this. When it spreads out in this fantastic way we experience it all, from the naive questioning of a Fool to the final elucidation of a Magician.

If you consider all this as one total effect, then it is complemented by its cause. What causes all this? Self-luminous *ātman* or the Self. The self-luminous *ātman* itself is not known, but its effect — all the pluralities of the phenomenal transformations and modifications that come into being — is all we see. What is, is not known; while what is not, is known. Hence it is called the grand magic.

Spiritual seekers are struggling to demolish all this magic and find the Magician. But when the magic is demolished you still do not see the Magician. The Magician is. That's a certainty; but you don't know him as a Magician when he is not playing his role. Thus we take away the possibility of knowing the source by merely denying the phenomenal. The being is to be known in the becoming, and becoming is known because of its beingness.

The Guru has given here the two aspects of a nondual reality. It is nondual, and yet it contains a duality. The dual aspects are the pure Self that hides in the dark as an unknown entity; and the so-called non-Self, consisting of this grand magical world of name and form placed in time and space, where there is a centralised 'I' identity which is asking questions, recalling memories, making judgements, and assuming roles and thereby getting into various peripheral identifications.

This is highly paradoxical. The non-Self should be the not known, but it is the known. The Self, the knower of everything, is not known. It is as if it is sitting in darkness. At least once in a while you should move away from the grand magic of your life, sit quietly and ruminate, and try to penetrate beyond the cloud of unknowing. You are seeking to know what is luminous there which casts its shadows in so many ways here. This is the eternal theme for the contemplative. Occasionally he revels in the magic, but all the same he knows it is magic and so he is not fully satisfied with it. He is fully satisfied only when he knows the manager behind the curtain, who is also himself. This is the grand theme of this verse.

Verse 28

aṭi muṭiyaṭṭaṭi toṭṭu mauliyantam
sphuṭamaṟiyunnatu turyya bōdhamākum
jaḍamaṟivīlatu cinta ceytu collu-
nniṭayil irunnaṟivallaṟiññiṭēṇam

Without bottom or top, from the bottom to the crest
where it terminates —
what is known vividly is *turīya* consciousness;
inert matter does not know; having understood this,
know that what is said to remain in between is not
knowledge.

The Self was defined in the last verse as pure awareness, which is born of itself and remains concealed in total darkness. This leaves us with the impression of two distinct entities: a darkness which doesn't know anything of itself, and a knowledge which fully knows that it knows.

When we consider our individuated being, we can see this dichotomy there very clearly. What we have is some knowledge of certain things of a certain kind and to a certain degree. In the world of form, our vision extends to the horizon and there it stops. We cannot see what lies beyond the horizon. If we fire a rocket into space, we can follow it with our eyes for a certain distance. Then it vanishes. We can see things of decreasing size until they become less than a dot. Then we can use a microscope to follow a ways further. If something becomes still smaller, we can no longer see it. Thus there is a spatial limitation to our knowledge of things. Our range of vision of forms in space is delimited.

If somebody reads out a passage of Arabic or Chinese or some other language with which we are not familiar, we can hear the sound just fine but the words don't have any meaning for us. If we put together the lexicons of all the languages of the world, we would not know even 10 per cent of the various articulated sounds used by our own fellow beings, let alone the various kinds of sound symbols other animals make. In the world of names also, our knowledge is very limited.

Again, if we look into our own past, we have only a faint idea of what we did only yesterday. Most of the details are forgotten. Generally, the farther in the past we think of, the more we will have forgotten. And when we look into our programme for today, we have only a vague idea of what we are going to do, who we might meet, and what we might talk with them about. So there is a circumlimited time span in which our consciousness operates. To those of us who have travelled about, our spatial limitations are all too apparent. So we can see that we are limited in the fields of name and form, as well as temporally and spatially.

In theology the existence of God is argued in terms of cause and effect: everything which is an effect should have a cause; the world is an effect and its cause is God. We know the relationships between certain simple causes and effects, but we come to an impasse when we try to push back to primary causes. So when we ask what caused God, we won't be able to answer. If you say God came by itself, then why have a causal theory at all? Then you can say the world came by itself also. The theologian will abandon the causal theory altogether at this point. When we come to ultimate questions we really don't have any certainty.

Up to now we have covered the limitations inherent in time, space, name, form, cause and effect. Furthermore, if we examine the knowledge we have, it belongs either to our five-fold sensory perception, our recollection of memory, or to a composition we make out of concepts. This is why Schrödinger called the world a construct of percepts and concepts. We have five sense organs, therefore we know five kinds of qualities. If we had ten senses, we would know ten kinds of qualities. From this it is evident that these five qualities do not exhaust all possible knowledge. Our sensory knowledge is only a projection of the properties of our sensory system, a projection that is made by the individuated being.

I like to compare the individual to a common insect, the spit bug. The spit bug is very tiny, smaller than a coriander seed. All the time it spits out a kind of foam all around itself. When you go for a walk in the morning, you can see its spittle all over the leaves and grass. It looks just like spit, but if you examine it you will find this tiny bug concealed in it.

Like that, individuation goes on spitting out constructs all around it. The tiny, fearful ego continually spews forth clouds of obfuscation in order to conceal its sense of insignificance, but its delusory images of glory appear to be no more than unwholesome excrescences to passersby. This is also what the single cell of the fertilized ovum is doing. It goes on spitting out more and more cells until it becomes a fetus. Then the fetus becomes a child, and the child a grown-up. We are still creating spittle all around. We spit out potentials; those potentials in us can be actualised at any time. Our daily wakeful experiences are expressions of motivations which lie buried in what is spewed out of an original programme

If we believe the geneticists, we come to this world with our blueprints in our chromosomes in the original cell. Then the programme is copied over and over, proliferating itself into a multicellular body. Within every cell is the same blueprint. There is a coordination between one cell and another because of the homogeneity of the plan.

We are equipped with a system that is self-agitated. If light passes into us, we are agitated in a certain manner. If a sound vibration falls on us, we get agitated in another manner. We react in other ways to the agitations of atmospheric pressure or the pull of gravity, for instance. We can even see simple illustrations of this in protozoa. Imagine a creature like a microscopic fish with no fins, a tail, and a head with no eyes, only a rudimentary nerve where an eye might later evolve, which can be agitated when exposed to light. When light falls on it, it jerks its head end and moves away. When it bumps into another object, it caroms off in another direction.

Our own behaviour, even though it seems very complex, is in

principle the same: a kind of agitation in response to a certain stimulus. Agitation in one field alone, when recorded, can fill volumes. More agitation produces more and more encyclopedias. We have already filled volumes upon volumes of encyclopedias, lexicons, histories and geographies. All the various elaborations of agitation: sensory agitations; agitations of the brain system, such as recall of memory, composition of memory, and dreams; and various kinds of glandular secretions creating panic, and by which you become angered, frightened, or harmonised, by which you feel love or empathy; all these are just magic created by some elaborating secretions.

When a man feels amorous toward a woman, he doesn't know what produces the amorous feeling. It happens despite himself. His sex glands are already stimulated and mucous formations occur even before he touches her. The woman can also have a similar secretory function in her just at the thought of a man. It may be only an idea, but the idea can produce liquids and chemicals. The bodily system is such a wonder; many rare enzymes are made by it which can't be manufactured commercially, even with millions of dollars and the most modern equipment.

Where do all these things take place? In between the light and the darkness. And what is the light we are speaking of? It is a pure light, one that transcends the concrete, gross world of wakeful experience, the subtle world of dream experience, and the non-activated potentials of the deep sleep experience. If we push these three states — tainted by darkness, by relativistic nature — away, what remains is a pure consciousness which witnesses the other three states. This consciousness has no beginning or end; it is not limited to any body. Everything that happens is within it. Such a state is called *turīya,* the fourth. It does not come within the three. Yet without the light of the fourth none of the rest can ever function.

Our consciousness is made up of two entities: the three states taken together, and the one that witnesses. The witnessing reality or pure consciousness alone is nonconditional. It is not a dependent factor in relation to anything. It is totally independent. The great saint and philosopher Madhva called it the pure principle of independence, *svatantra. Sva* means its own; it is its own *tantra* or tool, its own operation. The self-operating reality is called turiya, and the three states are called *paratantra*, dependent factors.

We go to schools and colleges and walk around with fat books under our arms, thinking we are learning. Certainly we are learning something, but our learning is confined to the world of agitations of the nervous system. We do not go beyond that. Narayana Guru qualifies this as the knowledge that happens in between pure darkness and pure light, and says that it is not worthy of being called knowledge. If you do call it knowledge, then the funny noises the little puppy makes when it is tied up and can't see its mom are also great knowledge. We have only refined that agitation or excitement or dissatisfaction more elaborately.

Once upon a time, earlier scientists thought they were getting definite knowledge with absolute certitude. Then along came some sober people with more honest minds, like Einstein and Heisenberg, who said, "Wait. Don't go that far. What we know is only from the standpoint of this individuated being who is using his senses and mind. All that we have to work with are data born of our sensory perceptions and our ability to calculate. This is understanding of a personal nature. We are unqualified to answer fundamental questions." Bertrand Russell calls this "piecemeal annexations of our impressions." That's all. Narayana Guru says it is what we articulate when we sit in between light and darkness, and that this is not the real knowledge we seek. So where do we turn when we wish to seek definite knowledge with absolute certitude?

This is the point where the need arises to transcend the triple states of deep sleep, dream and wakefulness. How do you know you have transcended? There comes a new clarity in the form of a transparency of vision where you see through the past, present and future. Your vision is not checkmated by any frontier: it is a frontierless vision. It is not confined to name and form. It does not come under the category of cause and effect. We cannot say it has a beginning or an end. In fact, words that we use and thoughts that we cerebrate are all of no use. This is the realm of infinite silence into which we can merge, where the present faculties which are very useful to us become of no use.

Now we come to a very difficult situation where we must go around a curve, so to speak, in our understanding. All the conditionings which we have so far called learning are no better than the salivating of Pavlov's dogs. All the rewards and punishments which you have had so far in the form of education help you only to salivate when the bell rings. Don't you want something better than that?

The Isavasya Upanishad says that those who rejoice in *avidyā*, ignorance, live in darkness; but those who rejoice in knowledge live in even greater darkness. Then it goes on to say that those who know the secret of the world of ignorance transcend death. To transcend death we must thoroughly review the world of ignorance, to which belong all the comedies and tragedies of life. An interesting exposition of this idea is given by the great playwrights of ancient Greece and later by Shakespeare and Shaw.

It is well worth knowing the secret of ignorance, but if you are indulging in that ignorance you live in the darkness and are not benefited by awareness of it. Most of us find ourselves oscillating somewhere between total ignorance and absolute enlightenment. What I try to do for one who is caught between these two worlds is to give a secret hint: that you go to the zoo only to marvel at it, not to get behind the bars. Perhaps one day a friend goes to visit the zoo and does not return. When we go to find him, he has gotten into one of the cages and is putting on a performance. We say, "Why are you here?" He answers, "I am experiencing the zoo." "Stupid man, come out. We sent you here only to have a look at the different animals in their cages, not to join them." He says "I am experiencing it. Give me a banana," and he becomes another monkey. We can only pity him and give him a banana and come away.

Another friend went to a department store to buy something. He found so many things to buy — it was very interesting. Soon he was spending all his time there. I asked him to come away: "You went there only to make some purchases. Enough. Come out. Your real nature is somewhere else." But he always found one more interesting thing to examine.

A compassionate man called Buddha once came and said, "Come out of this world of ignorance." A few people came away with him. Then along came another compassionate one. Unfortunately, he was in another part of the world. When he said "come out," people became angry and nailed him to a cross. They said, "This is how we come out." Still, compassionate people return again and again and ask, "Please, enough of this zoo business. Come out and be free."

So it is very important to know how you are ensnared and how to get outside of it.

Verse 29

manamalar koytu mahēśa pūja ceyyum
manujanu maṟṟoru vēla ceytiṭēṇtā
vanamalar koytumatallayāykil māyā-
manuvuruviṭṭumirikkil māyamāṟum

For the man who offers his mind-flowers to worship God
there is no other work to do;
pick flowers of the forest; or, if not that,
by ever-repeating the *māyā*-formula *māyā* will disappear.

In the very first verse of instruction in the Self we visualised a world of two opposite principles: the external, full of objects of interest; and the internal, like a stream of consciousness full of thoughts, sensations and all kinds of ideations. When the sun rises and illuminates the day, countless millions of things seem to exist. We become occupied with one task or another in order to actualise some hidden urge. Like waves on an ocean, these urges come one after another, and we are impelled, sometimes even despite our resistance, to do actions. Days and nights come alternately, and our moods and attitudes change accordingly.

It is hard for us to remember that we are of a divine origin and our pure state is of the Absolute. Our senses go out and feed on the fruits of enjoyment, and in this way we go away from the centre of our beingness. We begin to think the only thing in life is the gratification of our urges. The desire for gratification envelops our whole being like a creeper which is blossoming all the time with some modifications of mind. Somewhere deep down in us is a spark of consciousness which is consistently shining, but it is covered over with the great darkness of ignorance. Our light is feeble, and even what little light there is is coloured by our own egoistic tendencies. The Self itself is mistaken for our ego, and we get into various ego trips.

Our ego is motivated by latent urges. The actualisation of an urge takes place in the concrete world of phenomenal manifestation. There, objects of interest are considered to be the source of our enjoyment. In this way we cut ourselves off from the real source of all existence, knowledge and bliss, and make a fragmentary world. Like a man thrown into a desert land, we go from one mirage to another, always thinking that the water that can quench our life's thirst is outside of us. Search as we will, we never find it.

When we mistake an object as a source of joy, and having lost the inner vision to see the oneness of all, we fight with our own brothers and sisters. Since objects are limited we become competitive, elbowing into the thick of the fray, pushing people out of our path, and becoming totally selfish.

This is the scourge of maya, from which we want to escape. How do we go about it? In the twelfth chapter of the Bhagavad Gita, Krishna considers one possibility after another: if you can do this one, do it. If not, try this one. If you are not fit for that, there are still other alternatives. In the Bible, Jesus uses several analogies to describe the kingdom of God. If a certain analogy doesn't agree with you, there is another one. He embraces several paths leading to the same goal. If you have a temperamental difference with one of them, don't get disappointed. There is still a path for you.

In the present verse, Narayana Guru is offering three such paths. The first one is *manamalar koytu mahēśa pūja ceyyum.* Every word in it is pregnant with meaning. When a person comes closer and closer to his realisation, this world no longer appears to him as a terrifying experience. It is filled with pure joy. Everything appears as sweet, fragrant and beautiful as a freshly blossomed flower. Last night as we listened to music, everyone present appeared to be going into a state of their own inner melody. When we have a musical evening, the music in each one of us also comes to the surface. Even the little baby felt like singing when the others were. Everything was so pleasing.

This is the meaning of *manamalar.* When your mind is such that modifications of it become beautiful like a flower, consider it as worthy of being offered to the very Lord who is the gardener of your life. Your mind is so like a garden that is tended, nourished, watered and cared for by your master, *mahēśa*. *Maha* means more than just great. When you say *mahimā*, it means all the glories that you can think of, put together. Similarly the word *isa* means that which shines within you, animates you, gives you this never-ending supply of life's resources, and which functions as a definite, imperative law.

When you relate *manujan*, the man of contemplative nature, to his counterpart *mahēśa*, then you are establishing a bipolarity between man and God. Here the word 'God' is not to be taken in the ordinary sense, nor is 'man'. They mean a god that can be glorified as the light within you, and you as the one who is pondering on that all the time. Only in this way can all the passing moments become flower-like. Seeing all the passing events as moments of inner ecstasy, inner joy, can be experienced by anyone. On the other hand, if you are always haunted by fears you won't be able to consider those fears as beautiful flowers.

There is a certain state of excellence implied in the first part of this verse. This path is for one who has really advanced in spiritual growth, who knows the expressions of his mind are flowers to be offered. In the phrase *manamalar koytu mahēśa pūja ceyyum* you get the feeling of one who is ever engaged in a state of adoration or worship. One who is thus fully immersed feels no compulsion to be always engaged in work in order to feel in balance.

If you are an artist, everything which you see is appreciated as an ensemble of meaning. You look at the composition of it. Wherever the artist turns, there is always a potential picture inviting him to immortalise it. When a musician bops around, music is always humming in his ear. He hears new possibilities, new ways to express musical ideas. For a poet, life is a variety of themes for him to express how the golden threads of joy and the dark threads of agony are interwoven in the warp and woof of the universe. He can dwell on any of it to get to the very meaning of life. To a physician, the Lord is there providing an opportunity for service to those crying out in sickness and in pain.

It does not matter what vocation you have chosen or what kind of life you lead, there is always a deity to be glorified and a flower to be offered. When the artist paints, it is a real offering. When the musician composes or sings, it is done as a most wonderful offering to the Supreme. Every drop of ink that comes from the pen of a poet is an act of worship. It should fill our life with such joy that this is a temple where we have gathered to pay our homage to the Absolute that we experience as beauty, goodness, truth, service, compassion, dignity.

If you don't feel that way immediately you have to start from scratch. You should learn to cultivate beauty, love, service-mindedness in yourself. If a man has an idol or a picture of someone he adores, it is not only meaningless superstition. At least his mind is drawn to that thing as the central focus of his life. In *Les Miserables,* Jean Valjean always kept a candlestick with him which was given to him by the bishop, who was the first light to come into his life. For him the candlestick was the symbol of that light: Christian charity, the love of Christ, and the fearlessness of one who has turned to God for his guidance. He always kept the candlestick on the mantle, which he looked upon as an altar. He needed an object there. It possessed the magic to correct him.

To a person who is fully trained it may appear to be just a fetish, but to a beginner it is not a fetish, it is a spiritual necessity. You need a church to go to, a spiritual master to talk to, or something to adore and worship and revere as sacred, different from the rest of the world. You actually go and gather flowers and make an offering there. It may look ridiculous, childish, to go and stand before a picture, fold one's hands and say "aum." But it is not ridiculous when you are getting into this new mode of relating yourself to the Unknown. Certainly in the picture there is no one, but when you stand before it you are not thinking that God is in the picture, or that the brass piece or the stone idol actually contains the deity.

We say, "Close your eyes and look deep into yourself." What depth — the stomach? Is that all the depth there is in us? Physically we are not very profound — most of us anyway — but when we look deep into ourselves spiritually we see a real depth which has no end. When we say "sublime heights" we are not thinking of the sky. Within our own spirit we see a sublimity which soars high. You can spread out the wings of your imagination and soar like a lark into that unknown realm. So we need symbols like these only to gain the new dimensions of mind that we seek. Once you catch on they are no longer necessary.

If a man is in a place where he needs to build a fire, he takes two splinters and rubs them together. The splinters are cold and dead like everything else, but because of the friction he causes, fire is emitted. Once the spark comes and the fire is lit, the splinters are of no further use and he can discard them.

Sometimes when you want to start a water pump, you have to prime it. You have to pour a little water into it and then it will function properly. Once the water starts coming, you don't need to pour any more in. Like these examples, the altar you use is only to get started. This is the second way.

There is a third way mentioned by Narayana Guru here. Some people think, "This is too odd, too idolatrous, for me to put up a picture or some other image and worship it. Only primitive people do that. I am more civilised." Fine. If you are so rationally inclined there is a way for you.

Begin by asking what is the phenomenon before you that appears to be true? Come, have a closer look at it. When you come to have a closer look, you will need the guidance of some basic dictum. Descartes tried to do it, and he found he was going from confusion to confusion, doubt to doubt. There needs to be a stepping stone from where you can go further. He came to the idea "I think, therefore I am." You need at least some basis for thinking. "I think: I am." This is one way of getting into the secret of the phenomenality of our experience.

There are a number of such dictums given by the masters. For instance Jesus said, "Seek ye first the kingdom of heaven and all else shall be added unto you." This is a very clear instruction. Then you ask, "Which is the kingdom of heaven? How do I seek it? Who will show me the path?" Then you hear, "Come to me. Those who receive me receive my Father in heaven. Those who receive my Father in heaven also receive me. I am your light and your life. I am the way; I am the goal." Here you have something to ponder over. This is called *māyāmanu uruviṭṭu;* you have to repeat it again and again in your mind.

In *The Cloud of Unknowing,* such kind of a word or dictum is referred to as a hammer. In the Bible it says, "Knock and it shall be opened unto you." The anonymous author who wrote *The Cloud of Unknowing* says, "Take this word. It is your little hammer to knock against this big wall of ignorance. Ultimately it will give way."

The Vedantins use *mahāvākya.* The Guru calls his disciple and says, "*tat tvam asi,* you are That. Use this as your key and meditate on it." The student meditates: "How am I the whole Absolute? I am confined in this body." That is his maya. To get out of that maya, he has to ponder on the nameless in the place of what has a name, the formless in the place of what has a form, the imperishable in the place of what is perishable, formless beauty in the place of what is merely ugly or pretty, eternal joy in the place of mere happiness or misery. He goes on doing this in so many ways. Slowly he pushes away the transient, the fleeting, the momentary, the perishable, the superficial. Then that phenomenality will give way to him, and he will come to the numenon, the ever-numinous.

The Guru has pointed out these three pathways, but in between them are many shades and varieties of search. In all of them the central idea is the same. Philosophers in both the East and the West have written volumes and volumes of instruction, but when we carefully examine them they all boil down to the same thing.

For Sartre it was "existence precedes essence." He has to accommodate existence and essence. All the rest that he writes is only to elaborate on this one thing. So he is meditating on one dictum, one principle. For Jaspers, the seeming world before us is the only world that we live in. Yet the profound depth of truth, and beauty with all its musical excellence, cannot be just a fleeting experience. For him, to blend the two into one is his central theme.

We have to find out for ourselves what that central theme or dictum is, which we can endlessly repeat with fresh new insights and thus gain a key to get into the essence of any life situation. Then the world will change.

Verse 30

jaḍamaṟivilaṟivinnu cintayillō-
tiṭukayumillaṟivennaṟiññu sarvam
viṭukil avan viśadāntaranganāy mē-
luṭalil amarnnuẓalunnatilla nūnam

Inert matter does not know; knowledge has no thought
and does not articulate; knowing knowledge to be all,
letting go, one's inner state becomes boundless;
indeed, thereafter he never suffers confined within a body.

A child's first experience when it comes into this world from its mother's womb is being exposed to extremes of heat and cold and light. Birth itself is painful. The child is initiated into the world with a loud cry. Almost all of the child's initial behaviour patterns come from acceptance of pleasure and avoidance of pain. It reaches out and it withdraws. Pain and pleasure, strife and harmony, are the principles that are operative in the physical body.

And how many kinds of physical pain there are! Virtually every part of the body can experience pain, ranging from minor irritations to major, overwhelming sensations. The body is a bundle of pains. They are compensated for by various pleasures, but compared to the many possibilities for pain there are relatively few areas where pleasure can be evoked.

We have two polar aspects in us. One is the inertness of the physical body, the body we can see and which can be laid in a coffin and taken to the burial ground. The other aspect is the pure soul or the Self. We are not troubled by either of these. When a dead body is put into a crematorium and burned, it does not undergo any pain. The body as such is painless. The pure soul as such is painless. In between these is a region that is full of pain and pleasure.

When, for instance, a person has to undergo major surgery, and the surgeon plans to cut deep into the body, an anesthetic is administered so that the patient does not know what is going on. He does not feel anything. It is as if that part of the body has no pain of its own. When the dentist pulls out a tooth or drills into one, after the Novocaine has been administered we only know something is happening because of the sound. Inert matter as such does not experience pain or pleasure. What is the effect of the anesthesia? All awareness is taken away from the inert matter. As long as it remains as pure matter it experiences no pain or pleasure. What is it that is painful? It is not the tooth, eye, stomach, neck or back. There are certain sensory areas which become agitated, and there is a consciousness which accompanies these agitations. All our bondage to life and release from it are confined within this one region.

When we are physically hurt we live in the body. Most of the rest of the time we live in a social image of ourselves. We live in the physical body at the breakfast or lunch table, when some delicate dish is enjoyed. Even then, if there is good conversation, we attend to our social image and may not even notice we are eating.

Our social identity says: "I am so-and-so. In the eyes of my colleagues, my friends, my competitors and my enemies, this is the image I want to impress." Part of this image comes from the expectations of others. Other people expect you to wear a certain kind of dress, to have a certain kind of form, to speak with a certain kind of dignity. You watch all these social expectations and secretly try to conform to them. Thus, in about twenty years you build up a personality: your social image. Afterwards if any part of that image becomes tarnished, you get frightened. You think, "Now I'm going to be rejected because my social image is no longer perfect." Someone can now easily exploit you through character assassination or even blackmail. If someone's reputation is assailed, it is as bad as killing the body. One may even commit suicide. You should not confuse this social image with the soul or the Self; it is only the social ego.

We live in the body and the social ego. If we are not suffering from pains like a head or stomach ache we are suffering from the pains of what others think of us, or what happened to our trust in another person, or their trust in us, or to our love. This can become more gruesome and cause more suffering than physical pain. People have a remarkable resilience to physical pains, but when the social ego is tortured we may succumb rapidly to the pressure. This type of apperception is what was described in verse 28 as the knowledge in between. In between the bodily aspect and the soul aspect is an intermediary knowledge which includes the conditional states of consciousness. This alone is where we experience the awareness of pain and the awareness of pleasure.

We have four states of consciousness. One is wakeful experience, where we interrelate with other persons, things and events. We also have dream experience. Consciousness alternates between the wakeful and the dream, and both these regions of awareness are filled with painful and pleasurable experiences. This is the horizontal movement of consciousness.

There is also a vertical possibility in the movement of consciousness. It can rise to the transcendental heights or sink into deep sleep where we do not know anything. In deep sleep there is no pain, no pleasure, no physical ailment or any kind of social humiliation. It is a state where we merge into nature.

Nature, or prakriti, has the triple aspects of sattva, a pure-clear state of reflection; rajas, a turbulent state of distortion and conditioning; and tamas, an opacity where consciousness is veiled from everything. The inertial aspect of matter predominates in deep sleep; here the turbulent, kinetic aspect of the mind and its capacity to reflect or mirror are both enveloped by tamas or darkness. You do not know anything. Only when there is partial knowledge can you relate yourself to a quality. In sleep, experience becomes non-qualitative because nothing is perceived. You cannot say ugly or beautiful if you do not see. In silence there is neither dissonance or resonance. You cannot say someone is talking sense or nonsense unless they speak. So when you are completely enveloped by tamas you are in the deep sleep state. There you escape all pains and pleasures.

The deep sleep state is the negative aspect of the vertical potential of consciousness. The positive aspect is when you transcend all three qualities of nature, sattva, rajas and tamas. Then you are not in an unconscious state; you are all consciousness, through and through. Pure consciousness. This consciousness that transcends the triple modalities of nature is called turiya. The vertical axis includes all degrees of awareness, from none at the vertical minus to total at the vertical plus. Thus we have, in all, four states: wakeful and dream, deep sleep and the transcendental.

We need to cultivate an attitude in which we can clearly understand certain basic concepts. To begin with, we have a body. An aspect of Self or consciousness is illuminating this body. It is inevitable for the body to have the qualities of sattva, rajas and tamas. The body is constituted of five elements, which display their characteristics in experiencing sound, form, touch, taste and smell. The three qualities and the five elements interact. What you hear will be elevating and musical when sattva functions, agitating when rajas functions, and depressing and deadening when tamas functions. What you see may be luminous, inspiring forms when sattva operates, exciting forms which can put you through all kinds of agitations with rajas, or a kind of blackout where you cannot see anything clearly when tamas operates. In this way the three gunas operate in all five elements.

Our manifested form consists of the five senses and the mind, intellect, memory and the ego. Any of these may have errors and defects. There can be defective hearing, defective vision, defective discernment of various tactual stimuli. A mind can be retarded, abnormal, or subnormal, malfunctioning in many ways. Some people experience too much memory becoming available all at once. In certain kinds of madness, a person remembers many unnecessary things at all the wrong times; so many memories crowd into the mind that it is overwhelmed. The person is helpless to stop them. Again, if the door between memory and articulation is opened, the memories come out endlessly as many disconnected statements. You can have trouble with the mind bringing up unnecessary worries about the past, the present and the future, and then you have intellectual disquiet. When this happens, you cannot make decisions:

whenever you argue in your mind and come to a conclusion, a counter-argument arises. You are torn between two or more conclusions, and you cannot decide.

So you can have problems at any level: at the level of *manas*, the interrogating or questioning mind; *cittam*, the recalling mind; and *buddhi*, the deciding mind. Finally you can have trouble with the *ahamkāra*, the ego. This might make you personally self-conscious, wanting to be accepted by everyone. Often there is a great craving, a thirst for recognition. You look all around, thinking "who is going to admire me; who is going to recognise me?" You are always saying 'I and the other,' "I and the world," "I and the people." You are suffering from "I and the other" all the time. What a wretched life. Somehow you have to transcend all these maladies, because without doing so life becomes a horror.

Narayana Guru's suggestion is that we turn our affiliation from the physical body and the social ego to a third possibility, our own pure Self. He begins this verse by reminding us that the pure Self does not speak or even think: *jaḍamaṟivilaṟivinnu cintayilla*, know that the discursive thought going on in your mind is not your Self. When people like R.D. Laing say self, they are referring to this cogitating, thinking mind. This is what the Guru refers to as the not-Self. Not-Self is recognised in the Western world as self. Buddhists call it *anātman*, that which is not atman.

Here we are not saying that when a person has physical pain there is no physical pain. Certainly there is physical pain, but it is of the body, not of the Self. The body is animated by a fragmentary aspect of consciousness which is coloured and conditioned so it knows pain. Over time this becomes your major concern and major affiliation, until you cannot extricate yourself from it.

You must learn to free yourself from your absorption with your bodily and egoistic states. If you are a fully released person, you can still attend to your bodily states and social functionings, but with a certain amount of detachment. You attend to them just as you attend to your car or your computer or your radio or TV. You know your car or piano or radio are good things, so if something goes wrong you don't just say "Oh, it's only my car," and walk away and leave it. It's essential to get it repaired. In the same way, it is essential to take care of the body. Whatever is inevitable is inevitable, but if something can be corrected it should be.

The most essential thing here is to know that there is a third possible affiliation, one with your pure Self. After affiliating with the Self you can treat your relationship with the ego and the body with a normal attitude, rather than the exaggerated attitude of most people. The Guru says if you do this you become *viśadāntarangan*, a person with a expansive consciousness whose mind is no longer confined to one little thing in life, such as your headache or your toothache. You are still aware that there is a headache or a toothache, but you don't allow them to occupy your whole beingness to the point where you are nothing more than just an ache or a pain. You maintain your inner clarity in and through your pains and pleasures.

All the contemplation, meditation and discipline we do is only for this one purpose of disaffiliating ourselves from body identity and ego identity, and establishing an identity with our pure spirit. It is a pilgrimage. We are walking away from us to arrive at us. From where do we go? From the periphery of our skin and this feeling of ego. Where do we arrive? Deep down within us. The distance from our periphery to our centre, seemingly so close, is in reality very, very far. That's why the Upanishads say it is far and near, inside as well as outside; it is the farthest from all and the nearest of all. Nothing is nearer than your centre and yet nothing is a longer journey. It is very difficult to arrive at it, but once you do everything is expansive.

There is suffering in this world, but if you are too concerned with it you will miss your whole life. In spite of suffering, in spite of diseases, you should go on. Let the body drop off. One day it will drop on its own anyway. What do you do when your car won't go? You try everything, and when nothing works you have it towed to a garage. If the mechanic says its hopeless, it goes to the junkyard. You throw it away. With our body, it's the same.

When it comes to the ego, it is a hard nut to crack. Social acceptance has become a great necessity. A greater necessity, though, is your acceptance of your spirit, acknowledging your own truth, your real existence. Your primary and most valuable identity is not even recognised. Jesus asked what does it matter if you lose a limb? If you are losing your soul by saving your limb, that is a greater loss.

Only when we understand this can the paradox of the great suffering of the masters on the physical plane and even the social plane, juxtaposed with their calm, serene life in the spirit, be resolved.

There are many such examples before us, like Jesus, St. Francis, St. John of the Cross, Ramana Maharshi, Sri Ramakrishna, Narayana Guru. Physically they underwent the highest degree of intense pain. Some of them also had to undergo the mockery of the whole society. Jesus was abused and spat upon. Sri Ramakrishna was treated as a madman. Even Mahatma Gandhi, a man of great wisdom, who came and saw Narayana Guru and was convinced of his greatness, still went and wrote in his paper that he was to be treated only as a śūdra, an outcast. Such is this world. We are so socially conditioned. In spite of all these physical and social tortures and abuses, there comes from these masters the greatest peace on earth, the highest form of human consolation. They are our solace; in them we find our peace, our inspiration.

Clearly, it is the masters' identification with the spirit that calls to us, that beckons us toward our own pilgrimage. Jesus always referred to another entity he called "My Father in Heaven". The Upanishadic rishis always say, "Thus we have heard," or "Thus it is revealed." They don't say "I say," they say *iti śuśruma*, this is what we have heard which is very important, not belonging to any social ego.

To release ourselves from the clutches of the body and the society, we transcend. Thereafter, pain may be in your body but you don't suffer. Disgrace may be sitting on your name in the society but you don't suffer. This is a scheme given to us for working out our own release from a twofold misery.

This is really one of the most beautiful verses of *Ātmopadeśa Śatakam*. For years and years I have used this one verse for meditation. In all my troubles, physical as well as social, this verse has saved me many times. Again and again I go over it. Sometimes when there are bodily troubles, people around are upset, and the doctors are annoyed, giving me all kinds of medicines, I find over and above all this that the only medicine which gives me utmost relief is this one verse. It goes on saying, "This inert matter does not know anything. My pure soul is not the one which sits and thinks and worries. It is not the one which speaks to people. It's one all-pervading consciousness. This body is just one thing floating in that ocean of consciousness like a piece of cork. Sometimes it may be up and sometimes down." Thus there comes an expansive, transcendent consciousness. Is there pain? Yes, there is pain. Did someone say something terrible about me? Yes, he said I am a very evil man. Aum. Aum. "Are you not very evil?" Aum. Be it so. What of it?

You are really released. There is no greater achievement to make.

Verse 31

anubhavamādiyil onnirikkil allā-
tanumitiyillitu munnamakṣiyālē
anubhaviyātatukoṇṭu dharmmiyuṇṭe-
nnanumitiyāl arivīlaṟiññiṭēṇam

Without prior experience there is no inference;
this is not previously perceived with the eye;
therefore, know that the existence of that in which all
qualities inhere
is not known by inference.

Now we come to three verses which provide a methodology to assist us in our search for truth.

There are three fundamental questions we can ask about the world in which we find ourselves. The first is "what is matter?" Furthermore, how does it originate and how does it function? We see things which we consider to be concrete and existing outside of us. They are part of our experience and can be seen, touched, heard, tasted and smelled. Certainly they must have originated at some point. Where and when was that? And what really is the substance we call matter? How can things as different as air and earth be included under this one category? How can matter include both the living and the inanimate in its purview?

The second fundamental question is "what is life?" How does it originate? How do you distinguish between a biologic factor and an inanimate object? In other words, what particular quality in matter causes it to live? How does life evolve? What laws are operating and where is it taking us? Do evolutionary processes move according to special laws in order to achieve anything? Are they purposive? Does the world go by itself, or is it guided by something else?

The third main question is "what is consciousness?" How does it originate, and how is it different from life itself? What is the extent of consciousness? How deep is it, and how far can it be stretched? What are its foundations? Naturally the additional consideration arises of what is not consciousness.

The entire gamut of psychology comes under the question of "what is consciousness?" All of biology comes under "what is life?" and the entire world of physics and chemistry comes under the consideration of "what is matter?" These three questions lead us to make ongoing probes into the nature of our universe.

A fourth question comes as a natural corollary. "What do you want to find out?" If it is truth, how do you discern it? You set out to find some great truth. Are you sufficiently familiar with truth to know it when you come face to face with it? You see many things in your dreams which seem to exist, but when you wake up they are no longer there. What you experience in the wakeful state is not present in your dreams, either. So how do you know which of these is true?

Take an orange for example. How do we know an orange is an orange? What really exists, what is the truth of it? We see a spherical shape, orange colouring and a kind of skin on the outside. When we peel it, the inner contents are juicy. It has a particular smell and taste. We can analyse the orange into its many constituent properties. These are called dharmas. If we take it for granted these properties exist, only one thing will still be missing: the orange. Our analysis has only come across shape, taste, colour, touch and smell. We do not experience the orange when we touch it; we are only experiencing touch. Or we are experiencing colour and shape. Then where is the orange? It is only a composition we have made in our minds out of all its properties.

Thus, we have a synthetic understanding which integrates many divergent factors. If we go further into the constituents of a thing, they are synthesised of still more basic properties. So what you see is not what is inherent in a substance, but only what is inferred about it.

The need for a proper methodology to arrive at fundamental truths was demonstrated very early on by philosophers like

Parmenides and Zeno. Zeno is famous for his paradoxes that illustrate the limitations of our reasoning by showing how mathematical logic can sometimes contradict perceptions or common sense. In Western philosophy there was a great struggle over proper methodology up to the time of Descartes. He decided that philosophy would never be scientific and stand on its own unless a proper methodology could be developed. All credit goes to Descartes for laying the groundwork in this effort. But even the Cartesian methodology was not complete in itself. Afterwards, Immanuel Kant added a critique of pure reason and a critique of practical reason. He thought a theory should be feasible, acceptable to the mind, operative at a transactional level, and practical.

There should always be applied knowledge alongside pure, theoretical knowledge. The pure aspect is postulation. Applied science is performing something on the basis of that truth. Only when you have a proof, only when you see it with your own eyes, does information become convincing. In a physics class, for instance, a certain postulate expressing a natural law can be given by the teacher in the morning. Then, in the afternoon class, the instructor should show how it can be applied.

In this verse Narayana Guru is saying that in order to really know *brahman*, the Absolute, you have to experience it at least once. It should be as real as a berry in the palm of your hand. Only if you experience it can you truly be a knower of the Absolute.

In the previous verse we were given a very sweeping vision that inert matter has no knowledge, and pure knowledge does not cogitate or articulate. We are caught midway between two absolute forms of silence: the silence of inert matter and the silence of that unknown, inaccessible Reality. Both of these lie behind closed doors, so to speak. In between them is a twilight region in which we are living, moving around, making observations, yelling, shouting and carrying on. This the Guru has already discredited as non-knowledge.

There have always been disputes going on among people who are steeped in ignorance. And what is their method? They use inferences. Nothing is fully known to them. They see only a little bit and then assume the rest. Pedagogues in our university classes, schools, churches and other social institutions rant and rave solely on the basis of the blatant assumptions of their preselected inferences.

All that we notice here is only partial; the rest we imagine. Even when we think we have fully observed, we have only half observed. Our imagination, fuelled by our prejudices and predilections, fills in the gaps. Is this kind of methodology useful for knowing the Absolute?

Narayana Guru says no. You have to truly experience a thing in order to know it, and what you are here trying to discern does not come under that category. It is not a dharma, a property which sustains a thing as it is. Rather, it is that which contains all properties, *dharmī*. To arrive at the Absolute is a very frustrating challenge. All the pride of our understanding and learning must be taken away from us. To get over this hurdle, Kant brought in the idea of the main division between knowledge which is a priori and knowledge which is a posteriori. A priori knowledge is what is prior to your experience, while a posteriori knowledge comes after your experience. How does one get a priori knowledge? The Guru is going to tell us after a couple of more verses. At this point he just wants us to know that whatever knowledge we have gained so far is relativistic understanding which has some value in our interpersonal transactions but won't help us to know the Self. In order to realise the Self another kind of discipline and understanding is needed.

Two methods have been adopted by the rishis of the Upanishads to arrive at what is not known. They share the assumption that there cannot be many truths. Truth should be one, without a second. It cannot be one thing now and later something else. It cannot have a beginning and an end. Furthermore, there cannot be anything or anyone outside truth to be a witness; that imparts duality. All these are axiomatic reasonings, mathematically conceived. When you correctly arrive at the conception of theoretical truth by an axiomatic method, what you see cannot be anything other than the only truth. Otherwise, if you presume that it is not truth, you are assuming that truth can be many.

The first of the two methods of the rishis is to affirm everything. They go on repeating *asti, asti*, "and this, and this." They say, "What I see is also truth; what I hear is also truth; what I touch is also truth; what I think is also truth; what I imagine is also truth; what cannot be imagined is also truth". Anything which comes within the frame of awareness is affirmed as also being true. They know that each time they affirm something they are affirming only a part, which they presume belongs to a whole. This is in anticipation of someday arriving at a notion of the whole.

Even before that they axiomatically believe that there is a whole. From where did that arise? Who revealed it to them? How is the truth of axioms revealed to begin with? We do not know, and yet we experience it. This is called the argument of affirmation. The basis of the argument of affirmation is the revelation which comes in the form of an axiom that does not need to be proved.

The other method is to go on denying everything, *neti, neti*, "not this, not this." "Am I this body? *neti*. The senses? *neti*. The mind? *neti*. Anything visible? *neti*. Anything inferential? *neti*. Anything not visible? *neti*. Anything not inferential? *neti*." In the fourth quarter of the Mandukya Upanishad, there is a whole set of such denials. After denying everything, you come to a certain mystical silence in which you cannot further deny anything and yet you know that you cannot deny the existence of that state. You are enveloped and engulfed by an undeniable experience.

In the Brihadaranyaka Upanishad, Yājñavalkya uses the method of negation, while in the Chandogya Upanishad, Āruṇi uses the method of affirmation. With either method you arrive at the same truth.

There are two basic types of people, introverts and extroverts. Introverts tend to be withdrawn, introspective and contemplative; extroverts overt, externally minded and craving action. Clearly the method of negation is more suitable for introverts and that of affirmation more suitable for extroverts. In either case, both accept that there is truth to be found. Without ever having experienced the totality of truth, they intuit its existence. Such intuition is not supported by any reasoning. It doesn't come as part of emotional life. It is as if the very truth of being reveals itself through its own beingness.

This gives us a clue for our search. At first we may have been disappointed when we were told that pure knowledge does not think, reason or speak. How can we ever approach the unthinkable through thought? If we dismiss the world of our cogitations, the world of our inner reasoning, and the silent way of conversation within ourselves, what tool is left to us for our search? If all these inner voices and dialogues are not coming from the right source and we drop them, we become very quiet. With a kind of frustrated helplessness we take our hands off everything. We are surrounded by the din of silence. It may look as if we have lost our ground and are floating in thin air. We may even have to dismiss the very idea of a floating entity: there is no one to float, no one to know.

After all this tearing down and destruction, something still prevails. The seeker does not name it, he doesn't even call it an experience, but he knows he is That. It was with That he first spoke and first knew everything, and what he thus understands he cannot limit in any way. He cannot give any distinction, any name, any form to it. It overwhelms him and fills him. For him there is no 'I', there is only That. The very This which otherwise remains indistinct and indiscernible has grown to fill everything. Now there is no need for anything to illuminate because this is the same which remains in the darkness as the only luminous truth. It is self-luminous, an existence which proclaims its own existence, a knowledge which is knowledge through and through but not a knowledge of any thing. It is not deep; it is depth itself. It is not valuable; it is value itself. It is not making anyone happy or blissful, because there is no subject/object differentiation to say "now I am blissful." Yet it is devoid of all disturbances.

One who arrives at this comprehension is not assailed with any doubt. There is just Being. All that you can say is "It is." Even that is wrong to an extent, because 'it is' is a kind of judgement. If you can somehow compress Thisness and Isness into one and remain in the silence of pure Beingness, rid of all the colourations given by the sensory system, the mind, and your expectations and prejudices, that is the only reality.

If you are fully merged into that pure state, there is no ideation of the subject as 'I'. Words become useless. One knows the sublimity of height, the oceanic depth, and the boundlessness of infinity. Only after fully knowing what that is will you be able to look upon this world as a passing show, a shadow without substance. At the same time, once you are fully convinced of that, it is a sheer joy to come and play this game of Indra. You are a child playing the game called life on the expanse of nothingness.

This is only a preliminary entry into the true depth. We have to go a few steps more, and they are given in the next couple of verses. It requires more meditation and contemplation. If you touch it even slightly, it is the greatest wonder you have ever experienced. You are transformed.

Verse 32

aṟivatu dharmmiyeyalla dharmmamāmī-
yaruḷiya dharmmiyadṛśyamākayālē
dhara mutalāyavayonnumilla tāṅṅu-
nnoru vaṭivāmaṟivuḷḷatōrttiṭēṇam

What is known is not that in which all qualities inhere,
only the qualities;
as this, in which all qualities are said to inhere, is not visible
earth and all else do not exist;
remember that there is only a form in knowledge which supports.

In order to get the full implication of this verse, you will have to read Śaṅkara's commentary on the fourth section of the first chapter of the Brihadaranyaka Upanishad. It's a very elaborate piece, and as easily readable as Śaṅkara always is. Or you should very carefully read the *Critique of Pure Reason* by Kant. Both Śaṅkara and Kant want us to examine two aspects in knowledge. One is what we call experience, the other may be called the cause of experience. We are very familiar with experience: everybody says you should have experience, and that it is very important.

What exactly is experience? In short, it is the knowledge of "what is." This is different from "why it is." What is, is one thing; why it is, is another. I am now talking to you and you are listening to me. You understand that I am talking and you are listening. This is an experience. Why is it that you should experience that I am sitting here and talking while you are listening? Why don't you think this is a phantom sitting here and that you only appear to be listening?

Why don't you doubt like that? What necessitates a compelling feeling in you that this is true, that you are not sleeping and this is really a wakeful experience, that all of us are sharing the experience so it cannot be untrue? Where does that kind of compelling necessity come from? Is that also experience? When you and another person have experiences, what makes you feel that it is a universally shared experience rather than a private one? Kant draws a line between what is and why it is. He calls the 'why' an a priori judgement, and the 'what' an a posteriori judgement.

Śaṅkara asks, "What is the source of this thing you call *anubhava* or experience?" The source is the body. All your experiences are derivations of a sensation, a perception or a memory. Whatever grand name you give it, these things happen only as a result of certain bodily states. As they all come from bodily states, they cannot be called the Self. Their source is already contaminated with the properties of the non-Self. Śaṅkara wants us to turn away from experience itself to that which is the cause of experience.

Combining what Śaṅkara and Kant say, Narayana Guru draws a line between dharmi and dharmam, between the ground and what is manifested on it.

The Western conception of memory likens it to calling a person in from another room. He is not currently present and we want him so we call to him. From the next room he enters, and we identify him as the person we wanted. But is there really anything coming into one part of your brain from another part that we can call the memory bank? Is there a dark chamber somewhere in your brain that is kept locked up, from which something pops out and goes to another part of the brain, saying "here I am!" when you recall? Despite the theory, no such thing has yet been found.

The brain is made up of all this gray matter. When you examine it under the microscope you see nothing but some liquids in which nerve cells are floating around. The nerve cells have ends, called synapses, which interlock with other nerve cells. When something happens, your energy is tickled in a certain way. The only thing experimenters have been able to observe that might correspond to a memory recall is a change in the physical form of synapses. They observed changes in them which were very like ripples on the surface of water or a whirlpool being formed by ripples moving in a certain way. Otherwise everything remains the same. The quality and movement of the ripple, and the bulges and depressions that appear, are imagined to be memories.

This is as stupid as saying that Beethoven's Appassionata Sonata is caused by twangs on the strings of a piano which cause vibrations of certain frequencies. How can you say that? Naturally to play piano music you will touch keys that are connected to hammers that strike strings to produce vibrations of certain pitches. But it is putting the cart before the horse to say that music comes from the vibrations or that bulges produce memories.

The scientists do admit one element of truth: they say there is no special thing called memory sitting anywhere. There are only bulges and depressions. That is the most one can observe on the basis of the physical and chemical background of knowledge.

Narayana Guru further says *vaṭivu,* meaning a form. In your pure consciousness there is a certain form which comes. When you cut off that portion alone it is what you call empirical knowledge. People who call themselves empiricists concern themselves with the experiential part. Although we call Locke, Hume and Berkeley empiricists, this is an incorrect classification because Locke alone gave primacy to sensuous experience. Hume questioned it and Berkeley rejected it. Simply because of the context in which they were hitting at each other we call them all empiricists, applying a wrong methodology of classification.

If you do not have a background knowledge of all the philosophers, just making references is a waste of time, but I presume you at least know Locke, Hume and Berkeley. According to Locke there are no innate ideas. Man comes to this world with a tabula rasa, a clean slate of a mind. A child's mind has nothing written on it at first. Afterwards he gets exposed to the world through his senses. He formulates ideas from impressions of pain and pleasure, from pleasant and unpleasant agitations. People speak names to him and show him forms; in this way the coordination of names and forms are established in his mind. Slowly the child comes to relate cause with effect, and after some time it becomes fully indoctrinated in the cause and effect theory.

This is questioned by David Hume: is there any validity in formulating a causal relationship between two things simply because one comes after the other? For instance, we see water boiling and fire burning. The precedent factor was the burning fire, the antecedent was water boiling. So we relate one to the other and say the fire is the cause of the boiling water, and these concomitants always come together. Because of the concomitance of two things in a sequential order we think one is the cause of the other. He says this is only because we are psychologically impressed in this way and that there is no necessity for it.

Necessity is a principle which was brought to formal thinking by Descartes. He said there is one source of knowledge where your thinking is validated by an evidence which is inherent within, and called it self-evidence. This is found in mathematics. Whichever way you put two plus two, it is always four. It cannot be five or three and a half. There is an inner compulsion for everyone to agree that two and two make four. Such self-evident truth is a mathematical necessity. Hume accepted this, but he asked if there was any mathematical necessity in believing fire boils water. Since other possibilities can be imagined, it is only a psychological necessity.

Thus Locke's empirical stand was questioned and refuted. Even though it was not fully discarded, it was kept suspended by Hume. Then Bishop Berkeley said that what seems to be a universal experience is after all only your private idea. You formulate all your impressions using your own sensory system, so they are modulated within your mind and everything is your own idea. In this respect, although his theme was empiricism, Berkeley should actually be considered an idealist rather than an empiricist.

Kant started where Berkeley left off. When he wrote, he had before him Descartes, Spinoza, Leibnitz, Locke, Hume and Berkeley. Śaṅkara had before him the Purva-Mimamsa people, who said if you do a certain action it should yield a certain result, because every cause should have an effect. That means if you evoke a certain god with a certain mantra, that god should come before you and give you peace. They had formulated an elaborate system based on the psychodynamics of the Word. They saw the earth as a manifestation of water, water as a manifestation of fire, fire as a manifestation of air, air as a manifestation of ether, and the substance of ether as sound. Therefore the whole world is basically made up of sound vibration. If the vibration of sounds can become all the geometrical properties around us, then by hitting them with different kinds of sound their properties can be altered. The Purva-Mimamsa's research went on formulating and structuring sounds that could be used as antidotes. In other words, if one formulation of sound causes this, this other one will undo it. Then you can redo it in another way. You can create many parallelograms of forces with your sounds. Thus they evolved an elaborate semantic system of mantras. They claimed a relationship between chanting a certain mantra and rain coming, and everyone believed them. They were another kind of empiricists, basing their philosophy on action and experience.

Then the Buddhists came along and said that they didn't agree, that those people were making a duality of subject and object. To them, subject and object are both aspects of the same total reality. Any differentiation between them is at best a kind of quasi-truth, both true and untrue. They summed it all up as ignorance.

Then there were the Sankhyans, who believed neither in action nor the ignorance of the Buddhists. They argued: take anything. Take earth. Earth is an element. How many qualities does it have? It has the quality that it can be touched, tasted, smelled, heard, and seen. Then they would analyse its fundamentals until they arrived at the "thing in itself," *tanmātra*. Why does a thing in itself activate? There must be at least two principles, one which gives intelligence for an action and another which gives the capacity for action. A principle of self-luminosity and a principle of self-volition. They called these *puruṣa* and *prakṛti*.

Finally there came another school which maintained there should be some relevancy between one idea and another. Logistics is the most important structural secret by which the relations of things can be understood. They can be grouped by species, which in turn belong to a genus. Within a genus can be many coordinated species. These divisions are made on the basis of specific and general qualities. In this way the whole world was divided into generalities and specificities, and the relationships between them. This is the relation-relata complex. Philosophers of this school are called

Naīyāyika or logicians.

So Śaṅkara had all these schools before him. He put them all on one side and said, "You all line up here. I have to put questions to you." Kant also kept his six empiricists on one side and questioned them. After rigorous and thorough questioning, they both rejected all their predecessors' arguments. Kant said their arguments were all tainted by aspects of their physical and sensual experiences, which they mixed with their knowledge. Śaṅkara said essentially the same thing: "All that you say is tainted by experiences that can be traced to your bodily consciousness or an ego factor."

The cream of the best things said by these two grand philosophers, one of the East and one of the West, is expressed by this one verse of Narayana Guru. He says all our experiences are of the dharma and not of the dharmi, because the dharmi is not amenable to our experiences.

The other day we saw how we can affiliate ourselves with body consciousness and the social ego. These two affiliations can cause many modes of thinking and judgement within us. What we call our meditation is no meditation at all. It is only certain body postures; it is being self-conscious about many of our physical aspects such as breathing, sitting in a certain way, or imagining a certain part of the body. We think that directing the mind inward means actually looking inward at such and such a place, which is essentially an action. Thus we are doing an exercise, not meditating. Śaṅkara asked, "Why do you call it meditation? It is fun. It is some physical exercise. At best it is a psychological exercise. Even so, it has nothing to so with the Self."

Real meditation is not very easy. First you must drop from your mind all the names that you know, including your own. Drop not only the names of persons and things but also names of ideas, such as compassion, patience or whatever. I don't believe you've given up all names, but let us tentatively suppose you no longer know any nomenclature. Nomenclature means a label which you give with a sound or an oral or written sign.

Now drop from your mind all memories of forms. You should now not be able to say "Deborah" or recall a form which conforms to Deborah. Forget the distinction of past, present and future. Efface your location, such as Hall Street House, Portland. Next throw away all directions: north, south, east, west, and above and below.

When I ask you to give something up, you suddenly think of just that. It was not previously in your mind. You poor people are not thinking of your breathing at all until I say to forget it. Breathing is an action. Along with breathing, give up the whole world of action, any kind of movement. Now cancel away the duality of cause and effect. Forget that you are capable of knowing, feeling, breathing. Erase the distinction between 'I' and 'the other'. Make the usage of 'I' totally meaningless. In short, all the injunctions I have been giving you are not to do anything, but to do away with everything. You are not asked to think, but not to think. You are not asked to recall, but not to remember; not asked to win, but not to win.

Suppose we have achieved such a state, even though we clearly have not. It is evident that even in this ideal state there will be a presentation of consciousness. You can do away with virtually everything, but still a residual space and duration will remain for your awareness to exist. It is an irremediable impenetrability.

Kant says this has a categorical nature, a persistence that is unavoidable and universal. He argues two necessary conditions to go along with the quality of a priori judgement. One is universality, and the other is that it is imperative, categorically imperative. Śaṅkara quotes the Upanishads which say that to meditate should not be taken as an injunction. If you take it as an injunction you are merely thinking of a bodily function. How can knowledge be, other than by being knowledge? This is apprehended through what is called meditation.

The two qualities which Kant mentioned — the imperativeness of knowledge which is luminous through its own nature, and the universality which operates in and through all forms of manifestation all the time — roughly correspond to the images used by Narayana Guru throughout this work. At the core of all is the Karu, or the manifesting yolk which is shining both inside and outside as the supernal sun shining in the firmament of consciousness; as the one light that enables you to think your many thoughts, wake and sleep, eat and mate; as the one which is sitting as a witness beneath the tree of manifestation; as the one identity when two people say 'I'; as the one ocean which floods and fills the vast desert of our lives, turning every grain of sand into a pearl of priceless worth.

All through our study we have been seeing this one light which is us. But as soon as we act, we miss it. We pollute it with our sensations, with our body consciousness, with names and forms, time and space, cause and effect. In fact it is the most spontaneous thing, happening without any effort on your part to sit cross-legged, to concentrate on your heartbeat, or to breathe in a way that tortures your nostrils. It is always there by itself. You don't have to do anything. Yet it is the most difficult thing to know because you are already caught in the grip of the competitive world where body, mind and senses are focused on values which are extraneous to your own Self. To reclaim yourself from that feverishness, to bring you back to the pure, spontaneous happiness within: that is the only reason you have to sit cross-legged, turn inward or regulate your breath. It is all so you won't run into the marketplace again and again and hit your head against things which have no value for you.

First you imagine a certain necessity. It begins to haunt you. It comes like a devil and catches you. Then you get caught in the frenzy of it. Karma is waiting for someone to say there is a necessity, then it pounces upon them.

Not being caught up in action is not an excuse to be lazy. Please try to understand what the Guru is saying here. It is almost impossible, since for at least the last one hundred years in European universities the poor minds of every man and woman have been put on the anvil of conformity and beaten into the shape of the empirical religion. This verse looks so simple, so innocent, but in a way it makes all the difference. So at least for a fraction of a minute, enjoy the great freedom of your own Self by throwing out all this garbage called name and form, cause and effect, obligation and society.

Verse 33

aṟivu nijasthitiyiṅṅaṟiññiṭānāy
dhara mutalāya vibhūtiyāyi tānē
maṟiyumavasthayil ēṟi māṟi vaṭṭam-
tiriyumalātasamam tiriññiṭunnu

Knowledge, to know its own nature here,
has become earth and the other elements;
spiraling up, back and turning round,
like a glowing twig it is ever turning.

People of all ages and in all parts of the world have tried to account for creation. They have invented many stories in the attempt. For instance according to the Semitic religions, in the beginning there was nothing but God living in an abyss of darkness. Then he decided to make a world; in six days he created everything that is now in existence by his mere will.

The scientists who do not believe in a myth of creation think that there was a big bang. A highly condensed substance became spread out into various nebular, galactic, stellar and planetary systems. In due course life came about, and after a process of evolution consciousness appeared. Even today, both religious and scientific adherents are trying to ascertain a meaning for conscious, living being.

In this verse, Narayana Guru is offering his approach to this question. It is not merely to satisfy curiosity to know how this world evolved. The centerpiece of the discussion here is the Self. We have already established that the Self we are speaking of is not just the soul of one individual being. It is the only reality behind all manifestation, the very consciousness in us with which we see, hear, think, feel and experience. Everything is a manifested aspect of that supreme Self and, for that reason, only a feeble glow of its effulgence.

Through the agency of the Self we can look out upon the world, but we can also reverse our attentions and come to know its very source. When we look outward and perceive it is called knowing. When we turn inward, though, it is not-knowing. As we are conditioned to knowing things we have a feeling that realisation must be a similar kind of knowing, but it is not. It is being. Being of what? Being of knowledge itself. If in Realisation knowledge was knowing Knowledge, it would be a subject seeing an object. This is not the case. Being ceases precisely when a subject and its objects arise.

When being is turned outward, why does it seem to be all this? In the myths of creation we hear that God felt himself to be alone. He wanted to have company, so he decided to create all this. In some of the Upanishads, similar stories are related of the aloneness of the first spirit. The Brihadaranyaka and other Upanishads, which are highly philosophical and metaphysical rather than legendary, say that the same knowledge that is within us as being shows itself only by becoming *vibhūti*, specific manifestations.

So the Self itself changes, transforms. In those transformations are many new possibilities. It is like an artist who wants to express her artistic talent. If she does nothing, no one will be aware of her abilities. So she makes a sketch. But there are so many other possibilities. She can also paint, sculpt, build and combine materials, creating a tremendous variety of compositions. With a single pen or brush she can make innumerable artistic creations. All this variety is nothing but the expression of one single mind.

Similarly, when we speak we use only our single mind and our organ of articulation, but when properly manipulated it can produce an infinitude of sound systems. With the utterance of each word, a new concept arises, new meaning arises. These are also *vibhūti*.

A musician can make different kinds of tonal effects. With the aid of a poet, words and shades of meaning can be brought to expand the possibilities. By combining the rhapsody of poetry with the melody and harmony of music, a musician can make endless variations. Each variation is a revelation of the potentiality of his own musical nature.

The Self which we speak of is not a bland nothingness. Our very Self is like an ocean of potentials. Its own nature is just beingness; at the same time it is infinitely creative and expressive at the level of life. Where it expresses, it is as if knowledge, to know its own potentials, is changing into all this. Think for a moment of a beautiful sunrise in the mountains and no living being with eyes turned to see it, no conscious mind to appreciate what is happening. Doesn't it seem like a total waste of all the form, colours and beauty when there is no one to witness it? In the Spring all the flowers would come and there would be no one to be stirred by them, no bees to buzz deliriously.

When we consider all this, the human mind and senses are not the private preserve of the individual who wears them. They belong to the entire universe. They are the universe's way of perceiving itself.

Those who believe in evolution think of an earlier stage preparing for a more advanced form of organisation. They think of the body as nothing more than matter organised in a certain form. If we trace the history of life on earth over billions of years, it looks as if it has all been pointing to the development of man. If that is indeed the culmination, it would seem that the entire universe has been in the plight of trying to know itself by evolving matter into living matter, living matter into organisms, and organisms into more advanced organisms until consciousness was developed. After consciousness was attained it needed to be refined and expanded by developing the faculties of sensation, feeling and cognition, ultimately putting together all these into a framework of cause and effect. Only then could consciousness have a full comprehension of the universe. And who is seeing that universe? The universe itself is seeing it through the developed faculties which it created over billions of years. That's the scientific theory.

In our study of *Ātmopadeśa Śatakam*, we have learned how to go beyond time, space, names and forms. When considered from this perspective, the Self is beginningless and endless. It is not confined to any form or name. In spite of having no special attributes, every attribute that we can give to conscious life is part and parcel of it. So we may say that in order to know its own nature, the same knowledge has become all this. This is not very different in practice from the scientists' approach.

One key characteristic of consciousness is that it alternates. At one moment it goes back into the darkness; there is nothing, it just remains there. In the very next moment it becomes many subjective fantasies in the world of dreams. Then it wakes up and comes into the outer world of transactional awareness. Here it interacts as if it is separate from everything else. It goes into flights of imagination and thought, experiencing all sorts of moods. Then again it enters the stillness.

The Guru is here comparing the wonder of what we are to a person taking a burning twig and swirling it around in the darkness, making a figure eight movement representative of the movement of consciousness through its various states. There is just the one burning point where it glows, luminous, but when it is brandished about it looks like many fiery lines and shapes. It is like writing with a pen: there is only one tiny point from which a little ink is coming, but as you write the ink makes different formations, and each formation has a meaning of its own.

What is the difference between your writing and your thinking? Your own mind is a point of consciousness which moves like the tip of a pen. If you turn inward in your own mind, the point of your consciousness is just a glow. If that glow is allowed to operate and unfold, it is like the pen writing. It is more than just putting ink on paper, though. The ink can become a Ramayana, a Mahabharata, an Odyssey, a Divine Comedy — the magnum opus of a great writer.

All our philosophy, history, poetry and even art have passed through the tip of a pen. Like that, this whole universe which we see, with all its vastness, is the composition and organisation coming from our own individual consciousness. No one else sees for us or knows for us. Even what are considered to be the experiences of other people have to be recycled and made our own before we can truly know them. The vastness we see is what we have created out of something so small: a tiny spark.

This is one of the greatest miracles of life, that the very creator whom we praise for having made all this universe is still sitting here and creating the very nucleus of our own being. Your nucleus and the nucleus of the universe are not two. When you attain that identity in every moment of your daily life, you become the centerpiece of the universe; your actions, your ideas and your thoughts become the very thoughts, ideas and variegations in the composition of your universe. This brings you to an ultimate identity with the creating faculty. You are at once the Absolute and the very many relatives within it. You are the one unconditional Being who is also causing the many conditional states.

Verse 34

aranoṭiyādiyarāḻiyārnniṭum tē-
ruruḷ atil ēṟiyuruṇṭiṭunnu lōkam
aṟivil anādiyatāy naṭanniṭum tan-
tiruviḷayaṭāl itennaṟiññiṭēṇam

Mounted on the rotating wheels of a chariot which
have half-moments and such for spokes,
the world rolls on;
know this to be the beginningless divine sport
that is ever going on in knowledge.

When we think of the world as we experience it, we are aware of a vast space around us. We are always placed in the exact centre of a space in which it is equidistant to the horizon in all directions. We can never go near the horizon, and we can never be away from the center. No matter how hard you try, even if you run as fast as you can, you will always be in the center of the space bounded by the horizon.

We know that vast space, incomprehensible and ungraspable, lies beyond the horizon. We can only refer to it as the other side. In the spatial context, this is what is presented as behind and before us. Although we are experiencing only a part of space, we conceive of a whole to which the part belongs.

Space is only half the world picture. The other half is experiencing this moment. Just as there is a horizon around us delimiting our spatial experience, there is also a horizon of time. In space we have a front and a behind; in time we speak of a past and a future. In between the past and the future is the present.

In Indian mythology, time is looked upon as the son of Vivasvan, the sun. The sun begets time naturally. From its rise and setting we experience dawn, morning, noon, afternoon, evening and midnight. Time is considered a cycle of the sun, a recurrence of mornings and evenings. This is why Kala, or time, is considered to be the son of the sun.

In his *Confessions, Book II,* St. Augustine takes up the issue of time. He struggles very hard to understand the paradox of the passage of time or change in eternity. He addresses God, saying, "Oh my Lord of Eternity, why do you make time trickle drop by drop?" In his day hourglasses were used to tell time, in which sand drops little by little: the sands of time. He said, "When you call, the hours flee." Ever since St. Augustine's day, time has been a problem and a paradox to Western thinkers.

In his analysis of time, Augustine asks what is past? Is there anything called past-time? He argues there is no such thing. We have only memories of things that happened. Memory becomes a memory only when it is relived in the present. When you recall something you have once lived and then experience it again in the present, you see that its contents have become pale, the carcass of something previously alive. The nonsubstantiality of it is remarked as 'past'.

There is also nothing called 'future'. When we imagine in the present how it will be, the content of that imagination is called the future. Since we are imagining in the present, the time is present. But how big is it? Augustine says we can at least measure space and say it is 2 square miles or 10 square miles, but how big is the present? And before you have looked at even one moment to measure it, half of that moment has already slipped away from you. It's not even a full moment.

Narayana Guru says *aranoṭi,* half a moment, time is constituted of half moments. The Buddhist school of Vijnanavada thinks of this world as coming into existence in one-third of a moment, remaining as an experience for one-third of a moment, and disappearing in one-third of a moment. Before we recognise it, one-third of the whole moment has already gone by.

When it comes to time, we have to think in terms of eternity. The greatest paradox is that in eternity we experience something so fleeting. Although it appears to us as very minor, nothing has more confused the minds of philosophers and scientists alike than the very elusive problem of time. Everyone knows time, but at the same time no one knows time. You only know that there is a clock on your wall with hands that move. The clock on the wall is not time. The best minds in the world have all tried to figure out what it is.

Newton thought he could fix at least two categories of absolute in space and time. That started the trouble. Then came Lorentz' contractions and Einstein's special theory of relativity, which invalidated Newton's concept of absolute time. Minkowsky speaks of the rotation of the time-space axis, how the time axis and the space axis are to be taken together. These are very complicated issues.

St. Augustine's confusion was later attributed to what is called the confusion of passage: you think time is passing from the future to the present, that there is some hidden place called the future that time is popping up from. It comes rushing along like the rabbit in *Alice in Wonderland*, saying, "No time, no time!" and then it is already gone, into the hole. From where did the rabbit appear? Alice didn't know. Where has it gone? It has already disappeared into the hole. It looked at its watch and said "There's no time." That is called the present, only that much. The passage of the rabbit is the whole story of time. But if you read St. Augustine you will see he is putting both hands on his head, howling and crying, lamenting and calling to God to come and clear up the issue of time.

Others say that the old man is crying because he thinks of a passage of time. One part of the "myth of passage" is thinking of an ocean of time which we are walking into, conquering time moment by moment with our forward progress. The ocean of eternity is just lying there and we are entering into it. That is one fallacious way of looking at it. Another is that we are standing still and the stream of time is flowing past us. These are the confusions of the philosophers. When we come to the scientists, the confusion becomes not doubled or tripled but manifold.

Bergson brings in the idea of pure duration. He says you have already vulgarised the physical time you are speaking of by relating it to a machine. Thus you have spatialised your time, labelled it and made it convenient. This is not at all the same thing as time as duration.

Does machine time really exist at all? When you fly from Honolulu to Fiji, for instance, somewhere on the way our modern, packaged time inexplicably slips off. You can sit on the plane with your eyes open or whatever you want to try to hold onto time, but when you land a whole day is missing. What nonsense is this?

St. Augustine also wondered about how time could be measured. You cannot measure time like you measure space. If you want to measure a table, you just put a yardstick on top of it and read thirty-six by forty-eight or whatever. But you cannot use the same kind of measuring rod on events. When you try to apply it, some parts of the event are already past. They do not stand there for you to measure them, they change. How can you measure change in the midst of change, when you don't have a baseline to compare it to?

The sun — the original timepiece — is not stationary. It is moving at a very fast rate of speed, taking with it the whole of the solar system. The planets within the solar system have their own motions, while the galaxy that contains this solar system is moving in a completely different manner. Each system, from the atomic to the galactic, has its own set of relevant measurements. If you sit in a plane going five hundred miles an hour and throw something up in the air, it should be at least five miles behind you by the time it comes down. But that doesn't happen: it comes right back down into your hand. Outside the plane it would happen, inside it does not. Somehow the inside space is kept intact and separate from the space outside through which the plane is travelling very fast. The same happens with the planets in the solar system: despite the speed of travel there is a kind of immunity within the local system, where a neutral stasis prevails.

At each level of the system, different vectors are applied to what you are trying to measure. The more you take into account, the more complex the whole thing becomes. Eventually it seems to be nothing more than a vast, confusing flux. You can go mad trying to pin everything down.

The Guru says, "Don't be silly, don't break your head on this. The whole thing is a divine sport. Why do you worry about it?

Whoever had the fun of making the world just did it this way. So take it easy. It's only a joke." The ancient rishis didn't worry their heads about time. They just sang a song for it. The confusion started with St. Augustine, and by the era of philosophy we find Henri Bergson and Bertrand Russell calling each other names.

It was Einstein who promoted time as another dimension. A thing has not only a spatial relevancy but a temporal relevancy. Everything exists within a time-space continuum. Narayana Guru did not read Einstein or his special theory of relativity, but he saw the whole thing as being constituted of fractions of seconds and moments. He pictured the world as a chariot, with its wheels providing the movement. The wheels are made up of spokes of half seconds. Using half seconds for motive power, the world rolls along for all eternity.

In this verse the Guru brings in flux as the numerator factor, and eternity as the denominator factor. In the first half he speaks of fleeting time, and in the second half of *anādi,* the beginningless. The numerator and the denominator are brought together in such a beautiful way, one seeking the other out, that you get a numinous presence of the whole without any confusion about the time factor.

What is this *ādi*? *Ādi* means etcetera. We have already mentioned that what we call our world experience is constituted of name and form. We hear so many names. Many are identified with forms but some are not, and they probably never will be. For instance, everybody has heard the name God, but no one has yet identified him, pointed and said, "Here exactly we have that fellow called God. This is it." Of course, there's plenty of mistaken identity. Many are called God. God must be sitting somewhere and laughing, seeing the folly of people calling this man "God" or that icon "God." God says, "I will never reveal myself. They can go on looking all they want!" And God, why don't you want to reveal yourself? "Because I am not. Only if I *am* can someone find me out. I am not, yet these foolish mortals have invented names for me. It's their folly. What can I do?"

So there are billions of unidentified names. Also, there are many mysterious forms. We don't exactly know what they are, but we don't want to admit defeat so we give them names. We don't know what time is either. God only knows. We do know a little of space.

For instance, we know how to walk from here to the corner store. And that's about all we know.

Name and form, space and time, actor and action. I am speaking now, so I must be an actor. What I am doing is called an action. If you think of the world, you also have to think of who moves it and what kind of movement it has. Then there is cause and effect. Things are to be related as effect stemming from cause. We do not know exactly where cause becomes effect. Is the fruit the cause, or the seed, or the germinating seed, or the sprout? Aren't they also all effects? These are all just arbitrary distinctions we make, because we really don't know.

Universal and particular. The forest and the trees. How many trees make a forest? Fifty-two or fifty-three? There are so many categories. We assemble them all within this tiny glow or spark of our own consciousness. But they do not really exist, they are just postulates made by the tiny spark. They are the showmanship of the great magician. Whoever that is, it goes on making the projections of space and time, name and form, cause and effect, and so on.

This is my joy. I dip into the unconscious and come back into consciousness and make all these things, play with them for a time, and then go back. Then I come back and start doing it again. That's the joke which is going on. God is a little baby sitting in the centre of our own consciousness. Out of nowhere he creates an infinity of space. Out of half a moment he makes pure duration. With that infinitude of space and infinitude of time he fills a world of wonder and rejoices.

And yet, within that same world, fully knowing all this, we cry out, "I cannot adjust to that fellow. He has become so nasty." Or "Today has been a very negative day. It makes me unhappy." Or even, "I can't take any more of this life, so I'll just commit suicide. There's no other way." Knowing that all this is a joke, why don't you laugh at yourself? That's all that is to be done.

Verse 35

oru patināyiramādityēyar onnāy
varuvatu pōle varum vivēkavṛtti
aṟivine mūṭumanitya māyayāmī-
yiruḷineyīrneẓumādi sūryyan atrē

Like ten thousand suns coming all at once,
the modulation of discrimination arises;
the veil of transience covering knowledge is maya;
tearing this away, the primal sun alone shines.

We experience an external world full of objects of interest. Our five senses are drawn towards the magical charm of objects outside, such as the world of forms to see, the world of sounds to hear, and the many sensations of touch, taste and smell. But no attraction keeps you glued to it forever. If you always hear the same sound, no matter how sweet it may be, it becomes monotonous. You tune it out or move on to something else. The most pleasant touch becomes irritating if it goes on too long, and the same is true of the other senses.

Each sense brings momentary interests to the mind. The mind is delighted. The same senses also bring painful experiences which agitate the mind. Thus the world outside is the source of all pains and pleasures. Both pain and pleasure come and pass away alike. In the Bhagavad Gita, Krishna asks Arjuna, "Why do you lament about things which come and pass away? Both pain and pleasure are only momentary."

The senses relate to the external world. We also have an interior world we relate to with our mind, where we make ghosts of the objects of perception and experience nightmares of our own creation. Our fantasies help us to create a fool's paradise and revel in it, and our own fears assume definite shapes, which then haunt us and make us paranoid. This inner world is as transient as the outer one.

Our life alternates between the external world of momentary pleasures and pains and the internal world of fantasy and nightmare. In order to experience the external and fantasise the internal, you need consciousness. It is the same consciousness — the same knowledge — that is lending its light, ideation, meaning and value to be projected on the screen of the external and internal worlds. This is the same knowledge that is referred to in the first verse as the Knowledge that enters all other knowledge and that transcends all forms of fleeting awareness. The same knowledge is described as the supernal Sun that shines in the firmament of consciousness and becomes everything. The same was also shown to us as that limitless knowledge and the depth in which all untold values lie, and also as the light which was never lit and will never be extinguished. It shines and looks on. This is the one unchanging essence which is behind all the changing moods.

The wise one who knows the secret of aum knows this knowledge. He remains as That. It is considered to be the all-verticalising knowledge which shoots down the birds of sense enjoyment. It is described as the witnessing consciousness that sits under the shade of the tree of life. This is the one light that links everything and brings homogeneity to the world of multiversal identity. This light is described as having no base or crown. It is infinite. When it prevails, it makes this world as dear as a garland made of fresh flowers. When one is open to it, the world outside ceases to have any differentiation such as here and there; or sky, atmosphere and earth. As well, the internal world no longer has any divisions like knower, knowledge and known.

Pure knowledge transcends the three modalities of sattva, rajas and tamas. When it comes it is described as a flood of sound that transforms the desert land of our meaningless life into an oceanic treasury of the highest values, where every grain of the sand of our life is turned into a pearl of priceless worth. When one is tuned to it, it is as if he is suckled on the milk of the Absolute. To him, ten thousand years are just a passing moment.

This knowledge of all knowledge and light of all lights is described here as *vivekavṛtti*. Śaṅkara's *Vivekacūḍāmaṇi* opens with the insistence that one should have the power to discriminate between truth and untruth, the Self and the non-Self, and the fleeting and the eternal. As we are torn between the world outside and the world inside we always miss this centerpiece, which is the only reality.

Once in a thousand years, one among millions stumbles upon his own reality. Then it takes not even a fraction of a second for him to wake up to his own light. Prince Siddhartha, seeing the woes of the world, saw evil in the pleasures which he was fed in his own palace, so he discarded everything and went in search of wisdom. Not knowing where it was to be found, he went from guru to guru and country to country. With all his wandering and search and mortification of the body, he still could not find anything. At last, feeling it was completely hopeless, he decided to give up his life. He sat down under a tree and vowed to not get up until he either knew truth or left his body. Then, like a flash of a million suns rising all at once, illumination came to him. He became the Awakened One, the Blessed One, the Buddha. Until that happened the knowledge which had always been within him, which had never departed from him for even one second since his birth, was a closed book to him. In fact, it was this very light which prompted him to begin his search, led him from one insightful occasion to another, and finally revealed itself to him. At once all his doubts were sundered and he was shown what reality is. Its reverberation remains today as a consolation for the world, the eternal dharma, the noble truth.

A long time ago there was a young man who felt very distraught. He was drawn to a man who was preaching on the banks of the river Jordan. That man was giving baptism with water. This young man from Nazareth, called Jesus, also went there. When he was baptised it was as if all the lights of heaven were thrown open to him. The eternal spirit within him revealed to him the highest possible truth. By gaining that light he became the light of the world. It all happened in a fraction of a second, yet even today, in millions of hearts, he brings the message of light and love.

In the scorching desert land of Arabia a man was overwhelmed by the hot sun, so he took refuge in the coolness of a dark cave. He sat there withdrawn in reverie. Sleep overtook him. He was roused from that state by a strange vision. He saw before him a shining face asking him to read. He was about to plead that he was an illiterate who had never known how to read, but like a stroke of magic his eyes were opened to the secrets of the written word. He read books that had never been written, things that had never been recorded on any parchment.

Thus the Holy Koran came to Mohammed. He became the prophet of Truth, Love and Peace. How did it come to him? He did not go to any school or university. Nobody taught him. The whole fount of wisdom was within him all the time. Suddenly it blazed forth and he was filled with a light. From him, like a conflagration, it spread.

On the battlefield of Kurukṣetra, Arjuna stood dismayed, shedding tears in confusion. He did not know what he should do, or what he was doing with his life. He was a man confused about his own dharma. Then he had a cosmic vision. The world outside and the world inside all transformed into a series of values. He saw all values as emanating from one supreme source, Krishna, whom he had previously misunderstood to be only his friend and lifelong associate.

Like that, this knowledge is our own lifelong associate. We carry it around with us all day and sleep with it at night, not realising that the whole cosmos is lying buried in the unknown reality within our own self. There is essentially no difference in how the light comes to any of us, masters or simple folk. When we finally do discover it, it comes all at once in a flash.

To Sri Ramakrishna it came as the love of the Mother, tender, caressing, chastising, illuminating, opening up new secrets, gently showing him the path, teaching him how to behave, how to relate himself to the rest of the world. It resided in his lips as the answer to every question, the solution to every problem. How did it come to him? No one knows. He was a simple, illiterate person, who had never had any training under any guru, but when divine grace opened up in him he combined in himself the essence of all religions. His vision was that of a great seer, one of both the East and the West.

Narayana Guru describes the dawning of knowledge in this verse as the coming of ten thousand suns all at once. The intensely bright light puts a stop to the great sport of maya, which is beginningless but not endless. It always lives only in half second increments. Half a second is converted into millennia, while the history of a millennium is squashed into a single moment in the form of memory. It is so strange that you can go back in your mind through the memory of generations and generations of people who you do not know, and think of what happened billions of years ago.

Even scientists, who are supposed to be factual and down-to-earth, speak of the Big Bang and things that happened over a period of fifteen billion years with an air of "objectivity." It is as if our mind can unroll itself like a ball of twine and find, somewhere at the other end, the very beginning of the world. Or we can stretch our mind into the future and see what will become of this universe, of a sun which is slowly burning out like a celestial candle and a day when there is no sun, no stars. All these imaginations are possible right now in the span of half a second.

Thus in half a second our imaginary world of eternity resides and is rolling on. This fantasy can be stopped in a fraction of a second if we suddenly wake up to the light, which is what has allowed us the occasion to fantasise in the first place. Those who woke up from their reverie and found this light not only came out of the blues of their own lives, but also became the torch bearers of truth for the whole world.

This is possible for us to achieve. If we can relieve ourselves for just a little while of both the outside world and the inside world, so that we come to know the source, then all the external and internal will be flooded with that one light. That is all that is required. Then we can share the grace which was the Awakening of the Buddha, the descending of the Holy Spirit on Christ, the Revelation of Mohammed, the cosmic vision of Arjuna, the integral vision of Ramakrishna, and the unitive understanding of Narayana Guru. It is our heritage. We are That. We can share it in our daily lives. AUM.

Verse 36

aṟivinu śaktiyanantamuṇṭitellā-
maṟutiyiṭām 'sama' 'anya' yennivaṇṇam
irupirivāy itil anya sāmyamārnnu-
ḷḷuruvil amarnnu teḷiññuṇarnniṭēṇam

The power of knowledge is endless;
the end of all this can be marked as "sameness" and "the other";
thus, in this way, there are two divisions; in this, merging the other with sameness,
one should remain awake to that clear state of being.

The word 'knowledge' in the English language is used in a passive sense, so by translating *aṟivu* into knowledge we minimise its meaning. The dynamic power implied in the word *aṟivu* is not in knowledge. When we hear the word 'knowledge' we think of some impression being presented to the mind as a state of awareness, but this is only one small aspect of the word we are translating here.

We have already defined the Self as that knowledge which shines by its own light, and by which alone all our experiences are produced. When we say 'consciousness' we also imply the unconscious, which is the substratum of consciousness. In fact, consciousness is only a very fragmentary part of the general unconscious. Similarly, when we speak of *aṟivu*, we also mean that which is prior to a thing that is being known, what the state is in which it is known, in which direction it moves, the reason for such movement, what it can affect, how it can affect, what motivation arises, and what causes that motivation itself. All these implications are to be taken in one sweep to understand the word *aṟivu*.

When we say infinite are the powers of knowledge, our reference is to the totality of existence. The word 'existence' brings another limitation. From the very first dawn of our search for knowledge, we are confronted by the limitation of language. As soon as we express a thing, that expression remains limited within the boundary of a concept. For the sake of communication we attempt to express aspects of what can never be conceptualised by defining and presenting them in the form of concepts. The limitation of any one concept makes it necessary to amend it by bringing in more and more concepts.

Henri Bergson describes this as the gold coin which you can never fully match, no matter how much copper change you have. You can go on shelling out pennies all day long, but you still have the feeling that they can never be adequate recompense for the gold coin.

Let us start with the primary notions of knowledge. The very first knowledge, and the consistent knowledge I have, is what I term as 'I'. There is no other knowledge more intimate, more clear, more consistent and thorough, than knowing that I am. When I look into the content of what I call 'I', it's an awareness. When I say "I know I am," what is the difference between the first 'I' and the second? The first 'I' seems to be undefined. When you say "I know," the status of the 'I' changes into a knower. You conceptually use the idea of knowing to understand 'I'. The clear awareness that shines exactly where you have presupposed 'I', is now identified with it. In fact, you recognise an awareness, and you have now decided to call that awareness 'I'. It took an act of knowing to arrive at that decision. Furthermore, there is an act of awareness as well as a state of awareness. The act of awareness is in knowing the state of awareness. It is somewhat difficult to differentiate between these two.

Actually, the distinction is primarily a verbal one. 'I', the awareness of 'I', the state of being 'I', and the state of functioning as a knower, are all various ways of putting the same thing. In substance, only one thing is happening. There is an awareness of an awareness of an awareness. It can continue ad infinitum.

So much for the first part of the statement, "I know." The second part is "I am." A state of knowing and a state of being are combined into this second 'I', and you are underlining its beingness by saying

"I am." It is an existential statement. Just what is it that pervades the whole through all the different states implied in it? There is no real difference between being, knowing and inquiring. When you say "Who am I? I am so and so," you are making a presentation and a judgement. The judgement brings you a comfortable feeling that you have solved the problem.

One's consciousness remains always the same, over and above all differences and distinctions. For convenience we call this transcendence. Within that transcendence we have established existence. Philosophers like Husserl, Heidegger and Jaspers saw these two aspects as inseparable yet different. They felt the need to speak of both. Kant made a general distinction between pure reason and practical reason. Transcendence is a major factor in pure reason, while practical reason has to touch the empirical level at every point.

It is impossible for me to see you, unless I consider myself to be one person and you as another. I must become the subject and you are put in the category of the object. Seeing means I direct my eyesight towards you and I specify your form, your colour, and your distinction from others. I also have to separate you from your background. Thus, a number of empirical differentiations are to be made for me to know you. I not only decide that you are, but I also decide that you are not anything other than you. To arrive at this I use a process of elimination: I eliminate the other from you.

Even in a simple item of knowledge there are many differentiations. Still, we don't feel that it is a complicated task to know things; knowing is so simple. It only becomes difficult when I describe it. We look at the world and we immediately know it is there. We have no problem with it. Berkeley says that philosophers kick up dust and then complain of clouded vision. It is only because of the dust they have raised that they cannot see clearly.

Scientists do something similar. They look at a flower and are curious to know how one flower differs from another. They are never satisfied until they give the flower a family name. In order to do all this, they tear the flower open and take it apart. They compare the ovary, pistil and petals with those of other flowers. Only then can they classify and categorise it. And what have they added to knowledge by doing this? Nothing. But their curiosity is not satisfied unless they know all these things. So, we have taken upon ourselves the task of analysing everything. Does it have any value? It is only useful when we have to apply something at an empirical level.

We started this discussion with the primary notion of 'I': "I know I am." The second thing is "I am experiencing the world." This implies a major division: I am the subject and the world is the object. In the Bhagavad Gita, Chapter Thirteen, the knower is called *kṣetrajña*, the knower of the field. This is taken as a major principle for understanding our own Self as the knower of everything and the non-Self as the field of that knowledge.

This kind of usage can also be seen in the language of existential psychologists, who talk about the ego and its boundary. The ego boundary can be expanded or contracted. For instance, I sit here and look at one of you. I say to myself, "he's a very friendly person; I love him." I include him easily within my boundary as someone safe. Then I notice another person and think, "That man is a stranger; I don't know what he thinks of me. I'll bring my boundary inward a little so that he will be just outside the fence." So the ego boundary is not fixed; we are constantly adjusting it. It can be expanded or contracted, inclusive or exclusive.

This ego boundary is not the same as the difference between the Self as a knower and its field of knowledge, however. Everything coming within the ambit of knowledge is part of the field. It is in no way limited by the idea of mine and not mine. My lover and my enemy, what is strange, and even what I don't know are all within it.

Now let's go a step further. Can we imagine the existence of anything without knowing it? If I say I don't know Brezhnev or I have never seen Mao Zedong, I am speaking of my ignorance of two people. For me to do this, I have to postulate in my mind what I am ignorant of. So even ignorance is the knowledge of what we call ignorance. "I only know my knowledge" is a very misleading statement. I am again using the word 'knowledge' in a passive way. What is the 'I' but knowledge? It is knowledge knowing knowledge; it is knowledge that says "I do not know."

When we are seeking knowledge and finding it, who is it who seeks it, and just where does the seeker get knowledge from? These are really mysterious things. You presume that you do not know when you seek, and yet you seek in a certain direction. How do you decide this is the direction you have to move? Who motivates you, moves you? What intuition comes to you to say that there is a knowledge to be sought and found? Look at the millions of inventions we have made to make life so very comfortable. Look at all the technical devices, the artefacts. All these have sprung up from nowhere. They are all the creations of knowledge.

Knowledge can be just passive consciousness, a desire, a dynamic that makes you restless until you get up and seek and find and realise. Knowledge is a zest, a compulsion, a perseverance. It is the joy of recognition. It is fulfilment, accomplishment, effort. The whole of life and everything happening in it is nothing but that knowledge.

Knowledge is dynamic. Not one moment passes without the movement and transformation of it. And what transforms? There must be a substance that transforms. This substance cannot come from a fresh supply somewhere, since it already represents totality. A fresh supply would imply that it originated from somewhere and that it had been originated by something and that it gets expended somewhere else. It is not like that.

Physicists decided to say there is a conservation and a transformation of matter. The total mass is the same, yet within it many changes are taking place. '*A*' changes into '*B*', '*B*' changes into '*C*', and '*C*' changes back into '*A*' again, but on the whole it is the same. Indian philosophers consider the total substance the same as the conservation of matter. Within the total substance are countless possibilities for transformation.

We have to live both these aspects. I have to get up from my bed, look in the book and find the verse we will meditate on today. Then I read it, examining each letter separately, combining those letters into words and the words into sentences. I look into the logical structure of the sentence and get the meaning of it. All these are empirical activities, and I cannot neglect any of them in preparing for the class. I come and sit here. I recognise all of you and understand the situation of why I am here, why you are here, and what is expected of me. All these are again simple empirical matters. Irrespective of the great wisdom to which it may belong, there is action going on. I have to articulate meaningful things, and you have to listen and make meaning out of them by pondering over them. So we are all engaged in activities all the time. All these activities are happening with one consciousness.

We are always moving, shifting and changing our attention from the particular to the universal and from the universal back to the particular. The universal aspect is here called sama, sameness, and the particular aspect is called anya, the other. As you can see, sama is etymologically related to 'same' and anya to 'another'.

There is a likelihood of our making the mistake of getting caught in the particular. When this happens we stand always divided, treating 'me' as sama and 'you' as anya, and finding no way to come together in a common interest. The other possibility is to clasp our hands and sit together in silence, sharing the feelings of wonder. Then we forget that there are many. We also forget this 'I'. Then there comes a great peace, a great serenity, a joy that is not a form of excitement. In that joy everything merges. At least for some time there is no other. We need this, very deeply.

When we read the Bible, we always see Jesus walking away from the multitude. He goes to the mountain or he walks alone on the shores of Galilee. There he is one with the sea, the sky, the clouds, all of nature. It is as if he does not exist. We can imagine that serene moon-lit night, gentle waves with silver crests, musical rumblings of the ocean, and a lonely man standing there, looking into the vacant sky and feeling oneness with all. Even that very thought brings so much peace. Then we see him again with the multitude. There is a need for feeding people who are hungry. There is a need to heal people who are sick. There is a blind man who wants to see, a leper who wants to be cured, an unclean woman who wants to become clean and whole again. There are necessities and political controversies. There are people spitting on the face, reproaching; there is a trial, a heavy cross to be borne, the stark reality of a nail being struck, blood coming.

All this in the life of one person! Then it is as if it was all a dream. Like the passing of a nightmare or a sweet dream, it is all done with. It is all just phenomenality, yet within that phenomenality there is a noumenon, a continuous breathing pulsation of reality.

The unreal shadows are created by the real light. If you are contemplative, there comes an attitude of transcendence even in the thick of life.

Perhaps someone is getting into a heated argument with you, trying to start a fight. It can be any activity really, an encounter or a joyous relationship also. The empirical reality of the situation, which you term necessity, is very clear to you. You willingly offer yourself to play the game. In any case, a person of little wisdom forgets himself when he is fighting or relating positively. But for someone who is established in contemplative discipline there is an overriding resonance of an enveloping knowledge, which assures him of the general condition that is both the ground and the total environment of the specific game going on. Because of this, inwardly there is detachment and outwardly there is conformity to the demands of the situation. Yet there is no hypocrisy involved. You are not pretentious in your game and at the same time you are not affected by it in the way of a person who is fully infatuated with a situation.

When sama and anya, sameness and the other, interrelate in this harmonious way, it brings the quality of the highest kind of inner peace and calm to our life. When life is so protected with an integrated wisdom, there is no dissipation of your energy. It is all conserved. It is hard to even comprehend this state unless you are already established in it. But I assure you it can be attained. You can do this. You can be what you are, going on with all your games of life, and yet be detached from it. Deep within you is that aloneness which is not of the individual. It is the aloneness of the universal, the aloneness of God, the aloneness of substance, the aloneness of the real. Nothing happens to it. By retaining that aloneness, you can be the many.

When you touch, there is all the gentleness and care of the touch, but you are also not touching, because you know the beingness in which the touch and the touched are the same. The necessity to touch comes to assure you that you are already One. When you kiss, when you embrace, the urge comes because of a seeming forgetfulness saying, "Oh, what made us two?" We are not two, we are the same. It is as if your true beingness is broken into bits and pieces by the empirical nature of your sensory motor functions and changing transactional situations. Again and again beingness has to assert itself. It operates as a great love, a great caring, a great sharing, a feeling of wonder, a going back into serenity and reestablishing yourself in peace.

A garland is made up of a number of flowers and thread. We can appreciate and enjoy each flower separately. As we examine the colour, smell, texture and softness of each one we forget about the garland. If we treat it as a whole garland, the flowers blend together and lose their individual identities. It is also possible to think of it as both flowers and a garland: this is the integrated vision.

Narayana Guru is not asking us to run away from the particular to the universal, but to transcend the duality and live and accept both these games together. Then we will be living in our beingness and also allowing every little aspect of becoming to come to pass. In an earlier, very beautiful verse, the Guru said that knowledge, in order to see what it could be, becomes all this. This is what we are doing all the time. We don't relish eating the same food every day. The elements may be all the same: flour, sugar, rice, vegetables, but we make a new composition and serve it in a new way each time. So a new aspect of knowledge is revealed by the specific expression as it unfolds. It is placed as part of the universal, and the universal lives on through the particular we enjoy.

Although some have interpreted it this way, we are not advocating the negation of life and the running away from it. We do not say any of the luxuries of life are stumbling blocks to realisation. Nothing is to be thrown away. Rather, everything is to be seen with a new attitude. That new attitude is the old attitude that you know everything is One. It is a very joyous way of accepting life and a wonderful way of living it richly and beautifully.

Verse 37

viṣamatayārnneẓumanya vennu koḷvān
viṣamamakhaṇḍa vivēka śaktiyennyē
viṣamaye vennatināl vivēkamākum
viṣaya virōdhiniyōṭaṇaññiṭēṇam

The other is replete with difficulty;
and it is hard to win over without the power to discriminate the unbroken;
having won over the difficult,
attain to that discrimination which is opposed to sense interests.

What we seek is peace, the peace that can be associated with unbroken happiness. Where there is unbroken happiness there is also peace. This can be true only if the happiness is founded on truth. Truth does not change; what is true today should be true tomorrow also. Thus truth is consistent and continuous. Truth has an inner homogeneity, and if you are experiencing it, naturally you will be in a state of harmony.

Love is a state of great harmony. Stress or hatred is opposed to that harmony. Peace is opposed to restlessness; harmony is opposed to disharmony; truth is opposed to untruth; beingness is opposed to becoming. Thus we see there is the paradox of a dichotomy in our life, and we are looking for a solution by which we can get over it.

When our consciousness operates, a dichotomy arises from the very heart of it. One half of it is experienced as 'I', and the other half is experienced as 'this'. Another way to think of it is 'I' and 'the other'. The other, unlike 'I', manifests as manifold units. We can say "this is my friend," "this is a pot," "this is my hand," "this is knowledge." In all these we are referring to 'this'. And what is 'this'? It is a very indistinct thing. We only know what qualifies 'this'. If we take away all the qualifications, 'this' becomes too difficult to grasp. The whole world is a proliferation of 'this'. So we can either say "that is this" or "this is that." At a distance they are not two.

The idea of 'this' enters into the mind and goes on bifurcating consciousness into many units. The net result is that it brings interaction between the 'I' consciousness in us and thisness. The 'I' consciousness is not just a philosophical idea, it is socially structured with an egoistic status. This ego is monitored by our changing moods. Sometimes it is in a sublime state, sometimes it is in a passionate mood, and sometimes it is very depressed. It is not always the same. Its moods create a quality within our interactions, which very often take away our peace.

There are a number of things which we are exposed to in our lives over which we do not have full control. It is very peaceful to have a sound sleep, but if the mind is disturbed sleep won't come. You cannot force yourself to sleep. If you just say "let me sleep," it doesn't work. The mind has to become subdued from inside. The upsurges of consciousness have to become quiet. Of course, you can take a sleeping pill, but that is kind of a temporary suicide: you are killing your system with some poisonous medicine for a little while. You can also use the same medicine to put an end to all your misery by killing yourself completely, but then you have a permanent suicide. Natural death doesn't come like that. You cannot die at will, although you can kill yourself at will. But we are not planning to do any killing. If we die, we die gracefully. Like that, sleeping gracefully is different from forcing ourselves to sleep with pills.

How does sleep come? Nature has a rhythm. When solar energy goes to the other side of the Earth, we, being heliotropic people, experience a waning of energy. Activities become subdued, and sleep comes. If the mind is stimulated, either with stimulants or with thoughts, motivations, urges or passions, it will continue to be lively. Natural sleep is a blessing which comes only from inside.

Like that, we cannot forcefully love anyone. All religions exhort us to love, but if I walk into my neighbour's house saying, "Jesus said to love my neighbor as myself. I have come here to love you," they will probably get very annoyed and tell me to mind my own business. So you cannot force your love on anyone, it has to come in a very natural way. If someone comes and says, "I love you very much", that's OK. But if they were to say "I love you so much; why do you reject me?" I can't help that. If you love me I should also feel something reciprocal, and in this case I don't. One can't pressure another. Love comes only spontaneously. Of course you can create a situation in which love may grow, but all you can do is be available and wait for love to come. It is like sleep: both are natural occurrences.

Peace is also a natural thing that has to come by itself. Concentration is a natural thing. You cannot concentrate just by straining your eyes. Swamis from India may come and say, "Look at this candle. Put it on a stand at eye level and stare at it." Or they will ask you to breathe in a certain way. When you get exhausted from breathing hard, what else can you do but lie back? You might imagine you have gained something. The world is full of trickery. Someone finds out a way to trick your nervous system, and then they sell it and patent the technique. But there is nothing spiritual about any of these things.

The real issue here is how to win over anya. Anya means the tendency of proliferating otherness. We are disturbed only because of this anya, this otherness. Wherever otherness comes it interacts with the 'I' in us, affecting our balance. If the 'other' is not there, our 'I' has nothing to fight with. The cancellation of the 'other' and the ego brings peace.

And how can we cancel out the effect of the 'other'? The 'I' and the 'other' must be unified. By knowing what constitutes the 'I' is the same reality as that which constitutes the 'other' brings unification. We can also know that this 'I' is a fantasised modification of consciousness and the 'other' is a fantasised projection of consciousness. Both are false. Once we know that neither the 'I' nor the 'other' exist, there is no trouble. But it is not as easy as it sounds.

We have a body, and the body is equipped with its senses. Each sense organ brings a different kind of stimulus which acts upon our system. Many chain reactions come from just looking at a thing, say, or hearing a word. Thus we are bombarded from all sides with stimuli. In that bombardment it is next to impossible to sit quiet and calm.

Let us briefly catalogue the difficulties we have with this. It begins with this exposure to stimuli which create a number of reactions in us. Secondly, our mind gets into certain whirlpools; these mental whirlpools are called worries. We are exposed to two main kinds of worries. One is retrospective remorse, and the other is prospective anxiety. Retrospective remorse comes in the form of guilt: "I have done such and such a bad thing, now what can I do? My self image or my social image is tarnished. I am no longer the same honoured person in the eyes of my friends. Society is now suspicious of me; my integrity is questioned. Nobody will accept me as an honourable person any more. I have lost something precious in my life. I am deceived, cheated, defeated." We become bitter over our remorseful remembrances of the past and we feel worthless, annoyed, angry or vulnerable.

We also suffer from prospective worries such as feelings of insecurity. Our calculations have gone wrong. We see new factors rising up which we are uncertain about. We do not know how to deal with the new situation. The stock market may drop unexpectedly. Someone may corner the market on some product or raw material and make the supply dry up. If tomorrow the Egyptian president gets angry and closes the Suez Canal, all the shipping in the world will have to be rerouted and all the world's trade will be delayed. The same thing could happen in Panama. Some fool can even do something to unhinge the whole world. And who knows? Maybe someone is planning a sneak attack on us.

All these worries are in people's minds, but they can affect the whole world by making us act in certain ways. We are living in a society; we are not separate individuals who can fully insulate our lives from the onslaught of social trickeries. So we are afraid of the next one. How can we ever get out of these whirlpools of worry? They are empirically valid. They are not entirely our fantasies.

Another category of difficulty is the deep urges and passions in us that create various kinds of hungers. The hunger of the body itself is a great problem for the world. There are so many countries where the hunger for food is a daily experience. The hunger of the mind and of physical passions can be even worse than physical hunger in the sense that it can drive you to act inappropriately, to be a victim of your own drives. I have young friends who are very troubled because of their sex problems. They have not found a proper person to relate to, and so it has become a terrible conundrum. There are some others who have a hunger to be intellectually or spiritually nourished. They write me that they do not have a proper person around to talk to, with whom they can discuss anything serious, valuable, philosophical or spiritual. They feel as if they are in an arid desert land where there are no worthwhile values.

We could go on multiplying this catalogue of the blues of life. But what we need to know is the way out. Even a small pinprick in one of your toes is enough to affect you totally, taking you out of your mental and physical balance for at least a little while. Your body can develop so many kinds of diseases. It is actually a great wonder that most of us at least seem to be sane. It is easy to go insane in this world, yet there is still a fair amount of sanity left.

Anya, this differentiating factor, is always running amuck and creating problems for us. In fact, the whole world is in an eternal state of strife because of otherness. The Guru says that somehow we have to triumph over this great fear of the other and bring all to a sameness. He gives us a key idea here, *viṣaya virōdhini,* that which is opposed to a sensual orientation. *Viṣayam* means projecting the source of your happiness onto a thing and thinking it is the thing that makes you happy. Therein lies the crux of the problem. Once you think, "Without this thing I can never be happy," you have already alienated your happiness. You have created a chasm between your present state and a prospective future where happiness can be encountered. By default you have decided that at this moment you are not at all happy; you can be so only in the future. You feel that somehow you have to move away from the present to the future, and you won't be happy until then. You worry that you might miss this thing in the future in which your happiness is invested, and that your search will be a total failure and an absolute disappointment for you. Thus we alienate our happiness and postpone it via the *viṣaya* of the object of happiness.

If, on the other hand, you know that you are the source of all happiness and there is nothing to seek on the outside, the outer thing becomes associated with happiness only because you allow it to participate in your happiness. Discrimination is the key to making this happen. What kind of discrimination? The Guru says *akhaṇḍa viveka śakti,* it is not a discrimination which makes a thing different from you, but a discrimination which makes something also you or you also that. It is a unifying discrimination, not a separating one. If 'this' and 'this' and 'this' can all be brought under 'This', and then 'This' and 'I' are brought together as one, then you get it.

This is the reason Narayana Guru asked us in the very first verse to see the common link between the outer world and the inner world, which he described as Karu, a universal consciousness which is the divine manifestor of everything. He said we should withhold our senses and prostrate before That again and again. He asked us to look at the unlit light which shines within us. All that we see may look different, but it is the same light. When we turn to that light and allow it to guide us we get *akhaṇḍa viveka śakti,* an unbroken sense of discrimination.

Throughout all these verses the Guru has been telling us how we can get over our troubles. Back in the thirteenth verse he said, "Look at that Supreme One which transcends the three modalities: sattva, rajas and tamas. Pick the flowers of your mind and offer them to that Divine One. Turn your senses inward; cool the feverishness of your life; get your obligations unwound; merge into the glory of That." He told us of the blessed grace that comes to us like a flood, which fills the desert land and turns every grain of sand into a precious stone. He also told us to offer the flowers of our mind to the Divine if possible; if not, we should make a programme of actual worship and expression of devotion or we should philosophically meditate on great dictums to get over the illusions of life.

The ultimate thing is to become *saumya,* which means finding the quietness within you. It is by attaining sama, sameness, that you become quiet inside. This is to be cultivated throughout. Each day begins a new series of encounters. Each encounter is to be taken as a challenge to reestablish your inner serenity, inner quietness, inner sense of sameness through an act of adoration, an attitude of worship and a sense of the sublime.

There is no need for you to win all the time. Your greater victory lies in your acceptance of defeat, allowing the other to win. You may be in an argument. What does it matter if you win or not? Give the other person the chance to win. Even if he uses some falsehood, when you allow him to win he rethinks the situation. In his heart of hearts he knows he did not deserve the victory. He knows the truth of your silence. You do not become egoistic and you don't make the other person egoistic either. It will chastise him as well as purify him.

Thus, through the cultivation of silence, sameness and serenity, you come to a unitive understanding from within. This brings peace and harmony. Where there is peace and harmony, love spontaneously comes. When you give yourself into the hands of grace, the hands of the Divine, things which are difficult to attain become abundantly possible. Then you can say you have attained the discrimination of the unbroken, by which every 'this' is brought under the spell of the universal sameness.

Verse 38

palavidhamāy aṟiyunnatanyayonnāy
vilasuvatām samayennu mēlilōtum
nilayeyaṟiññu nivarnnu sāmyamēlum
kalayil aliññu kalarnnirunniṭēṇam

What is known as many is the other,
and that which shines forth as one is sameness;
having known the state, which is going to be spoken
of, and attained release,
remain dissolved and blended in the state of sameness.

These words are to be understood in a very special way. In the usual Malayalam sense, *nivarnnu* means a person becoming upright. In Nataraja Guru's commentary he has taken it in that sense. But I am taking it from the original Sanskrit source. In that there are two complementary terms: *pravṛtti*, the path of action and *nivṛtti*, the path of release. Those who are caught in the path of action get entangled in many action-reaction situations and bondages of karma. One who works out his release from this is called *nivṛtti*. I am taking the word *nivarnnu* in this sense, as one who is finding his release.

There are various differentiating prejudices in which our mind is caught. Regaining the mind from such bigotry is also to be understood as *nivarnnu*. A man may believe he is a Christian or a Muslim, that there is no other true religion, and that if you do not find your salvation that way you are doomed forever. His mind is caught in a certain way of thinking. It may be well and good for him, but it pits so many other people against him, and he cannot share his way of life with them. In this way we make factions and differentiations, which are the basis of conflict. How we release our minds from such kind of bigotry is what the present verse explores.

A special term here is *sāmyamēlum. Sāmyam* means likeness. Someone may be playing tennis and someone else football. Superficially it looks quite different, but if you look for identity you can see both are sports, and both give entertainment and physical exercise. The mode may look outwardly different; still there is *sāmya,* likeness.

Another word to understand is *kāla.* It is a term that comes in Yoga and Tantra. It is to be understood in the context of two other words, *nāda* and *bindu. Nāda* is the subtle vibration of sound. Our whole body itself has an unbroken sound, which the yogis call *anāhata.* The central locus of your psychophysical life is called *bindu.* When you are breathing up and down it is likened to a mantra which is said to be equivalent to the articulation of *haṁsa,* also an unbroken sound going on within you. It can find its own centre or *bindu.* When you concentre your consciousness in any of the synergic centres, it is as if consciousness is flowing or streaming centripetally and centrifugally, while keeping that locus as a monitoring force. One may find it in the centre between the brows, the heart centre, the throat centre or any of the other centres.

When a certain interest develops from the centre of your being, it enlarges and becomes a whole field of interest. As a function, this aspect of the self is called *kāla.* If you are looking for differentiation, the *kāla* will be seeing differences everywhere. If you are looking for unity, then you will find a hundred reasons for seeing all as the same. One has to cultivate the *kāla* of sameness as a functional reality, not just as an idea.

When we examine our external tastes, we see that they differ very much. One man's meat is another man's poison, as they say. In the Gospel according to St. Luke, Chapter Thirteen, Jesus says, "If you think I have come to bring peace, nay, that's not it. What I've brought is division. In a house of five people, three will be against two. In a house of three people, two will be against one. I have placed a discordance between father and son, between mother and daughter, between the son-in-law and the father-in-law."

What's with all this discord? When we think of Jesus, we think of unity, so its hard to understand this statement. We can find sense in it only when we think that the unifying factor is transcending the pettiness of all relativistic considerations. In this world everybody is full of relativism and therefore there is no agreement. The agreement can come only when you transcend this and see the Lord or whatever.

In the Mahabharata, the children of two brothers became a divided family, a divided home. There, one hundred people were pitted against five. The divisions multiplied. Those who were loyal to the five became one group and those who were loyal to the hundred were another. They decided to fight, and there was a great battle. When Arjuna came to the battlefield wanting to wage war, he was asked to look at his enemies. When he looked around, he was surprised to see his friends on all sides. He couldn't believe he was standing there bearing arms against his own grandfather, his own teacher, his cousins and best friends. He thought, "How can I fight these people? How could I go on living after killing my best friends, my close relatives? What is the meaning of life?"

So on all sides we have discord, division, strife. What Jesus said may seem very cruel, but it only acknowledges what is happening in most houses and most families. The husband is against the wife, children are against both. One year we may find them in great love, saying "God is showering his special mercy upon us." The next year they are at the marriage counsellor and then the divorce court. What is all this? It is called anya. Narayana Guru says that this tendency is seen everywhere, differentiating, separating, breaking away, alienating, rejecting. The rivers of tears that are shed because of this have no end.

There is a way out. It is called sama, cultivating sameness. In the Bhagavad Gita, Chapter Six, a whole series of verses is given to tell you how to cultivate sameness. First of all, there needs to be a basis for sameness. In the Bible the basis is to love your Father, your God, with all your heart, all your soul and all your mind. Then what happens? You find that all mankind has the same Father, which makes everyone brothers and sisters. Then we become responsible and committed to each other; we become each other's caretaker. We share and care for each other because we belong to the same Father. The first statement brings a corollary: to love your neighbour as yourself. Sama, sameness, comes where you say "as your own self."

So the very Jesus who said "I have brought division," also gives the antidote. The absolute nature of "all your soul and all your heart" means you have no selfish reservation. It is a total consecration. You are giving up completely.

Today I was writing to a person who occasionally asks for counselling from me, a very wonderful person full of love, piety, devotion, and great love for God and for other people. But there is always one spark of doubt in the mind. It is a very tiny spark that snowballs and becomes a big cloud of darkness and confusion. Then for six months everything turns out to be meaningless and frustrating. My advice was to give up that tiny little doubt and to be without any kind of a reservation: to love totally. When you whole-heartedly give, then you receive in full measure.

So, anyway, in the sixth chapter of the Gita Krishna says, "Be established in me. What makes a thing what it is, is its beingness. A thing becomes stable because of its beingness. Know me to be that beingness. Without me nothing can be, because I am the beingness. After having found it, feel devoted to it. Let your love flow toward it as the one beingness in all, as the one beingness which makes truth truthful, goodness good, beauty beautiful, love endearing."

You cultivate this through constant meditation. I am not speaking of meditation as sitting cross-legged with eyes closed, or some such. Life itself is a meditation. Everything passing in our life is a theme of meditation. When you say "this exists" and "this does not exist," what enables you to say it is that beingness. That is what we are asked to adore as the one God. It is up to your taste to call it God, or the Supreme Principle, or the one reality, or beingness, or what you poetically feel within you as the greatest empathy you can have, the sense of beauty you feel as an artist, the great love you feel as a lover. In all these there is a substantiality of beingness. You sense it from your heart.

Then the Gita says to see That as your own central reality. You are constantly saying "I am, I am, I am." What assures you of that "I am" is the light within you. "I am That" is just like saying "I am that I am." See it as the Absolute in you. Thus, having found beingness as the reality of everything, and as your own reality, it is easy to see that the real in you and the real in all other things are the same. This is how you gain the secret of sameness, *sāmyam*. It will bring you great serenity, great peace.

When you are seeing sameness but others are not, will you still have peace? Does this work when others do not see it? If your children are restless, and they are shouting and running around the house, you just think, "Well, it's their age. They are young and have a lot of energy. In my childhood we were all like that also. If I love my children I should allow them to have their free expression. Let them play. How happy are my children that they are so exuberant!" Then you don't feel annoyed. You rejoice that your children are healthy and cheerful, running around and making a lot of noise. So if you think of the others you are not disturbed, but if you think only of yourself in isolation it could be very irritating.

If the children are not yours but your neighbor's, they are even farther outside the small circle you draw around yourself. The *anyata* comes here: "They are not mine. They belong to someone else, the other." If they come running into your house and raising a ruckus you at once feel hatred. You drive them away. "Don't they have their own house to make noise in? Why should they come bother me when I have things to do?" You cannot bear them for even five minutes. Your *dṛṣṭi* — how you look at it — has changed.

When you know that the Self in you and the Self in others is the same, that knowledge brings *maitrī*, compassion. If someone is mentally upset, you don't just tolerate it. You embrace that person and share their feelings in order to help. Cultivation of this compassion brings about fellowship.

When your compassion becomes a functional reality, *kāla*, then it is as if you are melting into it. The idea of *kalarnnirunnu* in this verse is that you melt into the state of the functional reality of your vision of oneness. *Sāmyamēlum* is when the feeling of oneness is felt from within as an experience of universality. You don't see yourself as different from others. Everyone is free to advocate their own religion, their own way of life, eat their own kind of food and speak their own language. You have taken away all the barriers in your mind. You think, "It's OK, it's all mine. All the three worlds are mine and these are my kinsmen. I don't have any sense of differentiation." It has become *maitrī*, true fellowship.

You bring about oneness through wisdom, compassion and fellowship. At this juncture in the Gita, Arjuna says to Krishna, "This all sounds very fine, but I have to actually live it. My mind is not under my control. Like a wild wind it comes. Sometimes a ship lying quietly on the sea will be caught by a wind which drags it away and batters it and breaks it to pieces. This is exactly what my mind does to all my decisions and good intentions. I take a good resolve, but like a typhoon the mind comes and whips it away and wrecks it. What can I do?"

Krishna agrees. "That is so, my dear Arjuna. Mind cannot be forcibly controlled. Sometimes it is like a whirlwind. But don't you see that the mind is not a whirlwind all the time? Your mind may be restless for a little while. It may smoke and fume. But after some time it calms down, and when it does you have access to it. That is the time to show it the right way. When the mind is sitting calmly, show it there is no need to boil. Your true nature is divine, and everything is a manifestation of the Divine. Don't feel agitated. Deep down the mind understands. The next time it raves, somewhere it will know that this is not the right thing to do and it will settle down faster than the previous time."

In this way Krishna shows how to gently tame your mind by detaching yourself from the things with which you are infatuated. Also how, by continuous *abhyāsa*, continuous practice, you can make it learn to love everything as aspects of the one Being or the one Supreme. How, by maintaining *vairāgya*, detachment, and doing *abhyāsa* continuously, you will one day be able to make your mind fully in harmony with your vision of oneness.

The meditation of this verse is to watch for the many tendencies to close down or become narrow in your vision. Instead, enlarge your boundaries and thus find your *nivṛtti*, release. Only then will the functional reality of seeing oneness become a persistent way of life.

Verse 39

aruḷiya śaktikaḷettuṭarnnu raṇṭām
pirivivayil samatan viśēṣamēkam
virati varā viṣamā viśēṣamonni-
ttaramiva raṇṭu tarattil āyiṭunnu

To continue, of these forces just mentioned,
the second division, sameness, is of one quality,
while for the first, the difficult, there is no end to its qualities;
thus, these are of two kinds.

In verse 33 it is said that knowledge, in order to know its own potential, changes into the many known things. It enters into various states of clarity and obscuration. Sometimes it forms a pronounced dichotomy of the knower and the known. At certain other times it becomes the passive witness, where the knower aspect is not emphasised, watching the ongoing procession of known items flashing through consciousness as objects of awareness. Sometimes it leaves the world of the known altogether and sits by itself, ruminating "I am, I am," very much centered in the subject. Much of the time it alternates between the subject and the object: first clear, then vague. There are also moments when it withholds from the sphere of awareness entirely, where nothing is known. And lastly it is capable of effacing the duality of the subject and object, not negatively, but in a very positive way, by transcending the modalities.

When we examine this movement of knowledge, we can see that it always moves within itself. When you look at the flow of life horizontally, it passes sequentially from one thing to another. Each moment, or even less than a moment, the attention is fixed on one particular aspect; the very next moment the whole scene has changed and attention is with another interest. Narayana Guru uses the analogy of the spokes of a chariot wheel to describe the mind's movement from interest to interest. Even though the wheel has many spokes, the whole weight of the chariot rests on just the one spoke which is vertically below the hub. As the chariot moves the burden goes to the next spoke and the next. The image shows us that even though the shifting interests differ from moment to moment, the cumulative effect is constant.

Although we are drawn as though blindfolded by a negative or dark instinctive pull, we need not remain always in the state of negativity. There are two ways to deal with our lot in life. The lower animals, from viruses and bacteria up through most mammals, have a stream of development and a life plan that are fixed by nature's own devices. It is as if they have a set programme to go by. To them, life is a continuous passing show and they don't look back with any sense of regret or remorse. They don't have any assigned duties for tomorrow; they don't sit down and scheme and plan. A bird which needs to build a nest and hatch its eggs does not figure out how it is going to do it tomorrow. In the morning when it gets up it instinctively picks up little pieces of cotton and thread, leaves and broken twigs. Then it makes a nest. Just when the nest is finished, the eggs come. It's all so very well adjusted by nature. If someone breaks the eggs or pulls apart the nest, it flutters around for a little while and then forgets it.

Although they look mechanical, the bird's actions have an absolutism in them. Similarly, a drop of water in a stream goes on dancing all the way from the mountain top to the ocean. It merrily plunges ahead, unaware of what awaits it, whether there is a smooth bed or a plunging waterfall, whether it will always be pure and clear or contaminated by some city's effluents. It has no thought, it just goes.

We human beings have a different approach. Of course it's true that some of us are not so very different from animals or drops of water in a stream. We just go on, meeting contingencies as they appear in front of us. But in all of us there is one difference, present in varying degrees. The animal and the drop of water don't have any special obligation to anyone, but man makes promises and gets into obligations. When he drifts from one thing to another, there comes the constriction of previous commitments like the tug of a string wound about his limbs. Then he turns back. The alternative for him is to always be fully alive and wakeful to the whole situation. Then he does not allow any particular interest to infatuate him so much that he becomes blind to reality. The animal force which makes life mechanical is very strong. Most people cannot resist it. We just get into the mainstream and flow with it. Only here and there do we find the rare person in whom the whole meaning and significance of life has opened up, which brings a clarity like ten thousand suns shining all at once.

The Guru has said that our knowledge has innumerable powers, which can all be brought under the two headings of sama and anya, the same and the other. Sama is unitive consciousness. Even when you go from one thing to another, you know it is a continuation of the same interest, of the same consciousness, all within one ambit of existence. Anya is when the unitive aspect is blindfolded so you don't see it. You only see one thing at a time, and you get caught up in it and it fills your whole mind. For a time you are fully absorbed, not leaving even a little of your awareness on your transparency in time and space and the meaning of life.

Then he went further, saying that in our knowledge there is an indistinct aspect which calls for a clarity in every item of knowledge. This is called *viṣamā*, the difficult to discern, such as when you say "This is a pot," or "This is a friend." We do not really know what "this" is. We only know that it comes as a calling of attention to an awareness. When we specify "pot", "my friend" or whatever, our interest is immediately shifted to what we have specified. We don't bother about "this," because our interest is caught up in the qualifying aspect, *viśēṣam*.

We are speaking here of two pairs of ideas: sama and anya, the unitive and the differentiating; and a subdivision of anya, the difficult to discern, *viṣamā*, and the specifying quality, *viśēṣam*. Narayana Guru defines anya as that which is known as variegated, while what shines forth as the one whole is sama. He then asks us to keep our mind open and vigilant so that we can release ourselves from being blindfolded by the infatuating source of the specifying thing which comes in the form of 'other'.

In the present verse, the Guru is taking us a little deeper into the differentiating aspects. From the day of your birth to today, there is a constant return of consciousness to its core or centre. It always goes back and touches the centre. Then from the centre it goes to the periphery, where it deals with objects. No matter what the function is, the general nature of the experience is an illuminating awareness, a Self awareness. It is Self luminous. There is no other agent to throw light there.

Whether you sit with your eyes open or closed there is a consciousness that illuminates you, which brings awareness to you. It is always there, unbroken. Sometimes it takes the form of a wakeful consciousness. At other times it is like a dream consciousness. And sometimes it is a deep sleep. You are not wakefully aware or having dreams, but as soon as you wake up you remember it was a good time: "I had a good sleep." There is an awareness there which was very passive, and yet it lends itself to be recalled.

If you are so favoured to become a yogi who can transcend the three modalities and remain in a calm, serene state, where you are totally one with your Self, that transcendental state can also be related with the other three. Then the whole thing can be known as pure knowledge.

On some level, you have been experiencing pure knowledge all through until this moment. And what is its quality? It is just awareness, Self awareness. Within that state of awareness, two kinds of 'this-ness' are coming to you. One says, "This is me," and the other, "This is what I know." One 'this' pertains to the knower and the other pertains to the known.

When you said 'I' when you were two, four, ten and twenty years old; and what you will mean when you are fifty, sixty and seventy; you will always recognise as the same 'I'. You go on saying "I am this," and "This is me," and you have no doubt that the 'I' who said it yesterday is the same as the 'I' who says it today. The 'this' does not have a varying connotation from moment to moment and time to time.

The 'this' of the knower always remains constant, whereas the 'this' of the known can never be the same. It always changes, even if it sometimes seems repetitive. Infinite are the possibilities of the structuring of consciousness. Narayana Guru says there is a 'this' which is always one, and there is another 'this' which is infinite. *Virati* means termination; *virativarā*, that which has no termination. So we get *virativarā viṣamā*, that which is difficult to discern and yet has no termination. This pertains to the whole world of knowledge. Another *viṣamā* pertains to the 'I' itself. As we are flooded with the interminable interests of the passing objects to which our senses and mind are tuned, we are like children running to one toy after another.

If only we remembered that all of the passing show is an experience of our own consciousness. If we could sit back on the bank of the stream of consciousness, rather than drifting away like the water drops within it, we would have a different attitude towards life. Verse 39 requires us to be a constant witness of our own existence. This helps us not only spiritually, but on every level, in every way. When you are caught in an emotional situation, remember *virativarā viṣamā*, that difficult aspect which is interminable, which is taking you from one mood to another, one emotional state to another, one kind of appreciation to another; it has such a hold on you that you lose your power to restrain, to observe, and to be neutral and impartial in your observations. Instead you become identified with what happens to you each moment. Knowing this helps you to step back and free yourself from the entanglements of the situation.

When an actor is on the stage, appearing for all the world completely at home and alive in his role, deep down he knows that when the play is over he will no longer be that character. He doesn't carry the ups and downs of his character home with him. Even a person who dies on the stage gets up and walks away when the curtain is dropped. This brings a kind of lightness and freedom that are otherwise quite difficult for those who are attached to their personas to achieve.

In fact, our life is a continuous play, with continuous action and continuous staging. We have to get up and walk away from our roles moment by moment, but we forget. We are very deeply affected by events in our lives. We become so involved. But if we can have this little detachment, to sit back and see that this is a passing show going on, it will give us all the great strength and patience on earth. You are always just who you are. Somebody says you are good, somebody says you are bad — that belongs to the passing moment. Their remarks do not make you more good or bad than you actually are.

Detachment enables you to have a better appraisal of the passing moment. This is not only for your final salvation, but also for your salvation here and now. Your consciousness is flashing quickly between the knower and what is known. That which oscillates between them is the same consciousness, and it is you. So sit back firmly in your detachment, and yet also participate in the stream of life as it flows by you with its eternal rhythms.

Time has a mood. In springtime the mood is to dream, to plan, to make endless promises jubilantly and hopefully. You think it will always be spring. You are outgoing and optimistic. Then when fall comes, the mood changes. Your dreams change colours, going from bright to dry and brown. They break off from the main stem, flutter in the wind, and blow away into oblivion. The sweeper comes and they are all swept away. Your promises were of spring; in fall they are no longer valid. The mood changes again when winter comes. You withhold yourself from the periphery and sink into your own depths. You are one with yourself; you are now most important to yourself. It is very cold and still outside, snowing. Then once again when spring returns, you come out.

This is one possibility. It is good for the trees but not so good for us. The tree has no remorse about dropping its leaves, but we do. If you find a girlfriend or boyfriend in the spring and you drop them off in the fall, after six months when you see them again you will get a peculiar feeling about your fickleness. Man alone has this kind of funny feeling, not trees or slugs or birds. And as you have it, you have to be careful.

So cultivate this attitude. Once you've solidified a permanent mood and developed your ability to witness, then you can play around a little in your daily life. Always remember: we are aiming this study at our everyday life. It is not some far-off, exotic philosophy.

Verse 40

samayilumanyayilum sadāpi vanni-
ṅṅamaruvatuṇṭatatin viśēṣa śakti
amitayatākilumāke raṇṭivaṟṟin-
bhramakalayāl akhilam pramēyamākum

In sameness and in the other each one's
qualifying force always comes and becomes established;
by the fluctuating function of these two,
which comprises all, everything becomes the object of awareness.

"I want to give you a special instruction." "Let us meditate together." The first sentence centres around the idea of 'I'. The reference to 'I' is very specific. When I say "I want to give you. . ." I am differentiating you from me, and when I mention a special instruction the emphasis is on something very specific. So in the first sentence our minds are drawn again and again to specific notions.

When I said, "Let us meditate together," no limitation was set. The word 'us' might be a reference to all the people in the room or all the people in the world. There is an all-inclusiveness, with no reference to an 'I'. It is a very extensive way of looking at things. Furthermore, the quality of meditative awareness is a uniting, synthesising, pacifying one.

It is important to realise there is no contradiction between the first sentence, "I want to give you special instruction," and the second, "Let us meditate together." One is complementary to the other. Although one sentence refers to everything specific and the other to everything general, there is a perfect harmony and complementarity between the two. In this special context, the one is not opposed to the other.

There can be many other occasions when the notions around the 'I' are centralised and all else is excluded from it, and that becomes a selfish motivation where others are deprived of their proper integration in the situation. Similarly, if all-inclusiveness comes as a regimentation, such as "all people of the state should behave in a certain way," then we have a totalitarian dictatorship taking away individuals' inalienable rights to decide for themselves. So we have to be very careful with these concepts and understand them correctly, or they can very easily become evil.

The personal reference can be beneficial, since only when we turn inward and centralise ourselves do we get an orientation of knowledge. It is necessary to return again and again to the centre. Knowledge should also be able to expand its horizon to include as much as possible. In this way it becomes a pulsation, in which consciousness moves from the centre to the periphery and back again.

You can intensely think of yourself, gather your thoughts, your emotions and your sensations, and bring them all to the centre of your consciousness. Then you can change the locus of that consciousness by shifting the centre. For instance, you can bring it to the centre of your eyebrows. With your mind you meditate on aum. You place that aum exactly in between your eyebrows, and mentally meditate: aum . . . aum . . . aum . . . . It gives a certain special effect. Then you can shift it to the throat centre, making that source of sound the centre of your whole consciousness. There you can repeat the mantra aum . . . aum . . . aum . . . . It's different from what you do between the eyebrows. You can bring the centre of your consciousness to your heart. Your breathing, inhaling and exhaling, can be felt there. Having found the rhythmic movement of your respiration, if you centralise your consciousness there and say aum . . . aum . . . aum . . . it changes the tone of the experience, its texture and shading. You can then bring it to the navel, and experience your lower abdomen as the centre of the system. Within the navel you can meditate aum . . . aum . . . aum . . . . It can be further shifted to the genitals, aum . . . aum . . aum . . . and finally to the tip of the spine, aum . . . aum . . . aum . . . .

You have been repeating the same thing, concentrating the mind in the centre and saying the same mantra, but the effect is always different. Whatever we do, we alternate the unifying and differentiating effects of the mind.

Again, you can think of the several parts of your body separately, such as the head, trunk, hands, legs, the little finger as different from the thumb, sight as different from hearing, the experience of touch as different from taste. There is no end to such possible differentiations in the body. All these are united when you say "I am." In the knowledge of "I am" you don't experience the difference between taste and smell, body and mind, or whatever.

Individuals can be separately known, with the mind seeing each as a special person. Then you can forget names and peculiarities and generalise, along the lines of "those of us who gather here to meditate together." Then the names and features of each person vanish.

It is not advantageous to pay attention to only half of any dialectical situation.

A harmoniously balanced life requires us to go from the specific to the generic and then back to the specific. Both have their own special dynamism and their own special perspectives to add. For instance, if I do not think of myself as a separate individual with an 'I' as the agent of my knowledge, enjoyment and action, I will not be able to motivate and carry out action with any efficiency. But if I become stuck in the notion of 'I', I will become alienated from the rest of society. I won't be able to rise up and identify myself as also belonging to that which is in all other bodies. I will become helplessly self-centered. I need to release myself from individualistic imprisonment within the body, to cooperate with all and receive cooperation from all. Sharing with all is mutually beneficial, as I become an integral part of a composite whole such as the society, the world or the universe.

If I expand my consciousness from my physical self to my family, I can see how every member of the family is so dear. This feeling can be further expanded to include other human beings and even pets who share our life; then broadened to the collective community of the environment, the country, the culture as a whole, its history and future possibilities. The entire universe can even be included, with its millennia of history and its macrocosmic and microcosmic aspects, such as the musical dance of the galaxies and the miracles going on within the depths of atoms. From subatomic particles to galactic supergroups, it can all be brought under one scheme of understanding.

Then time and space fade out. Our consciousness is no longer within the body. We can meditate on a world without us in it, without any of the consciousness we normally confine in the body. It is so refreshing, so releasing, not to be tied down to a heavy body on earth: to become one with the evanescent wind and the blue expanse of sky, to dissipate ourselves into the vibration of the sound that fills the whole universe, to become part of the thermodynamics of the universe, to become an electrical wave in the grand electromagnetic field. Think of these great varieties and wide possibilities of identification. What is there you cannot become through the sheer power of identity?

All the great meanings and purposes we thought we had can fade away to nothingness. We see the whole world as a myth: you are a myth, I am a myth. In the next moment we can be very definitive. We can fill our minds with a certain purpose, become charged with a great urge, feel that something is the mission of our whole lives, that we have to do it. Thus comes compulsion, stress, urgency. But we can also say "there is no such urgency. Never mind. It's all okay. There is no such entity called 'I' anywhere. It's all an imagination."

Your consciousness can tighten up and make you feel like a bundle, a compact body. The same consciousness can also release you from that tightening up and make you feel as free as a passing wind. As Jesus said, "The wind bloweth wither it listeth." Such is your freedom.

Narayana Guru says even though the possibilities of these two ways of thinking are endless — one centralising in your 'I' and making everything specific and particular, and the other expanding you, identifying you with the cosmic whole, generalising and liberating everything — it all can be gathered under two categories, the unifying and the specifying. Consciousness is an eternal fluctuation between these two fulcrums. It zips about, now rotating around the hub of specificity, now changing to rotate around the hub of generality. In this way it enables you to know everything.

If you go on reducing the differences in consciousness, taking away one after the other, ultimately there is no difference at all between the knower and the known in the state of total transcendence. Then you are in a state of absorption, of samadhi, with no modulations, no modification of consciousness. The other extreme is that you become infatuated with a single idea. It captures your mind so much that you become blind to the rest of the world. It makes you idiotic, stupefied. We call someone stupid because they are stupefied with just one idea. They have lost their bearings and have no orientation to the bigger picture.

You should not get stuck in one single idea, nor get lost in generalities. In a healthy life there is a constant fluctuation between these two possibilities. Out of this fluctuating perspective arises our idea of the world. This doesn't come about through any effort on our part, it happens of its own accord.

In this verse we are not trying to do anything in particular. It is only a familiarisation with our own self, a familiarisation with the mechanism of how consciousness functions within us when it is left to itself.

Coming to the spiritual part of it, once you know that your mind is so engineered that it fluctuates between the specific and the generic, between a psychological and a cosmological orientation, and that all these are natural functionings, it is a great relief. It removes some of the load of responsibility you have saddled yourself with. Instead of forcing your mind to follow certain patterns, you can just think, "This is natural. It is my nature that my mind becomes centralised and the 'I' consciousness tightens up. And it is also my nature that I become sober and pacified." You become aware of consciousness as such getting involved in these two-fold functions. One who can cultivate the neutral attitude where he or she becomes a witness to the two-fold fluctuation of consciousness becomes a real contemplative.

Verse 41

"itu kuṭam" ennatilādyamām "ite" nnu-
ḻḻatu viṣamā; kuṭamō viśēṣamākum
mati mutalāya mahēndra jālamuṇṭā-
vatinitutān karuvennu kaṇṭiṭēṇam

"This is a pot;" in that, what comes first, "this,"
is the difficult to discern; "pot" is its qualifying
predicate;
for intellect and such *mahēndra* magic to manifest,
this itself becomes the *karu,* thus one should see.

This is apparently a very simple verse, but it summarises the whole process of semiosis in a few words. Semiosis is the process of consciousness transforming itself into specific ideas so that it can become a communicable language.

Even though we are all living in the same world, and in some cases are even part of the same society, life is presented to each of us differently. From each person's standpoint, we see certain things as important and do not notice some other things at all, which may be very important to someone else. Like the great Creator who is said to have created this world, each one of us is continuously in the process of creating our own world.

This creation always begins by specifying our consciousness so that we can start from one point and then develop it further. The first step is consciousness presenting itself a question, such as "what is this?" "who is this?" "why is this?" or "how is this?" The question occasions a search, which is imperative because of the lack of clarity. The mind is asking for certitude, for clarity. And what is not clear?

'This' is not clear. What is immediately presented to the mind is not clear. When you qualify 'this' it becomes clear.

In the question "what is this?" there are two aspects. One is the 'this'-ness, the other, the 'what'. 'What' is the qualification of 'this'. When you say "this is a pot", 'this' is qualified with the specific features of a pot. Now we know what 'this' is. It has become clear.

The mind doesn't stop there. It will present another 'this'. So another question comes: "What is that sound?" If we don't answer the question, the mind won't be satisfied. So we think "It is a child crying". Then it's okay.

The mind goes on continuously presenting 'this'. When it is presented, it is vague. We want an explanation of it. Then the mind gives the explanation. For the mind to explain a phenomenon, a 'this', it has to summon previous memories which have qualities that resemble the new experience. We also use our senses as instruments to search out more about the qualities that can be attributed to the present situation, in order to clarify it further.

All this belongs to what we call semiosis. It has three or four stages of development. One is intrinsically connected with our basic urges and interests. It reveals itself only at the termination of each unit of experience. In semantics this is called pragmatics. Every bit of information which the mind gathers is to fulfil a certain need. The need can be biological, psychological, physiological, logical, mathematical or social. The fulfilment of the need comes only through the process that triggers the interest to turn the mind in a certain direction and give it its powers of manoeuvering. We are not at all clear about the level where pragmatics enters consciousness, because it comes from the depth of our unconscious. In Indian psychology this is called vasana, the incipient memories or latent urges lying buried in the unconscious. Once the seed of a certain interest starts to germinate, it presents itself at the threshold of consciousness; like a bell it calls you to attention. You recognise that calling of attention as 'this'. Then the question comes, "What is this?"

Your ideas are subtle, and those ideas are prefabricated concepts. If you are working in a library and are asked to find a certain book, you can look it up in a catalogue, which will give you a number corresponding to a shelf in a certain section of a certain room. Like that, our mind uses a kind of cataloging. Information tags are attached to all the mind's nomenclature. For anything which is presented outside, there has to be a corresponding illumination within. You bring that from inside and see if it squares with the data that is presented by the senses. If there is a one-to-one correspondence, then you identify what is presented to you with the *pratibhā*, or corresponding concept. They become riveted together. Afterwards there is no separation of what has come from inside you and what is presented outside. In your mind it is a continuous whole, so much so that you do not even recognise that the psychic aspect and the physical aspect have now become integrated.

So from pragmatics you go on to what is called logistics. Logistics makes your ideation structurally meaningful. For instance, the subject and its predicate have to be related in a certain way so that your predication of the subject makes sense to you. Then if you want to communicate something to another person, you decide how you are going to express it. This is called the syntax. Only with all three of these aspects — pragmatics, logistics and syntactics — is the process of semiosis complete, even in such a simple statement as "this is a pot."

Now let's go back to the very first verse, in which the Guru said *aṛivilum ēṛi,* transcending or entering into the texture of knowledge. The term implies both transcendence and immanence. He says that withdrawing your senses and having surrendered your ego in an act of devotion, you should prostrate again and again to the Karu. Karu is that substance or that reality or that yolk: that causal factor from which this cosmos and its psychological counterpart have both emanated.

Instead of describing it theologically as God, we are making a philosophical appraisal. The idea of the Supreme Cause is an adorable concept of the Absolute. We are asked to show our appreciation of this concept by inclining before it with an attitude of reverence, prostrating our egos again and again. This refers to the cosmological level. On the everyday phenomenal level, the same appears to us in our daily life in a million forms, always beginning with the simple question, "What is this?"

The questioning aspect of the mind is followed by the

summoning of memory. Memory brings an appropriate concept to the surface, which is then linked with the presented subject. Then you make a judgement of predication. After the predication you become affected. Thus the four limbs of the mind — interrogation, recall, judgement and value appreciation — all line up. Only when a value appreciation finally emerges at the end of this process are the pragmatics presented. Although this ultimately is the cause which made your mind go through the whole process, it comes only at the end.

When a potter intends to make a pot, the pot is in the future. He has not yet made it, but the possibility of the future pot impels him to act toward it so that as the final realisation he can accomplish the pot. The *abhāva*, the absence of a thing, is present in our mind as a possibility which is taking us from the future to the present. Usually we think that we are moving from the past through the present to the future. But it doesn't happen that way. The future is dynamic. It makes you move from a possibility to an actualisation. That which is actualised thereafter remains frozen as an eternal event, an accomplished fact.

If you can see that this whole process is happening to you moment after moment, day after day, you will understand your inside and outside a little more clearly. This verse shows it to be such a simple thing: in "this is a pot," 'this' is the indiscernible, 'pot' is the qualifying aspect. You are participating in the creation of the entire world. My world has its own quality, and your world has another quality. My world is full of a transcendental analytic, while Nijinsky's and Van Gogh's is filled with a transcendental aesthetic, and Thoreau's and Whitman's, poetics, to say nothing of the rishis and all the great works of the rest of the globe. For you, it is likely to be another world. For a doctor the world is patients and redressing pain and bringing them to their normal state of health. For others it is the world of business and economics. So many things emerge from nowhere and become the facts of our individual value systems.

One thing that is hard for most people to understand is the concreteness they create out of a subtle mind. For instance, a typewriter sitting there is a concrete fact. If you lift it, it is heavy. When you touch it, it is hard. When you operate it, it functions. You can create a desired effect by working on it. It is a concrete fact, but the concreteness, the sense of weight and hardness and so on, are all experienced in your consciousness.

It is not only concrete for you, it is concrete for me, too. Thus, it is a concreteness we can share, called the universal concrete. The universal concrete is a participatory function of all minds. Because of the minds' homogeneity, we fully agree in a transactional sense. The universal concreteness we jointly create gives transactional validity to our world. In wakeful consciousness, where two people cooperate in a situation, they are dealing with the universal concrete, unaware that the psychic aspect and the physical aspect are amalgamated in their knowledge through the process of semiosis.

Philosophers have written pages and pages elucidating this idea. Narayana Guru has expressed the whole thing in the first half of a small verse: "'This is a pot;' in that, 'this' is the obdurate; 'pot' is its qualifying aspect." Putting them together you get the idea of a concrete pot. That is a universal concrete. Once you hit upon a universal concrete you have not only made a present, you have also made a past, because that experience will remain with you for the rest of your life as a recorded event. It is frozen and kept forever.

Thus, the whole of the past is generated at this very moment by the promises and potentialities of the future. Is it not a great miracle? Is it not happening like a great magician's magic? You are the magician. 'You' doesn't mean your ego. Your poor ego is only one of the tools used by this marvelous magician who is sitting inside you. That same magician is in an ant, a fly, a bee, a bird, in an idiot as well as a genius, continuously making things manifest.

In the next verse, the Guru is going to ask us to turn to that 'this'-ness with more clarity. It is adorable, a wonder within you. In this type of understanding you become more intimate with your God than when you relate to Him in the situation of a church, where you are analogically putting Him outside you as a foreign entity. Here it's you, the very process that is going on within you from moment to moment. You can never get nearer or closer than this to the very Creator, because the process of creation is going on here and now in what you call your mind, your intellect, your understanding and your affectivity.

Verse 42

"idamaṟive" nnatil ādyamām "ite" nnu-
ḷḷatu sama; tante viśēṣamānu bōdham
mati mutalāyavayokke māṟi mēl sad-
gati varuvān itinebbhajiccitēṇam

"This is knowledge"; in that, what comes first, "this",
is sameness; its qualifying predicate is awareness;
for intellect and all such to vanish, and for the true
path to come,
this should be meditated on.

The most elemental form of ideation is the presentation of a subject and the predication of that subject. When a subject is first presented we say, "What is this?" We answer by making a judgement. Even when there is no apparent question, one is implied in the indicative term 'this'. *This* is so-and-so. *This* is someone else. *This* is knowledge. *This* is non-knowledge. Whether the subject is concrete or not, true or not, the indicative is there, and it is a symbol for the question the mind has raised. Next the question is followed by a judgement, which is the predication of the subject. When you say "This is so-and-so," 'so-and-so' is the predicate. In "This is knowledge," 'knowledge' is predicating the subject 'this'.

In an earlier verse, Narayana Guru described 'this' as *viṣama*, the part of knowledge that is difficult to discern. If one person is sitting in a room and someone else is standing outside asking, "Do you see this?" the one inside will have to ask "What this?" He won't have any real interest until he knows what 'this' refers to. So just hearing 'this' is not enough: you have to explain what the 'this' is. In fact, the entire process of our mind is to be all the time explaining 'this'. We have no other business. We just go on interpreting every 'this'.

There is another aspect of our consciousness which comes to a decision: "This is such-and-such." The part making the decision is called the intellect. In Malayalam it is *mati.* In Sanskrit grammar we have *nirdeśika, pratigrāhika* and *sambandhika. Nirdeśika* is that which integrates, *pratigrāhika* is that which you grasp or learn or understand, and *sambandhika* is that which relates one thing to another. Corresponding to these three in Vedanta are three categories of mind: the questioning aspect, *manas;* the recalling aspect, *cittam;* and the deciding aspect, *buddhi.* In logic, these are called the subject, the copula and the predicate: the subject is interrogative or suggestive, the copula is relative, and the predicate is the decisive.

So these triple functions are universally recognised to be going on all the time. Then there is an agent behind them, and in whom all these take place, recognised as the 'I'.

Now, just what kind of decision is the intellect making? It is deciding what name should be given to what form. It is coordinating a name and a form, a mental image and a corresponding word symbol. When you say "this is a pot," there is an image of a pot, which is a concept. 'Pot' is a sound which revives an image from your consciousness. The image is then conjoined with the sound. The intellect is finalising, out of a series of concepts, one which is most appropriate for each situation. This is then underlined and promoted as "the" concept.

This does not take place in a passive mind with no interest. Every concept is marked with a certain colouration indicating a value. These values are very dear to the individuated self. "Here is a piece of paper." "It is not just a piece of paper, it is a dollar." When you say it is a dollar, it evokes more interest than a nondescript piece of paper. With each sound, each word, each evoked form, a certain value also comes to the mind. And when that value comes to the mind, you react to it. Our reaction can range from a high degree of infatuation to extreme indifference. Just hearing a certain sound or seeing an image can evoke a whole variety of interests throughout this range.

There is an old saying that a percept without a concept is hollow, and a concept without a percept is substanceless. A concept is either a processed percept, or it is what is mentally perceived. Regardless of whether it is mentally or physically perceived, it becomes a unit of value. That unit of value cuts itself off from other values and the rest of our knowledge. Consciousness is chopped into many fragments by our deciding upon the values of things — items of interest — upon whatever is presented. Through this process every item of knowledge decided upon by the intellect vivifies the world, vivifies consciousness.

Where does it all come from? Out of the one knowledge. From this one overall knowledge we modulate one little piece, and then label it and put it aside as a separate entity. We already belong to a world of unity of consciousness, of universal awareness, which has no specificity at all. Then when indicativeness tickles the mind, one definite piece is carved and forged out of consciousness. And it does not stop there. Every indicative knowledge points you to a certain possibility for gratification. When awareness becomes specialised, a special interest in you finds an opportunity for fulfilment. Groups of these special interests get related to each other. Someone might say to you: "There is a new film out at the Bijou Theatre." Then you wonder: "What time will it start? Is it tonight? How will I get there, and who will go with me?" A whole chain of reactions comes, at the end of which you decide whether or not to go to the film. Thus, the specifying of knowledge leads you to action, and each action itself leads to other actions.

The whole network of daily life is woven by a series of one 'this' after another, along with their meanings. It is all done by the intellect, correlated to the person's ego, *ahamkāra*.

Narayana Guru says *idam aṟivu*, "This is knowledge." In 'this' is sama. It is the same in all statements of individual units of knowledge: all knowledge begins by saying *idam*, this. Bertrand Russell, in his *Logical Positivism*, makes an analysis of what he calls atomic sentences. In them, the nuclear aspect is 'this'. A word is like a bomb. When I throw the grenade of a word to you it bursts into your mind, with the result that a meaning is evoked. In Sanskrit this bursting aspect of words is called *sphoṭam*.

We are shooting at each other with the bullets of words. They come and hit us and we react to them. So our world of conscious activity is caused by the bullets of words.

If we sit in silence, it is fine. It is not the silence of a graveyard. It is an all-filling silence. We are not being with one specific form of endearment, we are in a natural state of eternal bliss. In the present verse, the Guru puts it that all the specifying aspects that come are aspects of consciousness, nothing else. If the intellect which is causing these specifications can be removed, you get *sadgati,* the right path. While *durgati* is the path that leads you to trouble, to bondage, *sadgati* is the path which brings you liberation. Vedantins also have two paths. One is called *pravṛtti,* the involved, that which binds you to action, the action-oriented path, while the other is called *nirvṛtti,* the releasing way.

The Guru's point is that if you seek liberation, you should ask the question, "What is this?" You don't ask "What is this?" in the way that takes you to individual specifications and things. You are aiming at the 'this' in the sense of "What is the this-ness?"

Ramana Maharshi always instructed people to ask the question, "Who am I?" Between the 'this' and the 'I' the whole range of the mental process happens. Most often, a guru or teacher instructs a disciple *tat tvam asi,* "That thou art." 'That'-ness is identified as you. And what is 'that'? That which includes everything. Everything that can be summarised in the indicativeness of the mind is 'that'. 'This' and 'that' are not separate. The whole realm of indication taken together is 'that'. 'That' is none other than you. So you are instructed to meditate on 'that'. Other instructions include *ayam ātmā brahma,* "This self is the Absolute," where you are meditating on 'this'; and *aham brahmāsmi,* "I am the Absolute," where you are meditating on 'I'. Ramana Maharshi's instruction is to meditate on 'I' when you say "I am the Absolute," in order to arrive at the transcendental notion of the Absolute.

Narayana Guru gives here a form of meditation for arriving at the meaning of two of the great dictums of the Upanishads: "That thou art," and "This self is the Absolute." He combines both into one and says *itine bhaji ciṭēṇam,* "meditate on this." This will clear your mind of the triple functions of interrogation, relation and judgement. These are separated, but they originate from the all-comprehensive 'this'-ness.

In the previous verse, the word 'this' is indicated as the yolk or the substance which makes everything. In the first verse we were asked to kneel before that knowledge which is everything, cultivate devotion for it, consecrate ourselves to it, make obeisance to it, and prostrate ourselves again and again. If a person is contemplative, he should have a detached mind so that he knows that even when he is relating to many things, they are all born of one consciousness, called 'this'. Then we will not be caught in the magic that we ourselves create.

We are strange kinds of magicians that create a magic which we then get caught in the snare of. We need to be so clever that we create only to amuse ourselves, and do not get caught.

Once I painted a demon on one of the walls of a house where I was living. At night, I became so afraid of it I couldn't go down the hall where it was. I had done it with chalk, so I took a cup of water with me and when I passed by it I threw the water on it. Then I couldn't see the chalk while it was wet, so I could go past. The next day I was not afraid, but again the next night I did the same thing.

Like that, we are always creating demons out of our own minds and getting afraid of them. Narayana Guru says to not get caught in this delusion.

Verse 43

prakṛti piṭiccu cuẓaṟṟiṭum prakāram
sukṛtikaḷ pōlumahō cuẓanniṭunnu!
vikṛti viṭunnatināyi vēlaceyvī-
lakṛti phalāgrahamaṟṟariññiṭēṇam

Even those of good action are caught by nature
and whirled around in vicious circles;
one should know that non-action does not bring release
from perverted action,
only the non-desire for the fruit of action.

The mainstream of the philosophic life of India is constituted of six systems of thought that are considered to be orthodox. These philosophies naturally fall into three pairs: Sankhya and Yoga, Nyaya and Vaiseshika, and Purva-Mimamsa and Uttara-Mimamsa.

The Sankhya philosophy, whose principal exponent was Kapila, derives its name from the fact that its followers count and categorise. It is by no means a theistic religion; it is an out-and-out rational philosophy. There is no room for faith or dogma in Sankhya philosophy. All its convictions are derived from a mathematically precise understanding. To begin with, they think of a binary function: intelligence along with a field where that intelligence can operate, or a field which operates in the light of that intelligence. Corresponding to this, St. John's Gospel in the Bible refers to God and the Word. Word is considered to be the substance out of which all creations have come. It has the capacity to become flesh. So the substance has a homogeneous link with God: the will of God and the intelligence in the Word are not different. Sankhya philosophy has exactly the same idea, but does not present it in a legendary or myth-like manner, as the Bible does. The language of scientists is used.

Sankhyans speak of two primary realities, *puruṣa*, pure consciousness, and *prakṛti*, the field of creation. Prakriti is comprised of the three modalities: tamas, rajas and sattva, or inertia, kinetics and the sublime state. Of these, tamas and sattva are polar opposites. Tamas is the inertial state where things are held together; it is obdurate and does not easily yield. Being opaque, it has maximum opposition to spirit. Sattva completely resembles spirit, though it is not spirit. A mirror by itself is only matter. It is not luminous, but it can reflect light very clearly. If you reflect sunlight into a dark room with a mirror, that light can illuminate the room. The original quality of the sunlight can be conveyed by a mirror, which by itself is inert and non-luminous. This is precisely the nature of sattva. It can clearly convey the quality of pure intelligence into the world of manifestation, but is not itself pure intelligence.

So Sankhya philosophy has this dichotomy of matter and spirit, prakriti and purusha. Within prakriti, the polarisation between the pure, clear sattva and the dark, inertial tamas creates a lot of movement from one to the other. This kinetic aspect is called rajas. The science of physics mainly deals with the forces of inertia and kinetics. The states which come to prevail between the functions of inertia and kinetics can be understood in terms of intelligence.

Yogis apply this philosophy in their personal life. They look for an ideal state where sattva, rajas and tamas are brought to an equilibrium. This automatically brings an equilibrium between spirit and matter also. Then that duality is transcended and a unitive aspect comes. The whole system becomes quiescent. A beatitude springs forth from within. Inertia is not pronounced. Our normal idea of clarity, in the sense of a subject knowing an object, is absent. There is no longer any differentiation. In that differenceless state, in the absolute fusion of spirit and matter, one becomes the aloneness of the Supreme. Such aloneness is considered to be a very high state. It is a return from the world of activities to one's own original nature. This is the yogi's ideal.

There are many schools of Yoga, the most ancient of which is Patañjali's. His book, the Yoga Sutras, begins with the final goal. He states the final cause first, then goes into the material causes and the efficient causes afterwards. Yoga, union, is equated with samadhi, absorption. He wrote *yogaḥ citta vṛtti nirodhā*, yoga is the complete cessation of all modifications of the mind. With this he aims at the vision which may be called "arriving at one's own real state and getting established in it." The epistemology or the philosophy of this vision is given by Sankhya, and the application of it, including the methodology of applying the Sankhya wisdom, is given by Yoga. Thus, these two schools are a complementary set.

The second pair of complementary schools are Nyaya and Vaiseshika. Between them all the logical aspects of the mind are dealt with. They provide a methodology for thinking. Such methodology is the testimony by which one arrives at right knowledge.

For instance, perception is one testimony of knowledge. What I can directly perceive, I don't need proof of. This is called a *pramāṇa*, that which brings certitude. The first *pramāṇa* is direct perception. If I have an apple in my hand, I don't have to look into a book to know it. It is a direct experience, a *pratyakṣa*. The second *pramāṇa* is inference, where from partial knowledge one can infer the full reality. The third is analogy and the fourth is knowing a thing through the principle of contradiction. There is also a principle of sufficient reason. The final one is *śabda*, something stated by a wise person, a guru, or an authoritative book. This can tend to become dogmatic, but it is a priori. Some of their methodology is a priori and some is a posteriori.

The Nyayikas want to see how we relate a personal consciousness with the rest of the world. They consider that intelligence is that which deals with the objects of intelligence, and that our actions, non-actions, and life as a whole mainly depend on our knowledge. They study the logical relationship between things and ideas, and have come up with a set of categories. The first is *dravya*, things, which is usually translated into English as substance. The second category is *guṇa*, quality. A stone is *dravya;* its quality is heaviness. Water's quality is that it flows. Fire burns. Man is also a *dravya:* he has a concreteness. The world can easily be seen as a composite of concrete things with their qualities.

A number of things can be gathered together under one category because of their homogeneous nature. When things are related by gathering them together it is called *sambandha.* For instance, all human beings can be brought under the heading of man. That is *sāmānya.* Also, each individual can be studied separately and analytically. That is *viśeṣa,* the purview of the Vaiseshikas. Of course there are many other categories, such as time, space, action and absence.

The other two schools are Purva-Mimamsa and Uttara-Mimamsa, the anterior and posterior schools of critique. The anterior school assumes that absolutely dependable knowledge is a priori: that in order to have experience, there has to be within the person a certain revelation of an inner device by which things can be related. From the beginning of our knowledge of the world things have seemed as though they were spread out in space. No one needed to teach us that there is space. In the same way we see certain things as being above or below without being taught, and are also aware of the sequential passing of time as a part of experience. We are born with this knowledge. Therefore, these kinds of knowledge are not learned, but are part and parcel of an a priori revelation. Knowledge is being revealed to us. It is simply our nature, and we are realising our nature.

When knowledge comes to us, we tend to express it; and in order to express it we tend to use words. We think in terms of words, which are basically conceptual. For their articulation we take energy from the bodily mechanism. We use the energy in us, directed in a certain way to become conceptualised. This conceptualised energy becomes verbalised and is then expressed. It becomes a communicative force. When people interact and communicate, they create many new possibilities. For this reason, the Purva-Mimamsa school examines the process of semiosis in detail.

The potential possibility of consciousness in a person lies there like an ocean, out of which the waves of ideas emerge. Each emerging idea presents a vision to the person's own consciousness. So out of amorphous, unstructured consciousness arises a structured consciousness, which is described as *paśyanti* or vision. When the person wants to communicate his vision to someone else, he puts it in the form of words. For instance, when an engineer wants to explain her drawing of a structure to her clients she verbally articulates what she has drawn on paper, and through her sounds they begin to share her vision as a living possibility rather than a static blueprint.

According to the anterior critics of the Purva-Mimamsa school, the whole universe is nothing but a manifestation of the Word, which can be undone, redone and transformed through the application of words. The most important tool a man has is his word. The word is also himself. He is the tool. He makes the tool, and he and the tool can work together because of their homogeneity as consciousness.

The posterior school, known as Vedanta, accepts the two principles of Nature and Intelligence from the Sankhya philosophy. From the Nyaya-Vaiseshika schools they accept methodologies such as perception, inference, analogy, contradiction and word testimony. Narayana Guru belongs to this school, and he wants us to know how the knowledge which he has been describing operates in our daily life.

Your intention is to find ultimate release from all kinds of bondages that tie you down to the world of necessity, action and relativism, in order to attain absolute freedom. Absolute freedom means having no conditions. Your body itself is a limiting condition. There are physical, biological, psychological and chemical principles which limit you in various complex ways. For instance, your body is heavy and you cannot lift it into the air; it is tied to the earth by gravitational forces. From out of the domination of so many principles and laws you desire an autonomous status: to become the master of the situation.

In the present verse, Narayana Guru first mentions the person who has good intentions. The previous verse showed that our consciousness can be led in two directions — to see ourselves as part of the whole or to focus on the particular. If you only look to the particular and feel strongly that you are the particular, you become a self-centered person, giving primacy to your body and its pleasures. You get involved in acquisition, grasping for the things of others, and gratifying your latent urges. There is a strong impulse for action, action which is monitored by your individual desires. When such attitudes prevail, anya or otherness is operating in your mind.

The other possibility is to be dominated by a vision of the universal. You consider mankind as an organic whole. As long as your vision is that you epitomise the whole, and action moves you, your desire will not be self-centered but oriented to the well-being of the community, of Nature in its largest sense. You become an ecologist, a lover of the universe, one with the spirit of life. When you move in the direction of the welfare of all, sama or sameness is operating in your mind.

Between sameness and the other you can be pulled in different directions. If you commit yourself to the universal good, and your actions are all oriented in that direction, you become a *sukr̥ti. Suk* means good; *kr̥ti* means actor. This is a fine ideal. However, although you may be universal in your outlook, when you begin to act in the world many things interfere. You cannot do things just as you want because prakriti, the separating tendency, is found throughout Nature. So even a *sukr̥ti*, the best of people, has to conform to social principles, government laws, and all the rest. Perhaps the country is going to war and all are expected to contribute to the war effort. You can dissent and protest, but in some way you will be dragged into it. It will shape your life to a greater or lesser extent. Certainly, *sukr̥ta* is very good and you are going in the right direction, but limitations come from all sides and you also get caught by them. You may even find that your very goodness becomes an evil. In some situations, if you are too good people will kill you just for that. So your goodness has to be moderated, to be tailored to the situation.

The *sukr̥ti*, the man with the best intentions who identifies with the universal, will at times be compelled to do actions against his wishes. We can see that happening all around us: even the most broad-minded and generous people are caught by the mesh of nature, and go round and round feeling helpless. What is the way out of this dilemma? The Guru says *phalāgraham aṟṟariññiṭēṇam,* even when you are good and you are turning towards the sama, there is an impact of anya which gets in your way. You may want to see the effect of your work immediately or within a certain time limit. In this, although you seem to be a wise person, fully identified with the universal, you have limited your action situation to a context of anya. Your desire for good and immediate results has tainted the purity of your actions. The Guru recommends, along with the Bhagavad Gita, giving up the desire for the fruits of your actions. If you think you have made your contribution to the stream of events and that this will bring results not particularly to you but to humanity in its course of operation, then you are not held in any obligatory system. You have become both a witness and a contributor.

Another possibility is intending to not do anything, saying "I am in trouble because I act. Only a man who acts makes mistakes and gets caught. So I'll avoid that by not doing any action." This is called *akṛti,* nonaction. Will it help? If you do not act, will you become one with the Absolute? No. There are potentials in you which have their own dynamics to jump out and shape your behaviour. They may make you act in very strange ways. Mere suppression or inaction is not an antidote. *Vikṛti,* perverted action, comes out of you through reflex and instinctive urges. It spurts out and makes you act weird and crazy. This perverted action is sitting in all of us to some extent. We put on big cloaks of virtue and good action so it all looks very acceptable, but when we get hysterical we forget all that. Nonaction is no guarantee against this: it can actually make it easier for such perverted action to surface.

So you are not an *akṛti,* a non-actor, and you are not a *sukṛti* in the sense that you want to have good effected immediately. You are certainly not a *vikṛti,* because you do not allow perversion to take over. You are one who sees the good of all and intends the good of all. You contribute to the good of all to whatever extent you can, but you do not hold on to it with a desire to identify or to realise it here and now. Thus, your release is to be worked out by taking away the desire for the fruit but retaining the desire for the actualisation of good in a general way. You are still motivated, but your motivation is not bound to personal gratification. We will go more into the intricacies of this in the next verse.

Verse 44

pala mata sāravumēkamennu pārā-
tulakil orānayil andhar ennapōle
pala vidha yukti paṟaññu pāmaranmā-
ralavatu kaṇṭalayātamarnniṭēṇam

The many faiths have but one essence;
not seeing this, in this world, like the blind men and the elephant,
many kinds of reasoning are used by the unenlightened who become distressed;
having seen this, without being disturbed, remain steadfast.

This is a seemingly very simple verse, but it has a subtle relationship to previous verses. Verse 41 said that in the statement "this is a pot", that which comes first as *itu*, this, is difficult to discern. *Kuṭam,* pot, is its qualification, which is easily understood. The outgrowth of this situation is the magical phenomenal show of existence, which has its origination in the intellect.

Essentially, the intellect makes a decision about the nature of the total experience of what is presented to the mind. If it decides that a certain thing is very valuable, it is very valuable; and if it decides a certain thing has no value, it has no value.

At times we speak of certain people as being brainwashed. Some others we describe as exaggerating, and still others we say are underrating because they have not understood. In all these, we are finding fault with *mati,* the intellectual faculty. We are questioning its veracity. When a more intelligent person makes some claim, those who consider themselves inferior to him try to see what he sees and conform to the arbitrary vision which is being passed on to them. In this way, without deciding for themselves, many people make a decision on the basis of pure dogma. Here also it is *matam*, that which is born of *mati*. A mere intellectual assertion is accepted as the common faith.

Verse 42 says that when you say "this is knowledge," 'this' is the unifying factor in all the items of knowledge, and 'knowledge' is the qualification of that factor. Intellect vivifies knowledge into small spheres; for that to lose its hold on you so you can have a total vision of enlightenment, you should meditate on 'this'.

The very presentation of 'this' to consciousness tends to make two kinds of emphasis. One is on the side of sensory data, and the other is on the side of intellectual summation. You are receiving two lights into your organism. From the physical side you are stimulated, and from the psychic side you are stimulated. The first is a physical stimulation and the second is psychological. For the interpretation of both you need light, awareness. The source of this awareness is a common factor, one that is not only common to both of these aspects in you, but common to all beings also.

In all sentient beings, the illumination of the whole organism comes from one common source, but what it illuminates shifts from one focus to another. At one moment it may highlight physical data, then it will highlight psychic ideation, or again it will be the common source of all knowledge. In the first two, the function of interpretation is taken by the faculty called the intellect. We use our intellect for all expressions of judgement, and these have become more or less rigidly structured in the course of our development from childhood.

When the child asks questions and receives answers, he or she gets instructed not only in statements of fact but also in the nature of relation-relata complexes. Each answer actually teaches several things, most of them only implied. The child begins to think of cause and effect relationships, and to appreciate that there are general statements and particular instances; it learns it can arrive at particular or universal conclusions. Syllogistic and deductive reasoning become part of the intellectual functioning. When you become more inquisitive to find out why a certain general statement is accepted, you use inductive reasoning as well. By employing inductive and deductive reasoning, you make your intellect into an efficient tool to poke at the things which come from the external world as well as the ideations evoked by external events or memories. All too often, though, having used this tool and found it efficient for solving some of the riddles and problems of your personal life, you glorify it and make it your sole crutch for ever and ever.

Once you do this, you enter into another realm which is not directly related either to external stimuli or mere internal ideation. Now you are provoked by a basic need. When you think of your self-preservation, you begin to comprehend the hopeless situation in which you are placed. You see that beyond a couple of generations, none of your forebears is still alive. In fact, everyone who comes to this world eventually dies. So we see death all around us.

In your own case, when you look in the mirror you might see your hair turning white or new wrinkles on your face or colourations on your skin. Old age is inevitably coming, and the body will perish. You don't want to leave it, but then you are consoled by someone saying that only your body is mortal; your soul is eternal. But we don't know what that soul is. For our peace of mind we have to shift our camp from bodily feeling to this so-called soul or spirit, which is only conjectural. We can plainly see the body, but we have to imagine the soul.

The instrument with which we make our conjectures is the intellect. Admittedly it is very efficient when it comes to measuring the physical qualities of something. Whenever you can use a measuring rod or other gadget, you can be very accurate. But this is only on the material plane, and you have already found it to be without hope. It is always changing, deteriorating, falling apart. The only place where we can find some promise is in the immortality of the soul which someone has spoken of to us. And since we have no direct experience of it, our intellect is vastly less useful to us in this area. Still, it is the faculty we are most familiar and comfortable with.

So you take this same instrument, the intellect, into the new sphere and say "Okay, let's find out." In the Middle Ages, for instance, you might have asked your neighbour, "Who told you the soul is immortal?"

"I heard it at church. The Father said the soul is immortal."

"And everyone has one?"

"Yes, of course."

"Is it immortal for everyone?"

"Oh, no! He said only for those who believe in our saviour."

"You miss the relevant connections. If the soul is immortal and everybody has one, they must all be immortal."

The response is "No. Everybody has a soul, but it is in great peril if you don't believe in our Lord Jesus Christ."

"Who said that?"

"Oh, our priest said it."

"Is it in some book?"

"Yes, he has a black, hide-bound book from which he reads."

"Let us look into it."

"But it is in Latin."

"Why can't it be translated so we can all read it?"

By now the questioner is considered to be an agent of the devil. "You doubt because the devil is in you. We are giving you the teaching to immortalise yourself, but now you want to see it with your own eyes? The devil is in you!" So all those who wanted the Bible translated from Latin in the Middle Ages were burned alive because they wanted to discern for themselves the immortality of the Self.

Someone else says "Yes, it is assured by Allah." Another says "The immortality of the Self is declared by the Vedas." There are so many groups who all vouch for the immortality of the soul, but it is all written in some strange language or kept in somebody's special box, and you have no way to find it. Then there comes a person like the Buddha. If you ask him "Is there any immortality of the Self?" he will say "First there should be Self. Then only can it have any immortality. There is only immortality of the Self if the Self is assured." You are again confused, so he adds "*anātmā,* there is no Self."

All this is the sphere of *mati* or intellect. Narayana Guru has chosen to express faith in this verse as *matam,* that which is born of your intellect. It also means religion. Religion has two important aspects. One is using conjecture. What is the source of the major religions like Christianity, Buddhism, Hinduism, Judaism, Islam and Sikhism? They all come through a revelation. Usually the revelation can be traced to a single person. For the whole of Christianity, for instance, the authority is the word of Christ.

Again and again Christ turns to his own disciples, saying things like "Ye of little faith. Ye of little understanding." He is seeing a total vision, devoid of *mati*. It is something which needs no intermediary, no interpretation for him. Then he shows it to other people, to whom it is only secondhand knowledge. They see it through the distortions of their own intellects. This is why Peter interpreted Christ's teachings in a way which was very different from Paul. Peter understood emotionally and Paul understood logically. They never could come to an agreement.

This is a dangerous area. To see as Christ, Krishna, Buddha and Muhammad did requires a total vision. Anything less than a total vision is fraught with great peril. In *The Varieties of Religious Experience*, William James makes the point that he is not discussing secondhand religion, but firsthand religion. That is, firsthand religion as Jesus or Ramakrishna experienced it. Someone coming and saying, "Sri Ramakrishna might have thought like this," is experiencing *matam*, an intellectualised version of the original. What is invariably handed over to us is this secondhand version of a religious vision.

Once you go from the spiritual vision to religious belief, you have already strayed far from the truth. When we fight, the discord is about religion and not any spiritual vision. In two people who have a spiritual vision there is no difference of opinion: they melt into each other. But when you have only heard something and then you or a priest interpret it for yourself, you take a stand. Your position is rigid to precisely the extent that your vision is limited. You have to think of your loyalty to the man from whom you heard. He can express only one millionth of his total experience through his words or example, and your sole authority is that one little fragment. As it is not in any way yours, you are always afraid to move a little this way or that way from what you have heard. You don't want to blaspheme. You want to hold onto it, but you do not know either its intention or extension. The result is that we become victims of narrow religious thinking. In order to support our religion we know only argument. We go on reasoning endlessly, but reason is absolutely useless and meaningless, if not destructive, in this matter.

This is the only tool we know. But what else can we do? The Guru here says *pala mata sāravum ēkam,* the essence of all those intellectualised versions of total reality or the Absolute is the same. Our mind can be turned towards the spirit, towards the source of our own inner light, or it can be turned towards the world illuminated by our senses. One concerns the source of illumination, and the other concerns the objects which are illuminated.

When your mind is focused on the illuminated world, you are naturally tempted to segregate things, vivify things, and specify them. In that world, when you hold an opinion it will be different from another person's opinion. Then you come to a state like that of the several blind people who went to see the elephant in the famous story. You hold different views because of outwardness. If you always look through the wrong end of a telescope you will have a distorted view of things. It will bring much frustration. But in a sense this is exactly what we are doing in our daily life. We do not agree with each other, not only about the highest truth but even about simple truths.

We forget that in none of our mental functions are we in direct relationship with the original, we are always only interpreting sensory images received in the mind. When we intellectualise, our mind is giving its own version, its best estimate, not a total picture of facts or data. The data is only what we presume. 'Fact' is a fiction. There is no fact. There can be only a comparative range of fictions which are more or less useful or reliable. We make an approximation, even when we loudly swear our certitude.

Narayana Guru says, "First of all, come to know that you are living in a world of approximation, where you arrive at conclusions derived by the intellect." From the previous verses, we already know that this intellect is capable of making great magic, and unless you transcend it you are never with the total, with the whole. In the next five verses, he is going to tell us how this affects our social life.

Up to verse 20, the Guru was speaking of that primordial light which comes to us in so many forms. From verse 20 onwards, he has been telling us more of the individuated mind which is the recipient of that great light, and how it functions. Now begins a section dealing with how individuated beings in their interpersonal relationships get a social mind, and how we come under the influence of that social mind, which can bring about bloodshed in the name of opinion. If you want to have a peaceful life on earth you should know your social mind, your individual mind, and also the source from which your mind derives its light.

Later, Narayana Guru summarised all this in his dictum: "Man is of one God, one kind and one religion." The essence of our social values is one. The essence of individuation is one. The light that illuminates all this is one. This is his philosophy of unitive understanding, which will be elaborated in the next five verses.

Verse 45

oru matamanyanu nindyamonnil ōtum-
karuvaparante kaṇakki nūnamākum
dharayil itinte rahasyamonnutān e-
nnaṟivaḻavum bhramamennaṟiññiṭēṇam

One faith is despicable to another;
the *karu* described in one is defective in another's estimation;
in the world the secret of this is one alone;
know that confusion prevails until it is known to be thus.

The consistent behaviour of a person gives him his character. One of the main indicators of character is the predictability of a person's behaviour. We say, "He is a good Christian, so he will keep his promise," or "He will never fight with his neighbour." People can make such predictions about others' behaviour because they observe a consistency in their repeatedly choosing to act in a certain way in similar circumstances. If you know the situation, you can predict how a certain person is going to react.

A person's character becomes apparent through his habitual choices, and the habitual choices themselves come from our conviction of values. Conviction in values comes passively from an inner nonresistance, and actively through the exercise of our will, which selects out of many possibilities the one it wants to adopt.

Actions are actualisations of will. When you decide upon a certain desirable thing, that becomes your will. It is not easy to will. Sometimes you have to undergo a certain conflict. The conflict arises when there is more than one choice before you. When you consider the value of each choice, the advantages correspond to some of your latent urges. One urge may say you should have a good name. Another urge says somehow you should have the gratification of a secret desire. If gratifying the secret desire is going to be rated ignoble by society, you have to weigh it against how much you want to be respected by that society. If the social expectation and your individual gratification are at loggerheads, then sometimes, against your own deeper desires, you may agree to stand by the social standard because in the long run you deem it more worthwhile. The question is to decide between a small joy which is momentary and long-term happiness. In both cases the basic element is happiness. The question is how long or how short? How secure or how insecure?

All desires are born of the pleasure principle. The fact that someone can have many desires shows we have universes of desires. Each desire has a nucleus, which is the joy factor. Constellations of such joy factors come to us in structured groups, which make a collective impact on our minds. If your wife or husband, parents or neighbours like what you like, then the collective agreement gives additional impetus to your acceptance of it because you are gaining two things, personal gratification plus the support of so many other people. If you have to choose between an event you experience all alone and another which you share with others, you will naturally tend to accept that which is also acceptable to other people.

These kinds of choices have to be made from childhood on. When you are a child, you belong to grownups who take it for granted that they know better than you just because they are grown up. Saint-Exupery speaks of this in his book *The Little Prince*. Grown ups always think they know better, and that they have a right to impose what they consider better on you. The child does not see the good of something, but he has to accept it anyway because of his parents.

Fortunately or unfortunately, children belong to people with convictions. The parents say, "This should be your conviction, too." If the child struggles and fights back, it generally cannot win because the parents can always smack. Most children take the course of least resistance. The less resistance the better for a child, so it learns to agree with the parents.

Thus, long before the child knows what values are for itself, a number of external values are laid in its mind. Of these, at least eighty per cent are of the nature of Pavlovian conditioning. We pride ourselves on giving good teaching to children, but it is no better than what Pavlov did to his dogs. You push the button and give the food, and then they learn a reward will come every time the button is pushed.

Learning, especially in the West, is mainly conformity to socially accepted behaviour. The child is taught not to ask why when he is told to do something, like not putting his elbow on the dinner table. I also do not understand why the elbow should not be on the table. It is very comfortable. But the mother or father decides that is not how it should be. It is nothing but conditioning. There is no rationale behind it.

The religion Narayana Guru is speaking of here is not necessarily Christianity or Islam. It can be Communism or Free-thinking. It can be anything. But nothing is free. Free thinking means the child is conditioned to have free thinking. Life is full of such paradoxes. By the time a person is seventeen or eighteen they have already become a bundle of prejudices, and it is with these prejudices that one comes to estimate another person's character, their behavioural pattern and value system.

The Guru says *oru matam anyanu nindyam,* "Your religion can never be good for me. I have decided already." "Why?" "Because it is not my religion. How can it be good for me when it is not mine?" Then he adds *onnil ētum karuvaparante kaṇakki nūnam ākum,* "Whatever is said in your scripture or your book of faith must be defective." The Caliph once said "Everything that is good for man is given in the Quran. Whatever is not given in it cannot be true. If the same teaching is given somewhere else, it is superfluous." The Emperor Theodosius burned the great Library of Alexandria, saying, "What is the use of all these books? One will do, the Bible."

In a small way we all do the same thing all the time. The King James Bible is not acceptable to many American sects, because it is not an American version. Other people feel the American version is good for nothing because it is not the King James version. Yet it is the same book. Both kinds of people are Christians, dedicated to Jesus Christ, but still they argue over it.

Narayana Guru points out that we want to measure another's faith with our own measuring rod. Our measuring rod is our *mati*, our intellect. It is formed in childhood by the rewards and punishments we received. So I have made a measuring rod out of the balance between my rewards and punishments, and with that I want to measure your convictions. If they come under the category of those for which I was rewarded, fine. If I find in them something for which I was punished, bad. There is no universality in our measuring rods. They are all private ones, especially manufactured in the course of our life experiences, and based on our own understanding and interpretation of events. As a result, we fight. We have already decided to fight before we come together.

There is another possibility, another measuring rod which is not privately manufactured in one's individual mind. It belongs to *sat cit ānanda,* the existential verity of knowledge. *Sat* means existence; *cit*, verity; and ananda, value; so it is the existential verity of a value that is enshrined in one's very heart. In all experiences these three aspects are bound to be there: an existential factor, a knowledge of that existence, and the essence of that existence, which is a value.

The key is to have an attitude of neutrality. If you have an overall scheme of correlation in your mind by which you can see and decipher everyone's values from a neutral point of view, you have no problem. Your discipline is to gain this way of thinking. Then if you encounter someone else's prayer, for instance, you can decipher it and understand it in a transcendental language that is no-man's-religion. This is also the religious language of all. When we hold this key in our hand we no longer mock the ways of others. Otherwise, we are all the time estimating others and inwardly laughing at them. We want to suggest to them what the right thing to do is.

This verse is mainly aimed at a deconditioning of our behavioural patterns. The Guru uses very special words, such as *mati, matam* and *dhara,* which have great implications. He says *dharayil itinte rahasyam. Dhara* means the earth. Since the earth supports everyone there is a suggestion of universal support. Our basic foundation is the earth. When you know the secret of your basic dharma, which supports all your individual preferences, you have no need to fight.

From your individual preferences, which belong to *viśeṣa*, the 'pot', you are asked to move to *itu*, the 'this'. Usually you forget the *itu* because it is difficult to discern, but actually you should meditate on that and not on the pot. This helps bring about the attitude of neutrality you are directed to seek.

The religion you have been given has two distinct aspects. One is what Christ and the other masters experienced from within. That is the 'this'. The other aspect is what Peter noticed, the 'pot' aspect. You only know what Peter observed; the 'this' aspect you don't know. The 'pot' aspect is very evident; what was in the mind of the potter you don't know. You do know the pot he made, so you cling onto that.

After the death of every Guru there will be fights between at least five people, because each observed one particular aspect and the others do not conform to it especially. There are at least six or seven versions of Socratic teaching, since all the fellows around Socrates had their own versions of his teaching.

In one sense you should say "so many people, so many religions," because the specific factor of each individual is different. Or you should say there is only one religion. These are different from group religion, which is a political affiliation for the sake of social privileges and applying pressure tactics. When the Christians were not organised, the non-Christians rounded them up and killed them. So they had to make secret meetings in secret hideouts, and use the symbol of a fish to identify each other. Being acutely aware of the power of the Roman legions, they thought they could use the same pattern to bring about the kingdom of God on earth. So they said "Let us also get organised and be armed." But didn't Jesus say that those who took up the sword would perish by the sword? "That's OK, but for the sake of our Lord we can use the sword. Let us have crusades!"

Such is the stupidity in the name of religion that has been going on for ages. Not in just one religion, but in every one. In the name of the kindest, most loving masters, so much blood has been shed in this world. Narayana Guru is now making an appeal to the kind heart of everyone: Let us stop this bloodshed by recognising the common ground on which we stand; for instance, this *dhara*, this earth. Just as this earth is our common place to stand, happiness is the common denominator of all religions.

Verse 46

porutu jayippatasāddhyamonninōṭo-
nnoru matavum porutāl otuṅṅuvīla
para matavādiyitōrttiṭāte pāẓē
porutu poliññiṭumenna buddhi vēṇam

By fighting it is impossible to win;
by fighting one another no faith is destroyed;
one who argues against another's faith, not recognising this,
fights in vain and perishes; this should be understood.

Although this verse at first glance seems very simple, it has great inner depth and detail. Its implications would not be exhausted even if we were to dwell on it for many months.

Two of the six darsanas of the philosophical visions of India are Purva and Uttara Mimamsa, the anterior critique developed by Jaimini and the posterior critique expounded by Bādarāyaṇa. Jaimini's darsana is called the study of dharma, and Bādarāyaṇa's is the study of Brahman.

We have been speaking of sama and anya, sameness and the 'other'. The 'other' is where we encounter specific qualities. Dharma is one man's specific quality which distinguishes him from another. Salt is different from sugar because of their different specific qualities. You cannot take the saltishness out of salt or the sugariness from sugar, because those are their dharma. On the other hand, the very word Brahman implies all-inclusiveness. It does not allow for any separation or differentiation.

One is the differentiating, the other is the uniting. Those who see only difference and do not see unity cannot agree with one another. Those who see only unity do not see another to agree or disagree with. The *Dharma-Sūtras* of Jaimini presented the development of the ritualistic aspect of life, while Bādarāyaṇa's darsana gave rise to the doctrine of renunciation. Thus, these schools have two totally different outlooks on life. The householder stood by one and the sannyasi or renunciate stood by the other. In India they have been arguing over these ideas since the beginning, and their implications are pondered by people all over the world.

Religion is not merely one man's private opinion. A religion that rules a man's life consists of his total value matrix, which even he is not fully aware of. You do not know how deep the roots of your convictions are, how far they are going to take you, or with what other things they are entwined. The total matrix of life is lying unseen and often unimagined. It is very hard to discern its true or whole nature, which is shared collectively with our fellow beings, as most of our life urges are not only in the person but also in the collective unconscious or the collective wholeness of the society to which we belong.

Even in people who are not at all religious, or who are even anti-religious, there are subterranean currents of a religious pull. Two classic examples we can give are the thoughts and writings of Einstein and Freud, two of the most extraordinary people of our time. Neither of them had any leaning to the particular religious background in which they were born, Judaism. Yet the undercurrents of their thoughts contain powerful Jewish feelings. To some extent these were a form of reaction to being opposed as Jews by others, even though they did not think of themselves that way. The more someone attacks you, the more your dormant underlying traits become vigorous. Other traits were learned so early in life that they were not consciously perceived by them, or were so much a part of their culture as to be invisible.

This is a verse which we have to examine very closely. We will go step by step. First there is the statement of a general principle: *porutu jayippatasāddhyam,* it is difficult to win by fighting. You can overpower another person, but you will not win anything. What is the difference between overpowering and winning? There is an expression "he won my heart." You cannot win another man's heart by fighting him, but you can by giving yourself to him. When you give yourself to another in love, you win. But when you use force, you don't win. You overpower.

This is the first distinction we need to understand: by fighting we don't win, we only concentrate the opposition to a fever pitch. When an animal is at bay, pushed into a corner where it cannot go any farther, it has only one choice. With all desperation it will pounce upon you and bite you. What is happening in this situation? The life meaning of the animal becomes so concentrated that its whole system becomes filled with it. Every atom vibrates with the meaning of its life. When a man becomes angry, his whole body shivers. You can see hatred for you concentrated in his eyes, in his look, in his word, posture, everything. He gains a certain absolutist dimension at this time. There is no compromising. A dog, a cat, a rat, anything will become an absolute, total whole if you try to strike at the very centre or keynote of its life.

There is a story that when Mansur Hallaj was beaten, he became all the more convinced of his oneness with Allah. His hands and legs were chopped off, but he thought that it was only his hands and legs that were cut and not his love for Allah. Then he was hanged, beheaded and cut into pieces, and still every little piece chanted "an al haq! I am Allah!" When he was burned, the flames said "an al haq," and every particle of his ashes said "an al haq." Finally his ashes were thrown in the ocean. Each wave came crashing back, murmuring "an al haq, an al haq." So by fighting you don't win.

The next point in the verse is that if one person with conviction fights another person with conviction, it is not to the advantage of either. The dialectics of this situation produces either double loss or double gain. If you fight you get double loss, but if you come together you get double gain.

We can see from history that fighting between religions has not eradicated any of them. Many times the Jews have been decimated by various forces in different parts of the world, only to come back with renewed vigor. History recounts at least four or five thousand years of continuous tirade against the Jews, but the virility, inner strength, stamina, message and power of their religion could not be undermined.

The Roman Empire was at its height when poor Jesus of Nazareth came along. They thought he would be easy to crush, but instead the Roman Empire fell. The emperors converted to Christianity. The teaching of Christ could not be abolished. Luther and others tried to abolish Catholicism forever, but the Catholic Church still stands as strong as ever. And the Catholics thought they could defeat the protesters by hanging them and burning them, but that only increased the numbers of Protestants.

A recent example comes from a great superpower, America, deciding that communism is bad and democracy is good. Just what is communism? And just what is democracy? They could have discussed this in a university forum, but instead they sent a million young Americans to Vietnam to decide the issue. They thought that by fighting they could show that communism was wrong. They completely overlooked that they were going to an alien place where the people had ancient ties to the land. Above and beyond any issues of communism or democracy, the people there were fighting for their lives, their homes and their very dear land. On the other side the soldiers were conscripted, so they didn't have much zeal or zest for the war. So what happened? The Americans were not only defeated, but the Presidents and the architects of the war who were tied up with it are considered to have committed the one of the greatest evils in human history.

This is a recent example, but the same thing happened during the Medieval Christian Crusades. Did the crusaders finally do away with the Muslims and the Jews? The synagogue, the church and the mosque are still standing side by side in all those countries.

Let us look into the inner structure of this thing called religion in order to understand why it cannot be destroyed through fighting. Judaism has conceived a symbolic tree of life arranged with a top and bottom, two flanks and a centre. On the top are wisdom, reason and knowledge. On the sides are greatness, strength, eternity and majesty. At the bottom is sovereignty, and in the centre is beauty. The three words at the top look almost alike: wisdom, reason and knowledge. Yet we know they are not the same. Wisdom transcends reason. You do not know the depth from which wisdom comes. You do not know its scope of infinitude. You do not know its sublimity.

It is so vast, so deep. When you say reason, there is movement. You move from one vision to another, correlating one to the other and showing its relevance. If knowledge is like the whole ocean, reason is like the waves moving across the surface, one after the other. There is precision and order, arrangement and logic. So you are not only wise but also reasonable. You have the knowledge to argue and establish your case.

What is the difference between wisdom and knowledge? There is a saying, "he has the know-how." If wisdom is an eternal, continuous, never-failing fountain which is ever supplying the fuel of your life, knowledge has reference to a situation. There is a structural compactness which enables the situation to have a function that can be protective and creative, and to make total sense to you. Then you can say you have a knowledge of it.

So Judaism says, "When you come to us, understand that we care for wisdom, we have reason and know-how." That makes the religion invulnerable. If you go still farther, they say, "It's not about me. I may be no one, but I belong to an inestimable greatness which I glorify. That puts strength into my veins and muscles. The strength of this body, this mind, this spirit, is derived from a greatness that belongs to the Absolute. And it is not a brute force, because beauty is its centre." How can you fight that? Before beauty you become fully disarmed. If someone brings his might, his courage, his strength in the form of beauty, it doesn't just overpower you, it overwhelms you. You are filled with it, and the ecstasy of it makes you mad. You become drunk with it.

The Jews go on to say, "We belong to eternity and not to history. Only in history is there a beginning and an end. We belong to eternity. We see the majesty of it. This cannot be defeated because it's a law, a principle that rules our life, our sovereignty." When you see Judaism in this simple, yet intricate representation, it is overwhelming. You cannot fight it; you don't even want to fight it.

In any religion, similar principles are present one way or another. In the Vedic context, a world tree is represented in the fifteenth chapter of the Bhagavad Gita. It says:

> There is a tree. It has its roots above and its branches below.
> Those who know about it say it never expends. It is never

> destroyed. Its leaves are the songs of the Vedas. When a knower of wisdom becomes overjoyed and in exaltation, from him come the glorifying hymns; those are the leaves of this tree. A knower of this tree is the true knower.
>
> Its branches, which ramify in different directions, are the *guṇas*, the triple modalities of nature. They go on multiplying and multiplying. They are producing objects of interest. The mind branches off to different interests. The different interests are all implied by the different objects of desires.
>
> Just as it has roots above from whence it is nourished by the unknown, it has roots below which make it firm. The roots below are karma, the action and interaction which bind all of us into a compact whole. When you touch me, you touch another hundred people, because I belong to another hundred. When I touch you, I touch many unknown people. Our karmas bind us. To what depth and darkness they have gone, we do not know. No one can break this. This is what is called the dharma.

Just as beauty can overwhelm you, there is only one thing that can transcend this tree. It is given in the Gita as *asaṅga*, the sword of non-attachment. Instead of fighting you, I allow you to be. I do not merely allow you to be, I also include you. I accept you. When I accept you, I have already taken the zest to fight away from you. In the face of my calmness, you also become calm. So, if winning is your motive, win the heart. When you fight, not only does the other perish: you also perish.

There is an Indian myth that a certain demon came and challenged Balarāma, the brother of Sri Krishna. Balarāma accepted the challenge. He went, raising his fist to smash its head. Then the demon became twice the size of Balarāma. Seeing this, Balarāma, who had psychic powers, grew double the size of the demon. The demon doubled in size again, and started lifting hills to throw at him. Then Balarāma realised he could not overpower the demon. He turned to Sri Krishna and asked for help. Krishna smiled and said, "Brother, leave him to me. I'll deal with him."

The demon turned to Krishna and found that in his hand there was no weapon. Krishna stood with his hands open and smiled. Then the demon became the size of an average human being. Krishna still stood there with his bewitching smile and said, "Come on friend." He came close and became smaller than Krishna. Krishna patted him. He became very small. Then Krishna took him in his hand and stroked him. He became so tiny.

Then Balarāma came and said, "Brother, I don't understand this. How did he become so small? How did you tame him?" He replied, "Brother, don't you know this demon's name?" "No." "This demon's name is Krodha, anger. When you become angry, you are only feeding him. He thrives on somebody else's anger. When you take away your anger, there is nothing to nourish him. He becomes less and less. So when I give him love, there is nothing on which he can feed himself and he becomes very small."

This is also the central teaching of Buddha: with hatred you never appease hatred, but with love you win all.

Verse 47

oru matamākuvatinnurappatellā-
varumitu vādikaḷ ārumōrkkuvīla
paramatavādamoẓiñña paṇḍitanmā-
raṟiyumitinte rahasyamiṅṅaśeṣam

To become of one faith is what everyone speaks of;
this the proselytisers do not recognise;
wise men, freed of objections to another's faith,
know this secret in full.

The key word in this verse is 'secret'. The Guru says there is a secret which is known to wise men and not remembered by people who are enthusiastic about enforcing their religion. In Patañjali's Yoga Sutras, ignorance is described as mistaking the non-Self for the Self. This can manifest in several ways: becoming identified with a morbid state of mind and losing flexibility; becoming infatuated with a certain idea of pleasure or gain and then hankering after it; becoming hateful of those who do not agree with you or who thwart your intentions in a situation of competition or rivalry; or by becoming subjected to passions that come as psychological compulsions.

We can see all these in force in someone who becomes fanatical about an ideology. The ideology can be religious or political, a personal idiosyncrasy, or even a fad. When hate enters you, it is like you are possessed by an evil demon. It brings such a terrible block to your mind that you cannot see another's point of view. You become glued to one single stand, so that you can't move a little to one side to see that there could be another possibility.

When I was in my mid-teens I saw Mahatma Gandhi, the founder and father of modern India. He was revered as a great saint. He believed fervently in the nonviolence of Christ, and he taught that India should be converted to a creed of pacifism. He taught that one should win another's heart by love.

At that time, Britain was ruling India with full military force. To fight the British forces, which were armed with guns and bayonets, the Indians were made to march with slogans of nonviolence and peace. As a young man I thought this was very foolish. I had been extensively indoctrinated by the Marxist-Leninist groups, even somewhat brainwashed, to believe that the only possible redemption for India lay in a revolution organised exactly as the one in Russia had been. I had been made to believe that all of humanity could be divided into two groups: the exploiters and the exploited, the haves and the have-nots. However, it was difficult for me to decide whether my father was exploited or an exploiter.

This mythical division into two classes, two class interests, and class warfare all looked very reasonable to me. I thought that if only Mahatma Gandhi read a little of Marx and understood his true philosophy, India would be saved. Little did I know that he had lived in England and had every access to all the literature of Marx and Lenin, and that he knew all about revolution. I was so young and stupid, yet fanatically indoctrinated. So I found my way to the inner circle of the saint, and looked for an opportunity to present my gospel of class war to him.

When my chance came, I gave him a non-stop oratory on class warfare, as well as how useless his method of nonviolence was. He listened to me very carefully. That is my greatest surprise today. When I came to my final conclusion, he looked quite calm. Then he asked me, "Are you sincere?" That infuriated me: if I were not sincere, would I have gone out of my way to bring him this great message? I shouted that I was very sincere. He went on, "You are speaking with conviction?" "Of course!" "Do you think I have no conviction about what I say?" I had never thought of that before. I said, "Yes, you must have conviction." "Am I sincere?" "Maybe . . . ." "Are you not saying something which is in total contradiction to what I say?" "Yes." "Don't you see the possibility of two people with contradictory views both having full conviction and sincerity?" "Yes." "You are asking me to stand in your footsteps and look. Have you ever considered the possibility of standing in my footsteps and looking? If I stand in your angle of vision, I will see what you see. That's what you want me to do. Suppose I invite you to stand in my angle of vision and look at the same thing. Are you prepared for that?"

I was certainly not prepared, but I didn't say so. He continued, "Young man, truth is many faceted. You can look at it from a number of points of view, and from each angle you will get a different perspective. All that you have said is known to me, but what I see you have no patience to consider." I thought that was right. Although I had been listening to him for a week, waiting for my opportunity to pontificate, I had never really listened to him. I was only listening to myself, to my objections to whatever he was saying.

This simple incident was a great turning point in my life. It completely silenced me. Thereafter, when I talked with another person it always occurred to me that there could be one more way of looking at truth. I learned to step down from my pedestal and walk over to the other person's, to sympathetically get into his way of seeing. To me, this was the beginning of a great discovery of what a wonderful world we live in and how rich our human heritage is.

Once you take a position with a closed mind, it is as if the treasures your forefathers have amassed in all parts of the world are brushed aside as being of no meaning to you. Then Christ becomes meaningless. Muhammad, Buddha and Lao-Tze become meaningless. All the great thinkers, poets and artists of other cultures and perspectives are only to be reviled.

It took many centuries for the Greeks to imbibe the art that was developed in Egypt. From that the Greek culture rose slowly up, until they were able to bequeath many beautiful treasures to their gods of the finest carvings ever made by man. Then along came the Turks with a great slogan: "Every image made with a resemblance to anything on earth is against Allah." So they went around smashing all the beautiful marble carved by the master artists. That culture, its artistic production, those most beautiful expressions of the human mind, were all mutilated in the name of a stupid idea.

Still, that was only the destruction of dead matter. How often is it expressed with the cutting of throats in the name of the all-beneficent, the all-compassionate? In India sometimes a Muslim kills a cow. That's terrible, isn't it, to kill a cow, to kill a gentle creature that gives us milk? So a Hindu becomes very annoyed and very angry, and he stabs the Muslim. Isn't a man better than a cow? Should you kill a man because he killed a cow? The plea of the Hindu is that "life is sacred," but only when it is a cow. Is not life sacred in a man? This is what is called the blindness that comes from *asmita,* wrong identity.

When Narayana Guru came to the Sivagiri Mutt, there was already a small shrine there. In the shrine was a spear, representing Subramaṇya. Worship was offered to it by a priest. After a while another priest came who became very devoted to Narayana Guru. He said, "What are these stupid fools doing? They are worshipping a spear when our Guru is here? We should put something of Guru there instead of the spear." He threw the spear away and put a discarded pair of Narayana Guru's sandals on the altar and started worshipping them. The first man became extremely annoyed that his object of worship had been thrown away and replaced by a new thing. He went and complained to the Guru.

Narayana Guru called both of them and asked, "Why was this man worshipping a spear? Is the spear God?" "No, I know the spear is not God, but when I see it I think of God and become reverent." "So it stands for God?" "Yes". He turned to the other and said, "Why did you throw it away?" "Because it is superstition to think of a spear as God." "Why did you put the wooden sandals there?" "Because they are Guru's." "Am I God?" "There is the living God within you." "Am I those sandals?" "When I see them I think of you." "The other man is doing exactly the same thing." Then the Guru went on, "Do you think that I can only become wooden sandals? I can also become a spear."

The fetish is a psychological disease of the mind. In the twelfth chapter of the Bhagavad Gita, Arjuna asks, "How should I worship you? As the formless, nameless, transcendent reality, or as one with a form?" Krishna answers him, "The purest form of understanding is to know truth in principle, but for people with uninstructed minds it becomes very difficult. They need some medium of presentation. But then people tend to forget that it is a representation and not the original." No analogy to the Absolute can ever be complete; all analogies illustrate only a particular aspect of essential reality.

There is a wholesale difference between the Absolute and a relativistic version of it. That is why it is said that the Tao that can be spoken of is not the Tao. And yet it is spoken of in ten thousand and one words. So many words are needed because each one is only a partial expression. It can never be a total expression. This is the *rahasya,* the secret.

Henri Bergson puts this idea very beautifully using several examples. He speaks of the Absolute as the gold coin which can never be equaled by any number of copper pennies. Again, he discusses how a verse written in another language, which comes straight from a poet's inspiration and vision, can be translated many times, but the translations can only approximate the original and never communicate its full sense. Then he continues, suppose you go to Paris and walk around Notre Dame cathedral and take hundreds of pictures from inside, outside and above. Then you bring them home and juxtapose them all and show them to someone. No matter how the photographs are presented, they can never convey the overwhelming experience of actually walking into Notre Dame and being there, because each one is only a partial view.

One who knows the inner secret won't quarrel with anyone who is giving a partial view. Without exception, all the proselytisers are giving only partial views. Narayana Guru mentioned this in an earlier verse, when he brought in the idea of the blind men examining the elephant. Now he wants us to know one more secret. When I say, "Listen to me," it means that I have a piece of truth to show you. When I show it to you, you and I will be knowers of that one truth, and this will unite us.

Narayana Guru arranged for a Parliament of Religion which he called a confluence of all religions. There he displayed a watchword: "It is not to argue and win, but to know and let know." If you are arguing to win then you have already decided that the other person's point of view is wrong and yours is right. When you say, "Let me know from you," you have already admitted that there is a great treasure in the other person's understanding and it is valuable to share it. Through the sharing you can become one with the other person. The 'I' will change into 'we'. When you also offer, "I have something to let you know," you are seeing what treasure is in your possession, and the joy of sharing it with another person makes it all the more worthwhile. Thus, you share yours with another and they share theirs with you. You open up a tremendous opportunity. This is the wise man's secret.

Even when a Jehovah's Witness comes with his enthusiastic talk, he is so hopeful of the good that might come out of it — that both will become good witnesses of Jehovah — that a unity will arise where there is currently only duality. His intention is that if all the people of the world are brought to his point of view, there will only be one religion. Then the world would become very good and we would all become brothers, comrades, fellow men. So you can accept this from him, even though he may not accept anything from you.

When you walk into the lives of people of different faiths, and are not just watching them as members of some religion, but soaking into their minds, living the life they live and offering the prayers they give; when you really enter into the spirit of it, it enthralls you. It brings the same truth with another quality, another kind of sweetness.

Sri Ramakrishna tried one religion after another for his realisation. On each occasion the ecstasy he experienced had a special flavour of its own. When he wanted to know God the Christian way he constantly went to church, sat before the priest in all veneration, and read the Bible with earnestness. He fasted and prayed and thought of none but Jesus. When he wanted to experience the Absolute as Allah, he clothed himself as a Muslim, sat with their mullahs, listened endlessly to the Koran, and did the five kinds of veneration, *namas*, very strictly. He observed their fasts. He experienced the special quality of each religion in depth, but in spite of all the differences he could see the essence as the same.

Why should we give up such great treasures, when only superficial differences stand in our way? Nobody stops us except our own foolishness and fanaticism. In this there is double gain or double loss. Not only regarding religion. You can use this in your daily life, with your family, between husband and wife, among friends, neighbours, lovers, at the office, basically between you and any other person you come to transact with. You can see that there is another way of looking at things. Instead of a unilateral or linear way of thinking, there can be a dialectical coming together.

The key is being able to change positions to see the other person's point of view. You cannot have a vested interest in clinging to your own position. This approach was used quite well by Fritz Perls in his existential therapy, where he would have a person switch back and forth between two chairs representing two different sides of a conflict. It's really a wonderful way of teaching how identifying with two polemics can bring a new flexibility to the mind. A new lucidity can be achieved. It subtly brings you to a neutral zero. You are neither this nor that.

In the hundredth verse, Narayana Guru is going to tell us *atum itum alla,* it is neither that nor this. Try this in your own life, with your family and friends. You will make a wonderful world.

Nobody wants to have factionalism, but even as you are attempting to bring unity, you become part of a faction. It is in the name of unity that you are creating all these factions in the first place. Nataraja Guru gives the example of people making noise in a room. One man becomes very enthusiastic to bring silence, so he goes to the middle of the room and starts shouting, "Don't make noise! There is already so much sound here!" He is only adding to the hubbub going on there. Instead of contributing his own silence, he makes it worse by shouting.

So the true knower of this secret withholds from all disputes. The Guru made this so central to his teaching because it is in the name of this one dispute that we have been killing each other since the dawn of human history. There has been more blood shed in the name of religion than there is water in the seven oceans put together. It is such an important question for all mankind. If the dignity of man is to be enhanced, we need to find a solution to this eternal riddle of man killing man in the name of an opinion. There are two more verses before we reach the culmination of this line of thought.

Verse 48

tanuvil amarnna śarīri, tante sattā-
tanuvil "atente" "titente" tennu sarvam
tanutayoẓiññu dhariccitunnu; sākṣā-
lanubhavaśālikaḻāmitōrkkil ārum

The self encased in a body, in his eidetic consciousness,
understands all such as, "That is mine" and "This is mine"
bereft of body identity; on considering this
it is evident that everyone has truly experienced.

We all have various affiliations. We belong to ideologies of a religious, political, social, moral and personal nature. It is very important for us to establish an ethical norm for our everyday relationships.

A law cannot be enforced if it cannot be lived. For any ethical norm to gain social validity it should be clear enough for those who have to live it, and should be within their capacity to do so. From the first verse to this forty-eighth verse, Narayana Guru has developed his argument in such a way to keep it as close as possible to our everyday experience.

We can live completely withdrawn from this world in a state of absorption, where there is no time and space, no name and form, no actor and action, and no duality of knower and known or enjoyer and enjoyed. That is a state of pure transcendental beingness. In it there is no problem of interpersonal relationships, no problem of the world, no problem of any transaction whatsoever. Hence, there is no need for law. Law, or a norm, is only necessary when you come out of that state. Emerging from the transcendental means becoming conscious of your body. Once you are aware of your body as a separate entity, all other differentiations follow. When you say "I," 'this' also comes.

The first thing we have to realise here is that we are in a peculiar position of belonging at once to a transcendental state and an immanent state. In the transcendental state we can think of ourselves without the body. In the immanent state you feel that you are an embodied being. The Guru always chooses very appropriate words for the occasion. There are many synonyms for 'body' in Sanskrit, such as *sarīram, dēham* and *tanu,* but tanu has a special significance. When you physically think of a body, the minimum requirements are its extension, mass and weight. Extension means it occupies space. Mass is its physical content, and this is in turn subject to gravitational attraction, which we call weight. Yet it is possible to abstract the body so that the extension of it is not a necessity. It is not that it has no extension, you are just not emphasising that fact. Neither do you emphasise the fact of its having a mass, and you deduct from it its weight. If you do all this, it becomes almost like a mono-mark, a certain idea you have in your mind which stands for your body. This is called tanu.

The Guru could have used a more gross word like *dēham,* but he used tanu because it is more suitable to what he is trying to say. He means that when you sit in your body and think of yourself as 'I', the body becomes almost a negligible factor. You don't take into account your physical form, your colour, your weight, your state of physical health, your flabbiness or thinness. All these are made minimal, and yet you have not forgotten that you are an embodied being.

In the *Saundarya Laharī,* Brahman gathers the finest dust from the feet of the Mother to create the world. There *tanīyām,* related to tanu, refers to the very finite particles of the cosmic dust. Like that, when you consider your body as being almost akin to your mental state, you can easily pass from the mind into the body and from the body into the mind. Then you have a flexibility, a lucidity, a fluidity. The gross and the subtle become easily interchangeable.

Next the Guru uses the word *śarīrī,* which conveys the sense that you are not the body even though you have one. You have two body boundaries. One is your own physical body boundary, which falls within the law of impenetrability: you cannot occupy the same space I occupy. Even if two lovers try to get into each other, their bodies stop them from doing it. With all their fondness and affection, the body retains its impenetrability.

When you say, "This is my body, this is my mind, this is my intellect," you are seeing within the body itself an identity made out of things which can be placed within its circle. You say, "My mind." That exclusively refers to the ideations which are going on in this one particular body; feelings and sensations which are experienced only within this one unit.

It may look as though a person's experiences are within the limits of his body, but the same person says "my wife" or "my husband" or "my child" with the same ease that he says "my body." The relation established to another body is not of a physical nature. What does that "my" there stand for? At a value level, a level of affinity, you can forget the physical grossness of your body, as well as the bodies of your wife or husband, your child, your friend, or even of your car or your dog. Instead you establish a relationship, and in it you go beyond the body boundary.

There is an infinite range of what may be called the ego boundary. The state of the ego actually changes according to the expansion it attains. It becomes more a transcendental ego than an ordinary ego. A transcendental ego is not a social ego, it's only a centre of consciousness. Here the centre of consciousness is not just a passive witness, because the bond of affection is the one which makes the person go beyond his body limitations in saying "my child" "my friend" and so on. If you are a very altruistic person, like a mystic, you are so in love with everything that you can even say "my universe."

Examples of this attitude are plentiful. The French government plans to explode an atomic bomb in the Pacific Ocean, so Australians, New Zealanders and Japanese people have decided to go and stay where the test is planned to be. They are willing to die, saying "The nuclear bomb is bad for the world. Before you kill the world, kill us." They are saying "We love the world and humanity. We do not want humanity to be killed. We are in love with it, so we are prepared to die for it." What kind of identity is this? It is not like saying "This is my wife, I want to protect her," or "This is my child, I will do anything for her." They are identifying themselves with the future of life and the well-being of the whole world.

If you attach a body to your identity — the identity of your interest — it is called *sattā tanu,* the body of your existentiality. Your existence becomes a meaningful factor by the incorporation of values that you want to live by. When you say "I am," you are a living entity. In this there is a well-integrated, compact idea of beingness encapsulated as your existence. So your existence is your identity with values for which you live, for which you stand. Your freedom, your understanding, your validations of things — a number of these factors put together become your existential beingness.

Your existential beingness can be increased by including more and more values and items of value in it. It is within this body of interest that you say "he is mine," "she is mine," "this building is mine," "the car is mine," "this country is mine," "the world is mine." In this way, your body of interest enlarges. You don't have to become a Socrates for that. You don't have to become a Ramana Maharshi or a Yājñavalkya: you already experience it.

Narayana Guru says here, "I am not initiating a new law for you or an ethical norm for you that is not already known to you and experienced by you. If I am generalising and giving you an ethical norm, I am only deriving it from your daily experience. You already experience transcending your body limit and identifying with others. That being the case, I am only asking you to extend it a little more, to recognise it more consciously." People think realisation is a very rare thing that only one in a million might achieve. The Guru wants to explode that idea, saying "Don't give up your mind that way. You are as good as anyone. Don't think of this as being a rare privilege of someone else. You already have some realisation." Otherwise why, when your husband or wife is sick are you also affected?

I once heard a joke that a woman was in the hospital undergoing labour pains. Her husband was restlessly walking up and down. The doctor saw him and said, "Why are you so anxious? I have taken care of many deliveries in this hospital, and there has never been even one occasion of a husband dying. Relax, you have nothing to fear. Just go home." The doctor does not realise that the man's wife is part of his *sattā tanu,* his body of interest.

One has such an identity with his body of interest that this sort of thing is a common experience. And if you and your husband or wife or dear friend can be of the same self, you and the whole world can also be of the same self. You just have to extend it, extrapolate it a little farther.

Clearly, tanu is the key word in this verse. One is realising within the body of one's own interest, "this thing is mine," "that thing is mine," becoming oblivious to the bodily limitations of each thing. One neither thinks of his body nor of the impenetrability of the other body. They are all brought under one homogeneous reality.

This homogeneity is the integrating secret. When I talk to you and you listen to me, it is already with the realisation that at a certain level you can leave your peculiarities and idiosyncrasies, forget my peculiarities and idiosyncrasies, and enter into a world of ideas where my conceptual visualisation of an idea and your conceptual visualisation can become so alike, so identified with each other, that the word can make sense to you. We have to go beyond our bodies to communicate.

Next the Guru uses the term *anubhavam*, becoming like the other. It is not a mere resemblance, it is a factual identity. One becomes the other one. You transfer yourself from your bodily system to the bodily system of another. Within that oneness the duality of the body is no longer an issue. That's why, when a mother hears that her child has met with an accident, she becomes panicky. When she sits with the child, it is hard to tell who had the accident. The mother's and the child's faces look so alike in their sadness and pain.

This is reestablished in our lives everyday. When you pick up a cat and say "my dear kitty," you have already gone beyond your bodily limitations and your own body identity. People do not realise that this itself is part of your realisation. Of course, it needs to be further perfected. When you say someone is a realised person, it is not that she hugs a cat. There's a bit more to it. But you make a beginning just by hugging the cat.

A big myth is now exploded with this verse. You have now come so close to the experience of the Absolute. It is within your reach, in the palm of your hand, so to speak. When Jesus says, "The kingdom of God is at hand, close to you, within your own heart," people still doubt it. They say "If it is so close, where are the signs? Why are the clouds not becoming all pink and red? Why aren't the trees bursting forth in light and the sound of God's own voice?" Jesus says, "Ye hypocrites! I give you no signs."

All the religious words have frightened and confused us. Narayana Guru wants to give us courage, telling us, "Don't be afraid. You are as good as anyone. The essence of realisation is in your own daily experience." With this realisation you come to establish a universal norm for living that experience with others, not just in a state of absorption. When you are alienated and isolated it is easy to remain always good. There is no chance for the Pope to smack another person, for instance, because everyone stands before him with great politeness and reverence. Nobody even says one offensive word to him, so why should he get angry? It is easy for him to be pious and good. But bring him to the marketplace and expose him to all the troubles there. Then we will see his true tenor. There is no need for any ethics when you are in the state of a contemplative who is completely absorbed in the Absolute.

Your realisation is to be lived here and now in society where you touch and are touched by other people. Let us bring our realisation to the marketplace. But you think realisation is so holy and sacred that it must be kept separate, kept apart. That means you cannot live it. If you want to live it, it should be lived everywhere, at all times. Your perfection is a perfection for all time, not just for the church on Sunday. If you are perfect now you should be perfect in everyday life, too.

After the next verse there is a major change. If the whole one hundred verses is viewed as a garland, the first forty-nine present a kind of descending dialectics. From verse fifty onwards, an ascending dialectics is used. It is easy to go down, difficult to go up.

Verse 49

akhilarumātmasukhattināy prayatnam
sakalavuminńu sadāpi ceytiṭunnu
jagatiyil immatamēkamennu cinti-
ccaghamanayātakatār amarttiṭēṇam

All beings are making effort in every way,
all the time, for the happiness of the Self;
in the world, this is the one faith;
pondering on this, without becoming subjected to sin,
be controlled.

The central teaching of the Upanishads can be given in one sentence: *tarati śokam ātmavit,* the knower of the Self crosses over all pains. *Tarati* means crosses over; *śokam*, sorrow; and *ātmavit,* the knower of the Self. The mark of knowledge is *aśokam,* having no sorrow. Where there is sorrow there is ignorance, and where there is no ignorance there is no sorrow. You can easily find out whether you are ignorant or not by looking at yourself. If your mind has sorrow, if you are sad or in misery, it means you are in a state of ignorance.

The whole concept of Buddhism and the teaching of the Buddha is based on the redemption of misery. The Buddha does not go into a metaphysical inquiry of what this world is or what it is not. He only wants us to know that our common lot is misery and pain. This he calls the first truth about our own being. The second truth is that pain or sorrow comes from ignorance. The third truth is that this ignorance can be removed. The fourth truth is that the cessation of ignorance is called a state of happiness or nirvana. Of course, what he means by happiness has nothing to do with pleasure.

The central teaching of Christ is to love your neighbour as your own itself. Nobody wants his self to be misery. So care for the happiness of your self, then extend that to all.

Narayana Guru's main teaching is given in the form of a maximum or motto. If you go to India and ask what Narayana Guru taught, the first thing you will hear from any mouth is. "He taught that man is of one kind, he is of one faith, and he is one God." There are three factors here.

In the *Ātmopadeśa Śatakam*, the Guru first establishes what we might call one God. He does not assign any name to it. In fact, he never even brings in the word 'God' except by implication. In India, gods are referred to as Siva or Vishnu or Brahma. He never brings in any of those things. He used the word *Īśan*, which is used in the Isavasya Upanishad also, and only means 'the inherent principle'.

The first part of this book deals with the one God. That one God is explained to us as that which is shinning at once as the world which you see here and the world that you experience within. It is a very existential way of presenting it. Your very first experience is your existence and the world's existence. If you take the world that you see out there together with what you experience within, bracket them as one whole and then consider the reality of it, you can reduce it to one fundamental principle which is an unchanging reality that has within it the scope for continuous change. You see it inside as the stream of consciousness and outside as the changing phenomena. This is how the Guru first presents it.

Then he takes it further and gives both a structural as well as functional explanation of it. He begins with the very origin of consciousness where from an absolute state of inner darkness, as it were, consciousness comes in the form of an inquiry, extends itself as an observation, makes a judgement, and culminates in the reaching forward and experiencing of a particular universe of interest. Then it moves on to the next universe of interest. All the changes which take place from the primeval beginning of a question to a final satisfaction are all transformations of one consciousness. The Guru reiterates that the one God he speaks of is changing into all this, without changing. It is not a new idea. It's in the Upanishads. It's in the Bible. It's at the basis of all the great philosophies and religions.

Narayana Guru goes on to allude to the same one God as a treasury of immeasurable value which is like an ocean, on the surface of which is the manifestation of the changing modalities. Pain and pleasure abound on the turbulent surface, but when you vertically dive deeply into it, all those superficial experiences disappear and you become convinced of one total existence, one total awareness, and the value of all values. We have heard of the trinity in Christianity, the Father, the Son and the Holy Spirit. It is one and it is three simultaneously. Like that, the one God here is existence, subsistence and value, *saccidānanda*.

The Guru leads us from our initial experience of the world to the deeper core of the whole of existence until, in the sixth verse, we are told that hardly anyone knows the true nature of beingness. We are caught up in the conditional states of each passing moment, such as wakefulness, sleep, and wanting to eat or mate, that separate us from an understanding of the unconditional state itself.

As he proceeds with his elucidation of the one God or Principle, Narayana Guru brings in the next issue: how, from that very one God, is the self of the individuated person, as a nondifferentiated factor, derived. When we come to verse ten, we are asked to think of a person sitting in a dark room, who, suspecting the presence of another, asks "Who is there in the dark?" He receives the reply "I," which he understands in terms of his own 'I'. In this way the Guru introduces us to the second thesis that man is one in the Self, though not one in the body.

With the dark room, the Guru presents a kind of experimental situation where all differentiations can be annulled. In the darkness you do not see a person's form, colour or other superficial aspects. Everything is shut off except what is most central in each person, i.e. how one identifies himself. A person identifies himself with one monosyllabic sound, "I." That's enough. When another person says "I" and I hear it, I look upon the 'I' within me to know that someone is existing there. Thus, in a very subtle way, the Guru passes on from the question of one God to one mankind or one Self, the Self of all.

From that he brings us to a consideration of interpersonal relationships, and gave us an ethical code of aspiring for such happiness that includes the happiness of others. My happiness should be your happiness. Your happiness should be mine, too. He is not postulating either the oneness of God or the oneness of man for a metaphysical elucidation of some theory, but for the very practical purpose of living it here and now. He brings in the idea of one God so that we can meditate on that source and find our own unity.

In the thirteenth verse, he asks us to meditate on that Supreme Being which transcends the triple modalities of inertia, kinetics and sublimity, in order to transcend all forms of becoming. That very meditation will make our senses turn from the objects of enjoyment to the very source of the enjoyer. This cools us of feverishly running after sensual objects, and we become grounded in our own source. Narayana Guru proceeds in a very beautiful and subtle way, making God accessible to us and known to us as our very own source. He draws our attention to experiencing that God in our brother, in our neighbour, in the 'other'. On proper consideration, the 'other' is not an other. He uses special words to express this, like *aparan,* one who seems to be the other, but on consideration is not.

Then the Guru develops the third aspect regarding differentiations of opinions. He focuses on the structure of the mind and how it functions both analytically and synthetically, how it has an a priori function and an a posteriori one, how it stands by the nondifferentiated knowledge which is presented in a word like 'this', and from there how it goes off on the tangent of its qualification. The qualifying or the specifying aspect takes us to the individual, to the particular, to the details and the effects. On the other hand, consideration of that which is the same in all takes us to the primal cause. We can gather our thoughts from the many to the one and find our unity.

After explaining to us how we can either be experiencing the separate entities or the one, he also gave a correlation by which we can have a coordinated understanding of the many and the one as part and parcel of one life. From that he brought us two possibilities. One is when the vaporous substance of our breath strings together many organs and keeps us bolted together as one piece; we become identified with the physical body and feel our separation from everyone else. We become ego centered. By being ego centered, we become motivated by pain and pleasure. In this there is every likelihood of our rejecting or turning away from the 'other'.

The alternative possibility the Guru gave us is something that even a person of no understanding, in a very instinctive way, accomplishes. It is to go beyond the limit of the body and see our happiness as joined with the happiness of the other. There can be a unitive understanding in the very common man and even in animals. A dog loves its master and, in that love, transcends its own bodily limitations. It is very much influenced by the moods of its master. If even a dog can understand its unity with other beings, the superior man can certainly have a much better appreciation of this unity.

After showing these two examples to us separately, Narayana Guru now asks us to consider the very secret of all motivations, urges and drives that occur in all beings from bacteria to human beings. If you observe any species at any time, in any action situation, the primary motive is to move from a state of uneasiness to one of easiness, from discomfort to comfort, from maladjustment to better adjustment, from chaos to order, and from disharmony to harmony. This is a movement within the consciousness of all sentient beings.

We were taught earlier that the Self we speak of is that great knowledge which remains hidden within this seeming darkness. The consciousness we experience on the surface is only a tiny speck of the greater knowledge that remains hidden from us in the unconscious. We were also told that the world we see here is nothing but a manifestation of that supreme knowledge. We come to know this knowledge through its gradual manifestation and growth. After a very long period of development our earth was able to produce life, which became more and more organised through various stages. Its culmination so far is the human mind, with its very specialised sense organs supplemented by a higher understanding in which there is a mathematical unity on par with the mathematical harmony of the whole universe. Without leaving its own room, by its own meditations and calculations, that mind can see clearly how the moon moves around the earth and how the earth and other planets move around the sun. It can devise a mechanical instrument that can be accurately propelled from the earth to any other body in the solar system, or even sent beyond it to wander among the stars. How does it do it? The cosmos out there, the macrocosm, is regulated by certain laws that can be reduced to mathematical terms. Such a reduction is possible within human consciousness; thus all this movement is within consciousness.

If you are aspiring for happiness, that aspiration is happening within your *akatāṟ*, within your inner organ. Part of that inner organ is well-equipped to understand everything, because it is in liaison with the knowledge of the whole universe. This universe is a transient one. The Guru uses the term *jagat*, meaning transient, ever-changing. In all its changing it has a changeless law. Through the advancement of mathematics and physics we have come to know that the original matrices, the norms of measurement, which were used in studies like plane geometry, are no longer applicable once we go beyond the local stretch of space and time. We have evolved and are evolving a new methodology which focuses on the relationships between bodies moving at different velocities in different directions. By bringing in a topological approach, our understanding of the movement of another body in another plane means we have found a way to transcend changes and movement.

Using this kind of a mind, with its new eye, when you look at the changing world you see that all people, all beings, at all times and in all their endeavours, are motivated by this one drive for happiness. Narayana Guru says, "Know that to be the only religion." He builds up the whole thing in such a wonderful way that you can never escape its impact. If it is true that we are of one God, if we are of one kind, and if our drive is for one happiness, then restrain your mind so that you won't go off on a tangent where you differentiate your brother from you, where you alienate your happiness from the happiness of another. That will bring you to the mainstream of the happiness of all. Here the teachings of Christ, of Buddha, of Lao Tze — all teachings and no teachings — converge into one understanding, fully coordinated, fully correlated, unified.

Now we have a body of knowledge given to us in these forty-nine verses. The Guru uses another fifty verses to bring it to be a part of our life. Then he uses one final verse to sum everything up. That makes the total one hundred verses. With this forty-ninth verse, we close the section which may be called the pure aspect of the teaching. From the fiftieth on, we step into what we call the applied aspect. The application begins with the next verse.

Verse 50

nilamoṭu nīratupōle kāṟṟu tīyum
veḷiyumahaṅkṛti vidyayum manassum
alakaḷumāẓiyumennu vēṇṭayellā-
vulakumuyarnnaṟivāyi māṟiṭunnu

The ground, together with water, wind, fire and sky,
the functioning ego, right knowledge and the mind —
waves and ocean: what else is there?
All these worlds, having arisen, are changing into
knowledge.

The first reference in this verse is to the firm earth, where we sit, walk, work, and where we retire and sleep when we are tired. It is our ground. In fact, it is called terra firma, the firm ground. The Malayalam word Narayana Guru uses is *nila*, meaning firmness, solidity, existence. When you say it has a *nila*, it has an existence. The Guru could have used another word for earth, but he especially chose this simple one. It is that which you experience under your feet as your very base. We begin here with something firm and also the very basis of everything, the ground. Jesus says that you do not build your house on the sand, but on a firm rock. Nila has the same implication.

The Guru then moves on to something with a different quality, water. He has chosen the word *nīru*, meaning water in its functional sense: when it rains and makes pattering sounds on your roof, when it makes puddles, when it flows. When you turn on the tap, water gushes out. You can see it as a big river and as a gigantic, shoreless ocean. These are experiences which are very different from the firm ground. It is pliant, ever-changing.

When we breathe, it is so gentle and subtle an action that we hardly notice that we are passing air in and out. When a little stir is caused in the air it becomes an enjoyable breeze. It comes and tickles the leaves and flowers, and plays with the shrubs and trees in the garden. When it becomes a little stronger we call it the wind. With greater intensity it can become a whirlwind, and grow even more violent as a hurricane. Such is another experience, different from earth and water: the blowing wind.

If you take a match and strike it against the matchbox or the ground, it bursts into flame. Fire is our great friend. We cannot even live without it. It dwells within us, keeping our bodies warm. It fills the hearth, the fireplace, the stove, our lamps and lights. It is in the clouds as electricity. It blazes forth as the sun in the sky. Even the far-off stars are nothing but fire. This is yet another experience.

If you fling wide your doors and come out, you are in the open. For this Narayana Guru especially chose the word *veḷi,* meaning the open. When you go out into the open and look, there is no end to it. You can see the far distant horizon. The whole world is out in the open. To come out, you don't even have to get up from your bed and leave the room. All you have to do is open your eyes and you see the whole outside. What is not inside is outside, and it is paradoxically true that everything outside is inside.

Who has all these experiences? The Guru says *ahamkṛti,* there is an 'I' generating event taking place. It goes on generating 'I'. The 'I' generating thing is experiencing all this. It is just like when you light a lamp. The lamp not only shows itself, along with the light comes a world which is illuminated by it. Like that, when this 'I' is generated it does not stand by itself, it shines its light on everything and illumines it. In fact, once the light is turned on you almost immediately forget about it. What is illuminated becomes more important than the source of illumination. Similarly, as soon as the 'I' is generated, it becomes interested in whatever it sees, and focuses on it.

This is knowledge, vidya. Nataraja Guru calls it cognition. The cogniser cognises and has a cognition. And who cognises? 'I'. Who am I? That which cognises. How do I know 'I'? By putting together whatever is known to 'I'. Thus "I," "me," "my" and "mine" are being generated endlessly inside us. When we look at it we don't see any special 'I' in it, only whatever is being cognised.

If you put all this into one big circle, it becomes the greatest fiction we could ever think of. It is called the mind. What is mind? A fiction that is uniting all the facts. All the facts are held together by a fiction called mind. Can you see this mind anywhere? It is just like going to look for the ocean. You go and look for it, but it is completely cluttered with waves. There is not even a little space left where there are no waves so you can see the actual ocean. But you can send a frogman into it. He will dive deep and say, "Hey, there are no waves here. The vast ocean is underneath them." Philosophers and psychologists are commissioned as our frogmen to dive deep into the fiction called mind. Then they come and tell us, "It has a depth. It has more than what you see here as your thoughts, your perceptions and conceptions, your ideas, feelings and emotions. These are only surface things, waves and ripples on the surface. We have gone deeply into it. We found it is very deep and unconscious." They are our frogmen. We believe them when they tell us there is a depth.

So what have we come to ultimately? The firm ground, the water that flows, our experience of firmness and of movement, fluidity, viscosity; of warmth and wind, of the openness of the universe: all these have now become like waves. In Narayana Guru's prayer, *Daiva Daśakam,* he says, "Let me come to know this equation, that you are like these waves and your phenomenal power is like the wind that causes the waves. The depth of the ocean is unfathomable. Even so, let us see that your glory is unfathomable." Thus, everything becomes one unfathomable glory. When we ponder over all our experiences, ranging from the most firm, solid ground, to this ideation of a "me" here or an "I" there, with all its qualities, everything rises to one single experience of knowledge. That's the gist of this verse. We meditate on this for our onward march.

We have come to a turning point in Narayana Guru's instruction. In the last forty-nine verses, the Guru was speaking to us more or less from a transactional point of view. Of course, we were given an idea of what we are besides this body. He also saw us as part of a society in which there are other individual members just like us. There are various kinds of relationships existing between people. There is this world, the society, and the individual. All these were taken into full consideration. He worked out a system by which we first can find peace with our environment, with the social setup, and peace on earth and good will among people. These are the first requirements. Now we are going to have a more serious entry into our own real being.

In Patañjali's Yoga Sutras, after the initial discipline is given he asks you to cultivate a posture where you can sit peacefully and comfortably, to make yourself stable for your practice. He did not say you should sit in a *padmāsana* or a *mayūrāsana* or anything. Those were all invented by others. They may be good as exercises, but they don't especially aid your pursuit. All Patañjali wanted was a firm, steady posture so that you can forget about your body.

Likewise, in forty-nine verses Narayana Guru has prepared us to sit in peace so that now we can commence our search. We no longer have any quarrel with our neighbour. Let our neighbour be a Jehovah's Witness or a Hare Krishna, who cares? We have no quarrel with them, in fact we agree with them. If the Jehovah's Witness comes and asks, "Do you accept the only God, the true God?" you say "Oh yes. We have no quarrel with you." If the Hare Krishna person comes and demands, "Don't you agree that the only God is Krishna? Oh, Krishna, Krishna, Hare Krishna!" we have no quarrel. Now we can just sit very quietly.

What next? What comes next is very important. We commence the real probe.

You are sitting here firmly. Close your eyes. What is that firmness underneath that you experience? It becomes very strange as soon as you try to look at it. You take the firmness of the ground for granted, but when you isolate it as an experience and try to understand it, it becomes quite vague. Just what is that firmness? You can borrow clichés from the scientists and say it is a gravitational pull you are experiencing, but with equal plausibility you could say that in the middle of the earth is a great green demon that is pulling you down with invisible claws. If you were to make a tunnel to the centre of the earth you could see he is a very big, monstrous green demon. Who really knows? It may be the demon or it may be the force of gravity, but for us it is merely a strange experience. All you are sure of is your own knowledge. You know that there is a firmness. The firmness is your knowledge. Can you draw a line between the knowledge of the firmness and the one who is experiencing firmness? Can you say, "Up to this point is the knower of firmness and from here on firmness itself begins?" Not really. This is why I said that all the facts are put together by a fiction. They are all held together by what's called mind.

It is true, though, that you do experience a quality called firmness. When you turn on the faucet and water flows out of it, you know that this is very different from the solid spout of the pipe which just sits there and never moves. The water is flowing, and if you're not careful your cup or your sink will overflow. This is quite a different experience from firmness. Yet with all the difference, is it any different from your knowledge of the flow? Just what is this thing called flow, anyway?

In our everyday experience, all these things look very clear-cut, very definite. In winter we know it is cold outside and we should sit as close as possible to the fire. Its warmth gives us a very good feeling. In the spring we don't like the wind blowing; we keep the house closed up tight. When we go out it blows hard. We all know that experience, but what is it really? When we meditate on it, when we ponder over any aspect of our experience, we see that we have only one whole instrument: our knowledge. Arbitrarily we trifurcate that knowledge into the knower, the known and knowledge.

We have been asked to deal with the 'other', the other person. When you say "I" and the other person says "I," you can see that the 'I' in the other person and the 'I' in you are not two. Now we are asked to go still further. Not only the 'I' in you and the other person, but everything that constitutes the awareness centered around an 'I' is none other than consciousness. Somebody says you are very good and you are pleased. Somebody says, "I know you are an idiot," and you are suddenly very angry. Did anything happen? Nothing happened. Why are you so angry? "That's my nature." And what is your nature? "When my knowledge changes, I change. I was under the impression that I was a good guy, but now you say I'm bad. Now I'm meditating on badness. It makes me feel very negative." Can you not remain as free as before? "No, I cannot, because I don't stop at this one. As soon as you say something else it becomes part of me too." Why? "Because you are part of my knowledge, and I identify with that knowledge."

Is there no way out? Oh, yes, certainly. That is to know that if you say I am bad and I think I am good, it is all only knowledge. And because it is only knowledge, I can straighten it up even if you mess with it. All I have to do is remember it is knowledge and not get carried away by it.

The central pivot in all this is called *ahamkṛti*, the 'I' generating rascal who is sitting in the midst of it all. This is a tremendous problem. You don't know the nature of this machine that goes on clicking one 'I' after another — like drops from a leaky faucet — the consciousness of 'I'.

Let me share a secret with you. The Guru began with terra firma, something very firm and solid. Then he watered it down. He poured water onto the firm ground, to make it more flexible. So I say, "You stupid fools! Water down your 'I' a little. Why should you keep it so rigid? Why should your 'I' be so solid that you hold onto it as the dearest thing in existence? Let it go. What a great relief it can bring! You have no idea. So water down your ego a little." Then the Guru said, "Let it blow in the wind." First it was firm ground, *nila*, existence. Second, "Let it flow." Then he said, "Let it fly in the wind." Where is the answer? It is blowing in the wind. Then ultimately burn it! Bring fire upon it!

There is nothing more beautiful than this meditation. You have to do it every time this horrid 'I' comes and sits. Pour water on it, dilute it. This going around asking, "What did so-and-so say about me? What does he think?" Is it so important? "It is all-important to me." What is this 'me'? It's completely fictitious. If you can learn this much you don't need psychiatrists, you don't need mental hospitals, you don't need any of that stuff. It will bring you great peace by itself.

It's not that there shouldn't be a lovely device called an 'I' as the central orientation point of your world. That's very good. But it should only be for that one purpose of orientation, and nothing else. You don't really need other peoples' opinions in order to know how to feel. So don't make your 'I' your pet baby you're always fawning over. You make it your lap dog. You have to pet it all the time, taking it around for walks and asking your neighbour "how do you like my dog?" You feel very happy if somebody says "beautiful!" but you are upset if they say "I have seen better dogs than that!"

My friends, there is nothing more beautiful than this freedom of which I am speaking. Try to experience it. The whole day can be so wonderful! Whenever someone is making you turn and churn inside, causing a knot within you, remember it is time to add water and make things flexible once again. The world is so stupid! Someone or other may breathe poison in your ear — cast it into the wind or onto the fire. Do not take it seriously. Know that it is all happening where the generating of the 'I' is going on. This is the only place where real darkness prevails. Moreover, it is without our knowledge that the 'I' is being generated and passed on to us. We have no idea what tricky hand is doing it.

Narayana Guru could very well have said 'ego' in this verse, but he did not. He did not say just 'I'. He said *ahamkṛti*. *Kṛ* means to do; *kṛt* means one who does; *kṛti* is the doer. So *ahamkṛti* is "the doer of the 'I'," "the 'I' doing fellow." Karl Jaspers says that you cannot study philosophy, you cannot think of philosophy, you can only philosophise. Like that, you are always 'I'-ing. What do you 'I'? You 'I' this knowledge.

Cognition has the same meaning. It is from cogitation that Descartes derived the basis for his philosophy. He concluded, "I think, therefore I am." We have to go beyond that. Can you not say "If the thinking is me, then I am not. It is only the thought." Buddha came to that same conclusion. He said, "If you take an experience, such as a toothache, we grant that there is a tooth. We grant that the tooth has nerves. We grant that those nerves are rotten. We accept that the rotten nerves are agitating and that that agitation is painful." But when you say, "It is my pain," where did that 'my' come from? Buddha says, "I do not see any place for that. I agree with everything else." Only the thought content is there. Why should that thought content be an 'I'?

When you tune yourself to this inner mechanism in your meditation you get a whole new freedom: the freedom not to be agitated, the freedom to enjoy or not enjoy, the freedom to relate or not relate. From the most gross you can slip away to the most sublime, the most subtle. If you want you can go back to the terra firma and experience its solidness. When you open the window and the papers flutter, it is helpful to put a heavy weight on them. Like that, you have come to the most gross and found a use for it. In the world of uses, everything has its place. But don't get glued on to anything. Move freely within this whole realm of earth and water and fire.

In Nataraja Guru's commentary he placed the five elements and the three principles of 'I', knowledge and the mind in a circle on one side. Then he took the ocean and waves as the other, outer side, to show we are not only thinking of the subjective world but also of the objective one. In my translation and commentary, however, I relate the ocean and its waves to the first group of eight items as an analogy to decipher them. Both Husserl and Jaspers speak of deciphering, and I agree with their idea. First we have all the ciphers, and we use the analogy of the ocean and its waves to decipher them.

You cannot get rid of all the waves and just have a pure ocean. That is what everybody is trying to do — sit firm and close the eyes so that you get rid of all thoughts and ideas, and then finally you are left with the pure, pure ocean of the Self. Narayana Guru says this is like someone taking a cake of soap to the washtub and trying to wash all the lather out of it. No matter how much you wash, it cannot be done. The more water you pour and the more you rub, the more the lather comes. Trying to get rid of all the thoughts and ideas in the mind in order to come to pure consciousness is like that. It is in and through all this that you have to see pure consciousness. It is not that you kill everyone in the world and then find peace. Let your good neighbours be there. Their dog may bark, but you can still be peaceful. See how it works for you today.

Verse 51

aṟivil irunnorahantayādyamuṇṭāy-
varumitinōṭoridanta vāmayayūm
varumivaraṇṭulapaṅṅaḷ pōle māyā-
maramakhilam maṟayeppaṭarnniṭunn

Having existed in knowledge, an I-ness, in the beginning, emerges;
coming as a counterpart to this is a thisness;
like two vines, these spread over the tree of *māyā*,
completely concealing it.

Our most distinct and undeniable experience is that of an 'I' consciousness. The experiencing of "I am" is universal. When it comes, it is placed between two other entities: the world "out there" and the inestimable stretch of consciousness of which the 'I' is only a part. We are not very clear about the delimitation that is made of our 'I' consciousness, yet when we say "I am" we know it is not the whole of consciousness.

Thus, on one side is the physical world and on the other is consciousness. The individuality of our own self that we feel as our personality seems to be a confection of both the world and consciousness. This body can be touched; it is physical, like any other body. To that extent we belong to the world. Yet the non-physical consciousness of "I," "mine," "not mine" and so on is also part of us. How much of us is physical and how much is mental or spiritual? We cannot say, but we do know that both aspects are integral parts of us.

It is evident that before we started recognising ourselves as conscious entities, we must have been part of something very similar to the stuff of our consciousness. Narayana Guru presents this idea here as a basic substance out of which an 'I' consciousness manifests. Then the individuated 'I' simultaneously presents itself and what is other than the 'I' — the 'I' and the 'this' — to itself.

Next the Guru brings in the imagery, which he already introduced in verse 9, of a tree entirely covered with two vines, one called 'I' and the other called 'this'. This is one of the most important images of *Ātmopadeśa Śatakam,* one for us to return to again and again in our contemplation. Many times we have pondered how that person sitting under the tree can remain unaffected by all the intrigues of the vines growing all around him. But this time there is no person under the tree; he has become one of the vines itself, the 'I' vine, although the tree remains the same.

What is your main search? It is "Who am I?" or "What is this?" If you were to go to Ramana Maharshi, he would direct you to find out "Who am I?" If you went to Narayana Guru, he would ask you to find out "What is this?" Both 'I' as well as 'this' belong to one total reality. If you want to discover truth, you have to find out both. So if you are experiencing all this, what is the problem? The trouble is that your experience is not always correct. There is a possibility of error. If you do not avoid error, you can get into great difficulties.

For instance, right now when we look out the window we can see a magical world of our city through a swirl of snowflakes. It is so beautiful. There is every temptation to rush out into that beauty, but it is a snare. If we were not properly prepared, we would be frozen to death in no time. I remember being in Canada when I first experienced snow. There was a very bright sun outside. I thought it would be wonderful to walk up to the post office and back, so I set out. Then I thought all the water in my eyes was turning to ice, that my eyes were crystallising. I did not know how to save my eyes. I covered them with my hands and ran back as fast as possible to my room. I had never thought that the sun and snow could be so deadly. So like that there are many dangerous errors we can make when we don't fully understand the situation.

How do we avoid these errors? Narayana Guru presents us with a picture of a tree, which is to be looked at schematically. It has a base, or root, and it has fruit. The root and the fruit mark two poles. One is the basis, the alpha, and the other is the omega, the culmination or fulfilment. The origin in the root and the fulfilment in the fruit mark the vertical parameter. The horizontal component is the two sides. One is "I see the external world," and the other is "I have a mental image of the world." In other words, the objective and subjective aspects. For the most part the analogy of the tree stops here; don't press it any further.

We have pointed out four aspects of truth: its foundation, its meaning, its subjective appraisal and the objective experience of it. Of these, two belong intimately to 'I' and two belong to 'this'. The external world and the fruit we are looking for belong to 'this'. "I am" and my knowledge belong to 'I'. Thus, the four possibilities of error can be further classified under two headings, 'I' and 'this'.

When the fundamental truth of what I am is misunderstood it is an epistemological error. When the meaning of life is misunderstood it is an axiological error that is also called a teleological one, in other words an error in value assessment stemming from the misunderstanding of the natural design and end of life. *Teleos* means out there, in the future, what is yet to come, so teleology is an error regarding the future. We ask ourselves, "What should I become?" "What should I aim for?" and "What should I gain from my life?" If you are mistaken about these issues you might go on a wrong tangent, which is very serious. It is very important to know who you are and what you want to become. This marks the vertical parameter of life.

In order to know how to discern truth — what is true and what is untrue — you should have a normative notion about it. You need a measuring rod by which you can measure truth and decide, "This I accept as true, while this is untruth." This should be in your possession all day and all night, since at every moment you have to decide if things are true or not. If you make a mistake at this point it is called a methodological error. If something actual is taken as not actual or if something which is not actual is taken for actual, you are making a mistake at an ontological level. These are the purview of the horizontal parameter of life. So again we have the possibility of epistemological errors, teleological errors, methodological errors and ontological errors, and you need to be corrected of all four types of errors.

In the Upanishads we are given four great dictums. One is *aham brahmāsmi,* "I am Brahma." This is to correct the epistemological error, or the fundamental error by which a person thinks "I am the body." So much attention is given to a child's body, its clothes, its looks and its actions, that the feeling "I am this body," comes to stay. We do not give equal attention to making the child understand it is also something other than the body. By the time we are adults, our body consciousness is disproportionate to our idea of the spirit animating the body. This is an epistemological error in our understanding. The main question to address this is "Who am I?"

Narayana Guru says that phenomenal existence is totally covered over with 'I' and 'this'. The first dictum corrects this by answering the basic question, "Who am I?" with "I am the Absolute." To say "I am the body," is relativistically true, of course. We can see there are other bodies and that we are not pulsating within them as we are within this one. Our own body does have something special in a relative sense, but in the greater search this conception is an error to be corrected.

Before we consider the other two aspects, concerning the meaning of life and the actual world, we have to develop criteria to know truth. The only discerning instrument we have is our own mind and intellect. Yet we do not know how to differentiate between mind and intellect. We experience it all as part of our own totality of consciousness. It is within this consciousness that we experience a certain faculty which decides things for us, known as the intellect.

How does the intellect decide whether something is right or wrong? It certainly should not be by imitating others' opinions, though the fact is that we can be very much influenced by public opinion. Most of the things which we take for granted are not verified or critically examined. We just copy somebody else. But as Socrates said, an unverified life is not worth living. If you want to live a truthful life it must be verified, and for verification the evidence should come from your own self and not from someone else. This means the basic criterion you can adopt is the certitude of your own self, self-evidence. Ultimately it should be evident to your own self.

Gaining that kind of evidence means obtaining a normative notion. Norm means a measure; normative, pertaining to measurement. A notion is an idea. So a normative notion is an idea you can measure by. Furthermore, you can measure something only with that which truly exists. You are most convinced of your own existence. Therefore you own existence is to be made the basis for measurement. Even if a thing is true to all people, until it actually becomes your own experience the truth of it is only an a priori intellectual acceptance. It has not yet become part of your life. However, what is tested and found to be true in the lives of so many other people who have gone before you is certainly very helpful for you to accept as a working hypothesis. It's a fine place to start. So you don't have to say that you will not accept anything until it becomes your own experience. First you accept the universal truths that were found to be true by many before you. Then you try to integrate and experience them in your own life.

For this correction another great dictum was given by the Upanishads: *ayam ātmā brahma,* "this Self of mine is the Absolute." Narayana Guru has already defined the Self as "that which remains in darkness and makes things known to us, that is the Self." Now we say that Self is the Absolute. The light which is within us, which is Self-founded, which makes it known to us that we exist and also makes it known to us that other things exist, that is the Self. It is not contaminated with any relativistic notion such as "I am the body," or "I am in pain," "I am happy," "I am unhappy." These are colourations. If the colourations are removed and you understand the Absolute, the pure notion, then you have a very infallible measuring rod to discern what is true and what is not.

This does not happen in a single day, because your mind is already coloured with many preconditioned prejudices. To experience *ayam ātmā brahma,* this Self is the Absolute, many accretions of the mind have to be rubbed off and removed, many prejudices have to fall. You have developed many likes and dislikes because of your physical sense of pain and pleasure, the kind of food you have been given since childhood, the manners you were taught and the social values on which you were nurtured. Hundreds and hundreds of colourations have come into your life, constraining it and directing it in so many arbitrary ways, that to remove all these and know what the pure Self is is not an easy thing. But it is a great necessity if you want to adopt a correct methodology for the rest of your life, to make correct appraisals, and to not mistake the right for the wrong. Once you have that correct method, you have a testimony to measure the truth of things.

You have an immediate world to discern. There is snow outside, and it makes it difficult for you to drive your car. You cannot safely belittle that fact. It's an existence of a thing out there that has an ontological validity. In our transactional world there are a number of things which have this existential quality, and they should be properly discerned. The discernment comes from your own Self. There is an interaction between the Self and the non-Self. In that interaction you are always deciding the quality of the non-Self. If you fail here it can be disastrous.

The Upanishads give us another dictum to meditate upon: *prajñānam brahma,* "The external world is presented to you as your knowledge of it." To you, you have no other way of apprehending it; the external world and your knowledge of it are the same. Its existence is in the existence of your knowledge. Now, if there is not a one-to-one correspondence between what is out there and what is in your knowledge, you are bound to make mistakes. So, if the snow is cold you should know what that means. If the road becomes slippery when it is icy, you should know that. The truth that is in you is also the truth that has become manifest out there.

Don't just call it maya and dismiss it. Of course, the whole thing can be an error, but it is not a piecemeal one. If it is an error it is wholesale. You are within that wholesale error now. Do not mistake something wholesale for something piecemeal. As long as you are within the frame of reference called the transactional, you have to give full validation to every item in it. It is here that the spiritual life of some people fails, because in the name of spirituality, in the name of philosophy, or in the name of realisation, they belittle the validity of transactions. This ontological error is a big problem. To correct it, *prajñānam brahma* is given, to remind you that what is out there as your experience is born of the same reality that has produced you and your mind. Not until you realize this can you be at ease with the external world.

All this is in preparation for a final search, a search for the meaning of your own life. If you do not know the goal of your life, you might walk into many snares. If someone compassionate who has found out what can be most beneficial to a human being tells you, "Go this way, my child," a lot of trouble can be saved. People run after so many things in their lives, and by the time they realise those things are all meaningless they are too feeble in their bodies and shaky in their minds to make much of an effort. The intellect is no longer clear, and the memory is failing. Only when they are good for nothing do they realise that they didn't get anywhere. Since it is better to know this early, we are given a teleological pointer, *tat tvam asi,* "That thou art." This is the fourth great dictum.

"What is That?" and "How can I experience it?" To answer these questions you have to lift your mind from everything to which it is riveted. You are tied down to this body, this mind, to things. You need to loosen your hold to all those particulars to which you are now tied. This transcendence, this elevation, the sublimity to which you can rise, can be attempted day after day. By itself, this gives direction to your life. You may be an artist or a poet, an actor, a craftsman, a technician or a person doing service to other people. Your vocation can be anything. All paths lead to Rome. In other words, all paths lead to salvation, to your final emancipation. If the path is not leading you to this, then it is a snare and you should give it up. So with a little insight you can make any path lead to your salvation and emancipation.

Let's say you are an artist. What do you seek through your art? Call it beauty. How do you decide what is beautiful? You go to that normative notion of which we spoke. The artist says, "It is not by measuring anything with an external ruler, or weighing it, or using any other kind of brass gadget or electronic device that I come to know whether this is beautiful or not. When I look at it, my heart is filled. I get into a state of ecstasy. Then I know it is beautiful." Within you there is beauty. Only when a thing resonates with your true being, which itself is beautiful, do you know it is also beautiful. Every creation of beauty is a search to know more of you, more of your own self as the beautiful.

Suppose you care for children, not necessarily your own. The central value here is compassion. Compassion is your passion. The passion of you and the child become commingled and flow in a single direction. For this to happen, what is most dear to you and what is most dear to the child have to be brought together as one unitive meaning, in one common centre. That is the Self. It is the same Self in you and the child. One's happiness is the other's happiness. Every time you relate this way, you discover the greater secret of your own Self. So even though the meaning of life is given as teleological, that teleos is not very far off. It is in this very moment that you come to realise it. Then you go on to the next moment, and the next.

From the two aspects of *ahanta* and *idanta*, 'I'-ness and 'this'-ness, you come to the core of both. What is in both 'I' and 'this' is called 'That'. When you experience That in the Self as well as the non-Self, then the Self and the non-Self do not exist separately. This is a discipline which we need in order to go farther, the four-fold correction with four great dictums: a fundamental correction, a methodological correction, a correction of meaning and a correction of your apprehension of actuality.

Verse 52

dhvani mayamāy gaganam jvalikkūmannā-
ḷaṇayumatiṅkal aśēṣa dṛsya jālam
punar aviṭe tripuṭikku pūrttinalkum-
svanavumaṭaṅṅumiṭam svayam prakāśam

The sky will glow as radiant sound —
on that day, all visible configurations will become extinct in that;
thereafter, the sound that completes the three-petalled awareness
becomes silent and self-luminous.

We come to know our world by seeing the many things of which it is constituted. Everything we have seen from childhood to this day is put together to formulate the world for us. Whatever we have seen has also been named. We have heard the names of things as well as explanations of them in so many words from other people. A thing may seem simple when we look at it, but hundreds of words are needed to explain just one entity.

The experiences of people who have gone before us are passed on to us through words, either written or spoken. Thus, the great universe we think of geographically and historically, or spatially and temporally, is mostly made up of word content. If we dismiss from our minds all that we have heard so far, all the ideas formulated with the help of words, almost nothing is left. Such is the enormity of the world we have created out of words.

The word that is now coming to you from me is transmitted by a certain vibration I am producing in the atmosphere. There is truth in what the physicists say, that sound is transmitted to you through air. But it is not air itself that is creating the sound. It is a very mysterious force indeed. In the case of sunlight we are at least familiar with photons, but when it comes to sound it is far more mysterious. As the pitch and frequency vary, the sound gains many qualities, and what we call the psychodynamics of sound arises.

The psychic expansion of space, or the extensiveness of the psyche if you prefer, is called *ākāśa*. Everything has its place in akasa. Its intrinsic quality, or dharma, is sound. For this reason, sound can affect everything. It can influence, alter, build up or destroy. According to Jaimini's school of Purva-Mimamsa, this world is constituted of sound. They believe that since this world is created out of sound, you can change or modify it to your liking by using sound. They have made many sound structures called mantras. Mantras have a dynamic called *mantra caitanya*, the psychodynamics of mantra, which can bring about such changes.

We know that sound is very powerful. We can produce certain sounds that will hurt or please another person. With sound we command, lead, instruct, excite, express our grief, console, pacify, inspire. We can enchant with so many subtle varieties of music. Gentle sound can make you soar high into sublime heights. It can lead you to the depth of your own Self. Innumerable are the possibilities of sound.

Sound as such is called *śabda*, and a modification of *śabda* is called *dhvani*. In Sanskrit, the entire world of literature is called *dhvanyāloka*, a world that is seen through sound. A poet weaves an entire tapestry of a colourful universe using only words. The vowels and consonants used in language are called *varṇa*, colourations, in this case meaning the colour of the sounds. With the colours of the sounds we paint pictures of ideas.

What one person articulates, another visualises. This is one of the greatest wonders of life. An idea comes into my mind and I can convey it to you by breathing and moving my tongue and mouth in a certain way. I direct my prana, my vital breath, in such a way that it causes vibrations of sounds, and these vibrations convey meaning. The prana rises from my heart or the depth of my psyche to become meaningful. Here I am combining two things, prana and the word. If

I shorten or lengthen my prana, it changes the sound I am articulating. I can say aum, or I can say A . . . U . . . M. That way it becomes musical. Either way it is the same word and the meaning does not change, but the effect is different. The meaning part is called *ṛk*, and the musical quality produced by prolonging the breath is called *sāma*. When *ṛk* and *sāma* are coupled, it produces a psychic phenomenon. This world itself is a psychic phenomenon created out of sound.

Nobody knows what magnetism is. We do know that when a magnetised piece of iron is brought near another piece of iron there is a great pull, a great attraction. However much we carefully examine it, though, we don't see what's actually going on. When we pass on from magnetism to electricity, we speak of an electromagnetic field. Electricity has such a variety of qualities. It can emit fire, it can make something very cold, it can power the world, and it can even stop your heart from beating. We see what it can do, but do we understand electricity any more than we do magnetism? In the same way, we know something of the propensities and potentials of sound, but we are very much ignorant of its essential nature.

Sound in its purest form is called *para*, which is on a par with the Absolute. It is unmodified, unmodulated sound. In it we can see a certain possibility of visualising an idea and transforming the sound in such a way that the vision can be conveyed to another person. There needs to be a homogeneity of the visualisation and the unmodified sound for the visualisation to be communicated through sound. The homogeneity of the sound and the visualisation is called *paśyanti*, seeing; in other words the capacity to see in a medium which is essentially auditory.

Once a visualisation is expressed it undergoes some transformation. I have to wait for my idea to be expressed. If I want to express it in English I have to structure the sounds in a certain way, while if it is to be given in Sanskrit it should be structured in another way. If I know the language well I don't have to belabour myself. It comes of its own; the sounds get structured automatically. I don't have to think which sounds are dental and which are labial. I just decide to speak and all the sounds come. It's a great wonder.

The sound you have just expressed and articulated is called *vaikharī*. When you articulate a sound it is just like when a person bangs a drum once: *dhun*. When the drum is hit in rhythm, it makes a modulation, and when modulations come the *dhun* becomes a *dhvani*, which starts making sense to you. If a beat is given in a certain way, at once you can see a pattern in it. Then you can anticipate. Before the next beat comes, your mind is already there. If it goes wrong with you, it causes dissonance, but if it goes right it resonates with you because your spirit is already in tune with it. The *dhvani* out there and the *dhvani* within us resonate with each other. The mathematics of music is already within us because we *are* sound.

Dhvani is the whole world of sound, with all its richness. The artist's palette creates all the colours out of a few basic ones. Like that, we can combine a few basic sounds to make all the sounds and all their meanings. How many words are there articulated in the multitude of human languages with which our world abounds? Truly endless are the possibilities of sound combinations.

I sit here speaking plainly with you. But some other things which I might want only a certain person to understand I do not say explicitly. Thus a word has both a literal and an implied meaning. When I put an implied meaning into my words it is also called *dhvani*. As the implied meaning becomes more and more prominent, it becomes poetic. As long as it is a straightforward, square sound, like explanations in a physics textbook, there is no scope for any poetry in it. Two grams means two grams. But poetry is full of *dhvani*. There is a vibration, an echo of a vibration, in your soul. Creating that echo in your soul is another aspect of *dhvani*.

In this verse Narayana Guru is speaking of the possibility of the vast space of your consciousness becoming vibrant with one great sound, which will dissolve away in it all separate visions. I spoke of *vaikharī*, the articulated sounds, the word pictures you paint. You see all of these in your mind as separate entities. Such separations are totally effaced when the great sound becomes so vibrant.

Knowledge or consciousness may be compared to light. Light can vary from the most feeble ray to the brilliance of a million suns shining all at once. If there is no light, you don't see anything. If there is a little light, it makes a contrast between light and shadow. With more light there is a sharper contrast with the darker shadow. But if the light is coming from everywhere and there is no shadow left, you can't see anything. The most intense light effaces the distinction between the source of the light and the illuminated object. If you take the analogy still further, it also takes away the difference between the seer and the seen. The seer, the seen and the seeing are all just one light.

The Guru here says *gaganam jvalikkūm*, the sky of your consciousness is blazing forth in such brilliance. He began with the sound. Now he says the sound is blazing forth, leaping into flames. The very sky of your consciousness is on fire. It is radiant. Within that radiance it is so bright that you do not see any difference between things. The Guru says all those details of vision are effaced in this one radiance, this great splendour of light.

In another work describing his own experience, as well as elsewhere in this one, Narayana Guru says the highest discrimination of the Self comes like ten thousand suns shining all at once. Or, like a million suns rising all at once, thus comes the great experience of realisation. When such an experience comes, the individuations and differentiations of things are all effaced by it. After that the tri-basic consciousness (the knower, knowledge, and the known) becomes complemented and as one, so there is no distinction.

What causes this? A certain *svanam,* a certain sound. In the Mandukya, Chandogya and Katha Upanishads it is said that all we experience in the present, the past and the future is only modifications of aum. What we experience as the gross in the wakeful, the subtle in the dream, and the causal in deep sleep are all variations of the one sound, aum. If the secret of aum is open to us, then the gross, the subtle and the causal all merge into the pure silence that follows it. This is called turiya, the fourth state. When everything existing merges into that fourth state there is no longer the knower, the known and knowledge. They have all been completed and merged into the sound of aum. That place shines by itself as a pure light, *aṭaṅṅum iṭam svayam prakāśam*.

This is an experience, or *the* experience, which is on a par with what we hear of the Buddha getting his enlightenment under the Bo tree, the angel calling to Muhammad in the cave, or the Holy Spirit descending upon Jesus to confer on him the grace whereby he becomes the Son of God. It is equivalent to these — the highest possible experience one can have. The person becomes the all-embracing consciousness, which bursts out in a flame of such brilliance that it effaces everything. Thereafter, there is no sound. Or, the only sound is that which at one level is the wakeful world, at another level the dream world, and at still another level the deep sleep world. They are all now merged into the fourth state of pure transcendence. In that transcendence, nothing is left behind. It just shines by itself. This is the state to which a person comes at the height of his illumination.

Verse 53

itil eẓumādima śaktiyiṅṅu kānu-
nnitu sakalam peṟumādī bijamākum
matiyatil ākki maṟanniṭāte māyā-
matiyaṟuvān mananam tuṭarnniṭēṇam

The primal energy implied in this
is the seed from which everything here proliferates;
having understood that, without forgetting
to clear the mind deluded by *māyā*, meditation should continue.

Maya is described as *sadasad vilakṣaṇa,* in other words it is both real and unreal. Maya is not a thing, it is a situation. Whenever there is an event, an experience or a context that shows within it an enigmatic pull towards two opposites, it is an instance of maya.

For instance, when two people come together and feel attracted to each other, they experience something they have not had with anyone else. They find a tenderness, an easy flow between their minds, a mutual acceptance. Their hearts can communicate without words. At many levels of emotion they feel a sense of union. They marvel at the wonder of this, and think of it as a very special relationship that has never before occurred with the same beauty and joy.

Then, from somewhere, a small spark of doubt arises. The one having the doubt wants to dismiss it immediately. This causes a flicker of panic. In his frantic haste to disown the doubt he takes a step backward, and this is noticed by his friend, his beloved. This brings a note of dissonance. Misunderstanding comes. Soon it grows into a dark cloud, a fog that comes between them. As this increases it makes both of them aware of the separation. They become very apprehensive. The very love that was the source of all joy, all the sense of wonder, now has a new quality. It chokes them. It makes each other's company unbearable. Yet there is still the fear of separation. They want to cling to each other at the same time they want to push each other away. A terrible situation comes. Agony and pain suffuse every passing moment. At last, with all sincerity they wish they had never met, that this would have never happened to them. The very word 'love' becomes a synonym for defeat. At its worst, everything done before in love, in confidence, with a sense of sacredness, now looks very vulgar and profane. Memories to be cherished become haunting corpses of deceitful acts and treachery.

If you bracket all this intrigue together it is a single situation with two sides, one of grace and beauty, warmth and joy, and the other full of darkness. Whenever an experience has such a duality you can say it is subject to maya. In your life you can find hundreds of such situations where with great love you move toward a certain value, and when you are about to possess it you see a hundred other possibilities drowning you in unanticipated problems. You cling to it; you cannot have it and yet you cannot let it go. When such a duality comes, you become like a person possessed by an evil spirit. You don't know what you are saying or how to behave. You are at a crossroads, where turning one way is wrong and turning the other way is also wrong. We come to such crossroads in life again and again, and they are all situations of maya.

Narayana Guru asks where this comes from. Is it right to say this is only an illusion and there is no substance to it? No, you cannot say that. This is what you are living, and if you are living it, it has substance. It affects you. You cannot just dismiss it from your mind as being of no consequence. You must go back to the source. It is not far. It is right inside you, right where your consciousness originates. Looking inside yourself you can see that from out of unconsciousness, like little bubbles of consciousness, awareness is coming to the surface. This awareness is the illumination of a name, a form, a meaning. It brings associated memories of the past, the present and even the future. New dreams come, expectations come. You make designs in your mind to act. Soon you find you are in the thick of action. There is compulsion about it: you cannot put it off. You act.

If you watch all this, it's like a fountain gushing up from a great depth with tremendous force. You cannot plug it or stop it. It's a continuous flow. Narayana Guru says, "Know this to be a *śakti*, a force." When did it start? No one knows. Even before you were born, someone else was undergoing the same kind of thing. You yourself have come from that person or those people. Before you were born, what is now in you was lying in someone else as a seed. The desire of your father and your mother to come together caused your appearance. The intertwining actions of millennia are behind you. The history of ideas is within you. It's a continuous flow of great force, of which you are now a passing effect. This is what the Guru calls *ādi bījam,* the first seed of all this causation, of this great energy.

So what should you do to get rid of this kind of intellect, this kind of mind, that brings you to this terrible situation of duality? In the previous verses we were told that everything finally resolves in the still voice of aum. At the tail end of aum there comes a silence. A . . . u . . . m . . . . It ends in silence. In that silence is everything and yet nothing. Nothing is there because there are no names, no forms, no meanings, no situations, no events, no pluralities. Yet that which started out as 'a' and progressed through 'u' and 'm' culminated in it. Thus, everything is there.

When it begins at the level of 'a', that is, the wakeful, transactional level, there are thousands of names, forms, events and meanings. From this manifoldness the word tapers down in an unbroken continuum, passing through the dream state and the deep sleep state to end in silence. The step before coming to the great silence is deep sleep. The man who is sitting here and talking to you was in deep sleep at two o'clock this morning. At that time, did he have the philosophy, the ideas he is now explaining? Certainly. And what state were they in? At that time their state was purely potential. Everything was hushed into a potent state, so that when he waked up he was not newly creating all his words and ideas. They were all there even in the deep sleep, lying there like seeds in a granary or barn. When the wheat or rye is being stored it does not show any signs of life, but as soon as a little moisture is added the sprouts come out.

The stage before entering deep sleep is the dream state. All the ideation is there, but actions are not. That is, mentally actions are going on, but the physical organs are not moving. When this man we are speaking of dreamt he was walking, he was not walking with his actual legs. They were lying buried under the sheet. When he thought he was working with his hands, they were lying still. When he thought he was talking, his mouth was not moving. Still, everything seemed to take place just as if it were actually happening in the outside world.

When we come back all the way to the wakeful stage, finally action means physical action. Raising the hand means the actual hand raises. Talking means that a voice comes from the mouth. At this point, if I borrow ten dollars from you I become a debtor. Tomorrow when I wake up and you also wake up, you will ask me to pay you. But if I took a million dollars from you in my dream you wouldn't even know it, and I wouldn't have to pay it back.

So how can you say it is all maya? You cannot just brush it aside like that. At the transactional level it is a reality. But you forget all about your ten dollars as soon as you fall sleep. Then you excuse me because then I don't exist for you. We can go back and forth from the transactional to the dream, from the dream to the deep sleep, and from the deep sleep to what you cannot say at all. What really happens?

The One has this proliferating quality. It opens up and becomes transactional. It is like a pulsation. It opens up to the light, and then all this is laid out before you. Then it closes back down and nothing is there. By opening the eyes, the whole world comes. By closing them, it disappears. The pulsation of consciousness is like the eyes opening and closing. This is the beginningless and endless force, *śakti* or *ādi bījam*. You should meditate on this. But how?

There is a pure light in which all these actions are going on. Nataraja Guru, in his commentary on this work, gives the example of a stadium being illuminated with bright lights. People are playing games on the field. The light is only illuminating the games, only looking on in a sense, but without it the games would not be visible.

Like that, there is a consciousness that is illuminating everything, and within it there are so many games going on. We should be careful to take these aspects together, not separately. Even when I borrow ten dollars from you, I should also have the knowledge that this lender and I and the money all belong to one overriding whole.

When the One manifests into the many, it brings qualities that are not known to be in it. It is this issue that troubles us. When it is all one, it has no fault in it. A piece of cloth cannot be just one because it has two sides, but if you can efface that element it can be considered as one. When it is folded it has many new features — up and down, before and after, inside and out, big and small. All these pluralities come from one and the same thing. So which is more real, oneness or manifoldness? Even this very comparison is wrong. The one reality shows all these possibilities. When the cloth is folded you should treat it as folded, and when it is not folded you should treat it as not folded. There is no point in saying that when it is folded it is as if it is not folded. But you need to remember that it is the same as that which is unfolded, as that which has no qualities. To keep these two understandings together requires a dialectical method of looking, of critically seeing a thing with a unitive understanding, the one and the many at the same time.

The original sound 'aum', including the entire continuum from the silence where you merge through the 'a' where you transact, are all seen as one organic whole. Then you are not surprised by the eventualities in life, as you are when you see only one side. When you stand on one side of a hill it is physically impossible to place yourself at the other side also. But the knowledge that there is another side and that the vision from another angle could be different takes away from you the big fear, the big hatred and the big confusion.

Along the same line, if you know that a certain person under certain pressure will behave in a certain way, then you have no animosity toward them for their behaviour. They are not inherently good or bad, yet the situation has become drastic. If you can ease the situation somehow at the transactional level, do so. But even as you do that, think of the original state in which all these details are irrelevant. The relevancy and the irrelevancy are to be seen side by side. This creates a neutrality in your attitude.

The other person may be quite mad. Usually the immediate impact of this is you also go mad. But you can remain sane and save the situation, rather than proliferating madness by reacting to it. There is enough madness there already. Why should you add your own to it? Usually we are drawn towards it; there is every temptation to join in the confusion. This is called maya.

The intellect which is likely to be drawn into a dualistic situation is called maya *mati aṟuvān*. You should take this as a special opportunity to meditate on the oneness out of which all these dualities arise. This cannot be done in a lukewarm manner. Contemplation must become the main current of life. It is a twenty-four hour business requiring great dedication and sincerity. You also are living all your life as it comes, meeting all eventualities. This gives a new quality to life, an insight into things. It takes away the agony and helps you to have empathy with those who are not seeing it and thereby undergoing great pain. If we look at it properly, crime is a sickness. It is not a crime to fall sick. A sick person deserves sympathy. The problem is in seeing only one side of the coin. But you are seeing both sides.

When people brought a prostitute before Jesus and asked if she should be stoned, he could see both sides. He said, "Let him throw the first stone who has not sinned." He saw the implication of the law of the country. He also took into account the plight of the poor woman, and the animosity and wild nature of the people. And he could put the whole thing in a very simple way, with justice and fair play at the centre. Ultimately he brought compassion to prevail. Another classic example is the bishop in *Les Miserables,* by Victor Hugo. He always saw both sides.

Such kind of insight is what is called here meditation on that primal seed which proliferates as all this. When meditating on aum, we should go from our own transactional world through our dreams, into our deep sleep and beyond to the very source. From that we return, and then repeat the process. Thus, it becomes a continuous pulsation in our life. If the continuous pulsation is made meaningful, dualities will continue to be there but you will have taken the edge off them. They won't make your heart bleed any more.

When your thoughts get caught in a vicious circle and you go round and round and cannot escape from them, it is called *cintam*. When you make logical arrangements of thoughts as in a chemistry or physics book or an engineering manual it is *vicāram*. Neither of these forms of mind will help you. What will is *mananam*, going from the effect to the cause, bringing the many to the One, hushing the pluralities of things into their unitive nature, gathering your thoughts and getting into your centre, going to the greatest depth. The mind goes again and again to new subjects, but it is to be brought back to where it originated. All this is *mananam*. The fourth aspect is *dhyānam*. You don't do *dhyānam*, it comes naturally when your *mananam* or contemplation becomes real.

Narayana Guru here recommends the continuous contemplation of the primal seed of all this. If the cause is real, as the effect has come from the cause it also belongs to the real. You dismiss the effect as unreal because you see one part of it and another part is hidden from you. This falsifies its unity. But if you look to the unity, it cannot be false. Seeing unity in and through all the diversities, always, through a process of meditation and not of analysis, not one of fragmentary observation but instead always living it as a whole, is the message of this meditation.

Verse 54

uṇarumavasthayuṟakkil illuṟakkam
punar uṇarum poẓutum sphurikkuvīla
anudinamiṅṅane raṇṭumādi māyā-
vanitayil ninnu puṟannu māṟiṭunnu

In sleep the wakeful state does not exist
and when one wakes up no trace of sleep remains;
day by day, in this way, these two, having emerged
from the primal *māyā* woman, arise and alternate.

In verse 5, Narayana Guru said that people who are conditioned by nature's stimulation wake, sleep and think many thoughts. There is a light within which is like a lamp shedding its radiance and also witnessing everything. It has no beginning or end. One should contemplate on it.

In verse 6 he speaks of a natural block in the human mind to contemplation of this pure state, arising out of the alternating modes of waking and sleeping. He points out that in the wakeful state desires for nourishment and enjoyment come. Natural instincts for the preservation of the body and the perpetuation of the species impel one to eat and mate. He sees it as almost impossible for most people to break these habits, so he asks, "Because of these modifications, who is there to know the pure state in which there is no waking or sleeping?"

In verse 7 he suggests a neutral state which is neither of waking or sleeping, and he asks us to remain in it. If one is not capable of remaining in that state, then the suggested alternative is to seek the help of a contemplative who has attained it.

Now in the second half of *Ātmopadeśa Śatakam,* where the discipline is focused on actual experience, he hearkens back to these verses. In verse 54 he is highlighting the paradoxical counterparts which come one after another in our experience. In the wakeful state there is an awareness of a subjective self that marks the central focus of awareness, which we have designated as 'I'. A frame of reference is established with 'I' as the centre, providing a spatial extension where bodies are placed. One body is close and another is far, something is above and something else is below. It gives a spatial picturisation of the conscious world.

The dimensional partner of space is time. Time passes and there is no way of recovering it. There is a hopelessness about the way it keeps on running. Only the future is ahead, and what is lived is gone forever. This produces in consciousness a sense of urgency; thoughts like "I have to finish this before I go to sleep again."

The wakeful state is programmed and structured. There are places, things and events, as well as time. There are fixed identities such as "I do," "I know," or "I experience." Countless are the things we experience in the wakeful world, and millions are the names that we can give to them. The world of consciousness is extremely vast. We could go on elaborating endlessly on time, on sound, on form.

Think of this vast universe of all these properties and qualities. Then suddenly with a snap it all disappears. Is there something that sees it all disappear? No. It is simply a vacuity, absolute nothingness. Who is there to know it is absolute nothingness? No one. Then how do we know there was such a state? We don't know. All we know is there was a state when we were wakeful and now there is another state of wakefulness. In between something happened. And why do we presume that? Because we know we have gone to bed and then got up from it. Lying there, we have a remembrance of going to bed and a recognition when we wake up that we are in bed. If we look at the clock we see a difference in time, and when we look out the window we see snow that was not there previously. Putting all this together, we presume something must have happened and we were not there for a little while.

Thus, deep sleep is a presumption. In it there is no time or space, none of the identities. Is it also part of consciousness? Psychologists use the two terms, consciousness and unconsciousness, quite casually. If wakeful experience belongs to consciousness, its opposite is what is happening in deep sleep and so we call that unconsciousness. Do they both belong to the world of consciousness? If we take black and white, they are opposite in a sense but they are still both colours. Since they are within the same context they are not contradictory, they are only contrary.

Contrary and contradictory are not the same. Contrary means different but belonging to the same frame of reference, in the way that '*B*' is different from '*A*'. The contradictory of '*A*', however, is 'not *A*'. Something that is contradictory is absolutely different. The states of wakeful consciousness and deep sleep are absolutely different. How can they both coexist in the same entity? We can semantically coin a word 'consciousness' and place within it awareness and nonawareness. Does that allow us to experience them together?

In the previous verse Narayana Guru asked us to meditate on the supreme principle in order to get over the duality of maya. Here he is focusing attention on what we should meditate on. This is not an easy thing to do because we have taken refuge in word concepts. In India, most people do not know Sanskrit. If a Sanskrit word is used, it gives a sense of authority to the speaker. A person can thereby tyrannise others with it. When they say "I am now quoting from the Upanishads," everybody bows their heads. It is a kind of slavery, linguistic servitude. The same is done in the West with Greek and Latin, since ordinary people do not know those languages either. In fact, when you don't understand something, you say it is Greek to you. Scientists decided to give all their terms in Latin or Greek, just like the Indian Brahmin uses Sanskrit. If you use a word that no one can pronounce, everybody bows before you.

We have become victimised by such fancy language. The words sound impressive, but do we actually experience their meaning? No. We only think we do. It is just like saying "I believe in God." "Oh, did you meet that fellow somewhere?" "No, but I know all about Him. I hear about Him all the time." All this so-called familiarity with God is just having heard the word a hundred times, a million times even, from others. Is that God-experience? What do you mean by God-experience, anyway? Knowing the meaning of the word is only a dictionary experience.

Similarly, we have only a dictionary experience of consciousness and unconsciousness. If you want to go beyond that, try to place what you call consciousness and what you call unconsciousness together. If you can conceive them together and think of an all-embracing entity in which you can sit without contradiction, then you know what is being said.

This is difficult but not impossible. It's not like thinking of a square circle; in fact, it's not conceptual at all. When we try to contemplate, the main mistake we commit is in replacing direct understanding with intellectual understanding. We tend to imagine the unconscious in terms of consciousness, timelessness in terms of time, spacelessness in terms of space. This is an injustice, squeezing the unconscious into the mold of the conscious in order to try to understand it. It is also partisan: you are in favour of consciousness.

What is the faculty with which you contemplate, or, as the phenomenologists say, reflect? By the way, I agree with this term because you are most often thinking with your known tools of reasoning. You have to first suspend the mechanism of reasoning with ordinary logic. Then you allow the given — what is not conscious in deep sleep as well as what is conscious in the wakeful — both to prevail and be juxtaposed. You are therefore reflecting rather than manipulating.

The problem is one of getting over relativity. From the most unknown to the most known, there are shades of ignorance or shades of knowledge. Relative to something else you know this well or less well. To give this up and adopt an absolutist attitude is our main challenge.

When two opposites are brought together, validating both while not taking their contradiction into account, it is what the Vedantin calls maya. The problem we face here is maya. Time and timelessness, space and spacelessness, conscious 'I' and unconscious entity, things and no things, properties and no properties, are to be taken together. One cancels the other out. That which remains all through the cancellation is not maya, it is the Absolute. Maya and the

Absolute are not two, and at the same time they are two. They are two when you are facing the duality, but where the duality is resolved maya changes into the Absolute. At this end of experience it is maya, while at the other end it is the Absolute.

We face a certain amount of helplessness here. The tools which we have are specially made to serve us only for the dual half of our experience, and they are inadequate for the other half. Is it not strange that this very mind is capable of having timelessness and spacelessness, and of being devoid of the feeling of 'I' or any differentiating factors? Just a few hours ago it was in that state. Now we cannot imagine with our mind how it was accomplished, or how we have been doing it every night throughout our life and will be doing it in the future also.

We carry our body and mind with us everywhere, and yet we don't know anything about its secrets. Our greatest paradox is our own self. It is like a mobile box of ignorance with a candle placed on top of it. When blind men walk at night they carry a torch so that nobody will knock them over. We are just like that, a big unconscious with a little sign of consciousness riding on it. It's also like the big hill behind us here, that has a red light on top so planes won't crash into it. Does the light help the hill to know itself? Does our consciousness help us to know ourselves? No, it doesn't.

This brings us to the very crux of the situation. Hamlet's problem was to be or not to be. Ours is being and non-being. All that we have read and thought about and all that we philosophise becomes suddenly of no use to us. It is as if we are ignorant little toads who have wasted all our life till this moment, and now we cannot do anything. How terrible this is. Most people give up here. We have only come to the fourth verse in the second half of *Ātmopadeśa Śatakam*. We have another forty-six to go. It is very important to persevere at this point.

In the eleventh chapter of the Bhagavad Gita, Krishna tells Arjuna, "Boy, you cannot see what I am going to show you with your eyes. I will give you another eye." This is exactly what we need. With our eyes of wakeful consciousness we cannot look at that which is neither non-wakeful nor wakeful. The Guru gave us a clue in the fifth verse when he said that there is an unlit lamp that is shining and will never cease. We wend our way looking only at the things which are illuminated by the light of the lamp. The light does not see itself.

The question here is not one of knowing. When we hear "reflect" or "meditate" we are under the impression that we are being asked to know something. Not at all. We are not asked to know anything, but only to be. That being is different from knowing is a very difficult distinction for many to make. We don't have to do anything, accomplish anything. In that sense it is just like dying. People are afraid to die. Dying means leaving the world of knowing, of putting down all the instruments of knowledge. Socrates tried his best to let people know that that is not all. Jesus said if you do not perish, you will never attain immortality. What is this immortality you gain by perishing? What is the knowledge you get by not knowing? This is the theme presented to us here.

All the talks we give, the discussions we have, the reflections we make, are only to prove the inefficiency or the inadequacy of names. The seeming insurmountability of maya is a methodological error where we are trying to interpret the whole in terms of a part. If we can just give up that approach and allow the whole to prevail, that's beingness. But all these words such as beingness, meditation, etc., are to be treated as if they are not said. Once you conceptualise them you are on the other side, merely playing with the tools of consciousness.

There once was a man who came to the hills of Arunachala when he was only thirteen or fourteen. He did not try to read and write or listen to discourses. He didn't try to make money, make a living, or perform any manipulations so that someone would take pity on him and give him food. He just gave up, feeling it was all over. He didn't do anything. Then after twenty years the whole world turned to him. Around him was an atmosphere of transcendent peace that radiated to all. At least eighty per cent of the people who went there did not go to listen to him, because he wasn't saying anything. Occasionally someone forced him to talk, but most of the genuine people there weren't interested in any spoken words. There is another medium which transcends the spoken word, that prevails and is as positive or more positive than anything one could experience outwardly. Such was the hilltop retreat of Ramana Maharshi.

We are not in any way referring to a hopelessly difficult attainment. The mystical depth in question is in no way an intellectual exercise to be scientifically gauged. This is why at the very beginning, in the opening verse, we were asked to approach the whole subject with a sense of surrender, a deep devotion, with absolute reverence to the unnamable that shines by its own light both as the known and the unknown. The Guru recommends a greater acceptance of the sense of awe and wonder. We must stand before this seeming impossibility with wonder, allowing ourselves not to do, but to be done with.

Verse 55

neṭiya kināvitu nidra pōle nityam
keṭumitu pōle kināvumiprakāram
keṭumati kāṇukayilla kēvalattil
peṭuvatināl aniśam bhramicciṭunnu

A long dream is this; like sleep, this perishes every day;
in the same way, dream also;
the perishing intelligence does not see
what belongs to aloneness, and hence is constantly confused.

In the previous verse the two alternatives expressed were the deep sleep and the wakeful states. There was no mention of the dream state. There is one common feature between the dream and wakeful states, that in both we are conscious of a conceiving and perceiving 'I'. The notion of 'I' is operating as the central reference in both of them. Both have a time sense and a space sense, as well as the identity of knower, doer and enjoyer. All these disappear only in the state of deep sleep. In this verse, by contrast, primacy is given to the dream. Where before the wakeful was contrasted with deep sleep, now dream is.

When wakeful experience and the dream state are taken together, the whole of life can be treated as a single dream of experience. In it, our intelligence operates intermittently, since deep sleep is not a continuous thing. We have no use of our intelligence in deep sleep. We cannot discern with it by using it as an instrument or a critical faculty, as we do in the wakeful state. The question is why are the wakeful and the dream state put together here as if there is no difference between them, while at the same time transactional life is given only a secondary importance.

The process we are undergoing in this work is a transference from maya, the seeming first cause of the transactional world, to an ultimate cause. If maya both is and is not, it has no proper basis. For anything to be, it should have a real basis. So an existential ground is to be established for any experience. An experience may be an illusion of something, but there still should be a ground for that illusion. When you say something is superimposed, the question arises, "Superimposed on what?"

Here *kevalam* is given as the ground for the superimposition of whatever is experienced in the waking and the dream. We could still retain the wakeful experience, which is very prominent, instead of bringing in the dream, but Narayana Guru wants to point out one defect which affects them both and is important in the present context. There is an overall influence of an unknown entity which affects our mind when we are wakeful and think we are critically examining things. We assure ourselves of the certitude of what we are arriving at. In the dream state also we use the same kind of critical faculty: we assure ourselves that this is not a dream, it is really real. Even when we try to find out if it is true or not, we get every evidence that it is. We fool ourselves. After some time we wake up and contrast wakeful experience with what we have discovered in the dream state, and find out it is not true. Only then do we realise we have been fooled.

One difference between the wakeful and dream states is when we go from the dream to the wakeful there is some retention of the experience of the dream, and this can be deliberately recalled to be compared with the succeeding wakeful experience. But when we go from the wakeful to the dream, there is no retention of a memory cognised as a wakeful experience which can be kept at hand, ready for comparison. We do not decide that what we have experienced in the wakeful is after all not true. This is left unexamined.

The main conception of treating the wakeful as a dream originated with Gauḍapāda. Śaṅkara then brought in one characteristic of wakefulness that is different from the dream: you can connect one wakeful experience with another, thus making a continuity out of it in your life. But you do not make a continuous linking of dream with dream. This is certainly true but it is somewhat beside the point, since here Narayana Guru is treating both as one long dream. This can be accepted because we are not going to use transactional experience in this particular verse; at this point we are moving away from the transactional to the absolute state.

Earlier Narayana Guru said that where the still voice of aum concludes is a place of self-luminosity. From the "a" state, the transactional world where there are thousands of names, forms and interests, we go to the "u" stage where the forms and names and interests are all generated by one's own individual consciousness. Beyond this point the subject and object are left behind. In a sense everything perishes when there is no longer any 'I' or any 'this'. In this, the "m" state, the intelligence is extinguished, and everything dies away.

It is only after total extinguishment that we enter into the next state, that of the Aloneness. It is the Aloneness of that voice which has now lost all its dynamics of manifestation. There it is entering into the total realm of the unmanifest. We are confused when we come to this. We cannot remain there. We come back again and again to the familiar world of our experience. This final aspect could have been our realisation, but we are conditioned to expect a thing to be known, and we are in an operational field of knowledge only when the individuated intelligence can be applied to definite things. There you definitely see a thing as a thing, and an 'I' as an 'I'. If the distinctions of the 'I'-ness and the thing-ness are taken away, you don't know how to deal with it. Until you develop a new kind of appraisal of the situation this whole process is an impossibility. Only when one relative factor and another relative factor are both grounded on the Absolute, or at least on a normative notion of the Absolute, can the relative factor examine the other element and think of its existence, its awareness and its value, since these are all absolute notions.

When these separated entities are not there, only the Absolute is. Nothing is compared. Nothing is made a subject of study. Very soon you are thrown back into your position of a relativistic 'I' looking at a relativistic 'this'. This happens repeatedly. You become again and again confused. This confusion takes away from your mind the value and worth of what you have lived transactionally.

However vigorous your experience of the transactional world may have been, when you experienced along with it purely subjective things with no continuity, and now you sit back and recall the things which have happened and the things of which you have only dreamt, how do you differentiate the memory content of these two?

A thing which actually happened and a thing which was only seen in the dream both become memories. Both can be recalled, both can be revived, but no trace of either experience is left. They have become a knowledge of the past. Memory is a knowledge of the past. The quality of it in its essence is pain-pleasure, good-bad. This means the wakeful transaction loses its vigour. It no longer holds good. It has become a thing of the past. The dream has also become a thing of the past. When you put together these two things of the past, the wakeful and the dream which have blended together in memory, you have what Narayana Guru calls a prolonged dream. Your wakeful dream and your dream dream together make one big dream. The whole of life becomes like a dream.

Occasionally you fight with someone on some issue in wakeful life. Then after some time you make up, you once again agree and feel it was foolish for you to fight like that. The incident goes into the background of your mind as a discarded memory, and thereafter you treat each other as if nothing had ever happened. The phenomenologists call this a reduction. The reduction is that actual things and their values are reduced to an eidetic notion. The value or significance assigned to a thing at a particular moment is now considered only as a special feature of the reaction that was released in you because of your personality makeup. Or it may be that others were present in that situation and you were under the spell of a kind of mob mind or mass mind.

In the dream an unknown force influences your mind so that you behave in a certain way despite yourself, and yet you know that at that time it looked as if it were your decision. Like that, you can see that the wakeful experience is also not free of an overall dominating principle. This directing or dominating principle could be taken as the operation of a collective mind of which your individual mind is just a part. Or perhaps there were long stored up incipient memories which were looking for an opportunity to actualise.

What we are seeing as the here and now are the accumulated urges which were lying dormant for a long time finding opportunities to influence segments of your experience from within. Although it appears to be the individual's experience, the actual content belongs to many previously suppressed occasions in a temporal series; in other words, what you tried to accomplish on a subject four years ago, three years ago, one year ago, a few months ago, last week. The same thing has come up many times, but something in your ego repressed it. Finally it gets to a breaking point where that repression is no longer possible, because all the resistance is worn down. Then it comes out as an experience in the wakeful. In this way almost all our wakeful experience has an unconscious history behind it, which is impelling its operation.

The same thing happens in the dream state also: a subjective phenomenon desires to express itself in order to see how it looks, so to speak. Earlier, Narayana Guru said that knowledge, to know its own state, has become all this phenomenal world, so that through this intelligence it can see what it is. Human intelligence is considered an omega point into which knowledge has evolved, so that through it everything is seen. The alpha point of self-expression terminates with the omega of peak experience. This is what the first part of this verse describes: like the deep sleep which brings a daily ending to our lives, this discerning intelligence comes to a termination again and again.

Intelligence terminates like a wave. A wave is born where there is no wave, only water, as the product of several forces. After it arises it may travel for a long time as an invisible impulse in the ocean. Finally it reaches the place of its expression, where it comes to a peak, breaks into its full expression, and finally dissipates. After it has terminated there is once again no wave. Then it becomes another wave. The first wave has its own personality, and the second wave has another personality, but actually there is only water. In the water there is no duality. There is only aloneness. The aloneness of the water is called *kevalam*. The waves all happen within the all-oneness of water.

Our problem is we become confused about the reality of the

wave. Is it real or isn't it? When we saw it at its peak expression we thought it was very real, but where has it gone now? What is its status once it has merged with the water? Does the wave's essence remain preserved somewhere? No, it does not remain anywhere. Should we keep a record of it? We keep records of only the most powerful waves which wreak havoc along the shore. But that's all there is. The thingness of a thing is seen as a separate reality, but nothing really exists other than what we retain in the present.

Here, Husserl's phenomenological explanation becomes relevant. In it he examines the content of memory. Time is involved. For instance, with the wave rising and falling there is movement in space and duration in time. If the movement is happening to a thing by itself, without the human mind cognising it, it is as good as not happening with regard to our world of values and considerations. It becomes relevant to a human only when it is a part of his experience.

When one experiences something, it is an experience of the present. As the present moves away into the past, although the clarity of what was experienced becomes diminished, there is a kind of frantic endearment of the experience. It is not allowed to perish. This means your retention of it is forced into the present. The retention that is lived in the present is the memory of the past. It is not only a memory of the past: it is the past. Actually, there is no past. The past is the present retaining its own experience. Thus, in the present you can have a retention of a retention of a retention of a retention, endlessly, never allowing anything to pass away. There is a snowballing of retentions in the present of what is called the past.

The process of retention transforms things into shadowy substances. Rather than the actuality of a substance, we emphasise its historical, mythical, legendary or fantastic aspects, which are all shades of appreciation of only the content of retention. Because we are focused on the shadow rather than the substance, we become confused. We may be outwardly confident in our beliefs, but we are nonetheless confused at the core of our understanding. We cannot make up our mind about the value of anything. This is what is meant in this verse by *aniśam bhramicciṭunnu*.

This verse next mentions a state where what is objectively experienced and what is subjectively experienced are both annulled.

The subject/object aspects are gone, and what comes thereafter is a nonsubjective experience. There is no 'I'. As there is no 'I', you cannot say whether an experience is of the individual or the collective. Its universality cannot be determined and its individual relationship can never be stated because there is no centre of reference. We can say something is of an individual only when there is a focal point of consciousness to which it can be related, the centralised orientation of an 'I'. Where this is not, there is only aloneness. The *kevalam* or aloneness here is to be treated the same as where the still voice of aum culminates.

The effect of this in your daily experience is that you come to use a new kind of criticism. While there is a retention of the content of the past, there is also a criticism of the qualitative validity of that particular experience. If you are angry, or in a state of grief, or in pain, you can look at it critically. How much of this is my real anger? How much of it is real pain? Or in a positive experience, how much of this is my real achievement? Then there comes a pause. The psychological inflow of an overpowering dynamic, which makes the whole thing very real to you, gets suspended. It's as if you suddenly become ashamed of your enthusiasm, ashamed of your exaggeration. A lot of the fervour with which you had been accomplishing an act, appreciating an incident, or making a claim on something, drops away.

When we thus critically examine an experience, it proves itself to have the same kind of content which dreams have. If you continue to experience the mediocrity of a thing once it is shorn of all exaggeration, it takes on the status of a mere dream. If such a critical assessment of the past holds good for what is now entering your consciousness, you cannot get excited about it. You still make yourself as efficient as possible, as you did on a previous occasion, with all vigour and enthusiasm; you still perform the pertinent actions with great consciousness; but at the same time you know this is just a passing phenomenon. You do what is necessary because you belong to this system of embodied beings who are operated upon by natural impulses.

It is a little like a robot, a machine operating. Someone has switched it on, so it has to function, it has to perform its programmes.

You did not begin this machinery, it is just functioning by some natural propulsion. So you go on functioning, but personally you are disinterested in the whole business. When you lived it with interest and became very excited about everything, it did not persist as a matter of excitement. It proved to be of the same stuff as dreams.

According to this instruction, you come to a place where you are no longer excited about experiences. You do not treat them as good or bad even though previously that may have been very important to you. You no longer attach a moral tag that makes you feel guilty or benevolent. You don't treat things as bright or dull, or true or untrue in the relative sense. You just treat them as phases flowing past. And because you are no longer excited you are no longer terrified. There is no threat in anything. Insecurity could only be about the things that are passing away, so that ceases to eat at you. There is no gain you can retain. It is all just passing phenomena, to which you have a feeling of "Let it be."

This attitude brings you to live in the present, in this very moment, because that is all that is possible. There comes a kind of sameness. What once seemed very painful as well as what seemed very sweet become mere relative factors. The retention of the pair ful and the sweet are only two models. By themselves they are no longer sweet or painful when they are recalled to mind. The sameness that is in the recall of the retention is also experienced as it is taking place. That is how it should be. Narayana Guru says you fumble at the termination and do not realise it is all happening within the total oneness. You are still confused. He will examine it further in the next verse.

The meditation of this verse requires a very deep introspective analysis of one's personal experience, at a time when you are passing through a crisis. At the same time, the crisis can be seen as a phantom even while you are living it. This can be accomplished only when you can detach your mind in the thick of actual situations and can see how the exciting elements are passing into a retentive world even as you are living them in the here and now.

On certain occasions in my life when I had a physical or mental affliction, I took the opportunity for the meditative purpose of evaluating the actual pain, the actual agony to which the body or mind was subjected. I quietly watched the body's pain and wrote descriptions of exactly how I felt it to be painful. Immediately there came a psychological turnover of my interest from the pain itself to the norms of pain, intellectually conceived. That made the pain already a phantom.

The pain became less painful because my interest was of a critic making a critique of it. When you become a critic of your own pain, half of it goes away. Then you question whether the other half is real, because the first half already left. This is even more poignant when you are in an angry state and you make a journal of your anger. The bulk of the anger immediately dies down and becomes even humorous. You pose as the angry person and make a caricature of your anger. It becomes so satirical of your own state of mind that you see yourself as a big fool to get angry like that. There is so little content in it. It is blown all out of proportion. Once you see this, the whole thing leaves you and you wonder, "What is this thing called my anger? What is this thing called my pain? What are these things called my excitement, my sense of fame, my sense of importance?" All of it is reduced to an evenness. Somehow, up to now you have not cultivated that acumen. You can try it and see what kind of difference it makes.

Verse 56

kaṭalil eẓum tira pōle kāyamōrō-
nnuṭanuṭan ēṟiyuyarnnamarnniṭunnu
muṭivitineṅṅitu hanta! mūlasamvit-
kaṭalil ajasravumuḷḷa karmmamatrē!

Like waves arising in the ocean,
bodies one by one suddenly arise, then merge again;
alas! Where is the end to this?
In the primal ocean of consciousness potent action is
said to exist.

The analogy of the ocean and the wave is a poetic allegory and a very intriguing simile. Why doesn't the ocean remain without any waves? We can't see any reason why it should have waves, but somehow it is very restless. What makes it restless we don't know, but it is ceaselessly moving.

From all sides we see waves rising up. If you fly over the ocean in an airplane you can see so many waves appearing and disappearing for no apparent reason. You might ask yourself, "Is there anything really happening in the ocean?" You can answer yes. And what is it? New waves are coming all the time. But you can also say that nothing is happening. Whatever water is there remains the same. Waves may peak and subside, but nothing happens to the water itself; the ocean is essentially changeless.

Which perspective is true? They both are. The fact that waves arise and remerge is true, and the fact that the ocean never changes — that it is the eternal ocean — is also true. So what do we really have here? What is the whole question about if we lift the poetry out of it? It boils down to two logical terms: the universal and the particular. We exist here pondering over the many particulars that appear within the universal. What causes the particular to emerge from the universal? We do not know. Even shifting our attention from the visualisable example of the ocean and its waves to abstract calculables does not make the problem less difficult. Our inability to grasp how the universal is always changing into the particular, and how the particular cannot find its place anywhere other than the universal, persists.

Logically you can say "This seeming wave, when examined carefully — is it not only a change in the surface shape of the water?" Certainly. The surface could be flat, but it is undulating; the undulation of the surface is what we call waves. And how do we know this is happening? Our eyes see it. Undulation is an effect we see with our eyes, and we imbue it with a personality as if it is a separate entity. Its existence is merely appearance. So let us now at least get rid of one false notion. The wave is an appearance and the ocean alone is real; I think most of us will agree to that.

However, there is a far more interesting problem which affects all people: how can you be sure that the ocean is not an appearance also? It is certainly true that the waves are only apparent, but does that make it true that the ocean is not an appearance? What constitutes water? Very tiny molecules which we cannot even see. If you look beyond water molecules, then none of the characteristics attributed to a specific form of matter can be found. So the very substance out of which water is created is imponderable. Only because of the massiveness of the ocean are you impressed. But what is that massiveness? Where does it come from? It is all built up out of something infinitesimal. The very finitude of it is beyond the grasp of our imagination. If that is the primary cause, the ocean that you see is a much greater hallucination than just seeing a wave there.

One is a causal fallacy and the other is a consequential fallacy. The consequential fallacy is seen in the causal fallacy. Which is better? Neither of these is good. If you are seeking to go beyond fallacies you should reject them both forthwith, but you find you cannot. Why is that? One of the reasons is that you are affected by them. You are part of the same game. It doesn't matter whether we are speaking of water or skin and bones. Ultimately the categories are simply the universal and the particular.

And why is all this happening? Because things exist. It is only in the world of existence that we have this problem. Buddhists say there is nothing called existence other than action, and nothing called action other than existence. Existence and action to them are interchangeable concepts. Vedantins here agree with the Buddhists in saying that all this is action. Something exists because it has a functional efficiency.

What is the functional efficiency of, say, this piece of tissue? It holds itself out as a thin, paperlike substance. Each molecule of it is trying hard to keep its cohesion with the next molecule. So it's not a dead substance: it's trying hard not to perish, to keep up its substantiality.

I am using the tissue because it is very soft. The softness is my idea of its quality. Moreover, it looks pretty clean, with no stains on it. It is again my idea that this is clean. But with another kind of eye, a physicist's eye perhaps, I might see that this is a gigantic colony of bacteria, with each one preparing to pounce upon me and cause all kinds of diseases. Then I should throw it away and wash my hands a hundred times with antiseptic, imagining that in the antiseptic are some sworn enemies of these disease biotics which will kill them. On the mouthwash bottle it is written: "Kills germs by millions on contact." Do we see the millions? Do we see the big fight going on, the murdering, and then all the corpses of the bacteria lying dead on the battlefield? No, we don't see any of these things. We pretend. And yet, it is all scientific truth.

In *The Tao of Physics,* Fritjof Capra said that when he sat by the edge of the sea and looked out over the water he saw cascades of energy showering down on him from outer space and everything on earth spewing its energy back into space. Subatomic particles were shattering each other and creating new ones. He saw all these things happening around him on all sides, even in his own body. He had been lifted out of the mirage of seeing with his physical eye to seeing with the physicists' eye. He felt that he "saw" and he "heard". And what did he see and hear? He was not seeing what we normally see; he was seeing great sheets of energy coming from various cosmic bodies, bombarding the earth, and the earth transforming under the bombardment. Then he cried.

What made a poor physicist cry? Someone might think he was very sentimental. However, his sentiment is not born of any of the emotions we know in our social life, but by the enormity of this mysterious thing which he could not fix as being of matter or mind. He did not know where to say "this part is mind and this other part is matter."

I had the greatest revelation this morning — fantastic! We recently purchased a very big encyclopedia of science, so I decided to come to you well-informed about matter. I took down that big volume and looked for matter. That word has been removed from it. It is no longer a scientifically definable term. So that gave me great courage today to face all of you.

Narayana Guru says in this verse that from the ocean of *samvit* there arises body after body. You can look at it from outside and also from inside. Henri Bergson speaks of going around a thing and seeing it. When you do that, certainly one person is different from another. There are so many individual variations and differences between bodies. But you don't see your great great grandfather here with his characteristics. Where has he gone? And if we gather together again in a few years, instead of the baby who is with us now we might have some other friend's child. Where is that child now? Lying hidden here in the *samvit* ocean, looking for an opportunity to come up. The baby who is here now was not here last year. All these little waves are sitting in the *samvit* ocean, waiting for the proper conjunction of egg and sperm in the womb of some woman. Each child waits there for a long time as a possibility, a potentiality. But when it becomes an eight pound actuality it is no longer an idea. Now it has mass; or as we used to say, it is made up of matter. It has become tangible.

We have to combine these two elements: the world of ideas and the world of actuality. Some of our philosophers are responsible for perpetuating the nonsense that there are two separate things called matter and mind. We often put Descartes in the witness box, because he was partly responsible for this terrible misunderstanding.

Phenomenologists come and say that first you should suspend

judgement on whatever is presented before you. What I see before me now is a complex of people, made up of various ideas plus names and forms. The next step is to look for the substantiality of it. I reduce all of you to a single category, that of the perceived object. When the perceived object is one confection, there are no separate persons. All become the object of my vision. Then I question the distinction between subject and object. How much of the object is in the subject, and how much of the subject is in the object? Finally, once I reduce everything, I am forced to drop many things as inconsequential. Ultimately I arrive at the nondual entity, absolute being. Absolute being has no beard, no male or female differentiation, no inside or outside. It has no needs. It cannot be touched. It cannot be known. It is pure absolute.

To properly explicate this verse I would need at least seven or eight years. I would have to tell you all that Dignāya, Dharmakīrti, Asaṅga and Vasubandhu thought about it. There are others too. Many wise men and women have broken their heads on this, but the Guru puts it in a very simple way.

We need a fire here in the morning. Without it we wouldn't be able to sit together during the cold winter season. That is a fact. The factual world should find a place in existence, but the possibility of arriving at an absolute should also be there. If you can combine these two into one total vision it is called *samvit*. Is *samvit* cosmic consciousness? Yes. Is *samvit* matter? Yes. Is *samvit* pure Absolute? Yes. Is it God? Yes. Is it the devil? Yes. What is it not? 'Is' and 'is not' are both *samvit*. It is dynamic, and in that dynamism innumerable possibilities are happening.

Out of the ocean of *samvit* two possibilities emerge that are of general importance. One is the mind that perceives and the other is what is perceived. One is not the cause of the other: both are only consequential factors. It is not that the ocean is more real than the wave. The water and its agitations are both products of a total action situation.

We human beings have a number of prejudices. The questions that arise in our minds as to who is the actor and what is the action are only our prejudices. We think there needs to be an actor, who should have a purpose for action, a preparation for it and an instrument for carrying it out, who then performs the action. This is strictly anthropomorphism. Many of you think there is a God sitting in the heavens somewhere, complete with beard and arms and legs, who will gently touch your head and bestow his blessings upon you. Such images are born of your love for your grandfather. If you didn't have a benevolent grandfather you wouldn't think of a God-father who is sitting there patting you on the head. It is purely anthropomorphic — a very childish way of looking at it. At the same time it is very beautiful and sweet. But philosophically it is no more tenable than a cock-and-bull story.

Of course, cock-and-bull stories are very entertaining. They serve to keep us amused. Nobody stops you from imagining a fatherly God sitting on a throne who will give you manna when you ask for it. You can always rejoice when you get it. If you don't get it, it must be because you are a bad person, since God cannot be bad. It is only because of your demerit that you don't get it. All these are only tall tales, but people are afraid to call them stories because then religious people would lose all their patronage and the churches wouldn't get any money. So teachers, swamis, gurus, priests, everybody has to pretend to so many games.

Come out with the truth. Tear down all these stories. Then not only does the wave disappear, but the ocean also. We live in a world of make-believe, but does that mean that make-believe is not life? No, no, no! It's all life. Make-believe is life. This is all quite confusing, but confusion is very good for giving us a sense of the enormity of the absolute possibility in which you and I are caught. Narayana Guru says *hanta!* Alas, alas! Where is the cessation of all this? It is not just one body arising and subsiding. There is an infinite body of knowledge coming, endless clusters of ideas coming.

Once you understand the Guru's perspective, a great freedom is bestowed on you. There are no longer any boundaries. Infinite are the possibilities of change. You are no more bound to create a functional programme and then act it out. The big function, the great karma, is still going on endlessly, and you and I are part of it. Nothing else needs to be made to happen.

This is just like being put into a melting pot, where all our fixed notions are burned away. All our identifications are knocked off.

We are at once the Absolute and our own particular self. After all, this personal self only has its identity until its bubble bursts. We are really very funny people. We not only become enraptured with our bubble, but when it bursts we make a graveyard for it. We put up a big, impressive stone with a name on it, saying "This bubble was born on such and such, and died on so and so. It was really a very impressive bubble!" All it does is perpetuate the memory of a bubble. And where is it perpetuated? On the next bubble in line!

When he speaks of bodies endlessly arising in this verse, Narayana Guru is referring to ideas as well as material objects. We make a common mistake in thinking that an idea can never be gross, but as soon as it becomes a body it is gross. We have an idea of the gross, and the grossness is an idea. In fact, both are wrong.

Certain ideas are in the mind, certain ideas are touchable, certain ideas won't move. If you can piece them all together it is called *saṁghāta,* an aggregate. There are so many aggregates: forms, names, qualities, relationships, sensations. What you call a gestalt is only one aggregate of a living situation. If you can put all the possibilities of our experience into all the aggregates together, you have the *samvit.* Out of this ocean of possibilities all experiences emerge like waves.

To deny the wave and the ocean together, if you can, is wisdom. But if you then sit on what you have rejected, saying "I have realised; this is my realisation," you have only made a new slab of ignorance called "my realisation." I don't know if I am making sense to you. The very moment you realise that this is truth, you have falsified the whole thing. So where is the grace and where is the joy of the Absolute? It is all this. Don't be afraid: it's all still here.

Just suppose there is a possibility of your waking up and for a split second being aware of the state of deep sleep. Do you cry out, because at that time you have lost your body, you've lost your children, your parents, your possessions, everything? If you wake up only to know that much — that you are in the deep sleep state, which is a state of nothingness — have you thereby lost the possibility of picking up your child the next day and kissing it? No, it's all still there. It's just not in the deep sleep state, it's in another phase of your life, the wakeful. So there is nothing to be afraid of.

This is just one of the many facets of the aggregate of which we are speaking. To my mind, the ice-creamlike grace for which you crave is only one tiny little drop of the whole truth. The greatest grace is to have an insight into this great truth from inside, to know it as the wave, the ocean, the particle, the movement, the stillness, the ocean evaporating into the air, clouds forming, rain falling back onto the earth, forming rivulets, joining with other tributaries to form a stream, the big river flowing, the waterfall cascading, back to the ocean, the pure water merging with the saline of the ocean, losing identity.

What is this urgency about keeping yourself so pure, as if in a separate container? Doing this imprisons part of Beingness within what you call your identity. It's just like some childish people in India who go to the Ganges with a small bottle and fill it with water. They make it airtight, carry it home, and keep it for a hundred, two hundred years even. And what is the magic of this Ganga water? The Ganges' glory is because it flows from the Manasus River out of the highest peaks of the glorious Himalayas, down through thousands of miles of the world, nourishing and enriching everyone, only to pour back into the ocean, where it evaporates and returns to the mountains as snow. It is that endless cycle, the enormity of it, that makes the Ganges what it is. When part of it is put in a small bottle on a shelf somewhere, it no longer participates in the cycle of renewal. It is a pathetic mockery of its source.

Like that, you are breaking up the real grace, and throwing it away into meaninglessness, when you lift yourself out of the whole. I'm not taking grace away from you. I am asking you to trade in your childish grace for the real grace. You attain a greater freedom when you give up your small freedoms. So intriguing is this verse. Ponder over it.

Verse 57

alayarumāẓiyil uṇṭananta māyā-
kalayitu kalyayanādi kāryyamākum
salilarasādi śarīramēnti nānā-
vulakuruvāyuruvāyi ninnitunnu

In the waveless ocean, endless traits of *māyā* remain
as potent and beginningless effects;
water's taste and so on make a configuration,
and with such embodied forms world upon world
comes to be.

In the last verse we were considering the waves which come one after another on the ocean. When we think of the ocean, we automatically think of the waves also. We think of the ocean as the cause and the wave as the effect. The ocean is always restless, always causing waves. But imagine for a moment that there are no waves. What is important about the ocean if it has no waves? If you dip your finger into it and taste it, it is salty. The water of the ocean is saline.

We are going to an entirely different world of interest in this verse. We are no longer thinking of ocean and wave, we are thinking of the saline water and its salty taste. It is the same ocean, but our interest has been shifted from one possibility to another. Someone who sits and thinks about waves is focusing on only one aspect of the ocean. Another person experiences the taste aspect, which is totally different. A third person who comes to the ocean might think, "What a good place to surf!" Yet another might come on a calm day, see no waves, and think "Fine. It's a good time for oyster fishing, so

I will dive into it and pick up pearls." How many such interests there are, we cannot say.

This verse says that when waves cease in the ocean, do not think that all the possibilities have also ceased. The only thing apparent was the wave, and now it has ceased. Like the cessation of the wave of the ocean, our minds also at times become very still. For instance, a man who is sleeping looks very innocent. Maybe he isn't innocent, but for now he has given up all his activities. He is pacified, deep in sleep. But for all that serenity, he may be quite unpleasant or even dangerous when he awakens. Walpole used to say: "Let sleeping dogs lie." Don't go and tickle the dog. It may snarl and bite you. So let it be. Similarly, don't think that if the ocean is without waves it will be like that forever. You have no idea how many possibilities are lying latent it, nor how many different oceans there are.

The ocean of salt water is only one type of ocean. A philosopher who is thinking about the phenomenality of life and its dualities — pain and pleasure, becoming and being, truth and falsehood — sees the ocean of *samvit,* which is at once gross and subtle, conscious and unconscious. The possibilities of the ocean of *samvit* are many times more numerous than those of a saline sea. Again, a person in a mood of adoration, who is filled with a sense of reverence and who looks around and sees the abundant benevolence of nature, is filled with another idea: that of an ocean of compassion. One who is in a state of meditation, who is silently immersing into the unfathomable depths of his own self, sees in, around, above and below nothing but the ineffable ocean called *ādimahas,* the primal glory. So there are many oceans, and all of them have infinite possibilities.

Narayana Guru is here referring to the ocean of maya. Śaṅkara, in his *Vivekacūḍāmaṇi,* describes maya as the ignorance that is without a beginning, and that causes the dual aspect which conceals truth and projects untruth, with all its variegated names and forms, in a variety of ways. Since it has no beginning we cannot say "prior to the beginningless." We think of being first, and then becoming starts. We cannot conceive of a becoming that starts before being because we have already considered the process of phenomenality as beginningless. So there is no point in looking for something that is before it. Whatever beingness is there we have to see within the becoming itself, as being and becoming are inseparable.

In this verse the idea of endlessness is added to beginninglessness. Here maya is presented as a series of effects. Nobody can think of a cause without an effect. A cause is a cause because it affects something. Past is past because of the present. As long as the past is here, it cannot be past. It is the present. It is only in relation to the present that we can say something is past. Similarly it is in relationship to an effect that you say cause. It is only when you taste the saline water that you say it is salty: before you taste it that question doesn't arise. Thus all our experiences are clusters of effects. What we have seen so far is only a little, but it is nonetheless beginningless.

In the last verse the Guru called our attention to the shifting universes of interest: "Like the waves in an ocean, one embodiment after another comes and then disappears." You may be happy at one moment and moody the next, bright in the morning and depressed in the evening. Like the fluctuating moods of the ocean, the shifting patterns of the sky and the alternation of the seasons, consciousness is always changing. Changing from what to what? From one universe of interest to another.

Next the Guru says "no waves." We take our minds away from the interest in one thing followed by another. He is no longer speaking of the sequences of things: that is the temporal myth. Instead we should think of actualisation. When we taste water we are not thinking in terms of a sequence, we are thinking of the actuality of an experience. We can look at something in its latitudinal and longitudinal aspects, or we can locate it simply as a point in the here and now. This here and now experience is salty or sweet, bitter or pungent. All these possibilities are lying hidden here in the ocean which looks so calm on the surface.

You cannot judge anyone. You cannot even judge yourself. What a person may or may not do, may or may not think, may or may not understand, or may or may not like, has no limitations. They all belong to this phenomenal process called *kalya*. In that there are systems within systems. In terms of the collective consciousness, a mind is only one wave, but when we consider the mind separately it becomes itself an ocean, with all the interests arising in it as the waves.

Several types of disturbance can cause a wave in the water. The mechanical movement of a passing ship might initiate one, or the blowing of the wind. Perhaps a sudden change in atmospheric pressure might do it. Or again a cold water current sweeping into a warm one could cause the disturbance. We cannot decide exactly what causes a wave. It can be from above or below or within the whole structure. Like that, a person may react with me in a certain way and my mind gets into a turmoil. Or a hidden fear in me suddenly surfaces and my mind is upset. Or I see a new possibility of a gratification of a desire — my mind is again in a turmoil. My body contracts an ailment which it didn't have before — that brings more turbulence. Something of my great-grandfather which lay dormant for three generations and which lay dormant in me for another 50 years suddenly explodes like a time bomb and causes an upheaval in my psyche. When all these possibilities are there we cannot say which cause brings which effect at what time.

Innumerable are the possibilities of the *māyā kala*. Tantric Yoga speaks of *bindu, nāda* and *kala*. A *bindu* is a focal point. A point has no dimension, only location. But that location decides what is to happen around it. When you fix one end of a compass and inscribe a circle, the particular locus fixed as the centre decides where the circle is going to be. You can move the locus and then you will draw another circle. Of course, this is independent of the diameter you choose, which decides the size or the circumference of the circle.

What happens between a locus and a circumference decides the field. The operational function which originates at the *bindu* point and spreads all over the field is called *nāda*. *Nāda* means the vibration. There is a vibratory function which originates from the focal point and then fills the field. The field becomes permeated with that particular vibration. It can be a vibration of love, of hatred, of infatuation, of great joy, of serenity, of great peace, of beatitude, of anything.

When this happens it is called *kala*. Before it happens it is remaining there dormant. If the possibility is not in it, it cannot happen. For instance, if you put a fermenting substance into milk, it curdles. If you put the same into oil, it doesn't. Only if the possibility is there can something happen. In maya are many such potentials to produce ever so many *kala*. A *kala* is thus to be understood as both potential and actual: it is the total function which has its own will.

In this verse we are taking your experience, my experience and the experience of all of posterity into one, and saying it has no beginning and no end. Special notice should be taken of the words *ulakuruvāyuruvāyi ninnitunnu.* Narayana Guru again and again refers to this one word *ulaka,* the world where we are in pursuit of interests, where our sense interests have great relevancy. When we turn to sensory data and make out of it an ensemble of meaning, that becomes what we call one universe of interest. Each universe of interest has its own inner structuring, which is here called *uru*. A body is also called an *uru,* as in a body of interest. Thus *uruvāyuruvāyi:* one body and another body and still another body. In the previous verse the Guru said "wave after wave." Here he says "world after world" of interests, coming from the depths of maya *kala*.

In the *Yoga Vāśiṣṭha* is a story of a man who had ten sons. They decided to meditate on Brahma. It is said that what you meditate on, that you become. Here, Brahma means the Creator. When the ten boys started meditating, their identification with the Creator was such that each created his own world. Another boy came and confronted one of these Brahmas. He showed a kind of maturity which was beyond his age, and he was chastising him. The Brahma wanted to know where he got the authority to come and speak so to an elder person. The boy answered, "I know not only you as Brahma, but also all the previous Brahmas." He added that it takes four Catur Yugas, four great eons of several million years each, to make one cycle of time. That one cycle is when Brahma is keeping his eyes open. When he closes his eyes there comes the great dissolution of everything. Creation starts when he again opens his eyes. One opening and one closing together make one day. Three hundred and sixty such days make a year of Brahma. Only after a thousand such years does one Brahma go. The boy was saying, "This Brahma who is sitting here is one of the recent ones. There have been so many already!" He knew them all.

When you think of time like that, there is no end to it. I was reading in a physics book that recently physicists have found many new kinds of subatomic particles. There is one called a pion. For a pion to make a pilgrimage from one end of the atomic nucleus to the other takes ten particle-seconds. And what is a particle-second? If you put a zero, then a decimal point, and then put twenty-two zeros with a one at the end, that much of a second is a particle-second. Of course, the pion must be a loafer: it takes ten particle-seconds to cross the nucleus. The point is that the possibilities of time in its infinitesimal aspect also have no end.

Is any of this real or unreal? The Guru says don't put such questions. One story was told by a religious man, Vāśiṣṭha, and the other was told by a high pressure physicist. Both are equally fantastic and unimaginable. Imaginable or not, those possibilities concern just one factor, called time. In the phenomenality of becoming, time is only one element. So many other factors are there. And even within time there are so many varieties of possibilities. Then you have to think of space, of matter, mass, gravitation . . . on and on endlessly.

Narayana Guru gives us here a total vision where being and becoming are interlaced, cause and effect are inseparable, and the one and the many are the same. Interest and the cessation of interest are also to be taken as complementary aspects.

Do not try to understand this as a philosophy. Place yourself in the whole system. Look at the importance and unimportance of what is happening in life. Think of the great magnitude of potentials within a time-space continuum, in which your consciousness at the moment is in pursuit of one single interest. Also, think of yourself as the one consciousness which permeates all, envelops everything with a frontierless vastness. Thus you are both the tiny little interest that is running after gratification, and also you are that universal consciousness which is going on proliferating universe after universe within itself. What a grand vision this is!

Now think of your little gossips, bickering, petty likes and dislikes. We have such beautiful, fine, wonderful meditations in the morning, but once the closing chant is given the mood changes, the mind and its interest changes. You slip away into the world of gossip and innuendo, and say "I don't like that person sitting there; this one shouldn't be doing that; I don't like the way that person is behaving." How many such thoughts come and mar the beauty of this wonderful life! Where there is every possibility of great harmony, great joy, a sense of wonder piled on top of another sense of wonder, you invite frustration after frustration. This happens because you are shrinking into just one momentary point of awareness or interest and thereby isolating yourselves from the vastness. The 'me' in you becomes so very important and mean and dirty. It has become a scourge to annihilate the whole beauty of life. Learn instead to expand. Learn to permeate. Learn to embrace.

Karl Marx once said, "Workers of the world, unite, for you have nothing to lose but your chains, and a whole world to gain." We can also say, "Lovers of wisdom, unify yourselves, unite your understanding! You have nothing to lose but your stupidity, your madness, and you have a whole world of eternal joy to gain."

Verse 58

navanavaminnaleyinnu nāḻe maṟṟe-
ddivasamitiṅṅane cinta ceytiṭāte
aviratameṇṇiyaḻanniṭunnatellām
bhramamoru bhēdavumillaṟiññitēnam

Do not think in ever-new terms of yesterday, today,
tomorrow or another day;
all the endless counting and measuring is due to
confusion;
one should know that there is not any difference.

If you tell a story to a child, he will keep on asking, "What then?" Even when you finish the story by saying, "Finally the king died," he will again ask, "What then?" As in the child, in us too there is an irrepressible urge to live the new. We have the satisfaction of living a moment by experiencing it as the actualisation of a cherished desire. In fact, the so-called moment is the measure of the process of our achievement or the failure of our attempt to achieve.

If the mind is not filled with a holistic interest and the urge to act is not fully lived, dejection or boredom seeps in and creates an interlude between one main event and another main event. Time looms large as the fact of experience, when such interludes bring the drag of expectation and ask the mind to wait. Mind cannot wait endlessly for interesting things to happen, so it recalls past events which in some manner were exciting, agitating or disturbing. Another device which comes easily accessible to the mind is to fill the interlude with an interesting item such as a fantasy.

The Guru is asking us to take our recalled experience of yesterday and our "what's next?" anticipation of tomorrow and the day after, along with the now of today, and see how the objects and events in them are only configurations of the modalities of consciousness. He wants us to look for the difference in nondifference and the nondifference in difference.

According to Indian psychologists there are nine major moods, and all the shades of interest cluster around them. They are: erotics and compassion, heroics and hatred, fear and peace, humour and revulsion, and wonder. The dominant note of these moods can be seen as either coming under a positive resonance with the harmony of the Absolute or as tending to create disharmony. Erotics, compassion, peace, humour and wonder are in harmony with the perennial value of the Absolute, while the remaining four moods are opposed to cosmic harmony. With all the combinations and permutations of these positive and negative attitudes, the mind can get into processes that reflect innumerable states. At the same time, each mood or state has its own nucleus that is directly related to the value significance of the Absolute.

Everything belonging to the world of relativism has an origination, and hence is terminable. In the first vision of his *Darśanamālā,* the Adhyāropa Darśanam, Narayana Guru says:

> When Self-knowledge shrinks,
> then ignorance is fearful;
> substantiation by name and form,
> in the most terrible fashion, looms here, ghostlike. (v.7)

Forgetfulness of the Self or the Absolute is called nescience or ignorance. The feeling that a happy moment is gone or is only about to come indicates a rift or chasm in Self-knowledge. Although the sun does not go anywhere, for the people dwelling on the rotating earth it looks as though it is rising, travelling across the sky and then setting. For those who know that time and space are only creations of the mind, however, there are no limitations and there are no events.

The value of the Absolute is coexistent with the its beginningless and endless existence. The highest value of the Absolute as a living experience is identical with happiness, and the normative notion for deciding its validity is the unexpending nature of the *summum bonum*. In other words, the nature of the Absolute is eternal happiness. For this reason Narayana Guru equates imperishable happiness with the Self, and the Self with the Absolute. Perceiving or experiencing happiness is the same as knowing the Self, and to know the Self is to transcend all limitations, such as time and space, name and form, cause and effect, and the duality of subject and object. Therefore, we should remain Self-founded in the unexpending Beingness of the Absolute.

Verse 59

aṟivine viṭṭatha ñānumillayenne-
ppiriyukil illaṟivum prakāśamātram
aṟivaṟiyunnavan ennu raṇṭumōrttā-
loru poruḷāmatil illa vādamētum

Without knowledge I do not exist;
without me there is no knowledge; light alone is;
thus, both knowledge and knower, when contemplated,
are of one substance; there can be no doubt.

When we examine the content of the mind, we can see three main functional aspects. One is in the form of physical sensations being cognised. Sensations are either appreciated as pleasure-giving or painful. We cannot draw a line between a sensation as such and our feeling about it.

When I speak and then pause, what passes through your mind during that short interval is reasoning. You think about what you just heard. It is not a sensation, it's not a feeling that is aroused in you, but a chain of thought. Reasoning is the second functional aspect.

The third aspect is volition. I am now taking the resolve to talk to you. I can also resolve not to talk, but if I want to talk I have to decide to do it and then make an effort to come across to you by looking for the appropriate words and articulating them. For that, there has to be a steady preparedness on my side whereby I allow a compulsion to act upon myself. When I look for that compulsion, I find it is also myself. So I am compelling me to talk. The 'I' who is compelling and the 'me' who is compelled — how can we distinguish them? Both are subjective. Both are identified with the core of my own consciousness. Yet they are one as well as two. Sometimes when I compel myself, I groan under the weight of my own compulsion. Why should I do something which is not easy flowing? Why do I have to make it so difficult?

These three aspects, feeling, thinking and willing, all have one centre: the 'I'. "I feel," "I think," "I will." The quality of 'I' as a feeling consciousness, as a reasoning awareness, and as a willing agent, creates around each a whole universe of its own. The entire world of aesthetics has for its nucleus the feeling aspect. The entire world of logic has for its centre the reasoning aspect, and all of the moral life or ethics has for its centre the willing aspect. So there is a moral aspect, a logical aspect and a psychological aspect involved in the 'I'.

You cannot have a feeling aspect without associating it with a body. The sensations come through your senses. For that you need a central nervous system, a body and its sense organs. There also needs to be an external world where the stimulations come from, the world of forms. If another person is eating delicious food or drinking something refreshing, no matter how dear that person is to you it does not bring the taste or savour to your mouth. For that you have to put it in your own mouth. There is a distinction, a separateness, between one body and another. Still, that world of sensation that is so intimate to you is lying between a point of consciousness in you and a whole field which is outside your awareness. It is either by your choice or by an external compulsion that the consciousness within you relates itself to an entity which is external to it.

Philosophers like Kant want to make a clear distinction between a knowledge that is derived through psychological means and a knowledge that forms within you on the ground of pure logic or mathematics. A mathematical understanding is not a sensory one, it is a logical necessity which is felt within one's consciousness. Now, where in these two worlds — the sensory and the intellectual — do we see the willing element? Only in a very limited role. So actually you have within you the agents of three functions: an enjoyer, a knower and a doer. The enjoyer interfaces the world of sensation and feeling; the knower is the logician who calculates, differentiates, classifies and categorises; and the volitional function or the willing element in you is the actor.

So when you first say "I" it looks very simple, but it is not as simple as it seems. The simplicity is there because "I enjoy," "I know," and "I will" all spring from the same source.

In this verse we are asked to tie all the loose ends up in one single knot. The knower and the known are to be pieced together on the grounds that without the knower there is no knowledge, and without knowledge there is no knower. These are not two interlaced things: they are one and the same. And what is the nature of that oneness? Narayana Guru says it is a pure light. What is the advantage of knowing it is a pure light? The advantage is the very meaning of life.

When you feel there are many things that upset you, fill you with agony, struggle, pain and misery, your reason can become so confounded, so muddled and confused, that everything appears to be absolute darkness. The combined effect of a wrong stimulus coming into you and an unclear mind misinterpreting the meaning of what is coming in creates an apparent threat. The volitional agency — the person in you who has to act — has to face the consequence. You turn upon yourself. Your sensory and thinking aspects combine forces and turn against your volitional aspect.

You cannot act unless you have stamina which feeds you a continuous supply of energy. This energy is experienced as your interest. It is either a pleasure-giving interest or an interest in the preservation of your identity. If there is a threat and you have to fight to preserve yourself, then the very meaning of your life — the need for self-preservation — supplies you with the quanta of energy which you require to fight.

The source of sensation and feeling is also the source of all the energy. Previously I mentioned the nine kinds of moods: erotics, compassion, grief, humour, hatred, revulsion, fear, heroics and peace. They are all full of energy. When a person is aroused by hatred, seemingly out of nowhere comes the stamina and energy to be aggressive and to fight. When fear comes, it paralyses, freezes. Like that, all the moods are games of energy from the side of feeling.

In order to act you also need a direction to act in, a justification for your action, a strategy or plan of action, and a layout of the field before you. You need a visualisation of the whole thing as a mental image, a mental model of how you are going to proceed. For this your reasoning is your main tool. Although the knower, the doer and the enjoyer have equal status as parts of your personal self, as we have seen there can be strife between them. If there is no cooperation between your reasoning and your feeling, you cannot act. Any of these aspects can go against you. Your reason and your sensations can oppose you or oppose each other. Your volitional aspect can let down your reason or your feelings. Even though the feeling aspect might demand immediate action to gratify a certain desire which is purely pleasure-giving, and the reasoning aspect is giving you all possible justifications for those gratifications, the volitional element in you can still decide to let it go.

Thus the possibilities of the mind decide the whole meaning of life. If you do not have a unifying factor, you will be caught in one or another of the small loopholes of sensation, reason or will.

Some area in the body, some area in the mind, something in what you see or what you are — all can be sources of misery and problems. It is painful to see another person be miserable, and it is painful to be miserable yourself. The problematic area is lessened when you know that the misery that you see in yourself and in another person both originate from your own consciousness. This removes the first problem, the duality of the sources of misery. Then you only have to deal with the common source.

In this verse all the sources of trouble which were given in the last six or seven verses are brought under two common headings, the knowing mind and what is known. Śaṅkara calls this the *dṛk* and the *dṛśya,* the eye that sees and what is seen. Kant makes a division of pure and practical reason, while Descartes divides the body and the mind. After making such divisions, all these philosophers have had to find some methodology by which the duality could be bridged.

Śaṅkara's methodology first takes the physical eye seeing the world outside. If my eye is defective I will misinterpret the world accordingly. For instance, if I have jaundice the things I see will all be tinted yellow. Is it true that they are really yellow? No, it's the jaundice that makes them look that way. That means it is not the physical filament of my eye that operates as my eye. It is too unreliable. There must be another eye behind this physical one that is really doing the seeing.

This is why I can see in my dreams, even without the use of the physical eyes at all. I am sound asleep but in the dream there are so many colours, forms and meanings. How do I see them? With the eye behind the eye. Is it physical also? Yes. I have to be alive to dream. That means there is a bodily function connected with it. When I am seeing in the dream world, who is the seer and what is actually the seen? All the sensory stimuli connected with this organ called the eye have properties, such as shape, form and colour, and these are perceived in the dream. So it is not the things themselves but the impressions of things, the ideas of qualities, that are seen in the dream.

In deep sleep I do not see anything, and yet I am still there. I recognise afterward that I had a deep sleep. So what is the nature of that eye? It is not even my mind, but rather that which animates my mind. I can go from the physical world of experience to a dream experience to a deep sleep experience. If I go still farther I won't be able to make any distinction at all between the subject and object. The world of the seer and the world of the seen come together until both are canceled out and effaced. One comes to a neutral area of unity. Once we know that there is an aspect of knowledge which effaces or cancels out the physical world, the heaviness of phenomenality is not felt any more.

From this you gain a new freedom. The freedom is to relate yourself to the phenomenal world, with all the laws which operate in it, and yet to keep within a calm repose by which you can sit on your own seat of absolute certitude as a witness. For the purpose of deliberation, for the purpose of carrying out the transactions of the world, you can meet the contingency by becoming alive to the situation. It is not that you fade out as pure consciousness. You are in full alignment with that pure consciousness, but the retention of your ego enables you to meet the requirements of the world of transaction. This means you can laugh without moving away from the centre of total tranquillity, and you can cry your tears without the soul being affected by them.

There can be a real difference between two people who show the same behavioural pattern to our external eyes. One person acts out of a transactional model, consciously knowing the rules and what is required by the situation. For the other it is not a model. It is the original self transforming into the variegations to which it is subjected. Grief then means total grief; humor means total humor; confusion means total confusion. There is no inner poise, no place to stand, no inner stability. It is to be caught in the storm and to be mercilessly tossed around by it. In the first one, on the other hand, you sit firm on your own seat and live the storm as only a passing fancy. You can step back into your clarity at any moment. That makes all the difference.

In this verse we are told there is only one pure light, and yet that pure light provides for us the two spheres of the knower and the known. If we look at the previous five or six verses, we can see that each whole sphere is surrounded by what is called an ocean of phenomenality in which many traits lie hidden. Those traits of maya can bring an unlimited number of variegated worlds of differing name, form and meaning. These verses cannot be studied in isolation. We should retrospectively see the implication of all that has been built up in this section of the work. There is inevitable misery there. Detachment from that misery is only possible through the unification of our knowledge. This is done contemplatively, by practising withdrawal.

Of course, there can be a pathological withdrawal as well as a therapeutic withdrawal. A pathological withdrawal happens when you are afraid. You see a threat, you exaggerate the threat, you exaggerate the fear that is initiated in you, and so you want to run away from the situation and get back into the womb, so to speak. You become paranoiac. This is a pathological reaction taking the form of a withdrawal. When it expands to all its seriousness, it benumbs your faculties. Doors that are once closed you are unable to open again. Thus you become self-imprisoned, trapped in your own emotional state and locked in your own confused reasoning. The volitional element in you is so crippled that it has no initiative with which to break out.

The other withdrawal is that of the saint. It assumes the position of the witness rather than the actor. Here the agent of consciousness does not run away from any situation, but instead decides to go into an active form of silence. It is a silence not born of fear but of fearlessness. You are not escaping from someone, but at the same time you are not holding yourself obligated to anyone, either.

Then you should go one step further. On one side is the silence to which you go as a pathological trait; on the other side is the therapeutic silence. Through a dialectical synthesis of these two aspects you can come to your own natural Self, pure consciousness. Then you are the value or meaning of your own self. In this way the world show is all wound up and you remain steadfast in your own beingness.

This second half of *Ātmopadeśa Śatakam* is not meant to satisfy mere intellectual curiosity. It is a very difficult yet very profitable ascent. You may not see much difference between one verse and the next. To some people it might even be boring. But in each verse is a whole ocean of wisdom.

This morning I was looking at all the references that had to go into today's verse: the entire theme worked out by Kant regarding pure and practical reason, Fichte's ideas of the self and the non-self, Śaṅkara's theories of the *dr̥k* and the *dr̥śya,* the Bhagavad Gita's treatment of *jñāna* and *vijñāna,* the mind and matter of Descartes, Spinoza's naturing self — nature that is naturing and that is natured — and Leibnitz's blind, dull monad and the *monadum monadus.* There is a vast world to be unearthed that is lying dormant in just this one verse.

If you do not see all this related material, it is just a simple statement that without the knower there is no knowledge and without knowledge there is no knower. What is there to worry about? There is nothing to worry about, but there are so many things worrying you. This is a means by which you can get over all your worries. As I see it, its value is very great.

Śaṅkara finally comes to the conclusion *yathā dr̥ṣṭi tathā sr̥ṣṭi,* how your eyes are, so your world is. If you are pure, you see purity everywhere. If you are voluptuous, you see voluptuousness everywhere. If you are an egotist, you see the egotism of other people around you. If you are mad, you see madness in all. If you are peaceful, you see the occasion to have peace everywhere. If you are harmonised, the world is harmonised with you.

The advantage of this study is simply this: self-correction. When you correct yourself, the world is also corrected for you. That correction is possible only through seeing this oneness, this union. Very soon we will be told that the mere saying of it won't bring it.

As of the next verse we will have been at this for sixty days. For sixty days we have been continuously ruminating on the same subject. Did we go far?

Somebody wrote a reaction to this class and brought it to me, although I didn't ask anyone to write a reaction paper, saying that it has only stimulated the ego in people. I do not see how. But this is a good indication to show that even the best of effort and the best of intentions won't bring results by themselves, since by just going over the verses or repeating them we can still project our ego on anyone and think that *they* have a preoccupation with ego.

In spite of all this dirt that is coming up and madness that is aroused, we still have to find our way, gradually and steadily, to our own inner core, where we can finally discover and discern for ourselves the fountain-source of all peace and happiness. Nothing should stop us.

There are two key words in this verse. One is *prakāśamātram*, "that is light alone." The other is *oru poruḷām*, "substantially it is of one essential meaning." The essential meaning of the knower and the essential meaning of the known are the same. But how do we live it?

In his sermon on the mount, Jesus said if you say "Raca" to your brother and then go to the altar, you should first leave your gifts at the place of sacrifice and go to your brother and reconcile with him. Then come and do your sacrifice. He put it in a very simple, anecdotal way. He did not expound the philosophy of it. It does not matter whether you know the philosophy or not as long as you know what to do.

I do not know what Raca is; maybe it means 'rascal'. My only prayer is "God, never make me call my brother a rascal." Our self-righteousness can take us to such a putrefied state, full of pus and stinking horribly, that the whole soul becomes cancerous. Everywhere all you are smelling is your own stench.

To my mind, three examples stand in one line. The first is what I have just related of the teaching of Jesus: if you have already offended your brother, first reconcile with him before you go to God. The second is in Rousseau's *Confessions.* He says, "I agree I was a bad man. You have many things to accuse me of, but, my brother, come with me. Let us stand before our God who has the all-seeing eye. Before him, if you can, accuse me. That God who sees my action and your action alike, if you can conceal your actions and only hold out my actions before him, you are welcome to accuse me." He leaves it there. Finally, Henri Bergson, in his *Two Sources of Morality and Religion,* says, "When you point your finger at another and denounce him, you know in your heart of hearts that you are no better."

When I first came to my Guru, I had plenty of trouble with people, with my fellow disciples. Guru called me and said, "I shall give you a secret: allow the other to be victorious. If somebody fights you, let you be the vanquished and not the victor." I found there is nothing more helpful than this, to be vanquished and not to become victorious. Just say, "You have the upper hand. Let all the glory be yours. I shall lie in the dust." It is very difficult, but it works. You don't make any claim. You don't indulge in any feelings of martyrdom. You just give up.

The basic truth rests on this: there is only One and not a second. If there is someone to be punished, it is only you. If there is someone to be corrected, it is also just you. 'You' means 'me'. In my personal life I correct the other by correcting myself. I punish the other by punishing myself. I silence the other by going into silence myself. I bring peace to the other by making myself peaceful. I bring happiness to the other by making myself happy. It is a very intimate experience, to work with one's self. And it is the one place where you can conveniently work, where your volition, your knowledge and your feeling are all at hand, at the very source from which the idea 'I' comes.

Verse 60

aṟivineyum mamataykkadhīnamākki-
ppaṟayumitin paramārtthamōrttiṭāte
paṟakilum apparatattvamennapōlī-
yaṟivaṟiyunnavan anyamākuvīla

When knowledge is spoken of as subjected to the ego
without considering its ultimate truth,
even if that ultimate reality is spoken of in this way,
for one who knows, knowledge does not become other.

Man has a heritage of knowledge, which is presented through the expounding of various scientific truths. It can be seen applied in technology. Literature and the different forms of art also express it. It is within the various kinds of laws, such as the mathematical, logical, moral, natural and social. This body of knowledge has a central place in each person's life, and yet, on the whole, it is impersonal and universal.

When we relate this knowledge to truth, we think of truth as single. Truth has no limitation. We do not know the beginning or the entire scope of it. Those elements which limit anything, such as space and time, are all only constituent factors of it. We can have several kinds of attitudes towards truth — adoration, intellectual appreciation, a sense of practical utility, or even indifference — but our attitude, whatever it is, does not bring any change in the ultimate nature of truth, any more than any other constituent factor.

Nonetheless we are embodied beings. The body is equipped with senses and a mind. What is of great importance to each person is his experience, which is a reaction to what he imbibes as sensory data. The mind includes a rational intellectual function as well as an intuitive one. We really don't know what causes intuitive flashes and how they reveal certain aspects of truth, but they are undeniably present. Before our comprehension of any truth as such, all these things prevail upon us. Kant calls it the a priori synthesis. Before the operation of a logical analysis there is a presentation of all the relevant factors, and a general consciousness synthesises them into a coherent body of knowledge for us.

This individual experience of consciousness can be viewed from two perspectives: from the side of the knowing centre of awareness and from the side of the unknown where various data are presented. Philosophers make a division of this into the self and the nonself. In reality there is no such distinction; however, in order to understand our experience we have to look at it from the point of view of what is intimately and immediately clear to us.

What is most intimately known to us is the experiencing of the 'I' consciousness. If you draw a circle around it, keeping 'I' as the nucleus of knowledge, then what comes within that illuminated circle of consciousness is considered as knowledge belonging to that self or 'I' consciousness. Upon recognition of it, you say "this is my knowledge." When a person owns knowledge like that, consciously or unconsciously you are thinking of it as being other than your own. This is true of your knowledge, someone else's knowledge, or the knowledge that is not known, the unknown.

So, essentially we bifurcate knowledge into 'mine' and 'not mine'. There is no justification for making a cleavage in universal truth. Truth can never be mine; it can never be yours. It is universal. But in the actual experiencing and advocacy of truth we do make such a distinction, however unwarranted it may be. Even the great protagonists of the so-called highest truth, such as the propagandists of religions, claim to have an exclusive knowledge. They call it "my religion" or "my faith." In such cases there is a violation of the universality of truth.

In the world of actual transactions we have to reconcile with this inevitable limiting of knowledge. An embodied being has many limitations. One is that a person's sensory system cannot reach beyond a certain point in spatial extension and temporal recognition. Another is that our memory cannot go beyond the span of our own lifetime. It is true that we can incorporate the recorded experiences of others through a study of history, but these are of a secondary nature and do not come under the category of intimate experience. What is most clear to each person is the light that prevails around their own 'I' consciousness, and even this fades out at their own mental horizon. So the truth that is revealed to us is a very limited experience.

In spite of all these limitations, man is always communicating with others. Without alienating his own personal experience he is capable of expressing the truth as he sees it to another person, and under normal conditions it is more or less understood by the other person. Although each one has to use the symbols of his own concepts for the expression of truth, it is as if there is a recognised currency of concepts that can be exchanged. When people exchange currency bills like dollars or rubles or yen they are recognising a common truth behind the transaction. Behind the money — at least until it was recently fictionalised — was the gold standard, which is the absolute as far as money is concerned. Similarly, truth is the gold standard of our interpersonal communication. This communication occurs not only between people but also in different ways between all beings. To some extent even a plant understands the love that is given to it.

From all this we gather that ultimate truth is the totality to which we belong. It is not what we conceive. It is not what we ultimately or absolutely know. It is the total situation to which we belong. And the universality of it is not confined to living beings. Whatever is finds its ground, its stuff, its meaning all within the total reality.

Narayana Guru says here, "In everyday life, most people do not recognise this universality." Most people can speak only from their own standpoint. This he considers as bringing knowledge under the monopoly of one's personal experience. Although in principle this contradicts the very nature of truth, there is no other way for an individual person to know truth, to experience it, to live it and to express it. Thus there is a kind of transactional validity in owning truth and calling it "mine". Does it affect truth? Not at all.

Let me give you an example. Beyond the dateline the sun appears first in the Fiji Islands. Two hours afterwards it appears in Sydney.

Again, after three or four hours it is seen rising in Singapore, and after another two in India. So the six o'clock of Fiji is not the same as the six o'clock of India. At the same moment the inhabitants will be experiencing a beautiful dawn sun gently warming them and a brutal midday sun beating down in a fury. Is it a different sun in each place? No, we recognise it is the same sun, but it cannot be seen in the same way at the same time by all the people. So individual experiences vary in respect to local conditions, and they have a functional truth that differs from absolute truth. But this doesn't affect the reality of the sun at all. It continues to be the same sun no matter what people think.

In just the same way universal truth is unaffected by the partial experiencing of it by people. Of course there are often wrangles between people, when each holds out their personal experience as the sole truth with a bigoted, narrow conviction. The first thing to understand is the necessity of neutralising in our minds the contradictions between varying private experiences of truth, realising that there will always be different perspectives due to the individual approach we are bound to take. Then at least we will have no need to fight over truth.

The second aspect of the verse is that there is only one knowledge and that is the knowledge with which you know. Whatever you know belongs to the same knowledge that illuminates everything for everyone else. It is not necessary that you should always recognise it as such, since your recognition or nonrecognition is not going to affect the verity of it. The corollary here is: for the practical purposes of living truth there is a need to unify, coordinate and correlate truth as belonging to one homogeneous whole.

The physicist deals with many aspects of physical nature, but he has to reduce it all to one principle, such as a primal substance he may call matter. The biologist reduces everything to one principle of life, and then sees how it manifests in various ways so that he can place each manifestation in its respective position. Our business is the totality of life, not just an aspect of it, so we should similarly be able to incorporate the unitive principle of a whole truth into our life interest, so that existence, understanding and the evaluation of it can all be centralised.

This is very important. Many of the cherished human values are to be generalised and abstracted, at the same time that they are lived out as specific experiences. Love is one such generalisation. Justice is another. Goodness, all moral virtues — these cannot be separate entities. They all belong to one and the same truth. Only when they can be incorporated into one truth can my justice be your justice, or my love be meaningful to you. Whenever this universality cannot be experienced because of the private colouration that we put into it, people undergo great agony, such as when the authorities' sense of justice is at odds with the populace, or one person's love does not appeal to the object of his love.

The theoretical aspect of this verse may look bleak, removed from human life, outside of all our interests. But those who see the implications of it will be aware of how intimate a bearing it has on day to day experience. We stand divided in our opinions, and that is inevitable. But when you draw thick boundaries around your opinions and segregate the views of others as irrelevant and false, you are heading toward bigotry. This causes cleavage between man and man. You cast aspersions of a very derogatory kind, and thus bring total injustice to the evaluation of life situations.

Emotional people have a natural aversion to reason, while those who are logically structured often have a distaste for sentiment. If two such people were to evaluate a situation, each would consider their model to be the highest, best and most appealing, and the other's meaningless, shadowy and useless. They naturally lean toward their own preferences. They get into their own tiny compartments and say "this is mine and that is yours." The various religions have incorporated such compartmentalization, and each has its own protagonists. The more enthusiastic they become in giving adoration to the truth as they comprehend it, the more they become angry with someone else holding another view. Until this other view is destroyed they do not feel they are doing justice or giving their total loyalty to the kind of truth they adore. Someone else is to be removed from their neighbourhood so that they can live in peace, and there comes bloodshed. This approach leads to such kind of ridiculous ideas.

This particular verse is not to be treated as just a metaphysical abstraction. You should see how intimately it is related to your own peaceful life, to the joy of your own personal appreciations. There can be a more intimate relationship between things when you recognise the universality of truth and that there are many facets of it. When you see only one aspect and love or hate it, you need to remember that for sure there are many other angles of vision and many other possibilities.

The highest truth cannot be articulated, because as soon as you articulate you conceptualise. If you do not want to intellectualise it you should sit in silence. If you open your mouth you bring a concept. A concept is born of intellect. It is an intellectual appreciation of truth, and it is bound to be limited. Always behind that intellectual conceptualisation there is a person, an 'I', who is speaking. Since there can only be a transaction between two people, the person who listens also has the standpoint of an 'I'.

There are only two possibilities regarding the discussion of truth or philosophy: either one should opt to live in silence and be satisfied with silence, or accept that the moment you speak it becomes intellectualised. To hate someone for being intellectual is an example of truth being monopolised, and of your tendency to monopolise everything. Why does it prick you when I say that? Why does it hurt when a personal reference is made? It hurts people when you narrow a view. On the other hand, when you go to a more universal appreciation there is an elevation of experience. The important point here is that we are all intellectualising, only to different depths. So don't wrap yourself in smug satisfaction and think it's only something that other people are doing. Instead, see how that same process is going on in yourself.

Nataraja Guru, in his elucidation of this verse, asks us to consider two limiting points, the most transcendental aspect of truth and the most immanent. The immanent is where it pricks you, where it stimulates you, where it is your flesh, where it incarnates. The transcendent is where your ideas fade out, your individuation cannot continue, where you merge with the universal. Looking at this as the vertical parameter, when truth comes closer and closer to the side of the individual, the physical and the personal, it gains the richness of catering to your instinctive life. When it is removed farther into the transcendental it loses the blemish of all personal stains, but the intimacy that comes through the sensory and mental faculties fades out. At the same time you gain a spiritual glorification of truth, which is another kind of experience.

Verse 61

veḷi viṣayam vilasunnu vēṟuvēṟā-
yaḷaviṭumindriyamārnnu tante dharmmam
jaḷatayatiṅṅu digambarādi nāmā-
valiyoṭuyarnnaṟivāyi māṟiṭunnu

External objects appear to be different from one another;
it is the function of the senses to posit for each a distinct dimension;
nescience rises as sets of names, like sky and so on,
and changes into knowledge.

Life is like a procession through a fair: we do not know what is waiting for us around the next corner. And there are endless corners. Every passing moment has its own message, each its own surprise. One moment says, "Enjoy! I am here to give you fulfilment." The next moment says, "I will shatter all your dreams." It terrorises us. Then we come to another moment which creates a tremendous revulsion in us. We pass hurriedly on to something more pleasant. Then we may face a great horror, followed by something very consoling. There are moments of elation and moments of depression.

Within us we also hear corresponding responses to all this, saying "This is very good;" "Oh, this is not as good as that;" "This is heavy;" "That is hard;" "This is soft." There is always some judgement to be made, something to be appreciated, something to be admired, something to be reviled. The messages we get from the passing moments are in the form of promises, cautions, invitations. Some of them are very alluring. Some are compelling. Some create resistance in us. Thus we live in various kinds of moods. Where exactly are these moods created? Do they stem from something outside, or something inside us? No one can say.

A certain scientist in the old Soviet Union once said that revolutions and other changes in the world are happening more due to sunspots than because of dialectical materialism. Because dialectical materialism was part of the state religion at the time, the scientist was sent off to Siberia. But afterwards some psychologists in Montreal wanted to find out what caused hysteric upheavals in certain mentally disturbed patients, who were observed to have periodic increases and decreases in their unbalanced behaviour. They examined the food; they made a study of the temperature, the grouping of the patients, the attitudes of the nurses, the kinds of medicines given. Finally, in exasperation they compared the outbursts to the occurrence of sunspots, and found a striking correlation between them. So when we are sitting on our porches we do not realise what that terrible thing called the sun is doing with our glands.

Still, glands within us and stars and suns in the firmament may not be the ones to blame. There may well be other hidden and unknown forces operating which bring about turmoil or peace. The more you look at it and consider the possibilities, the less you can clearly say what is the cause of anything. It is also very difficult to say what is outside and what is inside: the cosmic vibrations of energy in outer space and the sweet symphony rising in the ear are not two. It is a single flow of energy.

When the cool breeze comes, the air we inhale through the orifice of our nose, the lungs that heave, the heart that pulsates, the neurons that carry the messages to the brain that cerebrates, and the soul that is delighted, are not separate. One prana operates in all of these. Outside it is the air, inside it is the vital principle, but it is always one continuous whole. There is a homogeneity of everything we experience. If something similar to light were not inside us, the eye could not see and recognise the light outside. If something similar to sound were not within us as well as without, we would not recognise any sound. The whole has to be homogeneous.

The present verse points out that when each object of interest comes, the corresponding sense is directed towards it. There is an underlying interest which finds its kinship with what is presented, allowing us to establish a relation between a thing 'out there', a name with which we recognise it, and the conceptual meaning of the thing we are experiencing.

In his *Advaita Dīpika,* Narayana Guru says, "A thousand names, a thousand objects of interest and a thousand concepts — when they are structured we get the world." And what is this world? It is woven together out of countless millions of names. Corresponding to every object, there is a name. Corresponding to every object and name, there is a conceptual image. These triads come along one after the other, endlessly. After a while we begin to substitute the name for the reality. If we look closely at some of the things we take for granted as objects, there is no object there.

The Guru gives one example here. He asks, "The space or sky — look for it. Where do you see it? Do you see space anywhere? Is there anything called sky anywhere? Yes. It is in the dictionary." Just like God, the only place where you can see it is on a page in the dictionary. It exists only as a name. Yet that name can move you. No other word has had so much impact on human hearts and minds as 'God'. But what is it? Mainly a name. Is it really a mere name? Yes. It's a name that moves you. It's a name that governs you. It's a name you cannot do away with. How many such names are there like 'God', which do not have a perceivable counterpart? Thousands and thousands. In fact, the objects which we have actually seen, felt and found tangible are only a very few.

Another example is the terms East and West. When we use them they have a clear meaning to us. But what actually are East and West? If we go far enough examining them, they each turn into the other. They are mere names appended to concepts. So we live within a much greater world which is created by names only, and we judge everything on the basis of our internal normative notions.

Now we have to think of a vertical parameter. At the base of it is darkness. From out of that darkness rises experience after experience. When each experience comes to the level of conscious awareness, it changes into whatever we are capable of appreciating. A thing may have many qualities other than those which can be seen, heard, touched, tasted or smelled, but those are all we can interpret. Suppose we had ten more sense organs. Then the qualities of all things would change. But we have only five senses, so we see all things in the world as if they had only five major qualities.

From this it becomes clear that we are not really seeing anything as itself. The thing is first of all transformed into a sensory experience. In order for us to know anything, we have to fit it into our own sensory system. So, when an unknown thing rises from the alpha of our consciousness, it is dressed up in our own familiar world of sensation. After it is made acceptable to our senses, we pass it on to yet another sphere, the nominal.

Once an experience goes to the nominal level, it can be categorised. A number of things with the same name can all be grouped together. When we look at each other, this friend is different from that one. But when I think of 'students', for instance, there are no longer any separate people here. 'Students' covers everyone. For a doctor, people are either patients or non-patients. We might not see which category we would come under, but for him we are clearly patients or non-patients. When you make a category like that, it is mainly based on the name you give the experience. Into that name you have to fit everything.

Between what is yet to be known — which remains in the unconscious — and that which is already known and has once and forever become a name, all the happenings of experience take place. We can visualise it as an ever-flowing stream that never ceases, continuously rising from the alpha of nescience into the world of names. If you meditate on this verse, the impact of it on your judgement, your personal behaviour, your interpersonal relationships, and your reaction to situations is very dramatic. The world which is out there and very substantial to you suddenly changes into a configuration of mental images. In a sense, the mind detaches from the body. Where stimuli from things 'out there' are believed to enter into the system called the body through the eyes and ears and so on, now the situation is reversed: "This thing called my personal life is always flowing out through my eyes and other senses into the external world. I am seeing only me — 'me' flowing and extending itself into the sky, the green forest, the mountains and the clouds."

The difference this makes is the difference between a detached observer looking at a picture and someone who is an integral part of the picture itself. We are endlessly creating a huge painting where the artist is part of the work itself. Can you imagine it that way? We have been told all our lives that things are outside and we are seeing them from a distance, instead of being told that all this is what we are. Vedantins do not believe that when you see a pot, the pot is "out there." They don't believe the pot is in your head, either. They say that you and the pot are somewhere where you are one. Neither do you or the pot have any existence "out there." Both you and the pot commingle and remain as an indefinable, indescribable entity. That's very shaky, but it serves to shake you out of the morbid establishment of a stagnant world.

I may hear a sound and imagine that it's a car passing by outside, but in reality it's just a disturbance I'm having. At the end of my disturbance, I perceive it as a sound and presume that the sound comes from a car on the road. I imagine the road and mentally put a car there, all to account for the disturbance I've just had. Thus, behind hundreds of our experiences there is an extension of our memory to substantiate them. Where subjectivity and objectivity mingle into one, we have a nondifferentiated world with millions of differentiations possible within it. There are so many possibilities with such inherent complexity, we should congratulate ourselves that we don't go mad trying to sort it all out.

So that is the first part of the meditation of this verse. The second part is that if all this is evolving out of the individual consciousness equipped with a sensory system, you already have a handle on it. If it is because of an excessive secretion of bile or adrenaline or something that you react in a certain way, you can tame your glands so they don't produce the excess. That may change the world for you. And this is true of more than the physical glands. In your psyche also are various kinds of positive and negative stimulations: jealousy and hatred and all such kinds of emotional disturbances. It is good to work there. You can moderate these emotions without repressing them.

The third part of the meditation is where your understanding, your awareness, everything is brought to a state of homogeneity. When you raise yourself to this level there is a great calm. There is a sense of peace coming from within. It is as if you have become one with the overlord of all.

There is a promise in the Bible that we will be provided with a seat on the right hand of God. If God has created all this, and all this is knowledge and you are seeing it as knowledge, you are certainly sitting on the right side of God and having a panoramic view of all that is below. It's very peaceful. It is like an endless magic. From nowhere you see it pop up and change into multicoloured forms, designs and patterns. These are all gathered up and become nominal. Then it spreads itself out into an infinitude beyond time, beyond space, beyond name and beyond distinction. It is just pure awareness. Such is the transforming panorama we are privileged to witness from our divine seat.

In the *Saundarya Laharī* of Śaṅkara we come across the same view. The Creator gathers dust from the feet of the divine Mother, out of which all this grand universe is continuously being made. The dust is what we might call today subatomic particles. Without stopping, this process is always going on: nebulae coalescing into stars and galaxies, some stars breaking up and forming planetary systems around them, some planets cooling and becoming moist enough to allow the proliferation of life. A mysterious power keeps each star away from its neighbours as they whirl through space, so that they don't collide, allowing time for sentient beings to develop. Then after some time the star system explodes, dissolving everything back into dust once more. Such is the wondrous cosmos.

The cycles of our consciousness are much the same. When we were lying asleep two hours ago, there was no *Ātmopadeśa* class, no Portland, nothing. Then we woke up and the programming began. As part of the programme, we now see all this. Again, in a little while all this will be gone and we will be in another world. By nighttime we grow tired and go back to bed. We have some dreams and then everything vanishes. Day after day the same pattern recurs.

If we put it all together in one picture, what we see is that from the alpha point to the omega there is a continuous rising of all the variegated forms, names, ideas and reactions, which change into one pure consciousness. It is all very peaceful.

Verse 62

paravaśanāy paratattvam entetennō-
rkkarutarutennu kathippatonninālē
varumaṟivētu varā kathippatālē
paramapadam paricinta ceytiṭēṇam

Do not think of the absolute truth overpowered by the sense of "mine";
what knowledge comes from merely saying "do not"?
This will not come by mouthing a phrase;
the absolute state is attained through relentless contemplation.

A spiritual search is generally considered to involve great effort along with feelings of frustration. It has been described as walking on the razor's edge. We have famous books like *Pilgrim's Progress* and, for an even more terrifying illustration of the whole path, Dante's *Divine Comedy*, full of all the nightmares of passing through Purgatory. The more suffering encountered on the path, the more likely the book will be a classic.

When Siddhartha, or Prince Gautama, became convinced of the pain and misery in which people live, he wanted to find a way out. With great difficulty he tore himself away from his dear wife, Yasodhara, and their newly born child, Rahula. He gave up his entire kingdom, and rode away to the forest with only one attendant. There he shaved off his hair, sent his horse back, and lived alone, going from one teacher to another. Each guru taught him whatever he knew, but Gautama was not satisfied. After a long search he decided there was nothing to be learned from any master. He had to find truth for himself.

Everywhere he saw ascetics undergoing all kinds of disciplines. Some had been holding their hands up for such a long time that the hands had withered and become like dried twigs. Some were hanging themselves upside down from the trees. With their legs up and their heads down their bodily forms had become very grotesque. Others had let their hair and nails grow long, and did not move from the place where they were sitting. Still others were trying to do away with their bodies by not eating. The future Buddha decided to outdo all of them. It is said he fasted so much that he became just skin and bones. When he touched himself on the belly he was touching his spine, and when he touched his back he was touching his belly. But with all this extreme mortification of the body he did not get anything, except perhaps a headache.

We can also read in the life of St. John of the Cross, how he would wear a robe with prickly hairs inside that would cause him great pain. He would cover it with another rag so that no one would notice that he was undergoing a painful discipline. Then he subjected himself to floggings from his fellow friars, and was humiliated by them. In this way he was trying to share the pains of Jesus.

You can resort to all kinds of mortifications, like the Indian yogi who sits by the wayside on a seat of nails and meditates, but does that bring you anything? It is all beside the point.

There are many people who have different kinds of religious infatuation. Some beat drums and cymbals, and sing and dance with hysterical frenzy. They think that by shouting God's name as loud as they can, that He will hear them and they will get realisation. Some become so enthusiastic about wanting to convert others to their faith that they take their scriptures in hand and parade proudly around the neighbourhood. Whether it is convenient for their neighbour or not, they just go and sit on their head and read from St. Matthew or Ezekiel or Corinthians. They won't leave anybody in peace, believing that the whole of salvation is to be found in verse such and such. They cause so much embarrassment and vexation for others, and yet never seem to notice the effect they are having.

And then there are those who assemble a whole army and march on others who do not share the same faith. They call out "Jihad!

Behead them! If they join our faith they will be saved, or if their heads are cut off in the name of God they will also be saved. This is our faith. Our faith is so important!" But it is not by frenzy or hysteria that you get to truth.

There are so many of these beliefs. Some people think that by going on a pilgrimage from one holy place to another, or going to every church or temple and paying to have special rituals performed for them, their sins will be expiated. Some learn how to twist and contort their bodies in a hundred and eight ways, how to sit in different postures, or how to breathe ten kinds of pranayama, some with grunts, some with hisses and some with hiccups. But with all this torturing of the body or the nostrils, you won't get anything.

Is salvation, or the highest truth, or realisation of the Self or the Absolute, or God-realisation, something you get by piling effort on top of effort? No. By working very hard you can make money and riches, get a house, an automobile, a position in society, and many academic degrees and other honours, but that kind of amassing of your labour will not bring any realisation. All those efforts are only egotistic trips; they only serve to harden the ego when treated as steps to salvation. That very ego will shield the truth you want to see away from you.

Often when somebody tells you, as I just have, not to indulge in all these various trips, that they won't bring realisation, you might adopt a negative attitude. You might think, "OK, then I won't do anything. Let realisation come whenever it comes. I will just allow things to be." If you take such an attitude, will it bring realisation? No, it won't work either. If you leave yourself to the mercy of natural events, your mind will be like a monkey, running from one fantasy to another, one mood to another, one depression to another. There are so many incipient memories in you wanting to find expression through the gratification of desires that urge after urge will come, and you will run after them. This will only take you to greater madness and greater darkness.

Then, what is the way out? How about going to the best libraries and reading the thoughts of the great masters in big books? That's one way of entertaining yourself. If you learn the vocabularies of all the religions and all the big words coined by philosophers, you can certainly impress someone. Śaṅkara said that if you become a great scholar someone might invite you to a good feast. They may honour you, but that is not realisation.

In the Upanishads it says, "I am Brahman." So why shouldn't I also say "I am Brahman, I am the Absolute?" As Śaṅkara also put it, a man who is crowned as king on the stage in a theatre cannot come out of the theater and rule over the people there as a king, because he is a king only on the stage and not elsewhere. So, if you say you are Brahman you are Brahman only in your own fantasy, and not in reality.

OK. We have discarded all the egotistic trips. We have seen that mere negativity won't help, and that there is no use in just mouthing phrases. What, then, is the way out? You should go back to the very first verse in the book, in which it is said, "Turn your senses inward; calm down. Calm your mind. Just watch what is going on. You see a world outside and a world inside. You can discern one thing from that: a knower is knowing. There is a field which is known, and there is a light which is illuminating that field. Behind your seeing, there is that light. Behind your hearing, there is that light. Behind every thought it is there. Every passing idea is illuminated by it." What is that nucleus of illumination which is in every experience? Invariably it is the self-luminous light which is experienced as the seer. It has no break. It is continuous. It takes no effort at all to know it.

In the Upanishads it is said: "That is far and near." It is far when you think of realisation as something which you have to achieve, God as something which you have to seek, the Self as something which you have to learn about. Then it is a far off thing which only seers have seen and wise men have spoken of. "I am an ignorant person. I don't see it. I don't get it. Will I get it in my lifetime?" When these kinds of thoughts are there, it looks very far. But, as Henri Bergson says, instead of going after knowledge and knowing it, if you just get into knowledge and be it, it is not at all far. It is here and now, in this very knowing. That which reveals to you that you are knowing — that is it. It is very near. It is inside and also outside.

The Isa Upanishad says, "It runs faster than the mind or senses, and before the mind or senses reach it, it is already there." The very light that illuminates the seer in you is also the light that has already illuminated what is seen. Before the eyes reach it and see it, the light is already there. The light of the Self has already illuminated as far as you can see in the universe. All the infinitude which you come to know is nothing but the same light.

It is not by breaking away from life or shunning anything that one finds realisation. Nature, with its illumination, its action and its obscuration, is going on endlessly. But that obscuration, action and illumination are only processes that are happening within the light. You are the light. You are the seer, and the process is what you are seeing. This differentiating process is what you call Nature. Nature is thus not an outside entity, not an outside factor. It is the seen. In what is experienced, there is no outside or inside. By relentless search, by continuous contemplation, one always knows this. Then you don't have to have this terrible struggle.

Ramana Maharshi told all the people who came to him to just ask "Who am I?" He didn't intend it to be turned into just another egotistic trip, with someone sitting for ten hours and asking "Who am I?" "What are you doing?" "'I'm doing my sadhana, asking myself who I am for ten hours." No, man, it's not that way.

You need to be a participant in all this. Live your natural life. But in and through this life, see the light which you are. When you ask, "Who am I?" it is not as a special discipline. And yet it is the only discipline, going deeper and deeper into everything you experience. You may be taking a cup of tea, eating a loaf of bread, or sharing an experience with a friend, being intimate with someone. In all these you just need your transactional mind. But that is only one aspect of the mind. There is a deep awareness in you which is silently witnessing, constantly questioning, and continuously flowing as an all-permeating consciousness. It is calm, serene, all-filling. It is both on the surface and in the depths.

Then the feverishness of your search drops away. It becomes steady, gradual, and very thorough-going. You no longer try to arrive at an event called realisation. You are not looking for one single experience of an overwhelming nature. In one sense you should always be overwhelmed, because there cannot be anything more overwhelming than this. You are tinier than a point, and yet in that speck of consciousness there is a vastness, an infinitude even, caught in a timeless, spaceless awareness. The infinite cycles of time and the vast space of the cosmos are all in an unutterable, silent consciousness.

This is called *paricinta* or *manana,* going from one depth to another depth, knowing a little more of everything tomorrow than you know today.

You should remember two things. One is when you see a form, that very form hides the reality out of which it has evolved. When you see bread, you do not think of wheat flour. When you see cloth, you do not think of cotton. When you see a pot, you do not think of clay. And when you see people, you do not think of the one evolving energy out of which they all have sprung up. When you see the world, you do not think of the Absolute. So forms operate as a kind of shield of a thing's intrinsic nature.

The other thing to remember is that when you think "my experience," you create a wedge between you and the other. This is because of the insistence on grouping things, saying things like "This belongs to my faith. That church there, the First Methodist, is *my* church. The one over there, the Presbyterian, is not the right church." "Those are all Christian churches, why should I bother about them? I am a Jew, and I have a synagogue to go to." The Hindu says, "My temple is in India. Until I get back there I won't have a proper place to worship." Conceptual islands like these spring up, which block off everything else from being a part of you. You should be able to break down all these barriers, not by going around and smashing them with a sledge-hammer, so to speak, but just by knowing.

This gentle way of knowing, rather than making feverish attempts, is what is recommended here by Narayana Guru. People understand the "Hallelujah" part of religion, the sensationalism, readily enough. They also understand the dreadful, tragic aspects, like a crucifixion, a crusade or a martyrdom. But they do not understand the gentle and beautiful contemplative. Jesus would withdraw from the crowd and sit in silence, gazing at the sky, or walk on the beach, having for his company only the winds from the sea or the waves lapping rhythmically on the shore. It's not very impressive, but it's a much more serene, profound and beautiful expression of what his life was really about. When he was stopped by a disabled man and spoke to him in a gentle way, it is not regarded as important. But when the same man, who had been suffering from palsy, got up and walked, that miraculous part alone has become associated with Christ's "real" life.

In this way we mark off areas in life which excite us, and think that there is where God manifests. Yet we don't have to make such exclusive boundaries around concepts like "God manifestation." The whole is one single manifestation. Lower the ego and turn it off.

In the Bhagavad Gita, Krishna says, "By just controlling from outside, inhibiting everything, you only make yourself a hypocrite." It's like putting on the brake and pressing the accelerator at the same time. First bring down the inner pressure. Then the outer will naturally come to a close.

The Guru is here suggesting to us the most gentle pressure in the search. At the same time it is not lukewarm. It is an out-and-out search, but that search is not directed to just one isolated area. Life itself is the search. It goes on until we come to what is called *paramapadam,* an absolute state.

The absolute state comes when all relative aspects are seen in their relatedness within the Absolute. Everything has its own niche and you don't have to dismiss anything. It all gets placed properly in its context. There has to be a reorganisation of the whole life so that things are put in their appropriate position and understood as being part of an organic whole. Once this is done, that's all.

The state of being the Absolute is continuous and simple. It's not a static experience or event. When you think of it, don't think of it as a great mass with the whole world inside it. A little baby smiling is a simple thing, but within that simplicity there is no shade of pretension. It doesn't smile to please anyone. It just smiles. A little flower tosses its head in the breeze — that's an absolute event. It is not a copy of a flower or an idea of a flower, it is an absolute flower. It shines of itself. So when you think Absolute, don't think it should fill the whole universe. There is a timelessness in it and an irrelevancy of the space occupied. It just is.

This is understood by the Japanese poets when they write haiku.

The quality of the haiku is the element of the Absolute in it which comes as just a little shimmering — of its beauty, of its plainness — in your heart. That's it. You don't have to explain it to anyone. You should never read haiku to someone and then give a commentary on it. That's the worst thing you could do with it. Instead, silently read it and close the book. Then just feel the serenity that pacifies you and makes you forget the world for a little while, even if only for a fraction of a moment. A fluttering leaf comes down and you gaze at it. Until it hits the ground you forget everything. It's an Absolute experience. You don't have to be ponderously meditating, "Who am I? Who is seeing this leaf which is fluttering in the autumn wind?" You falsify the whole situation by thinking that way.

Verse 63

aṟivil irunnaparatvamārnniṭātī-
yaṟivineyiṅṅaṟiyunnatenniyē tān
paravaśanāy aṟivīla paṇḍitan tan
parama rahasyamitāru pārttiṭunnu?

Apart from remaining in knowledge without becoming
other than it
and knowing this knowledge here,
struggling in frustration, one does not know;
who sees this supreme secret of the wise man?

For most people the concept of a spiritual life means going away from the activities in which they are normally engaged; to live an altogether different kind of life. Fully dedicated spiritual seekers, like Catholic monks, Buddhist bhikkus or Hindu sannyasis, seem to live a life pattern which is very different from the rest of us. They adopt a special lifestyle, often with rigorous discipline involved. Their behavioural patterns are not like those of others.

When we see all these things we tend to think that spiritual life means doing certain things and then achieving a result. The here-and-now aspect of life is considered to be not worthwhile. We think, "This time I have now is only for my training, so that someday I will become qualified to gain the great realisation." With these hopes, people enter spiritual pursuits. They believe they will be getting something down the road, or just around the corner, and their spiritual preceptors encourage such beliefs.

A whole lifetime passes like that. The great excitement which these people are expecting never comes to pass. Or, if something happens which is very exciting, they think "Oh, that must be the realisation I was looking for." But, like any other fantasy, it fades out. When it is gone they are no better off than they were before.

Yet people are struggling. Those who make spiritual realisation a commercial proposition only add to the struggle, since they gain from convincing their students that their efforts will bring results. We hear so many stories of great spiritual personalities like the Buddha, Christ and others. A story is only exciting if there is something spectacular in it. There has to be a very tragic situation or some other dramatic tension. Then suddenly something tremendous resolves the situation, a big light or whatever. If these things didn't happen it wouldn't be a very good story. But you cannot live someone else's story as your life. Your life is all you have, and it's a very simple thing.

Whatever realisation you are to get, you have to get in this life. It must infuse the very pattern in which you are living. There is no sense in pretending to be a Ramana Maharshi or a Sri Ramakrishna. You can't make a Kali temple here in America and sit before it undergoing all the devotional rites Ramakrishna did in anticipation that one day, suddenly, Kali will jump out of the stone image and give you the "big hit" on your head. No such thing is going to happen, but still we fantasise.

Let's examine the states of consciousness from the standpoint of how much control we have over them to bring about a desired result. The highest state, one we have only heard about, is called samadhi. Samadhi is not a state like eating chocolate cake. There are no sensations. There are no ideations. In samadhi, there is no modification of the mind. If there is no modification of mind, there is no question of knowing or not knowing. Is it possible to direct your mind in any way when there is no modification at all? Certainly not. It is just a state of being. There is no knower there, nor is there any knowing. What advice could be given if there is only a state of beingness? There is no scope for you to do anything, for the simple reason that you are not really there as an agent. If you were there, you could do something of course.

The next deepest state is deep sleep. Nobody can be instructed how to have a deep sleep, or how to cognise the experience of deep sleep. It happens where there is no cognition. Here also, effort is irrelevant. At least in two states, absorption and deep sleep, you are totally incapable of doing anything on your own. They are neither good nor bad. When they come, they come, and you just live them.

The dream state is very fascinating because now there is a cogniser. You can see what is going on. Many forms come, colourful, bold or frightening. But still you do not programme your dreams. You are only permitted to lie on your bed and witness all those things passing before you. Good or bad, there they are. That is all. You cannot do the least bit about it. Of course, you can get into a kind of self-criticism inside the dream, but the dream tricks you by supplying its own kind of reasoning. If you start examining your dream while you are dreaming, it knows just how to fool you. I try all the time, but I have never succeeded in maintaining a coherent logic in the dream state. I make all sorts of experiments to establish that it is a dream, but it defies my efforts and convinces me that it is not. Then I wake to find that it was a dream after all. So it seems that no discipline is possible in the dream state.

What is left to us as the field for our endeavour is only the transactions of the wakeful consciousness. Here things are very definite. If I want to read, I read. If I decide not to speak, I can remain silent. If I want to become self-critical or critical of others I can do that. If I just want to show my interest in you, I can show interest. If I want to withdraw, I just do it. This is a most convenient state of consciousness, where you can programme and do as you like.

In this world, where you have that kind of freedom, what kind of knowledge do you have? You have sensations of the body — heat and cold, physical comfort and all that. This is called *jīva-jñānam,* the knowledge of our biologic functions. Then you have knowledge which arises out of sense contact. "I see my spectacles sitting there; I see my wrap. It is a good wrap." These sensory images that one can experience are called *indriya-jñānam,* knowledge of the senses.

So we have a biologic knowledge and a sensory knowledge. Then we can think, "I am sure that the glasses sitting here are my spectacles and not my friend's. His are sitting on his nose." This is an exact knowledge, *yathārtha-jñānam*. The *yathārtha* or actual knowledge I have of my wrap is that it is a wrap and it gives me comfort. The difference between the transactional and the dream is that the dream is fiction and transactions are factual. The world of transactions has many factual entities in it. One entity is different from another because of its unique name, form, properties, meaning and significance.

If this experience is factual, why don't you call it your realisation? Because you have heard that in the realised state everything is one, and here you see everything as many. You have heard that truth is always the same, that it doesn't change. You have heard that in it there is no before and after, while here in the wakeful, transactional state things appear, are experienced, and then pass away. Thus there is a past, a present and a future. There is a process of becoming. Again, it is not one, but many. There is a knower and knowledge. How can all this be the Absolute? It cannot. There should not be any plurality in the Absolute.

So, then, where should you look for the Absolute? That's what you have to find out.

Now take this cloth I am wearing. Without pulling away the threads and making it useless, just by looking at it and knowing it, I can easily see it is made of wool. I can call it a wrap and use it as a wrap, but all the same it is just a cloth of wool. The wool, which was shorn from a sheep, is a biochemical substance that came from the sheep's body. On further analysis, the wool is made of chemical compounds. The chemical compounds themselves are made up of atoms, which themselves are forms of primal energy presented as particles and waves.

I have not done anything to my wrap, but now I have a knowledge that reduces my wrap — or my body or you or anything here — to one fundamental knowledge: that this has all evolved out of the same primal energy. This primal energy is one, changeless, of all time. So now I am seeing the changeless in the changing, the Absolute in the relative, the beginningless and endless in what is transient. This is the great possibility of the wakeful.

You have heard the Absolute is blissful, but you don't know what that means. It is delightful to see you. I am happy when I look at you. I'm also happy when I have a cup of some good drink or delicious food. It's a great joy to see the sunrise, to look at a flower, to read or write a poem, to listen to an interesting talk. In all these things we experience happiness. They are all the kind of happiness which comes from a particular subject or enjoying an object of interest. But this enjoyment of an object of interest is possible only if your knowledge can link together an existential factor and a value factor.

There is just one knowledge, and in that knowledge we have the assurance that at this moment this exists. We should also have the assurance that this is very delightful. It is the quality of our knowledge that it has an existential verity and at the same time is happiness through and through. The specific occasion that makes it a happy thing — such as good food, the touch of a dear friend, the word of someone loved, or the subtle nuances of music or poetry — can come only here and now in our present, actual life.

So if you want to look for the Absolute, this is the right place to do it, where you and I sit together and have a happy time. It is right in that happiness that you see the happiness which is called the Absolute. It is a very simple thing. It is not some blinding light which is going to knock you down. It is the happiness of right now.

Whether your joy is that of a yogi, one conjoined with the Absolute, or a *bhogi,* one conjoined to the light of the senses, you do not have any separate or different kind of experience from this here. You should see the blissful beatitude of the Absolute in sensual joy, and the joy of the senses in the Absolute. To the wise the eternal present is this here and now. What prevails in the state of supreme absorption, in the quietude of deep sleep, in the phantom shows of the dream, and in actuality, are all modulations of total knowledge. And never do you become so clearly aware of that knowledge as in the transactional, because here you can examine things and look for their deeper dimensions and significance. It is here you can reflect.

A thing sits solidly here before you. It is gross, concrete. But you can convert it into just your knowledge, because only your knowledge is there for sure. Then the concrete thing becomes very subtle. It is identified with your own consciousness, is part and parcel of your awareness.

It is up to you to make your consciousness bright or dull. If you decide, "Oh, this is the time to mourn, to sit and become boorish," you can. Or you can realise it's nonsense, just nonsense, to get into depressions. Instead you could think, "My Self is a treasure, and each passing moment is to be enriched with the treasure of my own Self. Every possible relationship I may get into here with the things that are presented to me in the wakeful, I will also enrich. If the Absolute is all joy, all bliss, there is no reason why this moment also should not be like that."

However there is one impediment, something called *vipati vijñāna,* seeing everything as its opposite. The Self is seen as the non-Self, and the non-Self is seen as the Self. It is not just because you are in the wakeful and the world is presented there and you can do anything that it becomes a happy occasion. No. From your side you have to do one thing. Certain kinds of understanding are to be reversed. For instance, what you experience as concrete you have to reverse and see how it is not concrete. It is only your idea of concreteness that seems to be so solid. Only your prejudicial view of a certain situation as inimical makes it so. You should be able to work on it to reverse the whole process.

The wise man inwardly sees the oneness, and that very cognition changes the external world for him. The problem arises when a person has to share the same with another person. Even if I see only the Absolute right here and now and I am delighted, you may look at me and see only a pot belly and a beard. So I also have to carry you with me. I have to somehow help you change your view so that even though you are seeing the pot belly and beard, you know those are only formal things which are impressed upon you by your senses and shaped by your ideas. The differences in the ideas are not in the substance of consciousness out of which the ideas are formulated. Give primacy to the substance of consciousness. It is ever there. Treat the modulations of it as a passing show. That will make it more comfortable.

The purport of this verse is not to take you away from the pragmatic utility or the transactional richness of life. It merely adds another dimension to them, the dimension of the Absolute. And in so doing they become infinitely more valuable.

An important word used here is *paṇḍitan*. We are familiar with punditry, a kind of bookish knowledge, but this is not the same as *paṇḍitan.* The Bhagavad Gita speaks of it, advising when you see a wise man, a Brahmin, a knower of the Self or a knower of the Absolute, who is worthy of being adored, who makes himself more worthy by being very humble, that means too much emphasis is being put on his values. Whatever his great qualities, such a person is to be equated with a cow. In Sanskrit literature the cow is always used as an example of a being with no intelligence. Whenever a person is foolish, it is said he is a cow. But in the Gita the Brahmin and the cow, as well as an elephant, a dog, and even an eater of dogs, are all to be equated. All of them are seen as one by the person with unity and sameness of vision. It is important to realise that the priest is not being reduced to the level of a dog-eater, however, but rather that you are seeing their underlying unity, that they have the same status as manifestations of the Absolute.

What is recommended to us here is this unifying vision. You cannot have a unifying vision in spiritual absorption, because you don't have to. In deep sleep you are not asked to do it because you cannot. In the dream also you are essentially helpless. But in this wakeful state alone, it is possible to become critical, thoroughgoing, penetrative, meditative, reflective and perceptive of this possibility of seeing the Absolute in the relative.

Verse 64

prativiṣayam pratibandhamēṟi mēvu-
nnitine nija smṛtiyē nirākarikkū
ati viśadasmṛtiyāl atītavidyā-
nidhi teḷiyunnatinilla nītihāni

Dismiss your memories of each object of interest,
which cause a state of obstruction;
the vast expansive memory, which can reveal
the priceless ultimate knowledge, is not unjustified.

Aldous Huxley calls our five senses the doors of perception. Life urges are always reaching out to the objects of desires through these doors. Once our attention is caught by any such object, it triggers many associated ideas in our minds. These associated ideas come in the form of memories.

We do not see anything without it being coloured by the memories that prevail at that particular time. The so-called ideal existence of a thing can never be isolated from the coloured glasses of our own memories through which we notice or observe the existence of everything. Because of this, pure existence is transformed into a phenomenological existence.

Heisenberg says that you cannot observe a thing without tampering with its structure. For instance, if you want to look at something under a microscope you have to have a bright light under the slide that holds the subject. We presume that the thing under observation will be the same even when it is exposed to the light, but the mere fact that light is a form of energy means that when it is turned onto something there is a collision of this energy with the otherwise functionally existing matter that is being observed. So only after disturbing its structure in some way are we able to look at it. Certainly it is no longer the same thing.

Similarly, our memory always brings its own colouration, and it is with this memory that we see a thing. Of course we are affecting everything we come in contact with. Narayana Guru says of this: "Your memory is an obstruction to having pure knowledge."

In modern physiological psychology they speak of two kinds of consolidation of memory, electrical and chemical. The electrical consolidation of memory refers to when you observe a thing and its image passes through your whole nervous system as an electrical reverberation or impulse. The stimulus goes through the external aspect of the eyes, for example, into the optic nerve and on into the brain, where a synaptic pattern is created for everything that is seen. Each particular reverberation has a unique pattern, and as you are experiencing it that pattern is established in your synapses.

In the brain each impulse is joined with associations in the form of memories, so that you can connect it with its name and related qualities. Whatever you have previously experienced or even heard of are contained in your concept, which comes from inside to be grafted onto the percept. Then alone does it become meaningful.

Within the brain are billions of synapses connecting the neurons. In each is a resistance which impedes the flow of energy through the system. It is only with a certain force that the resistance is overcome and the connection is made. Experiences come with the force necessary to open up thousands or millions of synaptic resistances, making a pattern. Each experience, with all its sensory qualities such as what is seen, heard, felt, and so on, creates a unique pattern of synaptic reaction. Once a pathway is forged in this way, if the triggering factor reoccurs it takes progressively less and less for the whole thing to be repeated. After a while there comes a stable chemical basis for such an occurrence to be registered easily, which is referred to as the chemical consolidation of memory.

According to the researchers, when there is only an electrical consolidation the whole effect of it can be altered in about two minutes, but once a chemical consolidation takes place it remains there for a long time, sometimes a whole lifetime. At least, this is the current theory.

The ancient theory of Indian psychology is that all happenings become samskaras. Samskara means processing or culturing. As in Western psychology, there is a processing or culturing of experience into memory. Each of the cells of our body has within it its own cultured state. In this way we are an aggregate of many processed individual units. Our actions are actually a collective behaviour.

If a society of people who dwell in a particular neighbourhood changes, the character of the place also changes. Similarly, the samskara or the processing that was going on for some time can be altered or changed when you are exposed to a new situation. Some of the previous conditionings can be erased and new ones made in just the way the Russian physiologist Pavlov spoke of negative conditioning or deconditioning.

Pavlov made a great contribution to psychology with his experiment of dogs salivating at the sound of the dinner bell. In their mind the dogs learned to associate various stimuli with food. This is actually a very good description of samskara. When anything happens in your life by way of an experience, it leaves an impression. The impression registers its impact on the mind and you can recall it afterwards. The very fact that you can recall it shows that it is already recorded there.

Whatever impressions come in the present life are known as samskaras. Indian psychologists also believe that samskaras can be further processed and consolidated to change them from a subtle to a causal state. A gross experience is first processed to become a subtle thing called memory, but this can be further processed to become part of our causal or seed consciousness.

It is believed that when life passes from one embodied being to another it leaves behind the gross body. It cannot take away even the subtle body, because it is linked inextricably with the corporeal body. All that it can take along with it is the causal body, which is known as *liṅgaśarīra,* the indicative body or individuation. The refined essence of memory that the life form carries over to its new body is called vasana. These incipient memories are the ones with which a newly born child begins to live.

We have within us these two kinds of memories. One is all the colourations and conditionings that have come in the present life, and the other is those conditionings we have brought over from our previous lives. Both of them are lying latent in us like a sprout within a seed. As soon as a proper environment is available, these memories wake up to create a new life situation appropriate to the new environment.

As Edmund Husserl put it, we live in the retention of retention of retention of retention. The memory of this moment is retained to live in the next moment, and then the next moment passes on to the next moment carrying the retention of the previous moment, and so on. He is right. But this is the same as saying that we live with our vasanas. This retentive aspect can be traced back through your whole family tree and genetically even back to what Carl Sagan calls the Dragons of Eden, or even beyond that to the kind of stuff out of which the first cells were made. Millennia of memories are in it. Schrödinger also says that if you take a simple living cell from your body, it has millions of footprints of memory in it. The footprints of the memories of the past, millions of them, are within every cell.

Regardless of the system you believe in, and in any case without your conscious knowledge, some mechanism is processing the whole of your experiences for your own benefit. Most of the irrelevant or nonessential elements are shorn off, and the essentials are put together so that when you recall it you can quickly remember the general anatomy of the event along with its vivid colourations such as grief, wonder, fear, and so on. These highlights are what are retained in an accessible form, so your recalled memory is not exactly the same as what you have lived. It is more like a caricature of it.

As you go from one memory to the next, there are no strong links such as between cause and effect. Even the slightest resemblance is enough for you to make the leap from one whole group of memories to another. How can it ever be stopped? It just goes on and on. Sometimes it leads to pleasant grounds, sometimes to evil ones.

Memory recall affects your nervous system. When I was writing *The Fable of a Yati,* my autobiography, and reaching deep into my memories, it was very painful. When I told Nataraja Guru that I was writing my autobiography, he said, "You are very young. You can wait until you grow old." Then on further thought he went on: "Oh, perhaps it's better not to write one's autobiography in old age, because it is debilitating. You are pulling all your nerves. If you pull nerves which have their roots in the past it may cause debility. It may bring some disease."

Here, in the first part of this verse, Narayana Guru is advising us to deny the memories which are associated with objects of interest because they colour our vision so that we do not see truth as pure existence.

There is a Sanskrit word for this, *smaraṇa,* one who reminds you. It is the same as Kāmadeva or Eros. Eros is now sitting outside, sitting in your nervous system, pulling at it and reminding you: "Look, are you not interested in this? Look, is it not like that?" It goes on reminding you. The enemy of Eros is *smaraharaṇa,* the destroyer of memory. It is also called Siva. What Siva brings is absolute peace, serenity and contemplation.

To enter into the state of Siva, you have to open your third eye and burn away Eros. Eros need not necessarily be associated with one's sexual urge. It is any urge, any remembrance. If you can nip the bud of a memory by not linking it to something else when it comes, you will slowly bring about the cessation of your mind.

Ouspensky wrote of a discipline of mindlessness given by Gurdjieff. He suggested living for some time without feeding the mind with memories. Like a bubble a thought will rise up in you, but you dismiss it. You don't follow it up. It brings a little disquiet. Then another thought is sent, like a feeler. You dismiss that. A few memories are waiting there to pounce upon you, but you don't encourage them and they fade out. Then, again, another thought comes. When you first stop feeding them, all the thoughts come crowding up like a challenge. If you don't pay any attention, the thoughts become fewer. Their pacing becomes more slow and feeble. Finally you no longer know what you are thinking or not thinking. There comes a magical pause in time when you are not thinking at all.

It is not an easy thing to reject all these memories. But the Guru asks us to at least break away from our personal memories, which bring regrets, remorses and anxieties; and, if we turn towards the future, to break away from the echo of our memory that comes in the form of fantasies.

Looking to the past brings memories of regret and remorse. Even the good things that have happened, the happy moments we have had — the very fact they are gone brings remorse. So should we give up all memories? In the Isavasya Upanishad it says *krato smara kṛtam smara,* meaning something like "you remember all my previous actions. I am not now in a mood to engage in action. I am too old for it. You remember whatever I have done by way of praise." This is calling attention to another kind of remembrance where it is not the individual who is asked to remember, but in its place a supplication is being made to God.

If you remember God and through him you are remembering who you are, you are going back to a real identity. The superficial remembrance that you are so-and-so is a memory which limits you, but if you remember you are the Absolute it will sublate all those binding, relativistic remembrances. Yet who among us can remember that original memory and truly say, "I am *saccidānanda.*"

Narayana Guru says here that by that remembrance which is vast and expansive, where you are related with the whole eternal universe, where the past, present and future are all taken as one whole, and your relevance to it is made clear to you, that kind of remembrance is a redeeming one. Live in your redeeming remembrance. In Vedanta this is considered to be very central.

There is a story that a certain lion cub somehow got mixed in with some sheep. Because it was in with the herd it believed that it was also a sheep, and it behaved like one. One day another lion came along and pounced upon the little lion. All the other sheep ran away. The little lion was very much afraid that the lion was going to kill it, because it was a sheep. Then the big lion asked, "Why are you bleating? You are a lion, not a sheep. Don't bleat. Roar!" He brought the little one to a well and had him look inside. When he saw his reflection he said, "Well, I'm not a sheep after all!" Then he roared.

Like that we are caught in the shadows and come to believe that we are a shadow. Then a Guru comes along and says, "Come away. You are not a shadow. You are *saccidānanda.* Look into this well." When you look, you roar. Your roar says "I am the Absolute. I am that I am." When you know "I am that I am," you are saved.

So we should either have the supreme remembrance, like this, or have no remembrance at all. Just forget.

When you meditate on this verse, if you use only one limb of it, that is, not following up the memories caused by the present environment, it becomes lopsided. This approach needs to be complemented by remembering your greater identity. If all you do is reject your personal memories, you become alienated from everything. But when you accept the higher memory, all the barriers of individuality leave and you become expansive.

What is being spoken of here should not be made into a destructive kind of meditation. As long as it is made expansive, there are no barriers between you and the other. This fosters a greater love and greater freedom. This is of critical importance.

For instance, a friend here is going to India with me soon. How does this apply to him? If he thinks of himself merely as an Oregonian doing business, then India will be a very foreign country for him, with an exotic culture and incomprehensible ways of life. On the other hand, if he can think of himself as an ordinary human being belonging to the whole world, he will be very much at home. All the checkpoints, borders, passports and immigration offices will look highly superficial, superfluous and phony. The unfamiliar culture will be intuitively familiar to him. Beneath the surface is the whole of humanity. Wherever he goes he will be meeting a brother or a sister with a mind remarkably like his own, and all the baggage he will need is his own smile, his own dreams. . . .

The realisation of the higher Self does not mean you should abstract everything and make it only a theoretical possibility. It is to be lived here and now in its most expansive sense. People who come to these classes here in America do not know my parentage; they know nothing of my school days. They know little or nothing of the particular culture in which I was raised. None of these things are necessary for us to relate in a free way with an open mind. They think, "This is a person who speaks of certain experiences of living truth." That's enough.

We have made our basis of friendship more broad than the relationship with any sister or brother within the family circle. Always, the narrow shell of relationship is to be discarded in favour of a wider one.

Verse 65

orukuṟi nāmaṟiyāttatonnumiṅṅi-
lluru maṟavāl aṟivīlunarnnitellām
aṟivavar illatiraṟṟatākayālī-
yarumayeyāraṟiyunnahō! vicitram

Nothing exists here that we have not known once;
veiled by form, all this is not wakefully known;
being boundless, there is no one who knows;
who is there to know this dear wonder? Alas! It is
strange!

In one of Plato's Dialogues, Socrates makes the same point as Narayana Guru puts forth here. He says:

> . . . the Soul, since it is immortal and has been born many times, and has seen all things both here and in the other world, has learned everything that is. So we need not be surprised if it can recall the knowledge of virtue or anything else which, as we see, it once possessed. All nature is akin, and the soul has learned everything, so that when a man has recalled a single piece of knowledge — learned it in ordinary language — there is no reason why he should not find the rest, if he keeps a stout heart and does not grow weary of the search, and learning are in fact nothing but recollection. —Meno, 81d

Socrates is very helpful in bringing out two points: that there is nothing in the world which we do not know, and that we believe that we know only very little. He says it just about as well as it can be said.

Many things are so perplexing that we don't see even the remotest possibility of some day understanding them. For instance, you might pick up Bertrand Russell's *Principia Mathematica,* but from just looking at the cover you will put the book down again. The cover design is such that it baffles your mind. When you open it and see the bizarre symbols with which it is filled, you imagine you could never understand even one page of it. But after all it was written by a man just like us. If it were totally impossible, he would not have attempted it. So if we were to take the time to decode all the symbols and study the arguments, eventually it would begin to make sense to us.

Narayana Guru says here that everything has been known to us at least once. His approach to the problem is different from Socrates', but the basic principle is the same. Socrates believes that if you did not already know something, you could never give your opinion. It was not immediately known to you only because you didn't recollect it. The Guru's idea is that what you experience is an effect produced by a complex situation. In the stream of consciousness new configurations of percepts and concepts are continuously arising. When we are presented with a new structure that looks different from anything previously encountered, we are momentarily puzzled. There is some familiarity, and yet we come to an impasse. We have the feeling we don't understand the situation, we don't know what is being presented.

Just what is it that is being presented to us, in the first place? Either sense data or concepts. Sense data means we are seeing something, such as a figure. Say I am seeing a shape before me. I see some colour in it. I know the figure must have content, that it is three-dimensional. So much is immediately presented to me. Still I do not recognise what the figure is. Then I put on my reading glasses and realise it is a human being sitting there. But even after finding out it is a person, I still don't recognise who it is. I put on my other glasses. Now the shape becomes more distinct, and I can see it is so-and-so.

In any configuration there are certain priorities. There is something more distinctive about shape than colour, for instance, and something more distinctive about the content than either shape or colour. We perceive colour, form and content, but we can give priority to any element. If we emphasise them wrongly, the elements no longer reveal things, but actually conceal them. They act to obstruct our recognition.

What we see here as forms is the formal recognition of those things with which we have associated in the present life. Those with which we have not associated in this life look strange, so we think of them as unknown. Even the known element in them comes to seem unknown. This brings a creeping sense of strangeness to our mind, which is one of the tragedies of the visual world.

The content we perceive in all given situations is consciousness, nothing else. The configurations are within your consciousness, aren't they? And the consciousness is all yours, isn't it? Yet suddenly you have forgotten whether or not the consciousness is yours because of the strange-looking configurations within it. You have drifted from a totally known situation to a seemingly unknown one.

If you sit with your eyes closed and look into yourself, look for what is unfamiliar. There is this consciousness, this awareness. It is not awareness of anything as such. It is just awareness. Within that awareness we observe certain movements. Things are moving, changing. There is also the passage of time, but that is also consciousness. The simplest consciousness has a tendency to weave fragmentary notions out of itself. These modulations arise like ripples on the surface of water.

Now go back from the wave to water, from the form to the sight, from the sight to the act of seeing, and from the act of seeing to the seer. If you go back in this way from the modulation to the consciousness from which it arises, you are going from the effect to the cause. Every bit of it is consciousness. From a pluralistic perspective it may seem that everything is not known to you, but if you look at it from the causal side — you being the whole consciousness — it is clear that everything is known.

Socrates goes farther in emphasising that everything is in fact known even in a pluralistic way. Another philosopher who presents this idea is Bergson. He asks what do you do when you listen to a person who is expounding a complex idea to you, like the most difficult of problems in mathematics or philosophy? How do you understand what you hear or see demonstrated? When somebody makes a certain statement and you say "I don't understand," what do you mean by that? What you mean is, when they speak a sentence you have to structure concepts in your mind that are equivalent to the words they have said. Then you put together all the concepts to make an ensemble or a meaningful gestalt. If at this point meaning does not arise in you, however, you say you are lost.

You are not really taking anything from the other person in your discussion, but it's good they have spoken because it gives you an occasion to make a meaningful structure using the order in which they put their word images. So many concepts are lying scattered around in you, and their words are only an occasion for you to pick these up, or rather recall concepts already known to you. Once you get your images organised you can say "I understand."

If you still insist you do not understand, then the person who is explaining goes from one part of his statement to another, recasting his explanation by bringing new word images together. At last you say, "Oh, I get it! In your way of configuring I didn't realise that the first word had associations with this and this other word, and this concept was associated with this other concept which I already understood. Why didn't you just say so at first? Part of it was concealed, that's why it didn't immediately make sense. Recast it and it becomes quite clear."

So even in understanding the individuated forms of things you are using your own hidden concepts. Nothing new is ever used, but there are ever so many possibilities of reorganising ideas so that they look new. You can always create complex situations and you can also understand all complex situations.

From the causal side of everything being consciousness and you also being that consciousness, nothing can ever be foreign to you. From the side of the logician as well, you can prove that all manifestations are nothing more than variations in the structuring of concepts. If they are put in a way that is familiar to you, you can go on annexing all the unknown areas until they are all known. And there is a third way of putting this idea, as presented by biologists. Although Schrödinger is not a biologist, but a physicist taking science as a whole, he very clearly demonstrates how everything is in everything else. The whole matter of this universe is the same.

When you structure it, it changes its character. Quantitative variation causes qualitative change.

Until recently it was believed that there was a conservation of energy, and all transformations happened within it. Even this notion has recently been exploded, and now it is believed that things can come out of total nothingness. Thus, even the difference between existence and nonexistence has been effaced in modern physics.

So, we can approach this problem from the point of view of the contemplative, that of the logician or psychologist, or that of the physicists, biologists or chemists. Whatever way we choose, it brings us to a sense of oneness with the whole world.

There is, though, one difficulty we should appreciate. When I sit with my eyes closed, how big is my world? Does it have only the spatial dimension of my skull? Or do I sense an unhindered, unobstructed world? Certainly I feel no barrier tc my mind because of having a skull around my brain. My world is as big as anybody's. In fact it is infinitely large. But when I open my eyes, my world suddenly becomes limited. Isn't it strange? Now, as I'm only in the living room, I'm limited to whatever I see here. My seeing something actually conceals everything else. The kitchen is concealed, the bathroom is concealed, my study is concealed, all by what I see.

The Guru puts this as *uru maṟavāl,* because of the body obstructing the sight of other bodies, you do not see everything wakefully. Wakefully here means if I am awake and read something and it makes sense, there is a great certitude, a great clarity. Such certitude doesn't come to me about my oneness with everything because some form is standing before me, occupying my attention. In this way I am redirected from the universal to the particular.

The Guru says that because of this you do not know what you are missing. "As this dear wonder is boundless, who is there to know it? Alas! It is strange." What you miss is the very dear Self. You are like a person who is sleeping with a great treasure under his pillow. If only you knew! But instead you feel so haggard and hungry and weary and poverty-stricken.

This verse should make you bold, happy and very enterprising. Bold in the sense that nothing can be hidden from you. You already know everything. But this knowledge is to be made certain in the language in which your mind understands it. There is a difference between having a knowledge and recognising it. The only difference between a seer — a realised person — and an unrealised person is that though they both have the wisdom, one recognises it with certitude and the other is still fumbling. It's not that he doesn't have it. In fact, he *is* it. When he looks into the mirror he sees his beard, or she sees her funny face. They think "How can I be That? How can I be the Supreme, the Absolute? Am I not that little mouse?" You are not the little mouse, that's only your form. Knowing there is nothing other than you, whatever your form, emboldens you, makes you fearless.

You also become enterprising, once you understand there is the possibility to go from the lack of recognition to the recognition of your inner vastness. You can not only be, you can recognise yourself to be. What we are given here is not just a generalisation, but how in the very world of the effect, the particular, the individuation of things, you can relate yourself to that Absolute, bringing the totality to bear upon what is presented here and now.

And, of course, happiness is a natural outgrowth of this increased understanding and identification with absolute values.

With this verse we close the Fall term. In January we will commence the next section. We have thirty-five verses to go.

This was certainly a wonderful experience for all of us to gather in the mornings and sit together and commune. Not all the days were alike, and everything you heard might not have been so inspiring, but here and there something must have gone deep into you. That little bit which strikes home, that makes a flicker of recognition and continues to shimmer in us, is enough to give us some direction in life. There is no need to learn each verse and then rationally apply it in everyday life. You can even hear it and forget it. Forgetting means it only goes deeper into you. Once you have heard it, it will go and work its way by itself.

The effect will be very subtle. It comes almost without you knowing that it is something which you heard that is enabling you to see things in a new light or make resolutions in a certain more helpful way. Nothing is ever lost. Even this very peace that comes to our mind during these verses is so penetrating that we feel the depth of the soul, the Self. It is indescribable. The indistinct part of it is as beautiful as the distinct. In a Chinese painting most of it is indistinct, but this does not make it in any way less valuable than a realistic photograph.

Verse 66

ira mutalāyavayennumiprakāram
varuminiyum; varavaṟṟu nilpatēkam
aṟivatu nāmatutanne maṟṟumellā-
varumatutan vaṭivārnnu ninniṭunnu

Food and all such always come again as a matter of
course;
that which remains free of becoming is one;
we are that knowledge itself; all others
also remain as its forms.

In the Chandogya Upanishad the sun is called *sūran,* meaning that which is going on. The vital breath, prāṇa, is also called *svaran*. They are both identified with aum. Aum is just like saying "It's okay." In the Sanskrit culture it is customary to say aum if you agree with something. It is a word of consent.

Aum is equated to *sūran* in the sense of what is articulated. The quintessence of all articulation is contained in it. So when you say aum, it is at once a consent, an articulation, and a going out of the breath. The breath that goes out does not come back. The word you speak does not return to you. It goes out, vibrating on and on. In all these senses it is *svaran*.

What is the consent that the sun is giving? It is both a direction and a consent. It is arousing everyone, saying "Wake up! Start living!" From one side of the globe to the other the sun is waking everybody up, asking them to do their thing. When I first stayed in Portland, some one gave me a radio. Around six a.m. the announcer used to say "Hi, you guys! Get up, lazy bums! It's six o'clock." That's exactly what the sun is doing to us. It comes every day and says "Get up you lazy bums! It's morning. Time for you to do your thing."

When we humans wake up we need a hot cup of tea or coffee. When the sun comes to the little ant and says, "Little ant, get up and go," it has to find something to eat, so it goes and looks for a spilled breadcrumb or a dead cricket. Fledgling birds wake up in their nests, look at their parents and cry. The parents' hearts are moved, and they fly out in search of food. The ant that leaves its hole and the bird that leaves its nest do not know where any food is. They are searching for it.

At the break of dawn the fisherman takes his net and goes down to the sea. He may pray to God for a good catch. He doesn't know exactly where the fish are hiding, but he has faith they will come to him.

Those of you who live in a more sophisticated society and have permanent incomes always feel sure that you can get into your car and drive to the store for food. You think everything is safely arranged, but this sense of security you have is to a great extent illusory. If you ponder over the many possibilities that are becoming actualised to bring you your food, you will see a number of imponderables. Even when you make a cup of tea, there are so many hands involved. The leaves are picked in Asia, dried in a factory, trucked to the coast and loaded on a ship. The sugar is harvested in Hawaii or Havana. There are so many ships plying the oceans, trains running with midnight cargo, people toiling hard in far-off places, and trade unions making bargains with management. So many things have to happen in order for these items to be on the shelf of your grocery store down the street.

We have to keep in mind the imperativeness of the need for food. There is no concession made here. Whether it is the little ant, the bird, the fisherman or the executive of a big industry, the imperative is the same for all. Each needs its own daily nourishment. We also have to take into account the chance factor governing the fulfilment of that need. The necessity which initiates action is almost mechanically rigid, and we cannot bargain with it. The world where fulfilment is to be found is very unpredictable. No one can say exactly where the ant will find the crumb of bread, where the bird will find the worm or where the fisherman will catch his fish. Yet while these are all unpredictable, the net result is that every day nearly everyone is eating three, four or even more times a day.

There are three elements here for us to take into consideration. One is the area of absolute necessity, where there is no concession. The second is the field of the operation of chance, and the third is the fulfilment that needs to be attained. A chance has to come in a way that is favourable for a link with another chance and then another and another, until fulfilment is reached. The net result of the fulfilment is satisfaction, but in between is panic and anguish — the pain and frustration of the search. Here Narayana Guru uses the term *ira,* which conveys the idea that one has the dire necessity to eat and then finds the counterpart: whatever is to be eaten.

The finding of food has a relatively great promise of fulfilment. If you badly want a piece of bread, you can just go into the kitchen and get one. But as you progress from this simple, basic need to more acquired, psychological needs — such as wanting to hear a symphony orchestra on a tropical beach at midnight under a full moon — your chances become progressively less and less. So there is a hierarchy, a gradation in the fulfilment of needs. The more sublime the need, the more scarce the opportunity for its satisfaction. Between demand and supply, or rather scarcity and fulfilment, there is an inverse ratio operating. Hardcore necessity comes face to face with the laws of probability. The former is certain, the latter more or less uncertain. Out of the dialogue between the certain and the uncertain there emerges a result which is satisfactory. This is called the world.

Phenomenologists like to ask, "What is our experience?" Edmund Husserl sums it up in one word, the world. And what is this world? He says it is a conjunction of several meanings. Many meanings are linked together to make a whole fabric of understanding, and each person's consciousness is spread throughout this fabrication of all meanings. This totality of meaning is what we call the world. This world is first to be recognised as what you perceive without assigning any philosophical meaning to the perception.

Husserl then goes on to examine the validity of this idea. His conclusion is that what we see of any given person or thing is only a partial perception. A person is not just a contour or a form; there are many other elements involved that are not perceptible. Thus the world we perceive is only a fraction of reality. His idea is that we first know a thing through immediate perception, then through an intuitional perception and finally through a sense of empathy. All three elements are important to the process of knowing.

A person will often behave in different ways and play different roles in different situations, but we can always identify them in spite of the superficial variegations. We do this by thinking of an essential person at the core of the complex of activities. That a person looks or behaves in a certain way at a certain time is only incidental. For continuity we rely on the essence, and for continuous comprehension of the world we are busy deriving the essence of every formal presentation and integrating it into the whole. If we were unable to do this we would become confused and disoriented.

When I'm teaching a class, how do I arrive at the idea that a mixed group of individuals — of different sexes, ages, moods, etc. — are a class? First I have to reduce all of them to the essential search they are making, and this provides me with a way to classify and systematise them. There are various categories of systems, and many criteria for making them, but each of them has their own characteristic essential nature by which we can link the systems together and correlate the categories with each other.

As Husserl went on examining like this he developed the two reference points of phenomenal existence and transcendent beingness. Heidegger tried to make it more explicit, with the result that phenomenal existence became one thing and transcendent being became another. Jean-Paul Sartre took this as his study in *Being and Nothingness*, and after a careful scrutiny he came to the conclusion that these two things are like closed boxes. There is no way of entering into them from the outside. You and I *are* the phenomenal existence we create and in which we participate, and we cannot get out of it. And since it is all produced by our consciousness there is no way of entry into it from outside.

If you introduce transcendence into phenomenality as Jaspers does, by sort of corkscrewing it in, you have immanent transcendence. Sartre disagreed with Jaspers, saying that when you say 'immanence' you are already agreeing to at least a very thin veil of separation between the transcendent and the thing in which it is immanent. There is an unbridgeable duality in all this. Thus these philosophers came up against a problem they did not know how to solve.

Here Narayana Guru overcomes that difficulty. The paradox or dichotomy involved only comes up when we conceive of transcendence as separate from phenomenal existence, but he doesn't see it that way. In the third verse he showed us that we have to conceive of the whole thing as a treasury of oceanic depth from which waves of phenomenality arise. The waves are not different from the ocean. In this verse he says the world of necessity that makes you pass through all these phenomenal bumps — the imperative need, the search and the fulfilment — is an eternal game that goes on and on. It has always been like that, and it will always be like that. But there is also a changeless reality which does not come and go, and it is the same as the knowledge in which the whole game takes place. They are not in any way separate things. It is within your knowledge you feel a need, within it you make your calculations as you go in search. The knowledge itself makes you gamble, take risks and have faith that what you seek will be provided and that somehow you will find it. The whole process, including its fulfilment, is all happening within knowledge.

The Guru says that that which is constant in all moods and changes is knowledge, *aṛivu.* The variables are the need, the search and the fulfilment; the constant is knowledge. He has already described knowledge as the Self: that knowledge which resides in the dark and knows by its own light is the Self, and not anything other than that. This is the constant, *aṛivu.*

He goes on to say we are That. He maintains we don't have to draw a line between ourselves and someone else, carefully delineating each one's territory. Everything we experience along with everything we can think of is a formation of That.

A key word here is *vaṭiva.* When the water rises up into a certain formation, we call it a wave. That it is only made of water in no way detracts from its wave-ness. As my friend put it the other day, a tidal wave can kill a hundred thousand people so you cannot say it is only a form. That's true, it is a form with a dynamic. By calling it only a form you take away from its actuality and its meaning within the transactional world, doing in the process a great injustice to the ontological understanding of things.

To underscore this point, Sartre called our attention to what he termed ontocontology. He thought simply saying "the ontological truth" was not enough, so he coined the term, saying we should not miss the ontocontology of things happening. He is right. If we don't insist on the ontocontology, we could claim that after all the wave is only an idea.

Sartre gave us a simple choice: either go with the idealists or with the existentialists and don't confuse their distinctions. To Narayana Guru this is an artificial separation: we have to recognise the wave, the water and also their oneness. To prepare us for this idea, in the previous verse the Guru said there is nothing we have not known at least once before. Thereby, the knowledge that has gone into us, our own stuff, is first made generic. Schrödinger comes to the same truth in *What is Life?* when he makes reference to the millions of footprints of memory each cell has.

How does this verse help us? We are subjected to various kinds of necessities in life. When we focus our attention on the world of necessity, there is a time factor which comes in between the beginning of our search and the moment of its fulfilment. The interim period is filled with a lot of effort and anticipation. Anticipation is not lived in a vacuum, it is filled with anxiety since we are not sure of the results. We are uncertain of the possibility, because probability and improbability are always vying with each other.

All our living moments are crowded with the intentionality of our consciousness. If we are always attached to intentionality, the peace, serenity and joy we look for are constantly being pushed away. In a sense, then, meaning is being transferred from the present to the future. We often speak of living here and now, but we don't realise the almost impossible pressure on us to not live in the present. We are always being made to wait, to look for, to expect, to anticipate. Half the time of our life is wasted in looking for and waiting for something to happen. If we can only establish a firm stand on the constant ground the Guru speaks of — the *aṛivu* or knowledge — our attachment and intentionality regarding the phenomenal world becomes a secondary interest. Our primary interest then becomes witnessing the game of life in the present moment.

To enjoy the game of life we don't just have to act out plans. I can ask my friend to give a performance and I'll just sit and watch. I am myself, but I am also watching what he is doing. This doesn't mean I'm not enjoying every shade of emotion he is creating through his words, gestures and expressions. I fully relish and enjoy every bit of it. I can even become tearful. But I'm not the performer, I'm the witness. And while I'm enjoying whatever he's performing, I'm also living the performance with him.

This is a very subtle thing. If you understand it, it makes a real difference in your life. You do and you do not do. You perform everything you are doing now and yet, at the same time, you do not do anything. The Gita expresses it as seeing action in inaction and inaction in action, but this can become a cliché. The whole meditation of this verse centers around not making it a cliché, but living it. Then you see the *vaṭiva*, the form aspect, the wave, and fully appreciate it while at the same time remaining as water.

When they were together in Colombo, Narayana Guru suddenly picked up an ochre-coloured robe and gave it to Nataraja Guru. Nataraja Guru had one moment of hesitation before taking it, because it meant a great deal. He was young. He had not decided whether he should live the life of a householder or that of a renunciate, or whether he should get his doctorate and take a good job or not. He had not decided anything. So he had one moment of hesitation. Then Narayana Guru said: "The colour is only on the surface of the cotton fabric. The cotton itself has not changed."

Do you get it? This meant everything for Nataraja Guru. Narayana Guru had called his attention to a very subtle difference. The colour was what appeared important, but the material was actually made of cotton. All the implications of the colour are only in the phenomenality of life. At no time does your real Self change, now or hereafter, whatever kind of life you live. You can be a sinner or you can be a saint; wearing holy robes will not alter who you are.

The day you go one step further to realise your becoming a great saint or a great sinner is not going to change your Self in any way, a great calmness will grow inside you. At least you will have gotten over the agony of your guilt.

Verse 67

gaṇanayil ninnu kaviññatonnu sādhā-
raṇamiva raṇṭumoẓiññoranya rūpam
ninavilumillatu nidrayinkalum mē-
linanagarattilumeṅṅumilla nūnam

One is beyond what can be counted,
the other is ordinary; other than these two there is
not any other form
existing in waking, or in dream,
or in some city of the gods; this is certain.

This around us is the ordinary world, and what is beyond cannot be subjected to any kind of study or approach. These are the only two — there is nothing else.

Let us consider these two categories. The first is called here the ordinary. The nature of the ordinary is that it is perceivable and conceivable. Anything we perceive we can count, measure, categorise or classify. We can do the same with our conceptions also. This is the world in which we live, and it has a transactional validity.

Transaction becomes valid in terms of norms and criteria. If I give you a measure of wheat and in return you give me three yards of linen, we are deciding that the value of wheat and the value of linen can both be brought to a normative exchange rate. As long as the norm is accepted we can make transactions. Furthermore, to make these transactions very efficient, physicists have evolved various kinds of measurements. Aided by mathematicians, they have formulated many physical norms and natural laws.

You cannot challenge a natural law without facing the consequences. The law of gravity is well known to all, but if a man takes heroin he might imagine he could take a space walk out of the fifteenth floor of a building. It's only in his mind that he can defy the law of gravity though, so his body accelerates downward to the earth's surface, and afterwards he can't remember a thing. The rule is inviolable.

Certain other laws are only socially conceived, and these are not as imperative or categorical as nature's laws. It is said, "Thou shalt not steal," but many people steal. If they do it with care they often get away with it. Many of the civil and criminal statutes are broken every day. Some of the offenders are caught and punished, some are not.

All these kinds of laws come under the category which Narayana Guru calls the ordinary. Everything in the ordinary world is relative. It can change or be changed. If you want happiness in the ordinary world, you should harmonise your life to its norms. If some of the norms are spurious and made by people only for the purpose of exploitation, you should question and correct them. Then the ordinary world will be improved.

You can occasionally see even natural laws defied by people with psychic or yogic powers. I once knew of a yogi in India who could touch a live electric wire without receiving any shock. Scientists tried to do all kinds of things with him to discover if he was using any tricks. He wasn't, but they were unable to explain what was going on. Such abilities are rare and unusual, obviously, and don't particularly alter our understanding of what is ordinary and what is beyond it.

That world which is called *sādhāraṇam,* the practical, the ordinary, has a snag: extraordinary things seem to happen, and unnatural events seem to interfere. If there were only objects and people we knew how to interact with and events we knew how to handle, the world would be fairly safe and unsurprising. But we tend to mistake one thing for another. We see in one object the properties of another. We mistake a person of a certain character and nature for someone different through our own projection, and try to deal with them in a way that is inappropriate to who they really are. When this doesn't bring the result we anticipated, weird situations are created, which are the seemingly extraordinary traits of the ordinary world.

We are familiar to some extent with our mind and its concepts, but from our consciousness there also arise certain urges we cannot control, certain emotions that cannot be bridled, along with depressions, negative feelings and even paranoiac fears. Here again we can lose our ground. We do not mean to belittle these aspects by calling the world they belong to simply ordinary. There is a lot of homework to be done in that world to keep things going harmoniously.

The other aspect mentioned by Narayana Guru in this verse is what might be termed the beyond. It is beyond the ordinary, in the sense that the world springs from it but at the same time does not modify it. It seems to be independent, self-founded and unitive, while remaining beyond adequate comprehension.

The distinction being made here by the Guru has an important historical precedent in the Upanishads. For instance, the Isavasya Upanishad begins by saying "As everything is enveloped by Isa, the Lord, what is there to aspire for? Whose is wealth? Be free and go on moving freely." There is no recognition of the transactional world in that. But afterwards an alternative is given. If you cannot be in that state of total freedom, then accept this as a transactional world. See how you are an embodied self and that you have a role to play. There are programmes in life. You should decide to live here a hundred years attending to them.

The Upanishad goes on to describe the peculiarities of that world, how you may come across things that are bright as well as dark forces that can envelop you and drag you away into worlds of unknowing where you do not understand anything. It describes how you can become addicted to ignorance and live in darkness, or become addicted to theoretical wisdom and live in even greater darkness.

This model is elaborated in other major Upanishads, such as the Brihadaranyaka and Chandogya, which go into all the details of life. No aspect is omitted, from the procreation of a child to its naming ceremony, baptism, growth, education, marriage and life as a householder. Then all that is put on one side. On the other they consider what cannot be considered — the pure.

Whenever you speak of an entity as 'I', 'you' or 'this', or the various states — wakeful, dream and states of meditation — inwardly you know there is something other than what you are experiencing and speaking about. At the same time you know it is not any other. It is so intimately one with you that it cannot be counted as one among many. All the many that you consider come within its ambit. You cannot say it has a beginning because however much you stretch your imagination you cannot conceive of a beginning for something you can't even comprehend. You cannot conceive of its end, either, since then all conceiving would be ended. So it is beginningless and endless. When you go on cataloguing its attributes you are merely deceiving yourself, making small conceptions of the inconceivable which you can hold on to, and trying to satisfy yourself by clinging to them.

What is the main purpose of this verse? In verses 63, 64 and 65, Narayana Guru repeatedly refers to the One as the ground of all: it is the existential ground, the only knowledge, the expansive memory, and the dearest of all values. In spite of the difficulty of visualising, conceptualising and perceiving this One, he wants us to know we belong to it.

Earlier he said that by exposing ourselves to great anguish and by struggling we cannot achieve an identity with the beyond. This secret is known to the truly wise. The wise person does not struggle, but lives in harmony. Is this a great thing? It's a very great thing.

If you read all the literature passed off as spiritual, and learn about the many techniques and gimmicks sold in the marketplace, and if you study the various kinds of exercises and disciplines people are trying to impose on themselves, you can see the importance of this caution. Contrary to popular belief it is not through any physical, mental or psychic struggle that we become endowed with wisdom. The Guru asks us not to look for it within the world of our thoughts or memories. Don't seek a reality other than the two mentioned here, the ordinary and the Absolute. You may read about psychic phenomena which excite you and charm you to run away from these two stable grounds — the transactional and the transcendent — and look for a third reality. It is the search for a third reality that puts you through endless struggles.

Many people seek growth and unfoldment in areas that satisfy them, such as the arts. They tune their life to certain values in a chosen field and work hard to develop their talents. This is how it goes in the first world, the ordinary world of transactions. Here there is a ground that sustains them, sustains their interest, sustains the laws governing their selves, as well as what they seek. In the perfection they are seeking, the evolution they are pursuing, there is an intimate relation between the ordinary and the unnameable.

Suppose someone reads about a man with psychic powers, like Lahiri Mahasaya in *The Autobiography of a Yogi*. He may take it as a model, since he read about it in a book which was written by an honest fellow with no ax to grind. Imagining such phenomena must have some reality, he aspires for it himself.

This is what I call looking for a third reality. If he was Lahiri Mahasaya it would not be a third reality for him. What, perhaps, music was for him, psychic phenomena are for Lahiri Mahasaya. He was seeking his growth in that just as this person is seeking his growth in music. If I were to seek my growth in music, it would be as false as this person wanting to become Lahiri Mahasaya.

Someone brought me the book *Seth Speaks* and told me, "This is it!" Yes, for Seth, but not for me. What Alice Bailey grew into was fine for him, but for me it's a third reality. What we have to become more and more conscious of in our life is the interplay between the one transcendent reality and the transactional world in which we have an assigned role. Only then can we give up the unnecessary searches.

Narayana Guru speaks of three wrong places in which many of us search. One is within our own thought sphere: taxing our brains to find a third reality. Another is living in wait for a vision to come, since we have so often heard of such visions coming to others. The third is striving for attainments. If you consult the Theosophists, for instance, they can give you the whole plan of aspiring to attain an astral body and fly to the seventh sphere. There are plenty of groups in the world with complicated plans for your life, but their ideas will only drag you into fruitless searches.

What, then, is this spiritual power or spiritual insight we are speaking of? If the Guru discourages us from seeking in all these places, where do we get it? It happens as simply as the little child getting breast milk from her mother, or the apple tree producing flowers and fruits in its proper season. It's as natural as that. If you don't think of yourself as only a creature of transaction, and if you keep yourself open to the greater ground in which the transactional occurs, something like an osmosis between your transactional world and the transcendent ground takes place.

Unfortunately, terms like 'transcendent ground' and 'Absolute' are misleading. No word can adequately represent what we are discussing here. You can say 'God'; you can say 'the Divine' or 'the Supreme Mother'. Such endearing terms are good because it makes you think of an adorable Absolute. 'Allah' does not mean anything, but Allah is adorable. The purest of all statements about this is to just say "Allah". Then you can add *bismillah al-rahman al-rahim,* "That which is not, is at the same time beneficent and merciful." This is the kind of attitude you can cultivate — a very deep trust, a great sense of adoration, absolute gratitude for whatever is happening in the transactional world.

Without asking for it we are given the air we breathe, the water we drink, the food we eat, the companions we play and associate with, the activities we engage in. Hundreds of thousands of things can be enumerated as the events of a single day, all issuing from what the Guru called earlier the Para, the Absolute. "For those who suck the milk of the *Para* — the Absolute — ten thousand years is only a moment." Every opportunity of transaction, every experience whether we are sleeping or thinking or enjoying in the wakeful state, can be an occasion to suck the milk of the Absolute.

We make a mistake only when we make That an object. It is not an object. In fact, it is the only subject of all subjects.

And again, what can we do? We can cultivate a great reliance, great trust and absolute dependence. Such absolute dependence is also the greatest freedom. This may look like a contradiction, but if you experience it there is no contradiction. As the Isavasya Upanishad says, move freely.

In Christian theology an analogy is given of a son agreeing to go for a walk with his father. If the son is as delighted as the father in going in the same direction and looking for the same experiences, then the father is not dragging him. He doesn't feel like an obedient slave in subjecting himself to his father's will, because his will and the father's are not two. His interest and the father's interest are not two. The direction he seeks and where the father goes are not two. His companionship is chosen in freedom and lived in freedom.

Only in a world of relative merit and relative choices can you feel a lack of freedom. Here you have a total acceptance of the One because it is not one and many. It is the only one. The recognition of this affects your awareness of your own existence. You place your existence in that One. Then right inside you, you feel that oneness.

The search is here and now. There is a togetherness in the search of the ordinary and the unnameable.

Verse 68

aravavaṭākṛti pōlahanta raṇṭā-
yaṟivilumaṅgiyilum katakkayālē
orukuṟiyāryyayitiṅṅanāry yayāku-
nnorukuṟiyennuṇarēṇamūhaśāli

Like snake-rope form,
the I-consciousness enters both knowledge and the body;
on one occasion the understanding is true, on another untrue;
thus one who can discern should understand.

This is a very crucial verse. It very correctly presents the kind of life most of us lead.

In our life there is an ambivalent pull. At one moment we conform to the requirements of this world, identifying ourselves with our bodies, our bodily needs, and the world of necessity. In this world we also look for pleasure, and get more or less satisfaction. Then a shift comes and we swing to the other side. We start questioning the validity of whatever we were just conforming to. The body seems to be unreal, and our identity with it is now shifted to an identity with the Unknown, the Absolute, the Ground, the Incomprehensible. If we look at what we have been doing with our mind, it appears absolutely meaningless, a sheer waste of time. Then the only meaningful value seems to be to turn to that unknown, secret beginning and try to understand it more. But you don't remain there long; you come back to the world of ordinary events and again join the fray.

If we accept this as the common lot, then all are schizophrenics.

There is not one person who is not split in this fashion. Schizophrenia is natural to all people.

Here Guru uses two special words. On one side he places *aṟivu,* pure knowledge, and on the other *aṅgī,* the possessor of the body in its animated state. In between is *ahanta,* the 'I' consciousness, which assumes two different dimensions. When it turns to the embodied state it assumes a particular status and when it turns to pure knowledge it assumes a different dimension.

To complete the picture we have to think of two more factors. Mind relates the ego consciousness to the identity with the body, and intellect relates it to an identity with the Absolute. So we can say an individual is composed of body, mind, ego consciousness, intellect and, as a total ground, the Unknown. This last is given many names, such as nothingness, beingness, existence or transcendence. Call it whatever you like — all these names suit it very well.

You should have a very clear picture of this scheme in your mind:

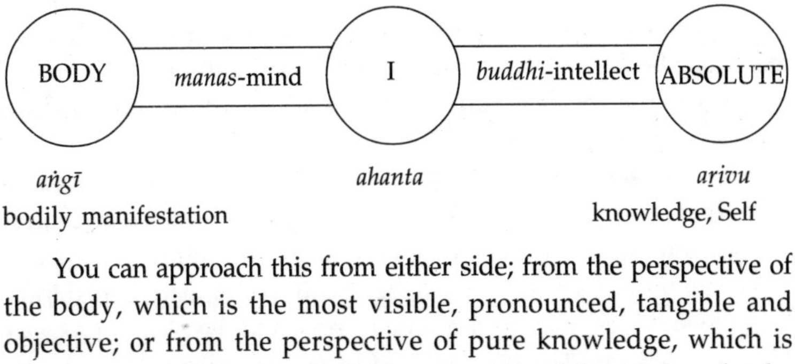

aṅgī *ahanta* *aṟivu*
bodily manifestation knowledge, Self

You can approach this from either side; from the perspective of the body, which is the most visible, pronounced, tangible and objective; or from the perspective of pure knowledge, which is sometimes symbolised as God. The argument of those who take the side of the body is: "Where is the individual without a body?" This is very true. If there were no bodies we couldn't distinguish one person from another. For there to be individual persons they have to have separate bodies.

It is irrefutable that we have bodily existence, but they are not just inert bodies, they are animated. The essential question is, is the mind coming from somewhere and animating the body or is the body so structured that it produces this thing called mind within itself? Physiological psychology tries to prove that the organisation of matter has built up everything necessary for the body to generate consciousness out of itself. From this viewpoint the body is primary and the mind is secondary. It's not that the body is animated by the mind, but the body's animation is called mind.

You can look into the whole setup, how physical and chemical operations create a system like this. What is called mind is nothing but a blanket phrase for various kinds of sensations. If you take away your eyes you don't have any sight. If you take away your ears you don't have any hearing. When you experience heat and cold, pain and pleasure, or when you experience a nonstop flow of all kinds of thoughts, muddled memories and questions in a mad procession, you call it mind. Fine. You are now on the side of *aṅgī*. *Aṅga* means limb; *aṅgī* means that which has limbs, the limb owner.

The limb owner with a mind has no motivation, no goal. But your life is purposive. You have goals and goal orientations. Your actions are all motivated. By whom? For motivation there has to be a central agency, called 'I'. Again, is this 'I' not the central focus of the mind? When the body perishes, what happens to the 'I'? Even before it completely dies, say if a person has a stroke and goes into a coma, there may be no 'I' functioning. But the body continues to live even without the 'I'. So it is not absolutely necessary to have an ego consciousness to be alive, but for purposive activity it is.

We are still looking at it from the side of the body. The more organised aspect of the body is the mind. The still more organised and central core is called the ego. That ego has motivations. Fine. What are they? Eyes are very delighted in seeing beautiful things. Ears are very delighted to hear good music and the pleasing sounds of loving friends. The nose is fond of goods aromas. We like the touch of tenderness and affection. Pleasure motivates, and the mind wants to be pleased in so many ways. But mind by itself is incapable of scheming or planning anything. A strong instrument of some kind is necessary. The body by itself has no light. The mind and the ego have no light of their own either.

From somewhere light comes, awareness comes. When awareness comes, the mind, ego and body can work. When it doesn't come, they don't work. At this point the scientists who uphold the theory of bodily organisation are at a loss to discover who organises, how the organisation is effected, or where the ingenious device of putting things together in a meaningful way comes from. That's the mysterious factor. Mystery or the Unknown is what we already put on the other side as *aṛivu.* Something close to that source of truth, light, intelligence and understanding has to come. We call it the intellect.

In a sense the ego hires the intellect. There are some illiterate millionnaires, but they hire people who have doctorates in economics and other helpful fields to handle their problems for them. Likewise, however foolish the ego is, it can hire the intellect. The intellect comes along and asks "What do you want?"

"I want a hamburger."

"That's all you want?!"

"I hired you only to get me what I want. Don't try to teach me!"

"Ok, if all you want is a hamburger there's a Super Beefo-Burger down the street. Just walk down there and hand them some money."

No matter what the ego wants, the intellect is willing to help. When it is employed in simple problems with mundane work, after a few days it becomes nostalgic for the realm to which it really belongs: pure knowledge and higher wisdom. It turns that way, and as it turns it drags the ego along with it to this new world. From the hamburger world the ego turns to the world of the Supreme. Then it says, "This is so different from all that I knew previously." A kind of shame comes upon it. "My God, how could I ask this intellect, which is always with this wonderful light, this blissful knowledge, to do such mean things for me? Oh intellect, will you please tell me a little more about this world?"

The intellect assumes the role of a teacher. It says: "Thus far you have had a wrong identity. You are identifying yourself with the body and things like that."

"What is wrong with the body?" asks the ego.

"It's not just the body. The whole thing out of which the body arises has a root aspect. You don't see it because it is lying buried. All the samskaras and vasanas — incipient memories and previous conditionings — are there in the root. They are what feeds you and so you become blinded. As you are blind you can only see the world of colourations. But I can show you how you can turn your identity to the original source of everything. Then you don't have to be bound to the world of necessity."

Then the ego starts questioning all the values it has been living so far. It says, "Oh, no. I don't want all those little things". The ego has no intelligence of its own, only this kind of borrowed intelligence. If it's with the intellect when it is on the bright side, it feels the calmness, peace, elation, sense of wonder, and great joy of that sphere. And what happens to the mind? It cannot stand alone with the body, so it also comes to the bright side, to the renewed identity with the Self. Then the hands say, "There's nothing special for us to do. We will also sit peacefully." The legs say, "Okay, we don't have to run around unnecessarily any more. It's very peaceful like this." All the body cooperates, and at last the mind, ego, intellect and the body are all together in the bright camp.

Eventually the momentum shifts to the other perspective, and the intellect is weaned away from the side of the pure once again. All the vasanas again act. The ego refocuses on the daily world and thinks, "What a folly that I wanted to leave my comfortable home, my spouse and children! All this stuff is so wonderful! It is all I want. That other state of mind was all just phony dreams. These gurus and swamis who come and say all those things — it's good for them, not for me. For me, this is the right thing: to be in my body and live this life."

Your attitude swings like the proverbial pendulum. For half the time you are with what is called *ārya*. I equate that with what the Isavasya Upanishad calls vidya. It is the side of the Self. Is Narayana Guru asking us to be only on this side, and to avoid the side of the body or *anārya?* No, not at all. It is here that his revaluation comes as a corrected form of Vedanta. Everyone else, except the ancient rishis, say to leave the body, leave the state of avidya.

But the Guru tells us we should know this is the way the whole thing operates. When the body functions have priority, we should see that as how nature operates. When the spiritual insight predominates, we should see that is how the supreme ground of everything lends its light, power, energy, sense of wonder, and truthfulness to infuse everything. These come again and again as a kind of pulsation. Like the alternation of light and dark, vidya and avidya always operate, but one who knows the secret of both rises above them. One who holds a central position, watching with an evenness of mind, can accept both.

You should take this as an invitation to intuitively keep yourself at a neutral zero in orientation. You are not asked to run away from home or commitments. You have a body, and until it drops away everything pertaining to it is relevant. The complaint here is about the lopsidedness that comes when you exaggerate the value of one side and become blind to the other, as is often the case. You should never be blind. When your bodily needs are to be met you should still be aware of your spiritual side. And when you are experiencing spiritual ecstasy or joy, don't forget you have a body and that many important laws pertain to it.

To have this fully balanced state is true wisdom. In this you do not give an exaggerated importance to your bodily comforts or your bodily pains. You don't exaggerate spiritual gains, nor do you negatively condemn the spirit as nonfactual or dreamy. This brings great peace to your mind. It is a peace that makes you efficient on both sides.

You know that some day the body will drop off, but until that time it is to be treated as an excellent instrument. It is magnificently equipped with both senses and a sensory interpretation system. When all is working harmoniously you have a healthy mind, a wonderful gift through which the great joy of the Absolute can be lived in a million ways and can be understood and appreciated in a million forms. Then as an artist, musician, writer, worker, engineer, doctor, housewife, mother, father — whatever your field or role, it all becomes deeply meaningful. You can appreciate it in all its richness. Yet as you know this is a passing phase, you are no longer threatened by it. Death no longer has its sting. You have already accepted it. If you know that you are hired for only eight hours a day at your workplace, you don't cry when the bell rings for you to go home. Your life is just like that. When death rings the bell, you just say it's all over. You know in advance what it's going to mean, so there is no fear. Death, the greatest of terrors, doesn't affect you.

Another great fear is that somebody may say something about you behind your back. But if you remember that when you are focused on the body side everyone's vision is naturally blurred and they all see only from their own point of view, you can just accept it. You know that those who look at you from above think you are below and those who look from below think you are above, those who look from afar think you are very small and those who look from inside think you are very big, and you just say, "That's your view. Fine." You don't have to get annoyed. You give complete freedom to everyone to have their own views about you. "You are moral." Fine. "You are immoral." Fine.

There is a story in *Zen Flesh, Zen Bones* by Paul Reps, about a grain dealer's daughter becoming pregnant. Since she was not married, her father became very angry. He asked her, "Who did this mischief to you?" She wouldn't say. He said, "Come on, tell me! Otherwise I will kill you." So she answered, "That Zen master who lives next door, he did it." The father was even more enraged. The Zen master was young and handsome, and everyone had great reverence for him. But the father thought, "This mischievous fellow is a black sheep."

He took his daughter, went there and said, "Hey, man! Take her! She's pregnant, and you did it!" The Zen master answered, "Is that so?" "Yes, that is so." "Fine." He said to the woman, "Okay, you can stay here. I'll go out and beg some food for you." But nobody would give him food because now they thought he was immoral, that he had impregnated this woman. So he became a woodcutter. He worked, brought food, and gave it to her to eat. Finally the time came for her to give birth. There was great shame and a deep sense of guilt in her, but the Zen master attended on her with great compassion, and the child was born.

Afterwards she went to her father and said, "I did a very bad thing. The Zen master is not the father of my child. He is a very pure man, very compassionate. I cannot bear this guilt!" "Then whose child is it?" "It was a fisherman from the market." Her father lamented, "Oh, what a terrible thing I have done to the great Zen master! How can I get any merit in this life? All my merit is gone!" He hurried to the Zen master and said, "Sir, you are not the person who fathered that child!" The Zen master answered, "Is that so?" "Yeah. I'm taking my daughter back home." "Fine."

This is where you have to stand. No matter what happens, no matter what anyone thinks, you can just say "Is that so? Fine." To be able to do this you have to be at a neutral zero, neither on the body side or the other side. This is the most central teaching of the Isavasya Upanishad. When you know the secret of avidya, you cross over death. When you know the secret of vidya, you enjoy immortality.

Verse 69

śruti mutalām turagam toṭuttorātma-
pratimayeẓum karaṇapravīṇan āḷum
rati rathamēṟiyahanta ramya rūpam-
prati puṟamē perumāṟiṭunnajasram

Hearing and such as horses yoked,
occupied by the self-image, the dexterous psychic
    dynamism drives
the chariot of *rati;* mounted therein, the ego
is continuously chasing each pleasing form outside.

Here we have the classical image of the chariot, which has an important place in Indian iconography. The Sanskrit name given for it here is *ratham*. The sound *ra* means happiness; *tha* means that which holds, conjoins or brings you to something. So *ratham* means that which brings you to happiness, or rather, is meant to do so. It is a vehicle, a *vāhana,* to carry you to *tha*. As an epithet, *tha* stands for Kubera, the Lord of Wealth. Not just financial wealth, but also wealth in terms of virtues or anything truly valuable. Thus we have the picture of the vehicle that conducts you to the great domain of values. The highest abode of values is the Absolute itself.

The body is another kind of vehicle in the sense of being an instrument to take you to the abode of the highest of all values. This chariot is yoked to the horses of sense interest, like *śruti,* what is heard. There is duality involved in the harnessing of your senses. The horses can be either divine or demonic, and life goes on alternating between them. Unless you can transcend the duality of this alternation, you will not be able to ride your chariot to the highest form of happiness, the Absolute.

The Chandogya and Brihadaranyaka Upanishads relate a story of the gods and demons, the devas and asuras, striving for ascendence over each other. First the devas revered the pure *udgītha*, aum, as the breath in the nose, with which sweet smells are discerned and enjoyed. But the asuras came rushing in and affected the breath in the nose, so that now people smell bad, noxious odours along with the sweet ones.

Since it is with the organ of speech we give the *udgītha*, the devas next concentrated there and tried to purify it. But the asuras had a plan and foiled the attempt. From that day, people have been speaking both truth and untruth.

Then the devas thought, "We have to conduct ourselves in this world with our sight. Let us now try to purify it so we can always walk carefully in the direction where it is always bright and never dark." Again the asuras entered in, and people started seeing both the bright and the dark. So that plan failed.

Next they thought, "This isn't working. Let's go to the *śruti*, what we hear through our ears. If we can always hear the supreme wisdom and keep ourselves in resonance with it we won't have any more trouble."

But before the devas could arrive there, the asuras went and spoiled that too. Now people hear good things and rejoice, but they also hear very bad things that tear their hearts to pieces and cause great disturbance. As we all know, if we hear even one bad word about ourselves it makes us quite upset.

So the devas thought, "What can we do now? We have been trying all these programs with our senses. Let's go to the mind, which controls all the senses. If we can purify that, everything will be all right." But the asuras arrived before the mind was able to be purified, and now we have depressing thoughts as well as elevating ones. You may direct your reason in the most wonderful way to sublime understandings, but you can also get into fantasies and delusory thoughts that keep you confused.

So at last the devas made up their minds to catch the prana where the asuras could not reach it. They looked for such a region and found it in the mouth, the space where the prana is before it enters the nostrils. They concentrated on it, and when the asuras came there they were dashed to pieces like clods of earth thrown against a granite rock. So the devas won the battle in the mouth. This prana inside us has a neutral status. That is why we don't smell good or bad things in the mouth, but only when they come to the nose.

Such dualism of the senses is what Narayana Guru is referring to in this verse. Prajāpati, the lord of our manifested individual self, resides in the midst of it, occupying the *ratha* or vehicle which is on a march in search of the great joys of life.

The word *pratimā* is significant here. *Prati* means corresponding; *pratimā,* that which corresponds to the original. A reflection, statue or image is called a *pratimā*. Vedantins give the simile of individuated selves as being akin to the foam on the ocean. When a wave breaks, the froth produced consists of millions of bubbles of various sizes. The sun shining above is reflected by each bubble, the small ones as much as the large. And not only the sun; anything the sun illuminates is also reflected on each bubble. When a bubble bursts, the sun and the world do not disappear. Only their images that were mirrored in that particular bubble are gone, forever.

You and I are the bubbles which mirror this cosmic show illuminated by a sun outside. There is only one supreme Sun, but we see millions of suns reflected uniquely in each individual bubble. Each of us has our own sun. This is called a *pratimā*. Thus, the self that is in the individual *ratha* is only an image of the Supreme.

The question is, how do we relate to that supreme Self? Again, you can refer to the first chapter of the Chandogya Upanishad, which deals with the spiritual aspect of the Word in a complex and symbolic manner.

The Word is called *akṣara* because it is imperishable. On the other hand, the articulating sound we use to pronounce the eternal Word comes and goes. It has a beginning and an end, and is only manifested in the middle part. So the Word is much more than the mere sound symbols we call words.

In the seventh khanda, the Chandogya speaks of the eye and the soul. That which is in the eye is called the shadow of the Self. The self that is shining in the eye and the self that is shining in the sun are both shadows of the unmanifested Self. The two unmanifested aspects are the sun which reveals the world to you and the seer in your eye which sees the world with the light of the sun. They are counterparts, and both of these counterparts are shadows of the supreme Self.

The *antaḥkaraṇas* are the four inner organs: *manas,* the interrogative aspect; *citta,* memory; *buddhi,* reason and intellect; and *ahamkāra,* ego. There is a certain way in which light comes to manifest, by way of the *tanmātras,* the five elements of earth, water, fire, air and ether. Three principles bring this about: *avyakta, mahātattva* and *ahamkāra.* The first is the state in which there is no differentiation between prakriti and purusha, the creative dynamics and the spirit. There is only a primordial unity. This is like the state of which St. John says, "In the beginning was the Word, and the Word was with God, and the Word was God." When you don't differentiate between the Word and God, that is the *avyakta* state.

When the Word begins to operate, it is called *mahatattva* or the great principle. The supreme principle has a logos, a reason about what and how it is going to manifest. Whatever is going to be brought into existence is not going to be done in a haphazard manner. It comes as a cosmic or universal manifestation of the law. The principle, the meaning, the relationship, the purpose — all these together can be called the reason of manifestation, identified with the *mahatattva.* In this, buddhi, the intellect, has a priority over everything else because it is nearest to the Supreme, in the sense that it brings the light of the Supreme to manifest in everything.

Until you come into manifestation you do not know that you exist. First of all your organs are put together in your mother's womb. You are not told how your eye is created or how your respiratory apparatus is built up. When you emerge at birth you don't ask, "Now what?" you cry, "I don't know!" Then your mother says, "Don't cry. Here is milk for you." She puts her breast in your mouth so you won't cry.

It is only later that the questioning aspect of the mind develops. Only when the mind gets disturbed is the affectivity felt by the person, the *ahamkāra.* Up to a point memory is not a conscious function. Rather it is what might be called habitual choice. As Schrödinger points out, no one has to tell the newborn calf where to look for milk.

It just gets up and totters over to the udder and in no time is contentedly sucking. Who teaches it? Thousands of footprints of previous memories are there. They are memories of whatever the calf is now created out of. Everything that has gone into the calf as a constituent part has these footprints of the repetitive aspects of life. Thus the *cittam* is both a recalled, consciously recognised memory, as well as a reflex, habitual operation.

The *ātmā pratima* or self-image is conjoined with the inner organ through the operation of reason. It rides in the *rati ratham,* in the vehicle which is meant to take you to the highest value. It is qualified as *rati,* which corresponds roughly to what in Western psychology is called the libido.

The ego, *ahanta,* is now bracketed and given special emphasis. Actually *ahanta* goes with the sense of *karaṇam* as psychic dynamics, not just as mind. Here it is *ramya,* that which brings you to a culminating joy. The word comes from *rama,* that which brings you to absolute happiness.

When happiness brings you to a state of absorption, it is called *rama*. This has two meanings. One is that you can become so infatuated by joy that you forget everything else, including sound reason. It can also be the highest joy of absorption in the Absolute. It can be the worst as well as the best.

The catch is in rupam, the form, of what seems to you to hold the greatest happiness. You are not discriminating the essence of it, you are just carried away by the outward form. The Guru referred to this in an earlier verse as *vaṭivu,* a form in knowledge, contrasting it with *aṟivu,* pure knowledge. When you give priority to the form and forget the essence, you are misled. Only the appearance is there. From the appearance you judge that something is going to make you happy, but of course it doesn't. You run after a pleasing form thinking it will give you happiness, but in the end you turn away with dissatisfaction and frustration.

This is a case study of Americanism. After six months or a year or two, they say "This doesn't work!" They begin by saying "she is the one," or "he's got it," but soon they say "I *thought* so!" They are misled by the rupam. When you find no satisfaction in an appearance, you naturally leave it and look for the next and the next and the next. You go on chasing such forms restlessly and persistently.

This gives you a picture of what Narayana Guru is representing with this verse. While there are slight differences in their metaphors, in the Katha as well as the Maitri and Mandukya Upanishads there are references to the body as a chariot, with the senses as the horses, the mind as the reins, and the ego as the driver. The Guru has combined what is given in these three Upanishads with the Bhagavad Gita, where Krishna holds the horses and Arjuna sits there as master.

If you understand all the implications of the principle that for all embodied beings everything — the body, senses, mind, intellect and so on — is made to seek happiness, it is very appropriate to call these *rati*. What we seek is happiness indeed, and we are equipped with an instrument that is well-suited to this purpose. As long as you remember that the horses harnessed to the instrument are *śruti* and the like, there is no possibility for the asuras or demonic forces to mislead you.

In this study we go by the direction of the Word of the Guru. The two main principles in this are *śraddhā* and *vairāgya*, faith and detachment. Adherence to sraddha means establishing a bipolarity with this principle of word wisdom, having one-pointed reverence, attention and acceptance of the essence of the word of the sastra, the Word of the Guru. You may not be seeing a guru in front of you in the form of a person. For instance, if you have accepted Jesus as your guru, he is not sitting before you in a physical way, but his word lives in the Gospels. The words in that sastra are the Word of the Guru. You don't see Krishna as such, but when you look into the Gita the Word of the Guru is there in the form of a written document. There again the sastra stands for the guru.

No matter how the Guru is represented in your life, it should be that guiding light within you, that great power within which can always direct you to the right orientation. *Śruti* here is most important, but we should also remember that everything connected with the senses is already defeated by our previous dark inclinations, tendencies, experiences and conditionings, and this makes us always mistake the appearance for reality. It is really a wonderful verse to meditate on!

Verse 70

oru rati tanneyahantayindriyāntah-
karaṇakaḷēbaramennitokkeyāyi
viriyumitinnu virāmamennu vēṟā-
maṟivavan ennaṟivōḷamōrttiṭēṇam

One *rati* alone is expanding into the ego, the senses,
the mind, the body and all that is;
where is an end to this?
Not until one knows that he is different, none other
than knowledge; remember!

The Brihadaranyaka Upanishad says that when the first being came into manifestation it was like a person, though it was neither male or female. When the person recognised its beingness, it said "I am," or in the original Sanskrit, *aham,* "I am That." The Upanishad says when a person introduces himself he first says "I am," and then adds his name. So first we say *aham,* "I am," and then we say whatever we want to add to it.

The Upanishad goes on to say when the person recognised that it was all alone, it was filled with fear. It says when you are alone, you are afraid. Then the thought came, "What am I afraid of if I am all alone?" With that the fear left. No one can be afraid if there is not any other thing. One can only be afraid of an other.

Then the person thought, "What can I do if I am all alone? I can't do anything." With that thought it split into two and became a he and a she. It split like the center of a pea seed, into two halves. According to the Brihadaranyaka, neither man or woman are a full person; each is a half. For each half, all space is filled with *rati,* the desire for the other. This means a person's space is filled with that which is to be sought and enjoyed. And who is it that experiences this enjoyment? The Eros in each person. Eros becomes the enjoyer, and *rati* is what is being enjoyed.

The primal instinct which sets all activities into motion is called the libidinal force. The term 'libido' was used around 1880 by Moll, and afterwards adopted by Freud. Moll was not very sure what it was. It was first brought up as a theory to explain instinct, but later the psychoanalysts did some astonishing work on the implications of libido which agrees in great measure with what Narayana Guru is saying here.

You have to look at yourself with the idea of you as the enjoyer, the one who is seeking enjoyment. To truly get into this, you have to understand yourself as a combination of the three agencies of knower, doer and enjoyer. We began today by saying "I am." That is the knower. When Descartes says "I think, therefore I am," he is giving priority to that aspect. When Romain Rolland says "I love, therefore I am," he gives priority to the enjoyer aspect. The third approach is when you say "I do, therefore I am."

We are knower, doer and enjoyer. The doing and knowing are goal oriented, motivated. But knowledge for its own sake is not very attractive. If you are given information about things you have no interest in, you get bored. Satisfaction is what attracts you. Whatever you are knowing or doing should therefore be satisfying. Thus the central role is that of the enjoyer.

We are made up of three aspects, *sat, cit* and *ānanda*. When we think of doing, there has to be an existential ground for it, an existential field for it, and also there has to be an ontologic factor. The doing part is primarily related with the existential reality, *sat*. Knowledge is *cit*. Both existence and knowledge should make sense to you, should be meaningful to you. The meaning comes from the value something contains or the value inherent in it. That value is ananda.

Narayana Guru, beginning here with *rati* as the ground for the aham to even operate, agrees with the findings of Freud about libido. Freud discovered that it is not just one instinct, but that we have a number of instincts operating in us. All of them are looking for gratification or some other form of actualisation. In his analysis

Freud found that although the initial movement of the mind is in search of the satisfaction of a particular desire, when a person comes to actualise it in the field, there is often a spontaneous change both in the object of the desire and in the understanding of its purpose.

Suppose a man feels very erotic about a woman. With every intention of expressing his desire and, possibly, satisfying it, he goes to her. When he arrives he finds that she isn't alone. There are other people there who greet him and then go on talking of poetry and art. While that is not the intention he came with, he cannot withdraw and thinks, "Okay, fine. At least she's here. Let's talk about art." Throughout the evening his enthusiasm mounts for the stimulating discussion. The stamina he would have expended in a sexual union is burned up by the intellectual investigations he is engaged in. He feels thoroughly satisfied by the end of the evening, even forgetting the purpose for which he originally came, and goes home relaxed and content.

What has happened here? This is a libidinal transference, where other instincts in him took over and shared between them the output of energy. Freud wants us to understand libido as operating in this way.

Freud also says that just as there is a flow from the individual's ego to pleasure objects, there can be a flow inward where the subject himself becomes the object of pleasure. In the Brihadaranyaka Upanishad, when the original person felt the need to have company it did not go in search of a mate. Instead, it turned upon itself and divided into two. The story goes that when the person divided itself into a male and a female, the male desired to mate with the female. The female thought, "How can I allow this? We are brother and sister and now he is after me. I will go and hide."

Space suddenly became full of her for him, full of his desire for her. She went and became a cow. He changed into a bull and mated with her. She changed into a mare, so he changed into a stallion. This went on through all of creation. In this way whatever beings are here have come from the many tricks of the original mother to escape the original father. All of space is now filled with the many different kinds of beings, and Eros or *rati* is toying with them all.

The libidinal flow from the self recoiling upon itself and falling in love with itself again is what Freud described as narcissism. In the Brihadaranyaka, when Yājñavalkya decided to divide all his wealth between his two wives, Kātyāyanī and Maitreyī, Maitreyī asked him, "With all this wealth, will I become immortal?" He answered "No. You can live like a rich person, but you won't become immortal." She said, "Then show me that by which I can become immortal." He gave her this great truth: "No love is greater than the love for the happiness of the Self."

This agrees substantially with what Freud said. Ultimately the object of your pleasure is your own self. It is for the sake of the self you desire everything. This identification of the libido with the aham, the self, becomes the propelling force for the expansion into so many other aspects. Those that Narayana Guru has listed here are the ego, senses, mind, body, and all that is.

A twofold operation takes place when the aham or the enjoyer-self is seeking enjoyment, one in the world of objects and the other in the world of subjects. The idea is to release your mind from these two attractions, remembering that there is nothing called mind anywhere other than this. Verses 24 and 25 of Chapter Six of the Bhagavad Gita make the same point:

> Abandoning completely all desires originating in the will for particularised ends, curbing the collection of sense-functionings on every side — slowly, slowly, activities should be brought to a standstill by reason steadily applied, establishing the mind reflexively in the Self, without thinking of anything whatever.

A person who wishes to effect the inner unition, yoga, is asked to give up all desires which cause *saṅkalpa*s within his inner realm. He is also asked to equalise his vision by withdrawing his interest from what is called *indriyagrāmam*. This is a very curious expression. When there are a number of houses in an area which make a village, it is called a *grāmam*. Like that, your desire can organise a number of interests into one living gestalt, which is then called an *indriyagrāmam*.

When the ego is turning inwards, seeking pleasure from itself, it uses fragments of the memories of previous experiences to make a construct. The construct thus fashioned is called *saṅkalpa,* meaning one's imagination or fantasy. You can fantasise a world within, and have your enjoyment there. You might elaborate the same fantasy semantically and create poetry. You may paint or sculpt it, or write it as a story or play. Thus, when the ego becomes motivated by the *rati* and you look for enjoyment within, the way it uses awareness — spread out in a pattern — becomes the mind.

There is nothing anywhere sitting by itself that is the mind. When I speak, mind becomes words. When I visualise, it is various images. When I feel, it is sensation. It has no definite form, texture, content or material. It assumes anything the self wants for its inner satisfaction.

The other aspect is when the mind turns outwards, so to speak, to focus on the *indriyas*, the senses. As explained in the previous verse, the properties of the senses belong to the five elements, so you experience sound, touch, taste, form and smell. It is impossible to say whether such forms of enjoyment are outside or inside you.

Vedantins have a theory of perception which is very different from those of behavioural psychologists, for instance. As the behaviourists see it, the object outside is a stimulant causing energy to flow through the senses, in the manner of light falling on the eye or sound vibrating the eardrum. But to the Vedantin there is only one reality, called *akhaṇḍa caitanya,* unbroken consciousness. The unbroken consciousness circumlimits itself and says aham, "I am." This broken fragment thinking of itself as a personal self is said to have *pramātṛ caitanya,* the consciousness of an observer or seer. The object towards which this observer is turned is also a circumlimitation within the same field of consciousness. The observer and the observed have both become fragments in the totality of consciousness. These are united by sensory acts such as looking or listening. Whether you are seeking enjoyment in the field of your own fantasy or with actual objects, it is always nothing more than a play in consciousness.

The self is turning to its own resources for enjoyment, either in the form of fantasies or overt empirical action. This necessitates an unfoldment into the senses, the inner organ, the body, the world, or what have you. What Narayana Guru is asking is how long will this search for individual unfoldment in the many worlds in which you live go on? The answer is, until you know that you are that knowledge which you are seeking. Until then the search is endless.

You can look at this from a more realistic angle. Imagine your birth. A certain man and woman were restless one day and became fascinated with each other, and inadvertently you were conceived. The original cause of your birth was *rati,* the sexual pleasure of two people. Throughout the Upanishads we again and again come across the words *rati* and ananda, which are equated in them with procreation. Procreation is not a sinful act in the Upanishads, it is most sacred. Only after Puritanical Christianity came along did it become associated with sin. Probably there was something wrong with St. Paul. He became very alarmed at the prospect of procreation. He made it sinful, where before it had been very sacred.

From the *ratirasam* came the essence of the man and the woman. As the geneticists see it, the chromosomes from both parents are paired into one total whole, bringing the qualities of both, along with their families, to the baby. The first things the child starts to use are the *indriyas*. It looks around in all directions. Then all the friends and family stimulate it by touching it, putting fingers into its hands and patting its cheeks. Some instinctive operation goes on inside, and slowly the child starts recognising things. Its identity of itself as a separate entity develops as it learns to distinguish one body from another. As the child becomes conscious of itself, the *ahanta,* the idea of 'I' and 'me', arises, and the eternal cycle continues.

In the next verse Narayana Guru takes this up again. It is a most natural thing he is describing. From a very minute particle the whole thing is blown up into a whole universe of interest. When it seeks, what is it after and what is its end?

In the previous verse we were told that we run after many things, thinking they will give us happiness. Doing this does bring happiness, but it also brings unhappiness. This experience of acceptance and rejection is examined by Freud also. He says that in the libidinal attempt at satisfaction there are two opposite forces operating: the death instinct, Thanatos, and the desire to live and love, Eros. The will to live and the will to die or destroy, love and aggression, go hand in hand.

When you realise this you withdraw from your chasing in order to have a better look at yourself. There is a realisation of the self that you are This, and there is nothing to seek, nothing to find. Then the circular chase comes to a close.

When people come to me emotionally charged, almost unable to speak, sit for many minutes finding no words, then become tearful, their face very red, often even shaking, usually I don't say anything. Although I am sympathetic, as I see that the whole thing is based on a flimsy, shadowy, stupid misapprehension, I don't have to feel sorry. The whole thing is a misunderstanding. After a bit they start speaking. They think they are saying something reasonable, but halfway through they become confused. Then they think that what they were saying was not right. I still don't have to say anything, they themselves will decide it was not right, something was wrong. They try to restate it, but they find it is no longer so important to them. The urgency with which they came is gone. Then they feel the situation is awkward, they are too uncomfortable to say anything. At this point I try to put in some words, but not about them. They may need something to hold onto, something that allows them to feel they can leave the shadowy thing behind. They feel very relieved it is gone, are happy to be done with it. "It was nothing!" they think. But can you say it was totally nothing? No. There is more to it than that.

If you take the whole content of what I've just told you, it will give you some picture of how *rati* operates. There is a great self-love in it. That self-love comes almost to a peak, and then you can see the so-called rejection. One person came to me bitterly crying, saying "nobody loves God. Why can't people love God?" Do you think she was crying because people don't love God, or is it that someone doesn't love her? Torrential tears flowing, saying, "Why don't they [sob] love God?"

At first it may not seem possible to relate it to libido, to our concept of libido. When Nataraja Guru used the word libido to translate *rati*, I was not very appreciative. But when I once again read Freud's own theory, his confusion about it affirms to me the very vague, uncertain areas that are covered by libido as well as *rati*. Even in the simple incident I just mentioned, the sunshine of knowledge finally breaks through the clouds. It's very soothing, very reassuring. When people get into it and bask, the clouds of darkness disappear. What Narayana Guru is referring to in this verse is a more definitive sunshine realisation, which dispels the clouds forever. Otherwise they go and come back over and over again.

If you have love for someone, if you are shopping, say, and see something and think, "Oh! This is what my love likes," at that moment the object is no longer just an object. It is the love. If you spend money on it, that money is sacrificed to the love. It is no longer just a dollar, the dollar has in it the fragrance of your sacrifice for love. It becomes a love object.

Think of the innumerable forms life takes. You write a letter. It is not just a letter but a piece of your love. When you think like this, everything becomes *rati* alone. No wonder Śaṅkarācārya said: "With a glance from your eyes, Oh Mother, this Eros wins the whole world. He has no proper bow; his bow is only a sugar cane. He has no proper string for his bow, only bees. He has no proper arrows to shoot; he has only five flower buds with him. He has no minister except the Spring season. His chariot is the southern wind. But that is enough — he is victorious."

Freud brings in a theory of Thanatos which represents the dark side of the picture. In place of this Narayana Guru says when your love is for the form, the form becomes deceptive. When you change what is from form to essence, you are the essence.

Let us take the example of a mother with an only son. All her love is concentrated on him. According to Freud, the relationship between a child and a mother in the early stages is purely sexual: the child sucking the breast and the mother kissing the child and seeing its facial resemblance with the father. There are so many things which evoke the reliving of the sexual pleasure with the father when the mother is handling the child. As this goes on over time, there takes place what Freud calls the sublimation of the libido. The mother does not treat the child as her mate, she treats him as a child and brings in many refined forms of love. It assumes the nature of a maternal protection with great tenderness. For her to become physically removed from the child is, as Harry Jacobsen recently wrote, "like death, because you are separated from your God." I like Harry's reference in which he said, "Your love and your God are not two. To be separated from your love is like being separated from God or from your own Self." There you bleed. Only those who have experienced it can understand it is the same as bleeding. It can bleed you to death.

For all of us, the presence of such a great love is always nurtured in the heart. It is only when we feel an outer event has taken it away from us that we feel the vacuum. But if we realise that our love was always an image in us — born of our own Self, our own consciousness — then we know that nothing really happens at any time. The same son is there where he was: in the same heart. There is really no separation.

If a mother knows this, she can allow her son a lot of freedom. He doesn't have to become a framed portrait sitting on her table all the time. Does she really want to put her son into a frame and keep him fixed there so she can always look at him? Of course not. She can give him all the freedom he wants, since she can say "My son continues to live in my heart, where he has always lived. I and my son are not two." Jesus also said, "I and my Father are not two."

We should be able to speak this way of all whom we love: "I and my love are not two". What great freedom it brings! What great relief it brings! And what great freedom and relief it gives to others, also. It takes away all the rivalry, competition, jealousy, bickering, insecurity — all with this one recognition, "That knowledge is me and everything is That".

The only difference I see in the libidinal theories of Narayana Guru and Freud is that Freud ended his study with a dismal feeling about the two warring tendencies of Eros and Thanatos, that they were eternally perpetuating tragedies. Narayana Guru sees the possibility of abolishing this duality in a transcendence capable of bringing permanent peace.

If a mother loves her son she should ask him what makes him happy. If he says, "To go to a baseball game with my father," she should say, "Fine. I'll put your knowledge of happiness into my sense of happiness." She doesn't have to manipulate his ideas into her ideas to feel happy. People can have any kind of idea about their own happiness. It's okay. You don't possess anyone. I consider this the great liberation. It is a liberation you can experience here and now.

Verse 71

savanamoẓiññu samatvamārnnu nilpī-
lavaniyil ārumanādi līlayatrē
aviraḷamākumitākavēyaṟiññā-
lavanatiraṟṟa sukham bhaviccituṇnu

No one in this world remains free from becoming,
in a state of sameness; this is said to be a beginningless play;
to him who knows this, which is unlimited, as a whole,
boundless happiness comes.

In the Bhagavad Gita, our life here is described as that which is not known in the beginning, known in the middle, and which is not known again at the end. What we call life is something which comes along and passes through our range of vision, just like a film of incremental images being projected at a normal speed to make a movie. We see a set of movements which elicits an idea, and then it passes on to the next and the next.

There are many theories about the past and the future. We can envisage the movement of time in two ways, either that the future is becoming the present and the present is passing into the past, or that the past is giving way to the present and the present is giving way to the future. In either case, we have a past which is beginningless, a future which is endless, and a present that is all we experience.

The process of the movement of time is called becoming. If we look at the way in which new things come about, it's as though they are being born out of the unknown. A continuous birth of incidents, events, notions, ideas and the like is taking place. The Brihadaranyaka Upanishad says that birth is given to speech, mind and the vital forces: *vāk, manas* and *prāṇa*. The *vāk* is not only the articulated sounds produced by human beings, it also includes the sounds of the wind, the ocean, or any happening you come to know through sound.

Manas is considered to be a medium to know what is happening in the so-called external world, as well as in the inner being. Sadness comes — the mind knows it. Happiness comes — mind knows it. The sun rises — the mind knows it. Anything that occurs as an external or internal event is known by the mind. When the mind is not present, none of it is known.

The pranas, or vital forces, are considered to be what you breathe through your nose, down to your heart, and from there to the navel and back. The vital breath between the heart and the nostril is called prana, and that which is between the heart and the navel is called apana. In between, and interlocking them, is the *vyāna*. The *vyāna* is considered to be superior because it permits us to speak. When we are in the process of speaking, we don't have to say, "Wait a moment, let me breathe!" in order to say the next word. Great orators and pedagogues can stand on platforms and go on talking for hour after hour, and they never need to stop for a breath. Why? Because *vyāna* is capable of regulating the prana and apana while they are speaking.

There are other vital forces as well. *Udāna* is a stabilising prana extending from the toe to the crown of the head. *Samāna,* supposed to reside in the belly, carries nourishment to all parts of the body. And the Upanishads add one more, *ana,* which is all these put together. It integrates the *vāk*, manas, and prana, which make up the process of becoming as the known, what is desired to be known, and the unknown.

Whatever is spoken is always known. The mind is always desiring to know. That is what keeps it moving all the time: it is not satisfied with what is already known. It says, "what next?" and then goes in search of it. And even the best physiologist who can describe the process of respiration in detail does not know how his *prāṇa, vyāna* or *samāna* operate. He can only conjecture about them, since the whole realm of vital forces is unknown. It's paradoxical that that which gives us the greatest sense of objectivity in life is even more subtle than the subjective because we don't know anything about it. The whole structure of the world of becoming is so fabricated that only a small part of it is revealed at any one time. There is a small part known, a search of greater or lesser intensity, and a vast unknown area.

Narayana Guru makes two points in this verse. One is that we should know that life is a *līlā,* a sport, and the other is that we should know this *ākavē,* as a whole, all together. These are the two saving factors.

If you do not know that this is a lila, this partial knowledge can be very tormenting. And it can be a nightmare if you don't know it as a whole. Understanding this as sport relates to what may be called the non-Self, while 'the whole' has reference to the Self. The whole panoply of life is played out between the duality experienced between the Self and the non-Self. This idea is made explicit in the opening chapter of Śaṅkara's commentary on the *Brahma-Sūtra*s, which are called a *mokṣa śāstra,* a science of liberation.

A friend was telling me the other day that we have screens before us so that we don't see what's going on in other people. We are partially blind in this sense, and it is this blindness that causes our misery. Śaṅkara says the same thing. He is a great philosopher, so he put it in a big way. My friend put it in a very simple way. But to me they are saying the same thing: there is partial blindness. We are cut off from reality, and to that extent we suffer. To remove this suffering we should take away the screen.

All the Upanishads, the *Brahma-Sutra*s, the Bhagavad Gita, the Bible and the Koran are attempts through the spoken word to remove darkness from the mind and the still greater darkness perpetuated by the vital forces. You are trying to conquer the unknown by annexing more and more of it through the spoken word which makes things known. You may not be able to know everything as a whole, akave, but at least you can know that it is like a sport.

Imagine you know nothing about football and you see twenty-two huge people coming with pads and helmets on. Then they beat against each other, push one to the ground and jump on him. If you were in a community where no one had ever seen this, what would you think of it? You would think of it as the most horrid thing, an evil, the worst of all spectacles. But people go by the thousands with their families to watch this all the time.

Or two people will go to an arena to punch each other's noses and make them bleed. Millions of dollars are spent to watch how they punch each other's noses for a few minutes. The audience is not terribly affected. They feel excited and happy about it because they know it's a sport. But if someone were to walk into our room and punch us, we would call the police and raise a big alarm. We might be terrified for the rest of our life by the possibility of another assault. So if you see it as a sport, it can take the shock out of it.

Mountaineers routinely suffer tremendous hardships of dangerous avalanches, icy winds and storms, and thin air. We sympathise with people in Russia who are sent to Siberia, but they are not suffering a fourth of what those who climb Mount Everest do. But going to Siberia is not taken as a sport, it is taken as punishment. So the lesser suffering is considered terrible, and the greater is seen as an ecstatic accomplishment. It's all in the attitude of seeing it as a sport.

And how do you take your tuberculosis as a sport? It can be done — there is a way of looking at it. Perhaps ninety per cent of the diseases we play out are sport. We know inside that it is not as bad as we pretend it to be. We want to get attention, so we overdo the game a little. I suppose I shouldn't let out my secret while my doctor is here. I have to be very careful, otherwise the next time somebody calls him to report I'm having an emergency he'll say, "Relax, the Guru is just having a sport."

In Carl Jung's *Memories, Dreams and Reflections,* he describes his first epileptic fit. He was attending the church where his father was a priest, when another young boy came up behind and pushed him and knocked him down. He could have immediately gotten up, but he wanted to show how mean the other boy was, so he just lay there. He pretended he couldn't get up so that others would come and give him lots of sympathy. He created a gruesome feeling around him, and reveled in it. His psyche learned the advantage of being sick and the kind of attention it brings. He started having frequent epileptic fits, and everyone sympathised with him.

One day he overheard his father talking with another friend about how much money he would have to spend to cure his son, how he had lost all hope for him, and how sad he was feeling. Remorse came to Jung, and he thought "I brought this upon myself. It's not really that bad." At the time he was having fits whenever he tried to learn Latin. As soon as he picked up the Latin book the fit would begin and he would fall down on the floor.

When Jung realised what was happening, he went to his room with the resolve, "I brought this disease upon myself, so I am going to cure it". He sat in his chair and picked up the Latin book. The fit started, but he thought "No. This time I am going to read Latin." It was probably his *udāna,* one of his vital forces, that picked him up and threw him from his chair. He lay flat and shivered for awhile, then got back up in his seat and picked up the book again. Once again the *udāna* came, but he sat firm. A third and a fourth time the crisis started, but he held his position. At last he got over it, and had no more fits.

Many of us do the same thing, but only a few of us can get free of the syndrome after it becomes ingrained the way Jung did. I know I do it . . . it's such a great joy that all of you suffer for my sake. With so many attentive friends, a heart attack is a kind of performance. So when you have such a realisation, even disease can be seen as a sport.

Disease, though, is your own game. You can do what you like, up to the point of no return. But how about something thrust upon you, like poverty? There are certain sects in the Catholic Church whose members take a vow of poverty. Indian sannyasis also take such a vow. When you accept a life of poverty as part of your game, then you enjoy it. Jalaluddin Rumi said, "Poverty is my pride and obscurity my refuge." Isn't it beautiful?

Once on the banks of the Ganges in the foothills of the Himalayas, Nataraja Guru and I went for a walk. We came upon a sannyasin's hut. Such huts are not made by the renunciates themselves. They take their advice from the book of Bhartṛhari, which says a sannyasin lives like a snake which makes no hole of its own. It goes into a hole made by a rat, eats the rat and makes the hole its home. From Kolkata to the Himalayas, all kinds of sannyasins live in huts on the banks of the Ganges which were put there through the work of a sannyasin called Kalikamblivala. His name means one who has merely a blanket, nothing else. He made the paths and bridges, and arranged for shelters and food along the entire pilgrimage route. Kalikamblivala adhered to his own vow of total poverty, but he was the richest of all. He took it all as a sport, a game. He set up a trust, to which people donate from all over India, to provide for any poor seekers who go there. A sannyasin can go into a hut and take it as a refuge given to him by the kindness of others. When he leaves, another will come along to occupy it.

We approached such a hut one evening as the sun was setting. It was very beautiful. All that was heard was the sound of the Ganges, like a liquid chanting of aum. Huge mountain peaks cast their shadows over the valley. The last golden rays of the sun were falling on the cottage, in front of which a man sat in meditation, listening to the gurgling of the river. Guru and I stood there. There was total silence for some time. Then Guru looked at me, and I knew he wanted to go to that man. It was like entering into a sanctum of great peace, great joy. It was not anything exciting, it was a joy which was so peaceful and calm.

Guru slowly walked towards the hut. I followed. We came quite close to the sannyasin. He opened his eyes and stood up. Without any introduction he came and prostrated himself before Guru. He had nothing to offer as a seat other than the plank of wood on which he had been sitting. He gave that to Guru and brought a small piece of towel for me to sit on. Then he asked us to sit. We sat. He was not in any hurry to find out who we were. He did not ask our names, or where we came from. He just showed his hands and we sat.

The man took his *kamaṇḍalu,* walked to the Ganges, filled it with water, and brought it to Guru. Guru held out his hands and drank. He gave water to me and I drank. Then he just sat down. The silence was such that after taking the cool, refreshing water of the Ganges we all became silent. It slowly became dark as the sunset progressed. After a little while Guru got up. The man once again touched Guru's feet, I gave my salutation, and we just walked away. He didn't give us any sweets or delicious food, no cozy seats — only just a plank of wood and Ganges water — but that was enough to remember our meeting for the rest of our lives.

For some reason we measure poverty by saying, "He has no television, so he must be very poor." I think he is so rich. He has the whole world: the sky above with all its stars, the sun and the moon, the pure water of the Ganges. The time of all eternity is his. He has no master, no servant, no one to say "Today you have to do this much work." He doesn't even have to bother about his food. One day when it so chances he will walk to a nearby centre and stand in line with others. There will be a basket of bread there which is again and again filled. He will also receive a bowl of dal and four chapatis, which he will take home. He will eat one chapati with the dal and save the rest. He doesn't want to have to walk the same distance again right away. The next day he will go to the Ganges and bring some water. He will put one chapati in it to soak, then he will eat it and drink the water. He has no income tax returns, no one to report to in any way.

Only when you experience this kind of life can you understand the word 'lila.' Poverty, disease, death — what is there more beautiful than death? Once you know what death is and how beautiful it is, it gives you no pain. It only takes the pain away, totally. It is so efficient. It takes not only your pain but all your problems completely away. Yet people are afraid of it. Death is such a wondrous thing, there is nothing to be afraid of.

So we have covered how to deal with pain, how to deal with adversaries as in football, and how to deal with death. The rest are all in your imagination. When you cry, I suppose your tear ducts are in need of stimulation. James Lange's theory says you are sad because you cry and afraid because you tremble. Of course, there are plenty of counter-theories, but no one has yet come up with anything satisfactory.

So what is known, yet to be known, and the unknown make up the whole thing. The word, the mind and prana — these constitute everything other than the Self: what is called the non-Self. The known makes a kind of shield. It becomes a screen against what is not known. What you desire to know causes all the restlessness, and the unknown is what frightens you. Still, these three can be made tools for happiness, too. What is known can make you happy because you know it, the desire to know allows for hope and gives life its promise, and what a great relief it is that you don't know a lot of things! You can look at it this way also. All that is required is akave. If you know all this, then you become very happy. It's not a great secret. It's really a very simple verse.

Everyone says you should resolve everything. The Brihadaranyaka Upanishad says that is the one thing you should *not* do. Thinking you know is a way of suppressing the beneficent flow of life. Once you resolve and make up your mind, things go against you and you have all the troubles in the world. The rishis advice is, "Don't resolve. Just be free. Feel free. Why should you resolve when you know you are not the master of anything?"

Once a fellow went to a great king and asked for a favour. The king told him, "Come back tomorrow." The man started dancing with joy, calling out "Come on, all you people, come out and celebrate!" The king said, "What do you mean by that?" He answered, "People do not know who you are. Everyone is looking for God, but they don't know that you are God!" "God?" "Sure. Otherwise, how could you say for me to come tomorrow? How do you know that tomorrow I will be alive and you will be as well? If you are so sure about it, you must know everything. You must be the Omniscient One!" So "don't resolve" means we do not know how it is going to be, so just let it be, let it go.

A whole chapter of the Brihadaranyaka is devoted to attaining the great freedom of knowing all. What is this meditation? The meditation is to know that there is a great paradox happening. Light is opposed to darkness. Light and darkness cannot be together; the quality-less and what has quality cannot be together. Yet light and darkness do come together in relative degrees. It is not an impossibility. We live in the midst of the paradox that light and darkness coexist and are interlaced. In the same way, the Absolute and the relative are not in two places, they coexist in the very same place. The transient and the intransient are not two: they are also interlaced. Because light and darkness make a kind of arrangement between them, forms appear. Forms are delineated by differences in light and dark areas. Opposites make many kinds of projections of forms; for instance, how do you appreciate the love shown to you?

Because you have experienced hatred, and compared to that love is great.

So the whole of creation is based on paradox. When you are lopsided and see only one side and not the other, you don't truly understand the game. You need to balance yourself at the neutral place where the two meet.

In the right eye is Indra, the master of the senses, and in the left eye is Virāj, the principle of sensation. They divide and then synchronise in the cavity of the heart. It is exactly like the copulation of a man and a woman. They are so completely lost in each other that there is no separate identity of man or woman. There is no other. There is only the pure joy of oneness, unition. In that unition is *hita,* that which you like.

Hita is considered to be a system of nerves as fine as a single hair split into its thousandth part. It is very subtle, but it fills your whole system, extending in all directions like a spherical radiation of light. It goes to the east, west, north, south, above and below — in all directions. If you close off all the avenues by which you are distracted and your mind asks "what next?" you say, "Nothing next, *neti,* not this, not this. Never mind." After a time you come to a stillness everywhere. On all sides you are filled with that great stillness, that overwhelming, all-pervading stillness. Do not try to give it a name. What operates then is your hita, what you like most.

The hita is affected by the blood, where the residual karma is said to be located. I was wondering how that could be, and then I found a reference in McCullough's *Embodiments of Mind* to Aristotle, who had before him Hippocratus. They spoke of the same thing. From their time to 1921 it was believed that you think with your blood.

And how does it work? What you are and what you are going to be are always in your blood. This karma comes again and again to afflict your hita, causing *ahita,* what you don't like. Whenever *ahita* comes you should not let it prevail upon you, you should say *neti, neti,* "not that, not that." In this way you can become absolutely doubtless about your hita, in other words, what you like to be or what makes you happy. If you meditate that you are all light and all happiness, no one can keep you from it.

This combination of Virāj and Indra brings you the highest happiness, which is becoming one with the Total. Remain in it. How about your hands and legs moving, your lungs breathing and your senses functioning? These never cease, but you can just say "I am not that." You experience everything, but there is a silence in it. You are not restraining or restricting, just allowing things to be. At the same time, your mind is in a state of total reflection.

This brings you what Narayana Guru calls the state of all-knowingness. When you know everything, you are That. What is seeming to be, like talking, walking, and so on — it's all lila, sport. Putting these together we get the beautiful gist of this wonderful verse.

Verse 72

kriyayorukūṟitavidya; kēvalam ci-
nmayi maṟukūṟitu vidya; māyayālē
niyatamitiṅṅane nilkkilum piriññа-
dvaya para bhāvana turyyamēkiṭunnu

Now there is action, which is ignorance,
and again there is pure consciousness, which is knowledge;
although these two are thus ordained by *māyā* to stand divided,
a non-dual vision of the Absolute brings about *turīya*.

This verse is to be understood in the light of the previous three verses. In 69 and 70 we were dealing with the libidinal force, and in 71 with the world of becoming. This verse says that maya institutes a certain alternation, ambivalence, or dichotomy. Yet maya is defined as that which is not, so how could it institute anything?

When we say the wind blows, there is really no such thing as wind blowing. When air is moving relative to the ground, we call it wind, and when it moves fast we say it blows. It is in this sense that we say maya institutes something.

Where does something which is not get any power to make things happen? It's a wonder. The Absolute is also known only as a wonder. There is a positive aspect of wonder and a negative aspect of wonder. If you are taken by surprise by an unexpected tragic situation, there is the element of wonder in it, but it brings threat and insecurity and creates fear. The other kind is a sudden promise of great joy. Between such excessive happiness and excessive agony, pain and fear, there is an alternation going on. The stuff which becomes modulated in both directions is your consciousness.

Regarding the functions of the brain, physiologists speak of nets, loops and circles. Certain formations in these neurofunctions determine how one's whole attention gets caught within them. The character of the formations impart qualities of particular sensations to us. The formations themselves are what we call vidya and avidya, and because of this the knowledge that is very pleasing to us as well as the knowledge that is unpleasant are both brought under the title of maya.

Since it has so much power to make things happen, let's look more closely at the special state we call maya. We tend to think of this as a world of facts because of its tangibility. We can perceive it with our senses. Simply because we can perceive a thing does not mean it is giving us pain or pleasure. A stone lying in the road doesn't affect us, except if it enters the context of action — if we fall on it, say, or someone flings it at us. Action situations are what call our attention to a specific area of focus.

Kriya, action, doesn't refer to only physical action. Thinking and conceiving are also actions. And just what is action? There is a sense of agency in you. The agent within has a motivation to change, to move away from the present state to another one. The present state holds dissatisfaction, boredom, anguish, a sense of worthlessness, satiation or monotony, so you look for novelty in the new. Any movement to anything other than the present seems to promise this.

Henri Bergson talks about what occurs if you already know something is going to happen. Say there is going to be a gathering. You can mentally imagine who the people are who are likely to come, where they are likely to sit, what their questions and comments are going to be. You already have a detailed picture in your mind. In spite of all that, when you go there you will find that the arrangement has an unanticipated novelty. Bergson says when you turn to even the most familiar thing, from moment to moment it offers you a novelty, and that novelty is enough to compensate you for moving from the present moment to the next moment.

People like Freud may attribute a libidinal interest to this movement. They say the libido in you is seeking gratification. It can either move outwards and get gratification, or it can move inwards, turn upon the self, and attain happiness. But whatever it does, it cannot remain still. There has to be movement.

The present verse begins with this condition of action, consisting of an actor, an action and a result of the action. The result of an action is called *karma phala,* as it is for the attainment of the fruit, or *phala,* the action is performed. The motivation for any action comes from thinking you are going to get something you don't have now.

This implies two items of ignorance. One is that you are rating yourself in terms of certain mental or physical conditions that are prevailing at the moment and not in terms of the pure Self. How often do we identify ourselves with the body and its names and forms, so that our individuated person can be compared with another? Then we think the other person must be happy because they have certain things going for them. We think, "If I get that condition then I will also be content." This first kind of ignorance is called *āvaraṇa,* the veiling of our real nature. We cover up our true nature with an unreal image of our own imagination.

Now you have an imaginary self-image of your happiness — "When I am like that, I will be happy." Your imagination is positing what you ought to be, what you want to be, what you desire to be. Thus your very future is already filled with an image. You compare your future image with your present one, and invariably feel unhappy with your present image. You feel that only when you come to that future state will you be able to be happy.

This type of projection is called *vikṣepa,* positing an image in what you consider to be your future. That future can be in the next moment, the next year, or in ten years, but once you have decided it is not now, you have already forfeited your right to be happy at this moment. "Until I attain that image, I can never be happy." Such an attitude is an important stumbling block to seekers of truth, who are often motivated by a desire to escape from present circumstances into a supposed heavenly future. This is why it is essential to befriend yourself in the present and not reject your own nature as a prelude to beginning the search.

Thus you invite unhappiness in two ways: by casting a veil over yourself, and by thinking of a future possibility. But if you have this moment your own happy image, and you are always asserting "this is fine with me," then there is nothing to annoy you.

Any noble sentiment like the search for wisdom or love or compassion, any of the higher values which can become your motivating force, immediately become affected by both vidya and avidya. Why do you love another person? What is the meaning of love? When love becomes very real to you, what you experience is the forgetting of the otherness of a person and also forgetting your own limitations. In the intensity of love you forget yourself as well as the other. There is only love and not the lover and beloved as two separate entities.

The most natural, most honest feeling that can come to a person is being drawn, not just to one person, but to all. Opposed to this you have images built up from inside of what you want to love and what is hateful. It is here the dichotomy comes, created by name and form. When your heart goes out to just one person in love, even that is fine because you are extending your self-identity beyond the limits of your body. You see your reality in the other person also. The other's happiness or unhappiness becomes your happiness or unhappiness. This allows you to cross the frontiers of physical limitation to which you have become riveted. This part is vidya. It is not nescience that makes you love; it is vidya, it is knowledge, it is wisdom that leads you to it.

When love pinches you, becomes filled with anguish and sorrow, it is because you have images about it. These images belong to avidya. The pursuit of love is engendered by vidya, but it often ends up in avidya. You smile and you expect a smile back; you touch and you want to be touched in return; you give and you want something to be given back to you. In this way you make it transactional. It becomes a contract, and if the contract is not carried out exactly as you want it to be you become very dissatisfied. Only when love is self-contained and has no hankering behind it does it belong to vidya.

Here Narayana Guru says we have to take for granted what is already there. Our very nature if we have a body is such that we will have limitations. The ideal love that is spoken of is hardly lived by anyone. Why? Because we all have our own natural limitations and abilities. However much we try to philosophise, some of these limitations will remain.

If a man is angry or mad and brandishing some weapon at you, this is not the appropriate time to say "No, no, no, I love you." It is not an opportune moment to embrace him or kiss him, either. As Sri Ramakrishna would say, "A hissing cobra is also Brahman, but keep away from it!" That isn't the time to play with it, despite its divine nature as an integral part of the whole. So there are certain transactional limitations.

What is the meaning of *advaya para bhāvanā,* the nondual vision of the Absolute? If it is natural for us to indulge in ignorance, and that ignorance has knowledge for its basis, how do we transcend both? We first have to think of three special areas: ignorance, wisdom and transcendence. Let us examine each separately.

There are certain inevitable aspects of ignorance over which we have no control. When a child is cutting a tooth it is very painful, and the child will often become irritable and cry all night. If the child cries in the night its mother can't ignore it, she has to do whatever she can to give comfort. No amount of philosophy will help in any way to alleviate the child's suffering. The philosopher's toothache is proverbial. When the pain is intense, simple propositions won't come to his mind, let alone far-reaching conclusions.

Buddha says that at the time when you are experiencing some such inevitable aspect of ignorance, you have to lock your fingers, sit firm, and suffer. If that does not contain the pain, then clench your teeth, make a fist, and suffer. If it is still too much for you, then lie on your belly and pound your fists and suffer. There is no other way. Such is the inevitability of ignorance. As Krishna said to Arjuna, "Whatever has no remedy, accept it. Only a fool will further torment himself." Already there is torment. Let it be. Don't add to it with your own mental agony. You can say, "My physical pain is there, and it will take a few days to go away. I just have to put up with it." Once you accept it, it doesn't cause you mental agony on top of the physical. That is the way to relate to the inevitable.

Still, if you look closely at the painful aspects of your life, only a very few items are actually inevitable. Most of them are minor things we exaggerate or things we bring upon ourselves. In the area of avidya there is a very large chunk you can just throw out, and by changing your thoughts and attitudes the rest of your suffering will be greatly minimised.

An area where this can have an important affect is love. Love can be so painful. "I love you. Why don't you love me in return?" "How much I love you . . . why don't you care about me?" It brings great agony. And what is this love? It is the love about which Khalil Gibran says, "Your thirst, your hunger. The hand you hold out in want." You are like a beggar. You are not the rich donor: "Let my heart flow to you." You are so thirsty and so hungry that you are in terrible need. You want the other person to give to you. It is this need, this thirst, you call your love.

"I want to love and also be loved." It's like a contract. If you truly love, you want to see that the person you love is happy. If the other person's happiness is to have their own way, why can't you be happy about that? Many people, like Victor Hugo, have tried to bring out this point, but they are dismissed as romantic dreamers. There is much more than a romantic dream in it.

In contractual love we do not elevate ourselves. There isn't much difference between an animal caught in an instinctive, reflexive need, and we human beings who think of ourselves as far removed from our animal life and yet react in highly predictable ways. At certain times dogs and cats come into heat. Then they suffer. They go about barking and sniffing and caterwauling through the night, but when their heat is over they immediately calm down. But human beings are in eternal heat. It doesn't just come once in a cycle. Humans go on perpetuating it, generating the heat out of their own minds.

There is a great possibility for us to relieve ourselves of this kind of pain. Suppose you finally get the man or woman you crave, or love, what will you do, put them in your mouth? You can't nibble them like a chocolate Santa — today the thumb, tomorrow the fingers — they always remain outside. However much you try to press them right into you, you are frustrated by what is called the impenetrability of matter. What you are seeing is lovability. You love the sunrise, but you don't reach out your hand to try to hold on to the sun. Instead you might take your camera and snap a photo, and then you can feel that you have kept at least a little of what you saw. Then after two days you forget all about it. That's much better than mooning about it for months on end.

If a rose is lovable, the idea of the worth or value in it is sufficient. The rest can stay in the garden. Once someone visited Rabindranath Tagore, the great poet of love, tenderness and beauty. In all his poems there are references to beautiful flowers. When this visitor came to his house, he did not see even one flower anywhere. He asked, "Oh, Gurudev, why don't you have any flowers here? You write so much about them. Why don't you have some flowers on your table?" Tagore answered, "I love children also. I write a lot about children. Do you expect me to cut off their heads and place them all around the house? I don't need that. Let them carry their heads. Similarly, let the plants keep their heads, the flowers. I can enjoy them more when they are alive. Let them be where they are." You can also think, "Let the one I love be where he or she is. My love is just the same. It is beautiful to love." Then that part of ignorance, the anguish, goes.

Now we come to the ground on which ignorance rests, vidya. It is only because of spiritual oneness that you love. It is only because your innate nature is wisdom through and through that you are trying to understand things through your senses, your intelligence and your mind. The senses are limited, but by turning them to many different things you can expand the knowledge that comes through them. The intrinsic possibility of knowing everything is there. In fact, you are knowledge itself; but as your senses are blind to that fact you can give them as many opportunities as possible to dwell on aspects of knowledge.

Your everyday mind is clouded. By removing the clouds from your mind you can bring illumination to it, because your very nature is knowledge. Ignorance comes and dwells in the senses, the mind and the intellect; and yet these are precisely the tools with which you go on expanding the area of your knowledge.

In the field of vidya, maya can function in a very funny way. If you think that after all it is the pure idea that matters and not anything that has manifested in name and form, then you have created a limitation or a frontier between the manifested aspect and the pure, ideational aspect. This may lead you to believe that the person who is actually standing there, smiling at you, is not what matters, but rather the pure idea of the person is what is significant. This is nothing more than another kind of ignorance. That is why in the

Upanishads it says the person who adores ignorance is living in darkness, but the person who adores only wisdom is living in even greater darkness.

You should be able to appreciate a rose which is actually offered to you, and at the same time you should be able to appreciate the idea of the rose, which is perennially beautiful. "A thing of beauty is a joy forever." You shouldn't say, "This rose is a perishable one, so I don't want it." The thing of beauty has manifested now as this rose. It may perish tomorrow, but now it is not an expired rose but a lovable one. So accept it.

When you have such evenmindedness that both in the field of ignorance and the field of knowledge you have a sameness of outlook, you have *advayam,* nonduality, in your attitude. You accept both with equanimity. This allows you to always remain serene and calm.

Narayana Guru says the experience of *turīya* can also come. What is turiya? We have four states of consciousness. One is wakeful consciousness, where there is a difference between subject and object. We also have a dream experience, where there is only a subject which is interacting with images born of the same subject. There is no objectivity in it. The third is a state of unconsciousness, where there is neither subject nor object. There is only a state of total blindness, absolute darkness. The fourth state the Guru is speaking of as turiya is that which is maintaining your beingness, your existence, within the state of total unconsciousness; and which is the ground of the operation of all consciousness in the dream as well as the ground of reality in the transactional world. This total ground remains unbroken through and through as the Self.

Yogis are supposed to experience the turiya in the state of samadhi, when they are not transacting with anyone, sleeping or dreaming. The turiya contains the best aspects of the other three states. In it the yogis' consciousness has a quality of wakefulness in the sense they are very alert, but at the same time there is no separation of subject and object, so it is not the wakeful state. In the dream state there is no objective world, and yet ideas can rejoice in ideas, and ideas can create ideas with ideas. The whole thing is a play of consciousness which is self-founded. The turiya is also self-founded, but it is in no way a dream state. In the unconscious state of deep sleep, there is absolute peace, with no problems. There is no 'I' and 'mine'. There is no separation from anything. Those qualities are also in the turiya, but it is not a state of inertness. There is no inertia at all.

Does the fourth state only come when you are in a state of absorption? There are many arguments about this, but at least the Vedantins and Yogis believe — and the Taoists have something similar to it — in a state called *jīvanmukta,* where you don't have to lie still or sit like an inert lump to experience the realised state. One experiencing *jīvanmukta* is also in the state of *sahaja samādhi. Sahaja* means natural, innate; sama means equipoised and *dhi* means intelligence.

Sahaja samadhi comes about through the same element of intelligence with which we appreciate a thing via our senses. The mind works by borrowing the light of that intelligence. It is the same intelligence by which one meditates, wills, acts. In fact, it is the only reality. That spark of intelligence belongs to a greater reality than we normally understand or appreciate. Usually our intelligence is moving around, oscillating, unsteady, so it is called *cala,* moving. When it is not moving it becomes equipoised, samadhi. When it is standing firm in the world of wakeful transactions and the world of subjective ideas, it is in samadhi.

And why sahaja samadhi? The Upanishads say that like a sword being put into its sheath, where it perfectly fills the entire sheath, this one reality fits everything of our beingness. If you are making bread with wheat dough you can say that through and through it is wheat. Like that, this manifestation itself is through and through of the same *dhi,* which we call *caitanya* and the Guru here calls *cinmayi,* that source of all light.

You are That. You can say you are born with it. Although you are born with it, by the institution of maya you don't see it. When you start seeing it, there comes the equipoise. Thereafter you carry that equipoise with you wherever you go, to whomever you relate. You appreciate everybody's excessive attitudes. You understand them. But you don't have to react to them unless you are called upon to do so as a physician or a teacher.

If you come to me with an ulcer, there is no need for any fear that I will put you on a table and take out a knife and start slicing into you, because I am not a surgeon. But if you come to me with an ulcer in your mind, I may do something like that to you because you have called me "teacher." If I don't play that role, then I can sit as quietly as possible and leave you and your ulcer alone. Then there won't be any trouble.

Teachers, even though they are wise, have to come to terms with avidya or ignorance. They have to come to terms with vidya when they are dealing with it. But on their own they stand with sahaja samadhi, the inborn equipoise of the pure state of consciousness, in which you and I are not different.

So these are the three areas in which you and I have to apply our intelligence and straighten up our lives. Don't think that by cultivating that attitude you will lose anything of this world. In fact, you will gain many times the happiness that you now have. The appreciation you have for this world can be greatly enhanced when you assume that state of neutrality.

The Mandukya Upanishad defines turiya as the fourth limb of aum. It is not 'a', the wakeful; 'u', the dream; or 'm', deep sleep. There was a silence before you articulated aum; it is on the background of that silence that you made a modulation of sound, and it is again the proportionate reacceptance of that silence that brings about the 'a' transforming into the 'u' transforming into the 'm' which then merges back into the all-embracing silence. In the beginning there was silence. Then there was a distinction from it in the form of sound, although silence was the ground of it. It is the silence which gives a musical tone to the sound, and it is again that silence which absorbs it back into itself. Finally there comes total silence. The silence which is all through is called the turiya.

You can have all the transactions of the world with that silence as the backdrop of your mind. You can have all the dreams and creativity of the world with that silence as the ennobling, stamina-giving, energising principle of your creativity. It is into that silence you can go just as you go to the lap of your mother or your most beloved person. Into that silence you can merge, because you are that. The one who is aware of this all through is having a sahaja samadhi, an experience of turiya.

Verse 73

oru poruḷiṅkal anēkamuṇṭanēkam
poruḷil orartthavumenna buddhiyālē
aṟivil aṭaṅṅumabhēdamāy itellā-
varumaṟivīlati gōpanīyamākum

In one substance there are many,
and in many things there is one meaning; reasoning thus,
everything becomes inseparably inclusive in knowledge;
not all know this great secret.

We live in a paradoxical situation of the one and the many. When you become self-conscious, you think of yourself as one surrounded by many others. Whenever you find yourself in a new place, a new situation, or a new environment, the consciousness of the 'other' is very intense. The idea "I am different" further intensifies the strangeness of the other. You feel like defending yourself, protecting or shielding yourself, veiling yourself. The immediate impulse is to withdraw into a shell and peep out through a little hole, staying hidden as much as possible while you look for some possibility of establishing a connection or even a friendship with someone in that strange environment. If you see a kind face, a greeting smile, a hand that reaches out to you — it brings a ray of hope, and you can begin to build a bridge to that person.

There is nothing more reassuring than the possibility of establishing a newfound friendship. In order to make that bridge, you have to recognise something in the other person with which your own feelings can be identified. Out of the many others you separate the one entity that looks most favourable. When once you smile back, shake hands and speak, if you find in their words a pleasing tone or a helpful meaning, the strangeness fades and the likeness emerges. When more and more of the strangeness is shed and unity is established, you and that person stand out from the rest as one among many. You begin to speak of "we" instead of "I" and "you."

"Let us face this world together." "Let us do this." Within that 'us' you have courage, confidence, strength and ability. When your new friend introduces you to ten other people from the strange crowd, even though you don't know anything about them yet, you have great confidence and trust in your friend. Her word is enough for you to include them also with "us". Here the *artha*, the meaning, you have found in your friend can be extrapolated, expanded, and projected onto others. This is a case of the many being brought together in the one.

Now let's look at a different situation. Imagine you are sitting all by yourself in your own home. There is nothing to fear from outside, so your preoccupation turns inwards. As soon as you look into yourself, you are facing a strange crowd. You are no longer just a single person. The seemingly solid 'I' in you dissipates into many separate elements. Your memories walk around like ghosts, and your desires take centre stage one after the other. You evaluate each in turn, examining the encounters each desire has brought you in your life, to what extent you have nurtured them and how much of them remains unsatisfied, the frustration each has already brought you, and what further frustration you anticipate.

In this situation, the single you has become many. You are faced with many internal elements all standing by themselves. Each has its own definite meaning. In a way it's like a colony of meanings of a heterogeneous nature. But here again you look for unity within yourself, for how many of those elements have similar aspects which allow them to be lumped together.

The problem of the one and the many is lived in entirely different ways when you are placed in these two situations. In the first case you are the one and all the other entities constitute the many, and in the second the whole world remains outside as one entity while you are divided within yourself into so many fragmentary pieces. The problem is how a unity can be established within so that you can become part of that whole world, with no difference between you and the rest.

This problem has been dealt with in so many ways by philosophers throughout history. Zeno and Parmenides were two of the Greek philosophers who gave it great attention, and in Plato's *Republic,* Socrates considers the one in which many are implied. It is also taken up as a major subject in the Bhagavad Gita, in Chapters 9-11.

This may look like a simple verse, but there are many aspects to be considered. All the shades of emotion that we experience, ranging from total frustration and depression to the highest forms of ecstasy, can all be placed on a scale of values. Imagine a scale, with 1 to 100 representing the positive side and -1 to -100 representing the negative. You can arrange your values of life on this scale in a graded order. All the criteria of the gradation are elements of value, artha.

In one sense artha means meaning, in another it means wealth. These are not such different definitions. When properly considered, wealth is that which is appropriate in a situation as a meaningful entity. If a dying person is holding in her hand an award of a hundred million dollars, she probably wouldn't even bother to sign the check. Of what use is the money to her? She might as well throw it away. A sympathetic hand to hold would be of far greater value. So the meaning or value of a thing depends on many subjective as well as objective factors.

You should look at your life. See what pinches you, and what gives you a sense of elation. What makes you feel happy, satisfied, content? These are the meanings for you, and the sum of your meanings constitute your life. Take into consideration the joy of possessing good health, the joy of having a good reputation, the joy of having wealth or a powerful position, the joy of having supremacy over others, the joy of having good companionship with someone who has a deep understanding, the joy of having the pleasures of the senses being gratified, and so on. All these seem to be entirely different, but who enjoys them? The enjoyer is none other than the one who calls himself 'I'.

Do you have separate criteria to measure these different forms of joy? Why do you call them all joy, or happiness, in the first place? How can so many different things have the same happiness for their meaning? Narayana Guru says here that in the many *porul,* the many things, there is one meaning. Also, in one thing you can find many meanings. That means we have to learn how to go in both directions — from the one to the many and from the many to the one — interchanging the characters of both. This is very difficult, but Parmenides considered it to be the most satisfying discipline one can have, and the Gita agrees.

Jesus said, "Those who are not against me are with me," and "Those who are not with me are against me." In the first statement, what does "with me" mean? Does it refer to becoming one of the close disciples who are directly serving his cause? Or only someone not actively fighting him. The condition in the first case is only that the person is not opposed to him. For instance, I do not belong to any Christian church. If I say I am not against Jesus, in fact I love him, I can claim that I am with him because I do not hate him. But one of his Christian followers might turn around and say, "You're not with him! If you were, you would have been baptised. You should be working for some church. You obviously are not with him, so you are against him."

This kind of paradox makes it difficult for us to establish ourselves in unity. We want to be friends with all, but there are psychological factors operating like the poles of a magnet causing attraction and repulsion. When the attitudes of some people are repulsive to you everything about them becomes repulsive: the sound of their voice jars on your ears, seeing them causes you to turn away in disgust, even their body odour sickens you. When they want to interfere in your life until it becomes a nuisance, how can you say, "Okay, I still love you. Come on and interfere all you want." It puts you off.

You cannot put sugar and salt in the same bottle. You have to keep them separate. The piano has many keys; they are not all tuned to the same pitch. When there are such diversities in the world, how do you effect unity in your own life? This is one of the primary problems we face. You can be very friendly, but the other person doesn't feel friendly at all. What do you do about it? You are trying your best to convince him you love him, but he is already convinced you hate him, and so believes you are being hypocritical or that you have some sneaky plans to deceive or betray him. He is paranoiac about you. However much you try to make yourself available to him, he is always moving away from you. What can you do?

What do you do with your compass when the needle is being deflected by a nearby anomaly? Can you tie the needle to some fixed point? No, you cannot. You have to take the deflection into account and compensate for it. You have to accept the diversities of things and the reasons which make them diverse.

In the United States it is very common for men and women to come together with great attraction. They feel so much closeness, such oneness as no one else has ever experienced before — probably in all of history. With the same force they split apart and become antagonists. They cannot see eye to eye. They go off in opposite directions. Then after rushing away from each other, sometimes they can come back together after a few months and become great friends. They say, "Now we have found a level where we can meet. All that we thought previously was wrong. Our love was wrong. Our enmity was wrong. But our new friendship is right." These are the same people. How can there be two kinds of unity, with different bases and different meanings?

It all comes back to meaning. In one meaning these people were lovers, in another they were hating each other, and in another they were friends. So what is the basis for determining the true meaning? This is what Parmenides, Socrates, Vyāsa and Narayana Guru want us to examine.

In the *Republic,* hearing is compared with sight in this way. If I sit in my room while a friend is playing the piano out in the living room, I don't have to switch on the light in order to listen. The music just goes in my ear and straight into my mind and soul. But if someone else brings me one of their best paintings, I do have to have light to see it. No matter how beautiful the artwork may be, I still require a third element. I have my eyes to see with and the object to be admired, yet the painting itself cannot get inside me the way the music does. I have to have light also. And light doesn't come by itself, there has to be a bulb or candle burning, a fire blazing or a sun shining. Light comes from some other object. So, many things are involved before you can say "I see it. I appreciate it."

An equation is sometimes made of the eye as the sun of the soul and the sun as the soul of the world. Without the sun, we do not see the world. Without the eye we do not see what is illuminated. Sight is the principle of unity. There is a homogeneity between the world and us, into which we read our meanings. And what is that homogeneous element for everything — for beauty and ugliness, goodness and evil, truth and untruth, kindness and unkindness, and love and hatred? Only your knowledge is common in all these. As aspects of knowledge, they are all equal.

You should make yourself familiar with that knowledge of which everything is a part. When you say "I," "I know," "I am," do you have anything other than knowledge to form those different images? No. The images themselves bring about the differentiation; in a sense they *are* the differentiation. And what makes the differentiations perennial? We attach a tag to them, in the form of a nomenclature or title.

Name and form go together. Forms are perpetuated by the names which are given to them. Some names are even given without any form to attach to. The mind then has to make up some form as a mental image.

Where is the meaning in all this? The name suggests a form and the form suggests a name. If the experience of listening to a name and reviving a form clicks with a certain affectivity which is more or less consciously felt, and that affectivity points towards either the positive or negative side of your scale of values, it makes meaning for you.

The same thing may have different meanings for different people. That which disgusts me may delight you, and vice versa. There really is very little uniformity in it. Our understanding has a long history behind it, and there are a great many factors constituting the social setup to which each of us belongs. Our cultural values and aesthetic sense are probably very different, and all these lend their weight to our assessment of the meaning of things.

Just the other day I heard two people speaking about the laser beam weapons the British are currently experimenting with. One thought it was the most unpleasant thing to hear about — why should you speak of warfare? Can't you use your energy to speak of something wonderful? Why should we have warfare at all? Why should man kill man? The other was very excited about it. You don't have to go out on the battlefield. You sit in your room with your controls, and the computer plots the path of the enemy plane. You just press one button and the anti-aircraft guns destroy the plane. A foolproof defense! From his side, a mathematical achievement, a great wonder produced by human ingenuity. From the other's perspective, proof of human ignorance and stupidity. Who can say who is right and who is wrong? It depends on your point of view.

The three primary principles of our universe are pure existence, pure knowledge and supreme value. Out of existence you can make millions of existential situations, and out of knowledge you can invent millions of miracles, but these only have meaning when the third factor is brought in. Only then can we decide which are good and which are bad, which are adorable and which are repulsive.

If the supreme value you care for is that which unites everything for the simple reason of what it is — that is love. This love is not the libidinal force of which Freud speaks. It is not even the first pole of love and strife which are seen as two contending forces by Democritus. Probably the word "love" itself is wrong. It can be considered as that harmony which can be brought about by the synthesis of pairs of opposites, like love and strife. Opposites can fall in such a way that they strike a balance, out of which an overarching harmony emerges.

Like this, music comes from the juxtaposition of different tones and pitches, which by their very differences strike harmony. The harmony itself becomes the overriding reality of the music. So this uniting of opposites is not anything foreign to you, it's virtually instinctive. You don't put the contending forces of your life side by side as some kind of logical proposition to be brought to unity. It is more as a wholeness into which you plunge, into which you give yourself.

Look at our wonderful world, with so many various kinds of climates, wildlife and vegetation; and people of different cultures, histories and languages, filled with myths and legends of all sorts.

There are so many gifted writers, poets, storytellers, playwrights, actors, musicians, artists and philosophers, all full of wisdom and absurdity. Is it possible for you to pick out of this vast ensemble one person or one philosophy or one piece of music and say it is the best and is the only truth? Of course, fanatics do that, but if you are sensible you cannot. Yet, shouldn't we have some scheme to which all this can belong? One in which the vision of every philosopher can be true from his or her own perspective? Where the love of every person can be justified from where they stand, and where all experiences have their own small niche to which they belong?

Certainly we should. It requires a large-heartedness and broad-mindedness, a great empathy and compassion — not just to live and let live, but to have a positive attitude of appreciation and admiration. This wonderful plurality of expression which has come from one and the same source — the omnipresent mind or light, or the all-animating supreme principle — the moment you recognise your kinship with it, your fraternity with it, you are like the Indian devotee who sings "Siva is my father, Parvati is my mother, all these people are my brothers and sisters, and the three worlds are my home." You can excuse his ideogram of Siva and Parvati and just understand the principle of the one fatherhood, the one motherhood, the one brother- and sisterhood to which we all belong, treating the whole world as your home, your mother land.

Verse 74

poṭiyoru bhūvil asankhyamappotikkuḷ-
ppeṭumoru bhūvitinilla bhinnabhāvam
jaḍamamarunnatu pōle cittilum ci-
ttuṭaliluminnitinālitōrkkil ēkam

Innumerable particles of dust inhere in earth,
and there is no difference in the earth that constitutes the particles;
just as inert matter exists in consciousness, consciousness finds its expression
here in the body; therefore, when contemplated, this is one.

During the course of our lives we are confronted by innumerable problems. When we are hungry we want food, and when we are thirsty we want something to drink. There are a number of pressing necessities like these. We also take the time to think of problems that are not so immediate, but are at the same time more serious and fundamental. Some of us give our whole existence in dedication to the greater issues of life.

If we take a contemplative renunciate like the Buddha, a wise teacher like Krishna or Jesus Christ, a rishi like Yājñavalkya of the Brihadaranyaka Upanishad, or a guru like Narayana Guru, who has given these hundred verses of Self-instruction — one common feature is they all have an air of certitude about them. They are absolutely certain of the ground on which they stand. They are not conducting experiments. They are not eager to prove anything. They are all well-established in a light which is the Light of all lights, on a stable ground which lends its stability to everything.

Until you yourself find that light and stand on your own stable ground, some of the references given by the great teachers may not make much sense to you. In this particular verse there is reference to the ground and also to motes or particles of dust. The *bhū* is the ground, and the motes are the elements of existence. The totality of the particles makes up the substance of the earth or the universe.

Although Narayana Guru is speaking here of dust particles, you should take this metaphor to refer to the finitude that constitutes each moment of your life. The hands and legs you use for movement, the body that sustains you, the seat on which you sit, the person to whom you speak and the words you use, even the air you breathe — all these are motes of dust.

My finger is as much a part of me as my nose, though the function of each is different. At the same time they belong to a single body. Like that you and I are dust, motes belonging to a greater universal reality, a universal substance. The motes vary because of their attributes, while from a distant perspective they all appear to be very much alike.

The motes are perceivable. Sounds can be heard with the ears, sights seen with the eyes, and aromas smelled with the nose. We can also conceive smell, conceive sight and conceive touch. From the actual extension of things we can go to an ideal conceptualisation of them, where we are able to interrelate things with their attributes conceptually.

Like many dust particles making one clod of earth, we can put ideas together to make a world of ideas. By knowing many particles of dust we can build an edifice with them by piling brick upon brick, so to speak. We can also pile argument on top of argument to build up theories. But there is a limit beyond which we cannot go with our senses. The area where they operate has a boundary. The area where the mind operates is also limited. It has its frontier too.

So part of our experience lies in our sensory perception and part in our mental conception — thought processes, reasoning and so on. Beyond these frontiers is a greater reality which cannot be reached with the mind or the senses. When you look at it in this way, the ground seems far removed, obscure and unknown. But the fact that the ground is actually within the mote, within your sensations and your reasoning, shows it to be nearer than the near. This is why the Isavasya Upanishad says, "It is farther than the farthest and yet nearer than the nearest." It is the most external, yet nothing is more internal. What fills the inside and the outside is that reality alone.

We can see two major attributes of the ground. One is the extension in space and time of the many particular formations known as bodies or material objects. But there is also a knowledge in us which is not spatial or temporal. It can assume any form, conceive any space, and observe duration. It has form and is paradoxically formless, at the same time finite and infinite. The nearest we can come in thinking of it is in terms of consciousness, but it is a consciousness which remains unconscious as it evolves into motes or the modulations of consciousness Vedantins call modes.

In this verse Narayana Guru calls the world of extension where things can be perceived, *jaḍam*. The totality of consciousness in which all our experiences of extension are placed he calls *cit*. They are so intertwined that they cannot be separated.

There is a necessary complementarity between the world above, of information about the motes and their attributes, and the ground below, which sustains all of them. What is above as particles is finite and discernible, while the ground is infinite and indiscernible. Within the substance there is a vast scope of attributes, and the very discernibility of these attributes makes the ground indiscernible.

A search for the Absolute or the Self — call it the Real if you prefer — cannot take us to a vision of the whole if it is confined only to the attributes of the various motes. We can have many discussions and arguments, and can make individual experimental cases, but we have to remember we are only dealing with the motes, or the modes, not the underlying substance.

If a man truly believes in God, then, it would be ridiculous for him to look for proof of God's existence. Only one who does not know what God is needs reasons and argumentation to establish his existence. Once somebody asked Narayana Guru when and where he had learned everything. His answer was: "First everything came to me as one knowledge, and afterwards I found it is also written in books or discussed by people." This is how it happened to the Buddha, to Christ, to Yājñavalkya, to Muhammad, to all the sages.

If two lovers get into an argument and demand of each other that they define what love is, the poor creatures can't do it. They don't know what it is because it is outside the bounds of definition. One who loves is already in the state of being established in love. It is not anything to be spoken about or elaborated upon or argued over. It comes only as a spontaneous flow. When we listen to music there is no need to have the scale explained or for the beauty of the lyric to be pointed out. It is an inward experience into which we melt, a spontaneous symphony.

This is the *bhū*, of which the Guru says, "It has no differentiation within it." It is not divisible. When we cater to the necessities of life at a surface level, keeping ourselves busy with the motes, we must also keep our feet planted firmly on that stable ground. It's like a tree having its roots deep in the unknown, out of which its sustenance flows. The water and minerals and whatever the tree needs enter through this invisible network in precisely the way in which the tree can make use of them. Like that you should have your own roots in the ground of the Absolute, while the inner nourishment you receive, like the tree's, is kept well hidden from the public gaze.

In Jesus' life we can see alternating phases of his going to the multitude and then retiring to the mountaintop or walking alone on the shores of Galilee. Following this way one seeks orphanage in God, in the Absolute, by getting lost in the indiscernible, which is the mystical ground.

When a poet writes a poem, she has to give her mind away to the Unknown. At first there is silence, while the mind sinks deep. Then suddenly it becomes surcharged with a tremendous energy. Inspiration flows in as a great tide, and words bubble up, motes of dust from the ground of the Absolute. They can be placed one after another, so the poet writes them down. Once the poem is written it is in finite terms, yet that finitude holds within it the legacy of the infinite: the richness of the spirit from which it has come. Beauty, love, compassion, anguish — whatever constitutes life is encapsulated in those words, and to those who have a similar transparency of mind the words give up their secrets in communication.

If the poet is the *bhū*, the words she writes are the *poṭi*, the dust. If the artist is the *bhū*, every stroke of the brush is the *poṭi*. If the philosopher is the *bhū*, every idea expressed through him becomes a finite mote as it is brought forth. Poets all over the world get the same symbolic vision, the same allegoric language, inspiration of the same order. With the roots of their souls they touch the life-giving water of the spirit, expressing motes of wonder out of the Absolute substance.

When a great Guru speaks of unity, it's not a unity you arrive at through equations. Physicists know that all forms of matter are basically one energy, but that does not necessarily make them wise. What they have is only information about the theory of unity. If they were actually grounded in that unity, they would experience it differently. They would witness modulations arising out of the one substance, and the infinite becoming extended in terms of the finite, with consciousness assuming the modes of the extended forms. Through and through they would be experiencing the absolute togetherness of the dual aspects of the All. Then they would be what is known in Sanskrit as *viśvāmitra,* a friend of the world, or *vasiṣṭha,* one who dwells in all as a dear value, rather than mere academics.

When you sit in meditation and slowly absorb yourself into your own silence, the world disappears. Your own physical attributes disappear. In one sense you are gathering everything together into your own centre. At the same time you are extending yourself within your consciousness in an unbounded, limitless expansion. The next moment some need of the body or a social pressure can bring you back instantly to the world of name and form. Then your consciousness seems so small. It is a finite flickering within you, like a shimmering spark which is visible . . . not visible . . . experienced . . . not experienced . . . known . . . not known. The wonder that makes consciousness so expansive as to include everything, and so diminished it becomes less, even, than a faintly glowing spark, gives us an inkling of the ground to which we belong.

When you attend to the nearly infinite number of finite motes, each in its own way gives you an experience of pain or pleasure. When you attend to your own ground, it is a deeper experience than what you have on the surface. It is a serene joy. Within it you are self-contained. There is no duality of 'I' and the 'other'. It is like returning to one's real home. It is one's own beingness.

This is not a mere philosophical state. It is a very rich experience, full of love. There is an all-filling grace and benevolence permeating it. The Lord's Prayer says: "Thy kingdom come . . . on Earth as it is in Heaven." There is an actualisation or realisation of that prayer in this experience. It can truly be said all glory and power belong to it.

Verse 75

prakṛti jalam tanu phēnamāẓiyātmā-
vahamahamennalayunnatūrmmi jālam
akamalar ārnnaṟivokke muttu, tān tān
nukaruvatāmamṛtāyatiṅṅu nūnam

Nature is water, the body is form, the Self is the depth;
"I am, I am" — thus, a restless repetition like a series of waves;
every inner blossom of knowledge attained is a pearl;
indeed, whatever each finds delight in is the nectar of immortal bliss.

In the transactional world our main source of knowledge is through perception. We perceive with our senses, and thus get what we call direct experience. When you directly experience something, it leaves no doubt in your mind about the validity of its existence. You don't have to consult anyone. If you drink water, you know it is water; if you are eating something, it is up to you to decide whether it is tasty or not.

When it comes to higher knowledge — knowledge of the Self or the Absolute — the perception of the senses is not considered very competent to give you right knowledge. And since you have not experienced the Absolute or the Self in a way that you can recall, the method of inference is also not valid. Your only recourse is to turn to another person you believe has experienced it. But if another person is to pass on to you an experience which he has had, he cannot enter into you and give it to you directly. He can only describe it in various ways.

One method which is considered to be very effective for this kind of description is to give analogies. Isaac Newton wanted to prove there is a gravitational pull towards the earth. We can't see the pull, so he proved it with an analogy. He took an apple, left it in mid-air, and it fell to the ground. That we can easily visualise. Is it gravity? No, it is the fall of an apple. He said, "What you see as the fall of an apple is only an external thing. The principle implied in it is the attraction of gravity." Although we still don't understand it, now we feel as if we have.

The heart of an analogy is an a priori revelation through word-wisdom. When a Master or Guru opens up a great secret to a disciple, on his side is a belief that what he has attained is attainable by others. He sees the one Self in himself and in all which is the source of all knowledge and which lends its light in the form of reason in order for us to comprehend. He puts his trust in that Self. He sees his unity with others via the link of the Self, and thinks, "Because of this homogeneity, what I have experienced I can reveal to others, and they will understand it. They may also even get the same experience."

The place experiments have in a science lab is the same that analogies have in Vedanta, and to some extent in Christianity. Jesus Christ taught with parables, stories, ideograms and analogies. He gave a number of examples to make it clear what the Kingdom of God is. Sri Ramakrishna taught everything using simple stories, while Narayana Guru relies a great deal on analogies. One of Narayana Guru's favourite analogies is the ocean. There are so many ways to appreciate it.

Analogies of the ocean have called to poets, writers and adventurers throughout the ages. Maxim Gorky, the Russian writer, wrote a beautiful short story about a storm petrel, a kind of bird which is very fond of storms. In it he paints a wonderful picture of the sky becoming overcast, growing dark, the wind blowing harder and harder and the waves roaring and leaping to the sky. Then as the dark clouds close in, the lightning shoots out of them like great snakes spitting their venom into the sea, where the waves are lunging and churning.

The little bird wanted to fly when the wind and driving rain made it almost impossible. Gorky describes how he flew on and on into the raging storm. On one hand is the vast ocean, the tempestuous sky, the roaring waves and the menacing clouds. On the other is only the little bird, the one beautiful thing in all the vast, chaotic world. There is a terrific struggle, but at last the wind subsides, the clouds dissipate, the sea becomes calm and the sun again bathes the scene. Only then does the bird fly to land, as if it has won a victory over the ocean. All in all it is a very thrilling picture.

When you think of the ocean like that, it is full of wrath and cruelty. Death and destruction lie in its depths. If you taste it, it is salty, bitter. It is dangerously deep.

In *The Rime of the Ancient Mariner,* Coleridge describes another kind of sea with no wind at all. A boat lies in mid-ocean, with emptiness on all sides. There is nothing but hopelessness, frustration, the ghastly visage of death. There is no water to drink, though the boat is surrounded by "water, water, every where."

So the theme of the ocean has been used by many different authors to bring home ideas about the world in which we live and the nature of our life. When the ocean is treated as an analogy for the great misery one has to deal with in life, it is called *bhava-sāgara,* the ocean of becoming. It is an ocean of duality.

The same ocean can be looked upon as an ocean of awareness. You can sit on the beach on a moonlit night and look up into the clear sky full of shimmering stars and out to the silvery crowns of each wave, soaking up the rhythmical music of the pulsating ocean. Each wave comes to your very feet, leaves a line of white foam with a gentle lap, and then recedes. It is so rhythmic; you can always anticipate how far it will come up and how it will slip away again. As it goes it leaves behind endless sparkling bubbles of foam, shining like diamonds. The waves come and go, soothing the mind.

As you look into the infinite range of the ocean, your mind also becomes very expansive. As the waves roll in, your time sense becomes on one hand limited to the event of one wave turning into foam. The relation of the next wave to the previous one, and those to the one which has already changed into foam, is the essence of the content of time. On the other hand you are aware that before you were born, and even before human beings came to exist on this planet, the sea was there. The waves were coming and going even as they are now. And even when we are long gone, the sea will still be changing into waves. Thus, eternity is there. In the heart of eternity is a temporal sequence, and in the temporal sequence is pure duration. This gives us quite another idea of the ocean.

This kind of picture comes when we analogically look upon the ocean as an ocean of knowledge. One becomes contemplative in such an atmosphere. We see that the ocean has a surface and that there is also a depth to it. There is water at the surface, in the middle and at the bottom. It has no special feature of its own, but when we look at its depth it gains a great deal of meaning. As in our meditation on the last verse, there is a ground and also a surface where the modulations take place.

In the analogy of the present verse, nature is equated with water. Each tiny little bubble of the white foam, which is so well-rounded and glossy, looking bright and dark at the same time, while on the surface of it we see many colours, is like a monad. Its inside is also the outside, in the sense that all that it reflects comes from the outside but is seen to be inside it.

Like that, although we are within the world, each of us contains a universe structured out of our own constructs, our own percepts. Even when two people seem to have great love for each other, how often does one turn to the other and say, "I don't understand you." How could they understand? How does one bubble get inside another bubble? One foam cannot be another foam. The world is just what is mirrored from your position. A bubble placed over there and a bubble placed here are both mirroring the same world, but from their own unique perspectives. There are many kinds of spatial and temporal differences, while relative factors make some things clear and some things obscure. We shouldn't be surprised by any amount of confusion, only by how much agreement actually takes place.

In one sense we are in the world. In another sense we *are* the world, each one of us, at the level where we equate ourselves with a simple bubble in a mass of foam. One bubble and another are basically water. We are all of the same ocean. In the Self we are one. In the content of the Self we are one. Only in the various formations, the different motes, do we have differentiating attributes.

Each wave symbolises a certain movement of consciousness as "I. . . I . . . I . . . ." "I am listening to you," — that's one 'I'. "I appreciate what you say," — that's another aham. "I don't like it." Another aham. "Oh, I like it very much." Another aham. "It depresses me." Aham. "It hurts me." Aham. The 'I' and 'me' which come one after another are as endless as waves on the ocean, while at the same time each formation of the 'I' perishes in the very next moment, just as waves expend themselves on the shore.

The perishable is also imperishable. Each wave perishes but in its place another comes, so it is as if it never perishes. Aham, aham — I am, I am. The Guru says of this, *tūrmmi jālam.* One of the senses of the word jalam is magic. The formations of the aham or 'I' sense are like magic. At one moment the 'I' identifies itself with a happy state and laughs. At another time the same 'I' identifies with something terrible and weeps unconsoled with anguish.

The ocean has in its depths lustrous pearls, *muttu*. Those who delve into it get the pearls. Pearls are not gathered from the surface of the sea; for that attainment you have to verticalise yourself. The verticality of our Self promises us the pearl of life.

The wave cannot do anything to reach the depths of the ocean without losing itself. When you lose yourself it doesn't matter, you become the ocean, because you are in it and you are of it. The same particles which constitute a wave are now finding their individual descent to the very depths of the ocean. The ocean subsumes the wave. When you are not separated from the ocean, you are the whole.

Your minds are so conditioned by contracts! Life is taught to us to be like a contract: you give something and then you get something; you produce something and then you are given some time off; you sow and then you reap. But in higher nature you don't get what you sow — you are reaping what was sown by someone else and you are sowing for someone else to reap. The key is there is no difference between that someone and you if you have a verticalised vision. Only when you look at it horizontally is there a difference between one person and another. That's why you need to have a universal vision to understand the full import of this verse.

Next the Guru says that when the individuated consciousness turns inward it finds something like a honey-filled blossom. The honey isn't on the tip of the petals, it is kept hidden deep inside. Like that, in your own depth is a honey which is as precious as a rare pearl. This turning inward is a difficult process. In the Katha Upanishad is a wonderful section where the sage finds fault with the Creator for creating all the senses turned outwards, so that the interaction between the individuated 'I' consciousness and external objects becomes very strong, and turning inward is very difficult.

But if the wave sees that its fate is to become a perishing foam, this externality is not so very tempting. Knowing one's own self, as Socrates put it, becomes of greater importance. Then turning inward, which is all the Guru asks, brings you to the pearl. He adds that the knowledge which comes from this is like the elixir of immortality. Here you truly relate yourself with your ground. In the perishable you truly find the imperishable. Change and the changeless are nowhere held so closely together. This is not really anything which needs to be elaborated upon. It is for you to see and understand where and in what sense this is your nature.

Outside it is spring. We can review the past and think of the millions and millions of spring seasons that have come and enriched the world, all the flowers that have blossomed and fruits that were borne, and feel how we belong to that nature and it belongs to us. Once we too were flowers and fruits, we were little plants and big trees, butterflies, fish swimming in running brooks, birds winging through the sky. We are the essence of all that. In us the whole universe has lived so many times before. These thoughts should bring us to a great kinship with nature, a great sense of belonging. It is no wonder we feel inspired when we walk in the forest. It is as if we hear the silent voices of the trees communing with our spirits. Possibly they were once human beings like us, or else we were trees standing with them, side by side, our branches gently swaying together in the breeze.

Franz Kafka wrote a story imagining his life as a dog among other dogs. Try to picture how it would feel to be a dog, meeting other dogs on your rounds through the neighbourhood. Children can more easily imagine it, but it is hard for us. Kafka of course could. What a beautiful mind he had, that could so clearly see itself in so many unusual situations!

Kālidāsa had that same ability. When Śakuntalā was being adorned by her ashram sisters to be sent to her husband, they wanted to pick jasmine flowers to decorate her hair. But she said, "No, No! It's also time for the marriage of the jasmine with the mango tree. So please, don't take her flowers." When an ashram deer that was pregnant came and tugged at her sari, she turned and looked at it, patted it, and then asked Anasūya and Priyamvadā to take care of her when she brought forth her little one. Thus the jasmine, the deer and the human could all blend into one life. Such was the lucidity of Kālidāsa's mind. No line was drawn between the human, vegetative and animal worlds. All was to be for the good of all.

You get a meaningful picture of the ocean of samvit only when you make yourself lucid like that. You have to take away the rigidity of your individualisation, that brick into which you are baked and made so brittle. You have become a block, brazen, stony, dead. Nothing can get inside you any more. You cannot be lively. This kind of understanding needs so much inner flexibility. You should melt. You should flow. You should soar off on the wafting wind like a sprightly fairy, playing in it, singing songs of joy. You should chase the stars and dance on the moonbeams. Why not? Such is the beauty we have within us if we want to live it.

But we have become boorish. We sit with heavy head and heavier heart, waiting for someone to do something for us. And who is going to do anything? Even sitting there and fantasising is better than boredom, boordom.

Narayana Guru brings two things together when he says *aham aham ennalayunnatu*. There is an agony in going on holding tightly to this identity of the 'I' and 'I' and 'I'. The same 'I' can become a great enjoyer by reversing itself, by turning inward and diving to the vertical depth of the ocean. How? By allowing itself to perish. The block must die to free the life inside. From Jesus we have this priceless analogy: the grain that tries to save itself will perish, and that which gives itself to perish becomes greater a hundred fold. This living truth manifests in manifold forms.

I admire the secret of this analogy, not the contract of it. Many are caught by the contractual element in it: "Oh, if I give this, then you'll give me that. Great!" This is how the church has become a commercial enterprise. They only look at the contractual part of what Jesus said. "If you praise in secret, you will be rewarded in public."

"Is that so? Then I shall pray three times privately and let everyone know I was being good so that I'll be sure to get my reward in public." The stress is once again outside with the ego. What does it matter if others know or not, if you are sipping the honey within?

I hope all the limbs of the analogy are clear now. Nature is water, the foam is us, and the restless waves are the ego sense, "I am, I am." The honey that wells up within is the flower of your own heart, and the knowledge flooding in is the pearl. Your act of enjoying it is the experience of immortality. This is all put together in one verse.

One very important point to note in Narayana Guru's work is that unlike many other teachers he does not brush aside any instance of joy if you experience it, no matter if it is inside or outside, or in things which are trivial or serious. To him every enjoyment brings a vertical relation between the ground and the mote. You tend to forget that there is a vertical participation in it, but if you remember it every item of joy is a joy of the Absolute.

Verse 76

maṇal aḷavaṟṟu coriñña vāpiyinmē-
laṇiyaṇiyay alavīśiṭunnavaṇṇam
anṛta parampara vīśiyantarātmā-
vineyakamē bahurūpamākkiṭunnu

As countless grains of sand ceaselessly blown onto
the surface of a pond generate ripple after ripple,
by untruths successively blown,
the inner self is transformed from within into various
forms.

The word for truth in Sanskrit is *satyam*. It consists of three sounds, *sa, ta* and *ya*. *Sa* stands for truth and *ya* also stands for truth, while *ta* means untruth. Thus, in the very heart of truth, untruth resides. It is not effective, because it is surrounded by truth. Untruth sits in between like a thief caught between two policemen — he has to be good. But, from another perspective, in the very concept of truth is a fear that untruth may appear at any moment.

Our life is like a great marketplace where everyone is jostling and elbowing each other, vying to be in the forefront. First one idea comes and sits prominently in our mind. Then another one comes and pushes it out of its place so it can have precedence. Then a third comes and elbows its way in. There is this continuous pushing going on within us, not of truth but untruth. This kind of malfunctioning is called *anṛta*.

When truth becomes functional it is called *ṛtam*. Satyam is truth in principle, and ritam is truth in practice. When a guru and disciple sit together and chant, they say *satyam vadiṣyāmi ṛtam vadiṣyāmi*, "I take the pledge to speak the truth in principle and also to practice it." In this verse we are dealing with untruth in practice. The word *anṛtam* as used here means a falsifying method.

The second-century rishi Nāgārjuna put this proposition: "When you say 'fire', does it burn you? No, it doesn't. Then it is not fire. If it were fire, it would burn you." The word 'fire' does not have the effect of real fire. So why do we relate something that doesn't have the quality of fire to fire? When you say 'sugar' your mouth doesn't taste sweet, so why do we call that white powder a name that doesn't have any quality of sweetness to it? If the word is only an image, why should you go with that? Why not go to the original? If the word 'fire' is not fire because it does not burn, what is it? If the word 'sugar' is not sugar, what is it? The point is, an image is a very poor substitute for the truth of the original.

The words you speak, the words you hear and even the words you think control your life from morning to night. Even when you aren't speaking or listening, words are filling your mind in the form of thoughts, and those thoughts rule your mind. Your whole life has become filled with concepts that are only images. Those images have no qualities of their own which qualify them to be related to one thing more than any other. So you are living in a world that is false through and through.

Spinoza calls this the 'affects'. Descartes, Malabranche and Spinoza revived the idea of affects which had been a part of European philosophy since Plotinus in antiquity. Their theory is essentially the same as what Nāgārjuna put forward.

The various modes of the horizontal forces always affect us to some degree. Spinoza speaks of three main kinds of affects: pain, pleasure and desire; which in turn create effects such as love and hatred. In our discussion of the previous verse we were speaking of the ground and the modes, and here the reference is the same. The ground is Brahman, the Absolute, the Self, pure knowledge. It is the ultimate truth. The life we experience is a consciousness that is superimposed in the form of modes onto this basic truth. Within this superimposition, various changes come day after day.

Rousseau, in *Emile,* uses the analogy of seeds germinating and coming up as shoots. He notes that at first they come up very straight, but then they encounter horizontal winds. To stand up to the wind the shoots need an inner stamina, and they sometimes have to bend in such a way that the wind blows over them. If they lack this strength they have to lean over onto a supporting wall or another tree. Either way the trees which started out so straight become crooked, gnarled and bent.

Narayana Guru presents the idea of anrita or falsehood here through the analogy of windblown sands rippling the surface of a pond. Vedantins conceive of certain formations called vasanas, which were formed prior to the present life. The formations that are accumulating in this life are called samskaras. The falsehood that creates the samskaras is pictured here as windblown sand falling on the surface of a pond. In certain coastal areas of India there are sands as white as a desert of sugar. Here and there within them are neglected ponds. Wind is always blowing in from the sea, and each time it blows some sand rises up and flies into the ponds. The wind is gusty, so it swishes in different directions. The ripples swirl and clash. The surface of the pond cannot reflect the sky since its clarity is so disturbed by all this activity. Meditating on just such a scene surely suggested this analogy to the Guru.

You have to consider this analogy as representing the events in your daily life. You are at the mercy of the world in which you are placed; extraneous things over which you have no control are creeping into your mind from all sides. You are not any special being. You can't be a state within a state, you are just part of the whole. Your world is full of horizontal winds that affect your equanimity: the actions of people and what they say about you, natural events and disasters, good and bad news, radios, television and all manner of public media. There is more than enough to disturb you, wherever you are. This is all the sand blown in to bring chaos to the serene surface of your personal pond.

If it were only a surface phenomenon you could say it was essentially harmless, but there is more to it than that. Whatever has caused the disturbance settles in to clog up the water. After blowing horizontally, the sand falls vertically down into the very depths of your life. First it affects your surface consciousness, then the water where your thoughts, ideas and emotions are, and then it sinks to the very bottom. The bottom is what has already been formed in you as your samskaras or the reactions through which you have built up your personality traits, innate dispositions and consolidated memory. Though it is invisible, this terrain of the very bottom is affected from moment to moment by the detritus that sifts down from our conscious experience. You can never remain precisely the same. You are not totally changed, but something is happening. Each day you are subtly different. You are still carrying all the previous sediments of your life, but something has been added and the contour of the terrain has changed. It changes day by day.

If you take only this life and look at what has happened from your birth to the present, there are a number of memories you are not very happy with. Certain inner formations you are not very willing to own. Some people even feel guilty and ashamed about this. They are afraid they cannot hide their inner terrain from the public, and that society might reject them if others saw the kinds of formations they have. There comes a fear of rejection which can lead to pathological cases. This is a very sad state at the end of the process the Guru is describing. Is it possible for us to avoid it?

Philosophers like Spinoza say we are not in a privileged class, we are like everything else in the *natura naturata,* the nature that is being natured, in that we belong and are subjected to a greater law. Our minds are not under our control; we cannot stop the formation of samskaras. On the whole, Vedantins do not take such a pessimistic view. They are much more optimistic about how much we can accomplish.

The Buddhists have taken the position that falsehood is only of this moment. By disowning what is momentary and by further disowning the falsehood of what is impressed on them, they get over whatever evil it brings. When you speak of Buddhism, the important thing to remember is that you do not exist. There is no 'I', no 'I' at all, only this thing which is happening, this moment. They accept being and not-being. At the same time, the being is not-being and the not-being is being. One is to be cancelled out with the other. This brings them to what they call *śūnyatā,* emptiness. It requires a continuous process of rejection. Through this continuous refutation, Buddhists get over the problem of affectivity.

Vedantins treat the whole analogy, that is, the environment, the wind, the sand, the surface, the water and the terrain, as one phenomenal superimposition on the ground of the Absolute. Then they don't bother about it. They say, "We are not that." Are we not living in it? "Yes, when you are ignorant you are living in it. If you are not ignorant then you take for granted that these are the things that are happening in the world of maya, but you are not that." The Buddhist position is, "There is no 'we'. We are not." The Vedantin's position is "We are not that." But what about those of you who are sitting here who are neither Buddhists or Vedantins? Are you affected? Yes, you are.

According to Nāgārjuna, you are affected by the concepts of things. According to Spinoza, you are affected by the states of your mind, such as pain, pleasure and desire. Can you imagine a way of life in which you can free yourself from both the states of mind and the affectivity that comes from word-concepts and symbol-images? Buddha recommends vigilance, observation, contemplation, and the constant, continuous rejection of falsehood when you detect it, thereby disowning what you are not. Whether you are or are not, my advice is to let it be.

I just received a letter from a young man in India — two pages full of his miseries. He said that he lost his job and he has to look after his father and mother, three sisters and two brothers. There is no way for him to get food for all of them. This is *anṛta paramparā:* not just one anrita, but a whole hierarchy of them are operating on him. He wanted me to give him some advice by which he can get over this problem.

His parents did not consult him when they were making three daughters and two other sons, did they? So how does he become duty-bound to find provisions for all these people? He thinks he *should*. What he should really know is that the other people came from the same womb as he did, and it is for them to take care of their lives just as he takes care of his life. As it stands now, he takes care of his own life and has taken over from his father and mother the entire responsibility of looking after the other children as well. This is just one anritaṃ. Where does it come from? His society says he is the oldest son and it is his duty.

I could write a letter to him saying, "You have no such duty.

This is a self-imposed nonsense. The responsibility you have taken on does not really exist." Then the whole society will say I am no longer a guru to give such terrible advice and make people irresponsible. If you suffer and are miserable, the society is very happy: "Look. He is the right kind of brother and a proper son," because he is suffering for their sake. "We are all suffering, so let him also suffer," they think, and then they are happy because he is sharing their misery. No one, it seems, wants to share happiness, but there are plenty of people willing to sit down with you and cry.

This may sound very callous, as though there is no compassion in what I say, but in the name of compassion we so often suffer needlessly. If maya had only evils in her stock we would long ago have overcome them. But maya takes some higher value such as love, compassion, justice, goodness or morality, and interlaces it with all kinds of false notions and false identities. When they are so well woven together it makes such an enchanting garment that you can't throw it away. But it is the kind of garment that Medea gave her rival, which burns when it is put on. It looks so beautiful but when you wear it, it eats into your system. Maya makes this kind of robe for each one of us. You are compelled to put it on; society approves of it. Everyone says, "It's wonderful! Put it on." But once you put it on you cannot get out of it; it clings. So you suffer for your own dear father and dear mother, dear brothers and sisters, your dear neighbor. You think, "Yeah, I am doing great sacrifice." No, you are not doing any sacrifice. You are just foolish.

Does this sound okay to you? If you produce your own child and that child is helpless, then of course you are responsible to feed it and care for it and raise it to the point where it can care for itself. That's what animals and birds do. But humans invented words, which birds and animals don't have. Huge tomes full of words have been written to confuse people. Once you read these books, you look at your own life and start suffering because it doesn't match the ideals set down in them. Then you read another book and get more confused. A crow doesn't go to the library and study up on how to get through life. Wherever it sees something tasty it goes there and pecks at it. Then it makes a big noise for other crows also to come and eat. It doesn't leave anything for others, especially, but if there is enough they are welcome to share. We don't have even the simple common sense that the wild creatures do.

The Upanishadic rishis see this barrier of words as a beautiful mask. In the Isavasya Upanishad it says, "Oh Pūṣan, Great Nourisher, remove this golden disk so I may see truth. I am a *satyadharma,* one who has taken upon himself the dharma of living truthfully." It is a golden disk, and it is so beautiful that you become attached to it and no longer seek the truth lying just behind it. This is the most skillful way to hide truth.

So where is the place for compassion in this? There is a difference between love and attachment; love is called *premam* and attachment is called *rāga*. *Premam* is the recognition of your oneness with the Absolute, along with your oneness with everything else within the Absolute. The recognition of that homogeneity brings an inner harmony. You feel at one with all. It gives you freedom. It is not a limiting love, it is freeing. In it, all is for all. Raga, on the other hand, is a binding love. The idea of the 'all' disappears, and the love gets confined to a single entity, whether a person, family, group or tribe. This produces a burning passion: "Without this person I cannot live," or, "This is *my* country." This type of fixation that is often called love can be seen all around us.

What is in the other person that is lovable? And what is in you that loves? If you see the ground of it, it is the one Absolute. But that ground is now covered by sediments from the continuous dropping of dirt, or anrita. You have to dive very deep and break through the built up deposits to arrive at your original state. The surface of the pond is your consciousness, just into the water is the subconscious state, and the dark terrain you cannot see from the surface is where your incipient memories are lying. Beneath those incipient memories is your real ground. If you can reach that real ground you can see the higher values such as love, justice, compassion and truth in their most pristine and pure form.

Like the word 'fire' that represents fire but is not it, and the word 'sugar' which has nothing to do with sugar, the so-called love, so-called compassion, and all the other conceptual things we live in social life, are only false images. In themselves they have no value, but as they are false images you can use them to exploit each other.

They become an accumulation of trash in which you live blindly.

Some of the words used in this verse are very special. One is *anṛta paramparā*. It's not just one falsehood: by the time you discover a certain thing is false, another comes along with its own set of alluring dynamics. I know several boys who have come to me with a girl and said, "She is precious. This is the *real* girl, the incarnation of love. All virtues are hers." Then the same fellow comes back looking dejected — she is gone. But then he appears with another one: "Now finally I've got the real one! The other one was all wrong, but this one is right!" Then she is gone, and again some terrible nights. Then he finds another one. This is called *anṛta paramparā*. There's not just one falsehood, they are all lined up waiting their turn. When one is gone the next comes, and so on. Where is the end to it?

You always think the last was wrong but the next is right. When you are deceived, you make up your mind not to be deceived again, but you do not know how you are caught. Maya knows her business. It is not the first time she has done it. She has been doing it forever.

This verse gives us a very comprehensive picture of the affectivity and effectivity of maya. Maya is not total untruth, it is called *sadasad vilakṣaṇa*, real and unreal put together. With the real aspect it catches you. With the unreal aspect it betrays you. "My mother." Very real. Then that "my mother" wants you to live exactly as she wants and not as you do. Once you accept that she is your mother and you are willing to love her, she makes demand after demand. Whether it is mother or father or anyone, it doesn't matter who it is, the situation is the same.

Spinoza says that nothing can destroy itself; only something else can destroy it. Other things are always ready to offer destruction. One thing is destroyed by another. But it is always mutual — each wants to destroy. Ultimately everything is destroyed.

You can meditate on your own self as a wayside pond. You should be a very sacred reservoir of wisdom, but instead the way of the world is such that you are like a neglected pond, and every gust of wind from the public media, school, university, church or home is blowing into you and filling you up with garbage. See all the rubbish that has accumulated so far!

But it's not quite all rubbish. Here and there you will also find some precious stones amid the trash: a heap of rubbish, then a pearl; another heap of rubbish, but then a diamond. There are some people who are successful in burning away all the trash and gathering together their pearls and diamonds to make an inside which is rich and beautiful. You can work that way on yourself.

Verse 77

paramoru viṇṇu paranna śakti kāṟṟā-
maṟivanalan jalamakṣamindriyārttham
dharaṇiyitiṅṅaneyañcu tattvamāy ni-
nneriyumitinte rahasyamēkamākum

The one beyond is sky, the all-pervasive energy is wind,
knowledge is fire, senses are water, objects of interest
are earth: thus, as five principles,
this is ever blazing; the secret of this is one.

This verse is difficult to understand just by reading through it. One needs to meditate on it to gain a unitive picture of what is being presented. It is to be understood in the light of the traditional philosophy and psychology of not only Vedanta but most of the other Indian schools of thought as well.

The Sankhyan theory views this world as a binary function of spirit, purusha, and a creative function, prakriti. The duality implied in this is acceptable to some schools and not to others. We are mainly following the school of Vedanta, which does not accept duality. At the same time, we do experience it in our everyday life, and it needs to be explained properly. For this reason Vedantins tentatively accept the Sankhyan hypothesis for reconsideration, reevaluation and restatement.

In the Seventh Chapter of the Bhagavad Gita, prakriti or nature is said to consist of eight basic principles: earth, water, fire, air, ether, mind, intellect and ego. These are actually the evolutes of prakriti, which in the evaluation of Vedanta can be combined with purusha into one *puruṣottama*, a cosmic being or entity. Prakriti in its unexpanded form consists of sattva, rajas and tamas taken as a whole. These three gunas are primeval causes, and not the effects of anything. Then there are the five *tanmātras*, things-in-themselves, which are the prakritis of the five gross elements: earth, water, fire, air and ether.

In this verse Narayana Guru is presenting a global picture. He says the secret of the *tanmātras*, which are ever blazing as five principles, is unitive, is One. Although we can only translate *eriyum* as burning or blazing, it is to be understood in the same sense as in the expression "the sun is burning," in that it remains as an unexpended reality while continuously radiating its energy. The five principles are forever operating in just the same way. So the final meaning we derive from eriyum is "functioning". one principle is functioning as five aspects.

The one principle is not given any name here; the Guru just says *ekam,* one. This is to be taken as the ground. The vertical pole is *param,* the beyond. Between these two everything is placed.

The beyond is here termed *viṇṇu,* a special word which both can and cannot be translated as ether. It means the sky as one experiences it above as the beyond; it is the farthest you can look into space, where you get an idea of its infinitude. Contrasting with this, *ekam* is experienced as the existential ground, subsistential ground, value ground, and the ground of everything. Thus we have transcendence and immanence coexisting in one single principle. The beyond has the force of transcendence, and the One spoken of here inheres within it all the immanent principles as well as this transcendence. It is transcendent and not transcendent, immanent and not immanent, all at once.

How do we conceive of the transcendent and the immanent as one and the same? Immanence suggests a content which is pervasive. It can be viewed as consciousness, or the content of consciousness, or consciousness itself can be the quality of what is immanent. There is a togetherness, a sense of closeness — very much of an identification with it. When you say transcendence, on the other hand, your consciousness is pushed to the farthest point to which it can go, beyond which it recoils upon itself. You have no grasp of it.

"Is it that or not that?" is a question that cannot be answered. All you can say is "I do not know." But remember there is still a certitude in saying you don't know.

You have to somehow conceive of a totality and then subtract from it all you are aware of, not only that which you are consciously aware of but also that which you have the possibility of somehow knowing. The known and the knowable are put together and subtracted from a conceived totality. What is left is an indescribable state, called the transcendent. Here the transcendent is considered to be just one aspect of the unnameable One.

We have now marked a ground for us to sit and meditate upon, as well as the farthest limit. Narayana Guru says we should understand that *param*, the transcendent, is symbolised by *viṇṇu*, what you perceive as the farthest distance in the sky, beyond which you cannot think. When you mentally produce a height or distance where you approach a horizon beyond which it is meaningless to make any supposition, that is to be understood as *viṇṇu*.

We have to give a content to the immanent. The Guru says *paranna śakti kāṟṟām*. *Paranna* is that which spreads out, radiates, distributes itself horizontally. *Paranna śakti* is any force that distributes itself, any force that goes from one thing to another, or any energy that radiates, conducts, or propagates itself.

Up to now we have been using only our own consciousness to make images of the two concepts of the transcendent and the ground. There was no sense of function in them. In this verse Narayana Guru introduces functionality, which is important to take note of. In us also there is a witnessing consciousness and a functional aspect, and you should clearly observe these two aspects in yourself.

When you laugh or cry there is an unaffected consciousness within you that watches while you are having the experience. As you cry you may sometimes feel that it is nonsense, but you can't help it. It's almost as if somebody else is finding fault with you. That fault finding is not coming from the witnessing consciousness, which is perfectly neutral; the witnessing consciousness reports to some other faculty within you that in its turn becomes ashamed of what you are doing. If you want to control your laughter and find you cannot, you think "What a shame I can't even stop laughing!"

The central awareness that is persistent throughout these experiences is the consciousness with which you arrive at the notion of the ground and the transcendent beyond.

Anything that has content, anything that is functional, anything that has structure, form and name — all come under the term *śakti*. *Kattam*, air, corresponds to sakti. It is not just air, but air that moves, that is energised. The analogy of wind is used here. Wind has force in it, and that force gives it content.

Next, knowledge is equated with fire, *arivanalam*. The knowledge by which you know immanence, the knowledge by which you know transcendence, the knowledge by which you know force, and the knowledge by which you see all modifications — all these are symbolised by fire. Fire can be an unseen thermal energy that keeps things warm. You don't see any fire in your body, but it does have a measurable warmth which indicates fire is present. Fire can of course also be seen: as a candle burning, smoke smoldering, sparks flying, or even a big conflagration blazing. In a red-hot iron ball, the iron is not fire, but the thermal action taking place at the molecular level is. Like the fire which manifests in so many forms, knowledge manifests in many ways, from unconscious reflex actions to the most profound thoughts and the highest forms of meditative awareness. Its nature cannot be fixed.

Water here is used to symbolise the sense organs. Actually each sense is associated with a different one of the five elements: the organ of hearing with the sky, the organ of sight with fire, the organ of touch with wind and so on; but here all the sense organs are grouped under the perceptual function, which is compared with water. Water is traditionally looked upon as the symbol of the vital functions. Although vitality comes from prana and is therefore usually related to the air or wind, because of the moods, feelings and emotions associated with the senses it is here linked with the water element.

This makes more sense in the context of the comparison of the objects of the senses, *indriyārttham*, with earth. Earth is considered the object of the senses. Take an object of sense such as the pleasure of touching a body. When you touch, you don't need your eyes or ears for the experience. You can turn away from whatever you are touching and look within for its effect: you may have a feeling of pressure, or roughness or smoothness, and the feeling of liking or not liking it. There is a physical content to it as well as a psychological content. The senses themselves should have a homogeneity with the objects of interest.

Just as water and earth can easily mix to varying degrees, the participation between the senses and their objects occurs in a variety of ways. The vibrations that make up the form of music come to you, you don't have to reach for them. The ear just catches them. Music is like an electrical energy that flows to you effortlessly. Enjoying a good meal is very different in this regard, although it is equally an object of the senses. One just comes to you, the other you have to grapple with, so to speak. But in both there is a flow between the psychic aspect which enjoys and the physical equipment of the body which has to relate itself to the corresponding objects of sense. They flow together, becoming almost identical. Therefore water and earth are put together here.

So in these five principles we have the sense object, the sense interest, the experiencing of that interest, the knowledge of experiencing the interest, the energy by which all these can be spread out within the limits of the beyond, and the ground. This gives a total picture, with nothing left out of the scheme. Nothing is either rejected or given an exaggerated prominence. Life and all its experiences are accepted, and are put together in such a beautiful way that they all fit in. Knowing this integrated scheme brings you great peace by unifying all the seemingly disjunct experiences. You are in the transactional world simultaneously with being in the highest meditative state, since you understand that one is not opposed to the other.

On the battlefield Arjuna was asked to meditate on the Absolute and also to fight. Fighting on a battlefield is the most immediate activity possible in the transactional world, with swinging clubs, shooting arrows and ruthless killing all around. Meditating means to be in a state of beatitude, of transcendence. These two look absolutely contradictory, but there is no such paradox existing in the mind of one who has a unitive understanding.

Narayana Guru is giving us a scheme with the help of certain analogies. When you piece all the analogies together you get a unitive picture, at least schematically. That unitive picture can then be used as a base for meditation, and it can be lived.

The first thing to meditate on is the beyond, the farthest to which you can go. Then bring yourself to the ground. Now you have a whole field to experience. If you consider the whole field as the total reality of the one who experiences, without creating a duality between the experiencer and the experienced, you get the idea of the One. This can be apprehended by an ascending and descending movement of consciousness, which also spreads out in all directions. This automatically brings you to all the horizontal forces which operate to fill the field.

Now give it a nucleus as the knowledge that knows, both in general and in all the special applications. Give tools to that central consciousness by allowing it to animate the senses. 'The senses' here means action as well as perception. They need counterparts for the eyes to see, the hands to work, the legs to walk, the tongue to taste, the nose to smell and breathe, and the ears to hear. When you put all these counterparts together, nothing is left outside. It is one compact whole.

When you look at it in this way, you become humble. You are filled with reverence, with a sense of adoration for all this which is happening. Something that is more than a cosmic function is operating within you, a tiny individual. The individual transforms into the totality, and the totality becomes epitomised in the individual. Both of these are happening side by side. This gives a sense of unity, the idea of the One.

Verse 78

maraṇavumilla puṟappumilla vāẓvum
nara surar ādiyumilla nāmarūpam
maruvil amarnna marīcinīru pōl ni-
lporu poruḷām poruḷallitōrttiṭēṇam

There is no death, or birth, or existence;
man, gods and all such are name and form;
what exists is like the water of a mirage in the desert—
it does not exist; this should be remembered.

This verse can appear totally meaningless to those who are caught in the thick of life and who have many obligations to fulfil. It says right off there is no death, but everywhere we see things that are perishing. Dead leaves are falling; paint peels off the side of the house; people are dying. Decay and death are on all sides, but here it says there is no death. It adds that there is no birth. Death is a consequence of birth. It is an effect which comes to something that exists. If you claim there is no effect, then you should turn to the cause. You die because you are born. If there is neither cause or effect, there can be nothing in between. Because of this, Narayana Guru says there is no existence, either.

Why does he make such a summary dismissal of everything? In the previous verse we came to a unitive vision. In it all experiences were placed in the flux, in the phenomenal. In and through the changing flux, we were invited to have a look at the changeless. Now in this verse we are shown a vision from the viewpoint of one who sees the changeless. What seems to be here has only a transitory existence from this perspective.

The Guru likens this to the water seen in a mirage. In the desert people become more thirsty than they do anywhere else. Water is not just something beautiful and enjoyable; it takes priority, it becomes a necessity. That object of your desire may appear to be before you, but when you try to walk towards it to quench your thirst, it recedes. It always looks like it is within your reach, but you can never get to it. This is a very good metaphor for existence here also.

Narayana Guru takes a very uncompromising position. He says the mirage should not even be called existence, the term is misleading. The temptation that comes to someone who enters a spiritual path is to hold onto the desires of the mind while seeking realisation. He will make many rationalisations to justify the cravings, trying to cast them in a spiritual light. But there comes a point in life when you have to take a drastic step. If you don't take it yourself in a philosophic manner, eventually nature will provide the example of the inevitable termination of life when the body perishes, proving irrefutably that you cannot depend on any promise from the flux of becoming.

This is something I personally experience as one of the major issues of life. It comes up in people with whom I have been talking or writing to for some time. Unknowingly they try to adjust their life movements in such a way that they can be with me more, have long periods of association with me, or even have their life dedicated to a certain cause which I somehow represent to them. But the "certain cause" is imaginary — what they are drawn to is an actual person with whom they feel a sense of security. When they begin to plan like this, I see the absurdity of it. I am after all only a bubble that may burst at any moment. They will also burst, but they are thinking of permanent possibilities, one being that this man will live forever or at least as long as they want him to. They don't think that this bag of gas can blow at any time. When they start planning like that, I also start planning — to get rid of them.

Some of you may be thinking, "Nitya may get a permanent visa and be able to stay in Portland, so I think I'll also be in Portland." I might get a permanent visa for this country, but not for earthly life. That is not within the ability of any government official. Even if you promise to pay ten thousand dollars to an attorney, he won't be able to secure a visa for me to have a permanent stay on earth. In this light, all such plans become meaningless. You base your life on hypothesis after hypothesis, but once you realise they are all hypothetical and reality lies in some other direction, you have to make an about-face and a quick march.

Somewhere we have to part company. It's inevitable. If not today, then tomorrow. When it comes it can be very painful. The best thing is to part company now, and continue to sit together in the waiting room awhile. You have already said good-bye but you are still sitting here visiting. But you know it is all over, that very soon we will all get up and go our separate ways.

Nobody really wants to accept this truth. It is very unpleasant. You want things to go on as they are just a little bit longer. You can rationalise it for a long time. But sooner or later a day comes when you have to part with everything. That parting can be effected here and now, even when the body seems to exist, the person and the world seem to exist; or it can be postponed until it is forced upon you by the final dissolution of the body.

When someone goes to a guru and asks to be initiated into the life of a renunciate, the guru will try to persuade him to continue the pattern of life he has been living, because it is not easy to turn away from one set of beliefs to another which is the exact opposite of the beliefs embodied in the social contracts of this world. If he persists, however, he will be asked to prove that he can die. He should die when he is alive. How is this possible? Isn't it a crime to kill? Yet there is a way of killing someone without the police coming after you.

The seeker has a certain name, a certain hairstyle, a kind of clothing, that he likes. The guru says, "Shave your head. Remove your clothes. Now burn your hair and clothes. Let us consider this as your cremation." He is declared dead — dead to society. Then his name is changed. He might plead, "Can't I keep my hair?" "No, no, no, you have died! That 'my' is no longer there. When you died, along with that your 'I' and 'my' also died." When the hair is burned along with the clothes, the real smell of a human cremation comes. For five minutes it is horrible, because he experiences the smell of his own body burning. Then he is either cast into a pond or water is poured over him. He stands there stark naked, as he was when he came from his mother's womb. Then the guru gives him a piece of cloth and a begging bowl. This means he does not belong to any world of contracts. He is no longer to think of making his own living. He lives by whatever comes his way. In fact, he is not even living. Life is only a pretentious thing, so he doesn't have to be serious about it. All the seriousness of life is taken away with that one stroke.

Narayana Guru says it appears to be existence, but it is not. Like a mirage in a desert, it seems to be there but isn't. After realising this, one's existence is only that of a burned corpse. The example is given in Vedanta of a burned rope. The charred ashes of a rope still keep the shape of the strands, but as soon as you touch them the shape disintegrates. It still looks like a rope even after it has been burned up, but it crumbles to ashes as soon as you touch it. A sannyasin is like the burned rope: if you touch him he goes away. His existence is a very ephemeral one, as he does not believe he exists. "Was that death you had real?" "No, it was unreal." "The new birth you had, was that real?" "No, that was also unreal." "Your present existence?" "That is also unreal." Like that, the birth, existence and death of the world you see around you is also unreal.

If you doubt this, the sannyasin asks, "Just what is your proof there ever was a world?" "History books in the library." "What is in those books?" "Some pictures and some names." "What is Napoleon?" "A picture and a name." "Hitler?" "A picture and a name." "Stalin?" "A picture and a name." "Jesus?" "The same." In one sense they are all just words in a book. In another sense, did Christ die because he died? No. If he died, how is he influencing us even now? Did Buddha die because he died? No, he is still influencing people. What is it that persists, and what is it that is gone?

Our relativistic perceptions are mostly opposed to what is true, because of the conditioning of our minds. When you are sitting on a train it looks for all the world like the trees are running past you, even though you know it is the train that is running past them. Your train may be stationary, but if another train goes by or starts up next to you, you will think it is you who are moving. You feel everything very realistically — the acceleration, the jolt, the clacking of the wheels

— but you are actually just sitting still. Like that you are mentally conditioned to plans, schemes and adjustments. To break away from all that, to have this wholesale vision of truth and accept its decree, is most difficult, even for those who accept this philosophy.

I had a friend in Madras, a very good scholar in Theravada Buddhism. He was fully convinced that this world is only an aggregate of impressions, that there is really nobody, there is no world or anything, they're all just aggregates of impressions. He was constantly reminding us that nothing here is permanent, that everything conjoined will be disjoined, that anything that has come to be will pass away, that all this is transient. We had many such conversations over lunch. He was a very pleasant man, friendly and happy.

Then one day when I came to see him he was in bed. He looked very moody and morose. I asked him what had happened. He wouldn't even speak. He just beckoned me to come close. Then he pointed weakly to an envelope under his pillow. I pulled it out. It was an X-ray of his chest. There was a note attached saying that he had TB and they had found a perforation in his lungs.

All his philosophy had failed him at that moment. He knew in his mind that nothing was permanent and any moment he could go, but when the summons came he was bewildered. He couldn't even speak. Tears were running down his cheek. I said, "What is this, Swamiji? It's only a medical report. Aren't you the same person who was sitting here yesterday, joking and laughing? Why should a medical report bring so much pain to you? It's only words." But then he said, "Don't you see that mark on the X-ray? That's a perforation." I said, "There are so many perforations, Swamiji." But he wouldn't buck up. Despite his philosophy, when the actual call came he just couldn't accept it. Poor fellow, he died in a month or so, without ever regaining his equilibrium.

This reminds me of some Greek stories where the hero goes to the nether world and is warned to not look back at all cost. Because as soon as you look back, you lose heart. You become like a pillar of salt, with no strength any more. But it is very tempting to look back. All your sincerity in the spiritual search is put to the test at this point.

Before arriving at the hundredth verse, Narayana Guru wants us to accept this absolutist stand. He is saying, "This is my real position. Do you want to come with me or not? Either way, don't touch me. I am already a burned rope. My strands will all disappear as soon as you touch me."

Can you accept that this is only a momentary arrangement? Can you accept that this is all ephemeral, without any compromise? If you can, it takes away all your burdens. You know that all your struggles are only until you wake up.

When you are having a nightmare you can sometimes realise it is only a dream, and that all you need to be finished with it and have peace is to wake up. Peace usually doesn't come during the nightmare, but you can cultivate that also. When I am dreaming I know I am dreaming, but I also know it takes some time for me to get out of it. Like that, you will all wake up some day. It may be soon or it may be after a long time. The time factor has no relevance to the clock of the Absolute. The clock of the Absolute is like the one the White Rabbit has in *Alice in Wonderland*. It is blank. There is no time marked on it.

The Hindus, Buddhists and Jains have developed a theory which lets you live in this system called the world and yet mitigate, even minimise, the suffering. They think whatever pain or misery you are having is the paying back of the debts of your karma. When you believe that your previous karma has generated the present situation, and that the present is an inevitable condition of past karma, then you feel it is meant to be. It takes away all their sense of responsibility, because how could you act any differently than what your karma compels? It takes the load off. And how about correcting your karma? There is no hurry about it, because we may have four hundred million lives and this may be around the two hundred millionth. What's the rush? You can take care of it sometime during the next two hundred million lives. So this is a supposition that gives a lot of ease to their minds.

It is really a pity that the Semitic religions have decided that life is only for seventy or a hundred years. Whatever you want to do has to be done right now. Then you will be taken to the other side and be frozen, to sit there waiting in suspended animation for the Day of

Judgement. But they also have a device: if you say you believe in God, God will put your name on the right side of the book and your accounts will all be settled. Probably you will even get one of the best rooms when you go there. This is another supposition.

The Guru is asking you if you are willing to throw all these away as nonsense — your karma theory, your rebirth theory, your salvation theory, your saviour theory? "Oh, that's very difficult." If you find it to be difficult, you are not fit for this study. If you opt for it, you should make a summary dismissal of everything as phenomenal. Does it exist? Yes, it exists, in the way a mirage exists. It has just that much existence. It *seems* to be so.

Nobody stops you from looking at a mirage and making your own fantasies about it. All the great poets and writers have known this secret. But if you are taking this study seriously, you should first experience your death and then come to understand that birth and death are irrelevant. When Fritz Perls said: "To die and be born again is not an easy thing," he was right. To die to the conditionings, to die to the suppositions, to die to the fabrications of the theories and to remain beyond the transitoriness of everything, without a name or a form, without any promise and without anything to hold on to, is very difficult, but it is also inevitable. In the long run you don't have a choice.

There is another way of not accepting what the Guru is saying. You can stand with Sartre and say, "This is nauseating. This is it, but it makes me sick." This is terrible. You are just helpless, and your existence is just the recognition of your anguish. If you can express the misery of your life, the dread and helplessness of it — that's it! That's all there is. So which is better? Either you can be in Sartre's camp and say everything is dreadful and then vomit, or you can join Narayana Guru's philosophy and forget your name and form. In between there are no schools.

You can turn to any school — Taoist, Zen Buddhist, Mahayana, Christian, Muslim, Vedantic — wherever you go there is a magic circle. If you want to enter into any of them you have to deny everything else. Jesus was a very loving person, so you might say, "I'll be with him." Then he shows you his crown of thorns and his cross and says, "Deny *yourself,* first." "Who, me?" "Yeah. If you want to follow me."

In the previous verse Narayana Guru showed us the five aspects of the phenomenal world in which we place ourselves, so we know he is well aware of the nature and structure of that world. He also told us the secret of all these is One. To pass on to that oneness, you have to forfeit the reality of all the five factors. You have to forfeit what you call the great goal of life. You have to forfeit the world of action. You have to forfeit all the little impressions that you have gathered in the form of awareness or knowledge. You have to forfeit the world of percepts. You have to forfeit all the interests of life. Then alone do you come to the Absolute. That means you cease to be. You cease to be in the absolute sense, not in the relative sense. Absolutely, you were not, even previously. You continue to be what That was or what That alone is.

You come to this not through any argument in your mind. It comes as an act of recognition, factual recognition. Think of the day when a man's mother was fondling him in her lap as her child, thinking about his future. Now he is sitting here, and where is his mother? They are just like any two people. Is she now capable of putting him through any programme she likes, as she probably did when he was two years old? No. Things have their meaning and apparent consistency during small situations, and those situations pass on.

A small child wrote: "You are the apple and I am the seed. I will follow the ways of my mother through all my life." Is it true? That's what she thinks now. Did her mother follow her mother all through? Were they not also an apple and a seed?

When young lovers meet, they also whisper to each other, "We will never part. I give you all my love. You are my only one." Very good, if those promises can hold true for even one lifetime. But there is no way you can extend them to the next life.

You have to push aside everything relative. Afterwards you can again sit there, but you will feel all the difference. It is a bit like an ex-wife coming back as a good friend. You can be friends then because there is a lot of detachment after all the previous attachment. You will clearly know the difference between the two experiences. Like that, you ask the supreme Attorney to arrange for a separation from this world, from all this relativism, and to effect your divorce. Then afterwards you can come back and live as a friend to the world of relativism. That makes you an *asaṅga,* an unattached person.

Verses 79 & 80

janisamayam sthitiyilla janmiyanya-
kṣaṇamatil illitirippateprakāram?
hananavuminnane tanneyākayālē
jananavumillitu citprabhāvamellām

sthiti gati pōle virōdhiyāya sṛṣṭi-
sthiti layamennoru dikkil ottu vāẓum?
gatiyiva mūnninumennumillitōrttāl
kṣiti mutalāyava gīru mātramākum

At the time of birth there is no existence; the one who is born
is not in another moment; how can such a state be?
Death is also like this, and there is no birth;
everything is of the power of pure consciousness.

Like rest and motion, how can contraries such as creation,
existence and dissolution coexist in one place?
There is no validity for these three anywhere; when this is considered,
earth and such are mere words.

We are presented with the day-to-day business of living our lives as a matter of necessity. From the first waking moment until we fall asleep, our day is filled with several activities which are physical or mental or both. They occur mostly in an action-reaction pattern. In order to act, you need to know what you are expected to do. There are impulses and urges coming to you all the time as compulsions to stimulate reactions. You can just react compulsively, or you can temper and control your actions to behave in a more calculated way. This is the horizontal perspective of life.

There is another way of looking at life, not merely viewing it from waking to sleeping, but as a series of days extending from birth to death. This gives a vertical perspective. When you take the vertical view, the emphasis is not on necessity but on the achievement of values which are considered to be desirable, values which lead to the highest good, the highest beauty, the highest truth. Compared to that, whatever you do on a daily basis is only incidental to the main pursuit of life, which is realisation, either as it is philosophically conceived or just generally felt within as a sense of the purposiveness of life.

For both these kinds of perspectives, the horizontal and the vertical, there is a need to be certain of whatever knowledge you have. Our lives are regulated by knowledge. When you turn to your daily affairs, the faculties you use to determine the validity of things are your senses of perception. You see, you hear, you touch, smell and taste. Those are your sensory data. Apart from that you have another faculty in the reasoning mind. The senses and the mind are put together to make a tool with which to conduct your life.

When you use your sense organs to decide the validity of something, you often find they are defective. They are not always giving you accurate versions of truth. You don't see everything presented before you, or hear every sound that falls in your ears. You don't want to taste everything. So you make a limited use of the capacity of your senses, selecting only what is pertinent and disregarding the rest. Who decides what is included and what is left out? The limitation comes from an unknown source. Furthermore, the very structure of the senses is such that sounds fade out beyond a certain distance, and sights become too small to see. The structure of our earth as a globe insures you can only see objects within the horizon. So even beyond your own selectivity there is another factor which limits your sensory apparatus.

Henri Bergson says that we pull our shutters against whatever it is inconvenient for us to see or against things that are not relevant to our own interests. The interest need not always be a favourable one. Fear is as strong an interest as love; pleasure seeking and pain have an equal impact on us. We can be attracted to both. Bergson asserts that we know by disassociating ourselves as well as by associating ourselves with the many elements of our interest. Either way there is a narrowing of our sensibilities in relation to our selective interest in the external world. We circumscribe our outlook by using only limited aspects of our senses at any time.

Philosophic people seek to move away from the quantitative enumeration of things by the senses to qualitative generalisations of the properties of things. The thing in itself is not what they look for, but rather the property of the thing which can be abstracted and then conceptualised. In this process the reasoning mind is given priority over the sensory function, meaning they prefer to philosophise rather than to live a more or less direct sensory experience. Although living comes prior to philosophy, it is made more comfortable, more feasible and more convenient by resorting to a series of rationalisations or philosophisings about whatever comes along.

This strain of thought began in the West with the Eleatic school to which Zeno belonged. To Zeno, reason was more acceptable than mere sensory evidence, because of the fact that you cannot simultaneously see everything. Also, if someone makes a loud noise from a distance, you see him make it before you actually hear it. The sight and sound are not coordinated. There are many such kinds of incongruities between the senses. You can only effect their coordination by putting them together logically. If you know that light travels at one speed and sound travels at another, taking longer to cover the same distance, you can mathematically conclude that when he was moving his lips he was also shouting, even though you heard him much later. The coordination of things can be ascertained in this way. We always use logic to explain what the senses cannot determine with clarity.

This idea was taken almost to absurdity by Zeno in his famous paradoxes. Narayana Guru is referring to the same thing in these two verses. These paradoxes come up when you look at things in terms of logical feasibility. In verse 79 he asks, "At the instant of birth you cannot say there is existence, and the one born is not in another moment. How can this be true?" Birth means something emerging out of nothing. *Sthiti* refers to a state where there is no range in time or space; motion means not remaining in the same place at the same time. These are basic concepts, but they are at loggerheads.

Zeno gives the example of someone shooting an arrow from point *A* to target X, asking if it is possible to shoot the arrow from A and strike X. He says, "No, it is impossible, because an arrow cannot move and be where it is not, and if you take it only at the point where it is, it is not moving. Either the arrow is where it is, or where it is not. Where it is it does not move, and where it is not it cannot move. Since it cannot be both where it is and where it is not at the same time, the arrow doesn't move." But the eye says it moves, and sees it strike the target. What about that? He says, "That may be true. You have so many illusions — this is another illusion. Logically, it is not possible."

Another famous paradox of Zeno is about the race between Achilles and a tortoise. Before the race the tortoise said, "Look here. I am a poor creature, well-known for my slow movement. Allow me a five minute head start on Achilles. He is a big marathon champion."

That was granted him. In five minutes the tortoise went a little distance. Then Achilles was given the signal to start. Zeno asks if he will be able to catch the tortoise? Everyone knows it is possible, but he didn't agree. He said it is not possible, because when Achilles covers half the distance between the start and the tortoise, doesn't half the distance still remain? And then when he covers half of that, isn't another half still before him? So no matter how fast he runs there will always be half of some distance yet to go, and Achilles will not be able to catch the tortoise.

What is the matter with this reasoning? Bertrand Russell took at least twenty pages to prove how it is wrong, and still no one was convinced, even Russell himself. But there is no need to argue about it. Narayana Guru says *cit prabhāvam ellām:* our consciousness is so structured that it can present through the senses a certain quantitative picture of dimensions, such as measurement, colour, form and gross attributes. Our logic can reduce those quantitative aspects into qualities and more subtle attributes, which then get another kind of structuring in terms of subject/predicate.

So ultimately no one can say what is right. We can only say the senses that perceive are also using consciousness. The mind that reasons is also using consciousness. The linear way of thinking is also consciousness. The dialectical way of thinking is also consciousness. In spite of the many similarities and contradictions we see, we know they are all within the field of consciousness. You only struggle because you want to look at parts taken away from the whole. If you see each as an integrated part of the whole you won't have this problem.

You have only to recognise that this is a wonder, this is a *cit prabhāvam.* You are unnecessarily kicking up the dust of skepticism, going from one possibility to the next and forgetting the issue at hand. The issue at hand is how to be happy, how to be at one with the totality of the situation with which you are presented. You keep forgetting that and getting sidetracked into the unnecessary fields of logic and philosophy. That's why Buddha didn't want to discuss them at all. He said, "If you are struck by a poisonous arrow and somebody comes along to pull it out, do you want to know the distance the arrow was shot from, what caste the man was who shot you, what metal alloy comprised the arrow's tip, and what specific type of poison it was dipped in?" Hardly. You just want it pulled out so you don't have to struggle any more.

You get sidetracked in your search either in the name of philosophy or by the actuality of the immediate pragmatic possibilities. You err on both sides, either looking at abstractions of things theoretically or rejecting the philosophic approach to seek immediate validation through an interaction with the world of concrete actuality. By examining relative points in isolation, you ignore both the concomitant factors that caused those situations to emerge as well as how they interrelate with the total nature of things. Because of this, when you try to correct one thing, three other problems crop up.

There is a story told of when the Moguls left India and the British took over. The British were delighted at all the valuable things which had been left behind, such as the Koh-i-noor diamond, which they sent to the British king for his crown. They took possession of the Taj Mahal. At that time it had a beautiful fountain that was continuously flowing, but the new occupiers couldn't find a source of water or even any pipe connection for it. They decided to dig up some bricks and have a look, thinking they could be easily replaced. When they pulled them out the fountain suddenly stopped. They couldn't find anything there, and they couldn't see how it worked. Even when they replaced the bricks the water didn't come back.

Like that, you tamper with your life, not knowing the full secret, and make a mess of it. You can make a mess on the side of the necessary aspects of life, or on the side of philosophic abstractions by clouding your intellect with more and more conceptualisations. Many writers and teachers have dealt with this same issue, but the greatest summation I have found is in the Bhagavad Gita, Chapter 2, Verse 29:

> A certain person sees This as a wonder, likewise another speaks about This as a wonder. Another hears of It even as a wonder, but even hearing no one understands This at all.

Narayana Guru says about this *cit prabhāvam ellām.* Understanding this concept is very important. The Absolute is defined as *sat-cit-ānanda*, existence-awareness-value. You can think of it as the existence of a value in terms of pure awareness, or you can say it is the awareness of the existence of the value, or you can say it is the value of an awareness which exists. It's all up to you; you have your own choice in structuring the meaning. But you cannot take away any one of the three elements. A value that doesn't exist cannot be a value. A value which you do not know is not a value. A knowledge which has no value — you don't want to know it.

In order to balance existence and value, *cit* has been put in between. Why? A value can exist and yet not be known to you. Until you know it exists it is not appreciated. So value and existence come together only when they are connected by awareness, or *cit*. The awareness spoken of here — is it an awareness of things? That is one special modality of it. We were speaking before of a ground and the various modes. *Cit* is the ground. The substance of that ground has the possibility of giving rise to a series of graded forms of knowledge, ranging from a total negation of the subject/object duality through all the subject/object distinctions. If there is no duality, then the subject cannot make anything else the object of its inquiry.

This means you virtually know nothing. That's the ground. From there you can come to a stage where there is subjectivity and the subject has ideations. Then it can extend all the way to the gross level where there is a clear distinction between subject and object. At this point the subject and object can be interrelated like compact, organised blocks.

From a mere ground on which you cannot predicate anything, you pass on to several distinctive possibilities. This is the horizontalisation of a vertical principle. When the vertical principle of pure consciousness, *cit*, gives room for horizontality, it is called *caitanya*, and when it is fully horizontalised as an individual being with body consciousness, feeling and sensibilities, it is called *cetana*.

So the *cit* undergoes great elaborations of its own powers, and when this is taken in its totality it is called *cit prabhāvam*. If you examine any aspect of what is presented in consciousness it will show within it contradictions like existence and nonexistence. The Guru says if you recognise that it is in such a wonderful way that this has come into being, then there is nothing to worry about. There is no problem.

I once visited a friend's home in Delhi. He had a small dog. It was only a little bigger than a squirrel, but it barked like hell. I thought of showing my love to it, so when it came close I patted its head. It bit my fingers! Then my friend said, "I am so sorry! I should have told you that he can be fondled, picked up, caught by his tail, taken by his legs, put in your lap. He does all those things. But he doesn't like to be touched on his head."

Once you know that, you have no more hatred for that dog. You just leave his head alone. But if you don't know it you think, "How can you keep a pet which bites you? It's a contradiction — a pet that bites. That's not a pet at all!" You can be reconciled to it once you know it acts like a pet as long as you don't touch its head. The contradiction even becomes amusing once you know it. Then you understand it is just the miraculous way in which this particular dog is made.

If you know this kind of information about your wife or husband, your child or your neighbour, you won't have trouble. You need to know where you shouldn't touch them. For instance, my grandmother was a very willful, strong woman who could stand anything, but we couldn't say "muslin" in front of her. When she heard that particular word she would get nauseated and feel like vomiting. It seems she was once given some muslin cloth, and the day she was given it she had some sickness. The illness became psychologically associated with the sound "muslin". So if we wanted to provoke her we would just say "muslin" and she would behave in a funny way. She shouldn't have — it's only a word. But after all, as Narayana Guru says, all that you think and believe is only words.

"Jesus Christ" — isn't that just two words? Have you ever seen him? No, you've just heard those words. The word 'Christ' was told to you, and now you love it and accept it. You have seen light and life in it, consolation in it. It's only a word, but saying that doesn't take away any of its psychodynamics. All that power still remains. If you whisper in someone's ear that you love them, it gives them a feeling of elation. If you whisper you hate them it can make them miserable. Some people smile outwardly, but inside they are repeating the negative mantra "I hate you," over and over. Words can have tremendous power, so you should use them carefully.

In verse 80 Narayana Guru brings up the psychodynamics of words. Before that, in verse 79, he tells us that everything is the miraculous power of pure consciousness, so there can be contradictions like birth and death seemingly coexisting in the same situation, even though logically you can't die and be born at the same time. If we take the modern physicists' word, it does happen. In *The Tao of Physics,* Fritjof Capra says there is a continuous emergence of subatomic particles from pure nothingness, and that this matter returns to nothingness when it is devoured by anti-matter. Then what exists ceases to exist, not just in the form of a transformation, but totally. So there is a total emergence out of nothing and a total remergence into nothing. Only in between do things *appear* to exist. He even says that you can't believe that, either. He has given the names of twenty subatomic particles and says that when one strikes against another they both change their nature and become something else. All this is possible in the world of subatomic particles. Once you accept it, the physicist can go to sleep. He thinks he has settled the issue, explaining that whenever these two things bump together they change into these two others. How? "Don't ask us how. We are just describing what happens." Why? "We don't know." You see, it's still a wonder.

In verse 80 the Guru says: "Like rest and motion, how can contraries like creation, existence and dissolution coexist in one place?" This is the same as Zeno's question. He goes on: "There is no validity for these three anywhere; when this is considered, earth and such are mere words." Here he calls earth *kṣiti,* elsewhere it is called *dhara*. These words are very important. They both refer to the earth, but have significantly different meanings. *Dhara* is that which retains, that which protects, contains, holds, supports. *Kṣiti* means that which decays, degenerates and dissipates.

Earth becomes the supporting principle, *dhara,* when you understand that everything emerges from it. Then the earth as *kṣiti* dissolves everything back into itself. If you bury a corpse and then look for it after some time, all you will find are bones. After some more time, they too will have become part of the earth. It has that power to make you decay, decompose, change and transform.

It is not the earth specifically which is under reference here, but the meaning we assign to words like earth. We do not know earth. We do not know anything.

We are fed on this food of reason, with words. We live and thrive on words. If we are unhappy, we go home and read some words. In America you pull out the I Ching, throw the coins, and look up your hexagram. If you don't like what it says, you throw your coins again. You are seeking consolation in the words. If they are not consoling, you try again. Or you might take the Bible and read a portion. But then you might come to a section where it says God became very angry and cursed. So you close that up and look for your Gita or call your best friend, who maybe is sitting there with a sore throat after a fight with her husband, so she puts all her blues on you.

You live in a world of words, and you consume words. It's not always bad. The other aspect of words is that they do console, otherwise you wouldn't go for them. A word can be a *dhara* when it consoles you and a *kṣiti* when it brings you misfortune. The essence is they both are words.

We are taking these two verses together because they deal with one picture of the world. It begins with the wonder of *caitanya,* which projects from the vertical into the horizontal, becomes fully horizontalised and truncated, and finally reaches its maximum extension, beyond which it cannot go. Then it perishes and returns to the vertical. This recycling is going on all the time.

You are again and again absorbed into pure consciousness. It happens every day. You wake into the world and perform many actions. After sometime the limbs become tired; you can't exact any more work from them. The mind becomes fuzzy and the eyes begin to droop. So you give up and go to sleep. There you are recycled, only to come back again fresh for another attack.

The secret Narayana Guru gives here is that on one side you should understand this is *cit prabhāvam,* this is the glory of that supreme consciousness out of which everything evolves, and on the other you should know that what irritates you and what delights you are just words. When you know you should not touch the head of the queer dog of idiosyncrasy, you know how to deal with the situation.

Once I became very annoyed with the position taken by my Guru in favour of a fellow disciple. I thought it was unjust, and that he was not seeing my goodness. Self-pity pushed me to the point where I decided to break away. I packed all my things into a parcel and put it on top of my head. When I came out Guru said, "Don't go away." I replied, "No, I should go." He said, "Madmen are not allowed to wander in the street." "But I am not mad!" "That's not for you to decide. It's for the doctor to decide whether the patient is mad or not. I am the doctor. It is not for the defendant but the judge to decide innocence. I am the judge." "You are neither the judge or the doctor, and I am going away!" "This is what all mad people say. I am a circus manager. I cannot let leopards and tigers loose in the road — I have to keep them in their cages."

I thought, "What a terrible man." In a fury I repeated, "I am going!" He said, "You can go, but you cannot steal my things and leave this Gurukula. I know that parcel contains many of my valuable things. I want the police to verify it before you leave." I pushed the bundle at him and said, "Take it!" I thought he would give it back, but he didn't. He just took it inside. When I went out he came to me and held my hand. He asked, "You are definitely going?" I said, "Yes." He said, "As your teacher I should punish you for this misbehaviour. So I am going to give you three slaps." I said, "Go ahead!" He slapped me twice on one cheek and once on the other. Then he said, "I slapped you so that nobody would slap you. And I want to give you one parting teaching." I cooled down and looked at him.

He said, "Remember *alapamātramakhilam*. This is Narayana Guru's word. Remember it. All that you hear is the vibration in the air. You are assigning meaning to it, and it is that meaning which disturbs you. All the words that you heard are only these vibrations in the air, mere words. You should never be offended by vibrations of sound. Keep this in your mind. It will save you for the rest of your life. You can come back whenever you want." I still walked away since my mind had been made up, but this started ringing in my mind, *alapamātramakhilam*. The vibration of that word has not left me even these many years later. When something upsets me, I always think of that.

There is a mantra contained in this verse, *gīru mātram ākum,* meaning it's only an articulated word. The whole edifice of life is built with the bricks of words. Universities are nothing more than places to cater these bricks and structures of words to you. You live in a house of words gathered from your teachers, your priest, your books, your friends, along with those of your own fabrication. If you really know this you are already saved.

In these two verses the Guru gives us two great mantras: *cit prabhāvam ellām* and *gīru mātram ākum,* everything is the wonder of consciousness and everything is only a vibration of a word. These should be enough to bring you total peace.

Verse 81

prakṛti piriññorukūṛu bhōktṛ rūpam
sakalavumāy veḷiyē samullasikkum
ihaparamamoru kūṛidantayālē
vikasitamāmitu bhōgyaviśvamākum

Prakṛti divides: on one side is the agent of enjoyment;
on the other, whatever shines outside
as the here and the beyond, as an expansion of thisness,
is the world of enjoyment.

In verse 79 Narayana Guru brought us to the conclusion that everything is an aspect or expression of supreme consciousness, *cit prabhāvam ellām*. In verse 80 he gave us another aspect, that everything we experience is only a word, *gīru mātram ākum*. In the present verse we are brought closer to these two aspects, the consciousness that holds within it everything experienced, and the world to which designations are given, in which things are known by name. There cannot be two separate truths. Both these belong to the world of experience and whenever we think of the word 'experience' we have to also think of an experiencer as well as what is experienced.

This verse takes us to the very core of our personal existence. Personal existence may at first look like a consciousness shining within a body, but that is a shallow understanding.

I do not know what others experience. Even when somebody describes their experience to me in detail, I can understand it only in the light of my own experience. When I hear something for the first time, I create a novel situation with newly structured concepts based solely on memories of my previous experiences. Although it looks new, the stuff of it comes directly from my own experience.

When we are confronted by a situation that is altogether new, however, we do not have any alternative other than to give into it. Before we are able to process the situation into our memory of previous experiences, there is a moment when it fills our whole awareness. It stands there like an all-encompassing wall. We do not immediately see any way to surmount it, because its bottom goes to the very bottom of our consciousness and its top to the very top. Its ends are beyond our reach. It becomes a This with a capital 'T'.

That 'This' is not "out there" as an impassive truth. We are intimately related to it because it concerns us, it challenges us. We cannot overlook it or forget it even for a split second. It fills every pore of our consciousness. It is not a thing, not just an event. It is a total This.

This great wall or confronting reality or undeniable existence does not appear as a historical consequence of anything else. It looks as if we are confronted with an otherness which has its base in the primeval reality. It extends to the boundless, unending future. It defies historicity by defying our categorisation of it using our memories of previous experience.

In this experience we are transformed from a miniature 'I' to an 'I' which is boundless. It is as if we are also beginningless and endless, capable of responding to the challenge in its totality. When we come to this state, the transformation of a particular 'I' with a dimension of finitude into this infinite 'I' is directly connected with the 'other'. In this particular case the personal 'I' transcends several of its limitations, such as age, name, sex, nationality and so on. All these are irrelevant little details of the modulation of 'I'. None of them now appear as the essential 'I'. The essential 'I' here establishes iself in the transcendent. The transcendent merges in to the immanent. The transcendence of this 'I' is given to it by the existential verity of the experience, which we naturally expect to come from the 'other'.

But these two aspects, the 'I' and the 'other', are related in one single consciousness, the consciousness we experience as the universal reality. The natural law that operates gives integrity to the 'I' consciousnesss as the respondent. That same law can necessitate the 'other' to hold itself together, to give itself substantiality as the correspondent. The same nature provides the 'I' consciousness with its faculty to reason, to feel, to recognise, to doubt, to fear, to enjoy, and also to make devices to overcome fear, to moderate enjoyment, to push forward and do or to restrain. The point is that there are not two separate laws, only a universal situation that we have split in two.

Some philosophers speak of human laws in opposition to natural laws. When we tear ourselves away from the notion of man-made or legislated laws, the discrepancies or the make-believes that are part of the 'other' become quite transparent, and we can see right through them. If these protected pretenses of a society cause an impasse in a situation — which they very often do — it is also to be taken as a part of nature's function. It is in no way an invalidation of nature's law. We need to notice how in nature there is flourishing forth, followed by disintegration and disorientation. This can happen to the individual human mind, as well as to the social mind to which several individual minds contribute. There you stand helpless, like the tree stands naked in winter. When its leaves start falling off, it has no way to resist. It can only accept. Likewise at a certain stage the human body degenerates, reason fades, emotions override and senility sets in. We have to stand and accept it also as part of the game of transformation.

When you truly grasp this you are left with an inside story of experience. You are no longer an individual who is planted deep into a system along with many other individuals, looking at particular things like a flower or a sunrise. You have become the universal person.

What is under discussion here is your existence and the existence of your world, which contains everything else — all the other people and things. In this experience you have grown from the status of an individual enjoyer of things to the universal enjoyer. The other half of your consciousness is seen to be universal enjoyment. You can think of yourself as the knower; then the other half becomes the known. You can think of yourself as one who acts or reacts; then the other half becomes the stimulus for you to act and the field in which your action becomes relevant. You become the knower and the actor. You become the experiencer.

There is a greater depth in the experience of enjoying than in the experience of knowing or even the experience of acting. There can be actions which are autonomous or reflexive, in which you act like a robot. All repetitious work, like daily chores, is also action, but it doesn't fill your whole beingness. Similarly there can be a lot of information fed into your system. We are in the so-called "Information Age," with billions of items of knowledge available to everyone. We are awash in a sea of information, but it is not the same as the overwhelming knowledge. Only in matters of enjoyment do we move from casual appreciation to a more direct involvement. The experiences of pain and pleasure absorb and transform our entire personality.

In the previous two verses we were considering the possibility of looking at everything as an adorable wonder of consciousness. Unknowingly we placed ourselves on the outside, as a little person standing in bewilderment, looking at the grand panorama and saying, "Wonderful!" And when we considered the possibility of treating everything as vibrations of sound or as mere words, it looked as if we could reduce everything to a casual experience of listening to something outside.

In this verse a correction is made: these are not two casual occurrences. The total scope of experience is taking place within the experiencer. There is nothing other than you as an experiencer; both the 'I' and the 'other' are within you. What you are experiencing is yourself. It's your nature. Or it's the nature of nature to see itself, to experience itself.

Early in this study Narayana Guru told us that knowledge, in order to know its own nature, changed into all these possibilities such as earth and so on. By changing and turning about, it knows itself. Like a spark which, when it is moved in circles, makes seemingly solid patterns in the air, your personal experience of the inward 'I' and the outward 'other' is to be unified under the category of looking at the totality from the angle of an experiencer experiencing.

When you touch the tip of a finger of one hand with the tip of a finger of the other, you are both experiencing and being experienced. Which finger is experiencing the touch of which finger? When you have a pleasant talk with a friend or when you embrace as lovers, kiss or make love, which one is the experiencer and which is the experienced? Who feels the joy of it? Of course each one thinks he is experiencing the love of the other, the touches and contact of the other. One person's object is the other person's subject. The category of consciousness in both is the same — an object experiencing a subject — but you only know the part which is your experience.

The far-off sky with its starry heavens and floating clouds, the great panorama of the snow-peaked mountains, and the pleasant feeling you get from a gentle breeze or sitting by a warm fire — all these blend into the 'other', which is intrinsically connected with 'I'. This 'I' has no existence apart from its seeing, touching, smelling, tasting, thinking, recalling, forgetting, its emotions of love or anger and its moods of depression or elation. It always exists as some experience.

When there is no experience there is neither the enjoyable world or the enjoying self. It's only through a philosophical abstraction you can even imagine it. You don't experience the non-experiencing of anything.

From the unreal that you postulate in the name of philosophy, you are now stepping onto the only reality to which you belong, the only reality you live. That whole range is an experience, and it is your nature, it is *the* nature. There is no longer any distinction to make between purusha and prakriti, spirit and nature, or of a 'you' as a visitor to nature. There is only nature: your total nature or nature's total you.

This meditation should take you to a very intense level of experience. You don't very often go into that state, it's true. When you sit in your own armchair and think of some other people as despicable or lovable, you have become a miniature 'you' thinking of miniature 'others'. There is a way of giving deliverance to that miniature 'I' sitting on that armchair with its little prejudices so that it becomes a universal 'I'. Then that despicable character can be seen as part of your visualisation, the 'otherness' of your nature, which is only presenting itself in a certain way. The feeling of revulsion you have is another despicable aspect of the 'I' consciousness. You cannot turn away from the despicable person, because he's inlaid in you.

When a transparent crystal is placed on a red carpet, there is no way of keeping it from turning red. Theoretically you can say a transparent crystal has no colour. That's true. But in that particular setting the red wavelengths emanating from the carpet are filling the crystal's transparency, making it appear red. Like that we can say in principle that you are not dishonest and the other person is, you are not ugly but the other person is frightful to look at, you are not a coward but the other person is afraid. But for you to see and experience those situations, the color of the carpet has to pass through the crystal of your mind, which takes on that colouration. To that extent it is conditioned.

There should be no eagerness here to disown the 'other' in order for you to become a very special person. You must face the 'other' with courage and totally accept it. You cannot escape it. Resisting and beating your breast only proves your ignorance of your own nature, your ignorance of your belongingness to nature. Here your earlier acceptance of everything as aspects of pure consciousness is no longer just a casual remark you have made, it becomes a living experience.

Earlier the observation was made that everything you can conceive of is a word-image of experience: experience is epitomised and put into word form. Here that word is releasing you back into the original experience. Words are considered to be sound entities which can burst in you like bombshells, filling you with their meaning. Saying, "It's just a word," does not lessen its impact on you. A word, properly directed and spoken, for which you are the target, has a particular impact on you. All the words you hear, speak and even think come and present themselves to you as the 'other'. Thus there is an integration of word dynamics with all the potentials of consciousness. The words become consciousness and consciousness becomes words. The 'I' and the 'other' are interchangeable.

We are not philosophising here; we are living it. And as we are living it there is this natural division of the experiencer and the experienced. This division is held to be true only for the purpose of understanding what we are experiencing. Otherwise the experiencer would have to soak into the totality in order to experience it. To experience sweetness your consciousness would have to penetrate into the sweetness of some substance and transform itself into that substance. Only when your consciousness had attained a full identification with the quality of sweetness would you be fully experiencing it.

Consciousness percolates into that which is experienced. It is a process of exosmosis and endosmosis where you cannot say which is which. Each penetrates into the other. Then all the dualities such as the ontologic and the teleologic, the immanent and the transcendent, the real and the actual, and the spiritual and the natural, are all fused into the one full reality, and you become the caretaker of it. You are the possessor of it, and you are That. There is no God outside to look for or to realize. There is no wisdom lying outside to seek and find. You are the law, a law unto yourself. You are the truth.

In Narayana Guru's "Universal Prayer", he says *nī satyam jñānam ānandam*, "You are the truth, you are the knowledge, and you are the blissful experience." In this context you come to that final state of saying "I am that I am."

Verse 82

araṇi katañnezumagni pōleyārā-
yvavaril irunnatiraṟṟezum vivēkam
parama cidambaramārnna bhānuvāy ni-
nneriyumitinnirayāyiṭunnu sarvam

Like fire that emerges from churning sticks,
the boundless discrimination that arises from contemplatives
burns as the sun that has attained the firmament of supreme consciousness;
to this everything is fuel.

When you enter into silence, two things may happen. All the functions of the body slow down, and as a result you might fall asleep. In this case the inertial state is increased until the whole organism comes under its sway. On the other hand the silence can enhance the intensity of the operation of the mind, because the senses are withheld from objects of interest and don't interfere. The entire energy of the body is directed to a single area — the reasoning faculty of the brain.

If you cut open someone's head and look around for their faculty of reason you won't see anything, except a kind of grayish cauliflower. Under a powerful microscope, though, you can see millions of neurons with billions of synaptic connections between them. In normal activity electrical impulses flow through this complex of cells. When your concentration intensifies it is as if the cells are refusing to get stimulated or excited by their neighbours, and as a result a whole series of excitements that might have happened in the neurons don't take place.

If the general interest or the central principle governing the organism is in favour of being excited and not inhibited, there is a ready response. Scientists are unable to tell us why this is so. They do know that when whatever is controlling the neuron (an imaginary supposition) does not give permission, it refuses to respond, but when there is interest the whole system goes into activity.

So we have two possible tendencies: either becoming alive to a situation or dead to it, either taking interest and accelerating or becoming disinterested and passive. The latter is a negative interest which causes inhibition. This is the "inside" story.

In the imagery of this verse, if you have a problem and you are intensifying your inner effort to find a solution to it, it is like rubbing sticks together to make fire, as was done by primitive peoples or by the Vedic rishis for their rituals. A rope is put around two sticks so they can be spun rapidly, their friction producing heat and eventually fire. The fire comes from the wood, but if you split open the sticks and look inside for fire you won't find any. Not only is there no fire in it, fire is actually opposed to wood: it burns it to ashes. How can that which is so destructive remain in a thing safely? How does the firewood keep fire inside without being consumed? Similarly, your nervous system by itself does not think. It has no luminosity or awareness. It is just like the dark bundles of sticks. When those bundles are excited, like fire emanating from the wood, consciousness is emitted from the nerve cells and you become aware of ideas.

This is called *araṇi*, the wood that you rub. *Katañññu* means to churn. You churn your mind, and when you do there comes the fire of discrimination. Narayana Guru says the fire of discrimination can become boundless. It can shine forth in the firmament of consciousness as a great sun. In the light of that sun all inertia, all darkness, all ignorance, is burned away.

There is a paradox in this. Our two "sticks" are a world of ignorance and an ignorant person who is seeking to enjoy that world. The paradox is when the ignorant person and the object of his ignorance are rubbed together, what is produced is not more ignorance but science, knowledge, awareness, even wisdom. Two mistakes are not making a greater confusion, but a bright light. It's very paradoxical.

We should relate this to the previous verse, in which we spoke of one half of nature as being filled with the enjoyer while the other half is the enjoyment of the enjoyer. Someone who is seeking pleasure or enjoyment outside, in objects, has no idea that what they are enjoying is the happiness of the Self. To that extent, at least, they are ignorant. When they think that the enjoyment of the Self comes from an object rather than the Self itself, that's also ignorance. So in the pursuit and in the experience we see two aspects of ignorance.

Thus the whole world is divided in two, one half being the enjoyer and the other the enjoyment. Totally, it is one nature, and out of that nature comes the all-filling spirit. What initially appeared to us to be a person seeking in ignorance an object that is to be ignorantly experienced, we now find to be pure wisdom prevailing. The enjoyer is the one who causes that wisdom, and what is enjoyed is the full expression of that wisdom.

This is hard to understand, but then, as is said in the verse itself, one should churn one's own mind to arrive at the meaning of this paradox.

What does this really mean to each one of you? It is common knowledge that when you don't have an answer to a question, when you encounter a puzzling situation, or when you meet one of life's challenges, you gather yourself together, you go in to the very core of your being and look for light. You do not know how to produce that light, so you struggle. As you go on struggling, you find new steps suggesting themselves to your mind. Perhaps you adopt them. There may be a lot of trial and error, but eventually, out of the many things that turn out to be successful and the few mistakes you make, you gain a wisdom which enables you to avoid making those mistakes. It is as if the seemingly random steps you are taking in the darkness are all being guided from within.

This doesn't happen of its own accord. There has to be a tremendous effort, an intensity, a yearning, a desire to find a way. You are always approaching the goal, the end you seek, with increasing confidence. Finally you emerge successful.

When your car refuses to move, you can't just ask it to tell you what's the matter. At first you have no idea of what is wrong. You open the hood and look at the engine. You don't start by dismantling the whole thing. You make some shrewd guesses, and you try out one after the other. Eventually you are guided to where the problem lies, and you are finally able to rectify it. Here you are dealing with a totally ignorant mass of stuff. In you also there is ignorance. Between these two forms of ignorance you are trying to find the way, and the light emerges from that.

In the previous verse we raised the personality of the individual into a cosmic ego, a cosmic enjoyer, having a cosmic enjoyment. Here also it is not just individual ignorance: the issue at hand is cosmic ignorance, the darkness pervading the whole system. Despite the prevailing ignorance, the whole system appears as a network of the most wonderful, precise interaction of laws. These are the two worlds in which we live.

We come to this world as a mass of flesh with a blind nervous system that is easily excited. A little light or other stimulation is enough to make it cry. Then there is total excitement and everything goes into chaos. This is followed by a slow sorting out period. It is as if matter is learning to live logically.

In Warren McCullough's *Embodiments of Mind*, he talks about what the frog's eye speaks to the frog's mind. He notes that, unlike human eyes, frogs' eyes don't move. They remain stationary. But they are structured in such a way as to cover a wide range. This allows the frog to be very still. As the frog makes its living by catching things that move, like flies, its eyes are more attuned to movement than other features. McCullough says if all the flies kept still the frogs would die, because they can't see anything stationary. They can only catch something when it moves.

Everything seems to be an extrapolation from this — our whole development of knowledge, intelligence, even wisdom. When there is a need for your organism to protect itself or preserve itself, that need becomes the problem. The solution of the problem is the evolutionary process of educating your blind nerves to find their own light. You begin from a very humble ground and bring light to it. It's just like in Cardinal Newman's prayer:

> Lead, kindly light, amid the encircling gloom,
> Lead thou me on;

> The night is dark, and I am far from home,
> Lead thou me on.
> Keep Thou my feet; I do not ask to see
> The distant scene; one step enough for me.

From the encircling gloom of matter the biologic need to live asks for a little light. For that it has to struggle, and from that struggle light emits. This is what is implied when the Guru speaks of churning sticks.

In the previous verse everything was equated with nature. The seeker, the knower, the enjoyer, the doer — all are part of that nature. And where is the enjoyer? Where the enjoyment is. The enjoyer and the enjoyment are not two separate things. The whole of nature can be considered as one enjoyer and one enjoyment put together. In this verse the same thing is put in another way: the dark, inert mass of matter changes into the all-knowing consciousness. That consciousness knows even the law by which the frog's eye can speak to the frog's mind in such a way that the frog's sustenance can be secured.

This is a verse which cannot really be explained verbally. In order to understand it, you have to first put yourself into the context. The context here is the struggle of life. If you see yourself as a bundle of nerves, muscles and bones, each part alone means nothing. They have to be integrated to be functional. Nor can you find in anyone's brain a region that produces poetry or that makes them humorous or depressive. It's a total function.

From your initial darkness you have to find out the laws of the whole universe, its physical operation, biological operation, the psychological evolution that takes place in it, and the consciousness of higher values towards which we are moving. The discovery of one law leads you to another and that to still another. Everything is part of one unified or unitive law. This doesn't mean you should study statutes and know all the rules and regulations. That's another matter. Here, your consciousness itself is the law. It is as if the law is revealing itself in the form of your own consciousness. You are gaining a transparency of vision of the whole universe of which you are a part. Rather, you *are* the universe, and you are the knowledge of the universe, too.

When you come to this level, all single items of experience are like fuel for the fire of your understanding. That is why the Bhagavad Gita says the fire of wisdom burns away all ignorance. And what is this ignorance we speak of? In Vedanta, ignorance is considered to be that which creates a desire.

Desires create the visualisation of ways to satisfy them. The visualisation of means to satisfactory ends initiates action; the idea of action builds momentum in you to act; and ultimately the action brings about an apparently new situation. As the new situation ebbs it is replaced by a sense of loss, which in turn initiates another desire. From the new desire arises the need to have another action. Thus one action leads to another, endlessly. This is called bondage.

What is the solution to this bondage? Vedantins first want to find out how they ever got into such a terrible mess. They seek to know the law that operates action, the law that operates desire, the law that operates the ignorance that causes the desire, up to the first cause of the ignorance itself. They view this knowledge as a kind of lever with which to pry themselves out of bondage. The solution is sought not in some unknown place but in the everyday world of experience, which itself is seen as coming into being as a result of our ignorance. Both the incentive to act and the object that attracts us arise in us as our agency to be an enjoyer or knower of what is outside as this experience.

So there is a wrong identification in your agency as a knower and a wrong identification in your agency as an enjoyer. You go into meditation about it, into a search for it. The search has to be in the very field where the action is going on: you can't seek something by going away from it. It's in the experiential world in which everything is happening, so you go there. It is the so-called wrong identification of the interest in the object that reveals to you that the projection of the Self's happiness was made on it in the first place. And it is the apparently wrong urge you think of as coming out of ignorance that opens to you the truth that it is the Self's nature to be by itself. Its nature is happiness, so it has to seek happiness. So through these two mistaken identities you come to the right identification, which shows you your true Self, both within your enjoyment and in the object you are enjoying. The only difference is the ignorance which had been surrounding it is no longer there.

In the process you don't run away from anything, nor is the world consumed in any fire of wisdom. The world remains as it is; you remain as you are. But you no longer have a smoldering problem in your mind — it has become a bright light. Another person may perform the same action or follow the same track with a sense of anguish, guilt and sadness, but now you walk that path as a ray of light, as happy as ever, unaffected by anything. Unscathed. That's all the difference.

You have to make a distinction between taking a relativistic path through life, with many compromises and half-baked notions about things — in other words, a pretentious life — and a thoroughgoing search made with great intensity, into which you put your whole mind and spirit, and where you will accept nothing less than complete understanding in every situation. This allows you to own your life entirely and live it with absolute clarity. Until it becomes totally clear to you, you refuse to take it. That changes your stature from a relativist to an absolutist.

The contemplative spoken of in this verse is not just a person who sits in lotus pose in a room with his eyes closed, meditating, but one whose whole life is engulfed in the white heat of a meaningful search. The search can take any form, but it is its thoroughness, the intensity of the pursuit, and the minute details to which one's best attention is given in all earnestness, that correspond to the churning of the sticks. You don't slack up even for a second; if you do the sticks grow cold again very quickly.

You keep up your vigil with all intensity. This doesn't mean that you make it intense in a way that exhausts your nervous system. Intensity here refers to the interest that is created. Many interests are on the order of infatuation, and in the long run they deaden you. But some interests, like dedication to a great cause, don't blindfold you. Rather, they open your inner eye more and more in all directions. They make you far-sighted or insightful. They take you both to the depths and to the heights. They enable you to transcend both cause and effect. Whatever pursuit you engage in — art, literature, science, anything that is your first love or your dearest value in life — when that overpowers you and you are given to it entirely, your sticks catch fire. Your interest flares up until you become like a great ball of fire. Half of the world becomes your fuel and the other half is the flaming fire. Though this consumption can be described as a great enjoyment, everything in you is consumed.

Here, as in the previous verse, you have to move away from the position of being just a private individual living in a city with many other people, where you have only a humble role to play. That may be true in society, but in the domain of your own spirit you are all in all and the only one. Everything is an object of interest to you, a fuel for your fire. In the previous verse you were the experiencer, while here you are the knower, and everything turns out to be your knowledge. The knower and the knowledge ultimately cannot be two. They are both aspects of the same knowledge. Seeing this unification in the coming together of everything will give you an idea of the purport of this verse.

For instance, a friend is having recurring doubts about whether he is doing the right thing. He wants to get into the full spirit of what is taught in the *Ātmopadeśa Śatakam*, and live it. At the same time he is drawn to public performance, where he will get his satisfaction from the satisfaction of others. He is recognised by others as a person of great worth. His worth is reflected in their looks, their words, their expressions. They are like a mirror held out to him. By looking into the mirror of public opinion he is convinced of his own value, and that brings him satisfaction. But occasionally he puts that experience on the side of ignorance and the word of the Guru on the side of wisdom. Then he struggles. He thinks, "I should leave that and come to this teaching."

If you understand Narayana Guru properly, the correction is to be made in the midst of the very action you like to do, rather than by giving anything up. If you like to give performances, nothing is solved by no longer doing them. You are to use the sticks of your own interests and rub them together until they emit the fire of wisdom.

So how is our friend to look at the problem? He should understand that the public mind which is giving him approbation is not a different mind from that of the total consciousness, to which his own consciousness also belongs. It's an extension of his own self. His mind and the public mind are like two hands coming together to do things efficiently where one hand is not enough. He as a performer and they as spectators of the performance should not be viewed as a duality. The joy he experiences in trying to move them and the joy they experience in being moved by him is one.

If he works to gain the best insight into the formation of their minds so that his performance will have maximum appeal to them, while retaining a clear understanding of the whole situation, he is not just aiming at getting their applause or admiration. The whole thing has become illuminated. He is not searching for a black cat in a dark room where it is not, but instead is creating the very value he is seeking. In fact, he *is* the value. Then he sees that value in himself, in his performance, and in people's appreciation. There is no area left dampened, dark, unilluminated. Light is brought into all corners, making everything fully enlightened. Then he can say he burns there as the sun in the firmament of his consciousness, and everything relevant to the situation becomes part of that illumination. All is illuminated by his light, and he is the central piece of the whole experience.

This can be true of anyone's life. When you do something half-heartedly, as a customary thing, a convention or a habit, you sink more and more into the morass of life's darkness. When you kindle a meaningful interest, light shines forth to illuminate the whole world.

Verse 83

uṭayumirikkumudikkumonnu māṟi-
ttuṭarumitiṅṅuṭalin svabhāvamākum
muṭiyil irunnaṟiyunnu mūnnumātmā-
viṭaraṟumonnitu nirvikāramākum

To break, to exist and to come into being is the nature of bodies here —
one goes, another takes its place;
remaining in the highest, the Self that knows all these three,
the indivisible one, is free of modifications.

We are now approaching the close of our study. It is time to fix our notion of Self-realisation.

The seeker of the Self is a consciousness that animates the physical body. This body, or the consciousness dwelling within it, is confronted by three kinds of obstructions or negative values: non-existence, darkness and death. The first *āraṇyaka* of the Brihadaranyaka Upanishad mentions a famous prayer which refers to these three aspects: *asato mā sadgamaya, tamaso mā jyotirgamaya, mṛtyormāmṛtam gamayati* (I.3.28). This means, "Lead me from untruth to truth; lead me from darkness to light; lead me from death to immortality." It is worth examining this in detail.

If you consider the experiences of your body-mind complex, you'll readily observe that you experience heat and cold, pain and pleasure, and sensations of elation and depression. There are many such dualities. But whenever you think that any one of them is a fixed quality which will exist forever, it is already gone.

In the Bhagavad Gita, Krishna advises Arjuna to turn away

from all dualities. Although they are inevitable, he points out that they come and go and have no permanent existence. And what is our true existence? What is nonexistent and seemingly existent is called falsehood. It is not true. If it were true it would be true throughout. Pain and pleasure are not true because they do not exist throughout. They are not untrue because we experience them. So their position is true and untrue; they both are and are not. If they were not at all true we wouldn't experience them. We do experience them, so they are true. But they are not permanent, so they are untrue. They come under the category of maya. Maya is *sadasat*, true and untrue. Most of the time we are focused on these kinds of transitory experiences, which is why we pray *asato mā sadgamaya*, "lead us from non-existence to existence."

From birth we carry this body around, yet we know almost nothing of its secrets. We do not know how sleep comes, or where dreams come from. We do not know how we wake up. Although the body is ours, its states of consciousness are not in our hands. They are all operated for us as if by some unknown entity. When you put food in your mouth the salivary glands salivate. Why? We don't know. There are any number of glandular functions which are autonomous and screened away from our consciousness. In fact, most of the body's functions operate out of our sight. Most of our lives are also steeped in darkness. We know nothing of what is going on in the next room. We forget the past. We don't know our future, what is destined for us. On the whole, our awareness is like a small island floating in an ocean of darkness. So for this we pray *tamaso mā jyotirgamaya*, "please take us from darkness to light."

Our bodies appear to be a single whole, but each one is actually a colony of billions of more or less autonomous units which interact like a corporation. Some of them have an affinity to work together, while others are opposed to each other. In the myriad forms within us is the principle of love and strife, shared by so many beings. They all come into being, remain for some time, and then die. When they die their places are taken by new bodies, which occupy the same niche for awhile. Then they, too, pass away, leaving the stage to others.

We think of the process in which cells die and are replaced by new ones as our growth. From infancy through childhood to adulthood there is a continuous transformation taking place. Since the birth and death of cells is invisible to us, we don't much notice until the time when dead cells are no longer being replenished. Eventually the vitality of the system begins to run short, and ultimately it collapses.

The body is like a big maternity ward, nursery school, marketplace, hospital and graveyard all rolled into one. It is a maternity ward for the millions and billions of little beings being created within it. It is a nursery school where they are all taught how to integrate, work together, collide or fight. It is a marketplace where they carry out all their transactions, and a hospital where broken tissues are lying in bed receiving maintenance and repair. For some time self-correction is carried out. Then finally the priest comes, the final prayer is given, and all life forces cease. Once the whole system becomes a graveyard, it is handed over to be buried somewhere. When we think of the perishable nature of the body, we pray *mṛtyormāmṛtam gamayati*, "lead us from death to immortality."

Whether it is buried or burned or whatever, nothing is lost. As it says in the Upanishads, the fire goes to the fire, the water goes to the water and the air goes to the air. Or as Gurdjieff put it, the acorns which do not become oaks become fertilizer.

We are all part of a system of nourishment for others. When we sit for meals, what is served on the table was all living beings a few hours, days or months before. Those living beings have now become food. When I see truckloads of pigs going down the road, I visualise how they all sit on plates on somebody's dinner table. While they are on the truck they all look around curiously. They are very emotional. But once they are a dish on the table you don't see their eyes, looks or emotions. I feel very sensitive about them; I still can picture them alive, so I wonder how people can eat them. But then the eggplant and the spinach may have their own thoughts — I don't know about those.

So, we are a part of this continuous transformation of birth, growth and decay. But is that all? If that is all, what is life? If our only significance is to fill a link in a biological chain, why should we bother to educate ourselves? Why should we take so much trouble to read Plato and Aristotle, or to learn those terrible things called logarithms? So that's not it. There must be something more to life.

We can see there is impermanence, darkness and death, and even continuation after death. When we look at nature, it vouchsafes two things. One is that when life begins as an entity in a body, nature provides for the continuation of that life for some time by giving it nourishment, a certain animation of consciousness, capacity for some self-repair and self-correction, and the power of adapting itself to its environment until its death. This is the short-term arrangement. Nature also has a long-term arrangement. Although the individual life eventually terminates, it can transfer its essence into a new body. This is why opposite sexes are attracted to each other. They procreate and produce progeny through whom the species is continued. In beings where sexual procreation is not possible, nature procreates by just splitting them in two. In any case the species is continued beyond the individual members.

If you take the theory of evolution as a reality, all forms of life are parts of the biologic mainstream. We are all part of one stream of life whose history is much longer than any human life. Nothing in this theory gives us any reason to discipline ourselves or have any kind of morality or higher values. There is no need to enlarge our intellect. So for us to commit ourselves to a higher form of life there should be a possibility of somehow moving from nonexistence to existence, darkness to light, and death to immortality. Then our life can have meaning.

Of course, it is out of the question to immortalise the body. Narayana Guru agrees here with the evolutionists that the very nature of the body is to break, then for something new to come and for that to continue for a while before it also breaks. Then its place is taken by another, and this will continue on and on. So there is nothing called the immortality of the body.

When Sri Aurobindo expounded his theory of spiritual evolution and the descent of the supramental, I don't know if he meant it this way, but what his devotees understood and we are likely to think when we read his book, is that the body, which is a receptacle of the spirit, is slowly changed by the supramental spirit to become an immortal vessel to hold life. He clearly seemed to imply a physical immortality rather than any theoretical one.

During his lifetime no one in the ashram was allowed to ask the question of what would happen after Aurobindo's death. It was taboo. They all believed he would not die and that his body was immortal. When he died, the ashram people wouldn't believe it. They refused to bury him. There was a French government at that time, and they did not subscribe to that belief. They had a law that a dead person should be buried within three days. The ashram people said "No, he is alive. He is in samadhi." After the third day the government decided to bury him forcefully, so the ashram finally allowed it after much dispute that he was still physically immortal.

Then they changed their theory. They said, "He is continuing now in the Mother. He has transferred himself to her. He is immortalising the Mother so she will not die." She did live to be ninety-seven. But when she died, nobody made any dispute. She was immediately buried. It is not a feasible theory that the body can become immortal.

So, then, where do you become immortal? In the mind? How could that be? After all, what is the mind? We can't say it is an entity by itself, because it is dependent on a biochemical system for its existence. Without the body we cannot think or know anything. You don't even have power over the different phases of consciousness. The alternating phases of consciousness come on their own. No matter how hard you fight, in a little while you will be snoring. So you can't immortalise the mind because you can't immortalise the body it depends on. Then what is this thing called immortality?

We should turn again and again to the very first verse, where Narayana Guru referred to a substance, a Karu, which has three modes. In one aspect it becomes the awareness, the knowledge, that fills the essential properties of everything and identifies them as the knowledge of a thing. The same Karu is all this concrete manifestation as well as the individual subjective consciousness. When what is objectively out there, what is subjectively experienced, and the consciousness of things both outside and inside are all reduced or traced to one common substance, it is unbroken. There is no cleft in it anywhere. We can't say whether it is a thing or a not-thing. It is both thing and not-thing. Basically we can say the Karu is a law that governs everything. That law is changeless, but at the same time it governs all changes.

There is one entity in us which bears a striking similarity to this: that which detects and recognises the law within us, the buddhi. When a physicist or mathematician makes calculations about the cosmos, the reasoning going on within the private shell of their skull somehow tallies with the astrophysical reality. The exact position of a star or planet and the trajectory of a rocket to reach it can be computed in the mind of a person when they are not even looking at the sky. Mathematics gives mind access to the principle of harmony or discord in the external world, whether in a musical symphony, the dance of heavenly bodies or the interactions of microscopic particles. Although our understanding of this principle grows and changes over time, the principle itself does not. This is called the principle of homogeneity, *samāna adhikaraṇa*.

It is in this *samāna adhikaraṇa*, this homogeneity, that the contents of consciousness and the contents of the material world become one total system. Change takes place within the system, but the system as such doesn't change. As we are already That, there is no reason for us to become immortal. We are part of an immortal system. When you know this from a peak state of consciousness you are only amused by the changes, not threatened by them, even though part of the amusement is regarding your own dissolution. You can just look at it and smile. Then you are ready to experience the sweet calmness with which a Socrates or a Buddha passes away, with no struggle, just witnessing the event. As the Buddha described it, it is like a dewdrop falling into a lake and merging with it. As if from above you are viewing the phenomenality of things. Thus, knowing is realisation, not any becoming. You don't have to become anything.

Our body is an object lesson. When we see how it changes and perishes day by day, it prepares us for its final dissolution. Dying with grace is as beautiful as living with grace. To live in grace and die in grace, one should have a vision of this great symphony of life, in which mortality brings so much variegation on an immortal stage.

Nataraja Guru, in his commentary on this verse, wants us to especially notice the ontological richness of life. Although this body is a decaying and perishing one and this mind is an ephemeral experience, within it is also placed this grand scheme of universal truth shining in all its resplendence. You have a mortal body to introduce you to the immortal theme, a stupid mind to lead you to the highest of all wisdom, and deep darkness to become the backdrop for the brightest of all lights. For all this you need a body, a life, a mind. When you see this it is not a paradox that frightens you but a paradox that surprises you and brings you so much beauty.

Verse 84

aṟivatināl avanī vikāramuṇṭe-
nnaruḷumitōrkkil asatyamuḷḷaturvī
niravadhiyāy nilayaṟṟu nilpatellā-
maṟivil eẓum prakṛti svarūpamākum

As modifications of earth are known, it is said they
exist —
this is untrue when considered; what exists is earth;
the countless entities remaining without foundation
are all innate forms of nature existing in knowledge.

What is your conception of the real world, the world of your actual experience? When you try to answer this question what comes to mind is a number of pictures pieced together, of such things as the house you live in, the trees around you, the streets where you walk and the people you see there, cars that drive by, shops in the town, the sky above.

You can go on extending your conception by recalling more things from your memory. Just as you know one city, you are also familiar with other cities you have visited or lived in before. You can piece them all together and bring to your mind what you have studied of geography, using a globe augmented by photographs of the earth taken from space. There are many such scattered images existing in your mind. You make a mosaic out of them and call it the world.

This is what Narayana Guru calls here *avanī vikāram*. There are several Sanskrit words to denote the earth. One is *avanī*, which means the abode of all beings. When you think of your abode, your mind is filled with all these pictures — all the familiar scenes of your dwelling place. The Guru says you think it is real becau you experience it, but it's not.

For the second earth in this verse the Guru uses another term, *uḷḷa turvī*. While *avanī* means abode, *urvī* means that which is extended, implying earth in the sense of its extensiveness. If you think of pure extension you do not attribute any content to it at all. But every specific reference you make within the extension also has its own intention: the actual city or geographic area being delimited. You have in your mind a very special reference, and the intention is the referral to a particular city and not some other one. When you say a person's name, the extension is their physical form and the intention is the specific person with a particular name, character and personality.

So intention and extension are two different aspects. Earth as extension only, without intention, remains without any modification. The intention brings the modification. The concept of earth as your abode has many intentional modifications put together. Narayana Guru says that pure extension is real, while the intention or the modification you give to it is unreal.

When you say clay is real because you see it, and pot is real because you see it, we don't see any difference between the two statements. But the Guru says the clay is real and the pot is unreal. A lump of clay is seen in the same way a pot is seen, so how can one be real and the other not real?

If you say the pot is unreal because it is a modification of clay, how is it unreal? It is unreal only in the sense that the substance of the pot and the substance of the clay are not two different things. They are one and the same clay. But with the pot, in addition to the substance of the clay a familiar shape has been formed and the name 'pot' assigned to it. The pot-shaped clay is the modification, the modulation of pure clay. The pure extension is the clay, and the intention that the potter has put into it is the pot.

You should be able to make this subtle discrimination of an unmodified state and a modified state. The unmodified belongs to the general and the modified belongs to the specific. The unmodified belongs to the thing in itself, whereas the modification is part of the subject's perception of the thing. You see everything in terms of gestalts, so you become a participant in the experience, not just an observer. Part of your mind has become the picture. Moreover, you are confused as to subject and object. When the subject and object intermix, if you do not recognise the subjective aspect of the picture but treat it as an objective factor, you are making an important mistake.

The world in which we live ranges from the most objective to the most subjective. In between there are several shades of intermixing. The criterion for discrimination is that which is absolutely true. What is absolutely true is an existence which is the same all through the duration of time. In the beginning, the middle and the end it should be the same. This is the *paramārtha*, the absolute meaning. In this world both the observer and the observed are undergoing constant change. It's a transitory world. Within the frame of reference of change we can have a conditional truth which is of a relativistic order. This is *vyavahāra*, meaning transactionally valid.

So we have two frames of reference. One is the absolute frame of reference of pure existence, pure knowledge and the absolute basis of value. Derived from this is another frame of reference in which there is a relative existence, conditional knowledge and a relativistic value system.

Relative existence is arrived at by the common consent of all participants. If what I experience as an existing factor is recognised by another also as an existing factor, we have an understanding that vouchsafes its relative existence regardless of its status as an absolute truth. If two children are playing and they imagine they are a father and a mother, maintaining a home, going to work and even raising babies, that is an existential reality for them. It's totally imaginary, but since they both agreed to think that way it is perfectly valid. If we go to a drama where the same person plays many parts, only changing his voice and expression a little, we all agree that now he is one person, now another. It's a shared supposition.

There is a physical basis in a situation where one person is sitting on a couch and other people see him sitting there, for instance. This is not imaginary. It seems to have a physical basis. But for us to come to a common consent there doesn't even have to be a physical reality. In our dreams we can have similar experiences, not knowing if it is a physical reality or not until we wake up. Similarly it could be possible that we will wake up from our empirical existence to still another state, and then the empirical experience will no longer be real.

What you should understand from all this is that this is a very tricky area. What you call the empirical world is not entirely empirical. As you mainly depend on your gestalt, and it is up to you to put the rich imagination of your fancy into each situation to make it interesting, the objectivity of it is minimal. Is there anything really objective?

Here the Guru says, *prakṛti svarūpam akum*, "for these countless imageries that fill the extension of the universe, the prime cause is prakriti." And what is prakriti? It is the pure attribute of sattva, rajas and tamas — knowledge, motion and rest.

On one side we have the universal concrete, where you and I feel the stability of the earth under our feet and the impenetrability of a wall or another body. It is a state of rest, stability, inertia. If more and more people were packed into a room, either the room would break or the people would be crushed. But that doesn't happen with ideas. Even if I fill my brain with all the knowledge of an encyclopedia, there still will be plenty of room for the acceptance of new ideas without my head being in any danger of bursting. So the world of ideas and the world of concrete bodies are different — one belongs to sattva and the other to tamas.

A third thing is also involved. If all the people in a room get up and run around, it creates a new situation. Movement changes the relationships of things. This is rajas, motion. Motion can happen to physical things and also to thoughts. It can be outside and inside, and it is homogeneous. So prakriti contains things which are stable, things without bodies, and motion.

Each of these three factors has its own dynamics, and one is not superior to another. Each has an important role to play. Pure extension is the same as pure, unmodified consciousness. Within unmodified consciousness, numerous modifications can be created and structured. When Schrödinger said that this world is a construct of percepts and concepts, he was right. But perceptions and conceptions are not static bricks. Even the most concrete reality changes and is no longer a reality for us in another state of consciousness. When you sleep, if you dream that you have fallen into the sea and are being carried away by a wave, you experience watery movement but you are on a stationary bed. The concreteness of the bed is not being felt. So, when you say concrete you have to ask, "Concrete for whom?" Concrete for a knowing mind. Concrete in consciousness. It is not stable, however.

The whole purpose of a spiritual pursuit is to learn to discriminate between truth and falsehood, so that what you consider to be happiness is not an illusion but a reality. Thus, discrimination becomes the most important part of the search.

Discrimination is to be made on at least three levels. One is to distinguish between illusion and transactional validity. Another is to discriminate between transactional validity and absolute or transcendental validity. And of course we need to distinguish between illusory and absolute validity.

Between tamas and rajas, various kinds of illusions can be created. Some of them are not illusions in the sense we usually think of, but they are nonetheless illusions of major importance. For instance, you may wake up some morning to find it has been freezing and raining all night. It's a concrete reality — solid ice coating everything like glass. You are cut off from other places, since you can't use your car and it is unsafe even to walk to the store for food. Because of the morbidity — ice as the inertial state of water — it does not move. Then the sun comes out, and after some time it has all melted and evaporated. You don't see anything. It's all gone.

You can say this is both real and unreal. It is an illusion for some time, created by an inertial state of matter. It's not that it wasn't matter. For all practical purposes it belongs to the world of empirical reality, but it is caused by inertia. When the inertia changes into motion, that state goes away and is replaced by another.

Similarly, a flood may come, which after a few hours subsides and is gone. The flood is not inertia but motion, but it passes just as the ice did. Thus at the concrete level, motion and inertia — rajas and tamas — cause states which can be threatening or dangerous. Yet after a little while there is no trace of them. They are ephemeral.

The same thing can happen in the field of consciousness. There inertia does not create any concrete event. Instead, you may get a feeling, perhaps that your best friend does not trust you, is hiding something from you, or is possibly even plotting with your enemy. The absence of your friend at a certain time and place combines with seeing her in the company of your enemy at another time to confirm your suspicion. Soon a darkness sets in, which can be just as bad and dangerous as ice coating the highway. Inertia here means your mind itself has become immobile, and no communication is possible until it thaws. You cannot put your thoughts across at all. This is another case of tamas, not on a concrete level but on a very subtle one. But just as the ice melts when the sun comes, the misunderstanding can disappear as soon as a certain word is spoken or a point is cleared up. Oh, she was just visiting her mother! Then you are ashamed there ever was such a state.

And like the flood of water on the concrete side, there can be a big emotional upsurge, a torment which shakes your whole body, making you weep or shout hysterically. It carries you along, helpless in its grip. Then it all drains away. It's all gone, and now you feel like yourself again. This is rajas acting at a subtle level.

There is also a pure light that shows things as they really are in the concrete world. It is matched by the pure light of intelligence, which clearly distinguishes truth from falsehood in the subtle world of ideas. This is the sattvic element.

When we speak of the modification of nature caused by sattva, rajas and tamas — pure knowledge, motion, and rest or inertia — you should think of the whole range that is possible. They can operate at what is considered to be an objective level, at what is considered to be a subjective level, and in the interlacing of the two.

In this verse, Narayana Guru wants us to know pure knowledge, and that the three dynamics — what he calls the modifications of earth — operate within the frame of reference of this pure knowledge. In their operation they produce endless specific modifications, which range from the illusory through the transactional to the transcendental. In this range are many degrees of difference, and these are very important to differentiate. Simply saying they are all modifications does not help you. You have to see in each piecemeal experience what kind of modification has come, what its essential nature is, and how you can see through it. This means a transparency of vision is to be cultivated, by which you can neutrally assess a situation that is superficially dismal or cheerful.

If you look outside and see that your car is buried in snow and ice, either you have to look for some special equipment to clear it all away or you can say, "This is not going to be a permanent feature. If not today, tomorrow the sun will come and melt it all." When you think like that you don't become panicky. If you don't know what causes a situation or how long it will remain, you are ill-equipped.

Most of us make our lives miserable by taking the illusory as transactional and by not seeing a way out of the transactional into the transcendental. If the transactional is binding and you do not see a way out, then you are fully committed to it. But it should not be binding. There are any number of so-called transactional commitments which are unnecessary. You can free yourself from them. You don't have to perpetuate misery by keeping yourself obliged in so many situations.

On the whole you should understand that you need a normative notion of the Absolute. The normative notion of the Absolute is that it is pure knowledge. Your personal self is the pure Self that shines by itself in the dark without anything else. It is self-luminous, and that light is knowledge, a pure state of knowledge. What you call the Absolute is also pure knowledge, so there is substantially no difference between the personal self and the universal Self. It is to the existence of that knowledge that you refer the existence of anything else. Thus, a conviction of validity comes from the existential reality you feel of your own self.

When this kind of existential validity is recognised by a number of people, the reference is then to a universal Self and not to a private one. The Self is an existence of knowledge which has no beginning and no end. It is beyond time. It is a timeless experience of pure being. It is not only existence, it is knowledge of pure existence. As it is self-founded, not lacking in anything, not needing anything to be added to make it complete or perfect, it is a value in itself. As it is a value in itself, it is the most dear experience.

When you come into your own in anything, you experience the

same endearment value. This is the measuring rod you can use for each modification to see if it is absolutely illusory, if it belongs to the transactional world where a number of people can interact on the basis of a common consent, or if it is a universal truth.

Now you are fully supplied with all the requirements: the Self or pure knowledge as your normative notion, the three dynamics of nature as the causal factor in all experiences, the triple phases of the transcendental, the transactional and the illusory, and the method of applying the principle of discrimination to distinguish the illusory from the transactional as well as from the transcendental.

Verse 85

niẓal oru bimbamapēkṣiyāte nilpī-
leẓumulakeṅṅumabimbamākayālē
niẓalumatallitu nērumalla vidvā-
neẓutiyiṭum phaṇi pōle kāṇumellām

No shadow exists independent of an actual form;
as there is no original form anywhere for the existing world,
it is neither shadow nor substance;
everything that is seen is like a snake painted by a master.

This is a very important verse. To properly understand it you should recall to your attention the correction given in the previous one, where the distinction was made between the unmodified and modified states as exemplified in a lump of clay and a pot. This leads us to several questions.

When you see a pot you experience seeing a real object. You call that real object a pot. Just what is this pot? Does it reside in the name 'pot', or in the specific form of the clay? We should first ask what constitutes an experience. An experience has two major factors implied in it. One is the beingness of what is experienced, and the other is the knowledge of what is experienced. Do you have a knowledge of pot? Yes, you do. Does the pot have a beingness? If you say yes, what does that do to the beingness of the clay? If you say the beingness of the pot and the clay are the same, does this mean there aren't two beingnesses? So if there is only one beingness, and that beingness is clay, why do you call it a pot?

Beingness is a substantial reality. There is an indisputable beingness of clay throughout. Before it was fashioned into a pot it was clay. When it is fashioned it is also clay, and even when the pot breaks it is still clay. Do you have knowledge of the clay before it is made into a pot? Yes. Do you have a knowledge of the clay even when it is a pot? Sure. Does that knowledge continue even when it is broken? Of course. All through this process, clay continues in your knowledge.

What truly is, is that which continues as knowledge and experience throughout. Then where did this temporary thing called a pot come from? It is an image, isn't it? But what is it an image of? If you say that the potter already has the idea of the pot in his mind, and he transfers the image from his mind to the clay, then the pot is only an image of the original image in his mind. Is the idea in the potter's mind a real pot, of which the actual pot is only an image? No, not at all. The idea is not a real pot, it is an image of the pot. It won't hold any water.

Experience consists of two factors, name and form. You can formulate a name without referring to any being. But if I hold up a book and say it has no being, you won't agree to it because you are experiencing a definite form. It's not like a name. The experience of form brings you to two fundamentals, knowledge and being. So there is this difference between name and form: you cannot experience a form without experiencing knowledge and beingness, while with a name you can.

Here is the difficulty. There is a pot; you have knowledge of it, but you have to establish a location for its being. Where you are trying to do this another being — the clay — is already there. Without displacing or disturbing that being, how do you place the pot's being? Obviously the beingness of clay is absolute. It does not have the conditional aspect of time in it. Origination, temporal existence and dissolution are not present as they are in the pot.

Why should we bother so much about a pot and its beingness? Why is this important? This question only arises when we do not know the subject we are dealing with. Many of our experiences are of a lesser degree of reality than the pot's. If you cannot establish the beingness of a pot, how can you establish the beingness of your husband or your wife? At least a pot can be seen; it has a certain form. But concepts like wife and husband, or friend and enemy don't have any form. You can't point out the wife in a woman, so how is it determined? Unless you establish the beingness of your wife, there is going to be great trouble. The solid foundation of the family, society, practically everything is built on top of this fictitious thing called husband and wife. Very many of your expectations in social life are based on notions which have their root in a wife image and a husband image. People are always looking for a social image.

Such images are the shadows the Guru is speaking of in this verse. He says *eẓhum ulakeṅṅum*. This is not just dealing with one object but with whatever people consider to be empirically valid or transactionally existing, in other words where there is a so-called objectivity and subjectivity. The world where there are conventions, customs and moral principles is called *ulaku*. This word appeared in an earlier verse with the special connotation of the world we perceive when we are earth-bound and mundane in our interests.

So is this world we perceive an image or not? If pot is an image, wife is also an image. We have already seen the difficulty of establishing the beingness of a pot, and if the beingness of a pot cannot be established, the beingness of a house or a car will also be hard to determine. This brings the very idea of form itself into question. All forms are images — images of what, we do not know.

To solve this problem, philosophers decided to invent another world, a world of models. Plato called this the world of the intelligibles, and placed the archetypes there. According to him, the horse you see here is only a shadow, an image of the archetypal horse. Then he conceived the cave allegory, where the world is likened to a shadowy cave, and everything you see in it is only a shadow. This does bear a vague resemblance to the Vedantic concept of maya. But Narayana Guru doesn't accept that there is a world of intelligibles away from the world of the visibles. He accepts that you understand things with your intelligence, but that is precisely where you see with your eyes also. None of this needs to come from some other world. If something were from another world you could just say that you do not see how it is reflected, but it is nonetheless a reflection. We do not subscribe to the Platonic theory of the visibles and the intelligibles.

The difficulty begins as soon as we accept the world of perception. In the world of perception we see form. For us to see form it must have existence and we have to have knowledge of it. In other words it must have beingness. But the place of its beingness is already occupied by the existence of another entity: the unmodified Absolute. Therefore it is suspended in midair, so to speak, without a footing. This is the crux of the problem.

How does Narayana Guru explain it? He says that when an expert paints a snake and the painting is placed in dim light, it can frighten a person. The dread can be so great that the person might even collapse and die. So the painting can function as a snake to some extent, but as soon as it is closely examined it will be found to be only a painting.

When it turns out to be a painting, it does not cease to be. The snake doesn't disappear. It continues to be what it always was — a painting done by a master. What changes is your reaction to it. You no longer react with fear but with great admiration. You say, "Look how lifelike it is! It's wonderful!" You might want to possess it: "Let me take it home. It's a terrific picture!" Once you accept it, it is no longer a snake. When you were dreading it, it was also not a snake. It all came from the mind's projection.

Now let's go back to the idea of 'wife'. The original clay is there: some flesh, a body. On it you project your dear wife, just like the potter projected the idea of pot onto the clay. The process is of course a little different. Here, a greater potter has done the first part of the work in fashioning the woman, but it only becomes meaningful when you project the idea of 'wife' on top of her, so to speak. Does this idea have validity or not? It has validity. Has it full validity? No. It is valid only until you telephone an attorney to effect a separation.

This doesn't only refer to the husband-wife business but is a handy way of understanding something general in life, where people get infatuated with so many things and then after some time effect a separation from them. Marriages and divorces are going on all the time between people and their relativistic values. They aspire to something, but when they get close to it they no longer want it. They think it is not what they were looking for. That's because the beingness of those things has the same status as a painted picture.

The painting is done from within. Is it real or unreal? The Guru says you cannot say it is real, nor can you say it is unreal. It's simply a wonder.

To apply this in your life, you have to look for the being which cannot be explained away. What is that being? It's called existence. You should also look for the knowledge which cannot be explained away. Such knowledge is awareness. Existence is called *sat*; the awareness of subsistence is called *cit*. *Sat* and *cit* never change, but you can fashion the *sat* like the potter fashions a pot, like the lover fashions the beloved, like the buyer of a commodity fashions its value, like the admirer of beauty fashions light into a beautiful form. The substratum is perennial existence. What you temporarily create out of it has existence only during the time when it is valuable to you.

This brings us to a third factor, the utility of a thing, its *prayojana* or value. The potter knows the clay will always remain clay, but he sees a utility in fashioning it in a certain way so it will hold water. Holding water is an important symbol. Every value should "hold water." It should serve your purpose. When it no longer holds water, when it does not serve your purpose, you throw it away. Its existence is finished.

A pot serves its purpose when you want to use it. At that point you don't have to say it is only clay. The pot has a transactional validity that you can accept. But in order to not become disillusioned you should always have a permanent notion beneath the surface operation. After all, the primary existence is not of a particular thing, but resides in another category.

The other kinds of pots I am speaking of, like husband and wife, friends, neighbours, enemies and so on, are fashioned out of an already transitory substance called the life process. The stream of life is moving, changing and transforming all the time. On top of this ever-flowing process you are making other suppositions. So there is every possibility that in the flow your suppositions will be dislocated. What you think of as permanent is really an impermanent fixation superimposed on an already impermanent substance. But that impermanent substance really does reside in a beingness which does not change.

So there are three levels: the changeless, the changing cosmic process, and, within that, an individual arrangement. It is in the individual arrangement within the cosmic setup we see what we call *ulaku*. If the image we see in the *ulaku* were copied from somewhere else, as Plato has it, we could transfer ourselves to that real world. But there is no such additional reality. This is not a copy of anything. Then, is it real? No, it's still not real at all. We have to learn to accept the transitory nature of life and the impermanence of all arrangements, while keeping in mind that every arrangement is valid for just as long as the ananda aspect is reflected in it.

The other day a friend from the class said, "The last three days when I have been sitting here and listening to the meditation, it has not been reaching me. I wish I were sitting at home instead." When it worked for him, he was here. When it doesn't work he wonders why he bothers. That is a failure of the ananda. The existence of the image really belongs to the ananda. When the ananda fails the image collapses. It fades out.

What is it that interferes with the ananda? The whole process is a search for happiness. What is opposed to happiness is called maya, darkness, or avidya, ignorance. Christians call it sin or guilt, or personify it as the devil. And how can ignorance come and take away the joy of something you have enjoyed? Because your basis for that joy was only a supposition. If you saw joy right in eternal existence itself, in eternal awareness itself, it would not have broken down. But we are forever fashioning something out of that and projecting our happiness onto this temporary creation, which is moving and changing all the time.

What we are saying is that you should not build your abode on transitory stuff. Jesus said the same thing: one who wants to have a strong house should build it on a rock and not on sand. You need to remember that your experiences are neither the original or a shadow of the original, but have only the status of a painted picture. You have to explore how you can get from a sandy foundation to one that is rock-solid. To do this you have to go beyond name and form, beyond the world of your senses, the world of your imagination, beyond the world of your fantasies.

In you there is a witnessing self, a *sākṣī*. It is the big eye which watches the visions of the two small eyes, one seeing the external world and the other the internal world. Only when that witnessing eye is relied on will you be able to transcend the other two. Until you come to that experience you will be alternately fearing the snake and admiring its beauty, and also losing interest again and again and again.

In the *Brahma-Sūtra Bhāṣya*, Śaṅkara's commentary on the Aphorisms of Vedanta written by Bādarāyaṇa, Śaṅkara deals with this subject. He speaks of a man in physical pain, whose leg is broken. Can you say the pain is only in his imagination? No. It's not imaginary, it is intense pain from a broken bone. But then why doesn't he cry out all through the experience? For two hours he sleeps and does not howl. If it is so real, how can he take a couple of hours off from it?

Śaṅkara then quotes a passage from the Kaushitaki Upanishad, which says that if you ask a person: "Did you see that sight?" they may say "no." If you ask why, they will answer, "Because my mind was not there." When your mind is not there, you don't see. The same can happen regarding hearing or smelling something. Someone may walk down the road reading. They know they are leaving one place and arriving at another, but they don't know how they get there. While their mind is on the book they are unaware of the movement of their legs.

So the reality or unreality of a phenomenon like a broken leg depends on the presence of the mind. If the mind is not present, the person is asleep, at least to the event. So where is the fracture? Is it in the leg or in the mind? If it were in the leg it should be there all the time, but it is only there when the mind is. What is the relation between the fracture and the mind, and the fracture and the body? That's a good question.

Next Śaṅkara takes it a step further. He says your leg is broken, but your wife's leg is not — why should she sit there with a long face? Why can't she sleep? What happened to her? Sometimes it looks like she is in more pain than you are. Her identity, her sympathy is so great that she suffers more than you. And sometimes husbands suffer along with the labor pains of their wives. This is the second question Śaṅkara raises. The pain need not even be in you. It can be in another body, and still your mind can take it on, making you suffer.

Ninety per cent of your suffering is imaginary. You sit there and imagine what must be happening to your father or mother, or your wife at home, or someone else somewhere else. While you're sitting there, from your last chakra or synergic centre, something goes to the next imagination and then the next. Then the whole thing burns inside. After posing these problems, Śaṅkara says, "Now find out the real basis of your experience. To make this experience real, you should tell me definitely what truly exists, what you truly know of this experience, that will not be altered at any time."

Even the idea "I am" is not there when you are in deep sleep. If you are in a yogic absorption, the central idea is not "I am." The distinction of 'I' and 'that' is gone. If what is behind these notions is real and unchanging, your greater insight should rest on that.

This verse is not of merely intellectual interest. It has a great spiritual import. To those who meditate on it and want to take benefit from it in their life, it gives so much. It is just like Jesus saying, "Come to me, those who suffer. Unload all your burdens on me." Why should you carry them around in your head? The whole thing is a supposition — leave it where it belongs. Feel right. Be happy.

Whether we meditate or not, we come to experience this in the long run. Let me give an example. A man sailed across the ocean. He was not with his wife and children. There was no society there. He was all by himself. How could he do it? It's a natural wisdom, a wisdom that comes just through maturity. The necessary attitude had to come not only from his side but from his wife and children also.

I know husbands and wives who can't keep away from each other even for one day, parents who can't tear themselves away from their children. But then after some time they learn it's okay: "My life is my life and their lives are their lives, but at the same time my life is not my life and their lives are not theirs. Our lives are in the hands of another great reality. I have an apparent responsibility, but that responsibility can be there or it can be snapped by the greater reality which is deciding things."

In the ocean a person can't make a wind. The wind should just come. But he can maneuver his sails when the wind comes. If the wind doesn't come he can't make it happen. There is a simultaneous resignation and acceptance involved. There is prompt action, too, efficiency to suit the situation. This is a living philosophy; it is a living annotation of this verse. The key difference is as between a painted picture and a series of painted pictures which are shown as a movie, and where you have some hand in directing it.

If one person can have that kind of inner freedom, others can also. You bind yourself so much with mere suppositions. It is those suppositions and images, called here *niẓal*, shadows, that you should be dealing with. Then alone can life become a harmonious flow. Otherwise it can spell tragedy.

Verse 86

tanu mutalāyatu sarvamonnil onni-
llanṛtavumāy atināleyanyabhāgam
anudinamastamiyātirikkayālē
punar ṛtarūpavumāy poliññiṭunnu

The body and all similar things have no being one in another,
and become untrue for that reason; another part,
remaining without setting from day to day,
once again, as the true form, attains perfection.

The previous verse brought up a very important point: it is essential to establish the true being of the items that are part of our experience. What is true is occasionally difficult to discern, but our happiness and in fact the very meaning of life depend on our doing this correctly.

Two special terms are used in Sanskrit to represent truth, *satyam* and *ṛtam*. Not only is there truth, but that truth is capable of asserting itself to the extent that it cannot be denied. When it is just truth it is called satyam. When it is also asserting itself and we are cognisant of the fact it is true, it is further qualified as ritam.

The truth of our existence is always there. Of course, when we are sleeping, the truth of our existence is not cognised by us, and when we are absent-minded the cognising of truth is not emphasised. But when we are awake we make judgements and assert the positiveness of every experience by saying "it is." Every time we say "it is," or for that matter "it is not," an aspect of truth is underlined. When we go on saying "is," "is not," "is," "is not," it is called ritam.

In the first part of this verse, the ritam or the undeniable truth of experience is examined. There is a reference back to the question discussed in verse 85. The pot has a body, but does it have existence? At first sight we agreed that the pot exists, that bodies exist. Then we looked for the beingness of the pot. We have the knowledge of 'pot', but what is the beingness of it? When we looked for the beingness of the pot, it became ephemeral and disappeared.

What is truly there is clay. Before the pot was made it was clay, while the pot exists it is clay, and when the pot is broken it will still be clay. There is a duplication of beingness in the being of the pot and the being of the clay. The being of the clay is transferred from our minds to the substance. If we are seeing separate entities like pot, jar, vase, plate, and so on, they are all separate ideations that we project on the one reality which continues to always be the same: the clay. Therefore they have no ritam. They are *anṛtam*, untrue. When things are taken separately, anritam is bound to be there.

Back in verses 36, 37 and 38 we discussed sama and anya. Knowing things separately is called anya, while knowing things unitively as one is called sama. Sameness and otherness are the two categories which decide what has satyam and ritam, and what does not have ritam.

At the age of six months Socrates had a small body, weighing perhaps 20 pounds. At the age of twelve he was maybe 4' 6" , and weighed about 80 pounds. At forty Socrates was a fat fellow of maybe 150 pounds, and towards his death he became an emaciated old man. These bodies all looked very different, and the stuff they were made up of was also different. So how can we say it was the same Socrates, materially or physically?

The physical aspect is anritam. Was Socrates not existing all through? Yes, of course. We don't look at Socrates as being different as a child from what he was as an adult. All the stages of life are to be taken as one, unitively. The separation of bodies, the separation of entities, is a violation of true beingness. The person who committed a crime yesterday is held responsible for that crime today. You cannot take yesterday's person as separate from today's person. In this, the world also knows the secret of taking things unitively and not disjunctly.

The *Kṣaṇika Vijñānavadā* of the Buddhists asks if you look at the burning flame of a candle, is the physical reality of the flame of this moment the same as its physical reality of a couple of moments before and a couple of moments after? After all, the flame is a transformation of wax into heat, carbon dioxide and water vapour. In this process the wax burned in one moment is not the same as the wax burned in the next, so physically the flame is made up of different components from moment to moment. Nonetheless in the whole event of the burning of the candle you can't draw any lines of separation. It is a continuous process, so we treat it as one.

The Buddhists say it is not one flame of a candle, it is a flame series. In each moment there is the birth of a flame, the presence of a flame, and the death of a flame. They divvy it up as the first third of the moment the flame is being born, the second third it is shining, and the third third it is going out. It is a series event.

All of us are serial in that same sense. But Narayana Guru says that if we look at things this way we are relegating them to anya, to the 'other', and then they have no truth. In the second part of the verse he says that if something does not become totally extinct, it has existence. That is, through childhood, adolescence, youth, and middle and old age, Socrates continues to exist, day after day, without disappearing. In this process the ground, the substance, persists, while the modes and modulations vary and change. The modulating part of it is anritam, but the substance is ritam. Here the Guru uses the term *poliññiṭunnu*, which means when you turn to that aspect of yourself there is perfection.

As a seeker, when you look at your daily activities, at how you feel fulfilled or dissatisfied, at how you are depressed one day and encouraged on another, you doubt the value of your life. You need to remember this is at the level of modulations. If each day you can find a deeper level, if you can get established in the firm ground of your beingness, then you stop worrying about the modulations. You know there is a pure being which goes on and on. Your status then is of a witness, not a doer. You are a knower, but not in the sense of one who gathers information.

Egoistic performance, egoistic knowledge and egoistic enjoyment, which are all in the transient field of modulations, are now considered as actions happening in nature, produced by nature's own laws. You do not take the responsibility of them on yourself and worry about them. The wind blows; therefore leaves flutter. It is a gnawing wind; the skin feels cold. As it feels cold, the body trembles and shivers. It's all part of nature. You do not have any responsibility for it because it belongs to anritam.

Where is the ritam then? There has to be something that persists all through for the cloud to rain, the fire to burn, the wind to blow, for you to breathe, your food to be digested, your blood to circulate, and so on and so on. This mainstream of life is where ritam is.

The triple modalities, sattva, rajas and tamas, which cause special attention, attraction and consequent binding between you and some thing, have their effect at the surface. You are to leave them and become the single large eye rather than the two small eyes. You become an observer of life's daily chores taking place in the outer world, and of the cyclic movement of your emotions, thoughts and memories which unfold inside you like a cinematographic film. You watch both the outer world game and the inner world game. You become the great witness. The transience is allowed to be, but as you know it is ephemeral and anyam, you begin to be more allied with what persists.

The persisting thing, out of which day and night, silence and articulation, rest and motion, and meaning and non-meaning come, is sama. The two main attributes, knowing and being, persist. When knowing and being come together as the knowing of all and the being of all, it brings perfection. You live in perfection all the time, while you witness pervasive imperfection on the surface. The first is ritam, the second, anritam. Anritam belongs to the 'other', to anya, while what belongs to sama is ritam. What belongs to the 'other' is imperfect, what belongs to the unitive way of knowing is perfect.

In yesterday's commentary I mentioned that a friend had talked to me about a change in his interest. He has gone from wanting to be at the meditation to wanting to be at home, and I referred to it as an example of the significance of verse 85, which deals with just such a dissipation or intensification of interest. Here I can elaborate a little. The existence of everything is borrowed from the one absolute existence. All individual information about things is also illuminated by the one light of absolute knowledge. All individual likes and dislikes come from the one supreme absolute value. When a state of mind causes a division, a separation of a surface modulation from the substantive ground, then you question the existence of the experience. Instead of clarity, doubts come. Instead of happiness, boredom sets in. This is symptomatic of moving away from the centre.

Moving away from the centre means becoming influenced by sattva, rajas and tamas. Even sattva as such is not very helpful. It operates mechanically with rajas and tamas in a cyclic manner. Nature, prakriti, always functions by rotating the three gunas. When sattva comes you feel interest. When rajas comes the interest changes into an emotional state. When tamas comes you forget what the interest was in the first place. You ask yourself, "Why am I doing this?"

There is no guarantee of how long each of the various states will prevail. There are biological reasons for a state to remain and influence your system. Nowadays you hear of so many things — biorhythms, sex rhythms, and the like. In any case, your mind is not always the same. Sometimes it is heavy and sometimes it is light. That belongs to nature. Your whole attempt is to wean your consciousness as much as possible away from the direct impact of these triple modalities.

On one side is *cit*, the pure light of consciousness. On the other side is the reflected world of consciousness. Most of the time you don't see how pure consciousness operates, because you live in the reflections, in the modalities, away from the substance. You are caught in a shadowy existence, a shadowy understanding, and a shadowy experience of values. Being shadowy and without substance, they fail you again and again. One has to remain quiet for the clouds to pass, and the sun of consciousness to shine again. Eventually it comes back, but you have to be patient. You cannot push the clouds away any more than you can push a river where it doesn't want to go.

In one sense we can say that realisation comes like ten thousand suns shining all at once. It is also true that you gain ground little by little, more like the sprouting, growth and unfolding of a flower. You can't tell how much the flower grows in a day, but it is nonetheless growing. Like that, you gain your ground in wisdom in invisible increments. Some days you make mistakes and prakriti wins. The next day you make amends for your shortcomings and go further. If nothing else you have learned how nature can come and assail you when you are weak or unprepared, and the next time you will be prepared.

This game is continuous. The pursuit is continuous, growth is continuous. Realisation is also continuous. Then why do we say that realisation comes like a flash? It's like a Chinese puzzle. When you look at one, for a long time you won't see anything. Then it flashes, and you suddenly see the figure that was hiding. Once it shows, it is hard for you not to see it.

This kind of realisation comes all at once in a big flash, and we can say it is coming like ten thousand suns. But that doesn't mean that you are realised once and for all. The next situation may be quite different. Another puzzle will be presented. Then again you will look for a long time, until abruptly, all at once, it comes.

Both kinds of realisation are happening. There is a gradual maturing, and also the sudden flash. It seems the flash gets most of the attention. The maturing part is also important, where you have to fight against the constant clouding of your intellect by nature. It's like the road workers clearing the roads of snow while it is snowing. As soon as they clear it the snow starts building up again, so they have to do it all over again every half hour or so. Like that, sometimes winter sets in in your mind, and the snow falls. What can you do? Just wait for spring to melt it for you? No. If you turn away from the clearing of the snow, it will become more and more heavily laid down. So get exposed to the discipline.

Verse 87

taniyeyitokkeyumunṭu tammil ōrō-
rinamitaraṅṅaḷil illayiprakāram
tanu mutalāyatu sattumallayōrttā-
lanṛtavumallatavācyamāyiṭunnu

Taking each kind alone, it exists;
mutually, each excludes the other;
when this is remembered, body and all such
are neither real nor unreal; that is indescribable.

Looking and seeing are two complementary aspects in the act of perception. The act of looking comes from the subjective side, while the possibility of seeing comes from the objective side. In other words, looking is what you do from your side and seeing is what takes in the other side.

What is there, you see. To see it, you look. What you look for and see can be a thing outside your body or something inside it. When you turn inward and look at your mind, the thoughts that pass and the emotions that come along are objects of inward, mental perception. They are to be added to whatever you look for and see outside.

You may ask "What is nature?" or "What is this world?" World is just another name for the comprehensive experience of nature. Sometimes we refer to the Earth as the world, but in a more general sense the world is whatever we experience. Whatever is experienced is part of this one entity we call the world. Even the 'I' consciousness — the feeling of 'I' — can be subjected to one's own inner perception. We know the 'I' consciousness directs thoughts and experiences many things, yet even it can become objectivised. The object matter can also include the subject as an object. Thus, 'object' is a very broad term.

So, then, nature is what we experience and the world is what we experience. Is this experience objective in the usual sense of the term? When we consider an object outside, we think of a concrete substance. The outside object is understood by us only in terms of the idea of concreteness. By itself the object doesn't get into our knowledge. What we have is an idea of its objectivity. In that sense we can say that nature is the idea of objectivity in our awareness. In another sense we can say the objectivisation of our ideas is the world.

A consciousness directed towards something becomes objectivised. What is perceived is the idea of an object. In either case, what we experience is a modulation. Modulations all have names.

Narayana Guru has been preparing our minds in the last four or five verses to arrive at the idea given in this particular verse. He says that to say a modulation or a modification is real because you know it, is wrong. We explained this through the example of the beingness of a pot. We found that the knowing of the pot is there, but the beingness of it is not, because there is only the beingness of the clay. This is why we say the pot is unreal: it is only a modulation in our ideas. The true being is in the clay. We need to bear this in mind now.

In verse 85 the Guru likened everything we see here to the masterly production of an artist, describing it as a snake painted by a master. In other words it has a marvellous form but no substance. The form is what gets a name. Even if you fashion the form of a flower in paper or plastic, the mind accepts it as a flower. It has no qualities of a flower, and yet we use the fake one in place of a true flower for decoration. We even call it a flower, since the name is so easily associated with the form. But it lacks any substance that would make it a flower.

To what category do a plastic flower and a plastic orange belong? You don't think of them as belonging to the same species, even though they are both plastic. One belongs to a flower species and the other to the citrus species — isn't it total nonsense? They are plastic lumps. How can one be a fruit and the other a flower? Since you have an idea of the kind in your mind, different categories are put under one class. You are once again seduced by the form over the substance.

Look at all your experiences, whether they are subjective or objective. They are all nameable. How do we decide to name a thing? By looking at its properties. If two things have the same major property, we tend to forget the little differences, the accidents. One person having a tall body and another a short, fat body are accidents. There can be permanent accidents as well as temporary ones. The shape of a man's nose is a permanent accident, but his wearing a red or yellow cloth is a temporary one. If there are ten people sitting together and if one is wearing a pink shirt, you might identify him as "the one in the pink shirt." It's only a temporary accident, but at that moment he stands out as one kind because of this very superficial thing. If we go a step farther and say "all those people who are about twenty," we are still referring to an accident, but we are including people irrespective of what they are wearing. When we say "human beings," it is not their age, dress, color or anything else that is particularly important.

There is one property without which people cannot be human beings, and with which they are human beings. This is called the *differentia*. Differentia is related to the word difference. Of the many possible differences, that difference that is the most essential is the differentia. A kind is decided by the differentia it has. *Homo Sapiens*, the thinking animal, is human. Among animals, the one that thinks is a man. So we classify all human beings with this one differentia. This kind of definition is called *genus et differentia*. The genus is animal, the differentia is the capacity for thought.

Our understanding of nature is mainly based on this one principle of differentia. Physicists, chemists, biologists, botanists — all scientists use classifications and categorisations. If you look at a botanical textbook or walk in a public garden, you will see a label on each tree and flower bearing the family name in Latin, which is the universally accepted nomenclature. One family is separated from another in this way. Even sentences are divided into several classifications such as nouns, verbs, prepositions, conjunctions, adverbs and adjectives.

In the objective world and the subjective world our minds work by pigeonholing, by classifying everything into kinds. Narayana Guru says one kind is not in another. The verb is not in the noun, and the noun is not in the adverb. Teak wood is not in ebony, ebony is not in fir, fir is not in redwood. The pig is not in the lion and the lion is not in the monkey. Even in music there are various scales which differentiate groups of related sounds. And so on. All the experiences we have are understood in terms of kinds.

One of the major ways to differentiate one kind from another is by form. There are many kinds of form, for instance physical, substantial, literal and etymological. Every form is a modification. You can draw a bird as small as a grain of millet or as large as an elephant but it will always be recognised as a bird. You can draw an elephant as small as an ant but it will still be recognised as an elephant. Form has this kind of magical power because our minds are conditioned to it.

I should confess that when I first came to the West I couldn't distinguish between people. Everyone looked alike. Now I wonder how that could have been, they are all so different. I can easily recognise the differences. The mind is very quick to learn to recognise individual forms. But just at first all white people looked alike, all black people looked alike, all Chinese people looked alike.

Porphyry made a system of classification which is now called Porphyry's tree. The categories get smaller as you go up, giving the scheme a tapering shape like a tree. At the base are the vast numbers of temporary accidents, and above that are the lesser numbers of permanent accidents or properties. Above them are differentia, groups, and then kind or species. At the top, just below the singular One or Absolute beingness, there is genus. All these, from the accidents to the genus, are different modulations.

This is the way our minds work. First we think in terms of the genus, then the species, the sub-classes, coordinate species, then smaller classes, and finally separate individuals.

Narayana Guru says *tanu mutalāyatu satumalla*. The word *tanu* has a very special connotation in both Sanskrit and Malayalam. It means just a sketch. If you take a pencil and make the barest sketch, without embellishment or shading, it is enough for our minds to distinguish what it represents. An exceedingly beautiful woman is called *tanvi*. It is as if she has no body — she is just a feminine formation. Your mind just sees the femininity. Her physical substance is just enough to create the apparition of a woman's form. The barest minimum requirement to recognise a body is called *tanu*. The rest is just padding.

So the Guru says *tanu mutalāyatu satumalla*, meaning that the central aspect of a perception, mental or physical, which brings you to pinpoint a thing as belonging to a class, is not real. Is it unreal, then? No, because it has functional validity. For all the transactions you make, you depend on this operational validity. Because it has an operational validity you cannot say it is unreal. Since it is neither real or unreal, the Guru calls it *avācyamāyiṭunnu*, indescribable or unpredicable.

I have been trying to understand what Husserl called pure or transcendental phenomenology. It bears some resemblance to what we are talking about. Husserl was trying to present a totally new science focused on the very core of human understanding, which is more the domain of philosophy. I don't know if Husserl finally arrived at the same vision the seers had, but as far as I have read he is moving in the right direction to reach the truth.

In presenting his trancendental phenomenology, Husserl was over-conscious of the possibility that someone might misunderstand him. He complained that for ten years whatever he had said about it was misinterpreted and misrepresented by many people, that he made more enemies than friends, and that hardly anyone understood him. He wanted to restate his case, so he began, "I am presenting here a totally new science." When you first hear this you don't think that this is possible.

So what is this new science Husserl is speaking of? There are already disciplines addressing everything we experience here. Physicists say they are making a science of the perceivable aspects of the objective world, and psychologists say they are building a science of actual experiences. Both the physicist and the psychologist deal with the facts of experience. Husserl says he is not making a science of facts. The science of facts relates to what I earlier called the "seeing" side of things, but he wants to call our attention to the "looking" side. This is the core to which he wants us to go: the subject in us who performs the great business of always looking at things — at itself, others, facts and ideas. You go to your own core, which is your very beingness, and this is what Husserl wants to make a science of. It's really quite wonderful.

Then he goes on: take your empirical experience, your very objective experience. Say you are enjoying a sunrise or a cup of tea. The sunrise and the cup are facts. Or you have a pain in your finger. That's a fact. Do you understand each of these individual experiences as a novelty when you experience it, or do you bring to your mind any recalled memories or things that are already known to you? Certainly you bring to mind a number of things you already know to understand every experience. Husserl says in that case you are making an eidetic judgement. The presumption of objectivity is only incidental. You project an eidetic judgement on the incident. Eidetic judgement means the memory you have as the seer of a previous, similar occasion which colours your vision of the present.

Husserl does not deny the world of facts. He says basically what Narayana Guru says, that the fact aspect is like a pencil sketch. The rest you fill in. Suppose you look through your window at night and see a man standing there with a gun. You are horrified. You don't know whether you should call the police or silently go back to bed and wait there for his next move. You close your eyes. When you look again he is still there. After waiting in agony for something to happen, you fall back asleep. The next morning when you wake up, you see what you thought was a man was really your overcoat, which you had hung in front of the window. Your fear of someone coming in the night supplied all the details: you clearly saw the man with the gun. Do you not do this in your everyday life?

Husserl gives another example which I thought was very good. You look at the sky and see three stars. The stars are probably hundreds of light years apart, but you see them as a triangle. You call another group of stars a bear and another one a hunter. Are there really any constellations in the stars? No. We make them all up and give them names. Similarly, if you put three dots on a piece of paper they look like a triangle. Actually there are only the three points, but your mind immediately constructs a triangle. Husserl asks what the difference is between the triangle you see on the paper and the one you see in the sky. In essence there is no difference, because that essence is the beingness of the triangle. He says this is not coming from the seeing side, but from the looking side.

Next, Husserl discusses what he calls 'regional ontology'. He says that there are two inseparable correlates. First, for you to see a triangle a figure should necessarily have three angles and three sides. Second, wherever this kind of formation comes it is inevitable that you comprehend it as belonging to that particular class. Thus, our lives are governed by the properties of modulations and the possibilities for their modulation. How this is, we do not know. It is a wonder. This same idea will be further elaborated in some of the upcoming verses.

In Sanskrit the looking side is called *pramātā caitanya,* and the seeing side is *prameya caitanya.* The criterion by which you relate the looking to the seeing is called *pramāṇa caitanya.* In these three is a common factor, *caitanya* or consciousness. The objective and subjective aspects of consciousness taken together with the criterion of consciousness, give you what you think of as a valid experience.

Facts are incidental in life, but operational meanings give facts validity for your empirical life. This is why the Guru says these forms are not anritam, they are not functionally unreal. They are unreal only in the sense that in themselves they have no beingness. Their beingness is only of consciousness, caitanya.

This whole mechanism called the functional aspect of consciousness is not something which should bring us to any depression, but to a state of elation. Accepting this takes a big load from our hearts. We no longer need to insist on having to understand everything. This whole creation-manifestation-projection is such that it is bound to be uncertain. That is the only certitude: the certitude of uncertainty. When we accept it we think, "I am not called upon to know everything. Fine. Now I can be a very simple person. There is no need for me to be as intelligent as God. It is God's creation." Or call it Nature if you prefer.

This is a world of wonder. The classes and categories that are relevant to our daily experience have an operational validity. This makes things very easy for us. When I assume I am a teacher and you are my students, it is functionally sound. I don't have to get confused about it. The uncertainty may be a wholesale uncertainty, but this part is certain: I am a teacher and you are my students, or this man is a doctor and his patients are receiving treatment from him. The pen is a pen and the computer is a computer because they all have their place, and thus are not anritam but ritam.

But I don't go to the other extreme and say each by itself is absolutely real. I have to be cautious, not taking everything for granted. It can be misleading. I am wakeful and vigilant because this is the field where I may encounter many snares.

The aspect which we say is a wonder is called *paramārtham*, ultimate meaning. Where there is a functional reality it is called the transactional, *vyavahāra*, and where it is illusory it is called *pratibhāva*. So there are these three aspects: the illusory, the transactional and the transcendental.

The transcendental is full of wonder, and it is uncertain. Why is it uncertain? Because the subject-object duality is effaced there. Husserl calls this the transcendental reduction. It is the ultimate reduction, by which you come to pure beingness, absolute and unquestionable. You are not there to question because you have merged into it, you have lost your face and your mind. This is not bad, because in its place you have gained the whole. In addition, you have the very workable field of transaction and the murky realm of illusions. It's all very beautifully laid out.

Verse 88

sakalavumuḷḷatu tanne tattvacintā-
grahan itu sarvavumēkamāy grahikkum
akamukhamāy aṟiyāykil māyayām van-
paka palatum bhramamékiṭunnu pāram

Everything is real in itself; one who grasps the basic truth
will understand all this as one;
if not known introspectively,
māyā's great enmity certainly creates much confusion.

After such a minute study of all aspects of the Self and its indivisible aloneness, even when we come to the eighty-eighth verse of *Ātmopadeśa Śatakam* the world has not disappeared. It persists, through all the reevaluations we have had. And we are the same people. We are engaged in the same kinds of activities, and we still react to each other the same way.

If the world persists must it be real? Is it real or not? Does it exist or not exist? Narayana Guru says have no quarrel — just take it for granted the world exists. Not only this world. Whatever there is. It's all okay. *Sakalavum uḷḷatu,* everything is real.

Next the Guru introduces a special word, *tattvacintāgrahan.* Usually translated as 'philosopher', the word means something like a lover of truth. A *grahan* is one who grasps and understands a secret, a reality. Of what? *Tat* and *tvam,* or That and thou. This is taken from the Upanishadic dictum *tat tvam asi,* "That thou art."

In the Upanishads, four great dictums or *mahāvākya* are given. One is called the dictum of instruction, *upadeśa vākyam. Upadeśa* means an instruction given by a guru to his disciple; *vākyam* means a sentence. Therefore it signifies a great sentence of instruction given by a guru to his disciple. Two other great dictums are given as methods for carrying out the instruction, called *manana vākya*, dictums for meditation. Then there is one called *annbhavam vākya*, the great dictum of experience. So the Upanishadic teaching begins with an instruction, then gives the methodology for carrying out the instruction, and finally describes the experience which is the achievement of the teaching.

The great dictum of instruction is *tat tvam asi*. *Tat* means That; *tvam*, you; and *asi*, are. Together it is "That you are," or "That thou art." Every guru whispers this great secret in the ear of his disciple, but you can shout it out loud, and still nobody will hear. The secrecy won't be lost even in a million tellings.

Then the disciple asks, "How do I go about it? You say 'That thou art', but what is That? And how am I That?" He is helped by the next two dictums. The first is *ayam ātmā brahma*, "this knowledge by which you know everything is the Absolute." If you want to find out what that is you should enter into your own knowledge and see how it is expansive, what depth it has, how it is the only luminous reality of being you experience, and so on. You have to do a lot of *manana*, which is not discursive thinking but going into the depths.

This is a good time to remember that our thinking processes can be circular, linear or deep. When you worry your thoughts go in vicious circles, which is why you can't easily get away from them. This is called *cintā* in Sanskrit, and is the worst kind of mental operation. In linear thinking you start with a statement, and then see what is connected or associated with it and where it leads to, before proceeding logically to the next item. You direct your thoughts with reason, called *vicāra*. It's a better way of thinking, but often is somewhat limited.

With the third way of thinking, you don't allow your mind to run away. First you decide what your standpoint is. Next you look at the field and decide what its scope is. You have to decide not to be carried away by anything you have previously heard, not allowing any kind of memories to come and distract you. You just repeat what you hear and penetrate into the heart of it, so that you can have an intuitive grasp of its meaning. This is *manana*.

The other of the *manana vākyas* is *prajñānam brahma*, "this knowledge is That." What you want to find out first of all is what 'That' is, what *tat* is. If this knowledge is That, what is That? Then you are told that all you experience here in this world in so many forms are modulations of consciousness, which are nothing other than the Absolute, brahman. So you do only two things. Either you turn inward and look at the subject who is knowing everything, or you look at everything that is not the subject and see the world of objects, which is also consciousness. These two things can be put together. The seer and the seen put together are That, *tat*.

When the teacher says *tvam*, 'you', you understand it as *aham*, 'I'. "That is me." The teacher did not say "You are That." If you first think 'you', you only think of your body and the rest of your individuation. To avoid that mistake you are first instructed to meditate on tat, and then place yourself in That.

Unlike *cintā* in Sanskrit, the word in Malayalam refers to contemplative reasoning. When you engage in the contemplative reasoning by which you can relate 'you' to that Absolute, you are called *tattva cintā grahan*, a knower of the secret of That and thou. Then alone do you become a philosopher. Such a person who is capable of relating the Absolute to the knower sees everything as one.

What is wrong with seeing everything as many? Nothing. Then why this insistence on seeing everything as one?

Whether you know it or not we are one, everything is one. As everything is one, there is an inner pull between things. That pull attracts one person to another. But we also experience repulsion. Within the One there are polarisations. The needle of a compass is one, but it has two poles. When you are drawn to an other, if you already know that you and the other belong to one and the same principle your behaviour is very different.

Here's an example. I have some books in my room, and I know they're mine. Then somebody walks in with another book that is not mine. I ask to see it, and I find it is a really wonderful book. I don't ask if I can have it, but because it is not mine I inwardly desire for that person to give it to me. It's all because I don't own it. If it were mine, why would I desire it? The ones that are mine are all sitting right there. Most of them I don't even bother to open.

So this otherness is the beginning of trouble in the world of the many. Any number of things we don't think are ours haunt our minds. The mind keeps on saying "How to get, how to get." We want to get things, people, and put them in our pocket. Then alone will we be happy. We want to be able to pull them out and say "You are mine. Jump around." Or walk around or sit around. "See. This is mine." Then we put them back in our pocket. It is so very comforting.

You want to possess. Then you want to dominate. You want to master. There is a powerful joy in all of this.

But to your dismay the other person wriggles away. It causes you great upset, heartburn even. You want to capture and hold on to that fellow, but they won't play along. It is just like when some silly cat almost comes to you, and then suddenly it turns and runs away. It's so soft and cuddly, but it never allows you to quite catch it.

We desire things only as long as we know they are not ours. Once something is in our possession there is no more desire for it. Does anyone desire that their father should be their father? No. They take it for granted that he belongs to them. Why should they desire their father to be their father?

So we don't have any trouble with our parents, since we know so well they are ours and we are theirs. But when it comes time for the child to leave home, the parents become torn and upset. At least in India it is terribly difficult to tear a son away from his mother or a daughter away from her father. So they simply never leave. What is wrong there? It is not desire, it is attachment. Desire is called *moha*, attachment is called *rāga*, and they are the main tools of maya. Maya makes differentiations of things so it can watch this great game going on, of someone desiring someone else or someone suffering the pangs of attachment to someone else. When they are thwarted, up comes anger and hatred. It makes good theatre.

When people go mad, they become angry with the very people they previously adored. Their adoration changes totally to bitterness. But most of the time they still behave well with strangers.

When a person lies in bed for a long time he gets bedsores, welts on the skin. Then the skin sloughs off and blood comes. The body becomes ulcerous. Like that, when people who are in love live very close together, short circuits come between their nerves. They also produce sores of a kind. When the other person comes near, the sores begin to creep all over. You get into a frenzy. You just want to get rid of that person. They may be just sitting there, but that's enough. Their very presence in the room is enough to make you miserable. You might have been sitting there all smiles, feeling pleasant, but as soon as you see them your whole face changes. It's as if the world has crashed. The sky is falling. You can't even breathe until they leave the room again.

Narayana Guru says this is known as maya's *vanpaka*, maya's great revenge. Brahman says, "Forget everything and just blend into me", but maya says, "Do not forget anything. Remember everything. Go on remembering."

In Tolstoy's story called "Love," a wife got angry with her husband. She started listing all the terrible things he had done during the previous ten years. The husband asked, "What is the relevance of that now? Why do you bring up all those things which happened so long ago?" "Because they are true! You are like that!" What could he do? She didn't remember one good thing he had done, but she hadn't forgotten any of the bad. Whenever it's inconvenient we want to forget everything, and when it's a convenient tool we rake up all the memories.

Maya has another name: prakriti; while brahman or the Absolute has three principles: sat, cit and ananda. In a circus, one man will perform a wonderful feat on the ground, then a woman will do something spectacular on the trapeze. When their big show is over a clown comes and imitates them, demonstrating how many blunders they could have made. His is also an artful act. Like that, when brahman comes and says sat-cit-ananda, prakriti comes and says "I also have three: sattva, rajas and tamas. That is my show — my three ring circus!"

First prakriti shows you a little of sattva. It glitters and shimmers, and you say, "Ah! That's good!" You are attracted to it. Then rajas comes along and says, "Isn't this bright? It's beautiful. Get into it. You don't have it now. You need to possess it!" Now infatuation comes. Sattva is gone, so there is no longer any light. You came and got committed, but now you wonder where the brightness went.

That beautiful, angelic glow is gone. It was the glow that attracted you, but now you see only a stupid man or a stupid woman standing there. They are not enchanting any more. But now tamas is increasing, and the light is going away. After awhile it becomes absolutely dark, but you are already committed. Hatred builds up from inside. You think, "My God! How could I get into this?"

I have actually heard conversations between husbands and wives that go like this: "You! Man! At the time I married you, even if some ass had come along I would have married it!" And he responds, "Sure! Do you think I would have married you if I were not an ass?"

When one unit of sattva, rajas and tamas is worked out, that's the moment you look around for a way out. Then sattva comes again and calls you. "What's that?" You are snared again. Everything you already learned is once more forgotten. When sattva jumps to another person, you think, "This is totally different. This time I won't be deceived. I'm too clever to get caught again."

Each time you feel it's different. Why? Because it is sattva that comes and attracts you, not rajas or tamas. Sattva is capable of mirroring something really bright, really true. So you are not mistaken when you say it's different. You are seeing a new value. Unfortunately you cannot keep the sattva. It slips away.

As you get interested, from below an energy builds up: rajas. It makes all your glands secrete, and your whole system starts to boil. When you're boiling, you fail to notice how sattva walks out. It escapes through the back door, and once again you find yourself caught in the same pattern.

Many people come and tell me of how the patterns repeat in them. And it's not just in individuals — the pattern repeats throughout the whole world. It doesn't end until the body wears out. The play goes on: sattva, rajas and tamas . . . sattva, rajas and tamas. What we were supposed to do was be in the camp of sat-cit-ananda. To move from the one to the other is a subtle alteration, but you gain a whole world of freedom.

That's why the Guru says if you are always seeing things as distinct and separate, you are in a world called anya. Sattva, with its attraction; rajas, with its infatuation; tamas, with its binding and darkness — this pattern will repeat again and again. So why don't you turn to the other possibility, to sama? Sama is seeing everything as one.

Does this mean that everyone will blend into one common material? Not at all. You are only asked to see things differently. When you see things outside you experience confusion, and this leads you to maya's revenge. But just as you have eyes turned outward to see things and facts, you can cultivate an inward eye to see how one consciousness is transforming itself to become the knowledge of things and facts.

In the fact world, things are bound to be distinct and different, but at the root it is your own consciousness unfolding. It was you who decided that that person had an angelic glow about them, and it was you who decided later that they no longer glowed. The transformation has come in your consciousness, and not to anyone or anything else.

If you know it is the nature of modulations to be transient, you don't expect them to be permanent. Then you can accept all modulations. If you know what is exactly where and how exactly it is going to behave, then you can adjust your life to it and it doesn't worry you.

Suppose somebody says, "I know there is a snake in this house, but I don't know where it is right now." It's enough to kill all your joy. You have no idea of where it might be. You imagine it is under or behind everything, and the hours drag by in a kind of nightmare. But if you know you have a harmless snake in your garden, you feel it is your dear little friend out there. It doesn't trouble you at all. Or if it is a dangerous snake that always stays in a particular place, you can just avoid going there. Then also it is no trouble. Similarly, if you know that each time you mention a certain thing in your household someone is going to get excited or angry, you can just avoid mentioning it. Here again your prior knowledge keeps you out of danger.

So you need to have an inside knowledge of the forms of transformation. This doesn't take you away from any external reality. Instead of seeing the external world as many disjunct, separate entities, you see it as organically related to the one common reality or beingness to which everything belongs. When you do, you can say you have become a *tattvacintāgrahan,* one who sees the root and all the manifestations as being the same as yourself. Now it is true that you are That. If you are That, you are the modulation, you are the substance and you are the attribute. This gives a unitive understanding.

This is not just a verse for philosophers. Anyone who wishes for peace, joy and harmony in their daily life should know it.

Nature gets angry with you if you violate any of her laws. I have a friend who fasted for ten days. On the eleventh day he stuffed himself. Afterwards he felt very ill. Nature had her revenge. If you go against her, she will ask you to pay for it in some other way. This is called *vanpaka,* nature's great enmity.

If you know the natural laws, though, you can work with them. Nature has a law of gravity: whatever you throw up will come back down. But you can use another natural law to create pressure, and you can launch even a very large metallic thing, a rocket, out into space. The one law can be used to overcome the other, if you know what you're doing. But make one tiny mistake and nature brings it down with a crash.

Not that nature isn't cooperative. If you understand maya, it will lead you to brahman. If you don't understand — crash! It's a good game and a terrible game. If you enter the game, be sure you know all the rules. If you don't, it will beat you.

There are so many laws and rules — how can you ever learn them all? When Śvetaketu, in the Chandogya Upanishad, returned from his graduation, his father asked him, "Did you learn that, knowing which, you know what is not known and understand what you have not understood?" He replied, "Father, no." "Boy, if you understand the iron in a pair of scissors, then you understand iron all over the world. You don't have to examine every piece of iron. You don't have to understand all the water in all the seven seas to know what water is. Knowing a single drop is enough." Although it looks like many, in principle it is one. You can get a master key by which you can open all doors, and that master key is the secret of *tat* or That.

Īśvaracandra Vidyāsāgar came to Sri Ramakrishna. He was a great scholar, highly educated, known as a Vidyāsāgar, an ocean of knowledge, a walking university. Sri Ramakrishna had been to no school, had studied nothing. But before him, it was as if Vidyāsāgar knew nothing. All wisdom was at the tip of Ramakrishna's tongue. Whatever he said was like a pearl of great price. People would come to him with problems, and he would listen, smile or shed tears, and say perhaps one word. It would be enough. Like a panacea, it would console and comfort in just the right way. How could he have such understanding without having studied anything? Without attending any university?

He had gone to the root. If you know the root, if you know the cause, then you know the effect also. The *tattvacintāgrahan* who goes to the oneness at the root knows more than all the analysts together in all their specialised branches.

Verse 89

aṟivil irunnasadastiyennasaṅkhyam
poriyiḷakibbhuvanam sphurikkayālē
aṟivine viṭṭoru vastuvanyamille-
nnaṟiyaṇamīyaṟivaika rūpyamēkum

Existing in knowledge, as the being of non-being,
countless sparks arise, causing the appearance of the world;
so, apart from knowledge there is not another thing;
thus one should know; this knowledge bestows the state of oneness.

In physical sciences like chemistry and physics, the operations of laws are demonstrated through experiments. Scientists postulate a hypothesis and test it, and arrive at an assessment of truth based on the results. Analogies in philosophy correspond to experiments in science. Both experiments and analogies are essentially examples.

The kingdom of God is illustrated by Jesus Christ using a number of examples. Analogy is one of his favourite methods, where each analogy highlights a particular aspect of the divine realm. Vedantins generally approve of direct perception, *pratyakṣa*. They also use *anumāna* or inference, *upamāna* or analogy, and *śabda* or word testimony. Two other methods are *arthāpattī* and *anupalabdhi*, the argument of noncontradiction and the proof by residue or by elimination. Of these, *upamāna* is the method relevant to the present verse.

Analogy is an a priori teaching. Actually it is not a priori to the person who presents it, but it is a priori to the person who listens or receives it. In analogy one has to take the word testimony of the person who gives it as true, and then try to see the way in which that person is seeing. What it boils down to is a person who has had a vision is inviting us to share it.

Here Narayana Guru is giving us a vision of truth as he sees it. From knowledge innumerable offshoots spring forth, like sparks leaping from a campfire. They burst out, fly up and disappear. What he means by knowledge is identical with the Self, God, the Absolute or whatever name you prefer to give it. This is related by analogy to the fire, the one common source from which all sparks come. What we see here as the world is nothing more than the continuous rising up of sparks from a common source. The sparks can be of different magnitude and brightness, and some may remain for a long time while others have but a brief existence, but ultimately they all disappear.

What is a spark? The spark that comes from firewood is a tiny piece of carbon. It is not luminous on its own. The carbon is being oxidised, so it is transforming and changing. It cannot remain as it was. Now it is glowing, luminous. And what is the significance of the glow in this analogy?

When we look at a book we see many tiny ink marks on the pages. If the book is in some language we can't read, like Chinese, all we see are beautiful forms and patterns. However, the so-called beautiful patterns are our projection. All that's really there is carbon molecules adhering to white paper. If the book is in a language we know we may never notice the ink at all. As soon as we look at it, each formation presents a familiar notion to articulate a sound. We start reading the instant we look at it. Each word flashes and bursts in our mind as a meaning. There are millions of sparks on the page which all come and burst into meaning in us. It is this meaning that bursts from the seemingly inert matter into the brilliance of significance that is being represented by the glow of sparks in the Guru's analogy.

Is there any difference between the tiny periods and commas on a sheet of paper and this great universe? The star up there is one mark; the period here is another mark. In both there is something that comes for a little while, reveals a certain idea, and then fades away. Each in its own way is a spark of the one fire. Narayana Guru qualifies the sparks as *asadasti*, unreal/real. The mode is unreal, yet the brightness they have is real. The whole world is like this.

So the whole world is nothing but an *asat*, an unreal medium which brings us meaning for the time being. The sparks may disappear, but our experience of their light is impressed on us first.

Another thing is that the sparks don't just exist individually, they can be correlated with each other. Although each has its own distinctiveness, our eye passes from one to the next, building up complex meanings as it goes along. The ideas grow and become continuous, and the whole thing shines in us as knowledge. From our very birth constellations of ideas are coming to us, like sparks becoming meaningful.

The whole universe is like a book, in that everything in it is a symbolic expression of higher truth. We are getting educated in that truth day after day. That truth grows, sustaining the meaning and value of life. If you turn to it, you see there is nothing devoid of knowledge. Such knowledge brings you to the oneness of everything.

This is a verse whose meaning is so simple it is difficult to elaborate. You just have to visualise the whole analogy as it is expressed: from knowledge, as both unreal and real, countless sparks are rising up to build the universe. But its simplicity is very rich in implications.

We start from a basis, *adhiṣṭhāna*. From the basis, an occasion arises. Every experience is like an occasion that is arising. Like a spark catching your attention, you are drawn to a tiny little luminous aspect in the experience. Then another spark comes and your attention is distracted. You go from one spark to another. The spark doesn't remain anywhere — it is always moving. All the sparks are moving. You cannot give your attention to many sparks at the same time, but you can shift it from one to another. By the time your attention has shifted, if you look back to the other one it's already gone.

A man I know was very worried about his wife, because each wanted to have their own way and they couldn't adjust to each other. Then suddenly he came to a realisation. He told her: "Hereafter we have no quarrel. You go your way — wherever you like — but don't expect me to sit here and wait for you. If you come back you may not see me, or you may find me with another woman. Let it be like that." Sparks don't wait. They just fly off. As you go from one spark to another, don't think that you can somehow get back. That's the way life is.

Life is both real and unreal. It is unreal to the extent that the stuff which holds the light burns away, so you cannot retain it. Time passes and slips away. Two things come together; they get separated. Flux — motion — movement: that is one reality. The other is the eternal source. We were told earlier that only a philosopher sees the eternal source as the same, while those who are not contemplative live disjunctly from moment to moment. This means only one spark is illuminated at a time. If you understand that sparks will continuously come and go, and that this is intrinsic to the game of life, then you will have no special expectation and therefore no anxiety.

The Bhagavad Gita says no matter what comes, one should accept it as profitable. If it comes, it comes. If it doesn't come, it doesn't come. Rejoice in it. Somehow one has faith that sparks will be continuously coming and there will be some joy in life all the time. It's just that when you try to capture one and possess it, expecting to get all you need for the rest of your life out of it, you make a mistake.

So we have a basis, an occasion, motion, simple luminous units that keep on coming, distraction, whole ensembles — so many things can be extrapolated from this small example. When you turn inward and look at it, relating your personal problems to it, it makes sense. But somehow it is difficult to have this passive view. We tend to exaggerate either the impermanence of all sparks, or else the glorious glow of a single one.

That glorious spark does not persist forever, and therefore you get frustrated. Either you become totally cynical, or you go from frustration to frustration. One who can transcend all the dualities, remaining unattached while enjoying the beautiful glow of the sparks, is well-established. Your attitude then is that life is incidental; people come and go; relationships will be established and then forgotten; that's the game of life. You accept it. A lot of inner tribulation is gone. Many knots inside are unwound. Life becomes easy.

This is the axiology or aim of this verse: to teach us that if we can see it is the same fire glowing in all the sparks, it will bring us to a unitive notion of the Absolute.

Three great philosophers of India, Śaṅkara, Rāmānuja and Madhva, refer to the same truth in three slightly different ways. Śaṅkara says *sva svarūpa anusandhānam bhakti,* one should have the knowledge of the true form of oneself. Rupam is form, *sva* means one's own. Isn't this body my form? No. When you were a child you had a different body, and all through your life it has been changing. After awhile you will die and your body won't even be around any more. So that is not your real form. Your real form is what persists in and through all these processes, without beginning and without end. It is ever there. You are in search of your own form. This continuous process of search, of meditation, to arrive at your own true form, Śaṅkara says is the greatest meaning of life.

Rāmānuja goes one step further. He says *svarūpa ānandam,* the pursuit of the ananda, the value or meaning of your real form, makes life meaningful. It is not just by knowing you are permanent or absolute, but that you are eternal joy, that your true beingness is present whenever there is joy or happiness. If your happiness is somehow concealed you do not see your form. Again and again you are brought to states of depression, disgust, distrust and misery. That means your true form has disappeared. The asat, the unreal, is intervening. Only when the ananda persists are you having your *svarūpa.*

Madhva says *svarūpa ānanda tāratamya.* The true form is the basis (like the fire in our analogy), but your individual manifestation is like a spark from that fire. In one spark there may be a little brightness, while in another there is greater brightness. As you move from one to the other you are constantly comparing them with the original source or basis. Therefore you continuously examine your small, sparky nature and compare it to the vast absolute nature, and wonder why you don't gain it. So you never feel you are the Absolute. That's why you can never become God.

According to Madhva, God is independent while you are a dependent factor. He describes God using the term *svatantra,* meaning that which exists by its own discipline, its own law. It is self-established. From out of this comes the *paratantra,* that which does not have a life or truth of its own. It depends on the Supreme for its existence. Your body, mind, intellect — everything you are constituted of is a little glow coming from the Absolute. Because of this seeming duality, you get caught up in a continuous *tāratamya* or comparison of your life with the Absolute.

The Sufis use this very methodology for their practice. They go on singing the glory of the Absolute, repeating "Allah hu akbar" or "He is beautiful, He is merciful, He is kind." They see in themselves a little kindness, and in God absolute kindness. They see in themselves a little prettiness, and in God supreme beauty. Through adoration and praise, they try to enhance their qualities to approximate those of the Absolute.

Rāmānuja says continuity is what matters. Even though the sparks come separately, before one dies out you should catch up with the next and keep up the continuity. That's also fine. Why should you allow any moment of your life to be wasted, to be barren and meaningless? Keep your life interesting. It's up to you. Life is so wonderful! Go on making it more wonderful.

You wait for things to happen to you. Why should you wait? It's not necessary. I pull out Plato, look into it, and say "Oh, wonderful!" Then that spark is gone. I put it back and pull out Heidegger. "Hi, Heidegger, how are you?" He says something very different from Plato. Wonderful. Then that spark is gone and I pull out another. Then I write a letter to a friend in London and say, "How about me coming to London?" I get him all excited about it. Then I write another letter: "I am coming to Australia". Isn't that a contradiction? Yes. But it stimulates me to think of the possibility of going to two places at the same time.

Is it not a joke? Yes. The sparks are all jokes. They come and the next moment they die. Who cares about it afterwards? I completely forget I have written to London and Australia. Until a plane ticket arrives in the mail. . . .

When we were in the hospital attending on Nataraja Guru, he would be on the bed. He was half paralysed. We would all sit there despondently, doing nothing. We would doze off. Then he would call someone and we would get up. He would say, "Get me out of this bed!" Then he would ask us to count each cleaning. He would ask "Is it the penultimate?" and we would say "Yes, that's the penultimate." "Now the ultimate." Then he would say "Put me back." We would all be wondering what the game was. He said, "There is nothing more boring than to be a paralytic patient and have people sitting around. To make life interesting you have to go on making programmes."

Then in the middle of the night he would suddenly cry out, "Call the nurse!" She would come rushing in, thinking he was having a heart attack or a stroke or something. Then he would ask her, "Have you read Kalidasa's Sakuntala? What do you think of Sakuntala? Can you be beautiful like that? Do you have any boys like Duṣyanta coming over the fence?" She thinks, "What kind of man is this? He calls me on an emergency and then asks if I have any boyfriends climbing over the fence?"

Narayana Guru says if you don't do this, if you don't make life interesting, the world becomes a *narakam*, a hell. Find out your own interests. Keep life exciting. Let new sparks, new joy come. That's how you make it interesting.

Śaṅkara says that unless you are in the *svarūpa* you are not happy. Rāmānuja says the continuity of happiness is important. Madhva says you should again and again refer to the very source of it. All three approaches are agreeable to Narayana Guru. He integrates all three positions into one with his analogy of the fire emitting ensembles of sparks to cause the appearance of a world. The three interpretations are possible if you conceive the whole of life as one perennial, independent factor. The Guru doesn't give any theory here. He only says if you visualise this it will give you the joy of your life.

You are so conditioned, so dependent on people! You think, "My happiness is hiding in your pocket. I will sit here and cry until I get it from you." But an infant wriggles and moves and just watches things. Until the age of about four or five, a child invents its own games. It goes on rejoicing by itself. Children live their glory in the little sparks that come along. You can do the same if you are able to retain that freshness.

A young man came to see me once, who was very confused. He said, "My teacher says one thing but others say other things. And they live a different kind of life." Isn't it interesting that there is more than one way of looking at life? He found it confusing, while I was thinking how wonderful it is that the mind is capable of projecting so many diverse thoughts and ideas. If you see that everything is patterns, formations, it is like the variegated brush strokes in a painting, and the whole thing is as meaningful as a work of art. Each stroke has a different hue and intensity. Taken separately some of them can be ugly blotches, like mud or dirt, but if you have the frame of mind to put them all together you can see the overarching beauty of it.

When you try to make everything uniform you create a hell world, but if you see the unity within the diversity it becomes instead a great wonder.

If you are a spark, how do you find out what is real in you and what is unreal? Maya is defined as *sadasat vilakṣaṇam,* that which has the special characteristic of being both real and unreal. Maya is often translated into English as "illusion", but this itself misleading. Professor Betty Heimann, in her *Facets of Indian Thought* gives a better interpretation:

> The Sanskritist must at the outset feel repelled when, for example, the Indian concept of maya is translated as 'illusion'. The western mind, according to the present use of 'illusion' sees here something unreal, deceptive and delusive. Yet this is not even the primary meaning of the Latin word *illusio,* from the root *luclere,* 'to play'. *Illusio* originally, though this is now forgotten, meant 'interplay'. As such, but only in its original meaning is it a near equivalent of maya. Maya, the 'world of the measurables' (from the root *ma,* to measure), is a relative and transitory display of forms. In this sense it actually corresponds to *illusio,* interplay in variant shapes and forms, manifestations of the underlying substance. *Illusio,* thus interpreted according to its original meaning, truly is analogous to the Sanskrit term *līlā,* 'play and display' of the creative urge for world-formation and elusive world-manifestation, as taught in Indian cosmogony.[1]

1. Betty Heimann, *Facets of Indian Thought* (London: Allen & Unwin, 1963), p. 172.

It is interesting Professor Helmann brings lila into her discussion. Lila has the additional meaning that life is to be taken sportively. A sport gladdens your heart and your mind. Within the sport there are elements of tragedy and comedy. For instance, in a game like basketball one side has to win and the other to lose. Winning is joyous and failure is tragic, and these are woven into the very fabric of the sport.

In the spark there is an interplay of these two aspects. The living glow of the spark comes from the very process of its dying out. The subject and object are intertwined: the body which burns away and the meaning of it coming as a luminous glow are both to be taken as part of the game. If it burns with the brightness of a Buddha, the body may perish at the age of eighty, but even after hundreds of years the afterglow lingers as if the spark were still in existence. The joy that we get from it becomes a perennial experience.

We have to accept the burning out part of us, and see how from the core we can perpetuate more and more interesting glows until such time as the whole thing burns out. Then the essence, the joy, the fragrance, the reputation of it can incite many people to have similar glows coming from them.

When you take maya in this sense, it is not just illusory nothingness. One half is provoking the other half. One half is exacting from the other half its meaning. One half is a challenge to the other half. Truth is a challenge to falsehood. The possible is a challenge to the potential, whereby the probable is asked to actualise itself. All this is revealed when we apply this in our own lives, and through it life becomes vastly interesting.

Verse 90

anṛtamorastitayē maṟaykkukille-
nnanubhavamuṇṭu sadastiyennivannam
anupadamastitayāl itāvṛtam sad-
ghanamatināle kaḷēbarādi kāryyam

The unreal does not conceal what exists,
such is the experience; what exists is; in this way,
at every step this is enveloped by existence;
therefore, body and such effects are existence through
and through.

In the second verse of the *One Hundred Verses of Self-Instruction*, Narayana Guru listed the important elements of our world experience. He began with the psychic dynamics, or what is called the inner organ, consisting of the questioning mind, the recollection of memory, the act of judgement and the experience of affectivity. The inner organ relates itself with several instruments of perception and action: the mind is in relation with the physical senses like the eye and ear, the will is in relation with the hands and legs or whatever has to operate, the judging faculty is in relation with the data brought to it from the external world, and so on. When the relationships of the senses of perception and the organs of action are well-established with the inner system, the body consciousness becomes a well-organised entity. This allows us to have a comprehensive idea of our personality.

When the inner organ, the senses and the totality of the person are taken as a whole, it is called *kaḷebaram*. Although *kaḷebaram* is sometimes translated as 'body', it is more than that. It should be understood in the special sense of the four aspects of the psychic dynamics, the senses, both of perception and action, and the personal identity with the body, all taken together. This makes one unit, which belongs to the knower. That knower stands in relationship to what is known, called *lokam*. *Lokam* is the whole field of the physical and psychic entities coming within the ambit of our conscious and unconscious experience.

In the second verse we were told that all these are modifications of the one primordial substance. The primordial substance was equated with a self-luminous entity, likened to a sun shining in the beyond or the Absolute. Thus, the substantial reality of everything manifested here was pointed out in verse two.

Now we have come to verse 90. We are once again brought to have a look at the several bodies that constitute this world. We are first told we have anritam, a wrong understanding of functional reality. When functional reality or ritam is understood improperly it is anritam. For instance, when a child is hungry and it cries, its mother may find it inconvenient to nurse it. Nowadays she may put a plastic nipple in its mouth. The child takes it for a breast, so it sucks. The child expects the false nipple to function like its mother's breast, but it is plastic and no milk comes out of it. For a while, because of the visceral pleasure of the lips, it goes on sucking. But when its stomach doesn't get filled, it starts crying again. It feels, "I don't want this thing! Give me real milk! Nurse me!" That protest, coming from within, rejects the falsification of the ritam.

In fact, we do this kind of thing to ourselves, nature does it to us, society does it to us. It is happening on many levels. There are many kinds of make-believe between people. There is a lot of scope for anritam.

The Guru says anritam can never satisfy you because truth will soon demand functional reality, and that whenever functional reality is belied the actual situation will expose it. If a man convinces you he is a very good plumber, but then he doesn't know how to fix something in your bathroom, it proves his claims are false. When what he says meets the acid test of functional reality, he has to confess he can't do it. The simple things in life can show this up very clearly. For instance, if you want to prepare a meal you should know how to cook, otherwise the result will not be edible.

This is a very important lesson to learn. If we get confused in situations in our daily life, like our interpersonal relations, it is because we are not paying heed to functional reality. This is different than abstracting the total truth in a situation. That also has a great value. But we live everyday in the manifest aspect rather than the unmanifest, so for that we need not the philosopher's truth but common sense truths which are valuable for everyday situations.

Before one gets the highest realisation, one should know how to listen to one's own common sense. It is at the risk of common sense that most people seek spirituality, and this heads them towards trouble.

Everything has an innate limitation as well as enormous potentialities. Sand cannot hold water. But sand can be melted and fused into transparent glass, which can hold water. If you look at a handful of sand and a glass bottle, you would never imagine there could be such a transformation. Enormous possibilities are lying concealed in the sand.

But however much you try you cannot get milk from sand, except in fairy tales. This is the field where charlatans thrive. When you abandon ritam, functional reality, they all rush in. "We shall help you! Now you have given up your common sense. Very good! That's an important requirement of our path. From here onwards we will be fast friends." This kind of spirituality is not safe.

I am reminded of a time when about thirty Australians were sent by their Australian guru to study with me at the Varkala Gurukula. Someone wrote back to their guru about something they feared might happen, so she sent a cable: "Return sooner than you can come." One of them brought it and showed it to me. He said they wanted to leave immediately. I said, "To go to Australia there is no way other than flying. You have to get tickets first. India is not like Australia, where you can just walk into an airport and buy a ticket. Even if you buy a ticket a month early they will say you are on the waiting list. It's five in the afternoon. By the time you pack it will be seven. The next plane from here is tomorrow at one p.m. You can all go if you want tomorrow morning. Why don't you take rest now?"

Then their chief took them all aside and said, "This man is against our guru! Our guru says 'return sooner than you can', and he doesn't allow us to go sooner than we can!" He came to me and asked, "If you got such a cable from your guru, would you wait like that?" I said, "My guru is on the next hill. You can find out from him."

So they all packed everything, took their packs and went to see Nataraja Guru. He was already asleep when they reached his hut, so they just sat there. Around 1 a.m. Guru woke up, hearing voices outside. He thought they were bandits! He turned on the light and shouted, "What is this? What's going on?" Then they told him why they were there. He said, "I really appreciate your great loyalty to your guru. It touches me very deeply. I have no right to correct your guru. You have so much faith! You should act upon her wishes. You want to go now, but even if you leave now the plane will take off only at one tomorrow afternoon. Why should you sit so long at the airport? Why don't you sleep?" Then he added, "I'll give you one piece of advice, because I am also a guru. With all your spiritual intuition and loyalty, also keep your common sense. It will be very handy in your daily life."

This plea for common sense leads us to the world of ontologic truth. What is ontologic truth? There is a distinction to be made between empirical truth and ontologic truth. Empirical means I can see something here and now with my own eyes and I am convinced of its existence. The ontologic is one step beyond the empirical, through a kind of reduction. There you arrive at the reality not only of one thing here and now, but of all things of the same class and the same order.

A pair of prescription glasses cannot be passed on from one person to another, because they are made according to the requirements of a particular person's eyes. There is an inner relationship, a pairing, a one-to-one correspondence between the lens and that person's vision. This is true because of a law governing real things, a law that governs everything we can experience through our senses, understand with our intellect and direct with our common sense. This inner structure of the psychophysical world gives us a foundation of truth on which we live our daily life.

This intrinsic structural unity is the ontologic reality. It is the ontologic reality of things that is exposed to you whenever you make an error at the functional level in any field, whether spiritual, social or material. In all of these is an inner structural reality that is well complemented by a functional reality. The structure and the function are two sides of the same coin. This is why a functional disturbance resonates instantly with the structural basis.

If a pianist plays a certain key and it makes a jarring note, he stops. He knows the string needs to be tuned. When a piano is properly tuned it makes the same kinds of tones in the same arrangement as all other pianos. So someone with the necessary skill comes, listens, and corrects the notes. Then the pianist listens and says, "Right. Exactly right. It's there." This is where the ontologic reality is touched. We can all see the piano with our eyes — that's the empirical reality. But we have to go one step further to make it fit the inner law and operate properly. Cosmologically and psychologically there are inner laws operating, and they are interlinked to govern the inner structure of everything. We need to be very clear in our minds about this.

Ritam and anritam are our guidelines here. There is a science of anritam. Even malfunctions adhere to certain laws. If this were not true a mechanic would not be able to repair a car, a plumber couldn't fix the pipes and a teacher wouldn't be able to correct anyone's grammar. Diseases are all anritams, malfunctions of the body. All the *materia medica*, all the pathological sciences, deal with aspects of anritam, but there is nonetheless scope for science in them, since even with a mistake you can see how it takes a certain inevitable course and brings a predictable wrong result. And by just examining a wrong result you can see what kind of mistake was made to arrive at it. So there is ritam working within the anritam. It is a universal law which guides you when it functions as well as when it malfunctions.

In our meditations or spiritual experiences, we should also make a search for the ontologic verity of the truth of what we experience. The seers' advice is if you have an experience and it is brilliant and very enjoyable but no one else has experienced it, it is hard to know whether you are going kooky or it is a real experience until you land in some terrible place.

Suppose something happens and you speak of it with your

personal teacher. He or she might ask, "Did you do such and such a thing? And did you get this kind of experience? Was it followed by this? And then came this?" If you say yes, then they might say, "Have no fear. That's exactly how it happens. To me it was also like that." At least now there are two people who have shared the same kind of experience. One thing then is sure: if the disciple is mad, the guru is having the same kind of madness.

Or perhaps your teacher picks up a book and says, "This work was traditionally followed by both teachers and disciples, and according to Sutra 37 you will first experience this, then this, then this. For at least two thousand years people have been following this and having the same experience you have." Then you can feel you are very safe. You have a living example in your teacher and also a tradition which supports it. They come in a straight line down to you. So it is almost certain to be a true experience.

When you don't have this kind of authentic reference point to see where you stand, you can be misled. You may be a very blessed person experiencing something no one ever has before. It might be wonderful, but it cannot be vouchsafed. If you want to take it at your own risk, fine. But mostly it can go the wrong way. As Narayana Guru says, anritam will not be able to conceal truth for long. Such is our actual experience.

Then the Guru says *sadasti. Sat* means it exists; *asti* means I know it is. In all experiences there is a cognition. When you perceive something it is immediately followed by the meaning of what you have cognised. You say, "This is such and such a thing." That is called *asti*, 'it is'. How do you know it is that? Because you are fully aware of the properties that go along with such an experience.

Then you are affected by the experience, *priyam*. The Guru is going to speak of priyam in the coming verses, but for now he is speaking of asti, the existential aspect. He says *sadasti*, 'This is'.

Then he says *anupadam*, your life is like a march to your goal. In that progressive march you proceed step by step. A step is called *padam; anu* means 'along with'. Along with each step there is a confirmation of truth. Each time you step, the good earth supports you, as if it were saying, "Walk on me. I am stable. I'll support you wherever you need to go." If there were an obstruction, you wouldn't be able to walk. A kind of confirmation is always coming from the path to the *pāda*, from the path to the foot. You turn on the tap in the kitchen — water comes. *Asti*. You look for a cup — it is there. You fill it. Everything you do goes on confirming that you are doing the right thing. You drink — it quenches your thirst. *Asti* again.

Where is there to go wrong, unless you are insane? It's not an imaginary thing. This truth is not anything alien. It lives within you. It gives confirmation, *anupadam*, with every step. Therefore Narayana Guru says at every step your experience is enveloped by truth.

The first mantra of the Isavasya Upanishad says wherever you turn, whatever you see, when it is all enveloped with God, then move free — not until then. The word for enveloping, *āvāsyam*, is used in a very special sense. Narayana Guru uses *āvṛttam* in this verse. The meaning is the same: enveloped by God or enveloped by truth. When the whole function is endorsed as truthful and you do not come across any snag, any hitch, then you can say you are living a truthful life. There is no obstruction anywhere. Everything is going smoothly. It's a gentle harmonious flow.

When malfunctions come, the *āvṛttam*, the enveloping aspect, is destroyed. Something comes in between to disrupt it. But when you do experience the confirmation of it from moment to moment and step by step, where is it coming from?

On one side is the seer, and on the other is its counterpart, the seen. Their complementarity makes an experience valid. When I confirm an apple is an apple, I am also confirming that I am a proper seer of the apple. The truth of an experience lies half in what is presented and half in the experiencer. It is not a one-sided truth. The truth belongs simultaneously to what you visualise and to who you are. Both are part of a single reality, called the Self, that envelops everything.

The Guru next uses the word *sadghanam*, meaning it is truth through and through. It is existence through and through and substance through and through. The same word is also used in the second verse to describe the one supernal sun shining in the firmament beyond, whose light transforms into all this.

The ultimate we search for and the immediate we live in are united. They are not two. Here and now we are living in the Absolute.

That's why Sir Arthur Eddington said that the Absolute could be defined as a relative which is always the same no matter what it is relative to. When there is such a degree of dependability, the relative becomes the Absolute.

We see two in relation to one, three in relation to two and one, and so on. The quantitative aspect of these integers doesn't change simply because they are relational. One and two always make three; three and two always make five. They are consistent, constant. The mathematical constancy we see operating functionally shows it to be truth through and through.

This verse is so closely related to verse two, it is well to recall it to mind:

> The inner organ, the senses, the body,
> the many worlds known by direct perception — everything,
> when contemplated,
> is the glorious embodiment of the sun that shines in the sky
> beyond;
> this should be known through relentless search.

What is experienced as the psychic dynamics, the senses, the body, and the very many worlds of interest are all modifications of the light of the one supreme Sun of knowledge, which shines in the firmament of the Absolute. This we should know by cogitation combined with proper discernment.

Now in the ninetieth verse, Narayana Guru brings us back. We have not gone anywhere; we are still remaining in this solid world where things have their thingness and their meaning. This verse is given for stabilisation, so you won't just take off. In the next five or six verses there will be another critical focusing on the verity of things here. You may lose your ground if you are not once again reminded to hold on to your common sense. This is just like telling a child to hold on tight while they are getting on a merry-go-round. The Guru says to hold on tight to the functional reality you know through your common sense, until you come to the other end.

This is the compassion of the Guru. Instead of making a fanfare of euphoria, he asks us to sit firm. There is a Malayalam proverb which says: "Sit firmly before you stretch your legs." If you suddenly stretch your legs while standing up, you'll fall with a bang! It is very bad for your buttocks. The ninetieth verse is chosen so you all will sit very firmly on solid facts.

The fifteenth chapter of the Bhagavad Gita serves the same purpose as the ninetieth verse of *Ātmopadeśa Śatakam*. In the Gita, an overwhelming mystical experience is presented in very raw and intense form in the eleventh chapter. In these Hundred Verses we have also encountered such mystical experiences as the whole sky blazing with the fire of the highest form of musical harmony, in which all names and forms disappear, or wisdom coming like a thousand suns rising all at once. The same thing happens to Arjuna in the Gita. Then in the twelfth chapter Krishna asks him, "Are you convinced of all these things now?" "Yes." "Great! Turn your mind to That and hold onto it with great reverence." The thirteenth and fourteenth chapters, along with the sixteenth and seventeenth, are a thoroughgoing scrutiny of Arjuna's inner traits. They are a kind of pathological analysis of Arjuna's personality after the big shakeup. But the fifteenth chapter is totally different from those surrounding it. It hearkens back to the eleventh chapter, reestablishing what occurred there on a proper foundation of fundamental philosophy. The cosmological, theological and psychological aspects of the mystical experience are all placed in context. Both the epistemology and the ontology of the philosophy are well laid out, so you are not left suspended in the midair of your mystical fervor. You can cool down and begin to comprehend what took place.

Before he leads us to the ultimate peace at the end of the work, Narayana Guru once again reminds us that God did not make a mistake in creating this world. God was justified in giving you a skeletal system, an anatomy, which is so structured that when you want to raise your hand you can, or when you want to make a fist you can, or when you want to point your finger nothing is simpler. It is a perfect arrangement with no mistakes. So don't say the physical world is superficial. There's nothing superficial about it. It's even a great thing that you can close your eyelids. Just the tiniest movement and the whole world disappears! Open your eyes and the world comes back. What a great wonder! Blinking is the simplest reflex action in the body. From the far-off stars to the grass beneath your feet, it all disappears and returns with a snap. What could be more wonderful than that? It belongs to the world called empirical, and the truth of it belongs to the ontologic world. Thus it is stabilised.

Geoffrey Hodson of the Theosophists has published a beautiful book of his African tour, with paintings of water nymphs, tree spirits, and all kinds of little fairies coming out of flowers. He does not say he imagined them. He says, "I see them just as I see you." He painted them all, and the pictures show them sitting there, posing properly for him to paint them.

If you put Hodson on one side and a materialist like B.F. Skinner on the other, a line connecting them will cover the whole world of conceptualisation. If you just hang on to Hodson you will be in a beautiful world, but there won't be any stable ground for you to walk on. If you're a partisan of Skinner, everything is physically measurable, countable and calculable. But you cannot calculate, count and get a measure of love for someone, or quantify a good feeling. So you need to know how to synchronise both these attitudes into a holistic approach. That will bring you a sound philosophy, sound mysticism, sound spirituality, and a whole life.

Verse 91

priya viṣayam prati ceytiṭum prayatnam
niyatavumaṅṅane tanne nilkkayālē
priyamajamavyayamaprамēyamēkā-
dvayamitutan sukhamārnnu ninniṭunnu

Whatever effort is made in relation to each
object of endearment it remains ordained;
this dear value — unborn, unspent,
unpredicable, one without a second —
remains established in happiness.

Back in verse 49, Narayana Guru gave us a universal law of axiology: In this world, all beings, always, under all circumstances, try to obtain the happiness of the Self.

What appears to be the final culmination of an experience is how we are affected by it, in other words the degree of happiness it brings us. And when we closely examine how we relate to things — how we envision and interpret them and how we select a stimulus or a group of stimuli — we can see that the consideration of happiness is to some extent an unconscious process. This was explained earlier as a selective structuralism which is implied in our behaviour.

In the structuring of any situation in our minds, we select certain of the aspects out of the multitude which are present. The criterion of selection is our happiness. If something promises happiness, our whole being is automatically attracted towards it. Even before our conscious intelligence decides that something is going to make us happy, an unconscious factor in us senses the possibility of happiness and we are drawn to it.

We also relate with other things which endanger the possibility of attaining happiness. A threat is negatively important because it concerns the removal of our happiness. So situations contain both attraction and repulsion, love and strife. Strife is only the negative aspect of love, while love is that which brings happiness. We don't love for the sake of love, but for that which brings us happiness.

In the last verse Narayana Guru spoke of the ontologic richness of what happens here. In all experiences he pointed to a law operating, namely a participation of the existentiality of every individual thing in the primal existence, or *sat* aspect, of the Self. Otherwise, transactional life has no meaning or order.

We discover natural laws in the transactional world, and they hold good in their applications. All the mathematical, physical, biological and chemical laws we have discovered are consistent, and are the same all over the world. This brings at least the perception of unity to mankind. The unity which is seen in the physical realm is further extrapolated to the social field, where we have evolved many social laws which are binding on all people.

Transactions take place in the world of psychophysical organisms. Certain aspects belong to the physical world, some to the psychological world, and some to the social world. In all these there is an endorsement of the validity of its truth, which enables us to come to a common consent. This, too, makes life rich and meaningful.

After referring to this existential aspect in the ninetieth verse, Narayana Guru now takes us to the axiological aspect. Axiology means that which pertains to the world of values. Something is present and it is valuable. The intermediary link between existential truth and its value or meaning is the knowledge by which you recognise the existence and interpret the value of something. The Guru says that wherever there is priyam, there is the cognition of an object that is both valuable and belonging to the non-Self. The individual self is immediately attracted to it.

The fundamental nature of the Self is happiness through and through. In individual cases we often stray away from our true nature and forget we are happy beings. As a result we become unhappy. We are on foreign ground. We are not grounded in our own true nature.

Any kind of grief, suspicion, distrust or frustration is an indication you have moved away from your centre. You have left your native ground. Then you see some sign of happiness somewhere. It reminds you of where you belong, so you immediately move towards it. This is a natural law. The Guru says it is always operating, unexpended.

Philosophers like Aristotle and Kant speak of the *actus pura*, or pure act. If you exert yourself, your body may become weak from the expenditure of physical energy, but as far as pure action is concerned, there is no expenditure of energy. It's a pure act, a pure law. Pure action is like a model for all being. Our individual actions in moving towards objects of interest are only in conformity with this natural law, which is engrained in pure action.

How does a thing become an object of interest, a *viṣayam*? In any group of people there may be many men and women, but we find that one man is attracted to a particular woman and she feels the same kind of attraction to him. Why don't all the men feel attracted to one woman, or are all the women attracted to one man? It doesn't happen that way. You may think a certain person has no attraction, but you will find that person is an object of great attraction to someone else. You might even wonder how that person could be loved by anyone. But this is not something which is based very much on the external forms of things. You know very little of the beauty of the inner psyche. There are many inner currents operating in our psychic world, and only when your own psyche is affected do you feel the pull.

In the previous meditation we were emphasising the very solid, gross, practical aspects of physical reality and what can be called the actual. From there we are going to another degree of truth which tends to be more spiritual or psychic than physical. There is a very alive core in us that is like a honeycomb in a beehive, in which there are newly laid eggs, eggs in the process of hatching, and busy bees engaged in building up the system. Our growing personality has many eggs that have not yet hatched, some in the formative stages, and some that are very much alive to the external environment. The eggs are called vasanas — innate dispositions or incipient memories — and they are all looking for opportunities to express themselves.

If you follow the Buddhist interpretation, they do not believe in a Self. Instead they believe in the affinity of action to produce results which follow from the preceding action. The precedents make up a kind of web they call a *sankhara*, an aggregate. According to Buddhist theory, we are all aggregates of dispositions which are produced by previous karma, previous actions and reactions. The actions need not be solely physical. Our thoughts are also a kind of movement from a cause to an effect, and they can have motivational forces operating in them. Motivation imparts motion. Emotions are also aspects of this motion. Thus, we are aggregates of our dispositions. All our actions, including our emotional life, are always perpetuating the continuity of these dispositions.

Like a bee that is attracted towards a flower and then instinctively goes to the very part where the honey is, we are also drawn to objects long before we consciously know anything about them. You start recognising you are in love with someone only after it has already gone deep into your system. At first you may even feel irritated by them, and try to avoid them. But recurring thoughts come. Images flash through your mind again and again, and eventually you become fascinated with them. Only then do they become what is called *viṣayam*.

Before you are aware of it, movements have already started in you to relate to a particular object. You are first unconsciously drawn to it and then later you recognize it outwardly. The recognition of it comes only when the link is already psychically established between you and the object of interest. Then it becomes a *priya viṣayam*. As Narayana Guru says, it is ordained that each object of interest compels you to act in one way or another.

And why is it ordained? There is an element of compulsion in it. When you are drawn towards something before you even recognise its value, that is compulsion. The compulsion comes because it is a natural law operating. The Guru calls it ordained because even if you are disillusioned about one interest, the life urge doesn't give up. It picks another object of interest and you are led towards that. It is happening all the time. It is a universal law, and you are part of it. This universal law does not give any credence to your one failure. It keeps on until you can no longer function naturally.

The Guru is speaking here of the normal cases. There are abnormal instances where a person is so shocked by the failure of one priyam that they become shy of putting forth any effort, and the whole psyche may withdraw into a shell. They become withdrawn, sometimes to the point of catatonia. But as long as you don't enter into such malfunctioning, you will continue to take interest in life.

Buckminster Fuller is in his nineties, but he is not at all tired of the many interests of this world. He still finds it awfully engaging. He says we have not come to stay but to pass on, so before passing on we should get to as many things as possible, one after the other. This shows he is not a pathological case. He is a very normal living being. What makes him and all of us continue is a dear value, unborn, unspent, unpredicable. It is within everyone.

Narayana Guru is referring here to the fourth state, or turiya, mentioned in the Mandukya Upanishad. The previous verse referred to our wakeful transactions, which belong to the first state or limb of consciousness. Within wakeful consciousness there are separate objects, and we function as the knowers of things, the doers of acts and the enjoyers of values. There is a one-to-one correspondence between the knower and the known. The same one-to-one correspondence exists between the doer and the action and the enjoyer and what is enjoyed.

There is a central core where the knower in you and the knower in me come together and unite. The doer in you and the doer in me are also united, as are the enjoyer in you and the enjoyer in me. This is what enables us to communicate with each other and make ourselves sensible. If my understanding is solely my own private one, I will not be able to put it across to you. There is a common ground where you and I meet. Similarly, we can cooperate only by doing action where my action can supplement and complement your action.

Our children can be the continuators of our action, and in that way our actions can go on endlessly. Like that, knowledge has been flowing through the ages like a grand stream of wisdom. The Upanishadic rishis, who lived three and four thousand years ago, still influence our minds. The words of the Buddha and Christ and Muhammad are keeping us alive in spirit. Nothing is lost. This means there is a common stream of consciousness, in which there is a common effort going on and a common happiness which we all recognise at once. These three strands unite in the one Self to which we all belong.

When you have this inner connection, the world is not alien and no one is a foreigner to you. The other person's joy becomes as much your interest as your own, and the other person's light becomes your own light, too. You come to a kinship with the whole world. Narayana Guru relates this to the fourth state, which is a translucent state where the 'I' consciousness is a kind of shimmering witness of all that is going on.

When you go into a deep sleep you are in a profound state of unconsciousness where you don't know anything. The dream state is also outside your control. These two states are kind of a given where you don't have much to do. You need to make a breakthrough in them so that the fourth state or turiya can be continuously brought to bear on the first or wakeful state. In fact, the fourth state is the pure consciousness lying buried behind all the conditional states of consciousness: dream, wakeful and unconscious. It is never far from you, but it is veiled by your dreaminess, your sleepiness and your daily activities so that you forget it. If this unborn, unexpending, nondual, unitive value of life, which is the eternal, blissful happiness of all can prevail in the wakeful also, then the quality of your transactions changes.

In the previous verse we were convinced that we are always in the truthful world of pure existence, and now the Guru wants us to be convinced that pure happiness always prevails. The problem is there are certain veiling principles which come between our awareness and this truth. If you make a breakthrough and get them out of your way, happiness will always be there.

You believe in productivity, in always producing something. Your thinking is that before you produced it, it did not exist; that with your own effort it was produced. Then you transfer this type of thinking to your happiness. If you are not in a state of happiness, you engage in some effort that you think will make you happy. You believe that happiness is produced, manufactured like a plastic wastebasket or some other consumer item. The Guru wants to correct this notion. He says happiness is your true nature, so it is not produced. It is unborn, *ajam*. It is also *avyayam*, unexpended. Just as it is not produced, it cannot be used up.

In daily activities, when you do something, even though it may be very exciting for a time, you eventually become tired of it. It becomes boring, and you want to put it aside. It has become *vyayam*, expended. But once you discover the true happiness of the Self you will find that it does not diminish. It is *avyayam*, unspent, undecreasing.

The Guru also describes it as *aprameyam*, meaning unpredicable. This is a little more difficult to understand. You cannot make the Self or pure happiness or pure knowledge or pure action an object of your ratiocinative thinking or your discursive reasoning. Any description or observation you make is inadequate to describe it. You can look at any object, though, and say it is a *prameyam*, an object of consideration, and you are making that observation, seeing and considering it. But both the dual aspects of the observer and the observed are to be transcended to arrive at the idea of *aprameyam*.

So why do you fail? You fail because you want everything to be put in terms of one limb of your consciousness, one quarter of your totality: wakeful consciousness. In the wakeful, everything has a definite name, a definite form, a mass, a dimension, and various specific qualities. When you are not interpreting events in this model you are at a loss. It is only the most gross aspect of your consciousness, but you hold on to it, you are riveted to it.

The Montessori schools are taking children's minds and riveting them to objects. The eyes are riveted to forms and colours, and afterwards the children can't get their eyes out of them. If a book has pictures, do we read it? There may be beautiful things written in it, but we just skip from picture to picture. That is their approach. Madame Montessori started her system to help handicapped children develop their sensory functions so they could share the world with normal children, and it worked very well in many cases. But now the schools treat all children as abnormal. Their spirits are drawn into the physical system and riveted there. They are never given the opportunity the enter into abstractions and generalisations, into the free flow of the mind to imagine. Even without this programme, most of us become riveted to objects far too early in life!

It is here Edmund Husserl makes a complete revolution in human thinking. He maintains that fancy is as valuable as knowledge, as the most solid, gross, external fact. He says facts have nothing to do with wisdom, nothing to do with knowledge. He puts this so emphatically you even get annoyed reading it. He goes on ad nauseum, telling us that fancy contains as much or more wisdom than facts do.

The transcendental reduction of which Husserl speaks is the same as Narayana Guru's *aprameyam,* but he probably never knew there were others who thought and wrote as he did. I don't know if he read any Oriental books. On the other hand, Karl Jaspers had a very good grounding in the Upanishads and Oriental mysticism. He frequently referred to Nāgārjuna, the Buddha and Plotinus, claiming you only had to restate what they had already said, that nothing else was needed.

When Plotinus spoke of the flight of the alone to the Alone, he already knew the possibility of going beyond all symbols, beyond all kinds of imagery and other crutches. So much of philosophy is merely an elaboration of this quintessential idea.

The *aprameyam* Narayana Guru is speaking of is a very valuable key for us. It means one without a second. One without a second is something you don't have to visualise.

In the Visvarupa Darsana of the Bhagavad Gita, Krishna said to Arjuna: "You cannot see this with your eyes of flesh, your physical eyes, but only with the eye of wisdom." When you try to transfer yourself from the physical eyes to the eye of wisdom, you want to carry the imagery of the physical eyes along with you.

Bertrand Russell puts it this way: it's just like after learning that spirit is entirely different from matter, in order to understand spirit a man makes a clay model of it. Will it ever be possible to make a clay model of the spirit? He gives another example. A turtle leaves his lake and goes for a walk on the land. After the walk it returns to the lake and says to a fish swimming there that it was very exciting to walk on the shore. The fish asks him what he did. "I was walking on the shore." The fish was disdainful. "Stupid! No one can do such a thing! Why don't you say you were swimming on the land? Do we not swim?" Fish can understand only what they already know, not anything new.

This is exactly what happens when you want everything to be put in terms of the language you already know. You need to make an effort to have another category of understanding.

There is a Sanskrit story about a swan that came from the lakes of the gods. It flew to an earthly pond, where it landed in the midst of some cranes. The cranes gathered around it and asked where it came from. It answered, "I come from the heavens, where the gods are." "What do you eat there?" "We have many celestial plants there, celestial lotuses with pollen dust and honey. We are fed on that." "Do you have any clams there?" "No, we don't have any of those there." "What kind of heaven can it be, then, if you don't have any clams? It cannot be a proper heaven, because those are the most delicious food for cranes."

The *aprameyam* aspect of the higher value, which is the value of the Self, is unexpended, one without a second. It is the other side of priyam. In it you get a unitive experience of supreme happiness.

Verse 92

vyayamaṇayāte veḷikku vēlaceyyum-
niyamamirippatukoṇṭu nityamākum
priyamakamē piriyāteyuṇṭitinnī
kriyayoru kēvalabāhyaliṅgamākum

Unexpended, the law of action operates outside;
therefore, it is eternal;
within, endearment is inseparable;
to this, action is only an external symbol.

Narayana Guru began the study of *Ātmopadeśa Śatakam* by presenting the primordial cause of everything, the cosmic mold or Karu, in its dual aspect of manifestation: shining outside as the world we consider external, and operating inside as our personal experiences and the knowledge we have of the world. He pointed out that in both the world outside and the knowledge inside there is an immanent as well as a transcendental aspect.

When we speak of knowledge, our idea is that it is an awareness we experience in our brain. We consider the concrete world as a reality by itself, standing in contrast to pure ideas. This is understandable, but in this presentation both these aspects are assigned to the Karu.

Now in our study we are returning to the world, which is specially emphasised in the first verse as the external world and its internal counterpart. Two kinds of action are taking place in these two realms. In the external world we see not only the action of the individual but many other kinds of action. For instance, we see the sun appearing in the east, traversing the sky and setting in the west. The rotation of the earth is bringing us day and night. Additionally, the whole solar system is moving and all the stars are moving away from each other. We don't actually see this, but arrive at the understanding by making calculations. As Eddington puts it, some of the major actions we see we know only as concepts. We have to accept these concepts or else we would not be able to explain certain things that take place. In fact, when examined closely most of the action in our personal experience will also be seen to depend on ideas passing through our mind.

At any rate, in the external world we see many actions going on, and they are continuous. The earth never stops rotating and revolving; the sun does not stop radiating its energy. Your body is also external in terms of your knowledge, and in it the same kind of continuous functioning is taking place. It isn't that the body is permanent, but the physical entities it consists of are continuously fulfilling their functions. Moreover, everything, including us, is constituted of simple elements, where each element has its own structure and function. Each element is also continuous, in that its atoms never stop their motions. There is no end to it, and we accept that. So the external world has a law of continuous action. The Guru says it is always going on, unexpended.

That covers the external factors. Now to the inside. We are drawn to things which please us. When we are drawn we see the potential of realising or experiencing our ananda by structuring or reassembling or adjusting things in a certain way. This is like what a sculptor does. She can see the form lying latent in the marble or whatever material, but the amorphous shape of the block veils the form she wants to bring out. Then she carves away whatever is extraneous so that we can see the true form without anything obscuring it. Like that, when you visualise your ananda, the true joy of your Self, in a certain situation, you inevitably associate it with things or people. Then you postulate in your mind that it will take so much effort and so much time to arrive at that happiness. The true happiness is now veiled and obstructed. The obstruction is to be removed so the happiness can again be experienced.

So mentally we conceive what we are going to find, and then we make efforts for the removal of the obstructions. But, as we have often pointed out, the realisation of the Self is not something that can be achieved through any action. A raw fruit is not edible until it ripens. You have to wait for the transformation of the green fruit into a sweet one. But in the case of the Self no such transformation is required. It is always ananda.

Because of the obscuring aspects of prakriti we spoke of earlier, the true nature of the Self is veiled to different degrees on different occasions. At times the veiling principle can be easily removed, and at other times it persists for a long time, leading you to get involved in more action.

There is no time when the aspiration to be with our own true nature is not with us. Our seeming alienation from it comes not in reality but in the individuated forms of our consciousness. When the Self manifests itself with a body, the body identity acts as a colouring or conditioning agent. This is the first veiling principle. Because of it, part of consciousness feels as if it is segregated from its true field, its true home, so it is always seeking to return to its native nature.

The inner quest continues in us, never leaving, perpetuated by the conditioning of the physical body. In reality nothing is alien to us, everything belongs to the Self and the Self is existence through and through. So in every existential factor there is a possibility of discovering the ananda aspect of the Self. This is why the mind is again and again drawn to individual things, people, events, possibilities. The existential aspect and the ananda aspect have become linked in our awareness, and are continuously operating within us.

So we have a great bifurcation or division into two: an outer manifestation where action never ceases, and an inner manifestation where the quest for being with our own true Self is also going on continuously. The Guru says what seems to be action outside is only an external reflection of this incessant quest we are feeling inside. All actions which happen outside mirror in themselves what is happening inside, that is, the eternal quest.

A wave is an action we see in water. Water is always the same. It never changes. But we can observe the continuous coming and going of waves in it, which is another example of the unexpended action instituted in the world.

Waves are the dharma of water, dharma being that which makes anything what it is. For fire to burn or water to flow and moisten, there are innate properties in them which function continuously and operate universally. That is why the Guru says in all that is constituted as the external world there is a perennial law.

Dharma and karma are inseparable. When all the individual dharmas are put together and seen as one total dharma, it still has within it the duality of cause and effect. When the cause and effect duality is transcended it is understood as brahman, the Absolute.

The things we are attracted to do not last. They are transient. So how can we say our inner effort is continuous? This is a subject on which Śaṅkara and Rāmānuja have different opinions. Śaṅkara speaks of the transience of the wave and the permanence of water. He says effects like waves are not to be looked into, because water itself never changes. It is the cause of the wave, and we should stay with the cause. This world is of the nature of *bhāvarūpa*, which is an innate law of constant modulation, and according to Śaṅkara those modulations are not to be recognised.

Rāmānuja says that's not so. If this world belongs to the Absolute, what is instituted as a permanent quality in it has a co-permanence with the totality. Wherever there is water there is always the possibility of ripples or waves or tides. Between a ripple and a small wave there is only a quantitative difference. In any case, it always happens in water. Rāmānuja says this is *bhāvarūpa svarūpa*, having the eternal nature of producing this kind of effect, so the effects should be recognised.

The body has a beingness, of birth, growth, change, decay and death, followed by a transformation into another body which again goes through all these stages. Here we are not looking at the segmented aspect but the principle behind it. The principle is not transient, it is a permanent feature. You become hungry in the morning, so you eat breakfast and your hunger is appeased. But hunger returns at midday and again you need to eat, and so on endlessly. So hunger is not to be treated as a transient event but as a continuous, perennial principle. It is to be understood vertically rather than horizontally.

The Guru says although the priyam or fascination with each

individual thing appears to be transient, you cannot help but go on seeking new *priyams*. The quest is continuous. It is as eternal as the action taking place in the external world.

In the Karma Darśana in Narayana Guru's *Darśanamālā*, he shows that all the cosmic functions such as the fire that burns, the wind that blows, the cloud that rains and the earth that supports, as well as the bodily functions such as the vital pranas that are going up and down, pulsating in the heart and communicating in the nervous system, are all to be treated as the functional ritam of the world order of which we are a part.

In the twentieth verse of this study, Narayana Guru says that this world has no reality other than the reality derived from what we have already seen as the cosmic mold or Karu. Then in verse 89 he says that everything exists and the philosopher sees it as one unitive reality. He has even said elsewhere that each thing taken separately has its own existence. When he says all these things he is recognising the continuity and the universality of the *sat*, or the existential aspect.

Our minds have to operate in two directions. We should cognise the ontologic verity of everything, as well as its teleologic aspect. Ontology is not just the empirical presence of things, what you see with your senses or what you experience with some immediacy in the here and now. To present the world there is an inner ritam operating that has an existential richness and validity. It is timeless and endless. We are always experiencing its reality in our actual life. Its presence is factual. The ontologic aspect is not each individual mote we encounter, but the essence of the mote comes from the ever-present ontologic reality. This ontologic reality is both in the external world with all its action and in the internal world with all its aspirations.

The problem of what necessitates the external world to function in the way it does and the internal world to aspire in the same direction brings us to the question of the teleology of the total situation. *Teleos* means perfection in Greek. Whatever is imperfect is aspiring to become perfect. This introduces a time factor. There is a movement over time from what a thing is to what it could be. If what the evolutionists say is right, over millions of years matter has gone on organising itself in increasingly complex ways, and in that organisation there is a continuous molding and structuring towards perfection. In your personal life also you are always moving from crudity to perfection. So we can see a purposiveness in the operation of the ontologic laws, both externally and internally, and that purposiveness is what is referred to as the teleological aspect.

When we look at the external world we can see a mirroring or a reflection of the progress toward perfection taking place within ourselves. You can also look at the evolution of the external world as outlined by Darwin and presented creatively by Bergson, and apply or interpolate it into your personal life. Then you see in your own life a process of evolution. Taken in that sense, you can say the external world is a *bāhyaliṅgam*, a symbol of what is going on within you.

In the last two verses Narayana Guru linked the existential aspect and the axiological aspect, the *sat* and the ananda, to awareness or *cit*. Awareness can embrace both sides. The fact I exist is my idea. The fact I want to be happy is also my idea. Thus consciousness has the special power to identify itself with two different sets of values: existential values and values of happiness. This gives a complete idea of the Self.

There is a generally held belief that because Vedanta treats this world as maya it dampens one's interest in everything here, making one ineffective. Many European critics think even now that the progress of India is retarded because of Vedanta's emphasis on maya as explaining away the need to do anything in this world. Narayana Guru restates Vedanta in such a way that every individual reaction, every aspiration which is ontologically valid, has a relevant place in life. There is no shying away from any responsibility or any efficient action, as long as it is done at the right time and in the right place. In this way we can say he corrects the notion of Vedanta in these verses.

Now by verse 92 the proper status of the transactional world is well established. Life is valid. It only lacks validity when we are confused regarding the *pratibhāsa* and the *vyavahāra*, or everyday aspects. *Pratibhāsa* means that within the transactional world there are possibilities for illusion. It's true those illusions are to be avoided, but this doesn't mean that because it gives rise to illusion we should neglect the necessary aspects of the ontologic world. That would be an unwarranted extrapolation.

Verse 93

calamuṭal aṟṟa tanikku tanteyātmā-
vilumadhikam priya vastuvillayanyam
vilasiṭumātmagatapriyam viṭātī
nilayil irippatukoṇṭu nityamātmā

To one detached from the changing body,
nothing is more dear than his self;
as the self-oriented value continuously remains
in this state, the Self is eternal.

In verse 12 Narayana Guru called our attention to the aspect of our being that is of a perishable nature, namely the body, which is constituted of skin, bones, and various kinds of dirt, as well as the many fantasies of the mind which have no lasting value. He contrasted this with another aspect of our being which persists throughout our life, the witnessing consciousness, which identifies itself as the occupier of the body and the master of the bodily instrument. Age does not cause any change in it, even as the body grows old. Despite intermittent lapses of awareness, such as when one is in deep sleep, one does not feel any disruption of its continuity. Alluding to this, the Guru said that when the body perishes, the consciousness that pertains to this persisting awareness will ultimately unfold itself into total perfection. The same theme now returns in this verse.

A contemplative is capable of withdrawing the mind from objects of interest and those bodily elements, such as the senses, where particular experiences of pleasure are found. When one withholds attention or withdraws from the bodily aspect, the mind doesn't totally lose interest. For instance when a person is sick, many attractions are disregarded for the time being. Life itself is more valuable than anything outside, so one foregoes the sense interests as being of little consequence.

A child may show great love for a doll it has, but if you show it a new one the novelty of it attracts the child's mind and causes an automatic detachment from the object to which it was previously attached. The mind is removed from its previous interest to a new one. In the shifting of interest, the child doesn't know that the value it was seeking in one object has been shifted to another, because the value always resides in the self and not in the object.

When the mind shifts its interest it has no awareness of devaluing something and promoting something else. But in effect we can say the person no longer cares for this or that. In the life of an open society like this one we can always see that a certain person is endeared very much by another. Pledges and promises are made, but when bitterness comes that person is no longer dear. All the promises are void. They find interest in some other person. What actually happens is that nobody is loved for their own sake. It is for the priyam, for the happiness of our own self, that we get into situations of endearment.

In the immediately previous verses Narayana Guru conceded to the transactional world whatever value can be allotted to it. From the existential point of view, he gave a relevant placement to whatever is ontologically real within the frame of reference of a relativistic world. Then, in the same frame of reference, whatever teleologic processes are going on were also recognised. After giving the transactional world what it deserves, he is now calling our attention to the transcendental state of the Self. He cites value as the most significant factor to explain both the existence and timelessness of the transcendental state of the Self, and its infinite, eternal nature.

All the Upanishads emphasise this same aspect at some point. From the ephemeral, the attention of the aspirant is directed to what is eternal.

The manifestation of the world is always explained in the Upanishads with the help of the five elements, which have within them a gradation from the most concrete to the most subtle. Earth is the most concrete, while water, fire, air, and akasa or space are increasingly more subtle. When you become individuated you have within that individuation the concreteness of a physical body, which is apparently separating you from all other objects and bodies in the existential world. But the vital principle is not confined to just one body. For instance, when you nourish yourself with food the vitality of other bodies interpenetrates and is incorporated into your body.

If you have the eye of a contemplative you can see that a stream of life is continuously flowing through you. Your own priyam, your own desire, is instrumental in how it is channelled through you. You desire food and you partake of it. Its nourishment is essential for you to retain your individual existence. You may not recognise on a daily basis that your love for food is a love for the perpetuation of the self, but in effect it is so. Of all instincts, self-preservation is the first and last. Everything else serves to aid in the preservation of the self.

The food you eat, the water you drink, the sunlight that nourishes you and gives you energy, the air you breathe, the emotional affinity you have for other people, plants, and animals, your intimacy with others — all these make dents in your concrete individuality. The external world flows into you and you flow into it. An exosmosis and an endosmosis are taking place whereby you become part of the world and the world becomes part of you. For all this the operational dynamics come from priyam, desire.

In the preservation of the individual self there is a bright aspect, which is the cream of your consciousness and can be called the intellect, and also a dark aspect, an autonomous, unconscious aspect that maintains the integrity of the physical organism and the harmony of the mental functions. These are symbolically known as Indra and Prajāpati in India.

Your life is afloat in the river of timelessness. A beginningless and endless stream of phenomenality is flowing along, and you are floating in it. You have a powerful urge to preserve yourself but you know your body wont last forever. One way you can do something about it, though, is by making progeny, by having your own children. Then you are passing your essence on to the offspring. Even biologically there is the preservation of part of your being through the continuation of progeny. This has been going on for time immemorial, and it will continue for at least that long.

Although there are many impediments in the stream, and it looks as if the organism might be broken up and dissipated by any number of physical and psychic events, there is one element which surmounts all obstacles and which is always victorious: when a sperm couples with an ovum and the cells begin to multiply in the mother's womb. There is nobody there to help its growth, but there is an urge to grow. The urge is not a conscious one. The embryo has to overcome many difficulties to become a fully developed child ready to be born. Birth itself is a very dangerous thing sometimes requiring outside assistance, such as in a Cesarean Section.

The urge to grow and persist is continuous. We can think of the embryonic urge as the beginning of a long and victorious march, yet while it looks very much like the beginning to us, we should not think it is the real beginning. The real beginning goes back at least billions of years, to the start of the first formation of stars. If we take it all the way back to the Big Bang the question arises: the big bang of what? And why and how? Even now physicists are beginning to suspect there must have been something preceding the Big Bang.

There really is no beginning. A beginningless urge becomes evident to us when a helpless child emerges from the womb and emphasises its needs with a loud cry — its needs to breathe, to be nourished, and to be protected. Often we only look at the external symbols and events. The Guru wants us to know there is an *ātmagatapriyam*, a dear value which is most central to the Self, and that it never breaks, never comes to an end.

The Upanishads speak of the Self as *aparājita*, the one which never concedes to any kind of defeat, which is ever victorious. The victory of the self, which continues its path by desiring one thing after another, is aided on the one hand by Indra, the devices coming from the intellect, including conscious planning, and on the other hand by Prajāpati, the autonomous and unconscious artifices. You are manipulating the situation both consciously and unconsciously so that you can always move ahead.

Part of the process of moving ahead includes coming to the realisation that there is a larger situation to which you belong. Then you enter into the apprehension of *vibhu*, that which was there even before it was manifested. In his *Symbols of Transformation*, Jung speaks of plunging into our childhood memories. The child is the beginning, the womb from which the adult has come. So the adult sinks back into the womb of childhood. Through childhood memories and dreams you reach the other world, which was present prior to your individuation. From the world here you enter into the world beyond. The Upanishads speak of this as entering into the Great Hall of Vibhu.

In one sense we can say the child has the mind of the beginning and the mind of tomorrow. Yesterday and tomorrow are bridged by the child's mind. When you alienate yourself from the unconscious you also become alienated from the total ability of both the autonomous and the pure intellectual functions. You begin to live in a contaminated world of relativism. It is in that contaminated world that we have chiselled out a niche we call the transactional.

The Guru is trying to help us to get back to our original state so we can reclaim the whole to which we naturally belong rather than getting stranded on the desert island of the transactional. When we find our way to the Hall of Vibhu we are given a throne to occupy. The throne is called *vicakṣaṇa*, the reference being to one who is capable of discerning right from wrong, true value from the imaginary value of fancy, and who is endowed with the dexterity, the expert ability, and the know-how to reach the full potential and bring it to fulfilment, rather than pursuing fantasies and facing frustration. If you are not capable of directing the right desire toward the right object and of employing the right method to realise it, then you cannot keep up what is expected of you: to be an *aparājita*, an all-conquering person.

When you enter into the world of *vibhu*, that which exists prior to manifestation, you are supposed to win and not to fail. What is prior to manifestation is the causal factor, and what you see here are the effects. If you do not know the cause, then you do not know how to deal with the effects correctly. To understand the tree you should know both the roots and the branches.

This study is a way by which you are guided from the branches back to the root. Your tools are a resting place, and a continuous supply of energy, the *amita oja*s. The continuous *ojas* can become discontinuous. The libidinal energy with which you are supplied and through which life has been persisting is beginningless, and it can be endless, too. But one should know how to conserve it and when to use it. Although its source is the Self, when it manifests it becomes bound by the limits of the body. There it can burn out.

In disciplines such as yoga, great stress is placed on the transmutation of *ojas*, the libidinal energy, for higher purposes rather than just wasting it. At a gross level it is identified with the sexual fluids and energies that are often expended for pleasure. This idea can be exaggerated so that it becomes a spurious or puerile understanding. But if it is understood properly, the *amita ojas* becomes the *brahma tejas*. *Ojas* is like fuel, and *tejas* is when that fuel burns in splendour. This can be either a temporary power release for the gratification of small desires or an intelligently directed exercise which can produce an effulgence like a torch of light blazing through time, like the simple glow of wisdom on the face of the Buddha.

How many thousands of images of the Buddha have been made just to try to capture that inward smile, that embodiment of serenity? Such radiance is called the *brahma tejas*, and in that form has become a priyam of the whole world. Everyone is endeared to the serene gaze of the Buddha.

The individual self has two consorts, *mānuṣī* and *cākṣuṣī*. It is like a man with two wives, or a wife with two husbands. *Mānuṣī* is the desires of the mind and *cākṣuṣī* is the desires of the senses. You should be able to tame the mind and the senses so they will appreciate the higher value, which is the value of the Self. What they should desire is union with the Self rather than the fragmentary images that come and go. But the mind distracts you, repeatedly showing you small, ephemeral images and urging you to hug this shadow and that shadow. You try to catch them, but you always encounter frustration. You burn out the *cākṣuṣī*, dissipating your energy through the senses.

The world you make for yourself is considered to be a garland strung by *mānuṣī* and *cakṣuṣī* with the flowers of values they pick up. Your life is a big garland, a *mālā*, of all the pains and pleasures gathered by the mind and the senses. The mind takes one little pleasure here, and the senses pick another little pleasure, and they are strung as an ananda, an endearment. Then the mind brings another and the senses bring another in an endless quest.

In the Kaushitaki Upanishad a certain mantra is given which has often been misrepresented as a kind of magical spell to be used to obtain the affection of someone desired. It has quite a different sense if you understand its spiritual import properly. You build a sacrificial fire and offer butter into it, calling out the name of the person. Then you chant: "The light of your eye I sacrifice in myself. The light of your ear I sacrifice in myself. The light of your fragrance I sacrifice in myself. The light of your touch I sacrifice in myself. The light of your thought I sacrifice in myself." You take the essence of the other person and sacrifice it in the flame of your own self.

The spiritual meaning of this is that the fulfilment of any desire is a blending of whatever essence or value you see in a thing with the essence of your own self. The attempt at blending is to be considered the alchemy of the sacrifice, where you burn out your individuality and the individuality of the person or thing you desire. You transmute your desire to the pure ananda of the self.

This same idea is presented in many different forms. There is an old story that focuses on the greatest of all desires. Once a seeker went to Indra and did something that pleased him. Indra said, "Ask a boon." He replied, "Whatever is good for me, you can give that as a boon." Indra said, "It is up to you to choose what is good for you. Whatever you ask for I will give you." The seeker protested, "I can not make such a choice. You being the all-knowing one, please tell me what is good for me and bestow that as a boon to me." Then Indra said, "Desire me, because I am truth. I am the truth of all things. I am the truth that is established in the heavens. I am the truth that is established in the atmosphere. I am the truth that is established on earth, and I am the truth that is established in the nether lands." The omnipresent truth, *satyam*, is the most desirable. Narayana Guru says the desire which never leaves the self is desiring the eternal truth that manifests everywhere in all forms. However different it may appear in its forms or by whatever names it is known, you should always go beyond the form and the name to realise it as the one truth and desire it.

This idea is presented in yet another way in the Brihadaranyaka

Upanishad. There a person is called a *nara*, an individual. What we see in our wakeful consciousness is the whole world. If we picture this whole universe as being a single entity, a *vaiśvānara* or cosmic person, that one person is enjoying everything. The hunger in each individual is considered to be a function of the hunger of this world spirit or cosmic person. As the cosmic person is full of desire and is living in all of us, we desire to eat in order to appease its hunger.

In the Bhagavad Gita, Arjuna says "O Lord, I see you with a million mouths." All forms of life are always searching for nourishment, and through their countless mouths the cosmic person is ever eating and drinking. Then Arjuna says "You are all legs and you are all hands. You are millions and millions of eyes." When you stop to consider it, the individuality of each item of desire cannot stand apart. It is all the total desire of the *vaiśvānara*.

At the manifested level, phenomenality itself is a process of desire fulfilment, and your life is nothing more than a participation in that process. At the same time the plurality of your desires can be unified into one single desire, the desire for the Self. Again in the Brihadaranyaka Upanishad, Yājñavalkya says to Maitreyī, "Nothing is more desired than one's own Self. More than a son, more than all wealth, more than anything you can think of, the Self is the most dear." The collective aspect of desire is thus given great importance.

The Bible gives an example of this idea in the parable of a man who has a hundred sheep and one of them is lost. He doesn't think, "I have ninety-nine, so I don't care." The sense of loss is felt if even a tiny part is lost. Nataraja Guru used to say the discomfort that can come to you on not finding a pin when you need one very much is the same as when your mother dies. Mother is a most dear value, and her death is upsetting and inconvenient. But you suffer the same kind of inconvenience when you can't find that pin when you most want it.

These examples are calling our attention to the significance of the totality of the desire manifesting in its individual aspects. Even though the singled-out value is a relative thing compared to the totality, you cannot say it is nothing. It is also to be seen as part of the Absolute. The way the Absolute manifests is through each individual desire. In the desire you can see the mark of the Absolute. So all desires are to be seen in the Absolute, and the Absolute is to be seen in each desire.

Of all earthly pleasures for human beings and other animals, the one that most excels is when a couple is in the deep embrace of love, experiencing orgasmic ecstasy. But the Upanishads say that experience is as nothing compared to the coupling of the cream of your intellect with the Self in the cosmic embrace. When that happens it is as if you have all the embraces of the world. You are in eternal union. It is this eternal union with the Self that you should see reflected in all other forms of embrace.

It may be just the eye caressing a flower or the finger giving a tender touch of loving care, but you should be able to see in it the coming together of the essence of your own life with the totality. The individual essence and the cosmic essence merge into one another. What pulls these two together is desire — a priyam or endearment — but it is that which brings you to the ultimate release, the absolute perfection.

In this verse, from an ontologic ground the teleologic finality of the soul's search is brought to its complete perfection. "This is a man's highest path. This is his highest achievement. This is his highest world. This is his highest bliss.[1]"

---

1. *The Thirteen Principle Upanishads*, 2nd edn., tr. Robert Ernest Hume (Madras: Oxford University Press, 1968) p.138. From the *Brihadaranyaka Upanishad* (IV, 3, 34).

Verse 94

ulakavumuḷḷatumāykkalarnnu nilkkum-
nila valutāyoru nītikētitatrē
aṟutiyiṭān arutātavāṅmanō gō-
caramitil eṅṅu cariccitum pramāṇam

The world and the truth exist intermixed;
this state is one of great iniquity;
in this, which is beyond the grasp of word and mind,
how can any right reason operate?

After establishing the validity of the transactional world on an existential and teleological foundation, Narayana Guru now leads us to a further critical examination of the world of appearance and reality.

The transactional world is generally looked upon as a world of appearance. The appearance of what? There should be something which causes an appearance. Even if the appearance is to some extent distorted or false, there should be something behind it to provide the occasion for it to appear. This is usually inferred to be the reality behind the appearance.

All we know is the appearance of things, and we can easily come to the conclusion that reality is just as it appears. For those who think that way, all problems are solved. Materialists think that the objective world is the real world, and that our sensory perception is the way of knowing reality. What you see is really out there, what you touch has tangibility, what you hear accurately describes the audible world — no problem.

But what one can perceive is only a small part of the whole. If you are thoroughgoing in limiting yourself to perception, the world becomes confined to the room you are in. You cannot even believe there is another side to the wall, because you can't see it. The so-called perceptual world is not really perceptual to any great extent. We complement it with our memories, hearsay, conjectures — any number of things are put together to supplement the limitations of the visible world.

So, if materialists were thoroughgoing in examining their beliefs they would admit only what was immediately perceived. That's why Narayana Guru once directed Nataraja Guru, as part of his discipline, to sit in a room and try to imagine there was nothing other than what he saw. If you can do this you instantly solve millions of problems. Right now in this room your mother and father, your brothers and sisters, neighbours, creditors, tax collectors, none of them are around. All the problems connected with them are irrelevant, because they aren't present. It's a very peaceful room.

To true materialists the area of the world becomes very limited. They only look to direct perception and equate that with reality. But they are not generally very rigorous about it. A great peace should come from the annulment of so many problems; since that doesn't happen it is evident they are not strict in their understanding.

Once you start adding complementary aspects to the world of immediate perception, it is hard to know where to end it. Should you stop at your own memory? Then you are cognising plus recognising. Or should you also admit input from other people? Then do you allow only what they directly perceive, or should you also admit their intuitive understanding or even their rational speculation? If someone gives you a model for an atom, you should understand it is just a figure postulated by them to explain some aspects of atomic behaviour. In the same way you use maps to understand the structure of the surface of the Earth, but you need to remember the map is not the territory. How many such crutches do we put on top of what we really know by direct perception?

The epistemology of knowledge is a very complex thing. Those who think that what they see is reality have to be careful to subtract all those unexamined aspects from their perspective. On the other hand, those who think that what they see is only appearance have to somehow account for the reality behind the appearance. If I see this chair and claim it is only an appearance, what is there to cause me to perceive the appearance of the chair? Many people think there is some energy source which stimulates the sensory system, causing the formation of an image. If a number of people have the same experience, we conclude there must be an identical source creating a similar experience for all of them. The idea is that the source is real and each of us experiences our own version of it as an appearance.

There are others who say reality is that which remains all the time as the very substance of our experience, and that reality is consciousness. Like the wave, which is a modulation of water, all appearances are modulations of consciousness. Therefore consciousness is the only reality, and whatever modulations there are are only appearances.

So many theories! Which should you choose, and where should you abide? There are schools of logic, like the medieval schoolmen, the theologians, who all swear by the logic of Aristotle. Aristotelian logic gives priority to objective experiences, to what is perceived through the senses. This school of thought believes that things possess essential qualities that make them what they are, their 'essence'. Buddhists disagree with this idea, contending there are no essences. They think that all namable things have a dialectical correlation with the idea of them, in other words that they exist solely as thought forms and not as essences.

The idea of essences was very important to the schoolmen because they maintained human beings have an essence that is real and remains even after the body perishes. The essence of the sin you have committed also persists along with your essence, so ultimately there is a need for you to redeem your sin. Simply by dying you won't escape. You have to kneel down before Jesus and say you accept him, otherwise you will never be pardoned. You will go immediately to the house of the Devil and be tortured forever.

So the schoolmen wanted to hold on to the idea of the essence, and at the same time they wanted to hold on to the idea of the objective reality of this world. They accepted both, saying objectivity is the appearance of the essence. There is a strong circumstantial link between appearance and essence: "It appears that you sinned, therefore the sin occurred." It's such a well-knit business you don't know how you are tricked. Narayana Guru says this is an injustice, that there is iniquity here. You are not given a chance to state your case since logically you have already been given the proof.

The Buddhists ask if there is something called "real" is there any way of knowing it? You say you are seeing a book, but do you see it? According to Dignāya you don't see a book. What is "book"? "Book" is a name. Out of your perception you are constructing categories called books, chairs, etc., which are all just names you have coined and given to the categories. In this way you have made a whole network of pigeonholes. You are satisfied when you can put any given experience into one of these categories with a definite name.

This is exactly what psychiatrists are doing. They think once they have given a name to a disease they have explained it. But all they really know is a name.

In the last verse we were speaking of *mānuṣī* and *cākṣuṣī*. They are the two wives who weave the whole garland of experience. *Cakṣus* means the eyes. When your eyes look at something, the first perception that comes to you can be called perception. In the second, third and fourth moments, and so on, you are no longer seeing it. When the first impression comes, the sensation, the *cakṣuṣī*, passes on the data to the *mānuṣī*. Sensation turns into cognition. You think about and interpret what you have seen. Cognition changes into recognition almost immediately. You recognise it to be a book. That means you have structured the meaning of your perception in your thoughts, and thereafter you see only the meaning of your perception in the object.

As soon as you start using words you are getting into dialectics, which belongs to the world of semantics. The first impression is only for a split second, then *mānuṣī* takes over and the whole thing is mentally created and stabilised. A name is given to what you have created, and thereafter it is a nominal perception. You are far removed from the real basis of your perception. All you can say about the real is that neither your sensation or your mind reaches it. Between the sensation and the mind you are busy structuring an understandable entity to which you can give a name.

Ultimately, all our understanding of sensations is a nominalistic understanding, dialectically conceived. On such a basis it is hard for right reason to operate. This is what Narayana Guru is saying here: what a person of common sense with a personal identity takes for granted as this transactional world of experience is very confusing.

Sir Arthur Eddington goes to great lengths in his study of the physical universe to understand the nature of it. He explains the table on which he rests his hand to write as being two tables. One is the common sense table which he can see and work on, and the other is the physicist's table which cannot be seen. The physicist's table is not a compact piece resting anywhere. It is made up of molecules that are flying around at tremendous speed, swarming and bumping against each other. Some cohesion is maintained by mutual attraction, since if they just flew apart there would be no table. Fortunately they do not take that liberty. They huddle around so a form is maintained.

Eddington speaks of how difficult it is for a physicist to enter a room. The earth is revolving in one direction at nineteen miles a second, rotating in another direction at a thousand miles an hour, and the whole system is moving through the galaxy. That door sill over which he has to put his leg is moving at a terrible speed in several directions at once. If he somehow manages to leap in, there is no guarantee he won't slip through the molecules, and if he doesn't slip through it's because the molecules of the plank of wood are bumping against his feet.

Who is more authentic, a first class physicist or the common man who knows nothing of these ideas? Naturally the physicist knows much more than we do, so the apparent chair or room or table is the confused one.

Whether you are a philosopher or a scientist you cannot escape this problem of discerning what is real and what is unreal. The reality you arrive at through reasoning and the reality or transactional facts that are presented to you through your senses are opposed to each other. Yet you see the one in exactly the same place as the other. The Guru says *nītikēṭu,* this is a great injustice.

The Katha Upanishad says that the Creator made a great blunder, a big mistake. When he created human beings he did not turn the eye inward, he turned it outward. Therefore we can only see things outside and do not know what is happening within. The Guru is using the same gentle kind of humour here in speaking of injustice.

So what is the outcome? We do not see any limitation to what is presented here. It cannot be grasped by the mind or described in words. The Upanishads say of that which causes all this, that when you try to grasp it with the mind, the mind recoils upon itself, and when you try to describe it the words recoil upon themselves. There is a transcendence which is very elusive. There is no way of discerning the truth of it. Narayana Guru asks if such is the situation, how can you bring any kind of logic into this field?

The two great schools of logicians in India, the Naiyāyikas and Vaiśeṣikas, claim that you can understand everything with the help of logic. To this the Vedantins respond no, your logic has its limitations. Within small fields of reference what you say is certain, but do not try to prove the ultimate.

There is a similar dichotomy in modern physics. If a carpenter measures a beam for a building, he takes for granted that lines are straight and right angles are possible and that parallel lines never meet. For all intents and purposes these are true. If an Einstein comes along and says, "Your line follows the shape of space, which is curved by gravity", the carpenter will reply, "Mr. Einstein, don't meddle with me! This works. I can do it this way and build a building. There is no question about it. So don't bring in your higher logic." But if you want to send a rocket to another planet, calculations on paper will help. If you aim right at the target you will miss by a tremendous amount. You have to take into consideration all the complex motions involved using a mathematical model.

Narayana Guru uses the term *pramāṇam*, which is here translated as right reason. *Prama* means certitude. That which gives certitude is called a *pramāṇa*, an authority. As we have previously mentioned, certitude is attained through the *pramāṇa*s of direct perception, inference, analogy, word testimony, noncontradiction, and the argument of residue. If you use one *pramāṇa*, one of these authoritative ways of arriving at certitude, to discern truth and also to make sense in the transactional world, it is going to contradict some other *pramāṇa*. This causes the enigma of paradox.

There is a horizontal aspect of life and a vertical aspect. If you don't know how to coordinate them properly you become confused. The Guru doesn't want to make a fixed scheme to put into your hands. If he did you would make another mistake. You would then have ready-made pigeonholes in which to place your ideas of horizontal and vertical. The next day what you found to be horizontal might have become verticalised and you won't be flexible enough to make the change.

There is a story about a Zen master who had a very clever novice who he taught to put koans properly. There was another master who had a novice who was not so bright, who couldn't catch the spirit of it. The two boys met on the way to the market. The bright boy asked the dull one, "Where do you go?" "To the market." "How do you go if you have no legs?" The dull boy burst into tears and ran back to tell his master that the other boy had defeated him. His master told him a clever rejoinder in case the boy asked him that question again. He strove mightily to commit it to memory. The next day they saw each other again, and the bright one asked, "Where do you go?" "To the market." "If there is no road, how will you get there?" The dull boy realised the answer he had memorised wouldn't work, so again he cried and ran back to his master. His master gave him a good answer for that question, which he spent the day repeating. The next time they met the boy asked, "Where do you go?" "To the market." "Have a good day!"

The world is not what you anticipate. You cannot just take an answer from a guru or someone else and use it blindly. You have to make learned wisdom your own, and then evolve your own way of applying it to things.

Verse 95

vipulatayārnna vinōda vidya māyā-
vyavahitayāy vilasunna viśva vīryyam
ivaḷ ivaḷ iṅṅavatīrṇṇayāyiṭum ta-
nnavayavamaṇḍakaṭāhakōṭiyākum

This extensive playful display is *māyā*'s
concealed energy of universal creativity;
again and again she manifests here; her limbs
are the ten million cosmic bodies.

According to the Christian concept, God is the bright Absolute who created a good world and the Devil is his relative counterpoint who is the source of great darkness. The Devil is continuously filling God's good world with evil, viciousness and sin. So there is a bright world on one side and a dark world on the other, with God presiding over the bright and the terrible Devil in control of the dark.

In the Vedantic context there is a similar division, but they don't have a God and a Devil. Instead there is the transcendental, unknown, incomprehensible Absolute on one side and manifestation on the other. The relation between these two is sometimes explained through Sankhyan epistemology in terms of purusha or the pure spirit on one hand, and prakriti or nature on the other. Prakriti has a bright aspect of divine reflection, a kinetic aspect of change, and a dark aspect of stasis. When the dark aspect is emphasised, it can account for whatever is assigned to the Devil in the Christian and Muslim religions. So sometimes māyā is looked upon as an evil goddess and sometimes just as nature.

In this verse Narayana Guru uses a number of terms to qualify maya. First, maya is given a very expansive area for its ambit. Then he qualifies it as *vinoda,* a very important term, meaning humorous or playful. It doesn't imply anything dark or demonic, but rather that maya is very bright and capable of tickling you and making you laugh. With *vidya,* science, she is in charge of the science of humour.

What if you said the Devil was in charge of the science of humour? Really, he is. Mark Twain and others have had that insight. In *Man and Superman,* George Bernard Shaw describes how Satan found that the number of people in Hell was increasing at a terrific rate. He took a roll-call to find out why there was such a burst of population, and he found that many were migrants from Heaven. He asked them, "What is wrong with Heaven? Why didn't you stay there?" Everyone answered it was very boring in Heaven. All you could do was be reverential and sit and mumble prayers all the time. But in Satan's world everything was very humorous and there was plenty of variety.

Likewise, the Guru is not depicting maya as an evil Satan, but putting her in charge of the science of humour. He also describes her as the operating manager or director of a grand drama. Like any director, maya stays behind the scenes, never coming to the forefront, but whatever the actors do has already been determined and structured by her. Then again she is *vilasunna,* shining, as *vīryyam,* the essence, of *viśva,* the whole cosmos. That essence of the universe which shines as the operator of this great science of humour over a vast, expansive area is maya.

Narayana Guru is really calling our attention to maya: *ivaḷ ivaḷ,* "Look at her, look at her!" Again and again she is descending here. *Avatāra* has many meanings. One is that from above something is coming down. Then again, when you first hold an idea it is a hypostatic principle, and when it becomes real it manifests here. A mother giving birth to a child is also an *avatāra.* Then he says her limbs are all these countless millions of cosmic bodies. They are all coming from her. She is giving birth to all of them, just for a joke.

We are coming to the close of our study of the Self. If you are making an inquiry into the Self to get away from all the miseries, pains and tribulations of this world, you must first know that all these tribulations are creations of maya. In this sense maya becomes a kind of enemy. A couple of verses ago there was a reference to maya taking revenge when someone tries to escape the world of manifestation and turn to the transcendental. That aspect is still there. But if you are a wise person — and the Guru expects that by now, the ninety-fifth verse, you should be wise — he wants you to also participate in the grand humour.

This is such a beautiful verse!

Just as you can meditate on God, you can also meditate on maya. The humorous part of the story is how someone is giving birth to things with limbs. When a man and a woman are attracted to each other, each is a plaything to the other. Probably that is why the American commercial experts decided to call one of their magazines "Playboy." Men and women are very playful. Their play only becomes serious when the woman goes to the maternity ward. But it all begins in great humour. They tickle each other and laugh together. They say light-hearted things and whisper sweet nothings into each other's ears. All this is part of the great science of maya. She creates big, bold things out of nothings, sweet nothings.

This verse is for all people to become light-hearted. We should see the light side of life rather than becoming so grumpy about everything. If you make a mistake it's because Mother Nature wants you to make it. So don't have any sense of guilt, make your mistakes gladly. If you don't make little mistakes, God will call out to you: "Fool! I gave you a chance. I sent you to the world, and you didn't make any mistake. Stupid! Get out!" If you are here in this world, make some mistakes. Maya is sitting there and asking us to do all these things. Nataraja Guru used to tell us in the Gurukula that we should make interesting mistakes, not stupid or clumsy ones. Whatever mistakes you make should be very clever and interesting.

Fritz Peters tells a great story about Gurdjieff. At his school one time he had to be away for a few days, so he put a trustworthy woman in charge in his absence. On his return she showed him a little black book in which she had kept track of all the offenses the students had committed. It was quite a long list. To everyone's surprise, Gurdjieff took out his wallet and started giving each one money, paying so much per offense. Fritz had been at the top of the list so he got the most money, but he was ashamed to spend it, feeling the old woman had been let down. She had carefully chronicled all the crimes, and now Gurdjieff was giving everyone presents for their mistakes. But Gurdjieff said life was like that, and if you didn't make mistakes life would never be interesting.

So here you are being given an invitation to make mistakes. And what kind of mistakes is maya causing you to make? Her mistakes are not freaks of nature. She has a system. We can see how comedy and tragedy come in such a way that over time they balance each other out.

For instance, she calls the mouse to the cheese. The mouse's nose is perfectly designed to alert it to food. It comes closer, sniffs, and bites through the package with its sharp teeth. Then maya calls the cat. The cat knows just how soft and delicious the mouse is, and how long it can play with it before sinking its sharp teeth in. While the cat is tiptoeing closer with its mouth watering, maya makes a little noise to alert the mouse that someone is prowling there. The mouse jumps up and runs and the cat scrambles after it. Then maya shows the mouse a small little hole, and it dashes in. The cat is left standing there, thwarted. But if the mouse is not alert or can no longer run fast enough or is not clever enough to find the hole, it loses the game and the cat will eat it.

It's the same with the caribou and the wolf, or anywhere in nature, in maya. All are part of her grand, humorous science. If you are clever and smart, you can get away. If you are not, you will be caught. Just like Nixon with his Watergate — he was not clever enough, or he might have escaped with the cheese.

Whether you are a mouse or a Nixon, maya makes no distinction. She says: "This is my game — the grand universal play of life." Her game is played by the stars, even. If they are all moving around in space without touching each other, fine. But as soon as they come too close they will break up into thousands of planets and meteors, or even explode. A subatomic particle can endlessly run anywhere it likes, but if it collides with another particle it is shattered or changed into another particle. So through all this universe, from subatomic particles through cats and mice to macrocosmic galaxies, including superior and inferior intelligence, whatever exists is part of a gigantic glass bead game. If you know how to play the game you enjoy it immensely, and the whole thing is a source of great humour to you. If you are ignorant, then you get caught.

In the *Yoga Vāsiṣṭha* and many other Indian stories, there will always be a terrible demon asking riddles. If you are wise you are rewarded, given the whole kingdom and great riches, but if you are not wise you will be eaten by the demon. In the *Vikramāditya* there is a story of a corpse and a king. The corpse puts riddle after riddle to the king, but he is capable of answering them all. These are wonderful metaphors for the science of humour maya is creating every moment.

In order to know the Absolute you should also know what is not the Absolute. If you want to know what truth is, you should also know what is not truth. Then you can exercise your *viveka*, your great discrimination.

Whatever is in the world has its own essence, and it is capable of producing something very similar to itself out of it. If you take a big tree, like a banyan tree, with its vast root system, its spreading branches, and all its leaves, flowers and fruit — it's huge. Yet its seed is not even as big as a mustard seed. Within the tiny seed resides the entire essence of the tree. Similarly, within the chromosomes which are passed on from a man and a woman to their offspring is condensed the whole essence of the child's being, the *vīryyam* of the new person. A man's semen is also called *vīryam* since it is the physical source of the progeny. The seeds are microscopic, but in them is the essence of all the possible details of the person, not only of their physical formation but also of all the functional aspects, as well as a chronological programme to be implemented over the person's whole lifetime.

When you think of something so tiny it's impossible to believe that hands and legs could be made out of it. This is called *avayavam*, all the cosmic bodies which are the many limbs given birth to by maya. We are all born in the same way from the *viśva vīryyam*, the essence of the world to which we all belong. When it is taken collectively we can readily understand what the *viśva vīryam* is. It is not just a joke. The joke is a meaningful game of continuing the phenomenality of the world. Phenomenality has a drastic aspect as well as a humorous one. The humorous aspect is when a couple is on the nuptial bed. The drastic part is when you call for the ambulance and rush to the hospital, where there are bright lights and the clang of instruments and forceps may be used to pull the child's head out. That part can be tragic and terrible.

Maya is sometimes depicted as the beautiful goddess Sarasvati, sitting in a white lotus and playing the vina. From one breast comes all the wisdom literature and from the other come all the creative arts. Thus she nourishes everyone. It's wonderful! That is one aspect of the role of maya as chief director of the science of humour. She is also depicted with garlands of skulls, holding a terrible scimitar in one hand while beckoning with the other as if to say "Don't be afraid!" Blood drips from her tongue and she is making terrible noises.

In his *Kālī-Nāṭakam*, Narayana Guru addresses her:

Adoration to you O Mother!
Dear to the four-headed god
Brahma and others of his order,
Who, emanating all the universe,
Holding sway over them,
With pleasing mien destroys all again.
Thus ever in joy delighting,
Now playful and now in ecstasy,
Raising repeated cries most agonising
While dwelling within the ground
Of my own great delight,
Brimfully filling this universe,
Lit up to view by the uttered word
Which, penetrating deep within
And remaining as a minute grain
In interiority ultimate,
Wriggling and wriggling while letting down a showering
Ooze of immortal bliss,
Fully aware of every pain
Befalling day by day to believers in your lotus feet,
Scorching effectively the seed of pain
Within those able for a while at least to fix
Their thoughts to rest on you,
So that they begin to ignore
Every other form of contemplation

Of the flight of the "alone to the Alone!"
In such a manner
Filling the whole universe
With the self-same substance uniformly all over,
To dwell therein excluding
The least taint of dross,
Knowing never the least decrease
Even on long lapse of time,
This day alas have we come to have
Awareness, somewhat at least,
Of this your tragic form.
Shall this same effectively block out the whole universe?
Able to know thus in this wide world,
Who could there be, alas?[1]

This gives us an idea of what the Guru has in mind when he speaks of maya as one who has supremacy over all this world of manifestation. We have to think of this in terms of the previous verse where he said appearance and reality are intermixed. There it was presented as a principle, while here it is personified as the mother of the universe.

Narayana Guru by no means personifies maya as Satan or the devil. The touch of humour with which he deals with it should brighten our minds and ease our spirits. The great secret of this is called *līlā*. If you understand the world as a lila, a play or sport, it lightens all your troubles. Even when the worst of the worst happens, you know that after all this game will be over in a little while. Then you can smile, not having the feeling that it is so dreadful.

In Jean-Paul Sartre's story *The Wall*, three political prisoners were ordered to be killed. Two of them became sick with the fear of dying. The third knew it was inevitable, that there was no way of reasoning with such people. He accepted he would be shot, and he did not want to die a mean death. He said, "I will die, but I will die

---

1. Trans. Nitya Chaitanya Yati

   Nataraja Guru's translation is available in: Narayana Guru, *An Anthology of the Poems of Narayana Guru* (India: Gurukula Institute of Esthetic Values, 1977) pp. 11& 12

in full consciousness. It is the inevitable end today or tomorrow I have to die. I accept it."

Here the Guru goes one step further. It is not taken just as inevitable, it is taken as the inevitable humour of life. If you are born, you have to die. It's part of the game, so you accept it. When you accept it as a game, a lila, the whole complexion of it changes.

We can see this attitude in the last moments of Socrates. Others were crying, but he didn't see what was wrong with them, why they should be upset. He could not convince even the best of his disciples that one can have a more even-minded attitude towards injustice and death.

So before you see that you are the Absolute you should examine your negative side. The negative side can be depicted as very dark and evil. In the Bible there are so many passages painting the negative aspect as so terrible. We are speaking of the same negativity, but you can take it much more lightheartedly. Then it doesn't oppress you so much.

I was recently reading the Psalms. They have such beautiful poetry in them, but after four or five lines of great beauty and joy comes something horrible to frighten you to the bone. I was wondering if someone could rewrite them, taking away the terror, dread and vengeance, and references to heathens and enemies. Then they could be songs for all humanity. It would be most wonderful. If the Bible was revalued in the light of Vedanta, we would have a very enjoyable book.

This is a happy day for us, being with maya.

Verses 96 & 97

aṇuvumakhaṇḍavumasti nāstiyenni-
ññane vilasunnirubhāgamāyi raṇṭum
aṇayumanantaramasti nāstiyennī-
yanubhavavum nilayaṟṟu ninnupōkum

aṇuvaṟivin mahimāvil angamillā-
taṇayumakhaṇḍavumannu pūrṇṇamākum
anubhaviyātaṟivilakhaṇḍamam cid-
ghanamitu maunaghanāmṛtābdhiyākum

The atom and the indivisible, both as being and non-being
shine from either side;
thereafter, being fades away
and the experience of non-being, having no foundation, will also cease.

The atom will disappear in the vastness of knowledge,
leaving no trace of its parts; on that day the indivisible will attain perfection;
without experiencing, one does not know this unbroken consciousness;
it is the silence-filled ocean of immortal bliss.

In the verses we have just covered special attention was given to the *sat* and ananda aspects of reality. In the present two verses attention is now turned to the *cit* aspect. What is existentially present, which has a value of some kind, we have always known with our knowledge. As we were giving special attention to the existential and value aspects, we did not have an occasion to know how they are effected in consciousness. Now we turn to consciousness. The Guru is pointing out two main divisions in consciousness: *sāmānya* and *viśeṣa*, or the general and the particular. All our experiences can be qualified under these two categories.

If a teacher instructs about triangles, he is speaking of the general triangle. When, to illustrate his ideas, he draws three lines on the board connected to form three interior angles, no matter how much he tries he will not be able to draw the general triangle. He can only make one or another particular version of it. He may draw other particular triangles with different dimensions and different angles. Then, after demonstrating the special qualities of the particular triangles he has drawn, he can ask his students to generalise the universal characteristics of all triangles from them. This general triangle can never be seen, but the experience of the general is so interconnected with the particular we hardly notice that we do not see it at all.

When we look at a forest we think of it in a general way, although we actually see only a number of trees. When we think of the forest we don't put any emphasis on the tree, and when we look at a tree we don't think of the forest as such, even though the idea of it is in the background. There is a kind of shifting of our attention back and forth between the particular and the general.

At the commencement of an Upanishadic class there is a peace invocation that the teacher and students chant together. It serves mainly to keep their minds tuned to the ideas of the present two verses:

aum pūrṇamadaḥ — Aum, that plenitude is perfect
pūrṇamidam — this plenitude is perfect
pūrṇāt pūrṇam udacyate — this plenitude arising from that plenitude is perfect
pūrṇasya pūrṇamādāya pūrṇameva avaśiṣyate — when this plenitude is annulled from that plenitude, the plenitude continues to be perfect
aum śāntiḥ śāntiḥ śāntiḥ — Aum, peace, peace, peace

It's an exercise in mathematics, but the rishis believe it will bring peace. *Aum pūrṇamadaḥ*, that is perfect. You can think "that triangle is perfect," or "triangularity is perfect." *Pūrṇamidam*, the triangle which you have now drawn here is also perfect. You cannot say it is an imperfect triangle. *Pūrṇāt pūrṇam udacyate*, it is from the conceptual general triangle that the present manifestation of the triangle is effected. That's clear enough. Then *pūrṇasya pūrṇamādāya pūrṇameva avaśiṣyate*, by deducting this particular triangle from the general — that is, by focusing on the particular and forgetting the general — it doesn't affect the truth of either part. If you take them together, as all the particular triangles constituting the general triangle, it will also be perfect. By taking them together or subtracting one from the other you do not affect the truth. If you know this you become peaceful.

From the time of Democritus, Heraclitus and Lucippus in ancient Greece and Kaṇāda in India, it has been believed that the world is constituted of minute particles, atoms or *aṇu*-s. When two anu's come together they become something new. Three anu's joined become something else. Quantitative variations therefore cause qualitative changes. As everything is made up of particles, all things here are a manifestation of very specific elements in particular combinations. This is one view.

The other view is that the great supreme God was filling the universe with his pure spirit. Then he desired to have manifestations, so he willed "Let there be light!" and the light came as a manifestation of his very word. Thus everything here is a manifestation of the word of God; it is all made up of the word. That's what St. John says.

When we look at it this way we are approaching the whole subject from the general perspective: *pūrṇamadaḥ*, that which is unbroken is all this. Or we make microscopes, place slides on them, focus and squint: "Look here, this is it!" *pūrṇamidam*. So we have a world of microscopes on one hand and a world of equations where we don't need any instruments other than our mind on the other. These are the two views from the intellectual standpoint.

In our everyday life the interplay of the general and the particular is very important. Suppose it is election time and you have to choose your president or your senator. People who have nothing to do with their citizenship suddenly feel they are Americans — or Indians,

French, Italians, Japanese — for a couple of days. Then right afterwards they forget again. If it is an election for Oregon senator, they become Oregonians for a bit.

Pascal once said, "Henry, I have to shoot you because you were born on the other side of the river. If you were born on this side we would be fellow countrymen, but unfortunately you are from the other side, so you are my enemy."

If you think of "my family," even though the members of your family are not present with you, your mind suddenly leaves the person sitting next to you and travels all the way to where your kith and kin are. They are all tied together in your mind as one general ensemble. "My family," "my countrymen," "my religion," "humanity," you can make a generalised picture in your mind by shifting your interest. But when it comes to the matter of brushing you teeth in the morning, no matter how dear your friend is you become very particular about having your own brush.

We are not speaking here of some abstract philosophy, remote from our normal concerns. This is something we deal with every day. When we think of the particular the general naturally becomes dimmed down, and vice versa. You can sit and argue for days whether the world is constituted of atoms or whether it all comes as the manifestation of the word of God, and it won't change much in your personal life. The general and the particular interweave all the time without having much effect on each other.

There are certain natural operations of the mind which are caused by the alternating states of consciousness. When you wake up, it is imperative to do certain things. Your sense of duty tells you to do them. Then when your eyelids become heavy and you fall asleep, you are introduced to another world with new demands and necessities. In the dream world perhaps a mad elephant may be glaring at you with a menacing look and you want to run away. But you find you cannot move. This was never a contingency in the wakeful world, but it has become a very critical situation in the dream. Then when you wake up, you laugh at yourself. What was so real in one situation is no longer real in the next.

This discrepancy does not occur only between the dream and the wakeful. Within the wakeful world itself you may exchange words with someone and put up a wall between you. They might cry out, "What am I, a sheet of paper for you to tear out and throw away? You still belong to me." "No I don't!" "Why not?" Then after some time you may feel bad about your attitude: "I shouldn't have been so cross. Sometimes I'm like that, so impatient. I got up on the wrong side of the bed this morning. I should discipline myself, learn to behave. I'll write a letter saying I was in a bad mood and I'm sorry." This clash of perspectives is part of our daily experience.

Here Narayana Guru says of the general and the particular, when one becomes real the other becomes unreal, in the sense that your emphasis is no longer on it. But both are shining. It's like two lights blinking alternately, where you get the illusion that the light is moving. First the light of generality is on, then the light of particularity. McCullough in *Embodiments of Mind* describes how this involves an actual change in the pattern of the brain's molecular operation. Just as in the Guru's description, there are two separate nets of cells in the brain, and when one shines the other is off. But they are mutually correlative. This needs to be understood dialectically.

In the light of this understanding, existence and value, which we have examined separately in the previous verses, are now to be brought together. There is no separate existence as such, and no separate value as such. There is only consciousness. The fact that consciousness glows is existence. The fact that the glow has a certain brilliance is itself the value. When you say *sat-cit-ānanda,* do not think there are three things sitting in the Absolute. There is only one thing, not three. You can either look at the one thing as existence or look at it as knowledge or look at it as value. The purpose of the present two verses is to synchronise our idea of existence and our idea of value as one idea of consciousness. The main thing is how exactly that consciousness operates.

We have now come to the last few verses, and Narayana Guru wants us to finally retire from this endless process of intellectualisation. We cannot go on discussing forever. We have to retire from where all these operations are taking place, and go into the very core, the very depth, to the place particularity emerges out of and remerges into, and the place where generality comes into focus and disappears out of focus again. We are to turn to that source.

"This." "Mine." "My child." "I am the mother." "I am the father." "I." "Humanity." After making a statement, if you allow silence to prevail and envelop you, the idea that comes with all its brightness becomes more spread out. The sharpness of its edges goes. It becomes vague. It fills the silence. Or the silence is interpenetrating into your thought. The next thought dissipates into silence, and at last the silence overcomes you. 'This' becomes a new pulsation of idea . . . no idea . . . idea . . . no idea . . . yes . . . no . . . yes . . . no . . . . Then comes a 'yes' that has no form, because it swallows up both the 'yes' and the 'no'.

The universality of things and the particularity of things, your personal preference and the preference of all, the love you give and the love you receive — all these ultimately subside.

The observer and the observed both blend into the observation. . . . The knower and knowledge, the doer and the action, the enjoyer and the enjoyment, all merge into this one silence. . . . The inner and outer . . . before and after . . . the one and the many.... All these differences are now effaced.

There is knowledge and there is the glory of knowledge. When you say "knowledge" it is a simple abstraction, but the glory of knowledge is a wonder that fills your knowledge through and through. In the final verse of Narayana Guru's *Daivadaśakam*, God is equated with the ocean and his glory is equated with its depth. This means there is a verticality of knowledge, and everything general and everything particular can be traced back to it.

Triangle ABC is true. Triangularity is true. Why? Because the truth of both belongs to a verity that axiologically exists with us. The Self approves of the truth. It's not a certitude which comes from any outside authority, the conviction comes from within, from one's own Self. The certitude of the Self is called *ātma nīścaya*. *Niscaya* means certitude. To the Self, that is sure. When you say "My God," it touches the same place. "My child," it touches the same. "Oh beautiful flower," "This great humanity," they touch the same. Whether they are general or particular, they all converge to one single point. Certitude is there, joy is there, knowledge is there, the sense of existence is there. All join together there.

To come to this you have to retire from all discursive reasoning, from applying any and all gimmicks and techniques, and from putting forth efforts, thinking that at the end of the effort you will get it. You retire from your role as an actor. You retire from your role of enjoyer and from your role as knower. You just allow yourself to be enveloped by whatever is. In fact, the 'is' and the 'is not' are both canceled out there. You no longer even look for what is or what is not. They are not relevant. It's only a question of giving up.

Then the Guru says there is no point in repeating this ad nauseum, either you know it or you don't. Either you are at one with this beingness or you are not. It is not consciousness of anything. It is not knowing anything. It's just knowledge, pure and simple. It is a deep, deep silence, where there is no question of change or transformation.

It is said whenever something occurs, it perishes. It becomes *mr̥tam*, mortal. Where nothing occurs, nothing perishes, so it is *amr̥tam*, immortal. *Amr̥tam ghanam* means through and through there is no separation.

Next the Guru equates God with the great ocean, just as in *Daivadaśakam*. He says that that into which you merge is an ocean of silence. As the amritam sound is there, existence and value are both to be seen in what is described as the ocean of silence. It *is*. It is amritam, but it is also *maunam*, the great silence.

Śaṅkarācārya has written some praises of the Guru Daḳsinamurti. In them he says that a guru sits under a tree. It's a wonder that he is very young and his disciples are all very old. He is not saying a word, but his silence is dispelling all the doubts of his disciples. His commentary on the Absolute is only his silence. And what is happening to the disciples? All their doubts are being shattered. This is the last lesson a guru gives.

Nataraja Guru writes, in his biography of Narayana Guru and in his own autobiography, that whenever the Guru and a disciple met the Guru always called the disciple's attention to some basic problem of philosophical or contemplative interest. They always had very interesting discussions. The last time he went to see the Guru, though he was sitting unconcerned. Nataraja Guru thought that was strange, because he always took such an interest in his disciple and brought up a question for discussion. But this time the Guru was sitting there completely indifferently. He thought, "Probably he is in some state of meditation. He has not seen me. I'll wait." He waited, but there was only silence. He ventured to put a question, but the Guru did not break his silence. He just sat there silently. Then he knew: "This is the last answer to all the questions, forever." It was into that silence he had to merge. It was from that he had to seek his answers.

For those who had the opportunity to be in the presence of Ramana Maharshi it was a very profound experience. Most of the time he sat in deep silence, but he was not meditating. He was sitting with his eyes open. He always looked just ahead. Several times I tried to determine exactly where he was looking, but I could never make out whether he was seeing outside or inside, something or nothing. At times I tried to catch his attention, but it made no impression. He was totally unaffected.

It is a little like being drunk, without normal orientation. There is no purpose, no questions or answers, no 'I' and no 'other', nothing to do. You have in a sense done everything, so there is nothing more to do. This is again the *kṛta kṛtyata*.

In the Nirvana Darśana of Narayana Guru's *Darśanamālā*, he says that when a person comes to a maturity of understanding he knows there is nothing for him to do. The body is there, hands, legs, eyes and the faculty of speech are all there, well adjusted. As there is a little power left in the equipment, let it be used for the good of the world. There is no personal gratification, but if someone needs to achieve something in the world he is capable of helping them. His action is performed only as a sacrifice. Then, gently, a whisper comes to him: "Get ready. Enough of all this." And that motivation also leaves. When this happens there comes an indifference, *udāsīna*, and he forgets about his bodily state entirely.

Towards the end of Narayana Guru's life, people would offer him lunch and there would be no response. They would wait a while and then say, "It's lunch time." Then he would touch his belly and say, "There is no feeling," and again go back into his state of absorption. He touched his belly as if to say that for the sake of the stomach he would take food, but there was no call for it from there.

This state is described in the Guru's Nirvana Darśana as *vedito veti,* if someone tries to call one to attention, he responds. Then nirvana proceeds a step further to *na vedito veti,* the state in which even when someone calls his attention there is no response. The person who is still doing some action for the good of the world, even while having nothing to obtain and nothing to achieve, is called a *brahmavit*. One who goes beyond this to a total neutrality of action is called a *brahmavit vara*. Finally, one who has totally entered into the silence, who knows nothing of this world, is a *brahmavit variṣṭa,* a most superior knower of the Absolute.

There is a state of spiritual attainment which in India is called *virakta*. Viraktas have absolutely no interest in anything. Once I went to Amritsar with Nataraja Guru for a Vedanta conference. Many great gurus and teachers from all over India were there, and an ocean of people. They would gather at 5:00 a.m. and sit until 6:00 or 7:00 p.m., listening to all the grand talks of all the great teachers. The conference had been convened by Swami Nirmal Maharaj, whose guru was a virakta. Whenever Nataraja Guru was not giving a talk, I used to slip out of his group and go see that guru.

On one side was a vast sea of people, and on the other a small room that faced the forest. There was nothing going on. He would sit there, very old but with bright, shining eyes. I couldn't say if he was smiling or not smiling, seeing or not seeing. He knew nothing of what was happening around him; at least that was my impression. With all the noise and chaos it was hard to believe that a person could be so totally withdrawn and not be catatonic or mentally ill. He was alert in another way. I could feel that alertness as soon as I came into his presence. It was as if I was sitting near a great power station and was caught in its energy field, as if I vibrated with the profound silence coming from that little hut. There was nothing negative about it. To me, it was more positive to sit in his presence for five minutes than to listen to all the talks of all the great teachers at the conference.

The best of all the meditations I know is not thinking or chanting or following some practice. It's allowing yourself to be lost, not directing your thoughts with any kind of motivated mind, not taking interest, not picking anything up, not feeding yourself on memories or paying heed to inner suggestions. It's not very difficult. It happens by itself, and then it affects others also. It's contagious. The silence envelops you and becomes very strong. You cannot say what kind of experience it is, unless you are caught in it. This is something we are carrying with us all the time. I'm not suggesting you get totally into this while you are still young, but short spells of it can be very refreshing and very reassuring. It will take you home, whatever that means.

The last verse of Narayana Guru's Universal Prayer is: "In that immeasurable depth of your glory, all of us should merge, gently, gently, and should remain there forever and forever in the unbroken peace of eternal happiness."

Verse 98

ituvare nāmoru vastuviṅṅaṟiññī-
lati sukhamennaniśam kathikkayālē
mati mutalāyava māṟiyalumātmā
svatayaẓiyātaṟivennu colliṭēṇam

We have not known anything here so far,
having spoken of great happiness;
even if intellect and such disappear,
the reality of the Self, without becoming disintegrated, will continue as knowledge.

The first stage of our life on earth alternates between a state of deep sleep and a dreamlike experience where the wakeful and the dream are not very distinct. The infant has no memory of an empirical world, so it sees for the first time various forms and images, and hears sounds for the first time as well. It does not immediately correlate the sounds it hears with any forms, so in its mind things have no names. They are only like moving pictures.

When the child closes its eyes we do not know what it sees. Perhaps the memories of similar shadows are passing through its mind. More than the memory of what it saw or heard, it is more likely to be recalling its memory of touches. Certain areas of the child's body, when tickled, produce pleasure. Freud has elaborated on this. The child's dreams are likely to be of being fondled, kissed, caressed, tickled, and either sucking its mother's breast or passing urine or feces. It does the latter along with the dream, so each time the child goes into a beautiful reverie you have to change its diaper.

So the first phase is deep sleep, and from that the child wakes into a world where the dream and the wakeful are bracketed. It enjoys deep sleep unitively, while the enjoyment of the dream depends on the kinds of impressions that come, either pleasurable or painful.

After a time the child enters into a more clear differentiation of the wakeful from the dream. By repeatedly seeing the same people, such as its mother and father and other family members, it starts recognising them. At a later stage it even begins the exercise of coordinating names and forms. Slowly the subject-object difference becomes more and more pronounced, until the wakeful stands out as a separate experience.

Now the child has three distinct types of experience: deep sleep, dream and wakeful. As there is a continuity in the wakeful which does not occur in the dream, because of the same forms and people appearing again and again, the wakeful begins to gain a higher status as what is consistently true. Whatever experiences you have in the dream, when you wake up they are all sublimated. They no longer have validity. What we experience in the wakeful likewise disappears in the dream, but we don't take that seriously because we can pick up whatever happened before and continue with it in the next period of our wakeful life. So the wakeful begins to seem more true.

This pattern of experience lasts to the very close of life. If someone has been having an enjoyable dream and then wakes up, they immediately devalue the joy experienced in the dream, saying 'Oh, it was only a dream!' In the same way, when you wake up from wakeful life to a higher state of consciousness, despite all the adventures you underwent and all the great pleasures you had, the validity of wakeful life ceases.

In this verse Narayana Guru says you have not known anything so far. We are in verse 98, and he is saying we don't know anything yet! By saying "we" he includes himself in this state of affairs. Until now, we have not known a thing properly. Why? Because we have been saying "Oh, that was excellent. It was wonderful, superb!" All these implied comparisons are there because you have never known your true state, in which there is no good and bad. There are no superlatives and nothing to compare anything to. It's just bliss through and through. Only if something has aspects could you say,

"In the morning it was like that, and after noon it became like this." There are no high and low tides in the joy of the Self. It's always the same. So we have to confess this is something we have not known.

St John of the Cross knew the Self. I have my genuine doubts about St. Teresa's experience, because she spoke of the many gradations of ecstasy she found as she went from one chamber to another. But St. John never admits any kind of comparison. At the bottom of Mt. Carmel there is nothing and at the summit also there is nothing. All he could say was, "Nothing, nothing, nothing!" The nothing of which he speaks is the same as what the Buddha called nirvana. It is the burning out of all the possibilities of the phenomenal, which brings you to a pure state. It is even a mistake to say you have come to a pure state, which uses the comparative language of the transactional world. The state was always there. You never left it.

Once a wandering monk came to the court of a great king, and said he wanted to show him his psychic powers. The king said, "Okay, show me!" As the courtiers watched the king, they saw his eyelids drooping. It looked as if he were taking a nap. The king saw himself going to a riverside to draw some water, and he found the river was in flood. On the other side he saw a beautiful girl coming down with a pot to also fetch water. He felt a powerful longing for her. Suddenly she slipped and fell into the water. She was drowning! The king jumped into the river and caught her, dragging her with great difficulty to the other bank. He laid her on the shore unconscious, but after a bit she recovered and was very grateful to him. She said, "Now you have saved my life you should meet my parents. They will be very happy."

The girl took him to her place in the forest. All her family were hunters and gatherers, so they didn't come back until the end of the day. She built a fire, and he sat there while she made a meal for him of simple, hunters' food. He forgot that he was a king and ate the food with great relish, even though by the rules of caste it was unclean, because she was so loving and so beautiful.

That night her parents returned, and she told them how he had saved her life. They begged him to stay, and later urged him to marry her. He stayed, and he married her. They taught him their livelihood and how to speak like they did, and gradually he became part of their community. Over the years six children were born, and they were all very happy.

Then one year there was a great drought and famine. The crops were all burning up and the family could not find food to eat. In desperation they decided to leave, and he carried the small children on his shoulders while his wife and the others followed on foot. They walked and walked. On the way one child died. With great grief he buried her. They continued on their way, suffering severe pangs of hunger and thirst, until another child died. He buried that one. Then another. Finally he was left with only two children and his wife.

Suddenly a huge brush fire swept through the forest. He ran, but the fire engulfed his wife and children. He couldn't stop to help them. The fire was getting hotter and hotter. It was starting to burn him, he could feel himself starting to die — and then he woke up. He saw he was sitting in the court on his throne. The magician was gone.

The king slowly shook his head and asked what happened. The chamberlain told him, "Your highness, a mendicant came and said he would show you some magic. Then we saw you sleeping." "How long did I sleep?" "Maybe three minutes." "Three minutes! I lived in the forest for twenty years. I had six children. So many things happened! And you say it was only three minutes?"

Nothing happened, but all those events took place. When the king woke up they were all as nothing. Then the king said, "I cannot take this as a trick. It was so very real." He sent some people to go to the part of the country where he dreamed he had lived. They found a forest fire blazing, and spoke to some hunters nearby. They told him, "There was a family that lived over there. A very unusual man married their daughter. They had six children, but they all went away when the big famine came. We heard that many of them died in the great fire." Then the king was really confused. This story comes from the *Yoga Vāsiṣṭha*.

Phenomenality comes as a series of such events, which are so convincing, and yet in the pure domain of spirit nothing is really happening. The Guru says here that that kind of knowledge comes only when we wake up from the wakeful. It is easy to awaken from deep sleep and it is easy to wake up from the dream state, but it is not so easy to wake from the wakeful. All spiritual pursuits are meant to bring about such an awakening. The word 'Buddha' means "the awakened one." He woke up from the wakeful world. We have just had two verses to get us to wake up. If you are still speaking of a wonderful joy you had yesterday at three o'clock, it shows you still have to wake up.

A little while ago a friend was speaking to me with great earnestness of a number of possibilities in his own personal life. He was absolutely sincere, very convinced of those possibilities, but after narrating an experience or describing a direction he would always come to a crossroads where his mind was seized by doubt. "Is what I am saying real?" he would wonder, and then an answer would come from his own mind, "Maybe not." How quickly the truth of what he had been saying with such sincerity was denied! Then he would go on to another theme, which was equally fascinating, very interesting, quite reasonable and thoroughly logical. He would come to another punctuation and the question would arise, "Is this real?" He himself says, "Maybe not. I don't know." Then the mind shifts and comes to yet another possibility.

I am not finding fault — this is typical. There are recurring patterns in everyone's lives. Many people do not retrospect and examine all the significant aspects of their life in order to learn and grow. They just walk on. They are not confused only because they don't think about things, not because they have resolved them. But they are really no better than the person who retrospects and is confused.

Such kind of a nonreflective way of life leads you to the most agonising kind of experience. The bright moments of life bring you, for a while at least, satisfaction in what you are doing. The next moment the whole thing appears to be futile, meaningless. Then come a few bright moments. Then doubt assails. The net result is living in a vicious circle.

In Mahayana Buddhism there are texts like the Lankavatara Sutra, the Prajnaparamita Sutra and the Diamond Sutra that deal with this problem. In them everything is presented in the form of a mental modulation, which is then examined, questioned and rejected. Paradoxically this process of rejection does not bring them to a state of darkness or confusion, but to a state of heightened clarity. Realising the emptiness or nothingness of the phenomenal world brings great clarity. But the phenomenal world persists so they go on to examine the next occurrence. That is also rejected, which brings them to the same confirmation once again.

Vedantins have the same method, as when Yājñavalkya resorts to the technique of negating everything, saying *neti neti*, "not this, not this." When this is done intellectually it brings absolute boredom. Sitting there and doing this as an intellectual process brings only darkness and frustration, because you are doing it in the wakeful and so it doesn't lead you to wake up from the wakeful. The transactional verity is to be rejected, but not from within the transactional frame of reference. This is where we fail. Without becoming endowed with a higher consciousness, we fail. Nothing you do while remaining in the ordinary consciousness takes you one step further.

This naturally leads us to the question, "How do you become endowed with higher consciousness?" There is no need for me to even mention that here, because no one is going to follow it. It's just a waste of time. You have to discipline yourself. Is there anyone who is willing to become a disciple? No one. Truly no one. Absolutely no one.

And why is that? You have your small likes and dislikes, your little pleasures. If a compromise could be made to include your special preferences in the plan of the discipline, then you would be willing to have it.

A good example is yoga. In America, if you go to a yoga teacher the class begins with a posture. That means you have already violated the spirit of yoga. Why? Yoga does not begin with a posture. That is the third stage of Patañjali's *Yoga Sūtras*. Before that there are two other steps, *yama* and *niyama*. *Yama* means five kinds of restraints, and *niyama* means five kinds of observances. It takes a long time to just accomplish the first two steps, and then the third step comes almost automatically.

I once met a very wonderful woman who has gone to a higher

state of consciousness. She doesn't claim she has gone anywhere, but she told me her story. She was the wife of a Muslim civil servant in India, but she had been born a Hindu. She had a great love for the Hindu sannyasins and gurus. After her marriage she expressed her desire to have a guru.

Her husband was very broadminded. He came to know of a certain man who was reputed to be a very good teacher. He went and invited him to his home, where he introduced him to his wife. The wife said, "Sir, I want to become a disciple. I heard you are a great yogi. Can you teach me?" He answered, "Yes. If you are sincere, I will teach you." "Can you teach me everything?" "I shall teach you everything I know."

He gave her the first step, *yama*. When she understood that, he told her the second step, *niyama*, in a somewhat hurried fashion. This happened over the course of two months. Then he died. The woman felt she had been deceived. The guru had told her he would teach her everything he knew, but he left her after only two months right on the brink of yoga instruction.

She used to sit alone and cry. Then one day he appeared to her in a vision asking her why she was crying. "Because you deceived me. You told me you would teach me everything you know." He said, "Are you not talking to me now? I can still teach you. I didn't go anywhere. It's not imperative to have a body to teach." So she was satisfied.

Then he said, "Why should I teach you the next step before you master the first two?" When I met her it was twelve or thirteen years after this incident. She said she was still going on with the first two steps, but she had a feeling the third step was coming to her automatically.

The third step is sitting in a posture. In Patañjali's *Yoga Sūtras*, the asana or posture is described as *sukham sthiram iti āsanam*. When you can sit steadily and comfortably, you are in a state of asana. But in order to sit steadily and comfortably your mind should have perfect rest. If needs come to your mind, you have to get up and go away to fulfil them. When the needs all drop away there is no more physical pain or mental agitation. Then alone asana comes. Other steps still lie ahead, namely *prāṇāyāma*, the regulation of the vital forces through breath; *pratyāhāra,* withdrawal from sense interests; *dhāraṇā,* concentration; *dhyāna,* meditation; and *samādhi,* merging with the Absolute; but these only come later.

If you fail it is not because there is no one to teach you or the methods are inefficient, but because you have not prepared.

When teachers come to a country like this they are no longer in their own place. If they want to get back to their native country they need to book passage. That costs money. While they are here they need food, and that also costs money. They don't have a visa that allows them to work, so the money has to come from those who patronise them. Those patrons, if they want to have an occasional beer and the teacher says "Don't take beer," or an occasional chicken fry and he says "Don't eat meat," will look for the next guru who will agree to let them do it. There is a big competition in the field of gurus. The gurus soon learn how to make themselves acceptable to the local wants.

I know I am almost a failure in the competitive world of the gurus. The "disciples" I have are the most down and out types who don't have fat checkbooks. At least that should make the quality of those who aspire through me better than the quality of the others. But there also I should say *ituvare nāmoru vastuviṅṅaṟiññī,* up til now we have not known anything. It's a very painful thing to have to say.

Even the very first step in Yoga, *ahiṁsā,* requires great discipline to be made a part of one's life. Ahimsa means not hurting, nonviolence. Many people are capable of adopting a pacific attitude which is superficially very goody-goody. That is not ahimsa. If you apply ahimsa to yourself there are many weeds, parasites that live on your own spirit. They are all hurting you, draining the very sap of your spiritual life. In a lackadaisical atmosphere where you don't bother about them they will thrive. And the same thing is also happening to other people. To see clearly the spirit of one and the spirit of another, and then to remove those parasites from a person's life, the methods we resort to may sometimes look harsh. It goes against the grain of our understanding of a passive life.

The best example of nonviolence or ahimsa I can think of is Christ. Mahatma Gandhi also accepted Christ as his model for nonviolence. We see Christ going into the synagogue in Jerusalem and overturning the tables of the moneychangers, pulling out a whip and demanding they leave his Father's temple. He calls people vipers and hypocrites, saying things to them like "Ye are like unto whited sepulchres, which indeed appear beautiful outward, but are within full of dead men's bones, and of all uncleanness." (Matt. 23:27) He uses words and even actions of a degree of violence, but their intention is to free people from demonic influences. Out of his compassion he is trying to purge people of their defects.

Christ also took upon himself the wrath of others, which was a thankless act. Sometimes in the Gurukula when Nataraja Guru was correcting some of us we would get very annoyed. He would say, "If the same treatment was given by a psychiatrist you would have paid his bill. I am doing it without billing you, so you should at least be thankful to me. Instead you are getting angry. It's a very thankless job."

So the very first step is hard to understand and difficult to follow. How about the next four?

Similarly, when you come to the *niyama* the first one is cleanliness. It's hard to know exactly how to become clean. An American bathroom is practically the cleanest spot on earth. The toilets are very well kept, but the people who use them cannot claim to be as clean in their minds. The concept of cleanliness, like that of nonviolence, is a very difficult one with many ramifications.

When can you say someone is clean? When nothing is misplaced. When your words are not misplaced, your thoughts are not misplaced, your spirit is not misplaced, your attitude is not misplaced and your appreciation is not misplaced, then you can say you are clean.

Today's verse is a reminder to us that if we are serious we should begin from scratch.

One of the students in the PSU class I am giving handed in a paper the other day about the life she has experienced growing up in America. It was very painful for me to read it. So much ugliness is there! Yet every day when I saw her in class she looked pleasant enough. We know well how to put on fronts while having all this garbage behind them.

She could write only what she has experienced, and it is not her fault that her experience is such. She lives in a society, and she is trying to live as best she can conforming to the prevailing pattern of behaviour. I should say, though, it is the most rotten, most stinking model of society. How can she ever aspire to be clean in such a society?

From these iron fortresses in which we are imprisoned, to make a breakthrough — that's the challenge. The sage Vāmadeva said there were hundreds of iron walls around him. Like a hawk he could pierce through all of them and fly to his freedom. The higher consciousness we speak of, which alone can help us to wake up from the wakeful, comes through self-discipline. When you are disciplined, you become a disciple.

People come to me and ask, "Can you take me as a disciple?" Are you willing to be disciplined? You have to prove your willingness by becoming disciplined. Nobody can make you a disciple. Only a disciple can make a disciple.

They ask me, "Will you initiate me?" The first initiation has to come from you. It's not that first you are given an initiation and then you start. First you take the initiative, and when you reach a certain height you will meet with your second initiation.

Narayana Guru closes this verse saying that which is not affected by inner or outer things, by discipline or no discipline, is always the same. Until you wake up from the wakeful you will not know this. There will always be these recurring dreams, like the king who dreamt all the twists and tortures of life, which will continue without ceasing.

Things of the world, such as the office where you go to work, make a certain demand on you. If you are late they mark you late. If you don't go they won't pay you, and if you stay away they will fire you. But when it comes to wisdom teaching you think, "After all, it is not as square and structured as my office. So what does it matter if I don't go one day?" You don't give that kind of excuse at your workplace. Then you think, "That man there who is the teacher, I don't pay him anything, so what does it matter? He is giving it gratis. If he were a man of worth, would he do that? He is a cheap fellow, and that is why he is giving that kind of teaching. So I can go whenever I feel like it. I can listen to the extent it pleases me. If it rains I won't go."

If you go to see even a police officer, you have to stand and wait until he is ready. But what about a teacher? "He is not as superior as a police cop. I can just push open his door and walk in without knocking. It should all be to my convenience. I cannot have any inconvenience in my wisdom learning. If he wants to teach me he should do it on my terms."

There was a man full of itches called Raikva. He lived under a cart. The great king Januśruti came to him to learn. He brought with him several gold chains, necklaces, pearls, horses, and a cart pulled by a mule, saying "Hey, Guru! I brought you all these presents. Teach me!" Raikva told him, "Go away, you sudra! You don't want Brahmavidya!" But Januśruti was a wise and determined man. He went back and brought everything he had, including his only daughter. He said, "Master, I give you all this." Looking at the innocent face of the king's daughter, Raikva said "The face makes me speak to you now." He still called him a sudra, one of the servile caste, but from that point he began to teach him.

The point is, you have to give every last bit to get the teaching. And it's not what you pay or what you give, but the attitude you have. Do you want it to suit you, or are you going to suit yourself to the situation? You have to make a hard search on this question. The best is always inconvenient, so the next best is preferred.

In the Isavasya Upanishad it says as everything is enveloped by God, move free. But if you are not finding that convenient, the next best thing is to be a person bound to a situation in life, and deciding to live one hundred years doing your action without becoming attached to it. That's the next best.

In Plato's *Republic*, the best of all possible states is described, but Socrates knew it wouldn't work because people were not prepared for it. He said, "This is the best. Even if it is not going to be lived by any people anywhere, I cannot say this is not the best."

We cannot change a country, its culture, its traditions or its heritage. If you are born there and have to live there, you probably have to look for what is suitable to that country. Of course, it won't bring about waking up from the wakeful; it only rearranges the wakeful itself a little more conveniently.

I am telling you the truth — accepting or not accepting it is up to you. Taking this into account the Gita says that only one in a thousand seekers is really serious about their search, and of those only one in a thousand finds truth. When spiritual life has to vie with Madison Avenue, competing for attention with lurid and exaggerated images, only Madison Avenue will win.

This verse is a challenge to us. When Narayana Guru says we have not known anything, we should be able to say we have known, we have learned from our substantial efforts. For that to be possible we should at least make a sincere attempt to raise our consciousness to another level. Such an effort cannot be made by someone else on our behalf, we have to do it for ourselves.

You have to bring your life to a white heat. Even in material things, such as splitting the atom or studying the depths of space, seekers have to make contrivances which look almost impossible, but they do it. And what do you gain by smashing an atom? If you want to know the least bit about a particle, an *aṇu*, you have to spend so much money and effort, keep a great vigil and constantly refine and sharpen your tools. Then, to know about the Absolute how much greater dedication should you have? How much more willingness should you have? How much more preparedness?

On your keyboard, if you make a mistake the next step is to consciously erase it. It won't go away if you just leave it alone. Then, with decision, after effacing the error, you have to type in the right thing. In our life also there has to be a reconsideration of each mistake followed by its resolute correction, before we go on with great resolve. Let us hope we will have the courage to make a determination in our own minds to start fresh and become more conscious of what we are doing.

Verse 99

a̱rivahamennatu raṇṭumēkamāmā-
varaṇamoẕiññavananyanuṇṭu vādam
a̱rivine viṭṭahamanyamākumennā-
la̱rivineyiṅṅa̱riyānumārumilla

Knowledge and I-consciousness — both are one
to him for whom the veil is removed; to another
there is doubt;
if knowledge, having separated from 'I', can
become another,
there is no one here to know knowledge.

Arivu is knowledge. Pure knowledge is different from the many conditioned forms of given knowledge. Like a salt crystal which is salt through and through, knowledge is knowledge through and through in spite of all its apparent modulations. This truth is given in the Brihadaranyaka Upanishad, which says that the Absolute entered in here even to the tips of the fingernails. In the context of the manifested world, the permeation of the Absolute is analogically referred to as a sword that is put into a sheath, where the sword comes to the very end of it. Like that, in manifested being — such as in the case of a human — the Absolute enters in even to the fingernail tip.

Every modulation has a name, which delimits the particular formation of knowledge to which it refers. A name differentiates one area of knowledge from another area with another name. Although the name is only a verbal modulation of sound, it is capable of producing rigid walls of separation between the specified aspects of knowledge. Names are only just sounds but the barriers they create sometimes cannot be broken, because we are so riveted to the ideas which are specified by the names.

It is precisely because we have assigned special names to each form that our experience seems to consist of interactions with a series of different forms. This is why some researchers in language think that word power or word dynamics are such that the way in which a language is structured influences behaviour.

In speech and reasoning we resort to words which are nominal identifications of forms of knowledge. Reasoning is always verbal. Either we are thinking or we are speaking and reasoning, and except for the sensations we cannot easily decipher, our minds rush to give a name to any experience. Because of the constant naming process taking place there arises the veiling of the part from the whole.

The Brihadaranyaka Upanishad (1.4.7) says of the Supreme Self or the Absolute:

> People do not realise it, for it is incomplete (when viewed as doing particular functions). When it only performs breathing, etc., it is called the vital force; when it speaks, the vocal organ (i.e., the speaker); when it sees, the eye (seer); when it hears, the ear (listener); when it thinks, the mind (thinker); (and so on). These are but its names due to functions. One who meditates upon each aspect of this totality does not know, because, being qualified by each aspect of the totality, it is incomplete.[1]

In other words, any kind of specification delimits the Absolute and can no longer be the Absolute. That is why Narayana Guru reminds us here that knowledge, *aṟivu,* and the knower, *aham* or 'I', are not two. If, however, the knower is carried away by the specification of the name, he loses his comprehension of this truth, substituting the incomplete for the complete. The Upanishad continues:

> One should meditate upon it only as the Supreme Self, because in it all these become one. Of all these, this entity called the Self alone is to be known, because one knows all

1. Nitya Chaitanya Yati, commentator, *The Bṛhadāraṇyaka Upaniṣad* (New Delhi: D.K. Printworld (P) Ltd., 1994) p. 170.

> these through it just as one can find (a missing animal) through its footprints. One who knows thus attains knowledge of unity and liberation.[2]

It is with such knowledge that we come to the absolute knowledge *aham brahmāsmi*, "I am the Absolute."

We have already mentioned the four great dictums: "That thou art," "This consciousness is the Absolute," "This Self is the Absolute," "I am that Absolute." Of these, the last is the dictum of experience. One comes to this last experience when there is perfect identity between the knower and the known.

The Brihadaranyaka Upanishad continues, in (1.4.10):

> And even now whoever knows That in a similar way, i.e., "I am *brahman*," becomes this universe. Even the gods are powerless to prevent such a one's becoming the universe, for one becomes their Self. On the other hand, one who adores another god thinking, "He is different from me, and I am different from him," does not know.[3]

It is in consideration of such a possibility of error on the part of the knower that Narayana Guru says *anyanuṇṭu vādam*, "for another there is argument." When one differentiates in one's mind, thinking "I am one and this is another," for such a person there is argument. There is a separation between the knower and the known. At no stage does knowledge stand separated from the knower, which is why the Guru concludes "If knowledge can be separated from 'I', there is no one here to know knowledge."

---

2. *The Bṛhadāraṇyaka Upaniṣad*, p.170.
3. *Ibid.*, p.179.

Verse 100

atumitumalla sadartthamallaham sa-
ccidamṛtamennu teḷiññu dhīranāyi
sadasaditi pratipattiyaṟṟu sattō-
miti mṛduvāy mṛduvāy amarnniṭēṇam

Neither that, nor this, nor the meaning of existence am I,
but existence, consciousness, joy immortal; thus attaining clarity, emboldened,
discarding attachment to being and non-being,
one should gently, gently merge in *SAT-AUM*.

It is not through the commentaries, the meanings, the explanations that we give to the Self, but by becoming very clear in our Self, that we attain this pure joy that is existing in pure consciousness. Knowing that, be courageous.

Let this understanding bring boldness and courage, and let there not be the dual preferences of *sat* and *asat*. Go beyond all arguments in mind.

Thus transcending all dualities, come to that deeply touching sense of the One. Know that to be the secret of aum.

In that, gently, gently merge, and let that silence, omnipresent, fill.

Aum

Appendix
Ātmopadeśa Śatakam
(free translation)

1. May the chanting be commenced, with the five organs of perception turned inward and pacified, again and again prostrating before that mysterious embryo, the Karu, shining within and without the knower.

2. By a relentless search one should realize that the inner faculties, the senses, the body, and all the worlds of our interest are but transformations of the glorious substance of the Sun shining in the void of the Absolute.

3. It should thus come to pass that all the differentiations encountered in the world of empirical perception be known as the same in their essence, like the uniformity of waves constantly arising on the surface of the ocean.

4. Knowledge, the object of knowledge, and one's cognition of both are in fact only variations of a beginningless Being. By merging in that knowledge of infinitude one should become undifferentiated with it.

5. One should conduct oneself in the light of the eternal Lamp which witnesses the sleeping, waking, and discursive cogitation of those who are wedded to their own worldly affairs, and which itself has neither any beginning or any extinction.

6. Alas! Who is there to know the one unchanging Reality, when all are subjected to the frequent rise of latent urges which ceaselessly compel them to wake and sleep, to eat, and to caress the objects of their desires.

7. One should remain without waking to distracting interests and without being asleep to the reality of the Self. If you cannot do this by realisation, you should offer yourself in service to those contemplatives who have gone beyond the dualities of birth and death to know the secret of aum.

8. This body is like a foul-smelling gun. In it reside one's senses, which are like five birds always looking for the opportunity to feed on chance gains. With right understanding and discernment one should break away from their enchantment, and should resolutely aspire to the good instead of being ensnared by the pleasurable. Then alone will one's inside be filled with the radiance of the unsurpassed bliss of the Absolute, which will foil all distractions generated by sensual attraction.

9. The phenomenal world is like a tree whose truth is concealed by a mysterious creeper, spread out in two directions and overladen with flowers. Living in the shade of this tree, a disciplined contemplative escapes the temptations that might otherwise lead to tragic consequences.

10. Someone sitting in the dark asks another, "Who are you?" and the other out of curiosity asks in return, "And who are you?" The answer coming from both will be the same — "it is I."

11. What are spoken of as 'I', 'I', when carefully considered, are not separate entities. Within the total Substance these are only modes, while the continuity of the ego is maintained by the connectedness of the attributes into which it is modified.

12. The ego clings to a perishing body composed of skin, bones, and all kinds of filth. This is the non-Self which is sure to decompose. One should aspire to transcend the limitations of the body and grow into the perfection of plenitude.

13. To become established in the Supreme Being, offer the flowers of your mind to the Great Lord, whose body is smeared with the ashes of the triple modalities of nature. Incline before Him in devotion. Turn your senses away from all objects of desire. Feel freed of all bondage. Become cool, and do not be excited even by the wonder of the Absolute.

14. Remember the secret of the Upanishads. The Self in its pure state is limitless and indivisible. It is bereft of divisions in time, and it fills the entire consciousness without the divisions of the knower, the known, and knowledge. One does not gain this state merely by making false claims to it.

15. To those fortunate ones who are enjoying the cream of absolute wisdom, ten thousand years appears no more than a fleeting instant. But to those who are caught in the snare of relativism, even a split second can seem an eternity.

16. To one well-established in the Self, the secret of the Word comes as a cosmic sound. It fills one's ears and drowns everything in them like a flooded river inundating a desert. Just as it opens one's inner ear, it also opens the eye of the inner self.

17. The Self is like a hanging oil lamp with two tiers, each with five wicks. It is of timeless origin and is always rotating. Its wicks are modes of the mind, and they are fed with the oil of preconditioned urges or vasanas. It burns as a shadow of the Self.

18. The Self is not darkness. If it were darkness, we would not have known and identified ourselves as 'I', 'I'. As we do know, we should let everyone realise that the Self can be known.

19. Not knowing that everything is a transformation of the primeval Being, people come into conflict, asserting "It is the base," "No, it is the crown," "No, no, it is this end," "No, it is that end," and so on. All perceptions regarding static and inertial forms are transient. How can there be any reality for a wave other than the water it is made of?

20. This world has no other reality. People who say it has are wanting in sufficient reason. Even if a dim-wit mistakes a garland of fresh flowers for a terrifying snake, does that make it one?

21. This thing is dear to me. To another, something else is dear. Thus there comes confusion in the appraisal of the correct value of the objects of endearment. One should know that his

experience of happiness is essentially the same as another's.

22. What is dear to another should spell endearment to me also. This is the correct policy. Therefore, whatever good one does should be so intended as to be beneficial to others also.

23. A compassionate person without any vested interest works day and night for the welfare of others. On the other hand, a selfish person, desirous only of his own advantage, toils endlessly but comes again and again to frustration.

24. What is known as that person or this person, when carefully considered, is the one undifferentiated form of the primeval Self. Whatever one does for the happiness of one's own self should also include the happiness of others.

25. What is good for one and might cause disaster to another is opposed to the unity of the Self. Those who grievously hurt others will consequentially bring upon themselves pain like hell fire.

26. The Self that owns the body bolts all the limbs together and animates it with a vaporous stuff. Once having become identified with the physical body, one loses right comprehension and fancies a separate reality for each person.

27. The Self is that knowledge which brings illumination to one's existence even when it is placed in the thick of darkness. This same knowledge assumes names and forms and engages in action equipped with mind and senses, for all the world like the miraculous performance of a magician.

28. That which has no beginning and no end and clearly sees everything from bottom to top is *turīya*, transcendent consciousness. The other extreme is the inert body, which has no knowledge. That which appears to exist in between, articulated as the output of cogitation, is ignorance.

29. For one who sacrifices the blossoms of the mind to the Supreme Lord, there is no other duty to perform. Otherwise one can do overt action, such as gathering flowers from the forest and engaging in ritualistic propitiation. A third alternative is to be

a contemplative who steadily avoids all snares of phenomenal illusion by exercising proper discernment.

30. The inert body does not know. It does not cogitate or articulate. One who knows all this to be only variations of knowledge becomes expansive in the transparency of comprehension, and does not thereafter suffer from body identification.

31. Without prior experience one cannot make inferences. As the Self is not a perceptible factor, one cannot infer the existence of any principle postulated as the basis of attributes.

32. What we know is only the attributes and not their source. As universal abstractions cannot be perceived, it is incorrect to say that earth and all such are factual realities. They are only compositions of modes.

33. As when a burning ember is twirled in a figure-eight movement and produces endless patterns, knowledge, in order to know its own potentials, modifies itself into endless eidetic modes, like earth and all such, and creates the phenomenal flux.

34. This is going on through beginningless time, this divine sport of the world, as if we are mounted on a chariot of becoming having for the spokes of its endlessly rotating wheels the infinite progression of milliseconds.

35. The function of Wisdom discernment comes like the dawning of ten thousand suns. This is the primeval Sun, which cleaves asunder the veil of maya that precipitates the transient forms of ignorance.

36. Innumerable are the powers of knowledge. They can be mainly categorised as two: 'sameness' and 'the other'. One should awaken to the clarity of vision in which all forms of 'otherness' merge and become one with 'sameness'.

37. It is hard to win over the obduracy of 'the other' without having achieved a vivid vision which leaves nothing outside of it. By conquering the power of the indistinctiveness of 'this', which forces consciousness to split into specificity, one should gain the wisdom of integral unity. That alone will gain one access to

pure wisdom, which leaves no room either to objectivise or to have the agency of a subject.

38. What is known distinctively as separate and specific entities is the 'other'. What shines forth as the indivisible whole is 'sameness'. This is going to be elucidated hereafter. Having known these states, verticalise knowledge and learn the art of unifying consciousness in the inclusivity of 'sameness'.

39. Moreover, of these two powers, 'sameness' is unitive, while 'the other' pertains to that which is never exhausted of its indistinctness and begs for clarification. They are of two separate kinds.

40. Their specific powers alternate between synthesis and analysis. Even though the contexts of operation are innumerable, the dual functions of the assumption of the agency of the subject and the knowledge of the object belong entirely to these two entities.

41. When one says, "This is a pot," what comes first as 'this' is difficult to discern, while 'pot' is its qualifying attribute. When the endless sense-oriented cogitations proliferate, one should bear in mind that the indicative pronoun 'this' is the fountainhead.

42. When one says, "This is knowledge," what comes first as 'this' is the unifying sameness; its distinguishing attribute is 'awareness'. For all mentations like discursive cogitation to cease, and to gain the path of liberation, one should contemplate on 'this', which inheres in the universal identity.

43. Even good people engaged in virtuous action are caught in Nature's repetitive compulsions, and they helplessly go round and round performing obligatory action. Mere omission of action does not cure the mind of its urge to modulate. Only unitive understanding, which is desireless, brings emancipation.

44. The normative essence of everyone's conviction is the same. Those who do not know this secret become fanatical in

establishing relativistic points of view, arguing like the proverbial blind men who went to "see" an elephant and couldn't agree between them in its description. Avoid all such disputes by cultivating the all-embracing attitude of sameness.

45. One person's faith will appear as unworthy to another. A basic tenet of another's religion is often rated unsatisfactory and looked upon with disdain. Such confusion is born of irrational prejudices, and continues in the minds of people as long as the secret of universal sameness remains unknown.

46. It is not possible to vanquish any religion by fighting it. By becoming competitive and fighting each other's religion, the zeal of the members of the persecuted religion only increases. By promoting religious feuds one is only destroying one's own integrity and succumbing to the evils of hatred. This should never be forgotten.

47. In principle all are aimed at arriving at the same faith. Disputants do not realise this. Wise people who are free of sectarian exclusiveness know this secret in full.

48. In spite of being identified with their own body, people do think of other people and things as their own and say, "This is mine," or "That is mine." On considering this, it is evident that everyone has some experience of the oneness of the Self.

49. All beings, at all times, everywhere, are exerting themselves to attain happiness. This quest for happiness is the one single religion in the world, of which no one has any dispute. Knowing this, one should not be lured into the sin of fighting one's own fellow beings.

50. The impressions of earth, water, fire, wind, sky, the ego-sense, knowledge, mind, and of all aspects of the one and the many, such as waves and the ocean — on entering into consciousness these transform into knowledge as they rise into the hierarchic series of states of awareness.

51. From pure knowledge emerges one's ego sense, simultaneously paired with the sense of 'thisness'. Like a twin creeper, the self

and the other entwine the maya-tree all over and hide everything.

52. When the sky of consciousness is enflamed with the vibrancy of sound (the Word), all perceptual forms disappear in its radiant blaze. When, in that splendor, the small voice that gives finality to the three-fold segmentation of awareness also ceases, there prevails only the radiance of the Self.

53. The primordial potency inherent in this is the seed which gives birth to all we see here. Bearing this in mind, and never forgetting it, one should meditate on its secret to dispel the thrall of maya.

54. In wakefulness there is no sleep, and likewise there is no sleep in the waking state. Day after day these twins are born of maya's womb, and they continuously alternate.

55. Our wakeful experience is also like a long dream. Both waking and dreaming terminate after a period of time. Because of the confusion generated by this alternation, no one sees the aloneness of the universal substratum.

56. In the ocean of consciousness, modulations arise one after another, causing the experience of perceiving embodied objects. Alas! Where is the end to this? In the sea of *samvit*, latent action is always ready to actualise.

57. Even in a quiescent state of consciousness there lurk many traits of maya. As in the ocean endless effects are produced from the many configurations of water — its taste and so on — world upon world is created out of the latent potentials of consciousness.

58. One should realise it is futile to ruminate on the past, be expectant of the present, and fantasise about the future. Without endlessly counting and measuring in confusion, one should cognise the One that always prevails, perceiving there is no differentiation.

59. I do not exist without my having any knowledge of it. Without me, my knowledge cannot exist on its own. The light that shines is the same, both in the knower and in the knowledge.

When contemplated it will undoubtedly be known that both are the same.

60. Even when a person, oblivious of the absolute status of knowledge, speaks of it as his or her private experience, knowledge does not become either differentiated from the truth of the knower or alienated from the Supreme Word that illuminates all minds.

61. Objects of perception appear to be of diverse attributes, in accordance with the innate quality of each sense organ. Gross objects of even faulty perception, such as the blue of the sky, when identified with a name, become part of the conceptual matrix and transform into knowledge.

62. Do not dispair that you cannot own the Absolute as your private experience. What knowledge can come by mere negation? Nothing. Nor does knowledge come by merely repeating the word "Absolute." It comes only by continuous contemplation.

63. The wise know there is only Knowledge, so they remain one with it and don't struggle. For them the truth to be known is here and now. But only a few see this secret. Those who do not know this think of it as an unknown entity to be sought and discovered, and under this delusion they struggle and agonise.

64. Every object of perception evokes a preconditioned memory, and one stumbles on its imagined consequences. Banish all such frivolous memories. The only memory worth cherishing is one's primal identification with the priceless, ultimate Knowledge.

65. There is nothing in this world we have not known at least once before (as pure Knowledge). When the same appears clothed in the garment of forms, it is thought of as separate entities not previously known. Who is there to wake up from his somnambulism and realise it is his own dear Self that is seen as all these? It is very strange indeed!

66. In this world of becoming, the food that nourishes the body and everything else come as a matter of course. Everything

undergoes transformation. Only one thing remains unchanged, and that is Knowledge. We are also that self-same Knowledge. Others too are none other than that.

67. All that comes within the ambit of experience can be divided into two. One is the ordinary, which can be perceived, calculated, analysed and categorised. The other is the transcendent, which is beyond the ken of one's mind to grasp. Apart from these there is nothing else, here or elsewhere. This is certain.

68. Like the presentiment of a snake evoked by a rope, the reality of the ego sense shifts from the body to the Self and back again. On one occasion it is experienced as profound, and when it alternates it is felt as profane. Only one who can discern this knows the Truth.

69. Our organism can be compared to a libidinal chariot yoked to sense perceptions, which are the horses. It is driven by the mind. Its occupant is the ego, the self-image, which is restlessly pursuing objects of pleasure in vain.

70. One pleasure principle (*rati*) expands and transforms into the ego, the senses, the mind, the body, and all that is, as if its proliferation has no end. It will go on operating till the cognising Self realises it is not any of the pleasure-pursuits but Knowledge, pure and simple.

71. No one remains established forever in a state of sameness. The process of becoming is ongoing, and all are subjected to this beginningless sport of the Divine. When all this is known in its entirety, one becomes happy beyond measure.

72. One aspect of life is action, and it belongs to nescience. There is another aspect which is permeated with consciousness, and it belongs to the sphere of knowledge. Although these two thus stand divided, as ordained by maya, to those who are successful in adopting a nondual attitude, the two together will give the pure experience of transcendence.

73. In one thing there can be many constituents, and many things can be encompassed by one meaning. Thus, when everything

is understood by complementary equations, nothing falls outside Knowledge. This secret of all-inclusive Knowledge is not known to all.

74. In the earth there are innumerable particles, and in each particle there is a world of the same earth-principle. Just as the body is conceptually envisioned by consciousness, consciousness is articulated by the body. When carefully considered, these are not two different things.

75. It is as if we are in an ocean of consciousness. Nature can be equated with the water. The Self is the ocean, while the body is like the foam. What constantly arise as 'I', 'I', are the waves. The flowerings of knowledge in the mind are pearls. What each person enjoys is the nectar of immortal bliss.

76. As sand in a wasteland is ceaselessly blown by gusts of wind, which disturbs the surface of a pond and makes it increasingly shallow, the sands of untruth are continuously disfiguring consciousness, and the inner self is cluttered with multifarious forms.

77. The Self and the world are not two. The transcendental is the sky. The horizontal blast of energy is the wind. Knowledge is fire. The senses are water. Objects of interest are earth. That which shines forth as the quintessence of these five principles is in truth only One.

78. There is neither death nor birth nor any manifested form of life. There are neither men nor gods nor anything of that sort. All of them are only names and forms. Their substance is only that of a desert mirage — and that is, for sure, no substance at all.

79. On the eve of birth there is no existence. The emergence from the womb is not a factual reality in a posterior moment. How can it be? Death is also like this. Everything seems to be only by the glorious presence of consciousness.

80. Rest and motion cannot happen in the same place at the same time. Similarly, creation, existence and dissolution cannot take place concurrently. When critically examined, these concepts

have no substantial validity. They are only words.

81. Nature divides itself into the enjoyer and the enjoyed. The conceiving self that illuminates all as counterparts of knowledge is the enjoyer; what is extended as 'thisness' both here and beyond is the universe that is enjoyed.

82. Like the fire that comes from rubbing sticks together, a wisdom of great discrimination arises from the minds of discerning contemplatives. It flames in the sky of consciousness, burning everything as fuel.

83. The changeless Self, from its vertical height, witnesses the flux of becoming, noticing how bodies exist and perish and come into being again, and how one is substituted by another.

84. From the mere fact that one perceives the transformation of forms, it cannot be maintained that the modifications, such as of clay, are real. When critically considered, clay alone is and the form is unreal. The very many entities that are seeming to be so are only nature's modalities transforming knowledge.

85. No image can exist without a model. If the world is a shadow it should have its archetype somewhere. No such original is seen anywhere; therefore, this world is neither a model or its image. Everything seen here is like a snake painted by a master artist.

86. The substance of one body is not in another. This fact contradicts the rejection of individual formations. As the verity of objects persists through time, their substantiality gains the status of the real.

87. When each entity is taken by itself, it has existence and it excludes other things by the law of impenetrablility. When this fact is considered, the body and such cannot be rated as real or unreal, they can only be termed indescribable.

88. In fact, all that we encounter is real as such. The philosopher in his contemplation sees everything as belonging to one unitive principle. If this inner truth is not understood, tribulations multiply like the snares of a revengeful maya.

89. From knowledge countless sparks emerge that are both real and unreal. The conglomeration of them appears as the universe. The understanding that nothing can be other than knowledge will give it homogeneity.

90. The unreal cannot conceal the real. That is our experience. Existence asserts itself at every step, producing all effects, such as the body.

91. It is a law that one strives to actualise what is dear to one's heart. As this impulsion to act is constant, its cause should be understood as a dear value, beginningless, never fully spent, unpredicable and one without a second. In short, this is the one happiness that gives reality to life.

92. The dynamic to act is eternal. As an unexpended law, it acts outside in correspondence with the perception of a dear value. These two are inseparable. By the action performed outside, this binary function is known.

93. To one who has withdrawn all interest from the changeful body, nothing is more dear than the Self. As this love for the Self never diminishes in anyone, it should be known as the eternal.

94. There is an inherent iniquity in the unreal world and Reality presenting themselves as one indiscernible whole. To these, which cannot be demarcated verbally or conceptually, how can any role of methodology be applied?

95. This world of manifestation is like a sportive display of maya, who conceals her forms and creates everything with her essence. Continuously she presents one limb after another, making this grand exhibit of the cosmos with millions of luminaries.

96. The finitude of the atom and the infinitude of the indivisible whole shine side by side as if they exist and also as if they do not exist, so it is not possible to determine with any certainty which of these two experiences is true.

97. On the day when the finite is fully absorbed in the glory of the infinite, that knowledge will attain the perfection of the Plenum.

One cannot even imagine the totality of the all-filling consciousness without experiencing its immeasurable magnitude. It is like an ocean of silence in which everything is submerged.

98. It is evident that we do not know what this august reality is; otherwise, how could we qualify every touch of pleasure as great happiness? The Self is not the sum total of dependent originations. Even when the intellect and such faculties are undone, the Self will remain unaffected as pure Knowledge.

99. Knowledge and the self spoken of as 'I' are one and the same to a person for whom the veil of ignorance is removed. To one whose intelligence is still veiled, there will be many hesitations to admit this identity. If the 'I' could stand apart from Knowledge, there would not be anyone to know Knowledge.

100. You are neither this nor that nor the content of what is perceived as being. Know yourself to be pure existence, all-embracing consciousness, and immortal joy. Being brave with such a clear vision, discard all attachment to being and non-being, and gently, gently merge in that Truth that fills all with enlightenment and serene joy — *AUM*.

Index